# The French face of Joseph Conrad

Joseph Conrad has generally been regarded as a novelist with 'dual' Polish and English national affinities. This study argues for a *triple* identity by introducing the French face of Conrad's work, demonstrating that his knowledge of the French language and its literature (which preceded his acquisition of the English language) has profound implications for the study of the novels. A survey of Conrad's literary and cultural background leads into a study of the impact on his writing of a number of French authors, notably Flaubert, Maupassant and Anatole France. Documenting these influences chronologically, Yves Hervouet builds up a picture of Conrad at work. In addition he discusses in more theoretical terms the aesthetic, philosophical and technical aspects of these influences and examines their implications for a reassessment of Conrad's creative originality.

The first large-scale account of Conrad's extensive involvement with the French literary tradition, Yves Hervouet's book will have a major impact on Conrad scholarship. As a study of cross-cultural influence, it will be of interest to all students of comparative literature in the period.

# The French face of Joseph Conrad

## Yves Hervouet

Formerly Lecturer in French Studies at the
University of Lancaster

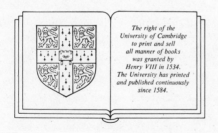

The right of the
University of Cambridge
to print and sell
all manner of books
was granted by
Henry VIII in 1534.
The University has printed
and published continuously
since 1584.

## Cambridge University Press

Cambridge

New York   Port Chester   Melbourne   Sydney

For
Ruth Bailey
with gratitude and love

Published by the Press Syndicate of the University of Cambridge
The Pitt Building, Trumpington Street, Cambridge CB2 1RP
40 West 20th Street, New York, NY 10011, USA
10 Stamford Road, Oakleigh, Melbourne 3166, Australia

© Cambridge University Press 1990

First published 1990

Printed in Great Britain at the University Press, Cambridge

*British Library cataloguing in publication data*
Hervouet, Yves
  The French face of Joseph Conrad.
  1. Fiction in English. Conrad, Joseph, 1857–1924.
  Influence of French literature
  I. Title
  823'.912

*Library of Congress cataloguing in publication data*
Hervouet, Yves.
  The French face of Joseph Conrad / by Yves Hervouet.
    p.  cm.
  Includes bibliographical references.
  ISBN 0 521 38464 8 (U.S.)
    1. Conrad, Joseph, 1857–1924 – Knowledge – Literature.  2. Conrad. Joseph,
  1857–1924 – Knowledge – France.  3. English fiction – French influence.  4. France in
  literature.  I. Title.
  PR6005.04Z7435  1990
  823'.912 – dc20  89–25401 CIP

ISBN 0 521 38464 8 Hardback

ISBN 0 521 38464 8 hardback
GG

# Contents

# Foreword

Yves Bernard Marie Joseph Hervouet died on 24 June 1985 in Lancaster Royal Infirmary. He was forty-nine and had battled against cancer with selfless courage and dignity for over two years.

Born in Nantes (the 't' in his name is sounded), he studied English at the University of Montpellier, where he completed a postgraduate dissertation on *Lord Jim*, which even in later years was to remain his favourite Conrad novel.

After teaching as a *lecteur* at the University of Birmingham and then at the University College of Swansea, in 1965 he joined a team working on the Nuffield Foreign Languages Project for primary and secondary schools. Based at the University of Leeds and later of York, he helped to write material for these pioneering audio-visual courses, but was chiefly responsible for the authenticity of the French and for the production of taped material in Paris.

On completing this assignment in 1973 he accepted a post in the Language Centre of the University of Essex before joining the University of Lancaster a year later. Appointed to the Department of French Studies as an applied linguist, he was well fitted to create new language courses at all levels and to inaugurate courses in stylistics. In addition he contributed to the teaching of nineteenth- and twentieth-century French literature (including narratology) and offered Maupassant as a special subject.

Endowed with abundant energy, an idealist and perfectionist, Yves Hervouet brought a passionate commitment to his work, expecting a like response from colleagues and students. Nevertheless, for he was a modest and private man, as a scholar he believed it possible to achieve objective truth and subordinated his own personality to that end. In discussion he was indefatigable, always perceiving fresh distinctions and shades of meaning so that his interlocutor's mind was stretched and sharpened. As an administrator he was disarmingly swift, for like all who pursue research he understood how to create the time needed for the central concern of his life.

He had retained his interest in Conrad and while engaged on the Schools Project at Leeds had been inspired by Donald Yelton's *Mimesis and Metaphor* (1967) to explore more fully for his PhD the French linguistic and literary influences on Conrad's work. Himself an *immigré* writing in a second language, Yves Hervouet could identify with Conrad's linguistic problems and his methods of resolving them. He also had the academic training to record and analyse his data and in the course of his wide reading, backed by a retentive memory, developed a sixth sense for models, echoes, or borrowings from the French. Thus the glorious hunt began, for he was fascinated on a linguistic level by the interplay between Conrad's prose and its sources.

In this book Yves Hervouet wished to assemble the evidence which would prove beyond doubt that Conrad was not merely a 'dual man', but a writer with a triple heritage, and he succeeds magnificently. The borrowings and other links recorded in part II, which was conceived chronologically to show Conrad at work, met stringent criteria and were considered by him as incontrovertible. The chapters in part III, though rooted in fact, are more speculative in their nature and hence will stimulate discussion. Part IV, which was intended also to weigh up the relative importance of art and life in Conrad's method of composition, was regrettably not completed, but the lack of these pages does not in any way affect the conclusion.

I must emphasize that the evidence, whether textual parallel or contemporary report, which is presented here, was regarded by Yves Hervouet, a scrupulous researcher, as objective. It did not enter his head that it might be interpreted as damaging to Conrad's reputation, for he knew, as the third section of the final chapter makes clear, that a creative artist necessarily assimilates and builds on the work of other artists. He himself, when writing this book, may from time to time have used other men's words which he had unknowingly absorbed, although he took every care to acknowledge his indebtedness.

The first draft of the manuscript took shape during the six months from July to December 1982. It was then revised and meticulously polished despite adversity and pain, which were in a realm beyond words, until the author's final collapse. By virtue of my post as *conservateur chargé des collections françaises* I had been closely associated with Yves Hervouet throughout and now was faced with a bulky typescript, which had to be cut and finalized for publication. This could not have been done without the help of three people: Dr Paul Kirschner, Owen Knowles, and Ms Bridget Cook, and to them I extend heart-felt thanks. With Dr Hervouet's wishes in mind, editorial intervention was minimized and pruning in the main restricted to excising repetitions or extraneous material. Dr Kirschner cut the introduction, chapters 1, 2, 3, 8, and the appendix (this was also re-shaped, having been intended for part I), while Owen Knowles was responsible for cutting the remainder. A very few bridging passages were rewritten, notably the final paragraph of the introduction and of chapter 1, the first two paragraphs of chapter 7, and the first of chapter 9, as well as half-a-dozen notes.

My own responsibilities, apart from co-ordination and initial copy-editing, were to integrate the notes and establish a bibliography. Their main cut-off point was December 1984, but relevant later titles have been added. Under my guidance Bridget Cook, who had been one of Dr Hervouet's students, carried out the enormous task of verifying the quotations and their sources. She also typed, with enviable accuracy, the revised version. Together we read the proofs of the printed book and compiled the index. The hours which she willingly gave to all this significantly lightened my own load and enabled us to finish in good order.

Likewise sincere gratitude is expressed to Professor Sylvère Monod for his helpful advice in respect of cuts and the overall structure. And the editors of the journals in which Yves Hervouet had published preliminary articles are thanked for their permission to re-use some of his material here.

The original uncut typescript can be consulted, if desired, at the Library of the POSK Joseph Conrad Centre, 238–246 King Street, Hammersmith, London, and at the University of Lancaster Library or borrowed from there through inter-library loan.

In conclusion I should like to record the admiration which Yves Hervouet felt for Flaubert, from whom he, no less than Conrad, gained inspiration, and whose spirit, it will be apparent, presides over this remarkable book.

Lindsay Newman

# Acknowledgements

Since it all started with a PhD thesis, 'French Linguistic and Literary Influences on Joseph Conrad' (Leeds University, 1971), my first thanks must go to my supervisor Mr Arthur Ravenscroft, then Senior Lecturer at the School of English in Leeds, who gave me invaluable encouragement and help as I took my first steps along what was to be a long road.

Given its range and synthetic character, this work is naturally indebted to a large number of scholars, not only Conradians, but also specialists of Flaubert, Maupassant, Anatole France, and others. My thanks are expressed to all of them. However, as the research was nearing completion, I benefited especially from the detailed criticism and support of five distinguished Conradians: Dr Paul Kirschner of Queen Mary College, London, who made numerous suggestions for improvements to the final typescript; Owen Knowles of Hull University and editor of *The Conradian*; Professor Sylvère Monod of the Sorbonne, who is responsible for the new translation of Conrad's *oeuvre* in the Pléiade series; Professor David Leon Higdon of Texas Tech University and general editor of *Conradiana*; and Mrs Juliet McLauchlan, Chairman of the Joseph Conrad Society (UK). I am also grateful to Professor Thomas Moser of Stanford University for allowing me to use as title a phrase which originally appeared in his review of Donald Yelton's *Mimesis and Metaphor*.

During my years in the Department of French Studies at Lancaster University, I have been touched by the many kindnesses shown to me by a number of colleagues, who, with considerable patience, have put my mind at rest on apparently endless queries about 'points of English'.

I should also like to thank the staff of the University Library there, not least the Inter-Library Loan service, for supplying the many documents on which this study has been based. In particular, as adviser, bibliographer, and finally as editor of the whole, Dr Lindsay Newman has performed a service which goes beyond the bounds of duty or friendship.

Last, who should be first, is Mrs Ruth Bailey. Her great contribution cannot be guessed at by others and certainly cannot be rewarded by mere acknowledgement from me, for it is to her that the work owes its very existence.

YVES HERVOUET                                        OVER KELLET, May 1985

# Abbreviations

Full details of the editions used are given in the bibliography.

*Primary works*

| | |
|---|---|
| AF | *Almayer's Folly* |
| AG | *The Arrow of Gold* |
| BA | *Bel-Ami* |
| BP | *Bouvard et Pécuchet* |
| C | *Chance* |
| CL | *The Collected Letters of Joseph Conrad* |
| ES | *L'Education sentimentale* |
| JCWD | *Joseph Conrad and Warrington Dawson: The Record of a Friendship* |
| LBM | *Letters to William Blackwood and David S. Meldrum* |
| LCG | *Letters to R. B. Cunninghame Graham* |
| LE | *Last Essays* |
| LEG | *Letters from Joseph Conrad, 1895–1924 [to Edward Garnett]* |
| LF | *Lettres françaises [de Joseph Conrad]* |
| LJ | *Lord Jim* |
| LL | *Joseph Conrad: Life and Letters* |
| LMP | *Lettres de Joseph Conrad à Marguerite Poradowska* |
| LRC | *Conrad to a Friend: 150 Selected Letters [...] to Richard Curle* |
| MB | *Madame Bovary* |
| MS | *The Mirror of the Sea* |
| N | *Nostromo* |
| NLL | *Notes on Life and Letters* |
| NN | *The Nigger of the 'Narcissus'* |
| OI | *An Outcast of the Islands* |
| PJ | *Pierre et Jean* |
| PR | *A Personal Record* |
| Res | *The Rescue* |
| Rom | *Romance* |

| | |
|---|---|
| Rov | The Rover |
| S | Suspense |
| SA | The Secret Agent |
| Sal | Salammbô |
| SL | The Shadow-Line |
| SR | Les Soeurs Rondoli |
| SS | A Set of Six |
| TC | Trois contes |
| TH | Tales of Hearsay |
| TLS | 'Twixt Land and Sea |
| TOS | Typhoon, and Other Stories |
| TU | Tales of Unrest |
| UV | Une vie |
| UWE | Under Western Eyes |
| V | Victory |
| WT | Within the Tides |
| YOS | Youth: a Narrative; and Two Other Stories |

*Secondary works*

Baines — Jocelyn Baines, *Joseph Conrad: A Critical Biography* (1960)

Chaikin — Milton Chaikin, 'Zola and Conrad's "The Idiots"' (1955)

Curle — Richard Curle, *The Last Twelve Years of Joseph Conrad* (1928)

Ford — Ford Madox Ford, *Joseph Conrad: A Personal Remembrance* (1924)

Gillon — Adam Gillon, *Conrad and Shakespeare* (1976)

Guérin — Yves Guérin, 'Huit lettres inédites de Joseph Conrad à Robert d'Humières' (1970)

Karl — Frederick R. Karl, *Joseph Conrad: The Three Lives* (1979)

Kirschner — Paul Kirschner, *Conrad: The Psychologist as Artist* (1968)

Knowles — Owen Knowles, 'Conrad, Anatole France, and the early French romantic tradition' (1979)

Meyer — Bernard C. Meyer, *Joseph Conrad: A Psychoanalytic Biography* (1967)

Morf — Gustav Morf, *The Polish Shades and Ghosts of Joseph Conrad* (1976)

Moser — Thomas Moser, *Joseph Conrad: Achievement and Decline* (1957)

Najder — Zdzisław Najder, *Joseph Conrad: A Chronicle* (1983)

NRF — 'Hommage à Joseph Conrad', *Nouvelle Revue Française*, XXIII, 135, (1924)

Retinger — Joseph H. Retinger, *Conrad and his Contemporaries* (1941)

| | |
|---|---|
| Said | Edward W. Said, *Joseph Conrad and the Fiction of Autobiography* (1966) |
| Watt | Ian Watt, *Conrad in the Nineteenth Century* (1980) |
| Yelton | Donald C. Yelton, *Mimesis and Metaphor* (1967) |
| ★ | Indicates that a borrowing was first noted by the author named |
| ★Hervouet | does not refer to a publication |

# Note on the text

For ease of identification, the textual parallels, which show the literal translations and close adaptations that Conrad made from French authors, are italicized.

# Introduction

'La phrase "qui est des notres" m'a touché car en vérité je me sens lié à la France par une profonde sympathie.'

Conrad to H. D. Davray, 10 July 1899 (*CL*, II, p. 185)

On 6 January 1908, a dejected Conrad reported to Galsworthy the 'honourable failure' of *The Secret Agent*, adding wryly: 'I suppose there is something in me that is unsympathetic to the general public [...]. Foreignness, I suppose' (*LL*, II, p. 65). And because of that foreignness he was viewed for many decades as an isolated phenomenon on the English literary scene.[1] Fifty years after his death, at the 1974 International Conference, Edward Said could still deplore the fact that he had been 'treated as everything *except* a novelist with links to a cultural and intellectual context'.[2] Since then his relationship to the Polish, Russian, English and French traditions, as well as to a number of novelists and philosophers from other cultures, has been extensively explored; yet there is still considerable disagreement about the respective importance of the traditions behind his literary cosmopolitanism. Gustav Morf was the first to attempt to link Conrad inextricably to his Polish background,[3] an idea which, as Frederick Karl notes, has become 'increasingly influential'.[4] Although in 1947 F. R. Leavis saw him as a 'cosmopolitan of French culture',[5] ever since the 1960s Conrad has been presented as having a 'double image' and 'dual identity' – Polish (or even Slav) and English.[6] The 'double image' survives in Cedric Watts's *A Preface to Conrad* (1982), where the concept of 'janiformity' of Conrad's texts reflecting the double nature of his character tends also to be linked to a double inheritance.[7]

This over-simplification has arisen through a decades-long neglect of Conrad's French background with a consequent persisting uncertainty about the exact nature and importance of his relationship to French authors. Although there have been countless testimonies to his unremitting interest in French literature, the question of French literary influence on Conrad's work has always been vexed. Some early critics flatly rejected the idea. G. Jean-Aubry, Conrad's first biographer, declared in 1923: 'Les oeuvres de Flaubert, de Maupassant, d'Anatole France lui sont familières, sans que cependant on puisse

1

relever dans son oeuvre rien qui y ressemble.'[8] More often, however, after a
brief acknowledgement that his masters were mainly French, their influence
has been dismissed as limited. In 1916, Hugh Walpole noted that Conrad's
early works, particularly *Almayer's Folly*, show the 'unmistakable' influence of
the style of 'the author of *Madame Bovary*', but quickly concluded that 'his
debt to Flaubert [...] can be easily exaggerated'.[9] In 1928, Richard Curle said
that although Conrad 'was vividly influenced by certain French writers it would
be an error to overrate' their influences, since 'they were soon transmuted by
his native genius. More and more the models fade into the background and
Conrad himself emerges.'[10] In 1960, Jocelyn Baines acknowledged that Conrad
had 'served his apprenticeship' under Flaubert and Maupassant, but added: 'It
was of course no more than an apprenticeship.'[11] Four years later, Najder
commented that the influence of Flaubert and Maupassant 'was in fact doubly
limited' since 'it concerned mainly matters of literary technique, and affected
almost exclusively [Conrad's] early and still immature books'.[12] Such superficial
judgements are still common in recent criticism. Thus, Andrzej Busza asserts
that for Conrad Flaubert's writings 'represent an ideal to be aimed at and
not material to be used, appropriated, or displaced'.[13] Even so meticulously
analytical and language-conscious a critic as Ian Watt follows Baines and Najder
when, having acknowledged that 'For Conrad the exemplary novelists were
French, and, in particular, Flaubert and Maupassant', he states that after
October 1898, Conrad 'was finally turning away from the French influence'.[14]
And his first statement is still too much for Robert Caserio who accuses Watt
of repeating 'an unexamined critical orthodoxy'.[15]

It is curious that so many critics have been, and still are, so quick to dismiss
Conrad's French inheritance, despite the evidence left by his friends, in particular by his collaborator and literary confidant from 1898 to 1908, Ford Madox
Ford. In *Thus to Revisit* (1921) Ford declared that 'what is cried out from every
page of Mr Conrad's romances [...] is that [...] the literary influence of France
is overwhelming over the style, the construction of the sentences, the cadence,
the paragraph or the building up of the effects'.[16]

Whatever the reason, the fact is that Conrad criticism still suffers from the
absence of a comprehensive account of his links with French writers. Although
valuable scattered contributions have been made, especially since the mid
1960s, they cannot build up an overall picture in a critic's mind. The consequences of the lack of such a picture can be plainly seen in three magisterial
works that appeared between 1979 and 1983: Frederick Karl's *Joseph Conrad:
The Three Lives*, Ian Watt's *Conrad in the Nineteenth Century*, and Zdzisław
Najder's *Joseph Conrad: A Chronicle*. Despite their impressive scholarship and
their avowed aim of relating Conrad and his writing to the Polish, French and
British cultural and literary backgrounds, these works are unable to convey
anything approaching the full measure of his involvement with, and indebtedness to, the French literary tradition.

The present study, benefiting from the findings already made and adding new ones, aims to remedy that lack. It is in four parts. The first, together with the appendix, consists of a survey of Conrad's French literary and cultural background, with a detailed account of his knowledge of French writers. The second deals with the textual, stylistic and thematic influence on Conrad's fiction of a number of French authors, especially Flaubert, Maupassant and Anatole France. The third is devoted to an examination of the aesthetic and philosophical aspects of the influence exerted on Conrad by those three writers. Finally, part IV takes up some of the psychological, ethical and aesthetic issues inevitably raised by the accumulated evidence, placing Conrad's methods of composition – methods which entailed transmuting other authors' fiction into his own – in a historical context of creativity and originality versus influence and tradition.

My purpose has been to remove from Conradian scholarship an important area of uncertainty which has generated nothing but sterile argument.

# Part I

## Conrad's French literary and cultural background

'a mind steeped in the modern literature of Europe, especially in that of France'

R. B. Cunninghame Graham, 'Preface', *TH*, p. ix

# 1 A part of Conrad's life

Whether French, English or Polish, Conrad's friends and acquaintances were all struck by his amazing familiarity with, and love for, French literature. The playwright H.-R. Lenormand, who met him in Ajaccio in 1920, recollected: 'C'était une joie pour moi de constater son amour des lettres françaises', and in his memorial tribute he stated that he spoke about French writers 'avec une tendresse filiale'.[1] In his own tribute, André Gide exclaimed: 'Comme il connaissait bien nos auteurs!'[2] John Galsworthy recorded that 'He was ever more at home with French literature than with English',[3] Ernest Dawson said that 'French literature made a stronger appeal to Conrad than English',[4] and according to Joseph Retinger, he regarded it as 'the most versatile, the most universal and the most cosmopolitan of all'.[5]

This remarkable intimacy with the French literary tradition had both national and family origins. As Conrad himself noted: 'of all the countries in Europe it is with France that Poland has most connection' (*PR*, p. 121).[6] As a member of the *szlachta*, or land-owning gentry, Conrad's early acquaintance with the French language was in no way exceptional. As in Russia, French was commonly used in Polish aristocratic circles throughout the nineteenth century as the language of cultured communication, 'a state of things', Georg Brandes says, 'which from the beginning of the century was promoted [...] by the continual intellectual intercourse with France'.[7] Retinger points out that 'in the upper strata of society' Polish children 'had as a matter of course a French tutor or governess [...] and were brought up on the French educational system, chatting in French from their earliest childhood'.[8] Such was the case with Conrad, who learned French at the age of five with 'the good, ugly Mlle. Durand' (*PR*, p. 64).[9] His early acquaintance with French literature, on the other hand, had much to do with his father, Apollo Korzeniowski, who not only pursued the task undertaken by Mlle Durand, but also encouraged his son to share his own 'strong taste' (*LL*, I, p. 3) for French literature. (Apollo, Conrad told Garnett, produced distinguished translations of 'V. Hugo, *Legende du Siècles. Travailleurs de la Mer. Hernani.* [and *Les Burgraves, Le Roi s'amuse, Marion Delorme*].[10] Alf. de Vigny Chatterton' (*CL*, II, p. 246).) Conrad recalled how Apollo, who was ill at the time, got him to read aloud 'from beginning to end' the proofs of his translation of *The Toilers of the Sea* (*PR*, p. 72). He also testified to his wide early reading: 'At ten years of age I had read much of Victor Hugo and other romantics. I had read in Polish and in French, history, voyages,[11] novels; I knew "Gil Blas" and "Don Quixote" in abridged editions; I had read in early boyhood Polish poets and some French poets' (*PR*, pp. 70–1).

Unfortunately, the last five years that Conrad was to spend in Poland after Apollo's death in May 1869 'constitute the period in [his] life about which the least is known'.[12] We do not even know with certainty where he was educated in Cracow, let alone what books he read,[13] and the same is true of his life in Lwów, where he was sent in August 1873. However, it may be worth remembering that, in the last decades of the nineteenth century, Cracow became, with Lwów, the seat of the literary movement known as 'Young Poland'. This movement, Avrom Fleishman observes, had 'a predilection for French Symbolism, Satanism, and other forms of neo-Romanticism from Hugo and Baudelaire to Mallarmé and Huysmans', and although it flowered after Conrad's departure, 'its roots must have been already planted in his student days there'.[14] That Conrad was already sensitive to his intellectual and cultural environment is beyond doubt: a young acquaintance from his stay in Lwów recalled that 'he was very advanced and serious for his age' and that 'he used to attend open university lectures on literature and natural sciences'.[15]

Although his account is somewhat rhetorical and contains demonstrable inaccuracies, Ford has claimed that Conrad continued his reading of French authors during his three and a half years of residence in Marseilles and while serving in French ships from October 1874 to April 1878:

Conrad was the most South French of the South French. He was born in Beaucaire, beside the Rhone; read Marryat in the shadow of the castle of the good king Réné, Daudet on the Cannebière of Marseilles, Gautier in the tufts of lavender and rosemary of the little forests between Marseilles and Toulon, Maupassant on the French torpedo-boats on which he served and Flaubert on the French flagship, *Ville d'Ompteda*.[16]

It was, however, mainly during his life as an English mariner from April 1878 to January 1894 that he acquired what Ford described as his 'amazingly wide' reading: 'And preceding, along with, and subseqent to this omnivorescence of English books went Mr Conrad's intense study of the great French writers'.[17] This recollection is supported by Richard Curle: 'He read omnivorously during his voyages – he has often described to me how he would pick up books before starting on a sea passage – and more particularly he read the best French novels'.[18]

After Conrad had left the sea to become a novelist, he strengthened his ties with French literature. Edward Garnett recalled being introduced, at the end of 1894, to Conrad's 'snug bachelor quarters' at 17 Gillingham Street, where he saw in 'the small firelit room, a row of French novels' (*LEG*, p. 5); and Emilie Briquel – whom Conrad met during his stay at Champel in May 1895 –

wrote in her diary: 'Like me he likes Pierre Loti, the poetry of Victor Hugo, and he advised me to read Daudet's *Fromont jeune et Risler aîné* and *Nabob*'.[19]

By the time Conrad started writing, he had not merely read but, as Ford pointed out, studied the views and techniques of most of the famous nineteenth-century French writers. In 1897, shortly after the publication of *The Nigger of the 'Narcissus'*, Henry Davray, who visited him several times in Essex, was struck by his knowledge of French literature: 'Il semblait avoir tout lu: il récitait des pages entières de Flaubert, il disséquait les personnages de Balzac, il citait nos poètes.'[20]

Throughout his career, Conrad continued to study the nineteenth-century French masters, and also kept in close contact with the works of his French contemporaries. Towards the end of his life, he amazed Jean-Aubry by his extensive knowledge and the 'recollection he retained of his reading, remembering many years later the names of the smallest characters and details', and this in a 'foreign' language.[21] In his introduction to *Lettres françaises* Jean-Aubry elaborated:

Il faut avoir vécu avec lui, comme je l'ai fait, pour savoir quelle étonnante connaissance il avait des romans de Balzac, de Flaubert, d'Anatole France, des contes de Maupassant, d'un grand nombre de nos ouvrages historiques: mémoires, journaux, souvenirs, et, aussi bien, des oeuvres d'écrivains plus récents, Henri de Régnier, Marcel Proust, André Gide, Valery Larbaud, Paul Morand. Des premiers auteurs que je viens de nommer, il se rappelait les moindres personnages et leurs plus minimes singularités: des paragraphes entiers lui revenaient, mot pour mot, au cours de la conversation: il en soulignait le trait comique ou dramatique, la tournure personnelle du style. Que de fois ne m'a-t-il pas surpris ainsi par des phrases du *Lys Rouge*, de *L'Education Sentimentale*, de *Fromont jeune*, ou du *Champ d'Oliviers*.                    (*LF*, p. 12)

Curle noticed that Conrad's 'French books' in his study at Oswalds (his home from September 1919 to his death) were 'falling to pieces',[22] a sign of their frequent use. It is clear that French works were always a part of Conrad's life from his early childhood; they remained his constant companions whether at sea or on land, in his cabin or in his study.

Paul Wiley's remark, made as long ago as 1954, that 'the full extent of Conrad's reading in French is not certainly known',[23] still holds true. It is time to provide a detailed and comprehensive record of Conrad's knowledge of, and response to, French novelists, poets, dramatists, critics, thinkers and chroniclers. Such a record can be found in the appendix (pp. 233–56); it shows that Conrad's French culture was no 'myth' (see note 6 to the introduction), but remarkable in its scope.[24] Three writers, however, exerted so profound an influence on Conrad that I shall deal with them straightaway. They were, first, Flaubert and Maupassant, and secondly, Anatole France.

Testimonies abound of Conrad's admiration for, and intimacy with, the works of Flaubert and Maupassant: 'Il admirait Flaubert et Maupassant, dont il se réclamait volontiers', said Gide.[25] Both Jean-Aubry and Dawson recorded that he had 'une révérence particulière' and 'the highest reverence' for Flaubert,[26] whom, according to Galsworthy, he read 'with constancy'.[27] Davray, recollecting a few hours spent with Conrad at the seaside, confirms this: 'nous vînmes à parler du style, et Mr Conrad, qui est des nôtres, sut dire avec une communicative ferveur toute son admiration pour Flaubert et tout son amour du style. Il citait des passages, avec une sûreté qui indiquait une connaissance intime du grand écrivain.'[28] As for Maupassant, Arthur Symons spoke of Conrad's 'enormous admiration' for his short stories.[29]

But, of course, the most extensive documentation is that left by Ford, who made it clear that what brought him and Conrad together was 'a devotion to Flaubert and Maupassant'. During their collaboration they discovered that they both 'had *Félicité, St Julien l'Hospitalier*, immense passages of *Madame Bovary*, *La Nuit, Ce Cochon de Morin*, and immense passages of *Une Vie* by heart or so nearly by heart that what the one faltered over the other could take up'.[30] Douglas Goldring's account of the weekend he and Ford spent with Conrad at Someries in November 1908 shows that Ford was not exaggerating. Ford and Conrad, Goldring said, devoted much of their night to talking – '*how* they talked! [...] booming about Flaubert, hurling great chunks of *Madame Bovary* and *Un Coeur Simple* at one another, with ever-growing excitement'.[31] Another recollection by Ford conveys the depth of Conrad's feeling:

Conrad had for Flaubert, years before he ever saw London city, an infinite veneration – an almost incredible passion for his writings, his power over phrases, his ideas of how books should be written, his berserker's literary personality. And ideas possessed Conrad with a passion that was almost an agony. It was painful sometimes to hear him read passages from Flaubert aloud, so immensely would he be impressed – and depressed – by the idea of that writer's impeccable unapproachableness.[32]

That dedication apparently never faltered: the last time he met Conrad, in May 1924, Ford recalled that, having agreed that they 'had altered very little', they recited by heart passages from 'Un Coeur simple'.[33]

Even more important, the references and allusions to Flaubert and Maupassant sprinkled throughout Conrad's correspondence and his critical and autobiographical writings make it clear that he learned his craft from them and constantly used their works (Flaubert's in particular) as his touchstone.

## Gustave Flaubert (1821–1880)

The first evidence of Conrad's intense and lasting interest in *Madame Bovary* appears in a letter to Mme Poradowska dated 6 April 1892 which pays tribute to Flaubert's powers of verisimilitude:

Dans la [omission] et saisissante simplicité de vos descriptions Vous me rappelez un peu Flaubert dont je viens de relire Mme Bovary avec une admiration plaine de respect – [...]

En voilà un qui avait assez d'imagination pour deux realistes. Il y a peu d'auteurs qui soient aussi créateurs que lui. On ne questionne jamais pour un moment ni ses personnes ni ses evenements; on douterai plutôt de sa propre existence.                    (CL, I, p.109)

On 5 October 1902, commiserating with Galsworthy about critics, he also invoked Flaubert: 'If you remember what tempest of anger Mme Bovary had raised by the sheer sincerity of its method alone you will understand perhaps that your sincerity [...] must prepare itself for a struggle.' (CL, II, p.445) He again used *Madame Bovary* as a point of reference when he objected to Ford's dating of the manuscript of *Romance* '1896–1903', arguing: 'Even Flaubert was not six years writing Mme Bovary which *was* an epoch making volume' (CL, III, p.59). On 23 December 1909 he wrote to Robert d'Humières, confirming the truth of Ford's assertions, that there was a time when he knew 'des pages entières de Mme Bovary par coeur', and called it 'un chef d'oeuvre'.[34] And on 12 March 1911 he referred to the same work when advising Garnett 'to execute a change of front' in choosing a subject: 'You know that it was from the discussion of the *Tentation de St Antoine* that the idea of *Mme Bovary* sprang up in Flaubert's mind. A complete turn about.' (*LEG*, p.228)[35] Clearly, Conrad's veneration for Flaubert's masterpiece never diminished: during his stay in Corsica, nearly thirty years after his praise of it to Mme Poradowska, he evidently spoke of it enthusiastically to Lenormand, who recollected: 'Ah! il n'était pas de ceux que *Madame Bovary* fait bâiller![36]

Conrad's intense feeling for *Salammbô* is also well documented. In a letter to James Gibbons Huneker of 16 April 1909 he affirms that he 'began [his] communion with Flaubert by *Salammbô*',[37] and, although chary of revealing his literary indebtedness, he acknowledged the influence of this novel on *The Nigger of the 'Narcissus'* in the above-mentioned letter to his translator, d'Humières:

Mais si Mme Bovary est un chef d'oeuvre, Salammbo frise le miracle. Je me rapelle bien, quand j'écrivais le N of the N Salammbo était mon livre de matin. En avalant mon café j'en lisais une page ou deux au hasard – et il n'y a presque pas de page ladedans qui ne soit merveilleuse. Et il n'y a pas a dire: l'influence de l'infiniment grand sur l'infiniment petit peut se voir. Dans mon traitement des marins il y a un pale reflet de la grande maîtrise de Flaubert dans son traitement des Mercenaires. Peut-être ce n'est qu'une illusion flatteuse. Mais je sais bien que j'étais sous l'influence de ce livre unique.[38]

And on 10 March 1911, while praising Galsworthy's *The Patrician*, Conrad admitted that it was not 'pure aesthetics', adding significantly: 'only Flaubert's *Salammbô* amongst novels is that' (*LL*, II, p.126).[39]

Many other references suggest the strength of Conrad's commitment to Flaubert. On 14 February 1899, when seeking a title for a volume to contain 'Youth',

12    Conrad's French literary and cultural background

'Heart of Darkness' and 'Jim' (which he hoped to finish for publication in April), he suggested to William Blackwood: 'Why not: "Three Tales" by Joseph Conrad. Flaubert (mutatis mutandis) published Trois contes' (*CL*, II, p. 167). And on 8 July 1903, he still had this title in mind for he wrote to Cunninghame Graham: 'Your delightful enthusiasm for les Trois Contes positively refreshed my mind' (*CL*, III, p. 45).[40] On 26 December of that year he congratulated the same friend on his depiction of Pizarro, and exclaimed: '"C'est *énorme* d'humanité" as the great Flaubert would have yelled to the four winds of heaven' (*CL*, III, p. 101). In August 1908 he cited Flaubert in defending himself against Arthur Symons's criticism of his treatment of the death of Kurtz in 'Heart of Darkness': 'Do you really think that old Flaubert gloated over the deathbed of Emma, or the death march of Matho, or the last moments of Félicie?' [Félicité] (*LL*, II, p. 73).[41] And replying to Huneker on 18 May 1909, Conrad revealed, in Yelton's words, 'something of the subjective basis of his attachment to Flaubert and the degree to which Flaubert figures in his mind as a heroic exemplar':[42]

your criticism where you overwhelm me with the mantle of Flaubert never came under my eye. Thanks for your intention – but it is an ominous garment to put on a man's shoulders. Yet there is one point in which I resemble that great man, it is in the desperate, heart-breaking toil and effort of the writing, the days of wrestling as with a dumb devil for every line of my creation.[43] And poor Flaubert had no wife and children, he had neither himself nor others to feed on the vain words which survive him for your delight and mine. Death had for him no terrors either in this world or in the next.[44]

On 8 November 1903, Conrad justified *Romance* to K. Waliszewski by arguing: 'Flaubert (un vrai saint, celui-là) s'est bien mis à faire une féerie' [*Le Château des coeurs* (1880)] (*CL*, III, p. 75). Five years later, in the opening of *A Personal Record*, he showed the same reverence:

and since saints are supposed to look benignantly on humble believers, I indulge in the pleasant fancy that the shade of old Flaubert [...] might have hovered with amused interest over the decks of a 2,000-ton steamer called the *Adowa*, on board of which [...] the tenth chapter of 'Almayer's Folly' was begun. With interest, I say, for was not the kind Norman giant [...] the last of the Romantics? Was he not, in his unworldly, almost ascetic, devotion to his art a sort of literary, saint-like hermit?          (*PR*, p. 3)[45]

Yet in June 1918 Conrad rejected the assertion, made by Hugh Walpole two years previously, that his early works show the 'unmistakable' stylistic influence of 'the author of *Madame Bovary*':

You say that I have been under the formative influence of *Madame Bovary*. In fact, I read it only after finishing *A.F.* [*Almayer's Folly*], as I did all the other works of Flaubert, and anyhow, my Flaubert is the Flaubert of *St. Antoine*[46] and *Ed[ucation]*: *Sent[imentale]*: and that only from the point of view of the rendering of concrete things and visual impressions. I thought him marvellous in that respect. I don't think I learned anything from him. What he did for me was to open my eyes and arouse my emulation. One can learn something from Balzac, but what could one learn from Flaubert? He compels admiration, – about the greatest service one artist can render to another.

(*LL*, II, p.206)

However, it is significant that in his own copy of Walpole's book, Conrad, despite his denial, marked 'very acute'[47] alongside the passage where Walpole noted the influence of the French language and especially of the author of *Madame Bovary* on his earlier style. What is more, critics have long discounted Conrad's declaration concerning *Almayer's Folly* by pointing to his letter of April 1892 to Mme Poradowska. Yet the rest of the passage is still quoted with little or no reservation: Conrad himself thus initiated the confusion about his relationship with Flaubert which persists to this day.

## Guy de Maupassant (1850–1893)

Conrad never hid his admiration for Maupassant. In May 1904, he wrote an enthusiastic preface to Ada Galsworthy's translation of a selection of the French writer's tales entitled *Yvette and Other Stories*, praising the art of Maupassant highly and declaring himself 'inspired by a long and intimate acquaintance' with his work (*NLL*, p.30). Indeed, as early as August 1894, shortly after completing *Almayer's Folly*, he wrote to Mme Poradowska that he was reading Maupassant 'avec delices' (*CL*, I, p.169), and later that year, after remarking how well Maupassant knew 'minor French clerks', he told her:

> Vous étes trop tard avec Votre avis Madame ma Tante. J'ai peur que je ne sois trop sous l'influence de Maupassant. J'ai etudié 'Pierre et Jean' – pensée, methode et tout – avec le plus profond déséspoir. Ça n'a l'air de rien mais c'est d'un compliqué comme mécanisme qui me fait m'arracher les cheveux. On a envie de pleurer de rage en lisant cela. – Enfin!                                   (*CL*, I, p.183)

In May 1898, he sent Garnett a copy of *Bel-Ami* (1885), calling it 'that amazing masterpiece' and adding: 'The technique of that work gives to one acute pleasure. It is simply enchanting to see how it's done' (*CL*, II, p.62). In January of the following year, he wrote to Mrs Bontine, in connection with Maupassant's first book entitled *Des Vers* (1880): 'I share your opinion of Maupassant. The man is a great artist, who sees the essential in everything', and he gave a discerning yet sympathetic assessment of Maupassant 'the poet': 'He is not a great poet, – perhaps no poet at all, yet I like his verses. I like them immensely' (*CL*, II, p.150). In August 1903, he recommended to Davray a selection of tales by Maupassant due for publication,[48] pointing out that he had been consulted on the choice of tales and felt a little responsible, and that this translation had been undertaken only 'comme hommage au grand talent, à l'art impeccable (presque) de Maupassant' (*CL*, III, p.52). His remark in a letter of December 1922 to George Keating, 'Certainly I have a great opinion of Maupassant' (*LL*, II, p.290), shows that his admiration never waned.

Finally, we have the clearest of statements from Ford that during their collaboration, he and Conrad relied stylistically on Flaubert and Maupassant to the point of translation:

> Our chief masters in style were Flaubert and Maupassant: Flaubert in the greater degree, Maupassant in the less. [...] We remembered long passages of Flaubert: elaborated long passages in his spirit and with his cadences and then translated them into passages of English as simple as the subject under treatment would bear. We remembered short, staccato passages of Maupassant: invented short staccato passages in his spirit and then translated them into English as simple as the subject would bear.[49]

More importantly, Ford claimed that Conrad, on his own admission, adopted the same approach when working by himself: 'Conrad held that a habit of good cadence could be acquired by the study of models. His own he held came to him from constant reading of Flaubert.[50] Ford's recollections are supported by Arthur Symons, who observed that one volume of Maupassant's stories, 'with some other French novels, was always thrown half open on one side of his [Conrad's] desk', and explained that 'this was a question of style'.[51] Most revealing of all, Conrad himself acknowledged in a letter to Davray of 22 August 1903 that at times he modelled his style on that of Maupassant: 'Moi qui suis, sans me vanter, saturé de Maupassant, j'ai été étonné de l'allure maupassantesque que l'on peut donner à la prose anglaise' (CL, III, p.52).

## Anatole France (1844–1924)

Unlike Daudet, who was one of his 'enthousiasmes de jeunesse' (CL, I, p.201), Anatole France seems to have been an enthusiasm of Conrad's maturer years. In August 1894, he wrote to Mme Poradowska that he had just finished Le Lys rouge (1894), adding simply 'Ça ne me dit rien' (CL, I, p.169). And yet we know from Jean-Aubry that, late in life, he often quoted whole sentences from it by heart. In July 1904, Conrad wrote a eulogistic review of 'Crainquebille' in which he paid tribute to France's 'distinction of thought' and 'princely command of words' and declared it 'difficult to read M. Anatole France without admiring him' (NLL, pp.35, 39). In a letter to H. G. Wells of 20 October 1905 pointing out France's allusions to him (Wells) in his latest book Sur la pierre blanche (1905), Conrad struck the same note: 'it cannot be denied that A F apart from being a great master of prose is one of the finest minds of our time' (CL, III, p.288). The following day he expressed to Mrs Galsworthy both his delight at her approval of France's short story 'Abeille' and his 'admiration of Thaïs' (CL, III, p.289). A letter to the Galsworthys from Montpellier on 31 December 1906, shows how well versed Conrad was in France's works and the importance he attached to all of them: 'There's nothing new – except (an important exception) that I've discovered a vol. of Anatole France unknown to us – a work of his younger days' (Jean-Aubry suggests: 'Probably Les Désirs de

*Jean Servien'*) (*CL*, III, p. 394). On 14 March 1908, he told Davray that he was completing a short novel 'à peu près de la longueur de *l'Histoire comique* de France. Cela s'appellera Razumov' (*LF*, p. 92). At the end of the year, he reviewed *L'Ile des pingouins* (1908), congratulating its readers on the 'feast of wisdom' in store for them (*NLL*, p. 44), and also expressing his admiration for *La Vie littéraire* (1888–1892), a collection of France's fortnightly literary *causeries* written when he was literary editor of *Le Temps*. Echoing France's own definition of the critic's task, he said that this work describes 'the adventures of a choice soul amongst masterpieces' (*NLL*, p. 41). During the last months of 1908 and the first half of 1909, Conrad wrote *A Personal Record* in which he called France 'the most eloquent and just of French prose writers' (p. 95). And when, in August 1919, *The Arrow of Gold* received adverse criticism from the press because such a book was unexpected from the author of *Lord Jim*, Conrad consoled himself with a memory of France, pointing out to his agent, J. B. Pinker, 'that when Anatole France wrote his *Lys Rouge* (something that nobody expected him to write) the reception by the press was very much in the same note; yet my copy, bought some time in the middle of the nineties, is of the twenty-seventh edition' (*LL*, II, p. 227).[52] Curle has left this recollection of Conrad's appreciation of the French writer towards the end of his life: 'I do not suppose that he thought that Anatole France [... was] in the first flight of creative artists, but he delighted in [his] beautiful clarity; [his] gift, seemed to him, within its scope, practically beyond criticism.'[53]

The wealth of evidence of Conrad's profound involvement with many French writers, particularly with the three just discussed, suggests a closer bond than mere admiration. In fact it has gradually become clear over the past two decades that Conrad not only drew inspiration from these writers, but imitated and even borrowed from them on an impressive scale. The time is due for a systematic and chronological examination of that debt, thereby helping us to understand Conrad's amazingly complex method of composition and the true nature of his originality.

# Part II

## Conrad's debt to French authors: description, style, psychology, philosophy and criticism

'Artists and philosophers [...] do not live in isolation, but breathe a common air, and catch light and heat from each other's thoughts.'

Walter Pater, *The Renaissance*, p. xiv

# 2    The early fiction

## Almayer's Folly

Ford recalled having seen 'the copy of *Madame Bovary*' from which Conrad had not only translated passages when at sea but 'upon the end papers and margins of which *Almayer's Folly* was begun'.[1] Whatever the truth of this statement, there are many similarities beween the two novels in subject matter and treatment which indicate an undeniable influence. Both protagonists, essentially mediocre people, suffer from the curse of an over-fertile imagination which isolates them in grandiose visions of a life at odds with what could reasonably be expected from their changeless, dreary and oppressive environment. Both are the victims of that form of 'bêtise' consisting of a fundamental delusion about oneself, which Jules de Gaultier called 'bovarysme'.[2] The theme of Romantic illusion, the 'bovarysme' of Emma and Almayer, represents a major point of contact beween Conrad and Flaubert. In response to Garnett's criticism of chapters 11 and 12 of *An Outcast of the Islands*, Conrad explained on 15 March 1895 that Willems was lying buried under his 'pet theory', which, as a previous remark suggests ('truth is no more immortal than any other delusion' (*CL*, I, p. 205)) refers to his view of man as a victim of his own illusions, a theme which is central in Conrad's work as it is in Flaubert's.

There exist also between *Almayer's Folly* and *Madame Bovary* a number of minor similarities some of which are worth recording, not on account of their intrinsic importance but because they illustrate the important part literary models played in the elaboration of Conrad's fiction from the very beginning, long before he came under the artistic and financial pressures that resulted from his becoming a professional novelist. If, as Guerard suggests, the description of Almayer's father grumbling 'all day at the stupidity of native gardeners' (p. 5) may be a faint echo of Emma's similar complaint: 'Mais le jardinier qu'ils avaient n'y entendait rien; on était si mal servi' (p. 30),[3] a stronger echo can be heard when Almayer shows some naval officers round his new house. Although it is empty, open to the wind and neglected, 'surrounded by a circle of glittering uniforms, [he] stamped his foot to show *the solidity of the* neatly-fitting *floors* and *expatiated upon* the beauties and convenience *of the building*' (pp. 35–6). During the visit the Bovarys, Homais and Léon make to the new flax-mill, which looks derelict before it is finished, Homais, undeterred by the fact that nothing could have been less 'curieux que cette curiosité', keeps talking: '*Il expliquait à la compagnie* l'importance future *de cet établissement*, supputait *la force des planchers*' (pp. 140–1). Nina's perception when, listening to her mother's recital of the deeds of the men of her race, she sees 'the narrow mantle of civilized morality [. . .] fall away and leave her shivering and *helpless* as if on the edge of some deep and *unknown abyss*' (p. 42), looks like a reminiscence of the passage where Emma, after her fruitless attempt to raise money in Rouen, feels forsaken by everything within and around her: 'Elle se sentait *perdue*, roulant au hasard dans des *abîmes indéfinissables*' (p. 413). And as Baines points out, after the elopement of his daughter, 'Almayer comes to resemble Charles Bovary after the death of Emma; there is the same helpless grief leading to a rapid decline and an undignified death on the last page'.[4]

There are, of course, important differences between the two novels. Many of them can be attributed to the fact that, as Watt states, *Almayer's Folly* portrays 'a markedly later stage of the vulgarisation of the theme', in which 'the will and the poetry which inspire Emma Bovary have dwindled into Almayer's dream of enviable consumer status'.[5] It seems appropriate to mention, in this connection, two novels by Maupassant which may also have played a part in the shaping of Conrad's conception of his subject – *Une vie*[6] and *Bel-Ami*. In fact, it could be argued that in some ways *Almayer's Folly* is closer to Maupassant's *Une vie* than to *Madame Bovary:* both novels share the theme of disillusionment which materializes in the downward trajectories of Jeanne's and Almayer's lives; both protagonists are essentially passive, doing very little towards the realization of their dreams, and showing nothing of that strength of purpose which animates Emma. Watt notes that the context in Amiel 'establishes the epigraph as more appropriate to Conrad's youthful romantic reveries than to Almayer's more material aspirations'.[7] It would be very appropriate, however, to Jeanne's romantic reveries, and would illuminate the theme of disillusionment which is explored in what claims to be – as the subtitle makes clear – 'the humble truth' of a life. The presence of *Une vie* in Conrad's mind could well account for this confusion.

The debasement of the Flaubertian theme is further manifest in the parallel which Paul Kirschner[8] has drawn with Maupassant's *Bel-Ami*: both Emma and Jeanne dream of great love, and so does Georges Duroy but primarily as a means of obtaining his main goal – wealth and power. In the evenings, as he leans out of the window of his squalid room overlooking the gare des Batignolles and watches the trains on their way to the sea, he imagines 'une aventure d'amour magnifique qui l'amenait, d'un seul coup, à la réalisation de son espérance. Il épousait la fille d'un banquier ou d'un grand seigneur recontrée dans la rue et conquise à première vue' (pp. 58–9). The 'shrill whistle' of a train waking him from his dream finds its equivalent in Conrad's opening: '"Kaspar! Makan!" The well-known shrill voice startled Almayer from his dream of splendid future into the unpleasant realities of the present hour.' (p. 3) Then, Almayer's 'dream of wealth and power' parallels Duroy's as he leans at sunset on the balustrade of his decaying house, watching an uprooted tree floating down to the sea. (*Kirschner, p. 207).

It is not arbitrary to bring Maupassant into the discussion. When Conrad wrote, after Almayer has had an angry scene with Nina, that *The sense of his absolute loneliness came home to his heart with a force that made him shudder'* (p. 102), he was probably echoing the passage from *Mont-Oriol* where Maupassant describes the feelings of Christiane Andermatt, abandoned by her lover: 'Et cette lune perdue dans ce ciel désert, et ce faible son perdu dans la nuit muette, *lui jetèrent au coeur une telle émotion de solitude qu'elle se mit à sangloter'* (p. 144). The French 'lui jetèrent au coeur' seems to be responsible for the unusual wording 'came home to his heart'. Also, when Nina is described fastening her eyes on Dain's in *'one of those long looks* that are a woman's most terrible weapon; a look [...] *that penetrates into the innermost recesses of the being'* (p. 171), one recognizes, despite the difference in meaning, the source of the italicized words in a similar scene from *Une vie* where Jeanne and Julien search deeply into each other's eyes: 'Ils se regardèrent d'*un de ces regards fixes*, aigus, *pénétrants*, où deux âmes croient se mêler. Ils se cherchèrent dans leurs yeux, derrière leurs yeux, *dans cet inconnu impénétrable de l'être'* (p. 78).[9]

As for Flaubert's influence on *Almayer's Folly*, it was not confined to *Madame Bovary*, as has always been assumed, but also included *L'Education sentimentale*. The scene when Dain sees Nina for the first time is certainly modelled on the first encounters between Frédéric Moreau and Madame Arnoux. Frédéric's famous first sight of her is as follows:

> Ce fut comme une *apparition*:
> Elle était assise, au milieu du banc, toute seule; ou du moins il ne distingua personne, dans *l'éblouissement* que lui envoyèrent ses yeux. En même temps qu'il passait, elle leva la tête; *il fléchit* involontairement *les épaules*                    (*ES*, p. 6)

When they part at the end of the journey, Frédéric 'lui envoya *un regard où il avait tâché de mettre* toute son âme' (p. 11). Later, when visiting her, he first sees her in shadow: 'par l'autre portière, Mme Arnoux parut. Comme *elle se trouvait enveloppée d'ombre*, il ne distingua d'abord que sa tête' (p. 65). After the meal, they exchange a few words in the salon and Frédéric 'regardait attentivement *les effilés de sa coiffure, caressant par le bout son épaule nue; et il n'en détachait pas ses yeux*, il enfonçait son âme dans la blancheur de cette chair féminine' (p. 69). At the end of the reception, she holds out her hand to him and with this contact *'il éprouva comme une pénétration à tous les atomes de sa peau'* (p. 70). Most of these details are found in Conrad: Nina appears to Dain after lifting a curtain and she 'now stood in full light, *framed in the dark background* of the passage', Dain 'struck by the beauty of the unexpected *apparition had bent low'*. He straightens himself and Nina looks at his face as it appears under 'the folds of a blue turban, *whose fringed ends hung gracefully over the left shoulder*'. The first surprise over, she sees his '*eyes fixed upon her* with such an uncontrolled expression of admiration and desire that *she felt* a hitherto unknown feeling of shyness, mixed with alarm and some delight, *enter and penetrate her whole being*'. Dain, '*dazzled* by the unexpected vision', forgets Almayer, his brig, his escort and 'all things else'. On parting, he again bends low '*trying to convey in a* last *glance* towards the girl the bold expression of his overwhelming admiration' (pp. 54–6).

These echoes in chapter 4 of *Almayer's Folly* are revealing. Conrad asserted to Walpole that he had read *Madame Bovary* 'only after finishing' his first novel, adding 'as I did all the other works of Flaubert' (*LL*, II, p. 206). John Dozier Gordan says that 'Apparently [Conrad] began the fifth chapter while staying with his uncle in the Polish Ukraine in the late winter of 1890'.[10] It now begins to seem that Conrad admired and imitated *L'Education sentimentale* before that date.[11]

In that context, the following parallel is also noteworthy. As a dejected Frédéric walks aimlessly one night in the streets of Paris, he suddenly contemplates his ruined hopes of a year earlier:

Toutes [ses espérances] étaient mortes, maintenant!

Des nues sombres couraient sur la face de la lune. Il la contempla, en rêvant à la grandeur des espaces, à la misère de la vie, au néant de tout. Le jour parut; *ses dents claquaient*; et, à moitié endormi, mouillé par le brouillard et *tout plein de larmes, il se demanda pourquoi n'en pas finir*? Rien qu'un mouvement à faire! Le poids de son front l'entraînait, *il voyait son cadavre flottant sur l'eau*; Frédéric se pencha. Le parapet était un peu large, et ce fut par *lassitude* qu'il n'essaya pas de le franchir.

*Une épouvante le saisit.* Il regagna les boulevards et s'affaissa sur un banc.

(*ES*, p. 110)

When Almayer thinks he has identified Dain in the mutilated body brought in by the tide, with the collapse of his hopes he sinks into 'the utter abandonment of despair':

A dead Malay; he had seen many dead Malays without any emotion; and now *he felt inclined to weep*, but it was over the fate of a white man he knew; a man that fell over a deep precipice and did not die. *He seemed somehow to himself to be standing on one side, a little way off, looking at a certain Almayer* who was in great trouble. Poor, poor fellow! Why doesn't he cut his throat? He wished to encourage him; he was very anxious to see him lying dead over that other corpse. *Why does he not die and end this suffering?* He groaned aloud unconsciously and *started with affright* at the sound of his own voice. Was he going mad? Terrified by the thought he turned away and ran towards his house [...]

Almayer felt *very tired* now, as if he had come from a long journey. [...] He took the tumbler with a shaking hand, and as he drank *his teeth chattered* against the glass

(*AF*, pp. 99–100)

We witness here Flaubert's impact on Conrad, at the outset of his career, as regards the duality of the self, a theme which became prominent throughout his fiction and which is also recurrent in *Madame Bovary*. For instance, when Charles is riding to Les Bertaux, half asleep, 'lui-même se percevait double' (p. 16), at once student and husband, lying in his bed and going through a wardful of patients. Moreover, Flaubert's influence here must have been strengthened by Maupassant's (see Kirschner, pp. 208–11).

## An Outcast of the Islands

During the composition of his second novel, *An Outcast of the Islands* (August 1894–September 1895), Conrad turned for assistance to Flaubert, Maupassant, and possibly Loti, in a variety of scenes dealing with sexual relationship, moral isolation or death.

Lawrence Thornton has pointed out that 'the capsule history' of Charles's family in the first chapter of *Madame Bovary* served as a model for the rapid retrospective view of Almayer's youth in the opening of *Almayer's Folly* (p. 5), and for the following passage presenting Willems's interior monologue about his wife at the beginning of *An Outcast*:

His wife! He winced inwardly. A dismal woman with startled eyes and dolorously drooping mouth, that would listen to him in pained wonder and *mute stillness*. She was used to those night-discourses now. *She had rebelled once* – at the beginning. Only once. Now, while he sprawled in the long chair and drank and talked, she would stand at the further end of the table, her hands resting on the edge, her frightened eyes watching his lips, without a sound, without a stir, hardly breathing, till he dismissed her with a contemptuous: 'Go to bed, dummy.' She would draw a long breath then and trail out of the room, relieved but unmoved. Nothing could startle her, make her scold or make her cry. She did not complain, she did not rebel. *(OI, p. 9)*

Sa femme avait été folle de lui autrefois; elle l'avait aimé avec mille servilités qui l'avaient détaché d'elle encore davantage. Enjouée jadis, expansive et tout aimante, elle était, en vieillissant, devenue (à la façon du vin éventé qui se tourne en vinaigre) d'humeur difficile, piaillarde, nerveuse. Elle avait tant souffert, sans se plaindre, d'abord, quand elle le voyait courir après toutes les gotons de village et que vingt mauvais lieux le lui renvoyaient le soir, blasé et puant l'ivresse! Puis *l'orgueil s'était révolté*. Alors elle s'était tue, avalant sa rage dans *un stoïcisme muet*, qu'elle garda jusqu'à sa mort. Elle était sans cesse en courses, en affaires [...] tandis que, sans s'inquiéter de rien, Monsieur, continuellement engourdi dans une somnolence boudeuse dont il ne se réveillait que pour lui dire des choses désobligeantes, restait à fumer au coin du feu, en crachant dans les cendres. *(MB, pp. 6–7)*

Thornton notes that in both cases Conrad failed in his imitations because they lack the richness, the 'ironic and tonal density' of the original.[12]

Conrad made use of *Madame Bovary* again by closely modelling the scene between Willems and Aïssa as their hands touch for the first time on the farewell between Emma and Léon when he leaves Yonville for Rouen:

*Lorsque le moment fut venu* des embrassades, Mme Homais pleura [...].
Quand il fut au haut de l'escalier, il s'arrêta, tant *il se sentait hors d'haleine.* [...]
Elle se détourna, le menton baissé et *le front en avant.* La lumière y glissait comme sur
un marbre, jusqu'à la courbe des sourcils, sans que l'on pût savoir ce qu'Emma *regardait
à l'horizon* ni ce qu'elle pensait au fond d'elle-même.
– Allons, adieu! soupira-t-il.
Elle releva sa tête d'un mouvement brusque:
– Oui, adieu..., partez!
Ils s'avancèrent l'un vers l'autre; il tendit la main, elle hésita.
– A l'anglaise donc, fit-elle, abandonnant la sienne, tout en s'efforçant de rire.
Léon *la sentit entre ses doigts,* et la substance même de *tout son être lui semblait descendre
dans cette paume humide.*
Puis *il ouvrit la main; leurs yeux se recontrèrent* encore, et il disparut.
(*MB*, pp. 164–6)

*When the* longed for *day came* at last, when she [...] *took his hand in hers,* he sat up
suddenly [...]. *All his blood, all his sensation, all his life seemed to rush into that hand*
leaving him without strength, in a cold shiver, in the sudden *clamminess* and collapse as
of a deadly gun-shot wound. *He flung her hand away* brutally [...] and sat motionless,
*his head fallen forward, staring on the ground and catching his breath in painful gasps.* [...]
Her face was grave and *her eyes looked* seriously *at him.*                      (*OI*, p. 77)

The telling link between the two scenes lies in the typically Flaubertian
perception, finely analysed by Jean-Pierre Richard, that 'desire "induces a
mellow limpness"', it makes one's being flow outwards'. In Willems the contact
with the loved one produces the same 'liquefying weakness'.[13]

Later, still dealing with the presentation of the Willems-Aïssa relationship,
Conrad recalled scenes from Maupassant's story 'Fou?' and from *Bel-Ami*. In
'Fou?', a jealous man describes his tortured feelings upon discovering that the
passion of the woman he loves has been transferred to a horse on which she
excitedly runs wild in the country:

J'avais compris! *j'étais* jaloux maintenant du cheval nerveux et galopant; *jaloux du vent
qui caressait son visage* quand elle allait d'une course folle; *jaloux des feuilles qui baisaient,*
en passant, *ses oreilles; des gouttes de soleil qui lui tombaient sur le front* à travers les branches
(*Mademoiselle Fifi*, p. 121)

When Almayer tells Willems, who has been deprived of Aïssa for a few days,
that he can come back if he wishes, Willems passionately exclaims: '*Do you
think I am mad?*' (Maupassant's character asks '*Dites-moi, suis-je fou?*') and
continues:

Without her! Man! What are you made of? To think that she moves, lives, breathes out
of my sight. *I am jealous of the wind that fans her,* of the air she breathes, *of the earth that
receives the caress of her foot, of the sun that looks at her* now while I... I haven't seen her
for two days – two days.                                                         (*OI*, p. 90)

And, just as Maupassant's character refers to '*la pointe rose et mouillée de sa langue* qui palpitait *comme* celle d'un reptile' (p. 117), so Willems's tongue is depicted, as he runs it over his swollen lips after being struck by Lingard, as '*a tongue whose pink and moist end* ran here and there, *like* something independently alive' (p. 266).

In *Bel-Ami*, when Duroy realizes that, to satisfy his ambition, he should have married Suzanne Walter, his director's daughter, instead of Madeleine, he decides to alter the situation and criticizes her suitor. Surprised, she asks him what the matter is; he then replies, '*comme si on lui eût arraché* un secret du fond du coeur', that he is jealous. In a severe tone, she tells him that he is mad; to this he retorts:

– *Je le sais bien que je suis fou.* Est-ce que je devrais vous avouer cela, moi, un homme marié, à vous, une jeune fille? Je suis plus que fou, je suis coupable, presque misérable. Je n'ai pas d'espoir possible, et *je perds la raison à cette pensée. Et quand j'entends dire que* vous allez vous marier, j'ai des accès de fureur à tuer quelqu'un. Il faut me pardonner ça, Suzanne!
*Il se tut.* [...]
Il se retourna brusquement vers elle, et il lui dit ...
– Si j'étais libre, moi, m'épouseriez-vous?
Elle répondit [...]:
– Oui, Bel-Ami [...].
Il se leva, et balbutiant:
– Merci ..., merci ..., je vous en supplie, ne dites 'oui' à personne! Attendez encore un peu. Je vous en supplie! Me le promettez-vous?
Elle murmura [...]:
– *Je vous le promets.*
Du Roy [...] s'enfuit, *comme s'il eût perdu la tête*, sans dire adieu.  (*BA*, pp. 512–14)

Conrad drew inspiration from this exchange when Willems explains his betrayal to Lingard and begs to be taken away from Aïssa:

He laughed. His laugh *seemed to be torn out from him* against his will [...].
'When I think that when I first knew her it seemed to me that my whole life wouldn't be enough to ... And now when I look at her! She did it all. *I must have been mad. I was mad.* Every time I look at her I remember my madness. *It frightens me... And when I think that* of all my life, of all my past, of all my future, of my intelligence, of my work, there is nothing left but she, the cause of my ruin, and you whom I have mortally offended...'
He hid his face for a moment in his hands, and when he took them away he had lost the appearance of comparative calm and *gave way to a wild distress.*
'Captain Lingard... anything... a deserted island... anywhere... *I promise...*'
'Shut up!' shouted Lingard, roughly.
*He became dumb*                                                           (*OI*, p. 274)

Baines's assertion that 'to no artist has isolation seemed so starkly to be a necessary condition of existence as it did to Conrad'[14] might be true were it not for the fact that this equally applies to that other 'eternal solitary', Maupassant, for whom 'the fundamental fact of human existence was "the black solitude of the heart, which rocks and deceives itself with dreams until death"'.[15] Indeed, in this respect, Maupassant had a strong impact on Conrad from the outset of his career.[16]

Among the many Maupassant characters who are a prey to invincible loneliness, one of the most prominent is the elderly poet Norbert de Varenne in *Bel-Ami*. In the course of a melancholy monologue, he confides to Duroy:

> *La solitude*, aujourd'hui, m'emplit d'une angoisse horrible: la solitude dans le logis, auprès du feu, le soir. Il me semble alors que je suis seul sur la terre, *affreusement seul*, mais *entouré* de dangers vagues, *de choses inconnues et terribles*; et *la cloison* qui me sépare de mon voisin que je ne connais pas, m'éloigne de lui autant que des étoiles aperçues par ma fenêtre. [...] le silence des *murs* m'épouvante.                    (*BA*, p. 212)

This passage (which Conrad used again in 'The Return') must have inspired his portrayal of Willems and Aïssa in part V, chapter 3, the chapter in *An Outcast of the Islands* for which he drew most heavily on Maupassant:

> Those two, *surrounded* each *by* the impenetrable *wall* of their aspirations, were *hopelessly alone*, out of sight, out of earshot of each other; each the centre of dissimilar and distant horizons; standing each on a different earth, under a different sky.    (*OI*, pp. 333–4)

Strongly influenced by Schopenhauer, Maupassant held the view that 'Miroir des choses et miroir des faits, chaque être humain devient un petit univers dans l'univers!' ('Un Fou', *Monsieur Parent*, p. 165).[17] He attributed our isolation to the limitations of our senses and to that 'little accident' called thought (*L'Inutile beauté*, p. 28) which is 'unfathomable' (*Monsieur Parent*, p. 264), and in many stories he explored the theme of a human being's inability ever to penetrate the mind of another, however near in affection they may be. In desperate attempts to understand each other, characters sometimes gaze long and deeply into each other's eyes, as do Duroy and Madeleine in *Bel-Ami*:

> Il s'arrêta en face d'elle; et ils demeurèrent de nouveau quelques instants *les yeux dans les yeux*, s'efforçant d'aller jusqu'à l'impénétrable secret de leurs coeurs, *de se sonder jusqu'au vif de la pensée*. Ils tâchaient de se voir à nu la conscience en une interrogation ardente et muette: *lutte* intime *de deux êtres* qui, vivant côte à côte, s'ignorent toujours [...].                    (*BA*, p. 466)

> Elle le regarda encore d'*un regard perçant*.[...] il évitait maintenant l'oeil pénétrant de sa femme.                    (*BA*, p. 470)

These passages, which inspired similar exchanges in 'The Return', also lie behind a scene between Willems and Aïssa:

> She stepped back, keeping her distance, *her eyes on his face*, watching on it the play of his doubts and of his hopes with *a piercing gaze, that seemed to search out the innermost recesses of his thought* [...]. He followed her [...] till at last *they* both *stopped, facing each*

*other* under the big tree of the enclosure. [...] He seemed to look on [...] as if moved [...] to screen this *struggle of two human hearts*                                    (*OI*, p. 154)

Such attempts, however, are doomed to failure, for love, in Maupassant and Conrad, proves no more effective in dispelling solitude than all the other illusions with which they see human beings trying to deceive themselves.

Kirschner has shown that Conrad was also receptive to Maupassant's ideas on mortality, expressed in Norbert de Varenne's melancholy reflections:

Il arrive un jour, voyez-vous, et il arrive de bonne heure pour beaucoup, où c'est fini de rire, comme on dit, parce que *derrière tout ce qu'on regarde, c'est la mort qu'on aperçoit.* [...]
Moi, maintenant, *je la vois de si près que j'ai souvent envie d'étendre les bras pour la repousser. Elle couvre la terre et emplit l'espace. Je la découvre partout.* [...]
*Elle me gâte tout ce que je fais, tout ce que je vois, ce que je mange et ce que je bois,* tout ce que j'aime, les clairs de lune, *les levers de soleil,* la grande mer, les belles rivières, et *l'air des soirs d'été,* si doux à respirer!                                              (*BA*, pp. 207, 209)

Still in part V, chapter 3, Willems experiences in the jungle the same sensation of the overwhelming nearness of death:

No! he was not alone, *he saw death looking at him from everywhere*; from the bushes, from the clouds – he heard *her* speaking to him in the murmur of the river, *filling the space,* touching his heart, his brain with a cold hand. *He could see and think of nothing else. He saw it – the sure death – everywhere. He saw it so close that he was always on the point of throwing out his arms to keep it off. It poisoned all he saw, all he did; the* miserable *food he ate, the* muddy *water he drank; it gave a frightful aspect to sunrises* and sunsets, to the brightness of hot noon, to the cooling shadows of the evenings.
                                               (*OI*, pp. 330–1; *Kirschner, pp. 199–200)

Conrad's borrowings do not stop here: the poet tells Duroy that the individual is alone in the face of death, that he can expect no help from any quarter:

– Mais aussi vous sentirez l'effroyable détresse des désespérés. Vous vous débattrez, éperdu, noyé, dans les incertitudes. *Vous crierez 'à l'aide' de tous les côtés, et personne ne vous répondra. Vous tendrez les bras, vous appellerez pour être secouru, aimé, consolé, sauvé! et personne ne viendra.*                                              (*BA*, p. 210)

Willems's feelings of helplessness and isolation are expressed in identical terms:

For the second time in his life he felt, in a sudden sense of his insignificance, the need to send a cry for help into the wilderness, and for the second time he realized the hopelessness of its unconcern. *He could shout for help on every side – and nobody would answer. He could stretch out his hands, he could call for aid, for support, for sympathy, for relief – and nobody would come.* Nobody. There was no one there – but that woman.
                                                                            (*OI*, p. 337)

Duroy is shocked by the mental picture conjured up by de Varenne: '*Il lui semblait qu'on venait de lui montrer quelque trou plein d'ossements, un trou inévitable où il lui faudrait tomber un jour'* (pp. 212–13). Willems, unable to break out of his isolation, has a similar presentiment of his end:

And, all at once, *it seemed to him that he was peering into a* sombre hollow, into a deep black *hole full of* decay and of whitened *bones; into an* immense and *inevitable grave* full of corruption *where sooner or later he must, unavoidably, fall.*                      (*OI*, p. 339)

And just as the poet had paused, thought for a few seconds, and then said with a weary and resigned air: *'Moi, je suis un être perdu'* (p. 211), Willems, after a time, murmurs with conviction 'speaking half aloud to himself in the shock of the penetrating thought: *"I am a lost man"'* (p. 340).

In the same chapter of *An Outcast* certain details seem to have their origin in 'Yvette', another work by Maupassant which Conrad admired greatly (cf. *NLL*, p. 30). Young Yvette, who has decided to commit suicide, suddenly visualizes her body in a state of putrefaction; the sunshine and the bustle of life around her make her aware that her death will change nothing and sadden no one:

*Morte! Je ne parlerai plus, je ne penserai plus,* personne ne me verra plus. Et moi *je ne verrai plus rien* de tout cela! [...]
Elle regarda son lit, et il lui sembla qu'*elle se voyait étendue,* blanche comme ses draps.
– *Morte.* Dans huit jours, cette figure, ces yeux, ces joues ne seront plus qu'une *pourriture* noire, dans une boîte, au fond de la terre. [...]
*Le clair soleil* tombait à flots sur la campagne et l'air doux du matin entrait par la fenêtre.
Elle s'assit, pensant à cela: Morte. – C'était comme si le monde allait disparaître pour elle; mais non, puisque *rien ne serait changé* dans ce monde, pas même sa chambre. Oui, sa chambre *resterait* toute pareille avec le même lit, les mêmes chaises, la même toilette, mais elle serait partie pour toujours, elle, *et personne ne serait triste,* que sa mère peut-être.
On dirait: 'Comme elle était jolie! cette petite Yvette', voilà tout. Et [...] elle songea de nouveau à cette pourriture, à cette bouillie noire et puante que ferait sa chair.
                                                                  (*Yvette*, pp. 115–17)

Like her, Willems visualizes himself dead, 'rotting slowly', and he, too, realizes that his disappearance will make no difference in the world and that he is doomed to oblivion:

After he had miserably died there, *all this would remain,* would live, would exist in *joyous sunlight,* would breathe in the coolness of serene nights. What for, then? *He would be dead. He would be stretched* upon the warm moisture of the ground, *feeling nothing, seeing nothing, knowing nothing;* he would lie stiff, passive, *rotting* slowly [...] till there would remain nothing but the white gleam of bleaching bones in the long grass [...]. There would be that only left of him; *nobody would miss him;* no one would remember him.
                                                                  (*OI*, pp. 331–2)

Finally, two passages show Conrad being inspired by Maupassant's descriptions of nature, a flight of birds in *Une vie* and a description of the night in *Bel-Ami*:

Lorsqu'elle [Jeanne] était loin du rivage, elle se mettait sur le dos, [...] les yeux perdus dans *l'azur* profond du ciel *que traversait vite un vol* d'hirondelle, ou la silhouette *blanche d'un oiseau* de mer.                                                                    (*UV*, p. 28)

Willems [...] threw himself down in the grass by the side of the brook [...]. The clear gap of *blue* above his head *was crossed by the quick flight of white* rice-*birds*   (*OI*, p. 74)

Paris était presque désert cette nuit-là, une nuit froide, *une de ces nuits qu'on dirait plus vastes que les autres, où les étoiles sont plus hautes, où l'air semble apporter dans ses souffles* glacés quelque chose venu *de plus loin que les astres*.                   (*BA*, p. 205)

*It was one of those nights that give the impression of extreme vastness, when the sky seems higher, when the passing puffs of tepid breeze seem to bring with them faint whispers from beyond the stars.*                                                                       (*OI*, pp. 336–7)

Although I have found no external evidence that Conrad had read Loti's *Le Roman d'un spahi* (1881), there are enough notable parallels between this novel and *An Outcast of the Islands* to suggest that he derived valuable hints from it, whether in respect of characterization, atmosphere or the treatment of certain themes.

As though under a magic spell, the two protagonists Jean Peyral and Willems become infatuated with a woman of a different race with whom they have nothing in common. As a result, they find themselves cut off from their own kind: for two years in the case of Peyral who is doing his national service in Senegal; in Willems's case forever. They each experience the same feeling of finality as they watch a boat going away, which signifies the end of their hope of returning to civilization: Peyral feels that 'c'était fini de lui' (p. 190) and later that 'sa vie était brisée' (p. 268); Lingard says to Willems: 'your life is finished' (p. 277) and, as Willems watches him go, he wants 'to call back his very life that was going away from him' (p. 281). In each case the spell is broken and the man's feeling towards the woman (Fatou-gaye or Aïssa) is one of horror followed by an intense desire to be left alone: 'il lui vint au coeur [...] une affreuse angoisse, dans laquelle il y avait [...] de la rage contre Fatou-gaye, de *l'horreur* pour la présence de cette fille noire, et comme un besoin de la chasser loin de lui; [...] il partit en courant sur les dunes [...] *pour être seul*' (pp. 190–1); '[Aïssa] clasped him round the neck [...]. He stiffened himself in repulsion, in *horror*, in the mysterious revolt of his heart [...]. "Don't follow me!" he shouted. "I want *to be alone* – I mean *to be left alone!*"' (pp. 285–6).

Peyral and Willems come to feel complete detachment and indifference, and looking back they both experience revulsion for the physical intoxication that had carried them away. This feeling of disgust stems partly from the conviction of the superiority of their white skins: after breaking off with Fatou-gaye, Peyral feels that he has regained 'sa dignité *d'homme blanc*, souillée par le contact de cette chair noire' (p. 245, original emphasis); Willems begs Lingard to take him away from Aïssa shouting 'I am white! All white!' thus 'proclaiming [...] his pure and superior descent' (p. 271).

Escape becomes the main concern of the 'outcasts'. Powerless to achieve it, they embellish in dreams the simple things of civilization: Peyral sees his return to his humble village 'sous des couleurs d'apothéose' (pp. 253–4); Willems hankers after 'the superior land of refined delights' (p. 329). Finally, both men die violent deaths, Peyral stabbed in the chest, Willems shot in the chest: 'Un jet de sang rose sortit de sa bouche [...] sa poitrine se dilatait comme pour *aspirer* plus d'air' (pp. 319–20); 'he stood *aspiring* in his nostrils the acrid smell of the blue smoke [...]. His mouth was full of something salt and warm' (p. 360). (Note the gallicism 'aspiring', apparently from Loti.)

There are also striking similarities in the cunning way the two native women enslave their man, in their worshipful attitude towards him, in the bafflement and despair each feels when he turns away and spurns her. They even have in common identical gestures: Fatou, realizing her fate is in the balance, falls on her knees '*enlaçant de ses bras les jambes* du spahi, et *se faisant traîner* par lui' (p. 187); in an attempt to hold Lingard away from Willems, Aïssa flings herself on the ground: '*She trailed* face downwards, *clinging to his leg with both arms* in a tenacious hug' (p. 261).

The themes of exile, solitude, and death form another important link between the two works. Peyral is described as in 'exil' (p. 191), 'abandonné', 'seul au monde' (p. 267), 'isolé', 'perdu' (p. 284); Willems, the outcast, is 'alone, small, crushed' (p. 329). In one scene Loti sees his protagonists as '*ces trois êtres jeunes et abandonnés*' (p. 187); Conrad also describes Willems, Aïssa and the old woman who lives with them as '*those three human beings abandoned* by all' (p. 328). Both authors stress the futility of human life seen against a meaningless death at the end of the road: Loti asks of his dead soldiers: 'dans quelques années, qui s'en souviendra' (p. 158), and Peyral sees 'toutes ces destinées d'exilés, follement dépensées, et guettés par la mort' (p. 207); for Conrad, too, the goal man reaches after the struggle is 'an untruthful tombstone over a dark and soon forgotten grave' (p. 197).

Finally, both novels are pervaded by an atmosphere of demoralization and failure largely created by the feelings of a European in an alien environment: note the similar evocation of the oppressive stillness of tropical nature in the following passages:

Et Jean regardait mélancoliquement les solitudes qui passaient après les solitudes. [...] des plaines maudites [...] lui causaient une impression pénible, un indéfinissable serrement de coeur [...].

Sur les rives mornes, par-ci par-là, marchaient gravement de grands vautours noirs ou quelques marabouts chauves rappelant des silhouettes humaines. – Quelquefois un singe curieux écartait des broussailles de palétuviers pour regarder filer le navire; – ou bien encore, d'une bouillée de roseaux, sortait une fine aigrette blanche, – un martin-pêcheur nuancé d'émeraude et de lapis, – dont le vol éveillait un caïman paresseux endormi sur la vase.

[...] de loin en loin passait un village, perdu dans cette grande désolation.

(*Le Roman d'un spahi*, pp. 277–8)

The water was gone, and he looked only at a curved track of mud – of mud soft and black, hiding fever, rottenness, and evil under its level and glazed surface. [...]

They slept or sat unmoving and patient. As the sun mounted higher the breeze died out, and perfect stillness reigned in the empty creek. A troop of long-nosed monkeys appeared, and crowding on the outer boughs, contemplated the boat and the motionless men in it with grave and sorrowful intensity, disturbed now and then by irrational outbreaks of mad gesticulation. A little bird with sapphire breast balanced a slender twig across a slanting beam of light, and flashed in it to and fro like a gem dropped from the sky. His minute round eye stared at the strange and tranquil creatures in the boat. After a while he sent out a thin twitter that sounded impertinent and funny in the solemn silence of the great wilderness; in the great silence full of struggle and death.

(*OI*, pp. 325–6)

Conrad's creative difficulty when handling love-themes may account for his probable exploitation of this novel for *An Outcast*. When he had little more than two characters in mind, Willems and Babalatchi, for what was then 'Two Vagabonds', he was lukewarm towards introducing a feminine interest; on 18 August 1894, he wrote to Mme Poradowska: 'Pensez Vous que l'on peut faire une chose intéréssante sans la femme?!' (*CL*, I, p. 170). During the months of September and October the story was almost at a standstill, and he complained to her: 'Il me manque des idées', 'Les idées ne viennent pas' (*CL*, I, pp. 173, 181). However, at the beginning of November, he described the action as 'chute, degringolade subite jusqu'a l'esclavage physique de l'homme par une femme absolument sauvage' (*CL*, I, p. 183). Although he goes on to say that he has come across this in his experience: 'J'ai vu ça!', he may have turned to *Le Roman d'un spahi*, a novel with the same basic theme, as a valuable artistic model, just as he relied on *Madame Bovary*, *Bel-Ami*, 'Fou?', 'Yvette', Alfred Wallace's *The Malay Archipelago*, the Brooke journals, and other travel books[18] to develop a story which, as he confessed, 'was never very near [my] heart' (*OI*, p. ix).

## 'The Idiots'

After laying aside *The Sisters* in March 1896,[19] Conrad took up a sea-story *The Rescuer*, but, in the following May, during his honeymoon in Brittany, he dropped the unmanageable fragment to write 'The Idiots', his first short story excepting 'The Black Mate'. Although his initial creative impetus was, as he pointed out, 'not mental but visual' (*TU*, p. vii) – consisting as it did of a brief encounter with some idiot children sprawling in a ditch on the road from Lannion to Ile Grande – the story is not, as Gordan believed, 'fundamentally the product of observation'.[20] Conrad himself hinted as much when, in the same note, he dismissed it as an 'obviously derivative piece of work' (p. vii). Indeed, it is very much a pastiche of Maupassant, Flaubert, and Zola.

Like Maupassant, who began more than half of his 300 short stories by setting up a frame in the form of a brief discussion or scene to introduce the main tale, Conrad begins with a narrator who describes his encounter with the idiots and explains how he managed to piece together their story. He then becomes an omniscient narrator, preserving, with rare intrusions of the Conradian voice, the detached stance of a typical Maupassant narrator. And the story ends in Maupassant fashion with a satirical coda on the themes of hypocrisy, selfishness and corruption in a meeting between Susan's ambitious mother and the intriguing Marquis de Chavanes.

'The Idiots' also reveals Conrad emulating Maupassant's atmospheric and symbolic presentation of landscape to set the stage for the ensuing drama and suggest the theme.[21] Milton Chaikin was the first to note the similarity between Conrad's description of autumn, where the chaos and violence of nature anticipate the human turmoil and tragedy that are later enacted, and the description of an autumn scene in *Une vie* which prefigures, by contrast with the beauty and excitement of the summer just evoked – a summer which has seen Jeanne's engagement, wedding and honeymoon – the desolation and emptiness awaiting her for the rest of her life:

Puis, après avoir regardé quelque temps le ciel où *roulaient des nuages sombres*, elle se décida à sortir. [...]

Les avenues *détrempées* par les continuelles averses d'automne s'allongeaient, couvertes d'un épais tapis de *feuilles mortes*, sous la maigreur grelottante des peupliers presque *nus*. Les branches grêles *tremblaient* au vent, agitant encore quelque feuillage prêt à s'égrener dans l'espace. Et sans cesse, tout le long du jour, comme une pluie incessante et triste à faire pleurer, ces dernières feuilles, toutes jaunes maintenant, pareilles à de larges sous d'or, se détachaient, *tournoyaient*, voltigeaient et tombaient.[...]

Les arbustes emmêlés, comme une dentelle de bois fin, heurtaient les unes aux autres leurs maigres branches; et le murmure des feuilles tombées et sèches que la brise poussait, remuait, amoncelait en tas par endroits, semblait un douloureux *soupir* d'agonie. [...]

Quelque chose l'appesantissait comme le pressentiment des longs ennuis de la vie monotone qui commençait.                                    (*UV*, pp. 118–19)

Autumn came. The clouded sky descended low upon the black contours of the hills; and the *dead leaves* danced in spiral *whirls* under *naked* trees, till the wind, *sighing* profoundly, laid them to rest in the hollows of bare valleys. And from morning till night one could see all over the land black denuded boughs, the boughs gnarled and twisted, as if contorted with pain, *swaying* sadly between the wet clouds and the *soaked* earth. The clear and gentle streams of summer days rushed discoloured and raging at the stones that barred the way to the sea, with the fury of madness bent upon suicide. [...]

And it seemed to him that [...] the earth [...] frowned at him like the *clouds, sombre and hurried* above his head.                                    (*TU*, pp. 70–1)[22]

Apart from bearing the seal of Maupassant, 'The Idiots', as Chaikin also pointed out, shows Conrad drawing from Emma Bovary's wedding procession and feast for his description of the procession and feast at Jean-Pierre Bacadou's wedding:

Les conviés arrivèrent de bonne heure dans des voitures [...] et les jeunes gens des villages les plus voisins dans des charrettes où ils se tenaient debout, en rang, les mains appuyées sur les ridelles pour ne pas tomber, allant au trot et secoués dur.

Jean-Pierre brought the two-wheeled spring-cart [...]. The gray horse galloped clumsily, and the bride and bridegroom, sitting side by side, were jerked backwards and forwards by the up and down motion of the shafts, in a manner regular and brusque.

Le cortège, d'abord uni [...] s'allongea bientôt et se coupa en *groupes* différents, *qui s'attardaient* à causer.

On the road the distanced wedding guests *straggled in* pairs and *groups*.

[Les messieurs] avaient des [...] habits-vestes très courts [...] dont les pans semblaient avoir été coupés à même un seul bloc, par la hache du charpentier.

The men advanced with heavy steps, swinging their idle arms. They were clad *in town clothes*; jackets cut with clumsy smartness, hard black hats, immense boots, polished highly.

Les dames, en bonnet, avaient des robes *à la façon de la ville*. [...] des pèlerines à bouts croisés dans la ceinture, ou de petits fichus de couleur attachés dans le dos avec une épingle.

Their women all in simple black, with white caps and shawls of faded tints folded triangularly on the back, strolled lightly by their side.

*Le ménétrier allait en tête* [...]; on entendait toujours *le crin-crin* du ménétrier qui continuait à jouer dans la campagne.

*In front the violin sang a strident tune.*

Le cortège, d'abord uni comme une seule *écharpe de couleur* qui ondulait dans la campagne, le long de *l'étroit sentier* serpentant entre les blés verts, s'allongea bientôt [...]. *Le bruit de l'instrument faisait partir de loin les petits oiseaux.*

The sombre procession drifted in and out of the *narrow lanes*, through sunshine and through shade, between fields and hedgerows, *scaring the little birds that darted away* in troops right and left.

C'était sous le hangar de la charretterie que la table était dressée.

In the yard of Bacadou's farm the *dark ribbon* wound itself up into a mass of men and women pushing at the door with cries and greetings.

Jusqu'au soir, on mangea. [Then follows the description of a Gargantuan feast lasting sixteen hours.]

The wedding dinner was remembered for months. It was a splendid feast in the orchard.

et toute la nuit, au clair de la lune, par
les routes du pays, il y eut des carrioles
emportées qui couraient au grand galop
[...].

Ceux qui restèrent aux Bertaux
passèrent la nuit à boire dans la cuisine.
Les enfants s'étaient endormis sous les
bancs.                         (*MB*, pp. 35–40)

Farmers of considerable means and
excellent repute were to be found
sleeping in ditches, all along the road to
Treguier, even as late as the afternoon of
the next day.                    (*TU*, pp. 59–60)

Two days after Emma's wedding, bride and groom leave Les Bertaux and
old Rouault accompanies them part of the way. As soon as he is alone, he is
overcome by sadness and 'les souvenirs tendres se mêlant aux pensées noires
dans sa cervelle *obscurcie par les vapeurs de la bombance, il eut bien envie* un
moment d'aller faire un tour du côté de *l'église*' (p. 42). Similarly, one night, as
Bacadou is driving through Ploumar 'some *obscure and drunken impulse* caused
him to pull up sharply opposite *the church*' (p. 68).

Thornton has shown that here again Conrad was 'not equal to the task of
recreating and particularizing' the material borrowed. Whereas Flaubert's
description of the procession gives us 'a genuine sense of excitement and color'
through the controlling metaphor of 'une seule écharpe de couleur' which first
undulates over the fields before it breaks up into different groups, and 'a sense
of humor' in the violin player's noise driving away the birds, Conrad's passage
has neither. The same applies to the description of the feast and its aftermath:
'with Flaubert's rendering of joyous drunkenness and careening carts fresh in
our minds, Conrad's imitation has about it all the excitement of a sentence in
a farmer's Almanac'. Thornton concludes that these early Conradian attempts
to reproduce Flaubert's magnificent rendering of things reveal that 'Phenomena
as phenomena is [sic] simply not in Conrad's stylistic range'.[23]

In 'The Idiots' the main textual indebtedness is not, however, to Flaubert
or Maupassant but, as was also revealed by Chaikin, to Zola's *La Terre* (1886)
and *La Joie de vivre* (1884).[24]

The connection between *La Terre*[25] and 'The Idiots' is noticeable in their
opening descriptions of the land:

*les* molles *ondulations de cette terre*
(p. 368).

*the undulating surface of the land.* (p. 56)

*les terres* nues, *jaunes* et fortes, *des* grands
*carrés* de labour, *qui alternaient avec les*
*nappes vertes* des luzernes et des trèfles;
(p. 367)

*The* small *fields*, [...] *lay in rectangular*
*patches of* vivid *greens and yellows* (p. 56)

*Au milieu, une route,* [...] *d'une blancheur*
*de craie, s'en allait* (p. 368)

And the landscape *was divided in two by*
*the white streak of a road stretching* (p. 56)

Both works share, as a major theme, the peasant's passionate attachment to the land, the fertility of which is emphasized repeatedly. On his return from the army, Bacadou is pained to find the farm work so neglected, and manages to persuade his old father to let him take over, arguing that it is not for himself: 'It is for the land. It's a pity to see it badly used' (p. 59). The same situation occurs in *La Terre*, with old Fouan being forced to give up his land to his children because, as he confesses, it hurts him to see 'cette bonne terre qui se gâte' (p. 383). Zola's characters fight fiercely for the land among themselves; Bacadou's father foresees the same enmity between his twin grandsons: 'They will quarrel over the land' (p. 61). Confronted with the crushing immensity and immortality of the land, the peasant is filled with a great desire for continuity and fiercely wants to keep his property within the family. The worst tragedy that can befall him is to be without a son to carry on after him, as is the case with Hourdequin, whose son is a Captain, and Bacadou, whose children are idiots: 'Il n'avait plus d'enfant, il finirait *solitaire*' (p. 452), '*Et la terre seule demeure*, l'immortelle' (p. 811); 'Having to face *alone* his own fields, he felt the inferiority of man who passes away before *the clod that remains*' (p. 71).

Other resemblances in characterization are worth noting: the portrayal of the peasants eating and talking is similar; the picture of Bacadou's father sitting in 'a kind of *raging* concentrated sulkiness' (p. 61) because he feels neglected by his son recalls old Fouan's '*rage* impuissante' (p. 732) when put on one side by his son Buteau; both Bacadou and Buteau are avaricious and quarrelsome, both beat their wives and give vent to their temper by riding their carriages furiously. Also indicative of Zola's influence is the introduction of the theme of heredity after Susan has stabbed her husband with a pair of scissors because she resents his continued sexual demands. On hearing the fatal news, her mother exclaims: 'You always resembled your father' (p. 76), and she rejects her, fearing that, like her father who died insane, she, too, has gone mad. Indeed, the vision of the rural community that emerges from 'The Idiots' is profoundly pessimistic and completely in accord with that of both Maupassant and Zola: the villagers are callous and concerned only for their own reputation, and their religious and political leaders are corrupt.[26] This is a world of emotional and moral idiocy of which the idiot children are fitting symbols.

The second part of 'The Idiots' shows the influence of Zola's *La Joie de vivre*.[27] Conrad found in its gloomy and ominous descriptions of the Normandy coast at night the details he needed for his own story which ends on the death of Susan by drowning at night:

| | |
|---|---|
| Et ses regards allaient au dehors, dans ce *gouffre noir* où les ténèbres s'étaient encore épaissies. (p. 828) | the bay of Fougère, fifty feet below the house, resembled an immense *black pit* (p. 71)[28] |
| et l'on entendit la mer [. . .] *qui battait les falaises*. A cette heure, *elle se trouvait* | At high tide the returning water *assaulted the ledges of rock* in short rushes, ending |

| | |
|---|---|
| *dans son plein*, chaque flot en s'écroulant ébranlait la maison. C'étaient comme les *détonations* d'une artillerie géante, des coups profonds et réguliers (p. 828) | in *bursts* of livid light and columns of spray (p. 72) |
| ciel livide, où le vent d'ouest emportait de grands *nuages noirs*, comme des *haillons de suie*, dont les déchirures traînaient (p. 809) | The heavens above the house seemed to be draped in *black rags*,[29] held up here and there by pins *of fire* (p. 72) |
| ils regardaient les étoiles pointer comme des perles *de feu* (p. 843) | |
| la *clameur des vagues* avait grandi (p. 816) | A sullen and periodic *clamour of waves* rolling over reefs (p. 78) |
| seule *l'église se découpait* encore nettement (p. 816) | Above it, [...] *appeared the* tower of Ploumar *Church*; a slender and tall pyramid shooting up dark and pointed into *the clustered* glitter *of the stars*. (p. 81) |
| Au ciel, *le fourmillement des astres* croissait de minute en minute, ainsi que des pelletées de braise jetées au travers de l'infini. (p. 843) | |
| *Le flot, qui commençait seulement à monter* [...]; la plage [...] cette plaine rase, salie de *flaques* [...] (p.809) | *The tide was creeping in quietly* [...]. Under the night the *pools* grew bigger with mysterious rapidity, while the great sea, yet *far off, thundered* in a regular rhythm (p. 81) |
| Mais, *au loin, la clameur* des vagues avait grandi (p. 816) | |
| C'était une écume blanche [...] recouvrant les dalles rocheuses, dans *un glissement doux* et *berceur*, dont l'approche semblait une *caresse*. (p. 816) | She [...] felt the cold *caress* of the sea (p. 80) |
| | Below her the sea *lapped softly* against the rock with a splash continuous and *gentle*. (p. 83) |
| | *Chaikin, pp. 506–7, and *Hervouet) |

These similarities of detail make it clear that Conrad, at this early stage in his career, read Zola attentively and was impressed by the pictorial quality of his writing, by his descriptions of light and darkness, his liking for silhouettes, and his general rendering of sense impressions. It is also apparent that description, be it of people or natural phenomena, was an area where Conrad felt the need of some authoritative model.

### 'An Outpost of Progress'

Conrad's next story, 'An Outpost of Progress', written in July 1896, is also, despite its greater depth and complexity, largely in the Maupassant manner.

The introduction of the characters is typical of Maupassant's way of portraying types in a few telling phrases, for instance, in 'Toine'. Toine is described as 'le plus gros homme du canton' (*Toine*, p. 2) and his wife as 'une grande paysanne, marchant à longs pas d'échassier, et portant sur un corps maigre et plat une tête de chat-huant en colère' (*Toine*, p.4). Conrad's opening lines read: 'There were two white men in charge of the trading station. Kayerts, the chief, was short and fat; Carlier, the assistant, was tall, with a large head and a very broad trunk perched upon a long pair of thin legs' (*TU*, p. 86). And the conclusion, with the hanged Kayerts 'irreverently [...] putting out a swollen tongue at his Managing Director' (p. 117) is also strongly reminiscent of Maupassant's ironic surprise ending and relish for the ghastly.

However, Wallace Watson argues that it is 'clearly modelled' on Flaubert's *Bouvard et Pécuchet*, 'both in the nature of its protagonists and in the brisk comic treatment it gives them':

> Echoes of *Bouvard and Pécuchet* are heard throughout Conrad's story. Like Flaubert's comic heroes, his European ivory traders isolated in the African jungle complement each other in physical appearance and temperament – Kayerts: short, fat, emotional, and effusive; Carlier: tall, thin, cynical, and taciturn. Like Bouvard and Pécuchet, who less than a week after first meeting 'se tutoyèrent' (p.10), Kayerts and Carlier within moments after the company steamship has left them at their inland station 'called one another "my dear fellow"' (p. 90). As in the opening chapter of Flaubert's novel, Conrad inserts brief, symmetrical biographies of his two protagonists early in his story. Flaubert's catalogues detailing Bouvard's and Pécuchet's endless projects (domestic fixing-up, reading, scientific inquiry, etc.) are recalled in Kayerts' and Carlier's 'pottering about with hammers and nails and red calico' (p. 90), and in their reaction to some old novels found in the house:
>
> > In the centre of Africa they made acquaintance of Richelieu and of d'Artagnan, of Hawk's Eye and of Father Goriot, and of many other people. All these imaginary personages became subjects for gossip as if they had been living friends. They discounted their virtues, suspected their motives, decried their successes; were scandalized at their duplicity or were doubtful about their courage. (p. 94)[30]
>
> Flaubert's terse, ironic narration alternates like clockwork its attention upon now one, now the other, protagonist ('Pécuchet contracta la brusquerie de Bouvard, Bouvard prit quelque chose de la morosité de Pécuchet ... Les métacarpiens désolèrent Bouvard; et Pécuchet, acharné sur le crâne, perdit courage devant le sphénoïde' (pp. 13, 74–5)). This is Conrad's characteristic narrative method in the story. For example, his heroes react further to those books:
>
> > Carlier cleared his throat, and said in a soldierly voice, 'What nonsense!' Kayerts, his round eyes suffused with tears, his fat cheeks quivering, rubbed his bald head, and declared, 'This is a splendid book. I had no idea there were such clever fellows in the world.' (p.94)[31]

Above all, the two works have the same basic theme, which Watt has defined as 'the practical incapacity, and the intrinsic moral and intellectual nullity, of the typical products of modern urban society'.[32]

To complete the picture of Conrad's involvement with Flaubert in this story, it should be added that the scene where Kayerts, having accidentally killed Carlier, sits by the corpse musing, looks like an adaptation of the scene where Charles Bovary, sitting opposite the pregnant Emma, feasts his eyes on her as she lounges wearily in her easy chair:

alors son bonheur ne *se tenait plus*; il se levait, il l'embrassait, passait ses mains sur sa figure, l'appelait petite maman [...]. *L'idée* d'avoir engendré *le délectait*. Rien ne lui manquait à présent. *Il connaissait l'existence humaine tout du long*, et il s'y attablait sur les deux coudes avec *sérénité*.                                                (*MB*, p. 122)

The violence of the emotions he had passed through produced a feeling of exhausted *serenity*. He had plumbed in one short afternoon the depths of horror and despair, and now found repose in the conviction that *life had no more secrets for him*: neither had death! He sat by the corpse thinking; thinking very actively, thinking very new thoughts. He seemed to have *broken loose from himself* altogether. His old thoughts, convictions, likes and dislikes, things he respected and things he abhorred, appeared in their true light at last! [...] *He revelled in his new wisdom*.                                    (*TU*, p. 114)

# 3    The first phase of maturity

## The Nigger of the 'Narcissus'

The presence of Flaubert and Maupassant is very conspicuous throughout Conrad's third novel, his first major achievement, *The Nigger of the 'Narcissus'*, written between June 1896 and February 1897.

Kirschner has shown that Conrad borrowed extensively from the rendering of Charles Forestier's illness and death in *Bel-Ami* in portraying the illness and death of James Wait. Forestier, who is dying of tuberculosis in Cannes, is domineering towards his wife and his colleague Georges Duroy who has just arrived from Paris in answer to her call. Engrossed with his condition, he constantly refers to his approaching death, thwarts all their efforts to take his mind off himself, and insists on having them at his beck and call. One evening, as the night draws in, he complains angrily: 'Eh bien, on n'apporte pas la lampe aujourd'hui? Voilà ce qu'on appelle soigner un malade' (p. 266). Like Forestier, Wait, who is also dying of tuberculosis, at first exaggerates his illness ('he worked his ribs in an *exaggerated labour of breathing*' (p. 35) just as 'Charles [...] *exagérait le fatigue de sa respiration*' (p. 221))[1] and takes advantage of his condition to tyrannize his shipmates, silencing any sign of cheerfulness on their part and rebuking them for lack of care: 'Some of you haven't sense enough to put a blanket shipshape over a sick man' (p. 39). Nearing the end, both refuse to accept the grim reality of death and show a complete change of front: Forestier asserts that his condition has improved, that he intends to return to Paris, and insists on a carriage drive; Wait tells Captain Allistoun that he feels better, that he is able to go back to duty, and decides to go on deck.

During his last days, Forestier has an aimless and restless habit: '*Il faisait avec les doigts de chaque main un mouvement nerveux et léger, comme s'il eût joué du piano sur les deux bras de son siège*' (p. 265) and so has Wait: '*the meagre fingers of one hand moved lightly upon the edge of the bunk playing an endless tune*' (p. 148). Shortly before Forestier's end, we read that 'chacun de ses silences était plus pénible que ses paroles, tant *on sentait qu'il devait penser à d'épouvantables choses*', and his death agony is described thus:

Il pleurait. *De grosses larmes coulaient de ses yeux sur ses joues décharnées*

39

Alors, ses mains retombées sur le lit commencèrent un mouvement continu, lent et régulier, comme pour recueillir quelque chose sur les draps. [...]

*L'haleine de Forestier était plus rapide que celle d'un chien qui vient de courir, si pressée qu'on ne la pouvait point compter, et si faible qu'on l'entendait à peine.* [...]

*Il regardait devant lui quelque chose d'invisible* pour les autres *et de hideux, dont ses yeux fixes reflétaient l'épouvante. Ses deux mains continuaient ensemble leur geste horrible et fatigant.*

*Soudain* il tressaillit d'un frisson brusque qu'on vit courir d'un bout à l'autre de son corps et *il balbutia:*

– *Le cimetière ... moi ... mon Dieu!* ...

[...] *Il traînait toujours ses doigts maigres sur le drap comme pour le ramener vers sa face.*

(*BA*, pp. 265, 276-8)

Conrad made use of these passages, first when he wrote that Wait '*panted fast like a dog after a run* in sunshine', and then when describing his death-throes:

*Jimmy's respiration was so rapid that it couldn't be counted, so faint that it couldn't be heard. His eyes were terrified as though he had been looking at unspeakable horrors*; and by his face one could see that he was thinking of abominable things. Suddenly with an incredibly strong and heart-breaking voice *he sobbed out:*

'*Overboard!* ... *I!* ... *My God!*'

Donkin writhed a little on the box. He looked unwillingly. James Wait was mute. *His two long bony hands smoothed the blanket upwards, as though he had wished to gather it all up under his chin. A tear*, a big solitary tear, *escaped from the corner of his eye* and, without touching the *hollow cheek*, fell on the pillow.

[...] Only his eyes appeared alive and *his hands continued their smoothing movement with a horrible and tireless industry.*                    (*NN*, pp.122, 153–4; *Kirschner, pp.201–3)

Forestier's death occurs as Duroy, who is sitting by him with Madame Forestier, begins to doze off:

*Le malade n'avait point bougé.* [...]

Duroy lui-même commençait à s'assoupir *quand il eut la sensation que quelque chose survenait. Il ouvrit les yeux juste à temps pour voir Forestier fermer les siens comme deux lumières qui s'éteignent.* Un petit hoquet agita la gorge du mourant, *et deux filets de sang apparurent aux coins de sa bouche*, puis coulèrent sur sa chemise. Ses mains cessèrent leur hideuse promenade. *Il avait fini de respirer.*

(*BA*, p.278)

Donkin is similarly startled by Wait's death as he is stealthily leaving his cabin after robbing him:

[Donkin] slipped the key under the pillow again, avoiding to glance at Jimmy, *who had not moved.* He turned his back squarely from the bunk, and started to the door [...]. He clutched the handle cautiously, but at that moment, *he received the irresistible impression of something happening behind his back.* He spun round as though he had been tapped on the shoulder. *He was just in time to see Wait's eyes blaze up and go out at once, like two* lamps *overturned* together by a sweeping blow. *Something resembling a scarlet thread hung down his chin out of the corner of his lips – and he had ceased to breathe.*

(*NN*, pp.154–5; *Kirschner, p.203)

We may add to Kirschner's discoveries that Conrad also seems to have found in the psychology of Duroy traits for the characterization of Donkin. Duroy soon realizes, after his arrival in Cannes, what he has let himself in for; but, as it is impossible for him to leave without losing the good opinion of Madame Forestier, he decides to stay, arguing with himself: 'tant pis, il y a des passes désagréables dans la vie; et puis, ça ne sera peut-être pas long'; and once Forestier is dead, he thinks with relief: 'Ç'a été moins long que je n'aurais cru' (pp. 268, 279). Watching the end of Wait, Donkin wonders in the same vein: 'How long would this blooming affair last? Too long surely. No luck' (p. 154). Both Duroy and Donkin are momentarily gripped with terror when faced with this reminder of their own mortality:

> Une terreur confuse, immense, écrasante, pesait sur l'âme de Duroy, la terreur de ce néant illimité, inévitable, détruisant indéfiniment toutes les existences si rapides et si misérables. Il courbait déjà le front sous sa menace.                    (*BA*, pp. 280–1)

> Donkin [...] felt the anguishing grasp of a great sorrow on his heart at the thought that he himself, some day, would have to go through it all – just like this – perhaps!
>
> (*NN*, pp. 153–4)

And they both, cowardly, turn away their eyes from the dead men: Duroy 'détourna les yeux pour ne plus regarder le cadavre' (p. 281); Donkin 'slipped the key under the pillow again, avoiding to glance at Jimmy' (p. 154).

Finally, just as Forestier speaks to Duroy '*avec un son de voix ennuyé et lointain, comme s'il parlait du fond d'un trou*' (p. 104), Donkin answers Wait '*in a bored, far-away voice, as though he had been talking from the bottom of a hole*' (p. 110).[2]

Flaubert's influence on *The Nigger of the 'Narcissus'* derives from two sources: *Salammbô* (see above, p. 11) and *Madame Bovary*.[3] Richard Curle first pointed out the influence of *Salammbô* as early as 1912.[4] Yves Guérin has shown that many passages in *The Nigger* are impregnated with the spirit of *Salammbô*, and, although the works are very different, they have much in common in style as well as in the choice and treatment of the characters.

In both novels the characters are simple-minded, rough, superstitious men. Mercenaries and Carthaginians alike are fascinated by the *zaïmph* to which they ascribe great powers; the sailors are equally 'fascinated' by James Wait: 'He overshadowed the ship' (p. 47). The Carthaginians have barely returned to their homes after the sacrifice of many children to Moloch when the clouds gather and the rain pours in torrents. This they interpret as an omen: Moloch has vanquished Tanit. At Jimmy's funeral, Mr Baker has hardly finished reciting the last prayer when the wind rises from the West, a coincidence which Singleton and the sailors do not see as fortuitous. Mercenaries and sailors also share a certain fatalism, which is no doubt partly due to the fact that they have to fight against irresistible forces: the mercenaries are mere toys against the blind

force and fury of the elephants; the sailors lead a 'hopeless struggle' against the
big seas which pursue them relentlessly.

In his opening scene, Flaubert enumerates the various nationalities of the
barbarians, less to distinguish them than to evoke the multiple faces of the
collective being into which they merge. The vision soon becomes general: 'les
soldats', 'les Mercenaires', 'La houle des soldats se poussait' (p.12). Conrad
also presents his sailors as a mass: 'Men in black jackets and stand-up collars
[...]. The group swayed' (p.5). Mercenaries and sailors have no individual
lives: they can find fulfilment only in the group to which they belong. Their
work can only be team-work, whether it be making an assault or fighting the
elements. Their affective reactions are also anonymous and governed by the
collective feeling. For instance, the revolt of the barbarians and the protests
when Captain Allistoun forbids Jimmy to leave his cabin are voiced in an
anonymous and collective form: 'Cependant les Barbares s'impatientaient, des
murmures s'élevèrent, chacun l'apostropha' (p.48); 'L'indignation des soldats
[...] éclata' (p.52); 'There were exclamations of surprise, triumph, indignation' (p.120). Both groups fall under the sway of a strong and cynical personality: Spendius quickly spreads doubt among an audience easy to convince;
Donkin soon exploits the sailors' credulity.

Both novels also treat the setting lyrically, emphasizing its limitless character
and the fact that it is forever renewing itself and yet always the same:

> La route s'allongeait sans jamais en finir. A l'extrémité d'une plaine, toujours on
> arrivait sur un plateau de forme ronde; puis on redescendait dans une vallée, et les
> montagnes qui semblaient boucher l'horizon, à mesure que l'on approchait d'elles, se
> déplaçaient comme en glissant.                                    (*Sal*, p.33)

> Round her [the *Narcissus*] the abysses of sky and sea met in an unattainable frontier. A
> great circular solitude moved with her, ever changing and ever the same, always monot-
> onous and always imposing.                              (*NN*, p.29; *Guérin)

Furthermore, the elements play an essential part in both works: in *Salammbô*
the movement of the sun punctuates the rhythm of most episodes, whether it
be the battle of the Macar or the last pulsations of Mâtho's heart; in *The Nigger*,
a sun with many aspects punctuates the course of the ship: 'For a moment a
livid sun shot horizontally the last rays of sinister light between the hills of
steep, rolling waves' (p.53), 'The sun was setting. A sun enormous, unclouded
and red, declining low as if bending down to look into their faces' (p.74;
*Guérin).

In addition to these similarities, Yelton has found a distinct verbal echo of
Salammbô's first appearance to the dumbfounded mercenaries: 'C'était la lune
qui l'avait rendue si pâle, et *quelque chose* des dieux l'enveloppait comme une
*vapeur subtile*' (p.14); in the appearance of the sick Wait before the startled
sailors in the forecastle: 'a black *mist* emanated from him; *a subtle* and dismal
influence; a *something* cold and gloomy that floated out' (p.34; *Yelton, p.115).

To this we may add the description of the houses on the banks as the *Narcissus*, at the end of her journey, goes up river, which derives from the description of the houses in Carthage:

A mesure que le ciel rose allait s'élargissant, *les* hautes *maisons* inclinées *sur les pentes* du terrain se haussaient, *se tassaient*, telles qu'un troupeau de chèvres noires *qui descend* des montagnes. (*Sal*, p. 21)

*On the* riverside *slopes the houses appeared in groups* – seemed *to stream down* the declivities at a run to see her pass, and, checked by the mud of the foreshore, *crowded* on the banks. (*NN*, p. 163)

*Madame Bovary* also provided Conrad with inspiration. Léon, after telling Emma how much he loved her when he lived in Yonville, looks closely at her face: 'Ce fut comme le ciel, quand un coup de vent *chasse les nuages*. L'amas des *pensées tristes* qui les *assombrissaient* parut se retirer de ses yeux bleus; tout *son visage rayonna*' (p. 324). Podmore's face, as he talks to Wait, is described in strikingly similar terms: 'Some *gloomy thought darkened his shining face*, fleeting, like the shadow of a *travelling cloud* over the light of a peaceful sea' (p. 114).

On a few occasions, the states of mind of Emma and Donkin are similar. At one stage Emma pretends to be a good wife and mother and discourages any advances from Léon: 'Emma *maigrit*, ses joues pâlirent, sa figure s'allongea' and she is 'toujours *silencieuse* maintenant'. But, although generally admired for her courteousness and charity, she is 'pleine de convoitises, de *rage*, de *haine*. Cette robe aux plis droits cachait un coeur bouleversé, et ces lèvres si pudiques n'en racontaient pas la tourmente' (pp. 148–9). This passage may have inspired the following presentation of Donkin:

No one knew the venom of his thoughts now. He was *silent*, and *appeared thinner*, as if consumed slowly by inward *rage* at the injustice of men and fate. He was ignored by all and spoke to no one, but his *hate* for every man dwelt in his furtive eyes. (*NN*, p. 143)

After her failure to obtain money from Guillaumin, the contemptible notary, Emma is in an indignant and rebellious mood:

Le désappointement de l'insuccès *renforçait* l'indignation *de sa pudeur outragée*; il lui semblait que la Providence s'acharnait à la poursuivre, et, s'en rehaussant d'orgueil, jamais elle n'avait eu tant d'estime pour elle-même ni tant de mépris pour les autres. Quelque chose de belliqueux la transportait. *Elle aurait voulu* battre les hommes, leur cracher au visage, les *broyer* tous (*MB*, p. 420)

The following two passages seem to derive from this analysis:

[Donkin] felt himself pulled up sharp by unrecognised grievances. He had been physically cowed, but *his injured dignity remained indomitable*, and nothing could heal his lacerated feelings. (*NN*, p. 147)

Donkin felt this vaguely like a blind man feeling in his darkness the fatal antagonism of all the surrounding existences, that to him shall for ever remain irrealisable, unseen and enviable. *He had a desire* to assert his importance, to break, *to crush*  (*NN*, pp. 149–50)

A fascinating example of literary relationship between Flaubert, Maupassant and Conrad appears in the link uniting the death scenes of Emma, Forestier and Wait. Roger Bismut has shown that in *Bel-Ami* Maupassant made a number of borrowings from *Madame Bovary*.[5] Although he does not mention the connection between the death scenes of Emma and Forestier it is unmistakable;[6] and there is much evidence to suggest that Conrad not only drew heavily on Maupassant's description for Wait's death but also found inspiration directly in Flaubert's text. Indeed, a number of details in Conrad's scene have an equivalent in Flaubert but not in Maupassant.

Both Emma and Wait sweat, shake, moan, and roll their eyes in their death-agonies. And just as Emma can only nod in answer to the questions that are put to her and smile two or three times, Wait can only nod and grin in response to Donkin's taunting remarks:

> Puis elle se mit à *geindre*, faiblement d'abord. *Un grand frisson lui secouait les épaules* [...].
> 
> Des gouttes suintaient sur sa figure bleuâtre [...]. Ses dents claquaient, ses yeux agrandis regardaient vaguement autour d'elle, et à toutes les questions elle ne répondait qu'*en hochant la tête*; même elle sourit deux ou trois fois. Peu à peu *ses gémissements* furent plus forts. Un hurlement sourd lui échappa  (*MB*, p. 436)

> His shirt clung to him. [...] *His* emaciated *back was shaken in repeated jerks* [...].
> [...] and hollow, *moaning*, whistling *sounds* filled the cabin [...].
> [...] Wait *shook his head; rolled his eyes* [...].
> The other [Wait] kept on headlong and unheard, *nodding* passionately, grinning with grotesque and appalling flashes of big white teeth.  (*NN*, pp. 150–1)

Emma is likewise presented '*roulant les yeux* autour d'elle' (p. 425), a detail which reappears when she is *in extremis*: '*ses yeux, en roulant*, pâlissaient' (p. 448). Both sit up most unexpectedly: 'Emma *se releva* comme un cadavre que l'on galvanise, les cheveux dénoués, la prunelle fixe, béante' (pp. 448–9); '"Blamme if yer don't look dead already." [...] And *sitting up*, against all probability, startled his visitor horribly' (p. 150). Emma loses her last hold on life when she sees her face in her mirror and realizes that death is upon her: 'elle demanda son miroir, et elle resta penché dessus quelque temps, jusqu'au moment où de grosses larmes lui découlèrent des yeux. Alors elle se renversa la tête en poussant un soupir et *retomba sur l'oreiller*' (pp. 447–8). Similarly, Wait feels mortally wounded when Donkin's cry 'Yah – you corpse!' brings home to him the immediacy of his death: 'He flung at Jimmy's head the biscuit he had been all the time clutching hard [...]. James Wait, as if wounded mortally, *fell back on the pillow*' (p. 152). Finally, the image of Wait's eyes blazing up and going out at the moment of death '*Like two lamps* overturned together by a sweeping blow' (p. 155), although part of a passage translated almost verbatim from Maupassant, is closer to the Flaubertian original: 'ses yeux [...] pâlissaient *comme deux globes de lampes* qui s'éteignent' (p. 448) than to Maupassant's variation *'comme deux lumières* qui s'éteignent' (*BA*, p. 278). The suggestion of Flaubert's presence is reinforced by Conrad's use of the word 'globe' in an earlier image: 'the fleshless head resembled a disinterred black skull, fitted with two restless *globes* of silver in the sockets of eyes' (p. 139).

After the death of their protagonists, Flaubert and Conrad emphasize man's insignificance by showing nature's indifference to his passing. Charles, alone in his garden, curses heaven, but 'pas une feuille seulement n'en bougea' (p. 453). When Emma's father arrives at Yonville for her funeral, he cannot believe she is dead because 'la campagne n'avait rien d'extraordinaire' (p. 463); and the funeral procession goes on its way to the cemetery surrounded by the 'bruits joyeux' of daily life (p. 466). Similarly, when Donkin sneaks out of Wait's cabin after his death he is 'perfectly astounded to find the world outside as he has left it': the men, the ship, the 'immortal sea', nothing is changed (p. 155).

The funeral services have also one distinct feature in common:

Les prêtres, les chantres et les deux enfants de choeur récitaient le *De profundis*; et *leurs voix s'en allaient sur la campagne*, montant et s'abaissant avec des ondulations.

(*MB*, p.465)

Mr. Baker read on, grunting reverently at the turn of every page. *The words*, missing the unsteady hearts of men, *rolled out to wander* without a home *upon the* heartless *sea*

(*NN*, p. 159)

Lastly, the description of the crew of the *Narcissus* as they come in their 'new shore togs' and with 'clean, radiant faces' to be paid off at the shipping office contains an obvious echo of the description of the peasants, clumsily dressed in their Sunday best, 'closely shaven' and with 'beaming' faces, who are guests at Emma's wedding. Flaubert pokes gentle fun at their 'habits-vestes [...]' dont les pans *semblaient avoir été coupés* à même un seul bloc, *par la hache* du charpentier' (p. 36), a picturesque detail which must have appealed to Conrad for he, too, presents his sailors dressed in 'smart jackets that *looked as if they had been shaped with an axe*' (p. 168).

Conrad's reliance on Flaubert in this novel is also reflected in its style. Yelton has called attention to his appropriation of an 'idiosyncratic Flaubertian usage: a double comparison of which one branch expresses a superiority of tenor over vehicle, the other an equivalence of the two terms'. The image of the triumphant Homais in his official regalia 'plus garrotté qu'un Scythe et splendide comme un mage' (p.475) is Conrad's paradigm when he refers to the stars which are 'more intense than the eyes of a staring crowd, and as inscrutable as the souls of men' (p. 29; *Yelton, pp. 114-15).

Moreover, the description of the laughter of the crew as 'dirty Knowles' delivers some opinion 'with an air of supernatural cunning' looks very much like a stylistic imitation of the description of the laughter of Charles's fellow students as he cries 'Charbovari' (one notes the similarities in both meaning and rhythmic patterns):

Ce fut un vacarme qui s'élança d'un bond, / monta en *crescendo*, / avec des éclats de voix aigus / (on hurlait, on aboyait, on trépignait, on répétait: *Charbovari! Charbovari!*, / puis qui roula en notes isolées, se calmant à grand'peine

(MB, p. 4; original emphasis)

a ripple of laughter ran along, / rose like a wave, / burst with a startling roar. / They stamped with both feet; they turned their shouting faces to the sky; many, spluttering, slapped their thighs; / while one or two, bent double, gasped, hugging themselves with both arms like men in pain.                                         (NN, p. 33)

Thibaudet quotes the sentence which concludes the description of Bovary's cap: 'Elle était neuve; la visière brillait' (p. 3) as an example of these 'imitative constructions' which abound in *Madame Bovary*. Indeed, after the big syntactic build-up depicting the grotesque construction, this sentence can be said to be 'as thin as a peak'.[7] Without always aiming for this kind of iconic effect, Flaubert often concludes his paragraphs on one or two such short, sharp notes, for example, in the first chapter of *Salammbô*:

D'ailleurs la dépense devait être excessive; il la subirait presque toute. (p. 6)

La clameur redoublait. Les lions blessés rugissaient dans l'ombre.(p. 13)

Les Barbares ne s'en souciaient; ils écoutaient toujours la vierge chanter. (p. 17)

Spendius les reconnut; il retint un cri. (p. 25)

Conrad shows a distinct predilection for this stylistic trait in *The Nigger*, which, again, suggests a deliberate imitation of Flaubert's practice:

They were great friends. (p. 20)

Donkin did not conceal his delight. We were dismayed. (p. 38)

It was a weird servitude. (p. 43)

His voice reached them in a warning whisper. They were startled. (p. 57)

He steered with care. (p. 89)

Every one stared at the nigger. (p. 141)

She had ceased to live. (p. 165)

The group broke up. The voyage was ended. (p. 166)

There seems to be a connection between Conrad's heavy textual and stylistic reliance on *Madame Bovary*, *Salammbô* and *Bel-Ami* in *The Nigger of the 'Narcissus'* and the verbal restraint which characterizes this novel by comparison with its predecessor. It is as if Conrad, who had been stung by Wells's criticism of the style of *An Outcast of the Islands*,[8] decided to forge a more economical tool, and found valuable models in Flaubert and Maupassant.

However, the charges of over-writing and grandiloquence still apply to a certain extent:[9] the author of *Chatterton* also left his mark on *The Nigger*, as Witold Chwalewik observed,[10] when, in a grand romantic image, Conrad compares England to a ship:

the coast, stretching away straight and black, resembled the high side of an indestructible *craft riding motionless upon the* immortal and unresting *sea*. The dark land lay alone in the midst of waters, like a mighty ship bestarred with vigilant lights [...]. *A great ship!* [...] *A ship mother of fleets* and nations! The great flagship of the race; stronger than the storms! *and anchored in the open sea.*                                      (*NN*, pp. 162–3)

In Act III, scene 6, Chatterton says:

*L'Angleterre est un vaisseau.* Notre île en a la forme: la proue tournée au nord, *elle est comme à l'ancre, au milieu des mers,* surveillant le continent. Sans cesse *elle tire de ses flancs d'autres vaisseaux* faits à son image, et qui vont la représenter sur toutes les côtes du monde. Mais c'est à bord du grand navire qu'est notre ouvrage à tous. [...] nous sommes tous de l'équipage, et nul n'est inutile dans la manoeuvre de *notre glorieux navire.*

It is impossible not to mention in conclusion the name of Pierre Loti, with whose work Henry James compared this novel in a letter of commendation addressed to the Royal Literary Fund. Conrad, he said, had recorded his experience 'in a form more artistic than has been given to *any* "Tales of the Sea" among English writers and that approximates more than anything we have to the truth and beauty of the French Pierre Loti' (*LBM*, p. 200).

A comparison between Loti's description of a storm in the China seas in *Mon frère Yves* (1883) and the famous storm in *The Nigger*[11] bears out the kinship felt by James; although it does not prove direct influence (the verbal correspondences indicated in my text by letters could be coincidental), it does throw light on the similarity of their aims and methods:

The sunshine gleamed cold on the *white curls*[a] of black waves [...]. She [the *Narcissus*] drove to and fro in the unceasing endeavour to fight her way through the invisible violence of the winds: *she pitched headlong into* dark smooth *hollows;*[b] she struggled upwards over the *snowy ridges*[c] *of great* running *seas* [...].
   [...] The watch on deck dodged the *sting of cold sprays*[d] or, crouching in sheltered corners, watched dismally the *high* and merciless *seas boarding the ship*[e] time after time *in unappeasable fury.*[f]                                                    (*NN*, p. 49)

Out of the abysmal *darkness*[g] of the black cloud overhead white *hail*[h] streamed on her [...]. It passed away. For a moment a *livid*[i] sun shot horizontally the last rays of *sinister*[j] light between the hills of steep, rolling waves.                        (*NN*, p. 53)

Outside the night *moaned*[k] and sobbed [...]. *Shrieks*[l] passed through the air. *Tremendous*

*dull blows made the ship tremble*[m] while she rolled under the weight of the seas toppling
on her deck.                                                        (*NN*, p. 54)

the coming wave [...] towered close-to and *high, like a wall* of *green*[n] glass  (*NN*, p. 57)

Their thoughts floated vaguely [...] while *their stiffened fingers* [...] *held with tenacious
grip against the violent shocks of beating canvas.*[o]                (*NN*, p. 92)

Depuis deux jours, *la grande voix*[l] sinistre *gémissait*[k] autour de nous. *Le ciel était très
noir;*[g] il était comme dans ce tableau où le Poussin a voulu peindre le déluge; seulement
toutes les nuées remuaient, tourmentées par un vent qui faisait peur.

Et cette *grande voix*[l] s'enflait toujours, se faisait profonde, incessante: c'était comme
*une fureur qui s'exaspérait.*[f] Nous nous heurtions dans notre marche à *d'énormes masses
d'eau,*[e] qui s'enroulaient en *volutes*[a] à *crêtes blanches*[c] et qui passaient avec des airs de se
poursuivre; *elles se ruaient sur nous*[e] de toutes leurs forces: alors *c'étaient des secousses
terribles et de grands bruits sourds.*[m]

Quelquefois la *Médée* se cabrait, leur montait dessus, comme prise, elle aussi, de
fureur contre elles. Et puis *elle retombait* toujours, *la tête en avant, dans des creux*[b] traîtres
qui étaient derrière; elle touchait le fond de ces espèces de vallées qu'on voyait s'ouvrir,
rapides, entre de *hautes parois* d'eau; et on avait hâte de remonter encore, de sortir d'entre
ces *parois* courbes, luisantes, *verdâtres,*[n] prêtes à se refermer.

*Une pluie glacée* rayait l'air en longues flèches blanches, *fouettait, cuisait*[d] comme des
coups de lanières. [...]

En haut, dans la mâture, on essayait de serrer les huniers, déjà au bas ris [...].

Il y avait deux heures que les gabiers étaient à ce travail, aveuglés, cinglés, brûlés par
tout ce qui leur tombait dessus, gerbes d'écume lancées de la mer, pluie et *grêle*[h] lancées
du ciel; *essayant, avec leurs mains crispées de froid* qui saignaient, *de crocher dans cette toile
raide* et mouillée *qui ballonnait sous le vent furieux.*[o]

Mais on ne se voyait plus, on ne s'entendait plus.        (*Mon frère Yves*, pp. 92–3)

Et puis le jour arrivait – un vilain jour, il est vrai, une étrange *lividité*[i] jaune, mais
enfin c'était le jour, moins *sinistre*[j] que la nuit.        (*Mon frère Yves*, p. 105)[12]

These short passages reveal two men who knew the sea intimately and placed
great emphasis on the visual. Each 'makes us see' but there was a significant
difference between them. The page from Loti is primarily a tableau (hence the
reference to Poussin) painted by a great seascape artist. In Conrad, the same
descriptive touches are scattered over many pages, forming, not a tableau,
but the background to the drama being enacted. For Conrad is not primarily
concerned with pictures but with exploring a moral problem through action,
with presenting 'a group of men [...] in a struggle [...] with the hostile conditions testing their faithfulness to the conditions of their own calling' (*LE*,
p. 94). With Loti the description of the storm is an end in itself; with Conrad
it is a means of conducting this test, since some hidden truths surface only in
men who are driven to the limit of human endurance.

Although there is no record of Conrad's having read *Mon frère Yves*, another
minor echo suggests his acquaintance with it. At the beginning of the novel,

Loti describes his sailors caught by a strong wind as their launch makes its way to the shore. Every time the launch leaps on the waves, a great sea 'venait se plaquer sur eux, *comme lancée par des mains furieuses*' (p.18). In *An Outcast of the Islands* Willems is caught in a tropical downpour and feels 'heavy big drops' striking him and 'dashing at him *as if flung* from all sides by a mob of *infuriated hands*' (p. 283). Conrad used this vivid simile again when describing the various moods of the West Wind in *The Mirror of the Sea* (1906) (in the above passage Loti was also referring to 'le vent d'ouest'): 'A shower pelts the deck and the sails of the ship *as if flung* with a scream *by an angry hand*' (p. 85).

## 'Karain'

In February 1897, with *The Nigger* behind him, Conrad started working on 'Karain', and the presence of *Salammbô* and *Madame Bovary* is again discernible in the first twenty pages.

Compare the end of Conrad's opening paragraph in 'Karain' with part of Flaubert's celebrated evocation of Carthage at sunrise:

> Mais une barre lumineuse s'éleva du côté de l'Orient. A gauche, tout en bas, les canaux de Mégara commençaient à rayer de leurs sinuosités blanches les verdures des jardins. [...] et tout autour de la péninsule carthaginoise une ceinture d'écume blanche oscillait tandis que la mer couleur d'émeraude semblait comme figée dans la fraîcheur du matin. [...] Les rues désertes s'allongeaient; les palmiers, çà et là sortant des murs, ne bougeaient pas; les citernes remplies avaient l'air de boucliers d'argent perdus dans les cours
>
> *(Sal, p. 21)*

> great trees, the advanced sentries of immense forests, stand watchful and still over sleeping stretches of open water; a line of white surf thunders on an empty beach, the shallow water foams on the reefs; and green islets scattered through the calm of noonday lie upon the level of a polished sea, like a handful of emeralds on a buckler of steel.
>
> *(TU, p. 3)*

> their steep sides [of the hills] were streaked with the green of narrow ravines;
>
> *(TU, p. 6)*

The similarities between the trees standing still, between the 'ceinture d'écume blanche' and the 'line of white surf', between 'la mer couleur d'émeraude [...]' comme figée dans la fraîcheur du matin' and the 'green islets scattered through the calm of noonday [...] like a handful of emeralds', between the cisterns looking like 'des boucliers d'argent' and the sea like 'a buckler of steel', between the canals which began to show their white curves streaking 'les verdures des jardins' and the hillsides 'streaked with the green of narrow ravines' reveal the hints Conrad could have taken from a close study of Flaubert's word-painting.

There are two other echoes of *Salammbô* at the beginning of 'Karain'. One day, a few members of the 'Grand Conseil' of Carthage decide to go to the mercenaries' camp which surrounds the town to seek peace terms:

*Ils s'avançaient d'un pas tranquille, jetant des saluts* aux capitaines, ou bien ils s'arrêtaient pour parler aux soldats [...].

[...] Au lieu de la confusion qu'ils avaient imaginée, c'était un ordre et un silence effrayants.

[...] *par les trous des tentes, ils apercevaient des prunelles fauves qui luisaient dans l'ombre.* [...] Ils se parlaient à voix basse. Ils avaient peur avec leurs longues robes de renverser quelque chose.                                                              (*Sal*, p. 72)

The naval officers that befriend Karain once saw him walking among the houses of the settlement:

*Karain walked fast, and with firm long strides; he answered greetings* right and left by quick piercing glances. [...] young boys kept up with him, gliding between bushes: *their eyes gleamed through the dark leaves.* The old sword-bearer [...] shuffled hastily at his heels with bowed head, and his eyes on the ground. And in the midst of a great stir they passed swift and absorbed, like two men hurrying through a great solitude.

(*TU*, p. 15)

During the banquet for the mercenaries (in a passage situated shortly before the description of Carthage) a violent incident occurs between Mâtho and Narr'Havas. After Salammbô has poured a cup of wine for Mâtho, a Gaul asks him when the wedding will take place because it is the custom with his people that when a woman gives a drink to a soldier she offers him her bed:

Il n'avait pas fini que Narr'Havas, *en bondissant, tira un javelot de sa ceinture*, et appuyé du pied droit sur le bord de la table, *il le lança contre Mâtho.*

Le javelot *siffla* entre les coupes, et, traversant le bras du Lybien, le cloua sur la nappe si fortement, que *la poignée en tremblait* dans l'air.

*Mâtho l'arracha vite* (*Sal*, p. 19)

The narrator, to illustrate the 'glimpses of a sombre, glowing fury' they caught in Karain, which he defines as 'a brooding and vague sense of wrong, and a concentrated lust of violence', recalls that, on one occasion, after they had been talking with him late in his campong, he *'jumped up'*:

He snatched the sword from the old man, *whizzed it out of the scabbard, and thrust the point into the earth.* Upon the thin, upright blade *the* silver *hilt*, released, *swayed* before him like something alive. He stepped back a pace, and in a deadened tone spoke fiercely to the vibrating steel [...]. *He drew it out*                              (*TU*, pp. 18–19)

The first reminiscence from *Madame Bovary* comes in the description of Karain's 'stage', when the narrator says: '*All that had* the crude and blended colouring, the appropriateness almost excessive, *the* suspicious *immobilitity of a painted scene*' (p. 7). The same memorable detail is to be found in the description of Rouen and the surrounding countryside as they suddenly appear to Emma during her weekly journey in *L'Hirondelle*: 'Ainsi vu d'en haut, *le paysage tout entier avait l'air immobile comme une peinture*' (*MB*, p. 364). The gallic 'immobility' for 'stillness' provides linguistic confirmation of Conrad's source.[13]

A few pages later, Conrad exploited the famous passage following Emma's surrender to Rodolphe:

*Les ombres du soir descendaient*; le soleil horizontal, *passant* entre les branches, lui éblouissait les yeux. [...] *Le silence* était partout; quelque chose de doux semblait sortir des arbres [...]. Alors, elle entendit tout au loin, au delà du bois, sur les autres collines, *un cri* vague et *prolongé*, une voix *qui se traînait*, et elle l'écoutait silencieusement, se mêlant comme une musique aux dernières vibrations de ses nerfs émus.

(*MB*, pp. 223–4)

*The darkness deepened fast*; torches gleamed fitfully, *passing* behind bushes; *a long hail* or two *trailed* in *the silence of the evening*; and at last the night stretched its smooth veil over the shore, the lights, and the voices.                         (*TU*, p. 11)

Conrad has again accurately reproduced familiar Flaubertian rhythms: a series of three precise notations in short, paratactic clauses separated by a semi-colon, and followed by a longer clause (introduced by the 'et de mouvement') which broadens the picture.[14]

The concluding sentence of the next paragraph is in fact a perfect pastiche of Flaubert's famous 'ternary period', his 'phrase type', according to Thibaudet.[15] In fact, as is often the case with the master's prose, Conrad has also used ternary rhythms inside some clauses:

He shared his food, his repose, and his thoughts; he knew his plans, guarded his secrets; and, impassive behind his master's agitation, without stirring the least bit, murmured above his head in a soothing tone some words difficult to catch.     (*TU*, p. 12)

Flaubertian influence has also been identified in Conrad's paragraph construction. As early as 1890, Emile Hennequin noted that Flaubert's 'paragraphe type' is made up of an *allegro*, an *andante* and a *presto*: short static sentences with a restrained character; a longer sentence which, usually thanks to an enumeration, becomes lilting and drags on a little; and the concluding period, in which a grandiose image, presented in sonorous and strongly stressed terms, blares forth.[16] James Huneker discovered the same musical pattern in a 'typical paragraph' of Conrad's which shows 'what might be called the sonata form: an allegro, andante, and presto'.[17]

Lastly, the closing scene of 'Karain' contains another reminiscence from Flaubert, this time from 'La Légende de Saint Julien l'Hospitalier':

Quelquefois, au tournant d'une côte, il voyait sous ses yeux *une confusion de toits pressés*, avec des flèches de pierre, des ponts, des tours, *des rues noires* s'entre-croisant, et *d'où montait jusqu'à lui un bourdonnement continuel*.          (*TC*, p. 116)

A watery gleam of sunshine flashed from the west and went out between two long lines of walls; and then *the broken confusion of roofs*, the chimney-stacks, the gold letters sprawling over the fronts of houses, the sombre polish of windows, stood resigned and sullen under the falling gloom. The whole length of *the street, deep as a well* and narrow like a corridor, was full of a sombre and *ceaseless* stir. *Our ears*

*were filled by* a headlong shuffle and beat of rapid footsteps and *an underlying rumour*
(*TU*, p. 54)[18]


## 'The Return'

After 'Karain' Conrad struggled with 'The Return' from April to September
1897. This was the first story that he began after his introduction to Henry
James early in the year, and critics have seen James's influence on it.[19] This
may be true; far more evident, however, is the influence of Maupassant which,
strangely enough, has gone totally unnoticed despite the fact that Conrad's
indebtedness to *Bel-Ami* and 'Un soir' extends over about thirty pages, afford-
ing an exemplary view of his working methods.

In *Bel-Ami* Conrad drew mainly from three important scenes between
Georges Duroy and his wife Madeleine (cf. *BA*, pp. 461–72 and *TU*, pp.
145–65), between M. Walter (Duroy's employer) and his wife (*BA*, pp. 544–9
and *TU*, pp. 163–4), and between Duroy and his mistress Mme de Marelle
(*BA*, pp. 557–9 and *TU*, pp. 166–70).

Madeleine's life-long friend, the Comte de Vaudrec has died bequeathing
her his fortune, but she cannot accept it without her husband's consent. Duroy
gives it on condition that he be given half, arguing that this would avoid a
scandal which would place his honour at stake. In 'The Return', Alvan Hervey
arrives home from the city to find a note from his wife telling him that she has
gone away with another man. However, later in the evening, she returns. In
the ensuing crises, despite the wide difference in contexts and the considerable
divergence in treatment (Maupassant's 'objective' method as against the inward
analytical method of Conrad), there are striking parallels beween the behaviour
of the four individuals. Each man, tormented by jealousy, tries to extract a
confession from his wife, carefully watches her emotions, attempts to justify
his actions and shows the same concern for public opinion. Both couples see
themselves in their true colours with the husbands and wives trying to read
their partner's thoughts in long searching glances; but all are beset by the same
fundamental loneliness and inability to communicate:

| | |
|---|---|
| deux êtres qui, *vivant côte à côte,* s'ignorent toujours          (*BA*, p. 466) | Thus Alvan Hervey and his wife for five prosperous years *lived by the side of* one another.                              (*TU*, p. 122) |
| Il prononça *d'un ton triste*, mais résolu, avec cet accablement feint dont on use pour annoncer les malheurs heureux: – Il y a que *je me marie.* (p. 303) | If she had only died! Certain words would have been said to him *in a sad tone*, and he, with proper fortitude, would have made appropriate answers. [...] But *every one married.* (p. 129) |
| Dès qu'elle fut seule, *elle alla*, par | *He caught sight of himself in one of the* |

instinct, *vers la glace pour se regarder,* | *looking-glasses.* It was a relief. The
comme pour voir si rien n'était changé en | anguish of his feeling had been so
elle, tant ce qui lui arrivait lui paraissait | powerful that he more than half expected
impossible, monstrueux. (pp. 544–5) | to see some distorted wild face there, and

he was pleasantly surprised to see
nothing of the kind. (p. 136)

*La solitude,* aujourd'hui, m'emplit d'une
angoisse horrible: la solitude dans le
logis, auprès du feu, le soir [...] et la
cloison qui me sépare de mon voisin que
je ne connais pas, m'éloigne de lui autant
que des étoiles aperçues par ma fenêtre.
Une sorte de fièvre *m'envahit,* une fièvre
de douleur et de crainte, et *le silence des
murs m'épouvante.* [...] Ce n'est pas
seulement un *silence* autour du corps,
mais un silence autour de l'âme [...] car
aucun bruit n'est attendu dans ce *morne*
logis. (p. 212)

And his thought, as if appalled, stood
still, recalling with dismay *the [...]
frightful silence* that was like a conspiracy;
*the grim,* impenetrable *silence* of miles of
*walls* concealing passions, misery (p. 136)

And right and left all the innumerable
dwellings [...] had presented, unmoved,
to *the loneliness* of his trouble, *the grim
silence of walls,* the impenetrable and
polished discretion of closed doors and
curtained windows. Immobility and
*silence pressed on him, assailed him* (p. 145)

Mais l'image de Forestier était rentrée en
son esprit, le possédait, l'étreignait. Il ne
pouvait plus penser qu'à lui, parler que
de lui. *Il demanda, avec un accent
méchant:* [...]
– L'as-tu fait cocu, ce pauvre Charles?
[...]
Elle se taisait, *choquée* comme toutes
les femmes le sont *par ce mot.* (p. 355)

Then after a pause the unconquerable
preoccupation of self came out, and he
raised his voice *to ask resentfully,* 'And,
pray, for how long have you been
making a fool of me?'
She seemed horribly *shocked by that
question.* (p. 146)

*Tout le monde le sait, excepté moi.* (p. 555)

'I want to know. *Everybody knows,* I
suppose, *but myself*' (p. 146)

Après un moment de réflexion, *elle
balbutia, d'une voix agitée:*
– Voyons... voyons... tu es fou ... tu
es... tu es... (p. 464)

'I have told you there is nothing to
know,' *she said, speaking unsteadily* as if
in pain. 'Nothing of what you suppose.'
(p. 146)

*Il s'arrêta en face d'elle et ils demeurèrent*
de nouveau quelques instants *les yeux dans
les yeux,* s'efforçant d'aller jusqu'à
l'impénétrable secret de leurs coeurs, de
se sonder jusqu'au vif de la pensée. Ils
tâchaient de se voir à nu la conscience en
une interrogation ardente et muette
(p. 466)

*He stopped and looked into her eyes* with
concentrated intensity, with a desire to
see, *to penetrate,* to understand, that
made him positively hold his breath till
he gasped. (p. 146)
There followed a period of dead
silence, during which they exchanged
searching glances. (p. 155)

Madeleine, à son tour, le regardait

*This arrested him, and they faced each other*

fixement, dans la transparence des yeux, d'une façon profonde et singulière, comme pour y lire quelque chose, comme pour y découvrir cet inconnu de l'être qu'on ne *pénètre* jamais (p. 465)

*wide-eyed*, uncertain (pp. 168–9)

Georges *restait debout, près d'elle,* suivant toutes ses émotions, comme un magistrat qui cherche à surprendre les moindres défaillances d'un prévenu. (pp. 464–5)

He came up *quite close to her, and [. . .] stood* looking down at her face for some time (p. 159)

*Il pivota sur ses talons* avec rapidité. (p. 201)

*He turned short on his heel* and *began to walk up and down the room* (p. 147)

Georges *s'était mis à marcher* à grands pas. (p. 466)

et *il évitait* maintenant *l'oeil* pénétrant *de sa femme.* (p. 470)

Her eyes followed the restless movements of the *man, who avoided looking at her.* (p. 147)

Elle le regarda encore d'un regard perçant. (p. 470)

Her wild stare clung to him, inquiring, wondering and doubtful. (p. 147)

*Il venait sans cesse ici* (p. 467)

'But *the fellow was forever sticking in here,*' he burst out (p. 147)

*Crois-tu que je ne voyais pas* que tu ne pouvais point rester deux jours sans le faire venir ici? (p. 544)

'But *if you think I was totally blind. . .*' (p. 148)

*Il vit deux larmes* grossir lentement dans les yeux fixes de sa maîtresse, puis *couler sur ses joues,* tandis que deux autres se formaient déjà au bord des paupières. (pp. 304–5)

*He caught a glimpse* of wet eyelashes, *of a* red *cheek with a tear running down swiftly* (p. 149)

Et, *brusquement, il lui murmura* dans le visage, *à voix basse:* – Allons, avoue que tu étais la maîtresse de Vaudrec. (p. 466)

'He made love to you [. . .]' *He lowered his voice.* (p. 147)

Ce mot, ce nom du mort sorti de sa bouche, *le surprit comme si* quelqu'un le lui eût crié du fond d'un fourré, et il se tut *brusquement* Au bout d'une minute, *il demanda:* – Es-tu venue quelque-fois ici comme ça, le soir, avec Charles? (p. 354)

*Suddenly he gave a start, as if* waking up, and *asked* very gently and *not much above a whisper* – 'Have you been meeting him often?' (p. 150)

*Sa pensée s'égarait dans ces angoisses et dans ces incertitudes. [. . .] ses idées*

He was wearied. *Thinking seemed a labour* beyond his strength. (p. 151) *devenaient pénibles*, troubles, lui faisaient mal. (pp. 545–6)

Le notaire reprit, *après un moment de silence* (p. 463)

He lifted up his head *after a moment of* brooding *silence*. (p. 151)

*Il paraissait hésiter* de nouveau (p. 470)

Looking at her *he appeared to hesitate* (p. 151)

et *il se mit à penser tout haut*, parlant pour sa femme sans s'adresser à elle:
– Eh bien! oui ... (p. 468)

At last she went on musingly, *as if thinking aloud*, 'I tried to understand.' (p. 152)

ravi de pouvoir se faire cette alliée dans l'existence, *il lui tendit les deux mains*:
– Je suis à vous, madame, comme il vous plaira.
   Elle sentit la sincérité de la pensée *dans la voix*, et *elle donna ses mains*.
   Il les baisa [...] puis il dit simplement en relevant la tête:
– Cristi, si j'avais trouvé une femme comme vous, avec quel bonheur je l'aurais épousée!
*Elle fut touchée*, cette fois, caressée par cette phrase (p. 177)

there was a suspicion of tears in his tone when he said almost unthinkingly, 'My God! I did love you!'
   *She seemed touched* by the emotion *of his voice*. [...] she made one faltering step towards him, *putting out her hands* in a beseeching gesture (p. 153)

*L'amertume de son coeur* lui montait aux lèvres en paroles de mépris et de dégoût. (p. 358)

He, with his features distorted by *the bitterness of his thought* (p. 153)

*Il frappa du pied*:
– Tu mens. Ce n'est pas possible (p. 467)

*He stamped his foot* in vexation [...] then exploded. 'What the devil am I to do now?' (p. 153)

Quand *il aperçut son visage* reflété dans le verre poli, il se reconnut à peine, et il lui sembla qu'il ne s'était jamais vu. *Ses yeux* lui parurent énormes; et *il était pâle*, certes, *il était pâle, très pâle*. (p. 238)

*He caught sight of himself* in the pier glass, drawn up to his full height, and *with a face so white* that *his eyes*, at the distance, resembled the black cavities in a skull. (p. 158)

*Dès qu'il* fut seul, *une rage furieuse le saisit contre* cette vieille rosse de mère Walter. Ah! il allait l'envoyer coucher, celle-là, et durement (p. 452) [Mme Walter had wound her hair round his waistcoat buttons and Mme de Marelle, finding it, had broken with him.]

'You've tried me to the utmost,' he said at last; and *as soon as he* said these words *he* [...] *felt himself swept away* [...] *by a flood of passionate resentment against* the bungling creature that had come so near to spoiling his life. (p. 159)

Elle parlait avec tant de naturel et de

Unexpectedly *he hesitated*.

| | |
|---|---|
| tranquilité que *Georges hésitait. [...]* *Elle murmura* avec douceur [...]. Il marchait toujours, et il se mit à penser tout haut, *parlant* pour sa femme sans s'adresser à elle (p. 468) | 'Yes... I see,' *she murmured.* 'Of course you would,' he said, looking at the carpet and *speaking* like one who thinks of something else. (p. 160) |
| Il n'a pas vu dans quelle *position fausse, ridicule,* il allait me mettre. (p. 469) | He said rapidly – 'My *position* is very *painful – difficult...*' (p. 161) |
| Il fut longtemps sans répondre, puis il prononça, en hésitant: – *Le monde* ne comprendra jamais (p. 469) | He looked [...] as though frightfully oppressed by a sudden inability to express his pent-up ideas. [...] *The world* is right (p. 161) |
| Elle répliqua un peu *impatiente* (p. 470) | He made a slight gesture of *impatient* assent. |
| Elle l'arrêta avec une nuance d'irritation: – C'est entendu. J'ai compris (p. 472) | 'Yes! Yes! It's all very well ... of course.' (p. 161) |
| Elle réfléchissait, troublée *comme on* l'est devant *les grandes catastrophes.* (p. 545) | He gazed down at her for a moment with a sombre stare, *as one* looks at ruins, at the devastation of *some natural disaster.* (p. 162) |
| *Il recommença à parler avec abondance [...]* Du moment que j'accepte la moitié de cet héritage, *il est bien évident que personne n'a plus le droit de* sourire. C'est dire hautement: 'Ma femme accepte parce que j'accepte moi, son mari, qui suis juge de ce qu'elle peut faire sans se compromettre. Autrement ça aurait fait *scandale.*' (p. 471) | *he recommenced talking very fast. [...]* 'For it is self-evident,' he went on with anxious vivacity, 'it is self-evident that, on the highest ground *we haven't the right* [...] to intrude our miseries upon those who – who naturally expect better things from us. [...] Now, a *scandal* amongst people of our position is disastrous for the morality (p. 164) |
| *Le monde a souvent des jugements malveillants.* (p. 464) | *The world is pitiless in its judgments.* (p. 165) |
| Il reprit: – C'est égal, nous ne pouvons accepter cet héritage dans ces conditions. Ce serait d'un effet déplorable. Tout le monde croirait la chose, tout le monde en jaserait et rirait de moi. Les confrères *sont déjà trop disposés à* me jalouser et à m'attaquer. Je dois avoir plus que personne le souci de mon honneur et le soin de ma réputation. (p. 468) | And yet those two had been engaged in a conspiracy against his peace (p. 159) the dishonouring episode (p. 160) 'Unfortunately there are always those in it [the world] who *are only too eager* to misunderstand. [...] any disclosure would impair my usefulness [...] in the larger sphere in which I hope soon to... [...] The ideal must – must be preserved |

Le monde ne comprendra jamais [...]
que j'aie admis cela, moi. (p. 469)

– Oui, *c'est clair comme le jour* (p. 471)

– for others, at least. *It's clear as daylight.*
[...] And there are the fools and the
envious – especially for people in our
position.' (p. 165)

One night, when Walter finds his daughter Suzanne's room empty, he
realizes that she has run away to join Duroy who wants to marry her. After the
first shock, being a practical man, he concludes that to avoid scandal he must
consent to the marriage but, on hearing this, his wife, who has been Duroy's
mistress, becomes hysterical. In the parallel scene, the same concern to avoid
a scandal is again uppermost in Hervey's mind, and he, too, upbraids his wife
for her lack of self-control and vents his anger and frustration in an outburst
against women:

*Il se mit à marcher* avec rage *à travers
l'appartement* et reprit (p. 544)

Dès qu'il l'eut vu [l'appartement de sa
fille], il ne conserva plus de doute. Elle
s'était enfuie.
*Il tomba dans un fauteuil* et posa sa
lampe par terre devant lui.
Sa femme l'avait rejoint. Elle bégaya:
– Eh bien?
*Il n'avait plus la force de répondre*; il
n' avait plus de colère, il gémit:
– C'est fait, il la tient. Nous sommes
perdus. [...]
Elle poussa une sorte de cri de bête:
– Lui! jamais! Tu es donc fou?
Il répondit tristement:
– Ça ne sert à rien de hurler. Il l'a
enlevée, il l'a déshonorée. Le mieux est
encore de la lui donner. En s'y prenant
bien, *personne ne saura cette aventure.*
Elle répéta, secouée d'une émotion
terrible:
– Jamais! jamais il n'aura Suzanne!
Jamais je ne consentirai!
Walter murmura avec accablement:
– Mais il l'a. C'est fait. Et il la gardera
et la cachera tant que nous n'aurons
point cédé. Donc, *pour éviter le scandale,*
il faut céder tout de suite. (p. 547)

Elle avait envie de crier, de *se rouler
par terre*, de s'arracher les cheveux. Elle
prononça encore, d'une voix exaspérée:

'Not you,' *he* said [...] and *began to
walk up and down the room. S*he remained
very still with an air of listening
anxiously to her own heart-beats, then
*sank down on the chair* slowly, *and sighed,
as if giving up a task beyond her strength.*
'You misunderstand everything I say,'
he began quietly, 'but I prefer to think
that – just now – you are not accountable
for your actions.' He stopped again
before her. 'Your mind is unhinged,' he
said, with unction. 'To go now would be
adding crime – yes, crime – to folly. *I'll
have no scandal* in my life, no matter
what's the cost. And why? You are sure
to misunderstand me – but I'll tell you.
As a matter of duty. Yes. But you're sure
to misunderstand me – recklessly.
*Women* always do – they *are too – too
narrow-minded.*' (pp. 163–4)

'Oh, nonsense!' he said, sharply. 'You
are perfectly capable of coming down to
dinner. *No one should even suspect*; not
even the servants.' (p. 169)

he felt such a tempest of anguish within
him that he seemed to see himself *rolling
on the carpet*, beating his head against the

– Il ne l'aura pas ... Je ... ne ... veux     wall. (p.130)
... pas!
Walter [...] reprit:
– Tiens, *tu es stupide comme toutes les
femmes*. Vous n'agissez jamais que par
passion. Vous ne savez pas vous plier aux
circonstances... *vous êtes stupides*!
(p. 548–9)

Mme de Marelle, having learned from her husband that Duroy is about to
marry Suzanne, realizes that she herself has been used as a stop-gap between his
divorce and his marriage and pours out her contempt until, half hysterical, she
accuses him of having already slept with the girl. Exasperated by this lie, Duroy
slaps her violently, and she falls to the ground where he strikes her again as though
hitting a man. Although Conrad toned down the physical violence considerably,
he reworked some of the reactions of these characters for the scene where Hervey's
wife bursts into hysterical laughter on being told he forgives her:

Il se leva, et la lèvre tremblante:
– *Tais-toi*, ou je te fais sortir d'ici. [...]
*Elle ne pouvait plus parler*, tant *elle
suffoquait* de colère, et brusquement,
comme si la porte de sa fureur se fut
brisée, elle éclata:
– [...] Crois-tu que je ne sais pas
comment tu as couché avec Suzanne
pour la forcer à t'épouser... [...]
Elle cria:
– Tu as couché avec, je le sais.
Il eût accepté n'importe quoi, mais ce
mensonge l'exaspérait. [...] cette
fausseté sur cette petite fille qui allait
devenir sa femme *éveillait dans le creux de
sa main un curieux besoin de frapper*.
Il répéta:
– *Tais-toi*... prends garde... tais-
toi... [...]
*Elle hurla*, décoiffée, *la bouche grande
ouverte, les yeux fous:*
– Tu as couché avec...
*Il* la lâcha et *lui lança par la figure* un
tel soufflet qu'elle alla tomber contre le
mur. [...] Il se rua sur elle, et, la tenant
sous lui, la frappa comme s'il tapait sur
un homme.
*Elle se tut soudain [...]. Elle ne remuait
plus*. Elle avait caché sa figure dans

'*Stop this!*' he cried [...]. He darted back
with *the idea of stifling that unbearable
noise with his hands*, but stood still
distracted, finding himself as unable to
touch her as though she had been on fire.
*He shouted, 'Enough of this!*' like men
shout in the tumult of a riot, *with a red
face and starting eyes* (p. 166)

*the woman gasped* and laughed [...].
He reappeared, striding at her, and
with a tumbler of water in his hand. He
stammered:
'Hysterics – Stop [...].' She laughed at
the ceiling. 'Stop this!' he cried. 'Ah!'
*He flung* the water *in her face*, putting
into the action all the secret brutality of
his spite, yet still felt that it would have
been perfectly excusable – in any one –
to send the tumbler after the water. He
restrained himself, but at the same time
was so convinced nothing could stop the
horror of those *mad shrieks* [...]. When,
*next moment*, he became sure that she was
sitting up, *and really very quiet* [...]. Her
face was *streaming with* water and *tears*
[...]. There was an utter unreserve in
her aspect (p. 167)

She pressed both her hands to her

l'angle du parquet et de la muraille [...].
Il cessa de la battre et se redressa.
[Duroy then goes to the bedroom to
wash and returns to see what she is
doing.]
*Elle n'avait point bougé.* Elle restait
étendue par terre, *pleurant doucement.*
Il demanda:
– Auras-tu bientôt fini de larmoyer?
*Elle ne répondit pas.* [...]
Puis, tout à coup, il prit une résolution
[...]:
– Bonsoir. [...] *Je n'attendrai pas ton
bon plaisir.*
*Il* sortit, *ferma la porte* (pp. 557–9)

temples. [...] *She [...] seemed incapable
of pronouncing a word.*
*Why didn't she speak?* [...] he began to
think of some effectual violence (p. 169)

'*I will wait for you*,' he said, *going to
the door.* [...] in the doorway he glanced
over his shoulder to say, 'It's rather late
– you know –' and saw her standing
*where he had left her*, with a face white as
alabaster and *perfectly still*, like a woman
in a trance. (p. 170)

Lastly, the influence of *Bel-Ami* can be seen in Conrad's extensive use of reflections in mirrors to externalize a psychological state, a device Maupassant exploited throughout his novel to emphasize its main theme, i.e. Duroy's advancement in the world. As Sullivan points out: 'at every critical point in his career he is suddenly brought sharply to an awareness of himself and his position by catching a glimpse of himself as others see him in the sudden apparition of his own image in a mirror'.[20] Similarly, in 'The Return' the theme of conventionality is emphasized by repeated descriptions of Hervey mirrored in his wife's pier-glass which produces a multiplicity of 'slavish imitators' and 'sham men' (pp. 124, 125).[21]

Towards the end of 'The Return', Conrad turned to another of Maupassant's tales, 'Un soir' (cf. *La Main gauche*, pp. 142–54, and *TU*, pp. 171–5 and 184–5). There are, of course, deep differences between Hervey's reaction to his wife's infidelity and that of Trémoulin, the main protagonist of 'Un soir': whereas the latter becomes morbidly jealous, the former suddenly develops a moral conscience. However, although the stories move far apart, they still have a number of points in common and there is clear evidence that Conrad wove some of the reactions of Maupassant's characters into his own work.

One day, Trémoulin sees a woman in the street who resembles his wife whom he has left at home complaining of migraine. Intrigued, he catches up with her:

Elle me regardait bien en face. Elle n'était plus rouge, mais plutôt *un peu pâle. Ses yeux clairs et limpides*, – ah! les yeux des femmes! – semblaient pleins de vérité, mais je sentis vaguement, douloureusement, qu'*ils étaient pleins de mensonge.* Je restais devant elle plus confus, plus embarrassé, plus saisi qu'elle-même, sans oser rien soupçonner, mais sûr qu'elle mentait. Pourquoi? je n'en savais rien.          (*La Main gauche*, pp. 142–3)

Having had 'the intuition of her falsehood' when facing her, he loses his mental balance until one night, demented by the idea that he will never be able to probe the mystery of his wife's mind, he feels like taking a hammer to break open her head 'to see inside'; he acknowledges that, of course, it would have been of no avail: *'Je n'aurais pas su! Impossible de savoir! Et ses yeux! Quand elle me regardait, j'étais soulevé par des rages folles. On la regarde – elle vous regarde! Ses yeux sont transparents, candides – et faux, faux, faux! et on ne peut deviner ce qu'elle pense, derrière'* (p. 148). Hervey, after his wife's escapade, looks at her in amazement that she should be only *'a little pale'* but otherwise 'unchanged'. And he wonders:

> What did she think? What meant the pallor, the placid face, the candid brow, *the pure eyes?* What did she think during all these years? What did she think yesterday – today; what would she think tomorrow? He must find out.... And yet how could he get to know? She had been *false* to him [...]. *Always false. She looked lies,* breathed lies, lived lies – would tell lies – always – to the end of life! And *he would never know* what she meant. Never! Never! No one could. *Impossible to know.* (pp. 171–2)

Later, at the dinner table, looking at his servants, he realizes that he will never know their secret thoughts either and he ponders on the 'impenetrable *duplicity'* of women (p. 173). Trémoulin holds the same view: 'Les femmes ont tant de subtilités et de *roueries* natives dans l'âme' (p. 146). Both men suddenly see life as full of deceit and uncertainty and have to face the destruction of their safe, comfortable little worlds. At first, the Frenchman tries to reason with himself: 'Chacun de nous n'a-t-il pas *le droit* d'avoir ses petits secrets innocents, une sorte de seconde vie intérieure dont on ne doit compte à personne?' (p. 145). This thought is reflected in Hervey's wife's reaction, who, when he insists that he 'wants to know', exclaims: 'Alvan... I won't bear this ... [...] I've a *right* – a right to – to – myself...' (p. 185).

At last Trémoulin sets a trap so that he may surprise his wife with her lover in a private room. But instead of finding her with the handsome young man he suspects, he sees her kissing a sixty-six-year-old general. He is so 'struck with amazement' at this sight that his anger subsides and is immediately replaced by disgust:

> Je m'attendais si bien à trouver l'autre, que je demeurai *perclus d'étonnement.*
> Et puis... et puis... je ne sais pas encore ce qui se passa en moi... non... je ne sais pas? Devant l'autre, j'aurais été convulsé de fureur!... Devant celui-là, devant ce vieil homme ventru, aux joues tombantes, je fus suffoqué par le dégoût. [...] Non, je n'avais plus envie de tuer ma femme [...]. *Je n'étais plus jaloux, j'étais éperdu comme si j'avais vu l'horreur des horreurs!* (pp. 151–2)

Hervey has a similar reaction after his wife has an 'uncontrollable burst of sincerity'. It completed *his bewilderment, but he was not at all angry now. He was as if benumbed by the fascination of the incomprehensible'* (p. 175). Later, they contemplate each other 'as if *struck dumb with amazement'* (p. 184).

Conrad was long tormented wondering how to end 'The Return' and 'Un soir' could have suggested the final twist. Trémoulin is now a settler in Algeria. When the friend to whom he has narrated the episode asks him what he did after the discovery of his wife's unfaithfulness, he answers simply 'Je suis parti'. Conrad's abrupt ending or 'coup de canon', to use Ford's term, is 'He never returned'.

The question remains: why was Conrad so attracted to these two works by Maupassant? In the light of the problems he encountered when he tackled his 'uncongenial subject' (the relationship between the sexes), the first suggestion is that they gave him material and models for the treatment of a marital conflict. They would also provide him with the appropriate bourgeois setting he needed. In a letter to Edward Garnett, he explained that he had 'wanted to give out the gospel of the beastly bourgeois' (*CL*, I, p. 393) and, no doubt, he found, in *Bel-Ami* in particular, the same bourgeois world, with its conventional values and shallow materialism, that he, like Maupassant, wished to castigate.

In August 1910, Conrad confessed to Mlle Séligmann-Lui, who had just completed the translation of 'The Idiots', that *Tales of Unrest* was, of all his works, the one that he liked least, adding: 'Je m'y vois "dérivatif" plus que de raison' (*LF*, p.103). We are now in a position to understand what he had in mind.

## 'Youth'

In 'Youth' (May–June 1898), a story based primarily on Conrad's own experience on the *Palestine*, his earlier experiments in narrative technique came to fruition with the creation of Marlow. Watson has argued that Maupassant's 'L'Epave' – a story included five years later in the Martindale selection – provided him with a 'helpful model' for the 'oblique narrative approach' needed to create the mood of 'wistful regret, of reminiscent tenderness' (*YOS*, p. vii) in an older man's recollection of a youthful experience, 'as well as for theme, tone, and many verbal details'. He explains:

Beyond similar narrative structures and their ironic treatments of youthful romanticism, the two stories have several important details in common. Most striking is the fact that significant action in each is set on an old ship, whose image remains vividly in the imagination of the narrator. Garin recalls feeling almost bewitched by the large wreck as he approached it across a wide beach at low tide: 'Je croyais assister à une féerie gigantesque et surnaturelle. [...] L'avant était entré profondément dans cette plage douce et perfide, tandis que l'arrière, relevé, semblait jeter vers le ciel, comme un cri d'appel désespéré, ces deux mots blancs sur le bordage noir: Marie-Joseph' [pp. 78–9]. Marlow of 'Youth' says of his first sight of the old ship *Judea*, her stern painted with her name, scrollwork, a coat-of-arms, and the motto 'Do or Die': 'I remember it took my fancy immensely. There was a touch of romance in it [...] something that appealed to my youth!' [p.5]. Furthermore, there are similar notes of regretful reminiscence both at the beginning and at the end of each story:

| | |
|---|---|
| It was twenty-two years ago: and I was just twenty. How time passes! It was | Oh! ce fut un singulier jour de l'an, cette année-lá. Il y a de cela vingt ans |

one of the happiest days of my life. [pp. 4–5]

... puisque j'avais trente ans et que j'en ai cinquante! [p. 72]

But you here [...] wasn't that the best time, that time when we were young at sea; young and had nothing, ... except hard knocks – and sometimes a chance to feel your strength – that only – what you all regret? [p. 42]

Elle doit être vieille, à présent ... je ne la reconnaîtrais pas ... Elle m'écrit que ses cheveux sont tout blancs ... Mon Dieu! ... ça m'a fait une peine horrible ... Ah! ses cheveux blonds! ... Non, la mienne n'existe plus ... Que c'est triste ... tout ça! [p. 92][22]

To this could be added a number of verbal parallels which show how closely Conrad was following his model:

Le père [...] la figure rouge *encadrée* de favoris blancs (*La Petite Roque*, p. 82)

[The skipper's face] was *framed* in iron-gray fluffy hair (*YOS*, p. 4)

Le jour [...] éclairait tristement ces sortes de *caves* longues et *sombres* (p. 79)

that vast hold, *gloomy* like a *cavern* (p. 6)

Tout à coup, *j'entendis des sanglots*. La plus petite des Anglaises *pleurait*. (p. 87)

One of the ship's boys [...] *wept* as if his heart would break. *We could hear him blubbering* (p. 7)

un jour gris, glacial, *sali* par une brume lourde [...]. Sous ce *plafond* de brouillard *bas* et sinistre, la mer jaune (p. 74)

a sky *low* enough to touch with the hand and *dirty* like a smoked *ceiling*. (p. 10)

l'épave, tellement brisée et *disjointe* que la première vague un peu rude *l'emporterait en bouillie*. (pp. 87-8)

She was *working herself loose* [...] the ship was *going from us piecemeal* (p. 11)

Le *Marie-Joseph* [...] naviguant au hasard *sur une mer d'écume*, – '*une mer de soupe au lait*', disait le capitaine (p. 75)

*The sea was white like a sheet of foam, like a caldron of* boiling *milk* (p. 11)

Two memories of *Madame Bovary* can also be traced at the beginning of 'Youth'. The description of Mrs Beard, 'an old woman, with *a face all wrinkled and ruddy like a* winter *apple*' (p. 7) echoes that of the old servant, Catherine Leroux, who is awarded a medal at the cattle-show: '*Son visage* maigre [...] *était plus plissé de rides qu'une pomme* de reinette flétrie' (*MB*, p. 208).[23] Similarly, Marlow's evocation of brown nations 'ruled by kings more cruel than Nero the Roman, and more splendid than Solomon the Jew' (p. 18) inevitably recalls the image of Homais 'plus garrotté' qu'un Scythe et splendid comme un mage' (p. 475). (*Yelton, pp. 114–15)

## 'Heart of Darkness'

Although 'Heart of Darkness' (December 1898–February 1899) is, like 'Youth', based primarily on Conrad's own experience, this time in the Belgian Congo in 1890, his wide reading played an important part in its elaboration. Norman Sherry and M. M. Mahood, in particular, have established a considerable number of non-fictional sources,[24] and extensive scholarship has made the story resonate with a multiplicity of historical associations, religious allusions to pagan, Christian and Buddhist traditions, and literary references to the *Aeneid*, Dante's *Inferno*, and the search for the Grail of Arthurian legend.[25] Aniela Kowalska has pointed to a source for Kurtz in Rimbaud's *Une saison en enfer* (see appendix, pp. 247–8). Mahood has also suggested that the origin of Kurtz as a symbol of European intrusion into Africa may lie in 'Le Vieux du Zambèse', by Pierre Mille, which appeared in *Cosmopolis* 'a month or so before "Heart of Darkness" took shape in Conrad's imagination'.[26] And Ernest Baker has noticed another parallel with Loti's *Le Roman d'un spahi* 'in the enervating and demoralizing effect of the African milieu on a European'.[27]

Finally, there are a few inevitable echoes from Flaubert and Maupassant. The opening scene of 'Heart of Darkness' seems to have been inspired by one from *Madame Bovary* also set on a beautiful evening:

*La vapeur* du soir passait entre les peupliers sans feuilles, estompant leurs contours d'une teinte violette, plus pâle et plus transparente qu'*une gaze* subtile *arrêtée* sur leurs branchages. Au loin, des bestiaux marchaient [...] et la cloche, sonnant toujours, continuait dans les airs sa lamentation *pacifique*. (*MB*, p. 153)

The day was ending in a serenity of still and exquisite brilliance. The water shone *pacifically* [...] *the* very *mist* on the Essex marshes was like *a gauzy* and radiant *fabric*, *hung* from the wooded rises inland, and draping the low shores in diaphanous folds. (*YOS*, p. 46)

The tell-tale word here is 'pacifically', instead of the normal 'peacefully'.

Watson has also pointed out that Conrad, when beginning this story a few months after writing 'Youth', may have remembered another detail from 'L'Epave': the ironic use by Maupassant's narrator of the Latin phrase *Ave, Caesar, morituri te salutant*, which Marlow invokes outside the 'door of darkness' in the sepulchral city.[28] Finally, Kirschner has noted that when Marlow, listening to the yelling savages, suspects there is a meaning in the uproar which he can comprehend because '*The mind of man is capable of anything* – because everything is in it' (p. 96), he is echoing Maupassant's remark '*L'esprit de l'homme est capable de tout*' (*Toine*, p. 131), the conclusion of the story 'La Chevelure', a terrifying illustration of this concept. (*Kirschner, p. 214)

**Lord Jim**

*Lord Jim* (May 1898–July 1900), 'Conrad's most Polish novel', according to Najder,[29] his most Jamesian novel, according to Elsa Nettels,[30] is also, together with *The Nigger of the 'Narcissus'*, the work where Flaubert's presence is most visible.

Once again Flaubert's famous study of the romantic temperament must have provided Conrad with a valuable model. Despite considerable differences, Emma and Jim have a great deal in common in their psychological make-up. Both have a taste for romantic and sentimental literature which, with their vivid imaginations, develops in them a distorted view of reality and an exalted conception of themselves. Both are narcissistic and, because of this concentration on self and its resultant feeling of personal superiority, are spiritually isolated, unable to respond to the needs of others and lack a genuine sense of commitment to their community. Because of the idealized role they embrace, they are incapable of learning from experience and so remain immature. Both fail to realize that, to alter the course of their lives, the change must come not from new surroundings and new adventures but from within themselves.

The congruence between the two works is most clearly seen in four areas. The first is in the parallels between Emma's life in the convent and Jim's training at sea; the second in the use of the sea as a symbol of the protagonists' aspirations and delusions; the third in the use of fog and mist to convey the vagueness that characterizes their dreams and their conception of themselves; the fourth in their suicides which are the natural outcome of their delusions.

The famous sixth chapter of *Madame Bovary* relates how Emma's romantic and sentimental nature was formed in her convent, how she acquired the habit of idealizing reality because she was susceptible to the symbolic illustrations in her missal, to figurative religious language, and later to romantic literature. Her tragedy arises from the fact that the romance and sentiment she found there so shaped her outlook that she can evaluate her experiences only by comparing them with those presented in her novels. The Ball at La Vaubyessard makes such 'a hole' in her life because she sees in it a confirmation of her romantic reading which has left her with three key terms for existence, 'félicité', 'passion', and 'ivresse' (p. 47).[31] Typical in this respect is her reaction after she has yielded to Rodolphe: she looks at herself in a mirror and, transfigured, exclaims: 'J'ai un amant!' (p. 225). She then recalls the heroines in her novels and is delighted because she feels that she has become one of them.

The same applies to Jim. He comes from a 'parsonage', another abode 'of piety and peace', and his vocation for the sea declares itself 'after a course of light holiday literature' (p. 5). When among his mates on the lower deck, he lives 'in his mind the sea-life of light literature' performing all sorts of wondrous feats, 'always an example of devotion to duty, and as unflinching as a hero in a book' (p. 6). After his interview with Stein, he confronts Marlow and exhibits 'with glee' a silver ring. He then explains that this was his introduction to an old chief called Doramin who had been Stein's friend, 'a sort of credential – ("It's like something you read of in books," he threw in appreciatively)' (pp. 233–4). Later, when he and Marlow attend a public function presided over by Doramin, he remarks 'triumphantly': 'they are like people in a book, aren't they?' (p. 260). The ring and Doramin's court are to Jim a reflection of his reading of adventure literature: triumphant proof of the reality of his own imaginings.

As dreamers convinced of their own superiority, both Emma and Jim are constantly seen, physically or mentally, above the workaday world. Jean Rousset has noted that Flaubert often places his heroine in a dominant position from which she has a plunging perspective.[32] For instance, Emma and Rodolphe watch the events at the *Comices* from the first-floor window of the Town Hall; their ride takes them to the top of the hill overlooking Yonville; she reads his farewell note in the attic; at the theatre, she looks down from her box at the audience and the stage; each week, as the stage-coach is approaching Rouen, she suddenly sees the whole landscape 'd'en haut' (p. 364); after the final break with Rodolphe, during her hallucinatory walk at nightfall, she again finds herself at the summit of a slope. Furthermore, Emma's dreams reveal the importance she unconsciously attaches to altitude. Fantasizing about Paris, she imagines the life of men of letters and actresses as 'une existence au-dessus des autres, entre ciel et terre, dans les orages, quelque chose de sublime' (p. 82). Embarking on her liaison with Rodolphe, she sees 'les sommets du sentiment' sparkling beneath her and ordinary life appears only as a distant phenomenon 'tout en bas' (p. 225). And when she is eloping with him in her dreams, they often catch a glimpse of some splendid city 'du haut d'une montagne' (p. 271).

Similarly, Jim is often placed in a dominant position and his natural home in his dream world is in the heights. As a child he lived just below a little church 'on a hill' (p. 5) and as a seaman his station was 'in the fore-top' from where he 'looked down' (p. 6) at the material world. The hospital where he recovers from a leg injury also stands 'on a hill' (p. 12) from which he has a splendid view over the roadstead. In the court-room, during his trial, he stands 'elevated' in the witness-box.[33] Marlow, in the course of his discussion with Chester, has 'a rapid vision of Jim perched on a shadowless rock' (p. 167). Later, in Patusan, we see Marlow with Jim 'high in the sunshine on the top of that historic hill of his', and he stresses the significance of this most emphatically: 'He dominated the forest, the secular gloom, the old mankind. He was like a figure set up on a pedestal [...]. I don't know why he should always have appeared to me symbolic' (p. 265).[34]

Such a conviction of personal superiority is bound to generate a contempt for others. On the death of her mother, Emma sends a bewildering letter to her father who hurries to the convent fearing that she must be ill, and Emma is gratified to feel that she has attained at the outset 'ce rare idéal des existences

pâles, où ne parviennent jamais les coeurs médiocres' (p. 53). After her unsuc-
cessful visit to the notary, it seems to her that Providence is bent on persecuting
her 'et, s'en rehaussant d'orgueil, jamais elle n'avait eu tant d'estime pour elle-
même ni tant de mépris pour les autres' (p.420). After his failure in the rescue
operation, Jim, instead of coming to terms with it, feels 'angry' with the
elements for 'taking him unawares'. But he also experiences a feeling of superiority over his mates: 'He had enlarged his knowledge more than those who
had done the work' and is even contemptuous of them, seeing in their account
of the incident 'a pitiful display of vanity' (p. 9).

Finally, a reminiscence from *Madame Bovary* is apparent at the beginning
of *Lord Jim*. Still in a languorous mood after her surrender to Rodolphe, Emma
slowly becomes aware of her surroundings and '*elle sentait* son coeur, dont les
battements recommençaient, et *le sang circuler dans sa chair comme* un fleuve de
*lait*' (pp. 223–4). As Jim's night watch on the deck of the *Patna* is drawing to
a close, he 'sighed with content, with regret as well at having to part from that
serenity which fostered the adventurous freedom of his thoughts. *He* was a
little sleepy, too, and *felt* a pleasurable languor *running through* every limb *as
though all the blood in his body* had turned to warm milk' (p. 21).

The sea is, together with the colour blue, Flaubert's principal symbol of
romance in *Madame Bovary*.[35] Its significance as symbolic of the ideal or infinite, especially the ideal love Emma is yearning for, is conveyed most explicitly
in her first conversation with Léon. When he happens to mention sunsets, she
adds that nothing is so admirable as sunsets 'especially by the sea'. Léon assures
her that he adores the sea; she then replies: 'Et puis ne vous semble-t-il pas
[...] que l'esprit vogue plus librement sur cette étendue sans limites, dont la
contemplation vous élève l'âme et donne des idées d'infini, d'idéal' (p. 112).[36]

Since Emma, like other romantic lovers, thinks of the sea as directly related
to the ideal, it is appropriate that her feelings and aspirations, which she regards
as the expression of perfect love, are often conveyed in sea imagery. Such a
connection is made early in the book when, as she begins to be dissatisfied with
marital love, she turns despairing eyes upon the solitude of her life 'cherchant
au loin quelque voile blanche dans les brumes de l'horizon' (p. 87). During the
ride with Rodolphe, her face appears in a bluish transparency 'comme si elle
eût nagé sous des flots d'azur' (p. 221) and, at the height of the affair, she
dreams of escaping with him to live forever 'au fond d'un golfe, au bord de la
mer' (p. 271). Later, when she and Léon are on their three days of 'honeymoon',
they take a covered boat to dine on an island and their bed in the Hôtel de
Bourgogne on the harbour at Rouen is 'en forme de nacelle' (p. 366).

But Flaubert reverses the meaning of the symbol from the euphoric to the
menacing, thus making it an ironic register of Emma's illusions.[37] The changes
in her fortunes are carefully recorded in important descriptions in the ominous
connotations of instability, in the sickening sensation of disorientation that the
sea suddenly suggests. Thus, after reading Rodolphe's letter of farewell, it

seems to her that the floor of the attic dips on end 'à la manière d'un vaisseau qui tangue' (p. 285). Later, when she retreats from his *château* shattered by his refusal to help her, the ground under her feet is 'plus mou qu'une onde' (p. 432). The cab in which she begins her affair with Léon, and which clearly stands for her own grave, goes round and round frantically and aimlessly 'plus close qu'un tombeau et ballottée comme un navire' (p. 338), thus anticipating the final image of her coffin moving forward in a series of jerks 'comme une chaloupe qui tangue à chaque flot' (p. 466).

Conrad made an equally complex use of this symbol. Stein's metaphor of the swimmer[38] is not merely the most striking in the book, but is also central to a cluster of images and symbols associated with romanticism.[39] Marlow, as Guerard pointed out, undercuts Stein's famous pronouncement 'A man that is born falls into a dream like a man who falls into the sea' and his advice on how to survive in 'the destructive element' (p. 214) by associating Stein and his 'conviction' 'with the half-lights of deception and menacing illusion'.[40]

The rest of the imagery also provides an ironic comment on the nature of Jim's fantasies and romantic aspirations. They are linked to the sea right from the beginning when he is in the fore-top of the *Patna* and again, a few pages later, when he is pacing its deck 'by the watchful stars':

his eyes roaming about the line of the horizon, seemed to gaze hungrily into the unattainable [...]. Jim would glance at the compass, would glance around the unattainable horizon, would stretch himself [...] in the very excess of well-being [...]. At such times his thoughts would be full of valorous deeds: he loved these dreams and the success of his imaginary achievements.                                   (*LJ*, pp. 19–20)

Jim reacts to the sea and the 'unattainable horizon' as Emma does imaginatively when she evokes its 'limitless expanse' whose contemplation 'elevates the soul, gives ideas of the infinite, the ideal', and just as Flaubert deflates Emma's reaction by placing it in the midst of romantic clichés, so does Conrad by juxtaposing Jim's 'imaginary achievements' with the 'unattainable horizon'. Furthermore, a number of sea images suggest unpredictability and mysteriousness and represent Jim's isolation in his dreams in the midst of the indifference of nature. Marlow describes Jim standing 'like a lonely figure by the shore of a sombre and hopeless ocean' (p. 173), and, most strikingly, evokes Jim 'perched' on the barren Walpole Reef, surrounded by an 'empty sky' and an 'empty ocean [...] simmering together in the heat as far as the eye could reach' (p. 167), a vision which ironically recalls the picture of the youngster whose eyes 'seemed to gaze hungrily into the unattainable' but 'did not see the shadow of the coming event' (p. 19).

In both novels extensive symbolic use is also made of fog. Emma, like old Guérin's daughter, suffers from 'une manière de brouillard qu'elle avait dans la tête' (p. 152), signifying inner vagueness, absence of social outline, and lack of identity. Words like fog, mist, vapour and smoke, with which her thoughts and actions are constantly associated, reappear either to refer to aspects of her environment or as part of an elaborate pattern of metaphor and simile. During the fateful ride with Rodolphe, there is 'du brouillard' over the valley below them which is intimately related to the 'sort of fog in her head': 'Des vapeurs s'allongeaient à l'horizon, entre le contour des collines; et d'autres, se déchirant, montaient, se perdaient. [...] De la hauteur où ils étaient, toute la vallée paraissait un immense lac pâle, s'évaporant à l'air' (pp. 219-20). At this crucial moment in her life, when she is about to take an irreversible step towards disintegration, the words 'brouillard', 'vapeurs', 'brume' (in the following sentence), 's'évaporant', 's'allongeaient', 'se déchirant', 'se perdaient', are, in Tony Tanner's words, 'as it were, internalized in Emma; or we may say that she begins to participate in disintegrative and diffusive processes that are operative in the realm of nature'.[41] When she is lying on her death-bed, the whole vocabulary of indistinctness gathers around her corpse one last time and it seems to Charles that 'elle se perdait confusément dans l'entourage des choses' (p. 459).

We also find an important strand of controlling images of mist and cloudiness in Lord Jim which conveys the shifting, unreal quality of Jim's inflated dream and idealized ego. Jim is an ambiguous figure: in many respects he is an ordinary young man with an open character and is 'one of us'; but he is also motivated by an obscure dream, a 'shadowy ideal of conduct', a misconceived view of himself and his destiny which places him 'under a cloud' (p. 416). Marlow emphasizes the fact that he sees him only intermittently and partially on several occasions. After recalling an evening spent with him, he comments: 'The views he let me have of himself were like those glimpses through the shifting rents in a thick fog – bits of vivid and vanishing detail, giving no connected idea of the general aspect of a country' (p. 76). Also, in order to present the ambiguity and elusiveness of Jim's personality, the physical setting itself is often described in terms of light and shadow, sunshine and fog, daylight and dusk or darkness.[42] The physical setting, therefore, also illustrates the ambiguity and elusiveness of his nature.

The similarity between Madame Bovary and Lord Jim can also be discerned in the deaths of the protagonists, who play a fictional role to the last. After Rodolphe's refusal to help, Emma, hurt and humiliated, becomes deranged almost to the point of madness as the motif of the fog and the nightmarish kaleidoscope of images whirling through her mind indicate. But her pride suddenly asserts itself and she feels the situation must be resolved. However, misguided by her damaged ego, the only course of action she can envisage is one more confused and romantic gesture – suicide, which she decides to accomplish 'dans un transport d'héroïsme' (p. 432).

With the death of Dain Waris and his men, Jim is also faced with disgrace and humiliation and a shattered conception of himself. As a result, it is 'at the call of his exalted egoism', as Marlow states, that he 'goes away from a living woman to celebrate his pitiless wedding with a shadowy ideal of conduct' (p. 416). That 'proud and unflinching glance' (p. 416) of his final moment shows that he dies with his heroic but egotistical conception of himself triumphant, all sense of disgrace and humiliation forgotten. He is, of course, very different from Emma in that he achieves what Marlow calls an 'extraordinary success' (p. 416) but the fact remains that the motivation for his 'suicide' is, in some sense, akin to hers. Both novels illustrate the dangers of romantic idealism, isolating the individual from the community in a dream of improbable grandeur whose inevitable clash with the humdrum reality of daily life can only end in tragedy.

Finally, the description of Stein's study when Marlow pays him a visit again shows Conrad emulating Flaubert's superb rendering of visual impressions as Emma, arriving at La Vaubyessard, is escorted by the Marquis through the dimly-lit billiard-room where portraits of his ancestors are hung around the walls:

Comme elle la *traversait* pour aller au salon, Emma vit autour du jeu des hommes à figure grave [...] et qui souriaient silencieusement, en poussant leur queue. Sur la boiserie sombre du lambris, de grands cadres dorés portaient, au bas de leur bordure, des noms écrits en lettres noires. Elle lut [...]. Puis on distinguait à peine ceux qui suivaient, car *la lumière des lampes, rabattue* sur le tapis vert du billard, *laissait flotter une ombre dans l'appartement.* Brunissant les toiles horizontales, *elle se brisait contre elles* en arêtes fines, selon les craquelures du vernis; et de tous ces grands carrés noirs bordés d'or sortaient çà et là, quelque portion plus claire de la peinture, un front pâle, deux yeux qui vous regardaient                                                                                    (*MB*, p. 66)

Late in the evening I entered his study, after *traversing* an imposing but empty dining-room very dimly lit. The house was silent. I was preceded by an elderly grim Javanese servant [...]. Only one corner of the vast room, the corner in which stood his writing-desk, was strongly lighted by *a shaded reading-lamp, and the rest of the* spacious *apartment melted into shapeless gloom* like a cavern. Narrow shelves filled with dark boxes of uniform shape and colour ran round the walls [...]. Wooden tablets were hung above at irregular intervals. *The light reached one of them,* and the word *Coleoptera* written in gold letters glittered mysteriously upon a vast dimness.                                            (*LJ*, p. 204)

The presence of *L Education sentimentale* in the opening pages of *Lord Jim* is also unmistakable. The beginning of chapter two contains a stylistic imitation of the passage which comes after the famous 'blanc' so admired by Proust. Flaubert's text sums up many years of Frédéric Moreau's life after the collapse of his marriage with Mme Dambreuse and the death of Dussardier; Conrad's gives a summary of Jim's life at sea after his two years of training:

*Il voyagea.*
*Il connut* la mélancolie des paquebots, les froids réveils sous la tente, l'étourdissement des paysages et des ruines, l'amertume des sympathies interrompues.
Il revint.                                                                                            (*ES*, p. 600)

*He made many voyages. He knew* the magic monotony of existence between sky and water: he had to bear the criticism of men, the exactions of the sea, and the prosaic severity of the daily task that gives bread – but whose only reward is in the perfect love of the work. This reward eluded him.                                                              (*LJ*, p. 10)

It is clear that Conrad reproduced Flaubert's powerfully foreshortened style in the short opening and concluding sentences and the use of nominal constructions.

It has been demonstrated that he again had Frédéric in mind in the following chapter when describing Jim's 'intoxicating' dreams on the *Patna*:

They had *a gorgeous virility*, the charm of vagueness, they passed before him with a heroic tread; they carried his soul away with them and *made it drunk* with the divine philtre of *an unbounded confidence in itself*.                                           (*LJ*, p. 20)

After Frédéric has agreed to fight a duel with the Vicomte de Cisy over Mme Arnoux, he experiences 'comme *un orgueil de virilité, une surabondance de forces intimes qui l'enivraient*' (*ES*, p. 319; *Kirschner, pp. 187–8).

These two reminiscences suggest that the conception of Jim may also owe something to Frédéric. For instance, both young men display the same inability to act decisively at crucial times in their lives. Furthermore, Jim's dream of greatness, although it destroys him, gives him a certain stature, and in this he is close to Frédéric whose dream, as Kirschner has noted, gives distinction to his otherwise mediocre life.

Yelton has shown that the trope which introduces the Suffete Hannon in *Salammbô*: '*On aurait dit quelque grosse idole ébauchée dans un bloc de pierre*' (p. 45) is the 'prototype of a half-dozen similes found in works extending over much of Conrad's writing career'.[43] Three such similes appear in *Lord Jim*: the Captain of the *Patna* looks '*like a clumsy effigy of a man cut out of a block of fat*' (p. 23), Doramin '*like a figure of a man roughly fashioned of stone*' (p. 260), and Jewel's white figure 'seemed shaped in snow' (p. 348).

Other evidence indicates that the grotesque figure of Hannon played an important part in the conception of the German skipper and, to a lesser degree, that of Doramin. Hannon's condition is caused by leprosy; the skipper, according to Marlow, 'seemed to be swollen to an unnatural size by some awful disease, by the mysterious action of an unknown poison' (p. 46). Hannon's 'difformité' is 'hideuse' (p. 45); the captain's figure is 'odious and fleshy' (p. 21). Hannon's lips are '*violacées*' (p. 133) and '*les plis de* son cou *retombaient* jusqu'à sa poitrine *comme* des fanons de boeuf' (p. 45); the captain's lips are '*purplish*' (p. 46) and '*the fold of his* double chin *hung* like a bag triced up close under the hinge of his jaw' (p. 21). Their eyes have a common 'burning' or 'devouring' quality: we read of Hannon: 'Deux charbons semblaient brûler à la place de ses yeux' (p. 133) and the captain is said to look at people 'with a devouring glare' (p. 22). Hannon speaks '*d'une voix rauque* et hideuse' (p. 152); the captain 'in a voice *harsh* and dead' (p. 21) and later 'in a voice *harsh* and lugubrious' (p. 38) (note Conrad's Gallic post-positioning of the adjectives). Both men have a vile temper: Hannon's rage caused by his suffering 's'exhalait en injures' against his prisoners (p. 133); the skipper frequently 'let loose a torrent of foamy, abusive jargon' (p. 22). When in a fury Hannon '*soufflait* comme un hippopotame' (p. 132); the skipper '*puffed* like an exhaust-pipe' (p. 24).

As these parallels make clear, animal imagery plays an important part in conveying the grotesque appearance of both characters. After being compared to an elephant, an ox, a hippopotamus, a vulture, Hannon's strange and frightening physique is said to make him look like a 'bête farouche' (p. 133). Marlow says that when the skipper found himself at the door of Captain Elliot's office 'some sort of animal instinct made him hang back and snort like a frightened bullock' (p. 39). Hannon's unnatural voice sounds like a 'rugissement' (p. 133); the skipper normally grunts and growls (p. 22).

Another possible influence on Conrad in the characterization of Hannon is his frequent portrayal as a dead or inanimate object. We first see him with bandages wrapped round his legs 'comme autour d'une momie' (p. 44) and the comparison to 'quelque grosse idole ébauchée dans un bloc de pierre' is followed by the explanation that leprosy gave him the appearance of a 'chose inerte' (p. 45). Later, his breath is said to be more nauseating then 'l'exhalaison d'un cadavre' (p. 133), and on his first appearance the skipper makes a professional remark 'in a voice harsh and dead, resembling the rasping sound of a wood-file on the edge of a plank' (p. 21).[44] Marlow's presentation of him as a 'thick carcass' (p. 42) trembling on its legs also implies dead animality. And just before disappearing for good in the 'ramshackle little gharry' (p. 47), the skipper gazes 'in an inanimate way between his feet' and then forces his 'vast carcass' (p. 46) into the little conveyance.

Although, as Fritz Gysin points out, the very features which the skipper and Doramin have in common 'distort the skipper into a grotesque figure, whereas they express Doramin's majesty and dignity',[45] there is evidence that Conrad also had Hannon in mind when creating his Malay chief, not only when he compared Doramin to 'a figure of a man *roughly fashioned of stone*' (p. 260) but also when he modelled the last appearance of the old *nakhoda* on the first sight we get of the old Suffete:

la litière s'arrêta, et Hannon, *soutenu par deux esclaves*, posa ses pieds par terre, *en chancelant*.

[...] *On aurait dit quelque grosse idole ébauchée dans un bloc de pierre* [...] *et ses petits yeux*, aux cils collés, *brillaient d'un éclat dur et métallique*. (*Sal*, pp. 44-5)

The unwieldy old man [...] made an effort to rise [...] and *his two attendants helped him from behind*. [...] Doramin, *struggling to keep his feet*, made with his two supporters a swaying, *tottering* group; *his little eyes stared* with an expression of mad pain, of rage, *with a ferocious glitter* (*LJ*, p. 415)

This parallel enables one to see how Conrad derived from the contrast between the bulk of Hannon, his appearance as an 'inert thing', and the extraordinary life concentrated in his small, brilliant and hard eyes, Marlow's impression of Doramin: 'With his imposing bulk and haughty little eyes darting sagacious, inquisitive glances, he reminded one irresistibly of a cunning old elephant' (p. 274).

The impact of *Salammbô* on *Lord Jim* can further be detected in two images that Conrad borrowed from the description of Carthage. The first, which he had previously exploited in *The Nigger*, appears in the description of houses in Patusan:

A mesure que le ciel rose allait s'élargissant, *les* hautes *maisons* inclinées sur les pentes du terrain se haussaient, *se tassaient, telles qu'un troupeau de* chèvres noires qui descend des montagnes.                                                                 (*Sal*, p. 21)

*The houses crowding* along the wide shining sweep without ripple or glitter, stepping into the water in a line of jostling, vague, grey, silvery forms [...] *were like a* spectral *herd of* shapeless creatures pressing forward to drink in a spectral and lifeless stream.

(*LJ*, p. 246)

The second has its source in the description of the rising sun: 'Tout s'agitait dans une *rougeur épandue*, car le dieu, comme se déchirant, *versait* à pleins rayons sur Carthage la pluie d'or de ses *veines*' (p. 21). Conrad used this violent image to prefigure Jim's death when setting the stage for his final act: 'The sky over Patusan was *blood-red*, immense, *streaming* like an open *vein*' (p. 413).

Lastly, in the light of Conrad's verbal saturation in *Salammbô*, the similarities between the description of the landscape surrounding Hippo-Zaryte as Mâtho sees it during the siege of the city and the description of Patusan as viewed by Jim and Marlow are almost certainly not fortuitous:

Mâtho allait *s'asseoir* en dehors des tentes [...] et, tourné vers Carthage, il regardait l'horizon.

En face de lui, dans les oliviers, les palmiers, les myrtes et les platanes, *s'étalaient* deux larges étangs qui rejoignaient un autre lac dont on n'apercevait pas les contours. Derrière une montagne surgissaient d'autres montagnes, et, au milieu du lac immense, se dressait une *île* toute noire et de forme pyramidale. Sur la gauche, à l'extrémité du golfe, des tas de sable semblaient de grandes *vagues* blondes arrêtées, tandis que *la mer, plate* comme un dallage de lapis-lazuli, *montait insensiblement jusqu'au bord du ciel.* (*Sal*, pp. 123-4)

*I sat* on the stump of a tree at his feet, and below us *stretched* the land, the great expanse of the forests, sombre under the sunshine, rolling like a sea, with glints of winding rivers, the grey spots of villages, and here and there a clearing, like an *islet* of light amongst the dark *waves* of continuous tree-tops. [...] The land devoured the sunshine; only far off, along the coast, *the* empty *ocean, smooth* and polished within the faint haze, *seemed to rise up to the sky* in a wall of steel.                         (*LJ*, pp. 264-5)

*Lord Jim* is, of course, a very different novel from *Madame Bovary*, and its originality is not diminished by saying that it contains a psychological analysis of romantic illusion in the tradition of Flaubert's masterpiece. Its links with *Salammbô* show that the material and the inspiration Conrad drew from Flaubert were not confined to the romantic. His own well-established interest in the grotesque[46] was fostered by his familiarity with Flaubert, who identified 'le grotesque triste' as one of his basic artistic tendencies.

Conrad was also indebted to Maupassant in two important descriptive passages. When describing the beginning of the voyage of the *Patna* on the Arabian Sea, he returned to 'L'Epave' and exploited the description of the steamer *Jean-Guiton* on its voyage from La Rochelle to the island of Ré:

Il partit en soufflant, d'un air colère, *passa entre les deux* tours antiques qui gardent le port, traversa la rade, sortit de la digue construite par Richelieu, et dont on voit *à fleur d'eau les pierres énormes*, enfermant la ville comme un immense collier; puis *il obliqua* vers la droite.                                               (*La Petite Roque*, pp. 73–4)

C'était un de ces jours tristes *qui oppressent, écrasent la pensée, compriment le coeur, éteignent en nous toute force et toute énergie*; un jour gris, glacial, sali par une brume lourde, humide comme de la pluie, froide comme de la gelée, infecte à respirer comme une buée d'égout.

Sous ce plafond de brouillard bas et *sinistre*, la mer jaune, *la mer* peu *profonde* et sablonneuse de ces plages illimitées, *restait sans une ride, sans un mouvement, sans vie, une mer* d'eau trouble, *d'eau grasse, d'eau stagnante*. Le *Jean-Guiton passait dessus* en roulant un peu, par habitude, coupait *cette nappe* opaque *et lisse, puis laissait derrière lui quelques vagues, quelques clapots, quelques ondulations qui se calmaient bientôt*.

(*La Petite Roque*, p. 76)

le capitaine [...] me montra, en pleine mer, une chose presque imperceptible, et me dit: 'Tenez, voilà votre navire!' [...] J'étais stupéfait. *Ce point noir*, à peu près invisible [...] *des phares* brillaient [...] pareils à des yeux énormes, à des yeux de géant qui nous regardaient, nous guettaient [...]. Un d'eux surtout m'irritait [...]. *c'était bien un oeil, celui-là, avec sa paupière sans cesse baissée sur son regard de feu*.  (*La Petite Roque*, p. 88)

*She was headed between two* small islets, crossed *obliquely* the anchoring-ground of sailing-ships [...] then ranged close to *a ledge of* foaming *reefs*. [...] the steamer pounded in the dusk the calm water of the Strait; and far astern of the pilgrim ship *a* screw-pile *lighthouse* [...] *seemed to wink at her its eye of flame*, as if in derision of her errand of faith. She cleared the Strait, crossed the bay [...]. She held on straight for the Red Sea under a serene sky, under a sky scorching and unclouded, enveloped in a fulgor of sunshine *that killed all thought, oppressed the heart, withered all impulses of strength and energy*. And under the *sinister* splendour of that sky *the sea*, blue and *profound, remained still, without a stir*, without a ripple, *without a wrinkle* – *viscous, stagnant*, dead. The *Patna*, with a slight hiss, *passed over that plain* luminous *and smooth*, unrolled a black ribbon of smoke across the sky, *left behind her* on the water a white ribbon of foam *that vanished at once*, like the phantom of a track drawn upon *a lifeless sea* by the phantom of a steamer.                                                                 (*LJ*, pp. 15–16) on each side of the *Patna* two deep folds of water [...] enclosed [...] *a few wavelets, a few ripples, a few undulations* that, *left behind*, agitated the surface of the sea for an instant after the passage of the ship, subsided splashing gently, *calmed down* at last into the circular stillness of water and sky with the *black speck* of the moving hull remaining everlastingly in its centre.                                                                              (*LJ*, p. 17)

This extensive borrowing shows Maupassant's decisive influence on one of Conrad's most characteristic stylistic features, that is, the repeated use of ternary structures and anaphoric parallelism, a device which was undoubtedly part of what Conrad had in mind when he referred to 'l'allure maupassantesque' he claimed to have given his prose.[47] It also provides a fascinating example of the intricate mixture of factual and literary elements which make up Conrad's fiction. The story of the *Patna* is based upon the desertion of the pilgrim ship SS *Jeddah* by her European master and officers, and the route it follows on Jim's first journey in her is that of the *Jeddah*. However, Norman Sherry has called attention to the similarities between the *Patna*'s passage and that of the *Judea*, suggesting that Conrad was not only making use of the same basic experience but was working with the text of 'Youth' in mind.[48] To this it must now be added that he was closely following Maupassant's description of the journey of the *Jean-Guiton*, making only the appropriate modifications demanded by the different geographical locations. The description of the voyage of the *Patna* in the above passage owes at least as much to his reading of Maupassant as to the maritime experience in which it is rooted.

The second passage indebted to Maupassant, as Marlow sets the stage for his parting glimpse of Jim, clearly derives, with its unmistakable sexual overtones, from *Une vie*:

*Le soleil, plus bas,* semblait saigner; et une large traînée lumineuse, une route éblouissante courait sur l'eau depuis la limite de l'Océan jusqu'au sillage de la barque.
Les derniers souffles de vent tombèrent; toute ride s'aplanit; et la voile immobile était rouge. *Une accalmie illimitée* semblait engourdir l'espace, faire le silence autour de cette rencontre d'éléments; tandis que, *cambrant* sous le ciel *son ventre* luisant et liquide, *la mer*, fiancée monstrueuse, *attendait l'amant de feu qui descendait vers elle.* Il précipitait sa chute, *empourpré* comme par le désir de leur embrassement. Il la joignit; et, peu à peu, elle le dévora.                                                                           (*Une vie*, p. 54)

under *the low sun*, glowing, darkened and *crimson*, like an ember snatched from the fire, *the sea lay outspread, offering all its immense stillness to the approach of the fiery orb.*
                                                                              (*LJ*, p. 334)

There are also some noteworthy reminiscences from Conrad's other French reading. Stein's warning: 'There is only one remedy! One thing alone can us from being ourselves cure!' prompts Marlow's famous reply. 'Yes, [...] strictly speaking, *the question is not how to get cured, but how to live*' (p. 212) is an echo of the Abbé Galiani's remark to Mme d'Epinay, in a letter of 8 February 1777: 'Il faut vivre avec ses maux. *Le problème est de vivre, et pas de guérir*'.[49] Whether Conrad had actually read Galiani's correspondence or had come across his saying in a secondary source, this borrowing again illustrates his remarkable ability to make use of everything that came his way.

We know from Jean-Aubry that Conrad read Louis Garneray's *Voyages, aventures et combats* (1851) with enthusiasm in his childhood,[50] and this work, together with other sea-stories, probably kindled his desire to go to sea.[51] Towards the end of his life, he expressed the wish to re-read it.[52] In the light of his lasting fondness for this book, two striking similarities between it and *Lord Jim* seem worth recording. Before young Garneray takes part in his first naval battle his cousin, who is captain of his ship and also his guardian, warns him:

> Louis, [...] j'ai peur que, jeune comme tu l'es et n'ayant pas encore assisté à une affaire, tu ne faiblisses, lorsque tout à l'heure la question s'engagera, devant un danger nouveau et inconnu pour toi, que ton imagination n'a pu te révéler tel qu'il est. Si tu aimes mieux, j'ai peur que tu ne sois surpris.[53]

Jim, on board his training-ship, is also faced with a new and unknown situation which his 'imagination' (p. 10) failed to reveal to him, and hence 'taking him unawares' (p. 9). Garneray tells of his strong 'emotion' when he first heard a cannon-ball hurtling by as the battle commenced but, remembering the captain's words, he concealed his fears because, he says, 'Je me figurais [...] que *tous les yeux de l'équipage étaient fixés sur moi*, et j'étais fermement résolu à *faire bonne contenance*' (p. 34). His conduct corresponds exactly to the psychological considerations uttered by the French Lieutenant:

> Man is born a coward (*L'homme est né poltron*). It is a difficulty – *parbleu!* It would be too easy otherwise. But habit – habit – necessity – do you see? – *the eye of others* – *voilà*. One puts up with it. And then the example of others who are no better than yourself, and yet *make good countenance*.                                    (*LJ*, p. 147)

Because of 'the eye of others' Garneray does not show his 'emotion' and acts courageously; deprived of the same support Jim instinctively 'jumps' away from danger. The similarities suggest that Garneray's book made a strong impression on Conrad in his most 'plastic' years and helped to form some of the views of the mature artist.

Conrad's extensive and varied reading played an important part in shaping the story of the *Jeddah* into a work of art. Seven travel books provided a great range of source material;[54] a passage of the letter Jim receives from his father was taken verbatim from a letter of the Reverend William Hazlitt to his own son;[55] one of Marlow's best-known sayings comes from Abbé Galiani's corre-

spondence. Very important, too, was imaginative literature,[56] including
Browning's poem 'Fifine at the Fair' as a highly probable source of some key
images and episodes,[57] a reminiscence from George Eliot's *Scenes of Clerical
Life* in the pink toads seen by the chief engineer of the *Patna* in his *delirium
tremens*,[58] two lines from Goethe's play *Torquato Tasso*, aptly quoted by Stein,[59]
an adaptation of words from *Hamlet* and the Hamletian theme,[60] an exploitation
of Maupassant in two important descriptive passages, and an imitation of Mickiewicz's *Pan Tadeusz* and *Konrad Wallenrod*. But throughout the novel it was
mainly in Flaubert's works that Conrad found the psychological, stylistic and
technical models he needed.

### 'Amy Foster'

'Amy Foster' is one of those stories in which Conrad's Polish cultural and
literary heritage is most conspicuous.[61] This, however, does not exclude the
use of other models, and indeed Richard Herndon has suggested, among a wide
range of sources, Flaubert's 'Un coeur simple', basing his evidence on 'rather
general parallels of character and action' between the two works, such as the
following: 'as Félicité, when walking in the road deaf to all warning, is whipped
down by the driver of the mail coach, so the distraught Yanko, who tries to
stop a milk cart to gain aid, is struck down. Deafness is the symbol and partial
cause of her isolation, foreignness of his'.[62]

The whipping down of Félicité may have given Conrad the idea for the
episode with Yanko, but for his treatment of it he relied on a similar incident
in *Madame Bovary*. As Emma's coach travelled between Yonville and Rouen,
an old blind tramp, hideously ugly and covered in rags, often thrust his hat in
at the window, 'tandis qu'il *se cramponnait* de l'autre bras sur le marchepied'.
His voice, at first a feeble whine, 'devenait *aiguë*' and rent the darkness 'comme
l'indistincte lamentation d'une vague détresse'. It upset Emma. When Hivert,
the driver of the coach, noticed a weight dragging on one side '[il] *allongeait* à
l'aveugle *de grands coups avec son fouet. La mèche le cinglait sur ses plaies, et il
tombait dans la boue* en poussant un hurlement' (*MB*, p. 370). Conrad used
some of these details in Dr Kennedy's account of Yanko's first appearance by
the side of the road. The poor 'horrid-looking man' frightened the children.
He had a voice that cried '*piercingly* strange words in the night', a voice 'that
was enough to make one die of fright'. And most relevant is the reaction of the
driver of Mr Bradley's milk cart:

[he] made no secret of it that *he had lashed his whip* at a hairy sort of gipsy fellow who,
jumping up at a turn of the road by the Vents, *made a snatch* at the pony's bridle. *And
he caught him a good one, too, right over the face*, he said, *that made him drop down in the
mud* a jolly sight quicker than he had jumped up.                    (*TOS*, pp. 118–19)

A few pages later two reminiscences from the same source appear in the portrayal of Mr Swaffer. Having been asked by the old man to enter his farm, Dr Kennedy sees Yanko *'lying on his back'* upon a straw pallet, blankets pulled up to his chin, breathing quickly, eyes restless, and while examining him he notices Swaffer standing silently by the door *'passing the tips of his fingers along his shaven upper lip'* (p. 126). In her death-agony, Emma also breathes quickly, her eyes roll, she pulls up the blankets, and when the celebrated Dr Larivière sees her cadaverous face as she is *'étendue sur le dos'* with her mouth open, he frowns and then, while apparently listening to Canivet, *'il se passait l'index sous les narines'* (p. 422), the kind of intensely visualized and particularizing detail which would have arrested Conrad's attention. On the next page, when describing the physical appearance of the old cattle-dealer, Conrad took another detail from the portrait of Catherine Leroux who has also spent her life 'dans la fréquentation des animaux': *'Quelque chose d'une rigidité monacale relevait l'expression de sa figure'* (p. 209). Indeed, his description – *'something rigid and monachal* in the set of his features *lends a certain elevation to the character of his face'* (p. 127), with its strange use of 'elevation' [relevait] and 'monachal' – bears the stamp of the French original.[63]

## Romance

In part IV of *Romance* (1900–March 1902) (the part written mainly by Conrad[64]) there are at least two borrowings from Maupassant's *Fort comme la mort*. In a moving passage (from which, years later, Conrad was to borrow again in *Victory*), the Countess de Guilleroy tells Bertin of her love for him:

> Elle *s'écria*:
> – Oh, mon Dieu, je voudrais vous faire comprendre comment je vous aime, moi! Voyons, je cherche, je ne trouve pas. *Quand je pense à vous, et j'y pense toujours*, je sens jusqu'au fond de ma chair et de mon âme une ivresse indicible de vous appartenir, et un besoin irrésistible de vous donner davantage de moi. [...] *J'aime en vous quelqu'un* que seule j'ai découvert, *un vous qui n'est pas celui du monde*, celui qu'on admire, celui qu'on connaît, un vous qui est le mien, *qui ne peut plus changer*, qui ne peut pas vieillir, que je ne peux pas ne plus aimer, *car* j'ai, pour le regarder, des yeux qui ne voient plus que lui. *Mais on ne peut pas dire ces choses. Il n'y a pas de mots pour les exprimer.*
>
> (*Fort comme la mort*, pp. 204–5)

John Kemp, narrating how he told Mrs Williams of his love for Seraphina, says:

> 'Mrs. Williams,' I *cried*, 'you can't know how I love her. No one in the world can know. *When I think of her – and I think of her always* – it seems to me that one life is not enough to show my devotion. *I love her like something unchangeable* and unique – *altogether out of the world; because* I see the world through her. I would still love her if she made me miserable and unhappy.'
> She exclaimed a low 'Ah!' and turned her head away for a moment.

'*But one cannot express these things,*' I continued. '*There are no words.*'

(Rom, pp. 324–5)

Conrad also used Maupassant's analysis of Bertin's feelings to describe the thoughts of Kemp as he looks back on the three quiet days he spent with Seraphina on board the *Lion*:

> Chez lui, ce fut une crise d'amour aigu, sensuel et poétique. Il lui semblait parfois qu'il s'était envolé, un jour, les mains tendues, et qu'il avait pu *étreindre à pleins bras le rêve ailé et magnifique qui plane* toujours *sur nos espérances.*   (*Fort comme la mort*, p. 55)

> How often the activity of our life is the least real part of it! Life, looked upon as a whole, presents itself to my fancy as *a pursuit with open arms of a winged and magnificent dream, hovering just over* our heads and casting its glory upon *our hopes.*   (*Rom*, p. 335)

David Thorburn quotes this passage as an example of these statements of 'deadly grandiloquence' in which 'Kemp tries to extract from his adventures some general moral signification', and with which the novel is choked.[65] Conrad seems to have failed to realize that Maupassant's analysis would indeed have a very different impact when transplanted from a psychological novel into an adventure story.

### 'The End of the Tether'

In 'The End of the Tether' (July–October 1902), Conrad's debt to Maupassant and Flaubert is again plainly visible.

The former's influence can best be seen in a borrowing that Conrad made from *Mont-Oriol*. Having discovered that her lover, Paul Brétigny, is unfaithful, Christiane Andermatt feels changed as though this crisis has altered her soul; she looks at past events with

> une clarté d'idées dont son esprit n'avait encore jamais été éclairé. Cette lumière qui l'avait envahie soudain, et qui *illumine* certains êtres *en certaines heures de souffrance*, lui montrait la vie, les hommes, les choses, la terre entière avec tout ce qu'elle porte comme elle ne les avait jamais vus.   (*Mont-Oriol*, p. 409)

In 'The End of the Tether' it takes the suffering caused by his increasing blindness to make Captain Whalley 'see' life:

> In the steadily darkening universe a sinister *clearness fell upon his ideas. In the illuminating moments of suffering he saw life, men, all things, the whole earth with all her burden of created nature, as he had never seen them before.*   (*YOS*, p. 324)

Another psychological detail has its origin in the same source. In a courting scene, Paul says to Christiane 'Liane, regardez-moi?', and the narrator adds '*Il l'appelait Liane parce qu'elle s'enlaçait à lui*, pour l'embrasser, comme une plante *étreint* un arbre' (p. 189). Similarly, the narrator says of Captain Whalley and his daughter: '*He had named her Ivy because* of the sound of the word, and obscurely fascinated by a vague association of ideas. *She had twined herself tightly round his heart, and he intended her to cling close to her father as to a tower of strength'* (p. 174).

Conrad's story also reveals several reminiscences from *Madame Bovary*. Although we know from Sherry that Captain Whalley was modelled on 'the dignified side of [Captain Henry] Ellis's character',[66] he acquired some of his most characteristic physical and moral attributes from Flaubert's Dr Larivière:

*Son regard, plus tranchant que ses bistouris, vous descendait droit dans l'âme et désarticulait tout mensonge à travers les allégations et les pudeurs. Et il allait ainsi, plein de cette majesté débonnaire que donnent la conscience d'un grand talent, de la fortune, et quarante ans d'une existence laborieuse et irréprochable.* (*MB*, p. 442)

*The first cast of his glance fell on you candid and swift, like a boy's;* but because of the ragged snowy thatch of the eyebrows the affability of his attention acquired the character of a *keen* and searching scrutiny. [...]
Once rather proud of his great bodily strength, and even of his personal appearance, *conscious of his worth*, and firm in *his rectitude*, there had remained to him [...] *the tranquil bearing* of a man who had proved himself fit in every sort of way for the life of his choice. (*YOS*, p. 187)

Captain Whalley's portrait concludes with another borrowing from the same work. The narrator says that it was impossible to connect his 'fine presence' and 'unruffled aspect with the belittling troubles of poverty; the man's whole *existence* appeared to pass before you, *facile and large* in the freedom of means as ample *as the clothing of* his body' (p. 188). This remark comes from the passage where Emma, lying in bed next to Charles, dreams of her approaching escapade with Rodolphe: 'et leur *existence* serait *facile et large comme leurs vêtements de soie*' (p. 272). (One notes the gallicism 'facile' for 'free and easy'.)

By contrast, Charles, who is also awake, dreams of the future of his daughter who lies in the cot alongside: '*Elle allait grandir* maintenant [...]. Enfin, ils songeraient à son établissement: on lui trouverait quelque brave garçon ayant un état solide; il la rendrait *heureuse; cela durerait toujours*' (pp. 270–1). Towards the close of 'The End of the Tether', Captain Whalley remembers how he and his wife often talked about the future of their daughter over her cot in their cabin on the *Condor*. Their hopes are conveyed in the typically Flaubertian use of free indirect speech: '*She would grow up*, she would marry, she would love them, they would live near her and look at her *happiness – it would go on without end*' (p. 327).

Five pages earlier, another distinct echo from the same source helps to account for an odd gallicism when a storeroom on the *Sofala* is described as 'that Capharnaum of forgotten things' (p. 322). 'Un capharnaüm' is the familiar French for a 'lumber-room', and the way Homais refers to his 'laboratory' (p. 340).

The conclusion of the story derives in part from the end of chapter 2 of *Madame Bovary* where, after the burial of his first wife, Charles goes to their bedroom and grieves for her: '*alors s'appuyant contre* le secrétaire, *il resta jusqu'au soir* perdu dans une rêverie douloureuse. *Elle l'avait aimé, après tout*' (p. 26). Upon learning of her father's death, Captain Whalley's daughter, too, loses herself in sorrowful remembrance; she slips his letter into her bodice '*and leaning* her forehead *against* a window-pane *remained there till dusk*, perfectly motionless, giving him all the time she could spare. Gone! Was it possible? [...] There had been whole days when she had not thought of him at all – had no time. But *she had loved him*, she felt *she had loved him after all*' (p. 339). Apart from the verbal parallels, there is again the tell-tale use of free indirect speech.

Finally, the strong impression which the figure of Hannon made on Conrad can again be seen in a striking image he used twice at eight years' interval. On hearing Hamilcar's gibe about 'elephants being afraid of the sea', Hannon denounces the indignity of the outrage saying that he has caught his disease during a siege; '*et des pleurs coulaient sur sa face comme une pluie* d'hiver *sur une muraille en ruine*' (*Sal*, p. 153). When Captain Whalley raises his eyes after reading the committal service for his wife, he sees 'old Swinburne facing him with his cap pressed to his breast, and *his* rugged, weather-beaten, impassive *face streaming with drops of water like a* lump of chipped red granite *in a shower*' (p. 173; *Hervouet). Yelton has noted the same image in a form closer to the original in 'A Smile of Fortune', again in connection with an 'old sea-dog' who is similarly moved during the burial of a baby; his '*tears* [...] *trickled down his* weather-beaten *face like drops of rain on an old* rugged *wall*' (*TLS*, p. 15; *Yelton, pp. 117–18).

Yelton has also found, in a sentence describing the movement of the *Sofala* up river, a reminiscence of the description in *L'Education sentimentale* of the steamer *Ville-de-Montereau* travelling up the Seine. Flaubert presents a harpist competing with the engines of the boat (the divisions illustrate the regularity of the rhythmic periods):

*les battements de la machine* / coupaient la mélodie / à fausse *mesure*; / il pinçait plus fort: / les cordes vibraient, / et leurs sons métalliques / semblaient exhaler des sanglots / et comme la plainte d'un amour / orgueilleux et vaincu.                    (*ES*, p. 8)

Conrad seems to have reproduced at the beginning of his sentence Flaubert's handling of rhythmic patterns to express the pulsation of the engines: '*The thump of the engines* / reverberated regularly / like the strokes of a metronome / beating the *measure* / of the vast silence'. (Yelton asserts: 'The image of the metronome is Conrad's own',[67] but I would suggest, on the contrary, that it derives from another boat scene in *Madame Bovary*, when Emma and Léon, during their 'honeymoon', come back from their island: 'les avirons carrés *sonnaient* entre les tolets de fer; *et cela marquait dans le silence comme un battement de métronome*' (p. 354).) The rest of the sentence, Yelton points out, 'falls into a quite different periodic structure, the more leisurely and extended movement of which serves to evoke the interminable forward movement of the steamer against the current':[68]

the shadow of the western wall had fallen across the river, and the smoke pouring backwards from the funnel eddied down behind the ship, spread a thin dusky veil over the sombre water, which, checked by the flood-tide, seemed to lie stagnant in the whole straight length of the reaches.                                               (*YOS*, p. 257)

Flaubert's scene presents the same contrast. After the staccato rhythms which fittingly convey the intense and chaotic activity on board the steamer at the point of departure, we also note 'the more leisurely and extended movement' of the boat during its journey:

Le tumulte s'apaisait; tous avaient pris leur place; quelques-uns, debout, se chauffaient autour de la machine, et la cheminée crachait avec un râle lent et rythmique son panache de fumée noire                                                        (*ES*, p. 2)

Both texts also have in common a few descriptive details worthy of note:

Des deux côtés de la rivière, *des bois s'inclinaient jusqu'au bord de l'eau*          (*ES*, p. 8)

The shores rose higher, in firm sloping banks, and *the forest of big trees came down to the brink*.                                                              (*YOS*, p. 257)

le pont *tremblait* sous une petite *vibration intérieure* (p. 2)

Sterne's body [...] *trembled* slightly from top to toe with the *internal vibration* of the ship (p. 257)

la surface de l'eau [...] se coupait à la proue en deux sillons, qui se déroulaient jusqu'au bord des prairies. (p. 5)

while two glassy folds of water streaming away from each bow of the steamer across the whole width of the river ran with her upstream smoothly, fretting their outer ends [...] against the miry foot of each bank.(p. 259; *Hervouet)

Apart from details for the description of the landscape and the movement of the boat, and possibly some hints for the delineation of the passengers, a close study of Flaubert's scene could have offered Conrad a model of descriptive writing. Christopher Prendergast has analysed the two following sentences from the passage:

La campagne était toute vide. Il y avait dans le ciel de petits nuages blancs arrêtés, et l'ennui, vaguement répandu, semblait alanguir la marche du bateau et rendre l'aspect des voyageurs plus insignifiant encore.                                        (*ES*, p. 5)

He comments that 'through their power of suggestion' these two sentences 'reach beyond the immediate context to integrate symbolically with some of the major themes of the novel: thus, the motifs of void and immobility, boredom and insignificance, adumbrate many of the central realities the hero will encounter in the course of his "education"'[69] It is significant that the descriptions of the *Sofala* plying her 'monotonous huckster's round' (p. 166) on a muddy river full of inhospitable reefs, and lined with occasional squalid huts and sombre masses of jungle vegetation, have been seen by Leo Gurko to fulfil the same 'expository' and 'symbolic' functions:[70]

Stagnation and confinement, a meanness of outlook and the monotony of routine are the features of the river in which the *Sofala*, appropriately, in her ugliness and meanness of shape, and the ugliness and meanness of the man who owns her, finally sinks. And with her Captain Whalley, trapped in the new age which the *Sofala* apotheosizes.[71]

It was Flaubert's view that description is crucial to the development of both character and action. Clearly, his example was not lost on an admiring and attentive Conrad who shared his belief that description, when it strongly conveys atmosphere and suggests the march of events, comes to assume a narrative function.

# 4 The second phase of maturity

## Nostromo

Conrad's next work, *Nostromo* (December 1902–August 1904), was to be both his 'largest canvas' and by almost general agreement, his masterpiece. A considerable amount of critical investigation has shown that Conrad drew many 'hints for characters, names, incidents, topography' as well as 'suggestions for important movements within the historical, socio-economic world of the novel' from several historical works on South America.[1] Only recently has much attention been paid to his use of imaginative literature in this novel, although his dependence on Anatole France, Flaubert, Maupassant, and possibly Hugo, is remarkable.

As Leavis said, in *Nostromo* Conrad 'is openly and triumphantly the artist by *métier*, conscious of French initiation and of fellowship in craft with Flaubert'.[2] This statement requires illustration, but also some immediate qualification. While the legacy of Flaubert may be felt as a general and pervasive fact in *Nostromo*, it should also be stressed that Conrad's main textual reliance was not on Flaubert or Maupassant but rather on Anatole France, a writer who plays an increasingly important part in the novels from *Nostromo* onwards. It is appropriate, then, to begin this section by focusing on that Francian legacy and the strikingly specific contribution to *Nostromo* made by Anatole France.

Conrad borrowed from *L'Anneau d'améthyste* (1899) – the third volume of France's *L'Histoire contemporaine* for the characterization of Pedrito Montero. In the following passage, France describes the psychology of Maurice Cheiral, a rather dull and shallow but ambitious young man who owes to his mother's influence the position he holds as principal secretary to his uncle, the minister of Justice:

> Cheiral n'était pas très intelligent. Il ne considérait jamais qu'un petit nombre de choses et *il se déterminait par des raisons que leur futilité rendait difficiles à démêler*. Aussi croyait-on qu'il avait, dans un âge encore tendre, des idées personnelles. Pour l'instant, il venait de lire *un livre de M. Imbert de Saint-Amand* sur les Tuileries *pendant le second Empire; il avait été frappé* à cette lecture, *de l'éclat d'une cour brillante et il en avait conçu l'idée d'un genre de vie où, comme le duc de Morny, il associerait les plaisirs à la politique et jouirait du pouvoir de toutes les manières.* (XII, p. 221)

Like Cheiral, Montero is a hollow sham, yet ambitious for power and pleasure. He is an incorrigible hanger-on and relies entirely on the success of his brother the General for his own advancement:

*His actions were usually determined by motives so improbable in themselves as to escape the penetration of a rational person.*
Thus at first sight the agent of the Gould Concession in Sta. Marta had credited him with the possession of sane views [...]. It could never have entered his head that Pedrito Montero, lackey or inferior scribe, lodged in the garrets of the various Parisian hotels where the Costaguana Legation used to shelter its diplomatic dignity, had been devouring the lighter sort of historical works in the French language, such, for instance as *the books of Imbert de Saint Amand upon the Second Empire.* But Pedrito *had been struck by the splendour of a brilliant court, and had conceived the idea of an existence for himself where, like the Duc de Morny, he would associate the command of every pleasure with the conduct of political affairs and enjoy power* supremely *in every way.*                    (*N*, p. 387)[3]

An echo of the passage by France can also be heard in *A Personal Record* written a few years later. Almayer's importation of a Bali pony into a trackless forest was, Conrad says, typical of the man, 'ambitious, aiming at the grandiose'. He adds ironically that it 'might have been part of some deep scheme, of some diplomatic plan, of some hopeful intrigue', and then applies to him Cheiral's psychology, as he had done to Pedrito: 'With Almayer one could never tell. *He governed his conduct by considerations removed from the obvious*, by incredible assumptions, *which rendered his logic impenetrable to any reasonable person*' (*PR*, p. 76).

Still in *L'Anneau d'améthyste* France discusses the value of work thus:

Madame Bergeret tira de ce labeur quelque avantage moral. Le travail est bon à l'homme. Il le distrait de sa propre vie, il le détourne de la vue effrayante de lui-même; il l'empêche de regarder cet autre qui est lui et qui lui rend la solitude horrible. Il est un souverain remède à l'éthique et à l'esthétique. Le travail a ceci d'excellent encore qu'il amuse notre vanité, trompe notre impuissance et nous communique l'espoir d'un bon événement. *Nous nous flattons d'entreprendre par lui sur les destins.* Ne concevant pas les rapports nécessaires qui rattachent notre propre effort à la mécanique universelle, il nous semble que cet effort est dirigé *en notre faveur contre le reste de la machine. Le travail nous donne l'illusion de la volonté, de la force et de l'indépendance!*                    (XII, p. 6)

Conrad shared France's view that work provides us with the best antidote to thought and represents the most effective way of dealing with the helplessness of our condition (cf. *CL*, I, p. 112). This passage struck a responsive chord in Conrad, for the subject lies at the heart of his view of life, and he used it in widely separated parts of *Nostromo*. After the death of his father, Charles Gould feels a 'mournful and angry desire for action', which leads to the authorial comment: 'In this his instinct was unerring. Action is consolatory. It is the enemy of thought and the friend of flattering illusions. *Only in the conduct of our action can we find the sense of mastery over the Fates*' (p. 66). Gould then makes the momentous decision to tie his fate to the success of the San Tomé mine. Towards the end of the novel, Conrad seems to echo France's view on solitude when he says that Decoud 'died from solitude, the enemy known but to few on this earth, and whom only the simplest of us are fit to withstand' (p. 496). He then returns to the theme of the value of action, having this time reshaped the second part of France's passage to make it fit into his account of Decoud's mental state in the solitude of the Great Isabel as he begins to entertain 'a doubt of his own individuality': *'In our activity alone do we find the sustaining illusion of an independent existence as against the whole scheme of things of which we form a helpless part'* (p. 497). Conrad again recalled the passage in his essay on 'Crainquebille' when he praised France warmly for his awareness that 'only in the continuity of effort there is a refuge from despair' and for his wish to see us *'preserving in our activity the consoling illusion of power and intelligent purpose'* (*NLL*, pp. 33–4).

However, action for France and Conrad is not simply an antidote to despair; it means a genuine commitment to life. And here again France's impact is irrefutable. In *Le Lys rouge* the poetess Miss Bell says to the sculptor Dechartre who has no desire to be immortalized: 'Monsieur Dechartre, *pour que la vie soit grande et pleine, il faut y mettre le passé et l'avenir. Nos oeuvres de poésie et d'art, il faut les accomplir en l'honneur des morts, et dans la pensée de ceux qui naîtront. Et nous participerons ainsi de ce qui fut, de ce qui est et de ce qui sera'* (IX, p. 144). Towards the end of *Nostromo* Conrad makes a sad and disillusioned Mrs Gould reflect: 'It had come into her mind that *for life to be large and full, it must contain the care of the past and of the future* in every passing moment of the present. Our daily *work must be done to the glory of the dead, and for the good of those who come after'* (pp. 520–1). That Conrad had really made France's view his own can be seen in his earlier statement in the Preface to *The Nigger of the 'Narcissus'* (1897) that the artist speaks 'to the [...] solidarity [...] which binds together all humanity – *the dead* to the living and the living to *the unborn'* (p. viii), and in a later remark, in a letter to H. G. Wells of 25 September 1908 where he declares: '*Your work, like all work that counts must have its connection with the* laborious *past and its bearing on the future'*.[4] This mature altruism represents a basic article of faith in Conrad's view of life and explains why those of his characters who are guided by purely self-seeking motives prove to be failures.

A few pages later, Conrad modelled the love scene between Nostromo and Giselle on a love scene between the black King Balthasar and Balkis, the Queen of Sheba, in France's story 'Balthasar':

Il n'en dit pas davantage. L'ayant saisie dans ses bras, il tenait renversé sous ses lèvres le front de la reine. *Mais il vit qu'elle pleurait. Alors il lui parla tout bas d'une voix caressante*, en chantant un peu, comme font les nourrices. *Il l'appela sa petite fleur et sa petite étoile.* [...]

Elle noua ses bras au cou du roi noir et dit de la voix d'un enfant qui supplie:-
*Voici la nuit venu.*                                                        (IV, p. 127)

Ils tombèrent tous deux *embrassés*. Ils crurent *s'abîmer* sans fin dans un néant délicieux
*et le monde des vivants cessa d'exister pour eux.*                          (IV, p. 133)

He could not restrain himself any longer. While she shrank from his approach, her arms
went out to him, abandoned and *regal* in the dignity of her languid surrender. He held
her head in his two hands, and showered rapid kisses upon the upturned face that
gleamed in the purple dusk. Masterful and tender, he was entering slowly upon the
fulness of his possession. *And he perceived that she was crying.* Then the incomparable
Capataz, the man of careless loves, became gentle and caressing, like a woman to the
grief of a child. *He murmured to her fondly.* He sat down by her and nursed her fair head
on his breast. *He called her his star and his little flower.*
    *It had grown dark.* [...]
    *He was lost to the world in their embraced stillness.* (pp. 537–8)

Thomas Moser has commented that Conrad's handling of the love affair
between Nostromo and Giselle 'very nearly wrecks the last few chapters'.[5] That
he needed a model to describe a first kiss is, to say the least, disconcerting, and
reveals his uncertainty about the presentation of the relationship.

    Perhaps the most interesting borrowing Conrad made in *Nostromo* is to be
found in his treatment of Decoud's last days on the Great Isabel. Decoud is
another complex Conradian creation. The initial source of the character is one
Juan Decoud, a journalist 'who lived outside Paraguay and was a mortal enemy
of Lopez'. Interesting similarities between the lives and personalities of Conrad
and Decoud suggest that in him 'Conrad drew close to presenting something
of his own nature'.[6] But at the same time Decoud, whose first language is
French, is also based to a large extent on Prosper Mérimée, as Owen Knowles
has suggested.[7] He draws attention to the fact that in *La Vie littéraire* France
concludes his review of a biography of Mérimée by recalling that the latter,
towards the end of his life, suffered from the effects of solitude and was subject
to 'le spleen'. France adds that his biographer, M. d'Haussonville, has searched
for the cause of this melancholy, and continues:

Il croit l'avoir trouvée dans *'l'instinct confus d'une vie mal dirigée, livrée à beaucoup d'en-
traînements, dont le souvenir laissait* plus *d'amertume* que de douceur'. Pour moi, je doute
que Mérimée ait jamais eu un *sentiment moral* de cette nature. *De quoi se serait-il repenti?*
*Il ne reconnut jamais pour vertus que* les énergies *ni pour devoirs que les passions. Sa tristesse*
*n'était-elle pas plutôt celle du sceptique pour qui l'univers n'est qu'une suite d'images incompré-*
*hensibles,* et qui redoute également la vie et la mort, puisque ni l'une ni l'autre n'ont de
sens pour lui? *Enfin, n'éprouvait-il pas cette amertume de l'esprit et du coeur, châtiment*
*inévitable de l'audace intellectuelle* [...]?                              (VI, p. 383)

Following the borrowing on the meaning of 'our activity', Conrad writes that
after three days in complete isolation Decoud had 'lost all belief in the reality

of his action'. On the fifth day an immense 'melancholy' descended upon him, and 'as if to escape from this solitude, he absorbed himself in his melancholy'. Conrad continues with this analysis:

*The vague consciousness of a misdirected life given up to impulses whose memory left a bitter taste in his mouth was the first moral sentiment of his manhood. But at the same time he felt no remorse. What should he regret? He had recognized no other virtue than intelligence, and had erected passions into duties.*

After seven days he is robbed of all energy and faith: '*His sadness was the sadness of a sceptical mind. He beheld the universe as a succession of incomprehensible images.*' On the tenth day, sad and weary before this meaningless spectacle, the brilliant *boulevardier* shoots himself and disappears in the 'merciless solitude' and 'immense indifference' of the Placid Gulf: he is '*A victim of the disillusioned weariness which is the retribution meted out to intellectual audacity*' (pp. 497, 498, 500, 501).[8]

Knowles has suggested that Conrad may not only have drawn upon this 'diagnosis of the exhausted sceptic' at a crucial time in Decoud's life, but that the borrowing from France 'represents only one vestige of a blueprint for the fashionably sceptical Parisian boulevardier and *esprit fort* which he derived from accounts of Mérimée's life'. Mérimée emerges from France's review as a *homo duplex*, that is, as Knowles puts it, a 'deracinated intellectual libertine whose entire life is a tragic record of impulses destructively at odds with each other – the romantic and sceptical, the sentimental and egocentric, emotional timidity and intellectual audacity, asceticism, and cultivated sensualism'.[9] Although he was sincerely convinced of 'la légitimité des passions' (VI, p. 378), he went through life in a 'roide et sarcastique attitude' (p. 380), hiding all his generous and affectionate feelings under a 'masque de cynisme et d'insensibilité' (p. 380), making it his study to suppress 'tous les dehors de ce qu'il regardait comme une faiblesse déshonorante' (p. 381). Nevertheless, for all his 'air brusque et dégagé' (p. 379), he suffered cruelly, unable as he was to disguise 'une sympathie ardente' (p. 378) beneath his affectation of irony. Conrad appropriated many of the symptoms of this *homo duplex* with his maladjusted sensibility and presented in Decoud a similar core of anguish. Like Mérimée, Decoud adopts a pose of dandyish scepticism which is at odds with, and threatens to destroy, his natural spontaneity: 'He had pushed the habit of universal raillery to a point where it blinded him to the genuine impulses of his own nature' (p. 153). He, too, has, in Knowles's words, 'genuine capacity for strong feeling – even faith – but cannot find it in himself to embrace a creed or the habit of instinctive action; hence, as with Mérimée, his growing anguish is indistinguishable from the experience of being surprised by a strength of feeling to which he cannot fully respond – that "tremendous excitement under its cloak of studied carelessness" (p. 212)'.[10] Ultimately, Decoud dies in the solitude of the Great Isabel because solitude 'becomes very swiftly a state of soul in which the affectations of irony and scepticism have no place' (p. 497).

Clearly, this 'invisible "parallel" sceptic' in the figure of Mérimée is of considerable importance in understanding Conrad's intentions for Decoud, and helps to explain the element of uncertainty in the treatment of his end, which has disturbed some critics.[11] Knowles has suggested that by relying closely on France's diagnosis, Conrad runs the risk of describing too rapidly and in too abstract a language the terminal psychological states Decoud undergoes for his inner collapse to be dramatically convincing. He may also be condemning him, in Guerard's words, for 'a withdrawal and skepticism more radical than Decoud ever shows'. Indeed, there must surely be a connection between the 'invisible "parallel" sceptic' and Guerard's other famous comment that 'Some of the irony is directed at a personage who is not fully in the book or not in it at all.'[12] Knowles concludes: 'the account of Decoud's disintegration and spiritual agony [...] does not finally yield the kind of summary which suggests that Conrad has fully probed Decoud's spiritual bankruptcy from the inside and in depth'.[13] The main reason for the deficiencies and contradictions involved in the characterization of Decoud and his suicide may well lie, as Kingsley Widmer has argued, in the 'unresolvable difficulties' of Conrad's own dilemma as conservative and sceptic: 'The skeptical author turns, illogically and inconsistently but poetically, against his own supposed skeptic in the desperate but pyrrhic effort to keep faith with his "simple ideas" '; the example of Decoud, along with others, shows Conrad 'ideologically pressuring for conventional faiths without real faith in them. In dramatic fact, he insists upon a drastic skepticism and destructiveness'.[14]

Of the Flaubertian legacy in *Nostromo* it may be said that it is everywhere felt – profoundly felt – but is not always easy to identify in terms of specific verbal or technical influence. The ways in which Conrad shared with Flaubert an enduring 'fellowship in craft' will, I hope, become fully evident in later chapters. Here we may begin by identifying some of the more concrete evidence of indebtedness. Comparison between *Nostromo* and *Salammbô* shows some striking similarities between them in their overall conception, as Wit Tarnawski observes: 'both novels were built within a scaffolding of prodigious research and reading', and continues:

> Both Flaubert and Conrad show a whole society, at a time of crisis and upheaval, with its national characteristics, its geographical environment and individual members against the vast, multilayered background. Both novels have a panoramic and monumental character, full of brilliant, dramatic scenes. Both tell the story of rebellion, revolution, and war. And both turn on the central theme of greed and the power of money.[15]

Furthermore, in terms of characterization, despite the presence of the equally magnificent and unsophisticated figures of Mâtho and Nostromo, both novels have no hero. As was pointed out in connection with *The Nigger*, Flaubert's real protagonists are groups, not individuals. In a like manner, neither Gould the idealist, nor Decoud the sceptic, nor Nostromo the man of simple faith occupies the front of the stage for very long; for Conrad, too, is not primarily interested in individuals but in the clash of conflicting ideas and codes of conduct as they shape the course of events. Lastly, both works are steeped in the irremediable pessimism of their authors' view of history, in the mood of despondency generated by their vision of 'the cupidity and misery of mankind' (*N*, p. 365).

Some of these aspects, especially the pessimism, apply equally to *L'Education sentimentale*, and it is inconceivable that Conrad, with his intimate familiarity with Flaubert, never turned, during the eighteen months of his struggle with *Nostromo*, towards this, his 'most cherished' novel and the cornerstone of the nineteenth-century French novel, a book so clearly similar in its scope and complexity. Indeed, both works, which are permeated by the sense of failure conveyed in the collapse of all dreams and the general degradation of all ideals, embody not only the same rejection of the notion of Progress,[16] but also the same disillusionment with life, the same overpowering feeling of the 'cruel futility of things' (*N*, p. 364).

That this comparison is not gratuitous is evidenced by two distinct borrowings, the first one making clear that *L'Education* was in Conrad's mind at the very beginning of *Nostromo*. Compare the portrait of Linda Viola and that of Mlle Vatnaz:

> *Et elle lui faisait la moue, en avançant ses* grosses *lèvres, presque sanguinolentes à force d'être rouges. Mais elle avait d'admirables yeux, fauves avec des points d'or dans les prunelles, tout pleins d'esprit, d'amour* et de sensualité. *Ils éclairaient,* comme des lampes, *le teint un peu jaune de sa figure maigre.*                                        (*ES*, p. 103)

> Linda pouted, advancing her red lips, which were almost too red; but she had admirable eyes, brown, with a sparkle of gold in the irises, full of intelligence and meaning, and so clear that they seemed to throw a glow upon her thin, colourless face.                        (*N*, p. 28)

The second borrowing occurs in connection with the composite character of Decoud, who, in one instance at least, owes an important psychological trait to Frédéric Moreau. Frédéric's love for Madame Arnoux is so deep that it almost becomes a general way of feeling, a new mode of being; as a result, '*toutes les femmes lui rappelaient celle-là, par des similitudes ou par des contrastes violents*' (p. 97). Ever since Decoud had been rebuked by Antonia when she was sixteen for 'the aimlessness of his life [a telling link with Frédéric] and the levity of his opinions', the impression left on him by this attack was so strong that '*all the girl friends* of his sisters *recalled to him Antonia Avellanos by some faint resemblance, or by the great force of contrast*' (p. 155; *Kirschner, pp. 188–9).

A specific area where the example of Flaubert, whether derived from *Salammbô* or *L'Education*, must have proved useful to Conrad was indicated

by Curle who declared that 'it is from Flaubert that Conrad gained his knowledge of managing a crowd'.[17] Karl discarded this assertion by saying that Curle
'did not have to look further than *Romance* to find a sharp prefiguration of those
ragged and disorganized mob-scenes in *Nostromo*'.[18] True, of course, but this
is not a convincing refutation since this is precisely the kind of scene for which
Ford and Conrad would no doubt have turned to Flaubert for hints on technical-
ities; witness Conrad's previous reliance on the treatment of the mercenaries
in the garden of Hamilcar for that of the sailors in the forecastle of the *Narcissus*.
Conrad (who shared Flaubert's dislike of democracy) would be attracted to
these scenes not merely on artistic grounds but also through the profound
accord he felt with Flaubert's aversion for what he saw as the appalling stupidity
and ferocity of human beings in the mass. Najder says that 'the fear of anarch-
istic destructive rabble turns up frequently in [Conrad's] letters and writings',
adding that its origin could probably be traced, apart from his own experiences
with the urban and port mobs, to 'the historical and sociological books he had
read (Taine, Gustave Le Bon)'.[19] Clearly, too, the influence of *Salammbô* and
*L'Education* can hardly be ignored in this context.

Lastly, it is worth examining here an important feature common to Flaubert's
and Conrad's writings. Flaubert, it has been observed, makes an anomalous
use of the iterative imperfect when he uses it to describe events which are so
detailed and clearly delineated as to be experienced by the reader as unique.
Roger Huss notes that this occurs, for instance, 'at several points in the fifth
chapter of the third part of *Madame Bovary* which describes Emma's Thursday
visit to Rouen'. He explains:

Here Flaubert appears to take advantage of the fact that the sequence of events described
(Emma's early rising, the trip to Rouen, her visit to Léon and return to Yonville) is
repeated, in order to extend the imperfect to actions within that sequence which it is
difficult to believe happened more than once. The blind beggar hangs on to the carriage,
his hat poking through the window, his voice fills Emma with melancholy, but Hivert,
noticing that the carriage is off-balance, lashes out with his whip, causing the beggar to
fall howling into the mud. This, surprisingly, is a frequent event, and the paragraph
begins: 'Souvent, on était en marche...'. Surely only in dreams and obsessive imaginings
are events of such specificity repeated.[20]

E. Stegmaier has analysed the same phenomenon, in what he calls the 'would-
scene', in *Lord Jim* and *Nostromo*. For instance, at the beginning of *Nostromo*,
Signora Teresa reproaches the absent Capataz for not having stayed to protect
them from the tumult and terror sweeping through Sulaco:

'Oh! Gian' Battista, why art thou not here? Oh! why art thou not here?'
    She was not then invoking the saint himself, but calling upon Nostromo, whose patron
he was. And Giorgio, motionless on the chair by her side, would be provoked by these
reproachful and distracted appeals.

'Peace, woman! Where's the sense of it? There's his duty,' he murmured in the dark;
and she would retort, panting –
'Eh! I have no patience. Duty!'                                                    (*N*, p. 17)

As Stegmaier comments, despite the direct speech which signals a particular
time and situation, 'this can no longer pass for a straightforward scene', for the
use of 'would' in 'would be provoked' and 'she would retort' makes it clear
that, although the scene 'remains scenic in form' it 'no longer stands for an
actual and unique fictional present' but for 'an unspecified number of similar
events'.[21]

Both Huss and Stegmaier arrive at very similar interpretations of the main
function of this technique, the former pointing out that 'From *Madame Bovary*
to *Bouvard et Pécuchet*, accumulation and repetition typify narratives which
convey an impression of inevitability and show new events to be essentially the
same as old' and that 'Flaubert's use of the iterative imperfect to convey highly
particularized events is consistent with a sense of *déjà vu* and tedium, with
an inability to believe in the originality of any event'.[22] And what about the
provenance of the device in Conrad? Stegmaier notes that, although he was 'the
first to have made any marked use of the would-*scene*', he had predecessors in
Smollett, Scott, Thackeray, and more especially the later Dickens. However,
given that this device first plays a significant part in *Lord Jim*, a work steeped
in Flaubert, it seems reasonable, as Stegmaier himself has suggested,[23] to trace
this aspect of Conrad's writing to the French master.

In *Nostromo* Maupassant's presence is conspicuous in two love-scenes and a
death-scene. In 'L'Héritage', Lesable, a young clerk, is invited for dinner to
the house of Cachelin, a colleague who wishes him to marry his niece, Cora.
After the meal, although it is dark, Cachelin opens the French window to show
the view over Paris from the terrace where Lesable and Cora are soon left alone.
In *Nostromo*, Decoud and Antonia meet at the Casa Gould; when it has grown
dark, the window is thrown open and they talk alone on the balcony. In both
cases, the young people gaze on the outside world: in Maupassant, there is
nothing to be seen except '*une lueur vague*' hovering over the town, with here
and there the more vivid light from a building; in Conrad's scene there is 'the
deep trench of shadow between the houses, *lit up vaguely* by the glimmer of
street lamps' with now and then 'the pulsating red glow of a cigarette'. They
also feel refreshed by the night air: 'Un souffle humide entra. Il faisait tiède
dehors, comme au mois d'avril' (*Miss Harriet*, p. 68); 'and the night air, as if
cooled by the snows of Higuerota, refreshed their faces' (p. 184). The similarities of the actions and emotions of the two couples are shown in the following
parallels:

| | |
|---|---|
| *Lesable s'était accoudé sur la balustrade* | She did not answer. She seemed tired. |
| *de fer, à côté de Cora* qui regadait dans le | *They leaned side by side on the rail of the* |

vide, *muette*, distraite, *saisie* tout à coup *par une de ces langueurs mélancoliques qui engourdissent parfois les âmes*. [Note the typical Maupassantian turn of phrase 'une de ces': 'Il [Norbert de Varenne] semblait surexcité et triste, *d'une de ces tristesses qui tombent* parfois *sur les* âmes' (*BA*, 206).]

little balcony, very friendly, having exhausted politics, *giving themselves up* to the silent feeling of their nearness, *in one of those profound pauses that fall upon the rhythm of passion*. (*N*, p. 185)

*Il s'était rapproché jusqu'à ce que leurs coudes* et leurs épaules *se touchassent*

*Decoud and Antonia remained* leaning over the balcony, *side by side, touching elbows* (p. 186)

Alors, il la questionna [...]. Et elle répondait sans embarras, en fille réfléchie, senseé [...]. Il la trouvait pleine de bon sens

All this could apply to 'the mature Antonia'. In this scene, Conrad simply speaks of 'her reasonable words' (p. 183).

*Il se sentait attiré*, ému par cette sensation de la femme *si proche*, par cette soif de la chair mûre et vierge, et par cette *séduction* delicate de la jeune fille. Il lui semblait qu'il serait demeuré là pendant des heures, des nuits, des semaines, toujours, *accoudé près d'elle, à la sentir près de lui, pénétré* par le charme de son *contact*.

He drank the tones of her even voice, and watched the agitated life of her throat, as if waves of emotion had run from her heart to pass out into the air in her reasonable words. [...] *she fascinated him* [...]. She *seduced* his attention (p. 183)

Their comparative isolation, *the* precious *sense of intimacy, the* slight contact of *their arms, affected him* softly (p. 188)

[Lesable hears Cachelin's sister talking about her fortune]
*Lesable*, tout à fait intéressé, *se retourna, appuyant* maintenant *son dos à la balustrade* de la terrasse. (*Miss Harriet*, pp. 68–71)

[At the mention of Montero, a clamour arises] *Decoud had turned round* at the noise, and, *leaning his back on the balustrade*, shouted [...], *'Gran' bestia!'* (p. 191)

The passage beginning 'She did not answer' has been analysed by Arnold Kettle who says that it shows 'several of the essentials [...] of Conrad's method'. The above parallels are further evidence that he learned certain of these 'essentials' from Maupassant – in particular, the presentation of the relationship of the two young people which is 'intimately yet objectively suggested' (Kettle's words)[24] and placed securely between the outside world and their immediate social environment.

Another interesting adaptation, this time from the scene when Duroy tells Mme de Marelle of his forthcoming marriage to her friend Madeleine Forestier, is found towards the end of the novel when Nostromo declares his love to Giselle immediately after he has agreed to become betrothed to her sister Linda.

The link between the two scenes is that both deal with a crisis situation in which a man has to make a confession to the woman he loves with a view to regaining his freedom. However, that freedom has a different meaning in each case; hence the interesting transposition Conrad made of Maupassant's material: whereas Duroy feels 'delivered' after the departure of his mistress and begins frantically to shadow-box, the 'captivity' with which Nostromo wrestles is not so easily dispelled despite his attempt at 'striking a heroic blow' for his freedom:

Si tu savais!... Il y a des jours où *j'avais envie de tuer* ton mari... (*BA*, p. 304)

In discovering that her beauty could belong to another *he felt as though he could kill* this one of old Giorgio's daughters also. (*N*, p. 534)

elle *respirait* toujours par secousses pénibles *qui lui soulevaient les seins* (p. 304)

The incorruptible Nostromo *breathed* her ambient seduction in the tumultuous *heaving of his breast.* (p. 537)

Et, soulagé d'un poids énorme, se sentant tout à coup *libre*, délivré, à l'aise pour sa vie nouvelle, il se mit à boxer contre le mur en lançant de grands coups de poing, dans une sorte d'*ivresse* de succès et de *force, comme s'il se fût battu* contre la Destinée. (p. 306)

In the exulting consciousness of his *strength*, and the triumphant *excitement* of his mind, he struck out for his *freedom.* (p. 540)

He wrestled with the spell of captivity. It was *as if striking a* heroic *blow* that he burst out – 'Like a thief!' (p. 540)

Puis *elle murmura comme tombée* dans une sorte d'hébétude:
– Oh!... mon Dieu ... (p. 304)

'A treasure?' she repeated *in a faint voice, as if from the depths* of a dream (p. 540)

Et *s'étant dégagée* d'un mouvement en arrière, elle s'en alla (p. 306)

*She disengaged herself* gently. (p. 540)

Il parlait de *sa voix* douce, voilée, *séduisante* (p. 304)

*Her* nonchalant and *seductive voice trembled* with the excitement of admiring awe and ungovernable curiosity. (p. 540)

Elle pâlissait, se sentant *trembler*, et *elle balbutia*:
– Qu'est-ce qu'il y a? *Dis vite*! (p. 303)

'A treasure of silver!' *she stammered out.* Then *pressed on faster*: 'What? Where? How did you get it, Giovanni?' (p. 540)

Mme de Marelle *tressaillit* de tout son corps, puis *elle demeura muette*, songeant avec une telle attention qu'elle paraissait avoir oublié qu'il était à ses pieds. (p. 305)

*She became quiet* (p. 540)

Demeuré seul, *il se releva, étourdi*

She listened as if in a trance. Her fingers stirred in his hair. *He got up from his knees reeling*, weak, empty, *as though he had flung his soul away*. [...]

He guessed at *her shudder* (p. 541)

*comme s'il avait* reçu un horion sur la tête
(p. 306)

The death of Nostromo, like that of Wait, again shows Conrad turning to Maupassant when writing a death-scene. In 'Hautot père et fils', the elder Hautot drops his gun while picking up a dead partridge and the second barrel discharges into his stomach. Realizing that he has not long to live, he confesses to his son that he has a mistress and asks him to see to her welfare. This confession over, he falls silent and ignores those around him:

> Mais le moribond avait *fermé les yeux*, et il refusa de les rouvrir, *il refusa de répondre*, il refusa de montrer, même par un signe, qu'il comprenait. [...]
> Il fut administré, purifié, absous, au milieu de ses amis et de ses serviteurs agenouillés, *sans qu'un seul mouvement de son visage* révélât qu'il vivait encore.
> Il mourut vers minuit, *après quatre heures de tressaillements indiquant d'atroces souffrances.*                                                                    (*La Main gauche*, p. 58)

Nostromo, having been shot point-blank in the stomach by old Giorgio on the Great Isabel, is brought ashore and asks for Mrs Gould. After confessing to her that he has stolen the silver, he goes through an agony which re-enacts that of Hautot senior:

> Nostromo *made no answer.* [...]
> Then his head rolled back, *his eyelids fell*, and the Capataz de Cargadores *died without a word or moan after an hour* of immobility, broken by short *shudders testifying to* the most *atrocious sufferings.*                                                                         (*N*, pp. 562–3)

The phrase 'after an hour of immobility' provides linguistic evidence of the influence of Maupassant's 'après quatre heures de tressaillements'.

*Nostromo* offers an interesting illustration of Conrad's interest in the *idée fixe*, a disorder of the mind from which a great many of his characters suffer, and which forms, as Kirschner has pointed out,[25] another important link with Maupassant. Conrad's treatment of Gould, Sotillo and Nostromo, all conspicuous victims of a fixed idea, may owe something to Maupassant. In *Fort comme la mort* Maupassant had written: 'Les idées fixes ont la ténacité rongeuse des maladies incurables. Une fois entrées en une âme, elles la dévorent, *ne lui laissent plus la liberté de songer à rien*, de s'intéresser à rien, de prendre goût à la moindre chose' (p. 277). Gould, whose fits of abstraction depict 'the energetic concentration of a will haunted by a fixed idea', brings forth the comment: 'A man haunted by a fixed idea is insane' (p. 379). And Maupassant is again recalled in Nostromo's advice to Dr Monygham to tell Sotillo that the treasure is sunk in the harbour and within his grasp: 'He will spend days in rage and torment – and still he will believe. *He will have no thought for anything else.* He will not give up till he is driven off [...]. He will neither eat nor sleep' (p. 460).

Finally, given the fact that Conrad went far afield in search of material when writing *Nostromo*, Wallace S. Watson's suggestion that he also made use of *Les Travailleurs de la mer* seems worth recalling. The list of elements which, according to Watson, seem to be 'deliberately echoed' is as follows:

descriptions of groups of islands or rocks which serve as symbolic preludes to narrated and dramatized action, in the manner of the carefully worked-over paragraphs on 'The Isabels' in Chapter I of *Nostromo*; slightly ironical but foreboding discussions of ancient legends of evil spirits haunting the locale of the story, similar to the allusions to the legend of the ghostly gringos on Azuera in Conrad's first chapter; the often-ironic mention of the invasion of formerly primitive and isolated Guernesey by various harbingers of progress, similar to the discussions of the coming of steamships and railroads to Sulaco, and of the revitalization of the Gould Concession; Gilliatt's heroic struggle on the isolated Douvres (observed only by sea birds) to save the engine of the steamboat and thereby gain the hand of Déruchette – an account that has a number of interesting parallels with Decoud's lonely vigil on the Great Isabel and the onset of Nostromo's corruption on the point of land between Sulaco Harbor and the Golfo Placido; the account of Clubin's lonely drowning, weighted with a money-belt of stolen money (but pulled down by an octopus), which may have suggested to Conrad the idea of having Decoud weight his body with silver ingots before his suicide on the water, and is also relevant to Nostromo's theft of the treasure; and, finally, a description of the shadows of Clubin and a co-conspirator on the inside wall of a deserted and solitary house on the Guernesey coast, as seen by two frightened bird-nest hunters, an image quite similar to Conrad's somewhat melodramatic account of Nostromo's view of the shadow of the body of the unfortunate Hirsch.[26]

Watson hastens to point out 'the vast difference' in the literary quality of the two novels, but even so, the evidence suggests that, at the peak of his writing career, Conrad may still have drawn some inspiration from his 'first introduction to the sea in literature'.


## 'An Anarchist'

As *Nostromo* was nearing completion at the beginning of July 1904, Conrad wrote a eulogistic review of Anatole France's 'Crainquebille', in which he described its opening chapter as 'a masterpiece of insight and simplicity' (*NLL*, p. 35). But his admiration seems to have found expression in a more significant way than mere praise. In his Author's Note to *A Set of Six*, Conrad lumped together 'The Informer' and 'An Anarchist' (November-December 1905) in one short paragraph, and was particularly evasive about the 'pedigree' of these tales which, he said, is 'hopelessly complicated and not worth disentangling'. What is more, he claimed to have 'forgotten for the most part' how their 'elements' came to be in his mind (*SS*, pp. vii–viii). Be that as it may, Sherry has established that 'An Anarchist' is based, in the main, on two accounts of a mutiny which took place on 21 October 1894 in the penal settlement of St Joseph's Island, French Guiana. But as there is no connection between these

accounts and the events in the first part of the story leading to Paul's imprison-
ment, he has suggested that they 'have their source in Conrad's imagination'.[27]
This may be so, but it seems likely that he also found some helpful hints in
'Crainquebille'. Two critics, at least, have seen a connection between the two
works: Ernest Baker, who called 'An Anarchist' 'A Conradian pendant to
"Crainquebille"',[28] and Baines, who described it as 'a savage, almost mad story
about a man who becomes a victim of society in rather the same way as does
Anatole France's Crainquebille'.[29]

There is, as these critics have noted, an obvious parallel between the victimiz-
ation of the two protagonists – both simple and law-abiding citizens – by society,
and their subsequent downfall: Crainquebille, the old street-hawker, is ruined
because of a policeman's error of perception followed by a ridiculous miscar-
riage of justice; Paul, the young mechanic with a 'warm heart' and a 'weak
head' (p. 161) is also inexorably caught up in a mesh of adverse circumstances
because, as he celebrates his birthday with his mates in a restaurant, he is
manipulated by two strangers whom he has invited to join his party. Both
protagonists are penalized by a harsh legal system, their young lawyers being
more interested in furthering their own careers than in establishing the truth:
Crainquebille tries to explain that he has not shouted 'Mort aux vaches' but
Maître Lemerle only shakes his head unbelievingly; Paul faces the same lack
of understanding when trying to assure his lawyer that he is no anarchist. At
their trials, both defendants are described as innocent victims: 'Crainquebille
est l'enfant naturel d'une marchande ambulante, perdue d'inconduite et de
boisson, il est né alcoolique. Vous le voyez ici abruti par soixante ans de misère'
(XIV, p. 29); '[Paul] was represented [...] as the victim of society and his
drunken shoutings as the expression of infinite suffering' (p. 147). Both lawyers
make magnificent speeches, and both defendants are condemned and
imprisoned. When released the two men find themselves in a similar predicament: Crainquebille is snubbed by his old customers; Paul is blackballed by
employers. Both take to drink and are then on the downward slope. Lastly,
both are taken advantage of because of their situation: when the housewife who
owes money to Crainquebille sees him being arrested, she pockets the money
'pensant qu'on ne devait rien à un homme conduit au poste' (XIV, p. 20);
the manager of the cattle station condemns Paul to servile employment while
similarly justifying his behaviour under the cloak of moral rectitude: 'you don't
think I'd employ a convict and give him the same money I would give an honest
man?' (p. 144).

It is also worth noting that the explicit moral of 'An Anarchist' seems to
derive from that of Maupassant's famous tale 'La Parure'. Mme Loisel, whose
life has been ruined by the loss of a borrowed necklace, sadly reflects at times
on the unpredictability of life: 'Comme *il faut peu de chose pour vous perdre* ou
*vous sauver!*' (*Contes du jour et de la nuit*, p. 72). This is precisely the 'principal
truth' discovered by Paul, namely that 'a little thing may bring about the

undoing of a man': "*Il ne faut pas beaucoup pour perdre un homme*," he said to me, thoughtfully, one evening' (p. 144). Years later, Conrad made Ricardo utter a similar observation: 'Strange what a little thing a man's life hangs on sometimes' (*V*, p. 133).

## The Secret Agent

The best known literary influence on *The Secret Agent* (written in 1906) is that of Dickens. It is understandable that, when working on his first city novel, with London as a setting, Conrad should turn to the most powerful of English city novelists. Dickens's impact has been identified, in particular, in the description of London, in the scene between the Assistant Commissioner and Sir Ethelred, in the cab-ride scene, and, in a more general way, in his treatment of broad social themes.[30] Elisabeth Gerver has also argued that '*The Secret Agent* [...] bears interesting similarities to, and may very well be influenced by [...] Henry James's *The Princess Casamassima*, Turgenev's *Fathers and Children*, and Dostoievskii's *The Possessed*', novels which 'provided Conrad with adaptable examples of fictional technique applied to the disparate facts of anarchism'.[31]

Furthermore, *The Secret Agent* offers ample evidence that the attraction of Zola was not confined to Conrad's earlier story, 'The Idiots'. Although the latter had voiced his disapproval of naturalism as early as Christmas 1898 ('*Tout ça, c'est très vieux jeu*'), the presence of naturalistic elements in the book was immediately recognized. An anonymous reviewer said that in portraying Verloc 'the author appears to have taken M. Zola as model, for he introduces him with a certain kind of respectability, making him decent in his indecency, and honest in his dishonesty',[32] and in 1954 Paul Wiley pointed out that 'In common with Zola and Maupassant, Conrad dealt with the popular naturalistic theme of individual failure, due either to circumstances or to inner weakness, and at times with abnormal states of mind as in tales like "The Idiots", *The Secret Agent* and *The Rover*'.[33]

Naturalism in its most superficial and sensational aspects is conspicuous in the novel's squalid background and the prevailing ugliness (as late as 1920, Conrad was defending himself against the charge of 'elaborating mere ugliness in order to shock' (*SA*, p. viii)), in the violence evoked through the sodden brutalities of Winnie's father (pp. 242–3) and the stabbing of Verloc, in the presentation of grisly details, such as Chief Inspector Heat's examination of Stevie's mangled remains. It is also conspicuous in the theme of hereditary insanity which is as prominent here as it was in 'The Idiots'. The capacity for violence in Winnie and also in her brother extends back to their father whose recurrent rages are mentioned twice. As she approaches Verloc with the carving knife, silently hysterical, her resemblance to Stevie grows with every step 'even to the droop of the lower lip, even to the slight divergence of the eyes' (p. 262), and we are told that into the 'plunging blow' with the knife she has put 'all the inheritance of her immemorial and obscure descent, the simple ferocity of the age of caverns, and the unbalanced nervous fury of the age of bar-rooms' (p. 263). In a more general way, Conrad was also influenced by the naturalistic approach to urban subjects which, as James Walton explains, entails 'the practice of treating lower class urban life with an air of scientific detachment and of presenting sordid or shocking details with an ostensibly moral or anti-bourgeois purpose'.[34]

It should be added, however, that Conrad's primary debt for material on degeneracy is to the work of the renowned criminologist Cesare Lombroso (whom Zola acknowledged in his preface to La Bête humaine) and to Degeneration (1892: English translation, 1895), the book which made the name of his disciple, Max Nordau. Lombroso referred all mental facts to biological causes. He held that the criminal population exhibits a higher percentage of anomalies than non-criminals, that these are due partly to degeneration, partly to atavism, and he argued that political extremism can be understood in terms of pathology. Though the references to Lombroso in the novel, which arise through Comrade Ossipon's fatuous invocations, are limited to the most trivial and popularly-known aspects of his theory, Walton has shown that there occur in Conrad's fiction 'certain observations which closely resemble Lombroso's published findings',[35] and many subsequent studies have clearly established that Conrad, when portraying Stevie and his anarchists, was adhering to the theories of Lombroso and Nordau.[36]

To corroborate Conrad's involvement with naturalism in The Secret Agent, we must consult the findings of R. M. Spensley who has demonstrated that 'parts of [Zola's] Pot-Bouille [1882] may have influenced [his] presentation of certain scenes involving the Verloc household'.[37] Spensley first notes that the pattern of relationship in the Vabre household, which is made up of Auguste Vabre, his wife Berthe, and her half-witted brother Saturnin, resembles that of the Verloc household:

In both households, the relationship of sister and half-witted brother is close, that of husband and brother-in-law – initially, at least – distant; Saturnin has been devoted to Berthe since helping to nurse her through an illness when she was a child; Winnie has been devoted to Stevie since their childhood, when she defended him against her father's violence. Saturnin is subject to fits of anger which only Berthe is able to calm: on one occasion, before Berthe's marriage, he waves a knife at Mme Josserand who is helpless until Berthe intervenes; after the marriage, Auguste appeals to Berthe to disarm Saturnin when, again brandishing a knife, he interrupts a domestic quarrel [pp. 45, 242]. Similarly, Stevie, over-excited by Karl Yundt's lurid tales of oppression, proves unmanageable to Verloc who appeals to Winnie to calm him [p. 56]. Winnie subsequently explains to Verloc how she was obliged to take a knife from Stevie when he was angered by an account in one of Ossipon's propaganda tracts of the cruelty of a German officer towards a recruit. 'Stevie would have stuck that officer like a pig if he had seen him then,' [p. 60] Winnie observes, using an image which is constantly in the mouth of Saturnin when his anger is directed towards Auguste. 'Si vous voulez,' he offers encouragingly to Octave Mouret, his sister's lover, 'à nous deux nous allons le saigner comme un cochon'; later he threatens Auguste directly 'Je te saigne, je te saigne comme un cochon' [pp. 238, 318]. One may well be reminded of Verloc's fate.[38]

Although the description of the cab journey has been called Dickensian, 'certain of its features', the same critic points out, 'recall a cab journey in *Pot-Bouille*' in which Auguste searches for his brother-in-law whom he wishes to be his second in a duel with Mouret:

In both novels, the physical details of the cabman, horse, and cab establish a tone of melancholy futility which is intensified by the interminable crawl through the streets of the capital. The effect is, in each case, symbolic; Winnie's mother is making a sacrifice which will prove to be pointless, even harmful, while Auguste will never in fact take part in the duel. Here is part of the Zola description:

> [Le] cocher, un gros homme très sale, le visage sang-de-boeuf, ivre de la veille, ne se pressait pas, s'installait, ramassait les guides. 'A la course, bourgeois?' demanda-t-il d'une voix enrouée [...] Le fiacre s'ébranla. C'était un vieux landau, immense et malpropre, qui avait un balancement inquiétant, sur ses ressorts fatigués. Le cheval, une grande carcasse blanche, marchait au pas avec une dépense de force extraordinaire, le cou branlant, les jambes hautes. [...] Le fiacre reprit son train d'enterrement. Sur le boulevard, il se fit accrocher par un omnibus. Les panneaux craquaient, les ressorts jetaient des cris plaintifs, une mélancolie noire envahissait de plus en plus le mari en quête de son témoin [...] Un silence régna, le fiacre se balançait mélancoliquement. (pp. 299–300, 305)

This is part of Conrad's description.

> Crawling behind an infirm horse, a metropolitan hackney carriage drew up on wobbly wheels and with a maimed driver on the box. [...] The passionate expostulations of the big-faced cabman seemed to be squeezed out of a blocked throat. [...] His enormous and unwashed countenance flamed red in the muddy stretch of the street. [...] In the narrow streets the progress of the journey was made sensible to those within by the near fronts of the houses gliding past slowly and shakily, with a great rattle and jingling of glass, as if about to collapse behind the cab; and the infirm horse, with the harness hung over his sharp backbone flapping very loose about his thighs, appeared to be dancing mincingly on his toes with infinite patience. (pp. 155–6)[39]

An assessment of the usefulness of Zola's assistance will depend, of course, on one's appraisal of the whole episode, and here reactions vary greatly, some critics judging it too much a caricature, others asserting, like C. B. Cox who quotes Hugh Walpole, that it is 'perhaps the most beautiful, touching and moving thing in the whole of Conrad'.[40]

The discovery of this literary source, together with that of the historical account of the Greenwich bomb outrage of 1894, gives another insight into the way Conrad's mind worked. Martial Bourdin, the victim of the outrage and described by Ford as 'half an idiot', provided the model for Stevie as a half-wit, and this, in turn, may have reminded him of Saturnin and the Vabre household. In a more general sense, it is understandable that Conrad, who was hankering for popular success after the comparative failure of *Nostromo* and identified 'an element of popularity' in his novel (*CL*, III, p. 439), should consider what naturalism could offer him in this respect, and think of *Pot-Bouille*, the novel of the *Rougon-Macquart* series which is closest in spirit to *The Secret Agent* with both novels containing strong elements of brutal and sordid farce.[41]

Conrad's relationship with naturalism is clearly more complex than his somewhat disparaging references to Zola might suggest. As Walton sums up in connection with this novel: 'He gives his old preoccupations a more conventional or "public" mode of existence by adapting them to derivative materials and techniques. But his use of naturalism remains double-edged. His own materialistic analysis of character and states of mind co-exists with a topical satire on that modish approach to life'.[42] On 12 September 1906, as the writing of his novel was drawing to an end, Conrad remarked to Galsworthy: 'As to the beastly trick of style I have fallen into it through worry and hurry. I abominate it myself. It isn't even French really. It is Zola jargon simply. Why it should have fastened on me I don't know' (*CL*, III, p. 355). His indebtedness to *Pot-Bouille* adds significance to this complaint which shows that he felt vulnerable to what he saw as Zola's detrimental influence on his style. What he really meant by that, however, must remain conjectural.[43]

Perhaps it is the farcical element in *The Secret Agent* which called to Conrad's mind one of Maupassant's farces, 'Ce cochon de Morin', of which he knew 'immense' passages by heart, but there can be little doubt of its presence in one scene. Morin, a shopkeeper, finds himself alone in a train compartment with a beautiful young woman as he returns home from Paris. To his distress, he discovers that he is unable to address her, she falls asleep, and he spends the night tormented by desire. When she wakes up, refreshed and happy, she smiles at him, which he misconstrues for a friendly advance, and, still unable to find anything to say, he decides to 'risk everything' by acting: 'et brusquement, sans crier "gare", *il s'avança, les mains tendues*, les lèvres gourmandes, et, la saisissant à pleins bras, il l'embrassa.' (p. 15) The young woman shrieks in fright, opens the window, waves her arms. When the train stops, Morin is arrested and prosecuted. Later, when the reporter on the case suggests to her that she could have changed compartments, she laughs and explains:

J'ai eu peur; et, quand on a peur, on ne raisonne plus. Après avoir compris la situation, j'ai bien regretté mes cris; mais il était trop tard. Songez aussi que *cet imbécile s'est jeté sur moi comme un furieux*, sans prononcer un mot, *avec une figure de fou. Je ne savais même pas ce qu'il me voulait.*                                                    (*Contes de la Bécasse*, p. 21)

On hearing of her husband's plan to emigrate, Mrs Verloc tartly tells him that if he goes abroad he will have to go without her. But immediately regretting her words, she gives him an arch glance over her shoulder saying playfully: 'You couldn't. You would miss me too much', to which the response is:

> *Mr Verloc started forward.*
> 'Exactly,' he said in a louder tone, *throwing his arms out* and making a step towards her. *Something wild and doubtful in his expression made it appear uncertain whether he meant to strangle or to embrace his wife.* (p. 196)

The amazing way Conrad picked up and retained every detail he read is again amusingly revealed in the reason given to explain why Sir Ethelred has adopted the nickname of Toodles for his Private Secretary, namely that he was '*hearing it on the lips of his wife and girls every day*' (p. 143). This is precisely the excuse M. Walter gives to Duroy when, inadvertently, he first addresses him by his nickname: '*Et puis, j'entends ma femme et mes filles vous nommer "Bel-Ami" du matin au soir*' (*BA*, p. 412).

Also worthy of note is a striking similarity between Winnie's perceptions and reactions as she walks to the nearest bridge where she intends to drown herself and those of Frédéric Moreau after Mme Arnoux has made him realize that his hopes are futile: Frédéric 'se sentait perdu comme un homme tombé *au fond d'un abîme*, qui sait qu'*on ne le secourra pas* et qu'il doit mourir' (*ES*, p. 287); Winnie feels alone in London and it seems to her as though the whole town 'rested *at the bottom of a* black *abyss* from which no *unaided* woman could hope to scramble out' (p. 271) (Conrad had already used a similar perception from *Madame Bovary* in *Almayer's Folly*).[44]

## Under Western Eyes

*Under Western Eyes*, Conrad's last great political novel, was written between December 1907 and January 1910. In a letter of 6 January 1908 to Galsworthy, he described what was then 'Razumov' as an attempt 'to capture the very soul of things Russian' (*LL*, II, p. 64), and in the 1920 Author's Note he presented the novel as 'an attempt to render not so much the political state as the psychology of Russia itself' (*UWE*, p. vii). Since it was the first time he had handled a Russian subject and since he denied in his letters to Garnett any knowledge of the Russians,[45] it comes as no surprise to find that during the composition of the novel he kept his sight firmly on the writer who, in his eyes, epitomized Russia and whom he once discarded as 'too Russian' for him (*LEG*, p. 240) – Dostoevskii. Indeed, the many textual similarities and thematic parallels discovered between *Under Western Eyes* and *Crime and Punishment* in particular give substance to the generally accepted view that Conrad's book was conceived as an anti-Dostoevskian novel.[46]

However, 'things Russian' in the novel are viewed by Western eyes, and here Conrad's immense reading in French fiction and non-fiction was brought to bear. In a note on Conrad and Pascal, David Leon Higdon comments:

Its extraordinary allusiveness sets *Under Western Eyes* apart from many of Joseph Conrad's other novels. Its echoes of and references to Dostoyevsky, Tolstoy, Rousseau, Hoffmann, Borel, and others [Turgenev, Mickiewicz, Poe and Shakespeare come to mind] place the novel almost in the context of a philosophical and literary quarrel with these authors.

And he concludes: 'In a novel "exclusively concerned with ideas" [Conrad's words] it is essential that we know what ideas and whose ideas occupied Conrad.'[47] The French authors to whom he alluded and from whom he borrowed are first Anatole France, who provided at least one distinct source, and then Stendhal, Maupassant, Pascal, Rousseau, Joseph de Maistre, Voltaire, Borel, with others, including Flaubert, whose presence can, at some point, be clearly identified.[48]

Anatole France's *Le Lys rouge* played a significant part in the composition of *Under Western Eyes* as can be seen in a number of borrowings of a descriptive, psychological or intellectual nature.

Several of these contributed to the characterization of Natalia Haldin. Her voice, complexion and 'vitality' she inherited from Princess Seniavine:

C'était la princesse Seniavine, souple dans ses fourrures qui semblaient tenir à *sa chair brune* et sauvage. Elle s'assit brusquement et, de *sa voix rude, pourtant caressante, où il y avait de l'homme et de l'oiseau*                                                               (IX, p. 8)

*Her voice was* deep, almost *harsh, and yet caressing* in its harshness. She had *a dark complexion*, with red lips and a full figure. She gave the impression of strong vitality.

(*UWE*, p. 102)

*Her voice*, slightly *harsh, but fascinating with its masculine and bird-like quality*, had the accent of spontaneous conviction. (p. 141)

The descriptions of her eyes and her healthy walk derive, however, from France's heroine, Thérèse Martin:

*et le soleil* penchant *faisait briller des points d'or dans le gris* profond *de ses prunelles.* (p. 327)

*and the* clear *sun put little points of gold into the grey of Miss Haldin's* frank *eyes* (p. 141)

L'ennui du ciel et de l'eau *se réfléchissait dans ses prunelles d'un gris fin.* (p. 6)

The light of the clear wintry forenoon *was softened in her grey eyes.* (p. 105)

Il lui dit qu'il l'avait reconnue de loin *au rythme* de ses lignes et *de ses mouvements*, qui était bien à elle. [...]
Elle répondit qu'elle aimait beaucoup *la marche* (p. 72)

Et, *la regardant de côté*, il lui trouvait l'allure souple et ferme qu'il aimait. (p. 74)

Her sincerity was expressed in *the* very *rhythm of her walk.* It was I who *was looking at her covertly* (p. 142)

Even a French phrase she uses could have been suggested by this fictional counterpart:

Mais elle ne pouvait plus retrouver les sentiments de ce temps-là, *les mouvements de son âme* et de sa chair quand elle s'était donnée. (p. 70)

'Admitting that we occidentals do not understand the character of your people ...' I began.
[...] She checked me gently – 'Their impulses – their ...' she sought the proper expression and found it, but in French ... 'their *mouvements d'âme*'. (p. 105; original emphasis)

Various small details can also be traced to *Le Lys rouge*. For instance, in two pages containing four distinct echoes from this work, we find a reference to the Geneva sky: 'the sky [...] swept and washed clean by the April showers, *extended a cold cruel blue*' (p. 141) which parallels France's description, also of a sky in Spring, but over Florence: 'elle vit le ciel qui, séché par le vent de la mer, *luisait d'un bleu pâle et cruel*' (pp. 184–5). And a detail for Peter Ivanovitch (a 'conglomerate of Bakunin, Kropotkin and Tolstoy, among others'[49]), in his 'black broad-cloth coat' which '*invested his person with a character of austere decency*' (p. 129) comes from that of a similarly 'inspired' character, the poet Choulette: 'Il était très grave; sa longue redingote *lui donnait un air de décence et d'austérité*' (p. 322).

More significant are the borrowings which contribute to the intellectual substance of *Under Western Eyes*. As will be shown later, France – before he became a socialist – and Conrad shared the same radical scepticism in their political outlook, and the fascination of *Le Lys rouge* for Conrad must have stemmed, in part, from its satirical portrayal of the French social and political scene. France tells how on 1 January 1814 Napoleon, violent and gloomy as the Empire was tottering, grabbed Count Martin's grandfather by the shoulders and, shaking him, cried out: '*Un trône, c'est quatre morceaux de bois recouverts de velours? Non! un trône c'est un homme, et cet homme c'est moi!*' (p. 42).[50] Razumov, after the failure of his mission with Ziemianitch, turns against Haldin whom he sees as a 'sanguinary fanatic' and, suddenly 'converted', believes in 'the man who would come at the appointed time'. It must be this idea of a providential strong man that evoked Napoleon in Conrad's mind for he made Razumov then argue with himself: '*What is a throne? A few pieces of wood upholstered in velvet.* But a throne is a seat of power too' (p. 34; *Knowles, p. 60). Later, when the teacher of languages refers, in connection with Madame de Staël, to 'Napoleonic despotism' as '*the booted heir of the Revolution*' (p. 142), he is echoing Jacques Dechartre's sally. To Thérèse's question: 'Et vous, aimez-vous Napoléon?' he replies: 'Madame, je n'aime pas la Révolution. *Et Napoléon, c'est la Révolution bottée*' (p. 56).

But the most important borrowing is found in Razumov's interview with councillor Mikulin. Having decided to make the high official 'show his hand', he makes for the door. When recalled, he says 'explosively':

You think that you are dealing with a secret accomplice of that unhappy man. No, I do not know that he was unhappy. He did not tell me. He was a wretch from my point of view, because to keep alive a *false idea* is a greater crime than to kill a man. I suppose you will not deny that? I hated him! *Visionaries work everlasting evil* on earth. *Their Utopias inspire in* the mass of *mediocre minds a disgust of reality* and a contempt for the secular logic of human development.                                    (*UWE*, p. 95)

For this declaration of political faith, Conrad exploited the tirade of the politician Garain:

Toute *idée fausse* est dangereuse. *On croit que les rêveurs ne font point de mal, on se trompe: ils en font beaucoup. Les utopies les plus inoffensives en apparence exercent réellement une action nuisible. Elles tendent à inspirer le dégoût de la réalité.* [In the preceding paragraph, reference is made to '*la médiocrité des esprits*'.]                  (IX, pp. 43-4)

Lastly, the description of the anarchist in Paul Vence's novel, 'Il n'est pas assez intelligent pour douter. Il est croyant. Il croit ce qu'il a lu. Et il a lu que pour établir *le bonheur universel* il suffisait de détruire la société' (p. 58), seems to have inspired two episodes in Conrad's work. First, an assertion by Sophia Antonovna in an exchange with Razumov:

'Everything is bound to come right in the end.'
    'You think so?'
    'I don't think, young man. I just simply believe it'.                  (*UWE*, p. 245)

Second, the angry thoughts of Razumov when he imagines himself accosting the revolutionary red-nosed student: 'Ah! you want to smash your way into *universal happiness*, my boy. I will give you universal happiness' (p. 302). One might imagine that Razumov is mentally confronting Vence's characters.[51]

Furthermore, France's influence was not confined to these borrowings alone and, in a more pervasive way, can be felt in many of the statements made by Razumov and the language teacher. The former's voice is unmistakable when the latter explains to Miss Haldin that in a real revolution 'the unselfish and the intelligent may begin a movement – but it passes away from them' and defines revolutionary success as 'Hopes grotesquely betrayed, ideals caricatured' (pp. 134-5). In the same way, the thoughts which dart through Razumov's mind as he faces Sophia Antonovna, 'the true spirit of destructive revolution', while undoubtedly Conrad's, have a distinct Francian ring: 'As if anything could be changed! In this world of men nothing can be changed – neither happiness nor misery. They can only be displaced at the cost of corrupted consciences and broken lives – a futile game for arrogant philosophers and sanguinary triflers' (p. 261). Indeed, both France and his mouthpieces would have approved such a conservative view. In *Les Opinions de Jérôme Coignard* (the chapter entitled 'Les Coups d'Etat') Coignard argues:

Songez, monsieur Rockstrong, que ces brusques changements d'Etat que vous méditez sont de simples changements d'hommes, et que les hommes, considérés en masse, sont tous pareils, également médiocres dans le mal comme dans le bien, en sorte que remplacer deux ou trois cents ministres [...] c'est faire autant que rien

(VIII, pp. 455–6)

Further evidence of Conrad's saturation in *Le Lys rouge* when he was writing *Under Western Eyes* (completed 22 January 1910) is apparent in a letter to Garnett of 20 October 1911. After protesting against the charge of putting his hatred of Russia into the novel, he goes on:

Is it possible that you haven't seen that in this book I am concerned with nothing but ideas, to the exclusion of everything else, with no arrière pensée of any kind. *Or are you like the Italians* (and most women) *incapable of conceiving that anybody ever should speak with* perfect *detachment, without some* subtle hidden *purpose, for the sake of what is said*, with no desire of gratifying some small personal spite – or vanity?          (*LEG*, p. 233)

The italicized words were taken from the following passage:

Le prince [Albertinelli] la regarda avec défiance. Il avait de la finesse, *mais il était tout à fait incapable de concevoir qu'on pût jamais parler sans but, avec désintéressement et pour exprimer des idées générales.*          (IX, p. 172)

The presence of France's sentiments in an informal letter suggests that Conrad knew them by heart.

Conrad's interest in France during the composition of *Under Western Eyes* was not confined to *Le Lys rouge*: he also seems to have derived a few suggestions on the nature of women and love from his *Histoire comique* (1903), a story in his mind at that time, as is shown by a letter to Davray of 14 March 1908 in which he says that he is completing a short novel 'à peu près de la longeur de *L'Histoire comique* de France. Cela s'appellera Razumov' (*LF*, p. 92).

When, in France's novel, Robert de Ligny helps his mistress Félicie Nanteuil to undress, he apologizes for his clumsiness in removing the pins which prick him. She answers laughingly:

Bien sûr que tu n'es pas aussi habile que madame Michon! ... Ce n'est pas tant la maladresse; mais tu as peur de te piquer. *Les hommes, c'est lâche. Tandis que les femmes, il faut bien qu'elles s'habituent à souffrir* ... C'est vrai! une femme, ça a mal presque tout le temps.          (XIII, p. 276)

This passage seems to lie behind two comments made by Tekla and Sophia Antonovna in their conversations with Razumov. Tekla, after offering him her help, assures him that she would know how to keep dumb if she was caught because, she explains, '*We women are not so easily daunted by pain*' (p. 237). Later, Sophia Antonovna acknowledges that sometimes men are inspired and that 'when you manage to throw off your *masculine cowardice* and prudishness you are not to be equalled by us' (p. 250).

Robert de Ligny then asks Félicie if she has heard of Claude Bernard. As she has not, he tells her: 'C'était un grand savant. Il a dit qu'il *n'hésitait pas à reconnaître à la femme la suprématie dans le domaine de la sensibilité* physique et *morale*' (p. 277). That France himself found the idea absurd can be judged from Félicie's reaction that if he meant that all women were sensitive he was 'un rude cornichon' [a real greenhorn]. Is it a coincidence that Peter Ivanovitch's 'new faith confessed [. . .] in several volumes' – and so ridiculed by the language teacher – should be based on *'the conviction of woman's spiritual superiority'* (p. 121)? And his explanation as to why 'women are not so easily daunted by pain', namely that they have 'blunt nerves or something' and that, as a result, they 'can stand it better' (p. 237), is very similar to the one on which Claude Bernard in his *Science expérimentale* based his assertion about women's superiority (and which France quotes in a footnote (p. 352)).

We may have here one more instance of Conrad's well-known practice of exploiting in his fiction ideas that were prevalent at the time. In the same connection, some Polish critics have pointed out that 'the "anti-Russian" sentiments of Conrad are not original but are almost word-for-word repetitions of the opinions of *Russian* liberal and revolutionary thinkers'.[52] Conrad was certainly a writer on whom nothing was lost.

Maupassant's continuous presence in Conrad's mind is conspicuous here in two instances. In the course of an exchange between Razumov and Sophia Antonovna, when she dismisses as 'nonsense' his suggestion that she must be a 'materialist', he mentions the definition of the French physiologist Cabanis (1757–1805) 'Man is a digestive tube'. To her disparaging answer 'I spit on him', he retorts:

What? On Cabanis? All right. *But you can't ignore the importance of a good digestion. The joy of life* – you know the joy of life? – *depends on a sound stomach, whereas a bad digestion inclines one to scepticism, breeds black fancies and thoughts of death.*

(*UWE*, pp. 251-2)

In 'Suicides', the character Mr X . . . says in his suicide note:

Car une bonne digestion est tout dans la vie. C'est elle qui donne [. . .] la joie de vivre à tout le monde [. . .]. Un estomac malade pousse au scepticisme, à l'incrédulité, fait germer les songes noirs et les désirs de mort.

(*SR*, p. 234)

Kirschner has shown that the perception of fear which pervades the works of Maupassant and Conrad, the true fear which is aroused not by any identifiable danger but the incomprehensible, is one of the areas where Maupassant must have had a potent effect on Conrad.[53] In one of his two stories entitled 'La Peur' Maupassant recalls a meeting at Flaubert's house with Turgenev who, telling a story on the theme of fear, stated: 'On n'a vraiment peur que de ce qu'on ne comprend pas.' And Maupassant adds: 'Avec lui, on la sent bien, *la peur* vague *de l'Invisible*, la peur de l'inconnu qui est derrière le mur, derrière la porte, derrière la vie apparente' (*La Petite Roque*, pp. 269, 270). After his thrashing of Ziemianitch, Razumov walks back to his lodgings 'holding a discourse with himself with extraordinary abundance and facility' (note the Gallic flavour). He then pauses and feels 'a suspicious uneasiness, such as we may experience when we enter an unlighted strange place – the irrational feeling that something may jump upon us in the dark – *the* absurd *dread of the unseen*' (p. 35).

Two dramatic episodes from Stendhal's *Le Rouge et le noir* have left a tangible mark on the harrowing scene of Razumov's confession to Miss Haldin. During the last night that Mme de Rênal spends with Julien Sorel before he leaves to enter a seminary, she is so paralyzed at the idea of their separation that she becomes like 'un cadavre à peine animé'. When Julien reproves her for her lack of response, she can find nothing to say except: '*Il est impossible d'être plus malheureuse* ... J'espère que je vais mourir ... *Je sens mon coeur se glacer* ...' (p. 196).[54] After Razumov's confession, the narrator describes Miss Haldin motionless in the chair into which she has sunk, with her hands 'lying lifelessly' on her lap, and the only words she utters – words which seemed to Richard Curle 'among the most tragic utterances in literature'[55] – are clearly those of Mme de Rênal: '*It is impossible to be more unhappy* ... [...] It is impossible. ... *I feel my heart becoming like ice*' (p. 356). And when, on the previous page, Conrad shows her pointing 'mournfully at the tragic immobility of her mother, who seemed to watch *a beloved head lying in her lap*', he is probably recalling in that gesture of 'an unequalled force of expression, so far-reaching in its human distress', the famous moment when, after Julien's execution, Mathilde de La Mole is described alone in her carriage holding '*sur ses genoux la tête de l'homme qu'elle avait tant aimé*' (p. 576).

In the light of these echoes, it is highly likely that Julien and Razumov have much in common in their intellectual and psychological make-up. At the seminary, the Abbé Pirard, when assessing Julien's character, acknowledges that in him 'l'esprit est supérieur' (p. 235). He passes for 'un esprit fort' (p. 217) with his fellow seminarists whom he keeps at a distance with a haughty and obstinate silence. Later, Mathilde notices with surprise that he seems to have lost 'ce ton de froideur impassible qui lui était si naturel; il n'avait plus l'air anglais' (p. 341). Similarly, Haldin, who, like the other students, has been impressed by Razumov's taciturnity, sees him as 'a superior mind' (p. 19), a view shared by Prince K— who refers to him as 'un esprit supérieur' (p. 49), and in the eyes of Councillor Mikulin he is 'an esprit fort (p. 296). And when he shows no sign of emotion on hearing that P— has been murdered, Haldin attributes this lack of response to his 'frigid English manner' (p. 16). The predicament in which each young man finds himself originates in a lack of parental affection. Julien believes that his estrangement from his father, who always hated him, is one of the great misfortunes in his life, and from childhood he has sought an escape in books. Razumov, the student, is also presented as a 'solitary individuality' with the vulnerability of a 'young man of no parentage' (pp. 10, 11). As a result of this absence of ties and allegiance, both are morally isolated and their ambition is purely self-centred.

In the last scene of part I, Razumov, as he begins to feel vulnerable to the irrational forces in his world, is moved to say disdainfully to Councillor Mikulin: 'I know *I am but a reed*. But I beg you to allow me the superiority of the *thinking reed* over *the unthinking forces* that are about *to crush him* out of existence'. And he continues to defend his right to be a thinking man, until Mikulin responds: 'I too consider myself a thinking man, I assure you. The principal condition is *to think correctly*' (pp. 89, 90). The metaphor of the reed, the verb 'crush', the assertion of the thinking man's superiority over unthinking forces, the emphasis on 'correct' thinking, all this echoes Pascal's famous *pensée* 347, as Higdon has suggested:

> *L'homme n'est qu'un roseau*, le plus faible de la nature, mais c'est *un roseau pensant*. Il ne faut pas que l'univers entier s'arme pour *l'écraser*; une vapeur, une goutte d'eau suffit pour le tuer. Mais quand l'univers l'écraserait, l'homme serait encore plus noble (puisque) que ce qui le tue, puisqu'il sait qu'il meurt et l'avantage que l'univers a sur lui; *L'univers n'en sait rien*.
>
> Toute notre dignité consiste donc en la pensée. C'est de là qu'il nous faut relever et non de l'espace et de la durée que nous ne saurions remplir. Travaillons donc à *bien penser*: voilà le principe de la morale.

Higdon comments that it is 'entirely consistent both in characterization and technique that Razumov, a third-year philosophy student and Conrad's man of reason, should turn to another man of reason, one within his purview as student, to assert his dignity and sense of being'.[56]

Rousseau makes two overt appearances in *Under Western Eyes*, with a reference to *The Social Contract*, and in the form of his bronze statue on the islet where Razumov writes his secret report to the Russian police. Najder, who has examined Conrad's relationship with Rousseau, shows that 'although [his] reaction to Rousseau was predominantly negative, the ideas he condemned left on him an indelible imprint'. For instance, Conrad 'saw radical social change, the modern nation-state, and democracy itself in characteristically Rousseauian terms'. This view helps to shed important light on the novel, especially on some of Razumov's reactions. As Najder further explains, it is, of course, pertinent that he should feel safe on the solitary islet 'devoted to the philosopher who maintained that man is innately good and that democracy is an excellent system but suitable only to people who are sufficiently mature'. Even more interesting,

Razumov's explanation of his betrayal of Haldin, like Jim's account of his desertion from the *Patna*, is that 'he was tricked by the circumstances' although 'his motives were pure and non-egoistic'. Thus, in both cases, 'we encounter a characteristically Rousseauian type of self-justification by reference to the exceptionality of one situation and (in Razumov's case) personality, and to one's good intentions'. And then, speaking about the novel as a whole, Najder comments:

> *Under Western Eyes* provides ample evidence of Conrad's opposition-obsession syndrome in relation to Rousseau. To begin with, Rousseau figures there in two roles: as a distinguished native of Geneva, an illustrious patron of Swiss democracy, exiled during his life-time but now honoured by the monument which plays such an important part in Razumov's actions; and as a patron of the revolutionary emigrants. Both roles are well-grounded in facts, because Rousseau signed his *Social Contract*, later to become a theoretical basis for revolutionary movements, 'a citizen of Geneva'. The first Rousseau is treated with a double-edged irony. The scoffing remarks about Swiss democracy have to be referred to him; and he provides a symbolic shelter for the *agent provocateur* Razumov. The ideology of revolutionary upheaval induced by terror and destruction is an object not only of implicit irony, but also of direct criticism raised somewhat naively by the narrator but given authorial support by the fact that most professional revolutionaries are presented as rather despicable figures.[57]

And here, in his utter rejection of the 'Utopian revolutionism' (p. x) which stems from Rousseau's belief that a change in institutions would bring about an improvement in men, Conrad found a powerful ally in Anatole France, who also detested Rousseau's ideas, and whose influence on the political views expressed in the novel has been shown to be both remarkably specific and pervasive.

Another opponent of Rousseau whose views are alluded to is Joseph de Maistre. In the same article, Najder observes that the main advantage of examining *Under Western Eyes* from the viewpoint of Conrad's relation to Rousseau is that it 'puts us on the right track' in looking for the origins of the novel's main intellectual sources. He explains:

> Thus the declaration of Mr de P—, the Minister of State, that 'the thought of liberty has never existed in the Act of the Creator. From the multitude of men's counsel nothing could come but revolt and disorder; and revolt and disorder in a world created for obedience and stability is sin. It was not Reason but Authority which expressed the Divine Intention' echoes, surely not by accident, the views of Joseph de Maistre, one of the most outspoken and influential conservative critics of Rousseau and the Enlightenment. De Maistre's voice can be heard also in Razumov's dispute with Haldin, when he pits historical tradition against radical change, and in Razumov's five principles, which he puts down after Haldin's arrest.[58]

That Conrad had 'great sympathy' for Voltaire's work comes as no surprise in view of the remarkable appeal Voltaire held for his intellectual heir, Anatole France.[59] It is of course appropriate that the shade of Voltaire should hover, with that of Rousseau, over the Boulevard des Philosophes, and Conrad's reference to him, like that to Mme de Staël (p. 125),[60] could hardly be casual. It does not seem likely that Conrad, when writing a novel where the ideas of the father of democracy and revolution play such an important part and where he gives him something of a drubbing, could have ignored Rousseau's most formidable opponent. Indeed, on one occasion Voltaire's voice is unmistakable. When Sophia Antonovna, in conversation with Razumov, exclaims, as she inveighs against 'the great social iniquity of the system', '*Crush the Infamy!* A fine watchword! I would placard it on the walls of prisons and palaces' (pp. 262, 263), she is echoing his famous war-cry '*Ecrasez l'infâme*'.[61]

Higdon has also analysed the relevance of Conrad's choice of the name Borel for the Château which, as he observes, 'Structurally and symbolically [...] dominates Parts II and III of [...] *Under Western Eyes* like the threatening, sinister castle of a Gothic romance'. He contends that Conrad had an intense dislike of French Gothicism, particularly 'black romanticism', and that Pétrus Borel (1809–1859), whose works are a mass of melodramatic extravagances and sensational horrors, 'provided an appropriate symbol for one wishing to discredit the movement'. Furthermore, Conrad also signalled his intentions by using many of the Gothic conventions which permeate the writings of Borel and his friends, like the references to ghouls, phantoms, automata, and vampires which are constantly applied to the revolutionaries. Most interestingly, Higdon also points out that Borel's home was called *Haute Pensée* and 'Château Borel houses a variety of *hautes pensées* which apparently victimize their thinkers. Indeed, the revolutionary actions planned at the Château border on caricatures and the house itself becomes a chamber of horrors inhabited by demonic creatures.' The sinister atmosphere echoes 'the hollowness of the revolutionary thought', and to Razumov it is 'a prison of the mind: "It offered no sign of being inhabited. With its grimy, weather-stained walls and all the windows shuttered from top to bottom, it looked damp and gloomy and deserted. It might very well have been haunted in traditional style by some doleful, groaning, futile ghost of a middle-class order" ' (pp. 210–11). Thus, the connection between Château Borel and Pétrus Borel reveals a typically ambiguous attitude on Conrad's part, similar to that found in his relation to naturalism, since, as Higdon concludes, he is 'paradoxically satirizing a style and cluster of conventions he himself employs repeatedly in his own work'.[62]

Finally, in this novel 'exclusively concerned with ideas' one must not overlook one of the most important problems it raises, that of the misuse and inadequacy of language. It is, of course, no accident that the narrator should be a language teacher since it is part of his main function as defender of rationality to be constantly aware of the excesses and distortions caused by, or reflected in, a misuse of language. In his preoccupation with language, Conrad found an impressive precedent in Flaubert, as we shall see in part III. At this stage, the following parallel will suggest their closeness on this subject. A well-known authorial intrusion in *Madame Bovary* analyses Rodolphe's jaded response to Emma's repeated protestations of love in conventional words: 'comme si la plénitude de l'âme ne débordait pas quelquefois par les métaphores les plus vides, puisque personne, jamais, ne peut *donner l'exacte mesure* de ses besoins, ni de ses conceptions, ni de ses douleurs' (*MB*, p. 265). The teacher of languages admits that when Miss Haldin asked him: 'I suppose you are wondering what my feelings are?' he could 'get hold of nothing but of some commonplace phrases, those futile phrases that *give the measure* of our impotence before each other's trials' (pp. 112–13). Despite the difference between expressing one's own sufferings and responding to another's trials, both statements reveal the same recognition of 'the imperfection of language' (p. 293).

The more we probe into the genesis of *Under Western Eyes* the better we understand Conrad's long and intense involvement with a book which he described in 1916 as his 'most deeply meditated novel',[63] and the better we appreciate his claim to Garnett that he aimed to achieve 'an effect of virtuosity before anything else'. It was certainly no mean feat to harmonize so many different voices into what he called 'the development of a single mood' (*LEG*, p. 234). That Conrad made an extensive use of books, fictional and non-fictional, particularly French, throughout his career, is by now abundantly clear, and in that sense *Under Western Eyes* is no exception. And yet, as Higdon rightly points out, its 'extraordinary allusiveness' sets it apart from his other works, for the allusions and borrowings (at least those of an intellectual nature) here acquire a special significance as they form an integral part of the overall design – that is, the confrontation, through the spiritual and ideological consequences of a betrayal, of Russian autocracy with Western liberalism, mysticism with rationality, and cynicism and nihilism with human values. And many of the allusions are sufficiently obvious to make it clear that Conrad intended his reader to identify them and see their relevance.[64] Furthermore, those references to the writings of others at the heart of this novel of ideas enable us to see how Conrad, whether as part of his original intention or not, would be led to explore in greater depth than in any other of his books what Jacques Darras calls '[writing's] power to distort as well as depict reality'.[65]

*Under Western Eyes* is, of all his novels, the one which best reveals Conrad's cosmopolitan background. In no other work is he so much the politically attuned European, and only a man of wide cultural background and range could have produced what is, despite a 'lack of finesse in some details',[66] a most subtle, complex and original novel.

# 5 The third phase of maturity and the last decade

## 'A Smile of Fortune'

Conrad started to write 'A Smile of Fortune' in May 1910 as he was beginning to recover from the severe breakdown he suffered on the completion of *Under Western Eyes*. As he was finishing it at the end of August, he wrote a letter to Galsworthy which shows how painful and unsatisfactory his first attempts had been: 'I did not really start till July. June's work was mere fooling, – not on purpose, of course. I was still too limp to grasp the subject and most of the pages written then have been cancelled in typescript. It was strangely nerveless bosh' (*LL*, II, p. 114). Paul Kirschner has shown that at this very difficult time, Conrad turned again for assistance to Maupassant, making extensive use of his novella 'Les Soeurs Rondoli' (1884).[1]

'Les Soeurs Rondoli', a story devised chiefly to titillate the readers of the *Echo de Paris*, relates the amorous adventure of the narrator Pierre Jouvenet[2] with an Italian girl, Francesca Rondoli. After a visit to the buffet-car, Pierre and his friend Paul Pavilly, who are travelling to Italy, find their compartment occupied by a young woman. Paul, a womanizer, winks and twirls his moustache with delight, but Pierre looks at her quietly, trying to guess from her appearance the kind of person she is:

> C'était une jeune femme, toute jeune et jolie, une fille du Midi assurément. Elle avait des yeux superbes, *d'admirables cheveux noirs, ondulés*, un peu crêpelés, *tellement touffus, vigoureux et longs, qu'ils semblaient lourds, qu'ils donnaient rien qu'à les voir la sensation de leur poids sur la tête.* Vêtue avec élégance et un certain mauvais goût méridional, elle semblait un peu commune.
> (*SR*, pp. 12–13)

In 'A Smile of Fortune', the Captain's description of Alice's hair is similar in detail and notable for its gallicism, 'nothing but to look at':

> it was a mass of *black, lustrous locks*, twisted anyhow high on her head, with long, untidy wisps hanging down on each side of the clear sallow face; a mass *so thick and strong and abundant that, nothing but to look at, it gave you a sensation of heavy pressure on the top of your head* and an impression of magnificently cynical untidiness.
> (*TLS*, p. 44; *Kirschner, pp. 221–2)

The picture of Alice is a composite one: her '*long, untidy wisps hanging down on each side of the [...] face*' come from the Italian girl's mother: '*Ses cheveux dépeignés tombaient par mèches sur* son front et sur *ses épaules'* (p. 52) and her 'dingy [...] wrapper of some thin stuff' which *'revealed the young supple body'* (p. 44) was suggested by the description of the Italian girl's younger sister: 'une grande fille parut [...] dépeignée aussi, et *laissant deviner*, sous une vieille robe de sa mère, *son corps jeune et svelte'* (pp. 56–7).

Both the girl on the train and Alice show themselves to be unsociable:

*Elle demeurait immobile à sa place,* les yeux fixés devant elle dans une pose renfrognée de femme furieuse. *Elle n'avait pas même jeté un regard sur nous.*

Paul *se mit à causer avec moi*, disant des choses apprêtées pour produire de l'effet, étalant une devanture de conversation pour attirer l'intérêt comme les marchands étalent en montre leurs objets de choix pour éveiller le désir.

*Mais elle semblait ne pas entendre.*                    (*SR*, pp. 13–14)

She leaned forward, hugging herself with crossed legs [...]. I detected a slight, quivering start or two, which looked uncommonly like bounding away. *They were followed by the most absolute immobility.*

[...] *I* [...] *began to talk* about the garden, caring not what I said, but using a gentle caressing intonation as one talks to soothe a startled wild animal. *I could not even be certain that she understood me. She never raised her face nor attempted to look my way.*

(*TLS*, p. 44; \*Kirschner, p. 222)

Pierre completely fails in his advances to the Italian girl, first in French and then in her own language. The Captain is no more successful with the peremptory Alice, whose *gouvernante* asks him if he thinks it his business to stare at the girl. Pierre then offers chicken and fruit to the Italian girl who, after several 'mica's' which gradually lose their harshness, accepts the invitation. However, after eating ravenously, she returns to her shell and repels all further approaches with a furious 'mica'. The Captain, on his first visit to Jacobus, stays to dinner, but Alice refuses to join them with 'repeated "Won't!" "Shan't!" and "Don't care!"' (p. 49). On another occasion, he offers her a plate of chicken which she again refuses with 'Don't care'. Pierre and the Captain adapt each girl's favourite retort as a nickname, Pierre calling Francesca 'mademoiselle Mica' (pp. 41–2) and the Captain calling Alice 'Miss Dont Care' (pp. 51, 66; \*Kirschner, p. 223).

When Pierre tells the girl that they will shortly arrive in Genoa, he is startled by her reaction:

Elle murmura, *sans me répondre, comme obsédée par une pensée fixe et gênante*: 'Qu'est-ce que je vais faire maintenant?'

Puis, *tout d'un coup, elle me demanda*:

– Voulez-vous que je vienne avec vous?

After more exchanges in the same vein, he asks her where she would like to go:

*Elle haussa les épaules avec une indifférence souveraine.*

– Où vous voudrez! Ça m'est égal.

*Elle répéta deux fois:* 'Che mi fa?'                                        (*SR*, pp. 26–7)

One day, the Captain, as usual, is gazing at Alice in the garden when he says:

*suddenly, without looking at me, with the appearance of a person speaking to herself, she asked* [...]:
'Why do you keep on coming here?'
'Why do I keep on coming here?' I repeated, taken by surprise. I could not have told her.

Watching her narrowly, he asks if she really cares to know:

*She shrugged indolently her* magnificent *shoulders,* from which the dingy thin wrapper was slipping a little.
'*Oh – never mind – never mind!*'                                        (*TLS*, p. 63)

In Genoa, Pierre, Paul and Francesca go to a hotel. She pairs with Pierre who, as she looks somewhat unkempt, pointedly places his toilet articles in sight and leaves her alone to wash. When he returns, he is met with a suffocating odour of perfume:

*L'Italienne était assise sur sa malle dans une pose de songeuse mécontente* ou de bonne renvoyée. *J'appréciai d'un coup d'oeil ce qu'elle entendait par faire sa toilette.* La serviette était restée pliée sur le pot à eau toujours plein. Le savon intact et sec demeurait auprès de la cuvette vide; mais on eût dit que la jeune femme avait bu la moitié des flacons d'essence. [...] *Un nuage de poudre de riz*, un vague brouillard blanc *semblait encore flotter dans l'air, tant elle s'en était barbouillé le visage et le cou.*                                        (*SR*, p. 34)

Though Alice does not use perfume, her attitude to her toilet is similar to Francesca's:

*She sat leaning on her elbow looking at nothing.* Why did she stay listening to my absurd chatter? And not only that, but *why did she powder her face in preparation for my arrival? It seemed to be her idea of making a toilette,* and in her untidy negligence a sign of great effort towards personal adornment.                                        (*TLS*, p. 58; *Kirschner, p. 224)

After a meal, Francesca consents to share a room with Pierre, but he is hurt by the complete indifference of her manner. When she wakes up in the night, however, her indifference ceases to bother him and leads him to have his way with her:

Mais, tout à coup, ma voisine se réveilla. *Elle ouvrit des yeux étonnés* et toujours mécontents, puis s'étant aperçue qu'elle était nue, elle se leva et passa *tranquillement* sa chemise de nuit, *avec autant d'indifférence que si je n'avais pas été là.*
Alors... ma foi... je profitai de la circonstance, *sans qu'elle parut d'ailleurs s'en soucier le moins du monde.* Et elle se rendormit placidement, la tête posée sur son bras droit.
Et je me mis à méditer sur l'imprudence et la faiblesse humaines.                                        (*SR*, p. 40)

Alice reacts in a similar fashion to the Captain; not even aware of his presence, which he sees with 'indignant eyes', she rises and stretches languidly in front of him, provokingly ignoring him: 'Leisurely and *tranquil, behaving right before me with the ease of a person alone in a room*, she extended her beautiful arms, [...] her body swaying.' This supreme indifference of the girl, behaving as though he were 'a wooden post or a piece of furniture', brings his anger 'to a head' and rouses him to action: he impulsively clasps her to him and the first kiss he plants on her lips is 'vicious enough to have been a bite'. As she does not resist, he does not stop, and she lets him go on *'as if she did not care in the least'*. All he can detect in her *'wide-open eyes'* is *'a slight surprise'* (pp. 68–70; *Kirschner, pp. 224–5 and *Hervouet).

For three days, Pierre drags his two bored companions from museum to museum, until Paul, irritated, decides to leave them. Pierre finds himself perplexed and embarrassed:

à ma grande surprise, *je m'étais attaché à Francesca d'une façon singulière. L'homme est faible et bête, entraînable pour un rien, et lâche toutes les fois que ses* sens *sont excités ou domptés. Je tenais à cette fille* que je ne connaissais point, *à cette fille taciturne et toujours mécontente. J'aimais sa figure grogneuse, la moue de sa bouche, l'ennui de son regard; j'aimais ses gestes fatigués, ses consentements méprisants, jusqu'à l'indifférence de sa caresse. Un lien* secret, ce lien mystérieux de l'amour bestial, cette *attache* secrète de la possession qui ne rassasie pas, *me retenait près d'elle.* (*SR*, pp. 43–4)

The Captain's reflections and his feelings for Alice prior to the kiss are almost identical:

*How weak, irrational and absurd we are! How easily carried away whenever our awakened imagination brings us the irritating hint of a desire!* I cared for the girl in a particular way, seduced by *the moody expression of her face*, by *her obstinate silences*, her rare, *scornful words*; by *the* perpetual *pout of her closed lips*, the black depths of *her fixed gaze turned slowly upon me* as if in contemptuous provocation, *only to be averted next moment with* an exasperating *indifference*. (*TLS*, pp. 56–7)

*Even her indifference was seductive. I felt myself growing attached to her by the bond* of an irrealizable desire, for I kept my head – quite.
(p. 59; *Kirschner, pp. 225–6 and *Hervouet)

However, despite the closeness of Conrad's text to Maupassant's, the apparently slight changes he made illustrate the difference in the sexual element in the stories, and in the approach to sexual matters of the four protagonists. In Pierre's case, love-making engenders a real attachment to Francesca; with the Captain, physical contact dispels his obsession and leads him to feel a 'complete detachment' (p. 79) from Alice. Both deplore a man's weakness in front of a woman, but, whereas for Pierre a man is carried away by his 'senses', for the Captain he is the victim of his 'imagination'. The bond linking Pierre to Francesca is 'possession'; that between the Captain and Alice is 'an irrealizable desire'. Pierre cares for Francesca's 'scornful permissions'; the Captain is seduced by

Alice's 'scornful words'. Francesca may 'consent', but she is not provocative whereas Alice's indifference seems like 'contemptuous provocation'.

Other details confirm the difference in the attitudes of the two men. Later, Pierre comments: '*Et je demeurais avec elle, le coeur libre* et la chair tenaillée, nullement las de la tenir en mes bras, *cette femelle hargneuse et superbe*' (p. 46). The Captain also calls Alice '*that girl, snarling and superb*', and later he, too, observes: '*I returned to her with* my head clear, *my heart* certainly *free* [...] but as if beguiled by some extraordinary promise' (pp. 58–9; *Kirschner, p. 226). Both are heart free, but whereas Pierre, with his 'flesh tormented', cannot keep his head, the Captain, who apparently feels nothing more than 'the hint of a desire', has no difficulty in keeping his 'clear'.

The first time Pierre sees Francesca naked, she is asleep on a bed, in a pose that reminds him of the famous painting by Titian. He looks at her calmly, with an aesthetic eye, and soliloquizes on the beauty of a sleeping woman:

> Quoi de plus joli qu'une femme endormie? *Ce corps, dont tous les contours sont doux*, dont toutes *les courbes* séduisent, dont toutes les molles saillies troublent le coeur, semble fait pour *l'immobilité* du lit. *Cette ligne onduleuse qui* se creuse au flanc, *se soulève à la hanche, puis descend* la pente légère et *gracieuse* de *la jambe* pour finir si coquettement au bout du *pied* ne se dessine vraiment avec tout son *charme* exquis qu'allongée sur les draps d'une couche. (*SR*, pp. 38–9)

Unlike Pierre's attraction, the Captain's is purely voyeuristic, and to watch Alice is the sole aim of his daily visits, a 'depraved habit' to which he becomes a 'slave': 'I loved to watch her slow changes of pose, to look at her long *immobilities* composed in *the graceful lines of her body*.' Later, further indulging his 'secret vice', he says:

> I looked her over, from the top of her dishevelled head, down *the lovely line* of her shoulder, *following the curve of the hip*, the draped form of *the* long *limb, right down to* her fine ankle below a torn, soiled flounce; and as far as the point of the [...] blue slipper, dangling from her well-shaped *foot* [...]. I seemed to breathe her special and inexplicable *charm* (*TLS*, pp. 58–9, 62)

In spite of its being an amorous adventure with a lighthearted and somewhat rakish ending, 'Les Soeurs Rondoli', with its prologue on moral solitude, shows a deep disillusionment with life, which is also experienced by the Captain at the end of his affair:

> *C'est en allant loin qu'on comprend bien comme tout est proche et court et vide; c'est en cherchant l'inconnu qu'on s'aperçoit bien comme tout est médiocre et vite fini*; c'est en parcourant la terre qu'on voit bien comme elle est petite et sans cesse à peu près pareille. (*SR*, p. 7)

> I felt in my heart that *the further one ventures the better one understands how everything in our life is common, short, and empty; that it is in seeking the unknown in our sensations that we discover how mediocre are our attempts and how soon defeated!* (*TLS*, pp. 79–80; *Kirschner, pp. 227–8)

Again, Conrad's small addition is illuminating: the extrovert Pierre refers to travelling far and seeking the unknown in life in general; the introvert Captain thinks in terms of a venture confined to seeking the unknown 'in [his] sensations', a remark which measures the degree of his self-centredness.

Kirschner points out that Conrad inverted the structure of 'Les Soeurs Rondoli', putting Maupassant's philosophical prologue at the end of his story. This corroborates Ford's remark that whereas he, Ford, preferred 'the more pensive approach', 'Conrad's tendency and desire made for the dramatic opening',[3] which he achieved here using the incident of the funeral of a child who died at sea. But Conrad may have preferred this inversion on other grounds: in 'Les Soeurs Rondoli' the disenchantment with life is felt prior to the amorous adventure; it may turn the adventure, in Kirschner's words, into a 'condemned man's jest',[4] but the jest sounds not too bad, whereas in 'A Smile of Fortune' the disenchantment stems from the adventure itself. As Wiley says: 'the erotic element which is everywhere permeated by a cunning tissue of insinuation, fades out with the rise of the concluding theme of the disillusionment of sensual love.'[5] At this point, one cannot help wondering what the Captain expected from his transient and somewhat perverse experience other than something 'common, short and empty'; in other words, it does not seem enough of a 'venture' to warrant the general philosophical conclusion he draws from it. This is probably what Guerard meant when he referred to 'Conrad's curious presentation and valuation of the experience itself'.[6]

Conrad's uncertain control over his hybrid material accounts for much that is unsatisfactory in 'A Smile of Fortune'. Here perhaps lies the reason for the ambiguously shifting attitudes of the Captain; for, whereas Pierre's attitude to Francesca is seen to be straightforward, rooted in an uninhibited sexual union which makes his attachment genuine, the Captain, who experiences nothing but a 'vague desire' towards Alice, seems sexually unfocused. Furthermore, the subject of attraction in two women as different as Francesca, an accepted member of society, and Alice, the social outcast, was bound to produce very different effects which Conrad does not seem to have foreseen. Very revealing is his statement that he had 'tried to make her pathetic' when, as a reviewer noted, she comes through as a 'sensual animal' (*LL*, II, p. 144). His confusion probably stems from a reluctance to deal with sexual matters, for it is a fact that, even in possession of Maupassant's frank and straightforward material, he still managed to display what Guerard calls 'clumsiness and evasion [...] in approaching the subject of sexual attraction'.[7]

Nevertheless, some of the borrowed material makes a positive contribution to the story. Guerard again points out that it picks up energy as soon as the slovenly and crouching Alice appears "snarling and superb and barely clad"'.[8] Clearly, the vividness with which she is presented owes much to Maupassant's model, and it is significant that she is one of the few women in Conrad who are not sentimentalized.

Ford said that Conrad was in the habit of modifying his stories according to his listener, and recalled the two ways he tried it out on Mme Poradowska and himself:

So the story afterwards used in a *Smile of Fortune* told to the writer alone was one thing and told to his [...] aunt, Mme. Paradowski [*sic*], was something quite different. It would be thinner, less underlined, more of a business-like subject for treatment if told to the writer alone: when told to the French lady [...] it would be much livelier, much more punctuated with gestures and laughs – much more *pimenté*; in fact, the story of a sailor's *bonne fortune*.[9]

This last version indicates that, at that stage, Conrad was still very close to his literary source, and confirms that, as he wrote to Galsworthy, he meant his story to be 'comical' (*LL*, II, p. 108). Although it did not turn out to be so, Maupassant certainly accounts for the generous dash of spice in it.

Critics still differ in their assessment of the autobiographical element in 'A Smile of Fortune'. No doubt, it is based on Conrad's seven-week stay in Port Louis, Mauritius, where, in 1888, as captain of the *Otago*, he met a young girl called Alice Shaw, the daughter of a stevedore. But whether the narrative adventure 'actually happened as described' (*LL*, I, p. 113) as Jean-Aubry firmly believed, is still a matter for dispute. Watt sees the story as 'largely autobiographical';[10] Karl warns that 'it would be a serious mistake to accept Jean-Aubry's account as biographical fact'.[11] Meyer has pointed out the improbability of Conrad's having two romances, with Mlle Eugénie Renouf and Alice Shaw, concomitantly and during so short a time.[12] Conrad's heavy dependence on Maupassant adds considerable weight to this view, and therefore to his own assertion in his Author's Note that, despite its 'autobiographical form', 'A Smile of Fortune' is 'not the record of personal experience' (p. ix).

## Chance

*Chance* (written mainly in 1907 and from May 1911 to March 1912) has been described by Moser as 'Conrad's most *English* novel'.[13] His examination of its sources shows how much it rests on notorious financial scandals which shook Paris and London at the turn of the century. A great deal of the book was also inspired by Ford: Conrad found 'considerable human detail for de Barral's story' in his friend's financial mismanagement of the *English Review*; de Barral himself, 'that cold, vain, self-deluded charlatan', 'looks, talks, and acts like Ford' and his 'situation at the time of his greatness [...] owes something to Ford's in his *English Review* days'.[14] Captain Anthony and his father, the 'poet-tyrant' Carleon Anthony, have real-life counterparts in Milnes Patmore, a sea captain who fell in love in his forties, and his father, the Victorian poet Coventry Patmore.[15] Moreover, Patmore's sentimental tribute to Victorian womanhood, *The Angel in the House*, is, according to E. E. Duncan-Jones, 'a frequent source of those generalizations about women which contributed so much to the early success of *Chance*.[16] In the light of this and other sources, Conrad's dependence on French originals is understandably limited, being apparently confined to Anatole France whose voice can nevertheless be heard distinctly on a number of occasions.

France contributed to a few of the observations about women sprinkled throughout the book. When Marlow says: 'For if we men try to put the spaciousness of all experiences into our reasoning and would fain *put the Infinite itself into our love*, it isn't, as some writer has remarked, *It isn't women's doing*' (p. 93), the writer he is paraphrasing is France who had written in *Le Jardin d'Epicure*: '*Nous mettons l'infini dans l'amour. Ce n'est pas la faute des femmes*' (IX, p. 413; *Kirschner, p. 233). In a later scene, Marlow detains Flora on the pavement while Mr Fyne remonstrates with Captain Anthony in the Eastern Hotel. He sees something comical in their situation as they await the outcome of Fyne's mission, which leads him to comment, in the words France uses in *Le Jardin*: '*Le comique est vite douloureux quand il est humain*' (IX, p. 412), '*But the comic when it is human becomes quickly painful*' (p. 206). Marlow then realizes that the girl is 'infinitely anxious', and he asks himself whether the 'tension of her suspense' depends 'on hunger or love'. This thought was probably inspired by France, who reiterated the view that hunger and love are the two main-springs of human action. In *Le Jardin*, for instance, he speaks of 'ce vieux fonds de faim et d'amour sur lequel [...] nous vivons tous' (IX, p. 459). Marlow continues: 'The answer would have been of some interest to Captain Anthony. For my part, *in the presence of a young girl I always become convinced that the dreams of sentiment – like the* consoling *mysteries of Faith – are invincible; that it is never, never reason which governs men* and women' (p. 206). Again, he is faithfully echoing France who, writing about woman in the same work, had declared: '*on se pénètre près d'elle de cette idée que les rêves du sentiment et les ombres de la foi sont invincibles, et que ce n'est pas la raison qui gouverne les hommes*' (IX, p. 412; *Kirschner, p. 234).

Other passages bearing the imprint of France's thinking will be presented in chapter 7.

### 'The Planter of Malata'

On 'The Planter of Malata' (written in late 1913) Anatole France, Maupassant, and Mérimée have left tangible marks.[17]

Although Renouard has resigned himself to the fact that he loves a woman who loves another, his resignation 'was not spared the torments of jealousy', which is described as 'the cruel, insensate, poignant, and imbecile jealousy, when it seems that *a woman betrays us simply by this that she exists, that she breathes – and when the deep movements of her nerves or her soul become a matter* of distracting suspicion, of killing doubt, *of mortal anxiety*' (*WT*, p. 34). Behind this analysis lies a passage from *Le Jardin d'Epicure*:

Au vrai jaloux, tout porte ombrage, tout est sujet d'inquiétude. *Une femme le trahit déjà seulement parce qu'elle vit et qu'elle respire.* Il redoute ces travaux de la vie intérieure, *ces mouvements divers de la chair et de l'âme* qui font de cette femme une créature distincte de lui-même, indépendante, instinctive, douteuse et parfois inconcevable. [...] Au fond, il ne lui reproche rien, sinon qu'*elle est.* [...] *Quel sujet d'inquiétude mortelle!*

(IX, p. 410; *Kirschner, p. 234)

The indelible imprint of Maupassant on the subjects of love, solitude and death can again be seen in certain of Renouard's reactions and attitudes. An echo of the passage from 'Fou?', already quoted in connection with *An Outcast*, can still be heard when he says to Miss Moorsom: 'Listen! I would never have been jealous of him. And yet I am jealous of the air you breathe, of the soil you tread on, of the world that sees you – moving free – not mine' (*WT* p. 74). His torment when facing her also echoes that of the haunted character in 'Solitude': '*Que pense-t-il? [...] Comment savoir [...] ce qui s'agite dans cette* petite *tête* ronde? Quel *mystère* que la pensée inconnue *d'un être*' (*Monsieur Parent*, pp. 265–6); '*He did not know what there was under that* ivory *forehead* [...]. *He could not tell what were her thoughts* [...]. He felt himself in the presence *of a mysterious being*' (*WT*, pp. 35–6). And his experience as he looks at the face of a friend is reminiscent of Norbert de Varenne's reflections on death:

Moi, depuis quinze ans, je la sens qui me *travaille* comme si je portais *en moi* une bête rongeuse. Je l'ai sentie peu à peu, mois par mois, *heure par heure*, me *dégrader* ainsi qu'une maison qui s'écroule.                                                                (*BA*, p. 207)

He detected a *degrading* quality in the touches of age which *every day* adds to a human countenance. They moved and disturbed him, like the signs of a horrible *inward travail*
(*WT*, p. 5)

The main source of inspiration, however, was provided by Prosper Mérimée, with Conrad engaging, as Knowles has shown, in a 'free adaptation' of the former's Venus legend. Knowles explains:

At some point in its germination Conrad seems to have found in 'La Vénus d'Ille' [1837] a presiding narrative legend which, in modified form, would be both flexible enough to carry all the 'implications and difficulties' of his material and yet simultaneously act as a simplifying framework for the tale as a whole. In transforming hints from Mérimée's story, he is likely to have been motivated by the technical challenge involved in fusing popular ingredients of romance, sensation and a ghostlike atmosphere with serious themes; but there seems little doubt also that he found in Mérimée a version of pagan myth congenial to his own semi-allegorical enquiry into 'the crude impulses of old humanity' which have been repressed and corrupted by a decadent civilization. (p. 77)

A key part of his demonstration reads:

Conrad's debt to Mérimée is most evident in the creation of Felicia Moorsom who in her own distinctive way combines the roles of Venus *turbulenta* and Venus in polite society. If not a statue, the statuesque Felicia has a form and fatally voiceless power similar to Mérimée's draped nude which is described as follows:

La chevelure, relevée sur le front, paraissait avoir été dorée autrefois. [...] Quant à la figure jamais je ne parviendrai à exprimer son caractère étrange, et dont le type ne se rapprochait de celui d'aucune statue antique dont il me souvienne. Ce n'était point cette beauté calme et sévère des sculpteurs grecs, qui, par système, donnaient à tous les traits une majestueuse immobilité. Ici, au contraire, j'observais avec surprise l'intention marquée de l'artiste de rendre la malice arrivant jusqu'à la méchanceté. Tous les traits étaient contractés légèrement: les yeux un peu obliques, la bouche relevée des coins, les narines quelque peu gonflées. Dédain, ironie, cruauté, se lisaient sur ce visage d'une incroyable beauté cependant. En vérité, plus on regardait cette admirable statue, et plus on éprouvait le sentiment pénible qu'une si merveilleuse beauté pût s'allier à l'absence de toute sensibilité.

[...] Cette expression d'ironie infernale était augmentée peut-être par le contraste de ses yeux incrustés d'argent et très brillants avec la patine d'un vert noirâtre que le temps avait donnée à toute la statue. Ces yeux brillants produisaient une certaine illusion qui rappelait la réalité, la vie. Je me souvins de ce que m'avait dit mon guide, qu'elle faisait baisser les yeux à ceux qui la regardaient.

This description and the ensuing debate about the statue provide a fund of motifs which haunt 'The Planter of Malata' with ghostlike persistence. The regal Felicia and the statue (both of whom take their revenge for being deceived by the male) belong to a pagan sisterhood, the former seeming to Renouard to be a centuries-old 'divinity' (p. 77), a 'strong-headed goddess' (p. 34) and a 'woman so marvellous that centuries seemed to lie between them' (p. 42). In his early description of Felicia, Conrad begins with the pagan and martial grace of her hair, 'chiselled and fluid, with the daring suggestion of a helmet of burnished copper' (p. 10), notes the mysteriously 'rhythmic upward undulation' of her figure (p. 9) and then moves on to the ambiguously daemonic charm of her face which, like the statue's, both threatens and attracts:

Her shoulders and her bare arms gleamed with an extraordinary splendour, and when she advanced her head into the light he saw the admirable contour of the face, the straight fine nose with delicate nostrils, the exquisite crimson brush-stroke of the lips on this oval without colour. The expression of the eyes was lost in a shadowy mysterious play of jet and silver, stirring under the red coppery gold of the hair as though she had been a being made of ivory and precious metals changed into living tissue. (p. 10)

While Conrad transforms Mérimée's statue into human form, he retains most of its otherworldly beauty and power in Felicia's outer appearance – particularly in her ivory forehead, crowning hair with 'the flowing lines of molten metal' (p. 10) and cruelly beautiful eyes which always threaten to destroy by their 'night-splendour' (p. 75). Other details in this description appear later in Conrad's story to intensify Felicia's radiant but destructive power. The account of the statue as combining extreme beauty with the absence of sensibility finds its echo in the description of Felicia as suffering from 'the insensibility of a great passion concentrated on itself' (p. 34). Yet both she and the statue are obscurely felt to express the ultimate truth about life: the statue stands for '*la réalité*', while Felicia repeatedly announces that she stands for 'truth'. Such truth in physical form appears to be so witheringly final that no man can bear to face it squarely, and both Conrad and Mérimée describe their male figures with instantly lowered eyes before the cruelly dazzling goddess-figure.

In a concluding section, Knowles argues:

'The Planter of Malata' has the interest of a technical experiment and the strength of a narrative myth which, in its carefully designed contrasts, borrows many of the strengths of Mérimée's 'La Vénus d'Ille'. In counterpointing the primitive and civilized to show how a myth fulfils itself destructively in modern conditions, the latter anticipates a familiar Conradian theme.[18]


## Victory

In *Victory* (April 1912–July 1914) – Conrad's last great novel for some critics, an inferior work for others[19] – his debt to French literature is once more striking. Three main contributions have been made in this area: that of Katherine Haynes Gatch on the links with Villiers de l'Isle-Adam's *Axël*, that of Paul Kirschner on the use of Maupassant's *Fort comme la mort* and 'Les Soeurs Rondoli', and that of Owen Knowles who discovered three sources: Anatole France's article on Benjamin Constant in *La Vie littéraire*, Constant's *Adolphe*, and France's *Le Lys rouge*.[20]

In this discussion, I intend to work chronologically through the novel in order to show how its French sources were used in the process of composition and revision. It would be fascinating to include Conrad's use of other literary sources from Shakespeare, Żeromski (*The History of a Sin*), Dickens, Emerson, Chaucer, Melville, and possibly Turgenev, but this would clearly be beyond the scope of this inquiry.[21]

After his elopement with Lena, Heyst signals from his island to Davidson to ask him to return a shawl to Mrs Schomberg. To Davidson's amazement, Heyst, who deplores having been drawn from the role of detached observer, greets him with this reflection: 'I suppose *I have done a certain amount of harm, since I allowed myself to be tempted into action. It seemed innocent enough, but all action is bound to be harmful*' (p. 54). These are the words used by Professor Bergeret in France's *Le Mannequin d'osier* (1897) (the second volume of *L'Histoire contemporaine*): '*Je suis méchant parce que j'agis. Je n'avais pas besoin de cette expérience pour savoir qu'il n'y a pas d'action innocente, et qu'agir, c'est nuire ou détruire. Dès que j'ai commencé d'agir, je suis devenu malfaisant*' (XI, p. 425).

The description of the 'music' which greets Heyst as he enters Schomberg's 'concert-hall': '*The uproar* in that small, barn-like structure [...] *was* simply *stunning*. An instrumental uproar [...] while a grand piano, operated upon by a bony, red-faced woman with *bad-tempered* nostrils, *rained hard notes like hail* through the *tempest* of fiddles' (p. 68), strongly recalls performances on the piano as described by Zola in *Pot-Bouille*:

Hortense, qui tournait les pages [...] restait *revêche* sous *la pluie battante des notes* [...]. Mais, brusquement, le piano trembla sous les mains frèles de Berthe, tapant comme des marteaux: c'était la fin de la rêverie, dans *un tapage assourdissant* de furieux accords. (p. 50)

– Tiens! c'est vous! dit-elle, lorsque ses frères l'eurent tirée de *l'averse battante des notes*, qui l'isolait et la criblait, *comme sous un nuage de grêle*. (p. 298)

Quand il revint, elle pataugeait dans des gammes, en déchaînant une *tempête* de notes fausses. (p. 311)

Early in *Victory*, there are intimations of a link between the psychology of Heyst and that of Benjamin Constant, the latter described by France as a man of divided sensibility who could live 'ni avec les hommes ni seul'. The first concrete evidence of such a link comes when Conrad, after mentioning again the conflicts tormenting Heyst, comments: 'Nothing is more painful *than the shock of sharp contradictions that lacerate our intelligence and our feelings*' (pp. 66–7). Similarly, France points out that it is impossible to trust a self-divided man like Constant, whose speech was nothing but '*le* brillant *cliquetis des contradictions acérées qui déchirent son intelligence et son coeur*' (VI, p. 72; *Knowles, p. 50).[22] A few pages later, we read that Heyst 'felt a sudden *pity*' for the poor members of the Zangiacomo band, for he was '*temperamentally sympathetic*' (p. 70), another trait he shares with Constant who was '*capable de sympathie* et d'une sorte de *pitié* réfléchie' (VI, p. 70; *Knowles, p. 50).

During his first meeting with Lena, Heyst looks with interest at her 'physiognomy':

*Its expression was neither simple nor yet very clear. It was* not *distinguished* – that could not be expected – *but the features had more fineness than those of any other feminine countenance* he had ever had the opportunity to observe so closely. *There was in it something* indefinably audacious and *infinitely miserable* – *because the temperament and the existence of* that girl *were reflected in it.*    (*V*, p. 74)

Strange as it may seem, this description of Lena was also borrowed from the same source. At the end of his article, France deplores the loss of a portrait of Constant which he had kept for a long time in his study:

Je m'étais pris de sympathie pour cette grande figure pâle et longue, empreinte de tant de tristesse et d'ironie, *et dont les traits avaient plus de finesse que ceux de la plupart des hommes. L'expression n'en était ni simple ni très claire.* Mais elle était tout à fait étrange. *Elle avait je ne sais quoi d'exquis et de misérable,* je ne sais quoi *d'infiniment distingué* et d'infiniment pénible, sans doute *parce que l'esprit et la vie de* Benjamin Constant *s'y reflétaient.*    (VI, p. 72)

When relating a later exchange between Heyst and Lena before they run away, Conrad drew again on Maupassant's prologue to 'Les Soeurs Rondoli'. Maupassant discourses on the painful loneliness which assails a traveller in a foreign town towards the end of the day:

Et on s'aperçoit soudain qu'on est vraiment et toujours et partout seul au monde, mais que, dans les lieux connus, les coudoiements familiers vous donnent seulement *l'illusion de la fraternité humaine. C'est en ces heures d'abandon, de noir isolement* dans les cités lointaines *qu'on pense* largement, *clairement* et *profondément.* C'est alors qu'*on voit bien toute la vie* d'un seul coup d'oeil *en dehors de l'optique d'espérance éternelle, en dehors de la tromperie des habitudes prises et de l'attente du bonheur toujours rêvè.* (*SR*, pp. 6–7)

Seduced by Lena's voice, Heyst 'seemed to see *the illusion of human fellowship* on earth vanish before the naked truth of her existence', and shortly afterwards, his vision of life before he felt 'the awakening of a tenderness' towards her is expressed in Maupassant's words:

Formerly, *in solitude and in silence, [Heyst] had been used to think clearly and* sometimes even *profoundly, seeing life outside the flattering optical delusion of everlasting hope, of conventional self-deceptions, of an ever-expected happiness.* (*V*, pp. 80, 82; *Kirschner, p. 220)

The same night, when the concert at Schomberg's hotel is over, Heyst paces to and fro, revolving novel thoughts in his head now that he has committed himself, 'accustoming his mind to the contemplation of his purpose, in order that by being faced steadily it should appear praiseworthy and wise'. The authorial voice then explains: '*For the use of reason is to justify* the obscure desires that *move our conduct,* impulses, *passions,* prejudices and follies, *and also our fears*' (p. 83). This comment bears the unmistakable mark of the author of *La Vie littéraire* who, in the steps of his master Voltaire, had asserted: '[Les hommes] ne se gouvernent jamais par le raisonnement. L'instinct et le sentiment *les mènent.* Ils obéissent à leurs *passions,* à l'amour, à la haine *et surtout à la peur* salutaire. Ils préfèrent les religions aux philosophies, et *ne raisonnent que pour se justifier* de leurs mauvais penchants et de leurs méchantes actions' (VII, p. 384).[23]

At the close of part II, chapter 2, we find the first evidence of Conrad's dependence on Maupassant's *Fort comme la mort* (1889). The Countess de Guilleroy, feeling ill and aged after the death of her mother, has gone to the country where the painter Olivier Bertin, her lover, pays her a visit. The morning after his arrival, she wakes up feeling much better:

Quand la domestique fut sortie, *elle alla se voir dans la glace.* Elle fut un peu surprise, car *elle se sentait si bien qu'elle s'attendait à se trouver rajeunie, en une seule nuit,* de plusieurs années. Puis elle comprit *l'enfantillage* de cet espoir, et, après s'être encore regardée, elle se résigna à constater qu'elle avait seulement le teint plus clair, les yeux moins fatigués, les lèvres plus vives que la veille. (*Fort comme la mort,* p. 208)

The reactions of Heyst (in the manuscript, Berg, as Heyst was then named, is also a painter) as he wakes up one morning feeling a new man after his decision to rescue Lena, are modelled on those of Mme de Guilleroy:

*He* got up then, *went to a small looking-glass* hanging on the wall, *and stared at himself* steadily. It was not a new-born vanity which induced this long survey. *He felt so strange that he could not resist the suspicion of his personal appearance having changed during the night.* What he saw in the glass, however, was the man he knew before. It was almost a disappointment – a belittling of his recent experience. And then he smiled at *his naiveness*.

(*V*, p. 90)

Conrad concluded this chapter and opened the following one by making use again of France's article on Constant. *'[E] chapper à la vie avec le moins de douleur possible'* (VI, p. 68): such is Constant's desire when his passionate days are over; in like manner, Heyst, 'by a system of restless wandering', has perceived 'the means of *passing through life without suffering*' (p. 90). Then comes a crucial passage in France which strongly influenced the conception and presentation of Heyst's father:

On peut juger sévèrement cet homme, *mais il y a une grandeur qu'on ne lui refusera pas: il fut très malheureux et cela n'est point d'une âme médiocre.* [...] *Il traîna soixante ans sur cette terre de douleurs l'âme la plus lasse et la plus inquiète qu'une civilisation exquise ait jamais façonnée pour le désenchantement et l'ennui.* [...] *Il veut toutes les joies, celles des grands et celles des humbles, celles des fous et celles des sages.*          (VI, pp. 68–9)

Thinker, stylist, and man of the world in his time, the elder Heyst had begun by *coveting all the joys, those of the great and those of the humble, those of the fools and those of the sages. For more than sixty years he had dragged on this painful earth of ours the most weary, the most uneasy soul that civilisation had ever fashioned to its ends of disillusion and regret. One could not refuse him a measure of greatness, for he was unhappy in a way unknown to mediocre souls.*          (*V*, p. 91)

Conrad then refers to his *'pale, distinguished face'*, features also derived from the portrait of Constant, and the paragraph ends on France's concluding note: like Constant, 'qui [...] *professa la liberté sans y croire*' (VI, p. 73), the elder Heyst claimed for mankind, in his last work, *'that right to absolute moral and intellectual liberty of which he no longer believed them worthy'* (p. 91; *Knowles, p. 49).

A reminiscence from *Bel-Ami* is apparent in a later exchange between Schomberg and Mr Jones: the very sick Forestier, we recall, sunk deep in his armchair, speaks to Duroy *'avec un son de voix ennuyé et lointain, comme s'il parlait du fond d'un trou'* (*BA*, p. 104); similarly, the sickly Mr Jones, 'lolling back idly in a chair', talks to Schomberg in a 'hollow' voice which *'sounded distant, uninterested, as though he were speaking from the bottom of a well'* (p. 110), and later *'in a voice indifferent, as if issuing from a tomb'* (p. 113).[24]

Conrad returned to *Fort comme la mort* in part II, chapter 3, and made

significant use of the love affair between Bertin and the Countess de Guilleroy
in the treatment of the Heyst–Lena relationship. But his exploitation of this
source was even more startling in the manuscript, judging by a number of
passages, which, like the following, were considerably reduced in the printed
text:

*He had always thought that love began in dreams, in poetic exaltation. What he had experi-
enced, however, had been an indefinite emotion much more physical than moral. He had been
nervous, overstrung, uneasy like on the eve of some disease, but there had been nothing painful
in that symptomatic agitation which had also extended his thoughts. In a short pause,* holding
her by the hand, *he descended within himself trying to understand. He could not say that she
corresponded to any of those feminine ideals which are created by the blind hopes of men calling
upon the desire of love to give them a vision of the moral and physical qualities destined to
charm and seduce their hearts.* He had renounced hastily that with the other desires of life.
*Neither had he felt impelled toward her by an irresistible impulse of his whole being. Yet now
he felt acutely her presence as though she had given him something nameless and subtle of
herself, something that is* (if) *she were to rise and go away* and vanish *would remain with him*
forever, while she would carry away something of his own personality which she had
appropriated and which he could not do without for the future.

(Barton Currie MS, pp. 581–2)[25]

Conrad translated here almost verbatim a whole paragraph in which Maupassant analyses the state of mind of Bertin, a sensitive and idealistic man,
uncomfortable in the presence of society women 'car il ne les connaissait guère'
(p. 23), who becomes aware, as the sittings for Mme de Guilleroy's portrait
progress, that he is disturbingly moved by her and falling in love for the first
time:

*Olivier avait cru que l'amour commençait par des rêveries, par des exaltations poétiques. Ce qu'il
éprouvait, au contraire, lui paraissait provenir d'une émotion indéfinissable, bien plus physique
que morale. Il était nerveux, vibrant, inquiet comme lorsqu'une maladie germe en nous. Rien de
douloureux cependant ne se mêlait à cette fièvre du sang qui agitait aussi sa pensée, par contagion.*
Il n'ignorait pas que ce trouble venait de Mme de Guilleroy, *du souvenir qu'elle lui laissait* et
de l'attente de son retour. *Il ne se sentait pas jeté vers elle, par un élan de tout son être, mais il
la sentait toujours présente en lui, comme si elle ne l'eût pas quitté; elle lui abandonnait quelque
chose d'elle en s'en allant, quelque chose de subtil et d'inexprimable.* Quoi? Etait-ce de l'amour?
*Maintenant, il descendait en son propre coeur pour voir et pour comprendre.* Il la trouvait charmante, *mais elle ne répondait pas au type de la femme idéale que son espoir aveugle avait créé.
Quiconque appelle l'amour a prévu les qualités morales et les dons physiques de celle qui le séduira;*
et Mme de Guilleroy, bien qu'elle lui plût infiniment, ne lui paraissait pas être celle-là.

(*Fort comme la mort*, pp. 33–4)

All that remains of this extensive borrowing in the printed version is a passage
where Heyst, who, as far as women are concerned, is 'altogether uninstructed'
(p. 222), experiences a similar emotion when Lena talks to him:

The rare timbre of her voice gave a special value to what she uttered. *The indefinable* *emotion* which certain intonations gave him, he was aware, was *more physical than moral*. Every time she spoke to him *she seemed to abandon to him something of herself – something* excessively *subtle and inexpressible*, to which he was infinitely sensible, which he would have missed horribly *if she were to go away*. (*V*, p. 188; *Kirschner, pp. 193–4)

It is strange that in the final stage Conrad should lapse into a gallicism – 'She seemed to abandon to him something of herself' – which he had avoided in the original version.

In the opening of the following chapter, while Heyst and Lena are still conversing, Conrad writes that '*She felt in her innermost depths an irresistible desire to give herself up to him more completely, by some act of absolute sacrifice*' (p. 201), thus transferring to her Mme de Guilleroy's feelings as, in a desperate attempt to remove the last barriers between Bertin and herself, she opens her heart:

– Oh, mon Dieu, je voudrais vous faire comprendre comme je vous aime, moi! Voyons, je cherche, je ne trouve pas! Quand je pense à vous, et j'y pense toujours, *je sens jusqu'au fond de ma chair et de mon âme une ivresse indicible de vous appartenir, et un besoin irrésistible de vous donner davantage de moi. Je voudrais me sacrifier d'une façon absolue*

(*Fort comme la mort*, pp. 204–5: *Kirschner, pp. 197–8)

The manuscript followed the italicized passage:

*She felt in the innermost depths of self, in her body and in her soul an inexpressibly intoxicating sensation of belonging to that man an irresistible desire of giving herself up to him more completely – by some act of absolute sacrifice.*                    (MS, p. 542)[26]

The first time the Countess returns to Bertin's studio after he has forcibly made love to her, she coldly repels his advances. Maupassant then describes Bertin's reactions:

il eut tout à coup une de ces fureurs d'amoureux *qui changent en haine la tendresse. Ce fut, dans son âme et dans son corps une grande secousse nerveuse, et, tout de suite, sans transition, il la détesta.* Oui, oui, c'était bien cela, la femme! [...] *Elle était fausse*, change-ante, *et faible* comme toutes. Elle l'avait attiré, séduit par des ruses de fille, cherchant à l'affoler sans rien donner ensuite [...].

*Lorsqu'il eut marché quelque temps, d'un pas rapide et irrité* [...] *sa grande fureur contre elle s'émietta en désolations et en regrets.* [...] *il se souvint*, en voyant passer d'autres femmes, *combien elle était jolie* et séduisante. Comme tant d'autres qui ne l'avouent point, *il avait toujours attendu l'impossible rencontre, l'affection rare, unique*, poétique et passionnée, dont *le rêve* plane sur nos coeurs. N'avait-il pas failli trouver cela? [...] Pourquoi donc est-ce que rien ne se réalise? [...]

*Il n'en voulait plus à la jeune femme, mas à la vie elle-même.*

(*Fort comme la mort*, pp. 50–2)

Conrad used this penetrating analysis to convey Heyst's feelings when Lena fails to show any sympathetic understanding of the part he played in the Morrison affair:

*In his soul and in his body he experienced a nervous reaction from tenderness. All at once, without transition, he detested her.* But only for a moment. *He remembered that she was pretty,* and, more, that she had a special grace in the intimacy of life. She had the secret of individuality which excites – and escapes.

*He* jumped up and *began to walk to and fro.* Presently *his* hidden *fury fell into dust* within him, like a crazy structure, *leaving behind* emptiness, *desolation, regret. His resentment was not against the girl, but against life itself*          (V, p. 215; *Kirschner, pp. 195–6)[27]

Again, the manuscript was closer to *Fort comme la mort.* Among the deleted passages, we read: '*He experienced in his soul and in his body a nervous reaction which changes tenderness into hate. He saw her weak and insincere*' (MS, p. 594); 'the abominable thing [. . .] which had beguiled him into this unrest and injustice by some unconscious *dream of rare and unique perfection. For he was* not *conscious of having ever dreamed of the impossible*' (MS, pp. 596–7). Conrad had also written that Berg 'seemed to discover in her words, acts, movements, tones in all her impulses and in he [*sic*] shynesses, in her shrinkings and in her caresses *the obscure mental reserves of a* sensitive *being which thinks itself to be of an* inferior *essence*' (MS, p. 595), a comment based on Bertin's perception of Mme de Guilleroy at the beginning of the novel: 'Derrière les sourires et derrière l'admiration [. . .] il devinait *l'obscure réserve mentale de l'être qui se juge d'essence* supérieure' (pp. 23–4). The following borrowing was cut from the final text, too:

*Tant pis pour elle, après tout; il l'avait eue, il l'avait prise. Elle pouvait éponger son corps et lui répondre insolemment, elle n'effacerait rien, et il l'oublierait, lui. Vraiment, il aurait fait une belle folie en s'embarrassant d'une maîtresse pareille*

(*Fort comme la mort,* p. 50)

*So much the worse for her then. He had possessed himself of her. She might* shut herself up as much [as] she liked, present to him her veiled eyes which refused to speak in the moments of passion, *nothing could do away with that fact.* So much the worse for her. And so much the worse for him too; *a perfect imbecile saddling himself with a woman in a moment of emotional folly.*

(MS, p. 596)

It seems likely that the next paragraph, which concludes this chapter and shows Heyst forcing his attentions upon the reticent Lena (p. 215), was also inspired by the scene leading to Bertin's first love-making with the Countess (p. 40). (The manuscript's greater closeness to Maupassant probably accounts for the fact, noted by Dwight Purdy, that it treats the sexual embrace 'a bit more boldly'.)[28] But, whereas it is the tears in Bertin's eyes which break down Mme de Guilleroy's last defences, it is Lena's tears which finally overcome Heyst's reserve (p. 215). Both love scenes end on similar notes: Mme de Guilleroy rises suddenly and picks up her hat which has fallen on the carpet; Heyst scrambles quickly to his feet and goes 'to pick up [Lena's] cork helmet, which had rolled a little way off; once in the street Mme de Guilleroy feels completely 'écrasée, les jambes rompues' (p. 41); on Lena's still face is depicted 'the infinite lassitude of her soul!' (p. 216). Conrad may have followed his model too closely here, for, whereas the reticence of Mme de Guilleroy is perfectly natural, that of Lena is less understandable after we have been told of her 'irresistible desire to give herself up to him more completely, by some act of absolute sacrifice'. And the same applies to the subsequent reactions of the two women, with Lena's moral weariness being hardly convincing. Conrad himself admitted in response to Christopher Sandeman's criticism: 'My fault is that I haven't made Lena's reticence *credible* enough – since a mind like yours (after reflexion) remains unconvinced' (*LL*, II, p. 184).

A few pages later, the scene where Lena reproaches Heyst for his aloofness is again remarkably close to the one in which the Countess, who has given herself to Bertin without reservation, reproaches him for his reticence:

*Elle murmura*:
– *Vous ne m'aimez pas comme je vous aime!*
– *Ah! par exemple!* ...
Elle l'interrompit:
– Non, vous aimez en moi [...] une femme qui satisfait les besoins de votre coeur, une femme qui ne vous a jamais fait une peine et qui a mis un peu de bonheur dans votre vie. [...] Vous avez aimé, vous aimez encore tout ce que vous trouvez en moi d'agréable, mes attentions pour vous, mon admiration, mon souci de vous plaire, ma passion, le don complet que je vous ai fait de mon être intime. *Mais ce n'est pas moi que vous aimez*, comprenez-vous! Oh, cela je le sens comme on sent un courant d'air froid.Vous aimez en moi mille choses, [...] *mais ce n'est pas moi, moi, rien que moi*, comprenez-vous?
*Il eut un petit rire amical*:
– Non, je ne comprends pas très bien. *Vous me faites une scène de reproches très inattendue.*                               (*Fort comme la mort*, pp. 203–4)

'You should try to love me!' she said.
*He made a movement of astonishment.*
'Try!' he muttered. 'But it seems to me –.' He broke off, saying to himself that if he loved her, he had never told her so in so many words. [...]
'What makes you say that?' he asked.
She lowered her eyelids and turned her head a little.
'I have done nothing,' she said in a low voice. 'It's you who have been good, helpful and tender to me. Perhaps you love me for that – just for that; or perhaps you love me for company, and because – well! *But* sometimes *it seems to me that you can never love me for myself, only for myself*, as people do love each other when it is to be for ever.' Her head drooped. 'For ever,' she breathed out again; then, still more faintly, she added an entreating: 'Do try!'
These last words went straight to his heart – the sound of them more than the sense. He did not know what to say [...]. But *he managed a smile* [...].
'My dear Lena,' he said, '*it looks as if you were trying to pick a very unnecessary quarrel with me* – of all people!'                    (*V*, p. 221; *Kirschner, pp. 196–7)

The description of Heyst's discomfort which follows, 'he was twisting the ends of his long moustaches, very masculine and perplexed, *enveloped in the atmosphere of femininity* as in a cloud' (pp. 221–2), was also inspired by Maupassant who then shows Bertin walking between the Countess and her daughter 'possédé par elles, *pénétré par une sorte de fluide féminin* dont leur contact l'inondait' (p. 206).

Conrad used *Fort comme la mort* for the last time in Part IV, chapter 2. As Bertin's exhilaration subsides after Mme de Guilleroy's shocked flight from his studio, he wonders what her subsequent reaction will be. In order not to raise her husband's suspicion, she decides to continue the sittings, a decision Bertin wrongly interprets as an unspoken consent to become his mistress:

> Du moment qu'elle pouvait le revoir, entendre sa voix et supporter en face de lui la pensée unique qui ne devait pas la quitter, c'est alors que cette pensée ne lui était pas devenue odieusement intolérable. Quand une femme hait l'homme qui l'a violée, elle ne peut plus se trouver devant lui sans que cette haine éclate. *Mais cet homme ne peut non plus lui demeurer indifférent. Il faut qu'elle le déteste ou qu'elle lui pardonne. Et quand elle pardonne cela, elle n'est pas loin d'aimer.*                    (*Fort comme la mort*, p. 53)

Similarly, although Lena has violently repelled his assault, Ricardo misconstrues her silence with Heyst as a promising sign:

> *A woman* that does not make a noise after an attempt of that kind has *tacitly condoned the offence*. Ricardo had no small vanities. But clearly, *if she would pass it over like this, then he could not be so utterly repugnant to her.* He felt flattered.

But, again, Conrad gives a twist to Maupassant's psychology:

> Out of the unfaded impression of past violence there was growing the sort of sentiment *which prevents a man from being indifferent to a woman* he has once held in his arms – if even against her will – and still more so if she has pardoned the outrage. It becomes then a sort of bond.                    (*V*, pp. 294, 295–6; *Kirschner, pp. 194–5)

In part IV, chapter 5, Conrad made use of France's feminine psychology once more when describing Lena's state of mind as she decides, for love of Heyst, to act for his protection: '*A great vagueness enveloped her impressions, but all her energy was concentrated on the struggle* that she wanted to take upon herself, in a great exaltation of *love and self-sacrifice, which is woman's sublime faculty*' (p. 317). Conrad has conflated here two separate passages from *Le Jardin d'Epicure* in which France refers to women's '*faculté sublime d'aimer et de souffrir*' and asserts that when a woman is jealous '*Un grand vague enveloppe ses impressions, et toutes ses énergies restent tendues pour la lutte*' (IX, pp. 402, 410).

The most extensive borrowing so far discovered in the final version of *Victory* comes in the opening of part IV, chapter 12. The passage describes Lena's thoughts while waiting for her momentous meeting with Ricardo after Heyst's departure, and is a remarkably close borrowing of a long passage from *Le Lys rouge* where France depicts the mood of Thérèse Martin, as she anticipates a meeting with her lover, Jacques Dechartre:

*Elle ressentait une angoisse qu'apaisait un sentiment* inconnu, *d'une douceur profonde.* Elle ne retrouvait pas la stupeur de la première fois qu'elle s'était donnée par amour, la vision brusque de l'irréparable. *Elle était sous des influences plus lentes, plus vagues et plus puissantes.* Cette fois, une rêverie charmante trempait le souvenir des caresses reçues et baignait la brûlure. Elle était abîmée de trouble et d'inquiétude, mais elle n'éprouvait ni honte ni regrets. *Elle avait agi moins par sa volonté que par une force qu'elle devinait meilleure.* Elle s'absolvait sur son désintéressement. *Elle ne comptait sur rien, n'ayant rien calculé. Sans doute, elle avait eu le tort de se donner quand elle n'était pas libre,* mais aussi n'avait-elle rien exigé. *Peut-être n'était-elle pour lui qu'une fantaisie violente et sincère. Elle ne le connaissait pas.* Elle n'avait pas fait l'épreuve de ces belles imaginations vives et flottantes, *qui passent de haut, pour le bien comme pour le mal, la médiocrité commune. S'il s'éloignait d'elle brusquement et disparaissait, elle ne le lui reprocherait pas, elle ne lui en voudrait pas;* – du moins elle le croyait – *Elle garderait en elle le souvenir et l'empreinte de ce qu'on pouvait trouver* au monde *de plus rare et de plus précieux.*          (IX, p.217)

While lifting the curtain, *she felt the anguish* of her disobedience to her lover, *which was soothed by a feeling* she had known before – *a gentle flood of penetrating sweetness.* She was not automatically obeying a momentary suggestion; *she was under influences more deliberate, more vague, and of greater potency. She had been prompted, not by her will, but by a force that was* outside of her and *more worthy. She reckoned upon nothing definite; she had calculated nothing.* She saw only her purpose of capturing death – savage, sudden, irresponsible death, prowling round the man who possessed her; death embodied in the knife ready to strike into his heart. *No doubt it had been a sin to throw herself into his arms.* With that inspiration *that descends* at times *from above for the good or evil of our common mediocrity, she had a sense of having been for him only a violent and sincere choice* of curiosity and pity – a thing that passes. *She did not know him. If he were to go away from her and disappear, she would utter no reproach, she would not resent it; for she would hold in herself the impress of something most rare and precious* – his embraces made her own by her courage in saving his life.          (*V*, pp. 394–5; *Knowles, p. 55)

Furthermore, this borrowing was not produced out of the blue; other textual parallels make it clear that Conrad had had France's novel in mind for a long time. During one of his first meetings with Lena, Heyst, under the charm of her voice, 'seemed to see the illusion of human fellowship on earth vanish before the naked truth of her existence, and leave them both face to face in *a moral desert as arid* as the sands of Sahara, without restful shade, without refreshing water' (p. 80). This strange perception seems to have been suggested by the statement Thérèse reads in a novel, that 'la passion est *un désert aride,* une Thébaïde brûlante' (IX, p. 92). After his father's death, Heyst observed that it did not trouble '*the flow of life's stream, where men and women go by* thick as dust, revolving and *jostling* one another like figures cut out of cork' (p. 175). The basic image probably derives from a comment made by Thérèse, by way of excuse, in a letter of farewell to her first lover: 'Elle parla obscurément *des âmes emportées dans le flot de la vie,* et du peu qu'on est sur l'océan mouvant des choses' (p. 223) and her later remark: 'On est jetée, *poussée,* ballottée' (p. 239). After his interviews with Mr Jones and Wang, Heyst says to Lena that during her sleep he sat 'to consider all *these things* calmly, *to try to penetrate their inner meaning*' (p. 321). Likewise, the writer Paul Vence says of the poet Choulette that he was 'Habile à concevoir les symboles et *à pénétrer le sens caché des choses*' (p. 85).

Both novels also contain many suggestions of a final cataclysm. Knowles comments:

Forebodings of the world annihilated are, in fact, a constant motif throughout *Le Lys rouge*, with Thérèse at one point discussing 'la fin du monde' with a friend (p. 94–6) in a way strongly reminiscent of Lena and Heyst who contemplate the 'vision of a world destroyed' (p. 191). At moments of crisis, the two heroines react similarly: there is a common tone of resigned expectation in Lena's thought that 'the heart of hearts had ceased to beat and the end of all things had come' (p. 373) and Thérèse's feeling that 'c'était le moment qu'elle vînt finir le monde pour la tirer d'affaire' (p. 184).[29]

Nor can it be wholly fortuitous that Thérèse and Lena, who have much in common as lovers in their semi-religious impulse towards self-sacrifice, should also be remarkably alike in their appearance (note the parallel of their splendid teeth: '*Ses lèvres s'entr'ouvraient sur l'éclair de ses dents humides*' (p. 244); '*the* red *lips parted slightly, with the gleam of her teeth within*' (p. 187)), their musical voices which lull their lovers, and their statuesque forms. There is also a striking similarity between the description of Thérèse as she gives herself to Dechartre: '*Il la porta inerte*, comme la dépouille précieuse de celle devant qui il avait pâli et tremblé. [...] Renversée sur le lit, *elle noua ses bras autour du cou de son ami*' (pp. 243–4), and the account of Lena's death, with Heyst being frightened by the '*limpness* of her body' as he '*carried her off* into the other room' and the comment, as the end is near, that 'she had no longer the strength *to throw her arms about his neck*' (pp. 404–6).

Finally, a last echo from Constant's own work, *Adolphe* (1816), has been detected by Knowles in the novel's concluding pages:

The tragedy linking Adolphe and Heyst is that they fully realize their emotional impotence and suffer from it – as do those with whom they come into contact – but are powerless to remedy it. Indeed their debilitating habit of reflective self-consciousness forms the basis of the cautionary moral offered by each story. *Victory* warns against the 'habit of profound reflection [... which] is the most pernicious of all the habits formed by the civilized man' (pp. x–xi) and ends with Heyst's lament: 'Ah, Davidson, *woe to the man* whose heart has not learned while young to hope, to love – and to put its trust in life!' (p. 410). An unused fragment of one of the Prefaces to *Adolphe* speaks of 'cette analyse perpétuelle, qui place une arrière-pensée à côté de tous les sentiments, et qui par là les corrompt dès leur naissance,' a sentiment implicitly echoed later when Adolphe cries out: '*Malheur à l'homme* qui, dans les premiers moments d'une liaison d'amour, ne croit pas que cette liaison doit être éternelle!' (p. 66).[30]

On 7 April 1924, only a few months before his death, Conrad wrote to Henry S. Canby that in *Victory* he had 'tried to grasp at more "life-stuff" than perhaps in any other of [his] works' (*LL*, II, p. 342), a claim that many later critics do not find successfully achieved in the novel. But if we leave aside the question of the novel's artistic merit, the mass of published criticism on it suggests that the claim is not exaggerated. As Gurko remarked over two decades ago, '*Victory* is a teeming warehouse of materials'.[31] Indeed, the cultural range Conrad displays in this 'bit of imagined drama' (p. ix) – undoubtedly his most philosophical work – is again bewildering, and, of all his novels, it must be second only to *Under Western Eyes* in its extraordinary allusiveness.[32]

The very range of these appropriations and allusions is clearly a part of the novel's representative 'life-stuff', its urge to confront ultimate questions about man's estate, the problem of 'how to be', and the individual's relationship to the world and the conditions necessary for his fulfilment. Conrad's major protagonists – Heyst the elder, an idealist, misanthropic and nihilistic philosopher who has bequeathed to his son a doctrine of non-involvement; and Heyst, the 'man of the last hour' (p. 359), 'a man of universal scorn and unbelief' (p. 199), and an exemplar of modern Western man – speak with the representative tones of late nineteenth-century sceptical philosophy. It was clearly Conrad's aim to probe the problematic nature of this philosophy, and whatever reading of the novel – realistic or allegorical – one may adopt, it is also obvious that he exposes its crippling nature and tragic implications.

While imagining a drama of conflicting ideologies, Conrad's mind was considering, and responding to, a number of literary models. Villiers de l'Isle-Adam's *Axël* – one of the most celebrated works of the French *fin de siècle* aesthetic movement – offered, in the words of Edmund Wilson, the 'type of all the heroes of the Symbolists'[33] who, believing in the nothingness of life like Laforgue's Lohengrin and Huysmans's Des Esseintes, withdraw from an unworthy world. Once Conrad had seen the connection with his own work, he could derive many useful hints for the treatment of his life-drama and the fate of his hero: philosophical detachment, physical isolation, invasion of the hero's solitude first by a woman suggestive of the female principle, and then by a corrupt and malevolent enemy in search of a fabulous hoard of stolen treasure and embodying The World at its most evil (Commander Auërsperg to Axël: 'Je m'appelle la vie réelle'; Mr Jones to Heyst: 'I am the world itself, come to pay you a visit' (p. 379)),[34] leading finally to his suicide.

Judging by the volume of textual borrowings, the example of Constant's life was even more valuable, as it provided a specific source for Conrad's philosophic 'Storm and Dust' (*V*, p. 219), as Knowles demonstrates. The latter shows that 'Even more importantly' France's article provided 'a suggestive synopsis of a problematic life and career' which, in conjunction with the expansion to be found in the autobiographical *Adolphe*, supplied 'an important source for details of Heyst's character, dilemma, and involvement with Lena'. Conrad had at his disposal the detailed record of the life-history of a major nineteenth-century figure who, because he had been subjected by an ironic father – an 'observateur froid et caustique' (p. 47) – to a lonely and harsh education 'qui desséchait son coeur en exaltant son amour-propre' (p. 60), later turned out to be:

fundamentally mistrustful of life, a despiser of mankind and floating observer who, while he is 'aussi incapable d'aimer que de croire' (p. 63), is subject to an ambiguous impulse of pity which betrays him into fresh ties – 'liaisons nouvelles' (p. 65). Like Heyst, Constant is a bewildering compendium of detachment, cold charity, repressed sensuality, world-weariness and perpetual nervous anxiety which makes him in France's view a prototype of the modern, neurotically self-divided man who is lost because he lacks the simple trust in life to make even the most basic commitment.[35]

As usual, Conrad also looked for assistance when dealing with the Heyst-Lena relationship and the subject of female psychology. *Adolphe* was probably helpful on this score as well, for, as Knowles points out: 'The opening stages of the [Adolphe–Ellénore] relationship are remarkably similar to those between Heyst and Lena'. Adolphe may also have supplied 'hints for a concrete plot, a patterned contrast between male apostate and female devotee'.[36] But Conrad's main reliance was, once more, on his two favourite 'authorities', Maupassant and France, and the very substantial borrowings from *Fort comme la mort* and *Le Lys rouge* show how easily amenable to adaptation he found these models. *Fort comme la mort* was particularly helpful for the treatment of the sexual aspect of the relationship – 'the type of thing' as Karl observes, 'he usually avoided altogether or handled awkwardly'[37] – especially in part II, chapter 3 to part III, chapter 5, offering straightforward material for the characterization of both partners.

The part played by *Le Lys rouge* in the composition of *Victory* was, as Knowles has shown, much more complex.

*Le Lys rouge*, while dramatizing the failure of the relationship between Thérèse Martin and Jacques Dechartre, explores, in Knowles's words, 'the "carbon" of the male and female identity which, as the novel progresses, largely takes the form of a patterned contrast between the woman's semi-religious impulse towards sacrifice at the altar of love and the male's more fastidious, earthbound egotism'. The extensive borrowing Conrad made in part IV, chapter 12, shows 'how generally dependent' *Victory* is on *Le Lys rouge* 'for its conception of female "dreamy innocence" (p. xvii) and for a kind of prose with which to describe religious imaginings'. Knowles observes: 'If Lena fails to carry conviction as a character with a distinctively felt life; it is mainly because Conrad remains content with the semi-idealized postures of womanhood and a sculptured, iconographic prose style which have a long history in nineteenth-century French fiction and which France picturesquely elaborates'.[38] Finally, the conception of Heyst may also owe something to the figure of Dechartre, who, as Knowles points out, can be regarded as another 'tragically "lost" modern man' whose 'potentiality for passionate commitment is [...] vitiated by sceptical mistrust'. Both men are the victims of 'a sensibility scarred by *fin*

*de siècle* life-negation which, rooted in adolescence and the habits of the dreamer, has become an ingrained feature of the middle-aged mind'. In both, 'the
undisciplined imagination attracts them to areas of instinctive passion which
they later come to distrust'. Both are 'foredoomed [...] because in their "masculine fussing" (p. 308) they are products of an age too old and wrinkled to
come to terms with the female's child-like faith. Heyst confesses to being of a
later date in the world's history than Lena, while Jacques feels – speaking of
all men: "Nous étions déjà si vieux quand nous sommes nés!"' (IX, p. 262).[39]

In his Author's Note, Conrad said: 'Since this Note is mostly concerned with
personal contacts and the origins of the persons in the tale, I am bound also to
speak of Lena' (p. xv). In the light of this statement and the record of his
meeting with the original of Lena in a café in Montpellier, in which he stresses
how intently he gazed at the girl, the unsuspecting reader would be entitled to
think that he was writing from memory. He was, however, emphasizing once
again the importance of observation whilst disguising his indebtedness to other
works. Katherine Haynes Gatch says: 'The mystifying reference to the original
of Heyst [...] is obviously intended to conceal more than it reveals.'[40] Indeed,
Conrad admitted: 'He was not the whole Heyst of course; he is only the physical
and moral foundation of my Heyst laid on the ground of a short acquaintance'
(p. xi), a statement verified by the many aspects of Heyst's character, dilemma,
involvement with Lena, and philosophical views which he inherited from Axël
d'Auërsberg, Constant, Adolphe, Bertin, Dechartre, Bergeret, and other
sources. This also applies to the fictional Lena who owes much of her identity
and appearance to Thérèse Martin, Mme de Guilleroy, Villiers de l'Isle-Adam's
Sara de Maupers, and Żeromski's Ewa. [41] Once more, one cannot but view
with amazement the remarkable alchemy that went into the making of this
perhaps defective, but highly intricate, novel.

## The last decade

After *Victory*, Conrad turned back to his past more consistently and intimately
than he had done before, so that much of the work of his last phase was, as
Karl observes, 'an extension of *A Personal Record*: reminiscences, autobiography, and memoir material'.[42] Perhaps for this reason, and as far as one can tell,
the late work appears to show very little dependence on imaginative literature
in general or French literature in particular,[43] and only a couple of borrowings
from Anatole France seem worth mentioning.

Conrad's statement in *The Shadow-Line* (February–December 1915) on the
*'unknown powers that shape our destinies'* (p. 62) echoes a passage from *La Vie
littéraire* where France, talking about 'l'action romanesque', remarks: 'C'est
peu que d'y montrer les hommes: les hommes ne sont rien; il faut y faire sentir
*les puissances inconnues qui forgent et martèlent nos destinées*' (VI, p. 606). It is
probable, of course, that France is echoing Hamlet: 'There's a divinity that

shapes our ends / Rough-hew them how we will', (V.ii.10), but the exact verbal correspondence between Conrad's statement and that of France makes it clear that it was directly inspired by the latter.

Conrad was still relying on *Le Lys rouge* when dealing with the subject of love in *The Arrow of Gold* (August 1917–June 1918). Dechartre's confession to Thérèse of jealousy after discovering that he is not her first lover prompts her to say that he is 'absurd'. He then replies:

> – Oui, je suis absurde, je le sens mieux que vous ne le sentez vous-même. *Vouloir une femme dans tout l'éclat de sa beauté et de son esprit, maîtresse d'elle-même, et qui sait, et qui ose,* plus belle en cela et plus désirable, *et dont le choix est libre,* volontaire, instruit; la désirer, *l'aimer pour ce qu'elle est et souffrir de ce qu'elle n'a ni la candeur* puérile, *ni la* pâle *innocence qui choqueraient en elle,* s'il était possible de les y rencontrer; lui demander à la fois qu'elle soit elle et ne soit pas elle, *l'adorer telle que la vie l'a faite et regretter amèrement que la vie, qui l'a tant embellie, l'ait seulement touchée, oh! c'est absurde.*          (IX, p. 265)

In a conversation with Monsieur George, Doña Rita recalls asking Blunt 'whether he didn't think that it was absurd on his part' to be jealous, and telling him plainly that

> to want a woman formed in mind and body, mistress of herself, free in her choice, independent in her thoughts; to love her apparently for what she is and at the same time to demand from her the candour and the innocence that could be only a *shocking* pretence; to know her *such as life has made her* and at the same time to despise her secretly for every touch with which her life has fashioned her – that was neither generous nor high minded; *it was positively frantic.*
>
> (*AG*, pp. 210–11)[44]

Again, the literal transposition from France has led Conrad to use a gallicism: 'artlessness' is what he means here, not 'candour'.

Pending further research, this assessment of Conrad's debt to French literature during his last decade can only be regarded as provisional. However, in addition to the shift of emphasis in the nature of his subject matter, other factors may explain Conrad's waning dependence on imaginative literature. That he needed to dictate some of his later tales may have reduced the practice of using books. Or perhaps he had exhausted what he could draw from his French sources? Whatever the reasons – and assuming, of course, that no substantial findings will alter the present evaluation – it is tempting to wonder if there is some connection between Conrad's sharp artistic decline during this period and the sudden absence of the support which had been so necessary to him throughout the two previous decades of great creative activity.

# 6  Critical writings

Conrad wrote the Preface to *The Nigger of the 'Narcissus'*, his well-known literary manifesto, sometime between January and August 1897. A number of sources have been suggested, both French and English, the latter including Walter Pater's *Marius the Epicurean* (1885, rev. edn 1892), his essay 'The School of Giorgione' (1877), and especially his essay on 'Style' (1889), and also Henry James's 'The Art of Fiction' (1884). It is, of course, Conrad's debt to nineteenth-century French literature which will be examined here, and that means primarily his debt to Flaubert (the hero of Pater's essay on 'Style'), Maupassant, and Anatole France.[1]

The first studies of Maupassant's influence on Conrad appraised the impact of 'Le Roman' (the introductory essay to *Pierre et Jean* (1887)) on Conrad's preface. Edgar Wright showed that 'the main themes of [the Preface], the stress on temperament, the denial of any formula for the novel, the demand for sincerity and originality, the importance placed on the handling of words and style, the personal vision, the presentation of actual events so handled that the reader can arrive at the contained meaning, all these repeat Maupassant'.[2] Conrad's intimate knowledge of 'Le Roman' may also account, as Wright has noted, for the wording in a letter to Miss Watson on 27 January 1897. Just as Maupassant speaks of 'les personnages dont nous prétendons *dévoiler* l'être intime et inconnu' (*PJ*, p. xix), Conrad says that in *The Nigger*, which he had just completed, he had tried '*to get through the veil* of details at the essence of life' (*CL*, I, p. 334).[3] Similarly, in the Preface, he refers to 'the *unveiling* of one of those heartless secrets which are called the Laws of Nature' (pp. xi–xii).

George Worth, too, has pointed out some telling parallels:

He [Conrad] follows Maupassant, and here there is a similarity of phraseology too striking to be entirely coincidental, in urging the writer to ignore the clamor of the multitude and to pursue his artistic aims steadfastly and with a clear conscience.

En somme, le public est composé de groupes nombreux qui nous crient:

– Consolez-moi.

– Amusez-moi.

– Attristez-moi.

– Attendrissez-moi.

– Faites-moi rêver.

– Faites-moi rire.

– Faites-moi frémir.
– Faites-moi pleurer.
– Faites-moi penser.
Seuls, quelques esprits d'élite demandent à l'artiste:
– Faites-moi quelque chose de beau, dans la forme qui vous conviendra le mieux, suivant votre tempérament. (p. ix)

Conrad, too, insists that the writer must endeavour to achieve his 'creative task' undeterred by those who, 'in the fulness of a wisdom which looks for immediate profit, demand specifically to be edified, consoled, amused; who demand to be promptly improved, or encouraged, or frightened, or shocked, or charmed' (pp. ix–x).

The same critic also draws attention to the 'fundamental theme' common to both artists, which he defines as 'their mutual concern for the supreme importance of craftsmanship, their mutual abhorrence of cheap, shoddy work'.[4]

That Maupassant's views on this subject made a deep impression on Conrad is shown in the later appearance of two echoes from 'Le Roman'. In a paragraph contrasting men of genius who, because they are endowed with irresistible creative energy, are spared the anxieties and torments of mere conscious and tenacious workers (note Conrad's reference to 'the worker in prose' in the Preface (p. ix)), among whom he places himself, Maupassant says that the latter should fight against 'l'invincible découragement [...] par *la continuité de l'effort*' (p. xxi). And later, he declares that the writer must search relentlessly for the right word 'et ne jamais se contenter de *l'à peu près*' (pp. xxiv–v). In his essay on 'Crainquebille' (1904), Conrad said that France knows that 'only in the *continuity of effort* there is a refuge from despair' (*NLL*, pp. 33–4), and in a letter to Mrs E. L. Sanderson of September 1910, he warned: 'In writing and especially in descriptive writing one must guard oneself against the "*à peu près*", – the horrid danger of the "near enough"' (*LL*, II, p. 118).[5]

In his rejection of all approximations, Maupassant was, of course, repeating his master Flaubert, the supreme exemplar of the indefatigable artist, to whom he paid such vibrant homage in 'Le Roman'. Similarly, Conrad's references to 'complete, unswerving devotion to the perfect blending of form and substance' and to 'an unremitting never-discouraged care for the shape and ring of sentences' (p. ix) show how completely he, too, had made Flaubert's ideals and practice his own. When confronted with this exacting task both novelists voiced their dissatisfaction with their medium in strikingly similar terms. On 18 February 1859 Flaubert wrote to Mlle Leroyer de Chantepie: '*Mais la vie est courte et l'Art est long*, presque impossible même lorsqu'on écrit dans une langue *usée jusqu'à la corde*, vermoulue, affaiblie et qui craque sous le doigt à chaque effort' (IV, p. 314). Conrad also quoted the famous Latin tag 'Art is long and life is short' and he, too, complained of 'the old, old words, *worn thin*, defaced by ages of careless usage' (pp. xi, ix).

The example of Flaubert is also implicated in the emphasis Conrad placed on what Ford called 'visibility'. In 'Le Roman' Maupassant gives Flaubert credit for helping him to develop visual penetration and for teaching him that the least thing has 'un peu d'inconnu' (*PJ*, p. xxiii) in it. The passage reporting Flaubert's own words to his disciple ends on this note: 'et *faites-moi voir, par un seul mot*, en quoi un cheval de fiacre ne ressemble pas aux cinquante autres qui le suivent et le précèdent' (*PJ*, p. xxiv). Conrad – after his re-fashioning of Maupassant in the passage noted by Worth – then adopted an expanded version of Flaubert's injunction: 'My task [...] is, *by the power of the written word* to make you hear, to make you feel – it is, before all, *to make you see*' (p. x). And Conrad's expansion makes fully explicit what is implicit in Flaubert's view – that the power to 'see' extends beyond the merely visual aspect of things.

The Preface is also deeply indebted to Anatole France, especially his review of Maupassant's *Notre Coeur* in *La Vie littéraire* (see following quotations from VII):

| | |
|---|---|
| It is an attempt to find [...] in the aspects of matter and in the facts of life what of each is fundamental, *what is enduring and essential* (p. vii) | Il faut beaucoup d'observation [...] pour démêler au milieu de l'infinie complexité des choses actuelles *les traits essentiels*, les formes typiques. (VII, pp. 403–4) |
| The *changing* wisdom of successive *generations* discards ideas, questions facts, demolishes theories. (p. viii) | Oui, sans doute, M. de Maupassant a raison: les moeurs, les idées, les croyances, les sentiments, tout *change*. Chaque *génération* apporte des modes et des passions nouvelles. (VII, p. 402) |
| there is not a place of splendour or a dark corner of the earth that does not deserve, if only a passing glance of *wonder* and *pity*. (p. viii) | les choses humaines n'inspirent que deux sentiments aux esprits bien faits: *l'admiration* ou *la pitié*. (VI, pp. 213–14) |
| [The artist] speaks [...] to the subtle but invincible conviction of solidarity that knits together the loneliness of innumerable hearts, to *the solidarity [...] which binds men to each other* (p. viii) | [La femme moderne] sert la société sans le vouloir, sans le savoir, par l'effet de *cette* merveilleuse *solidarité qui unit tous les êtres*.(VII, p. 409) |
| [The artist] speaks [...] to the solidarity [...] which binds together all humanity – *the dead* to the living and the living to *the unborn*. (p. viii) | Nos oeuvres de poésie et d'art, il faut les accomplir en l'honneur *des morts*, et dans la pensée de *ceux qui naîtront*. (IX, p. 144) |
| [The artist] speaks [...] to the sense of *mystery surrounding our lives* (p. viii) | une inquiétude du *mystère qui enveloppe* la destinée. (IX, p. 53) *Le mystère* de la destinée *nous enveloppe tout entiers* (IX, p. 424) |
| *To snatch* in a moment of courage [...] a | Il faut beaucoup d'observation [...] *pour* |

| passing phase of life (p. x) | saisir le caractère de l'époque dans laquelle on vit (VII, p. 403) |
| To arrest, for the space of a breath, the hands busy about the work of the earth (p. xii) | cette multitude humaine vouée à la tâche auguste et rude de gagner le pain de chaque jour. (VII, p. 409) |

In *Notre coeur* (1890) Maupassant gives this portrait of the novelist Gaston de Lamarthe:

Gaston de Lamarthe [...] c'était avant tout un homme de lettres, un impitoyable et terrible homme de lettres. Armé d'un oeil qui cueillait les images, les attitudes, les gestes avec une rapidité et une précision d'appareil photographique, et doué d'*une pénétration*, d'un sens de romancier naturel comme un flair de chien de chasse, il emmagasinait du matin au soir des renseignements professionnels. Avec ces deux sens très simples, *une vision nette* des formes et *une intuition instinctive* des dessous, il donnait à ses livres [...] le mouvement *de la vie même.*                    (*Notre coeur*, pp. 17–18)

Conrad had certainly read *Notre coeur* by 1897 but his attention must have been directed to this passage by France who adds that no one could succeed in this ideal better than Maupassant because he has 'l'oeil juste et *l'intuition sûre*' (VII, p. 404) and, like Lamarthe, 'une vision nette des formes et une intuition instinctive des dessous' (VII, p. 407). The corresponding double aim of outward clarity and inward depth also represents Conrad's well-known artistic tenet: 'And art itself may be defined as a single-minded attempt to render the highest kind of justice to the visible universe, by bringing to light the truth, manifold and one, underlying its every aspect' (p. vii).[6]

Maupassant concludes the portrait of Lamarthe with this assessment of his achievement as a novelist: 'Il donnait à ses livres, où n'apparaissait aucune des intentions ordinaires des écrivains psychologues, mais qui avaient l'air de *morceaux* d'existence humaine arrachés à la réalité, *la couleur*, le ton, *l'aspect*, *le mouvement* de la vie même' (*Notre coeur*, pp. 17–18). This passage must have been in Conrad's mind when he gave his definition of the novelist's task: 'The task [...] is to hold up unquestioningly, without choice and without fear, the rescued *fragment* before all eyes in the light of a sincere mood. It is to show its vibration, its colour, its form; and through its *movement*, its *form*, and its *colour*, reveal the substance of its truth' (p. x).[7]

On 16 May 1904, while composing a preface to Ada Galsworthy's Maupassant translation, *Yvette and Other Stories*, Conrad wrote to Galsworthy 'I get on slowly with the Maup^t preface' (*CL*, III, p. 138) which suggests that he was experiencing some difficulty with the writing. Under these circumstances, he looked for assistance to France, a writer whose admiration for Maupassant equalled his own. In the opening of 'M. Guy de Maupassant critique et romancier', France wrote: '*Quant à l'esthétique, elle est telle qu'on devait l'attendre d'un esprit pratique et résolu, enclin naturellement à trouver les choses de l'esprit plus simples qu'elles ne sont en réalité*' (VI, p. 359). Conrad used the first part of this statement as his opening: '*Maupassant's conception of his art is such as one would expect from a practical and resolute mind*' (*NLL*, p. 25), and used the second part later, together with another of France's opinions ('Et puis, *il ne raisonne pas*' (VII, p. 407)): 'It cannot be denied that *he thinks very little. [...] His view of intellectual problems is perhaps more simple than their nature warrants*' (*NLL*, p. 30). The rest of the essay confirms that France may have acted as Conrad's *maître à penser*. Both underline the 'impersonality' and the self-denial which they saw as the outstanding features of Maupassant's writings, for he was concerned with facts, with giving life to characters, and not with moralizing. Both were struck by his honesty and his frankness and by what might even appear to be a certain callousness. But they believed that, in spite of his apparently detached attitude, Maupassant felt what France calls '*une pitié profonde*' (VI, p. 60), or in Conrad's words '*a profound pity*' (p. 29) for his characters. They also emphasize his intense Frenchness.

*A Personal Record* (1908–1909) also offers evidence of the influence of 'the most eloquent and just of French prose writers' (p. 95) on Conrad's critical outlook. In *Le Lys rouge* Princess Seniavine asks the novelist Paul Vence what was the subject of his last novel; the answer is:

C'était une étude, dans laquelle il s'efforçait d'atteindre à cette vérité formée d'une suite logique de *vraisemblances* qui, *ajoutées les unes aux autres*, atteignent à l'évidence.
– Par là, dit-il, le roman acquiert une force morale que, dans sa lourde frivolité, n'eut jamais *l'histoire*.                                          (IX, p. 57)

Although this long-standing debate as to whether the novel and poetry are not in the last analysis 'truer than history' can be traced back to Plato and Aristotle, these lines by France seem to have inspired Conrad's own definition of the novel: 'And what is a novel if not a conviction of our fellow-men's existence strong enough to take upon itself a form of imagined life clearer than reality and whose *accumulated verisimilitude* of selected episodes puts to shame the pride of documentary *history*?' (p. 15). As a result, both writers believed that the creative artist is the real historian of human experience: just as France describes Paul Bourget as the 'historien des affaires de l'esprit' (VI, p. 143), Conrad defines James as 'the historian of fine consciences' (*NLL*, p. 17).[8]

France insisted on the merit of imagination because 'On n'est grand que par elle' (III, p. 401), but he discarded what he called 'invention'. Reviewing *Le Cavalier Miserey*, he rejected the contention that the officers portrayed in it have been 'copied' from nature: 'Ils sont inventés' (VI, p. 78). Conrad used the same critical distinction, stressing that 'Imagination, not invention, is the supreme master of art as of life' (p. 25). And it is significant that the 'great French writer' to whom he alludes when he writes of 'the much larger band of *the totally unimaginative*, of *those* unfortunate *beings in whose empty and unseeing gaze [...]* "*the whole universe vanishes into blank nothingness*"' (p. 92) is France. In *Le Mannequin d'osier*, Professor Bergeret, on his way to see the dean of his faculty, confides to a colleague that this visit is painful to him because the mere fact of approaching a person '*dépourvue de toute espèce d'imagination*' makes his blood run cold. He then explains: 'ces âmes mornes, *qui ne reflètent rien, ces êtres en qui l'univers vient s'anéantir*, voilà l'aspect qui désole et qui désespère' (XI, p. 273).

Recalling the day when the desire to start writing took hold of him, Conrad asks himself why the memory of Malays and Arabs he had known should demand to materialize in the shape of a novel, except 'on the ground of *that* mysterious *fellowship which unites* in a community of hopes and fears *all the dwellers of this earth*?'(p. 9). He had already used similar words in the Preface to *The Nigger* which have been traced to France. Recalling that day again later, Conrad says that the books then lying about in his room were not the works of great masters where '*the secret of clear thought and exact expression can be found*' (p. 70). This echoes France's 'Auguste Vacquerie', an essay in which he speaks of his reverence for Racine, whom he claims to know by heart, and of whom he asks, nearly every day, '*le secret des justes pensées et des paroles limpides*' (VII, p. 345).

Finally, Conrad makes it clear that he is largely in agreement with France in his subjectivism on literary matters. Because of his conviction that we are prisoners within ourselves, France declares in his introduction to *La Vie littéraire* that we should recognize that '*nous parlons de nous-mêmes chaque fois que nous n'avons pas la force de nous taire*' (VI, p. 6). Conrad repeats these words approvingly: '*failing the resolution to hold our peace, we can only talk of ourselves*' (p. 95). As a result, France claimed that 'Il n'y a pas plus de critique objective qu'il n'y a d'art objectif', and defined the good critic as 'celui qui raconte *les aventures de son âme* au milieu des chefs-d'oeuvre' (VI, p. 5).[9] Again, Conrad quotes this 'memorable saying' approvingly, and also views literary criticism as a 'well-told tale of personal experience' (p. 96). And just as France expresses his conviction that it 'survivra à toutes les autres formes de l'art' (VI, p. 514), Conrad states his 'inward certitude' that it 'will never die' (p. 96).

The concluding section of Conrad's review 'The Life Beyond', written in July 1910, was indebted to two of France's essays. Conrad first drew from 'Pourquoi sommes-nous tristes?', a review of Loti's *Japoneries d'automne* and Maupassant's *La Main gauche*:

> Nous sommes plus affinés, plus délicats, plus ingénieux à nous tourmenter, plus habiles à souffrir. En ornant nos voluptés nous avons perfectionné nos douleurs. [...]
>
> Ne nous flattons pas d'avoir entièrement inventé aucune de nos misères. *Il y a long- temps que le prêtre murmure en montant à l'autel: 'Pourquoi êtes-vous triste, ô mon âme, et*

*pourquoi me troublez-vous?'* Une *femme voilée est en chemin depuis la naissance du monde: elle se nomme la Mélancolie.*                                                               (VII, p. 20)

We moderns have complicated our old perplexities to the point of absurdity; our perplexities older than religion itself. *It is not for nothing that for so many centuries the priest, mounting the steps of the altar, murmurs: 'Why art thou sad, my soul, and why dost thou trouble me?' Since the day of Creation* two *veiled figures*, Doubt and *Melancholy, are pacing endlessly* in the sunshine of the world.                          (*NLL*, p. 69)[10]

Conrad then turned to 'Joséphin Péladan', who, France begins, '*est occultiste et mage. [...] Le Mage*, selon la définition de M. Péladan lui même, *c'est le grand harmoniste*'. Later, France acknowledges that he can be incomprehensible, '*absurde*', even a little 'fou' if you like; but he has a great deal of talent, and his book contains '*des pages d'une poésie magnifique*', pages which show 'l'élégante mélancolie de cette prose d'artiste et de poète'. France concludes on Péladan's last invocation to '*les esprits de l'air*', transcribing '*cette magnifique invocation*' almost in full:

Ô nature, mère indulgente, pardonne! Ouvre ton sein au fils prodigue et las.

J'ai voulu déchirer les voiles que tu mets sur la douleur de vivre, et je me suis blessé au mystère... Oedipe, à mi-chemin de deviner l'énigme, jeune Faust, qui regrette déjà la vie simple et du coeur, j'arrive repentant, réconcilié, ô menteuse si douce!

                                                                                       (VII, pp. 226–34)

After saying that 'during this transient hour of our pilgrimage, we may well be content to repeat the Invocation of Sar Peladan', Conrad continues:

*Sar Peladan was an occultist*, a seer, a modern *magician*. He believed in astrology, in *the spirits of the air*, in elves; he was marvellously and deliciously *absurd*. Incidentally he wrote some incomprehensible poems and a *few pages of harmonious prose*, for, you must know, '*a magician is* nothing else but *a great harmonist*'. Here are some eight lines of *the magnificent Invocation*. Let me, however, warn you, strictly between ourselves, that my translation is execrable. I am sorry to say I am no magician.

'O Nature, indulgent Mother, forgive! Open your arms to the son, prodigal and weary.

I have attempted to tear asunder the veil you have hung to conceal from us the pain of life, and I have been wounded by the mystery... Oedipus, half-way to finding the word of the enigma, young Faust, regretting already the simple life, the life of the heart, I come back to you repentant, reconciled, O gentle deceiver!'      (*NLL*, pp. 69–70)

In September 1911 Conrad wrote 'A Familiar Preface' to *A Personal Record* where the influence of France's *La Vie littéraire* is again strongly felt. France begins an article entitled 'Maurice Spronck' with the comment that

M. Maurice Spronck étudie quelques excellents écrivains du XIX^e siècle *qui ne cherchèrent jamais dans la parole écrite autre chose qu'une forme du beau* et dont les oeuvres furent conçues d'après la théorie de l'art pour l'art.                                (VII, p. 179)

Conrad used the italicized words to proclaim his artistic aim:

*I, who have never sought in the written word anything else but a form of the Beautiful –* I have carried over that article of creed from the decks of ships to the more circumscribed space of my desk, and by that act, I suppose, I have become permanently imperfect in the eyes of the ineffable company of pure esthetes.                                    *(PR*, p. xvii)

In the light of the borrowing, 'the ineffable company of pure esthetes' no doubt refers to Théophile Gautier, Charles Baudelaire, and others who make up the subject of Spronck's study.

In a scathing attack on Zola's *La Terre*, which was bound to attract Conrad's attention, France had said: '*les choses humaines* n'inspirent que deux sentiments aux esprits bien faits: '*l'admiration* ou *la pitié*. M. Zola est digne d'une profonde pitié' (VI, pp. 213–14). Conrad probably echoes this passage when he writes: 'The sight of *human affairs* deserves *admiration* and *pity*' (p. xix). He then appropriates a statement France had made in an essay on Edouard Rod:

s'il nous est impossible de découvrir un sens quelconque à ce qu'on nomme la vie, *il convient de vouloir ce que veulent les dieux, sans savoir ce qu'ils veulent, ni même s'ils veulent et que ce qu'il importe de connaître, puisque enfin il s'agit de vivre, ce n'est pas pourquoi, c'est comment.*                                              (VII, pp. 257–8)

*I think that the proper wisdom is to will what the gods will without, perhaps, being certain what their will is –* or *even if they have a will of their own. And in this matter of life* and art *It is not the Why that matters so much* to our happiness *as the How.* (p. xix)

Lastly, Conrad's 'quotation' from *The Imitation of Christ* was drawn from France's essay on Paul Bourget's *Mensonges*, as the close echoes will indicate. France thought that the author of *The Imitation* '*connaissait profondément la vie*' (VI, p. 309), and applied his words to the hero, René Vinci: 'Cette parole de *l'ascète* se vérifia pour lui: "Il arrive que, sans la connaître, *on estime une personne sur sa bonne réputation, et, en se montrant, elle détruit l'opinion qu'on avait d'elle*"' (VI, p. 312). Conrad also writes: 'And I cannot help thinking of a passage in the "Imitation of Christ" where *the ascetic author*, who *knew* life so *profoundly,* says that "there are *persons esteemed on their reputation who by showing themselves destroy the opinion one had of them*"' (p. xiii).[11]

Why did Conrad borrow so much in his critical writings? The references he made to himself as a critic are invariably modest. In September 1910, he wrote to Mrs E. L. Sanderson: 'I am a poor critic, – and what's worse, I may be a misleading one. You see I've nothing but my instinct to guide me and no great facility in expressing my point of view' (*LL*, II, p. 117). And as late as March 1921, he was writing to Garnett: 'I am glad you like the "Maupassant". I was never satisfied with it but shall think better of it now. After all the things in that book [NLL] – it is not my trade! There's not a single one (with the exception of the Censor) that I haven't done unwillingly – against the grain' (*LEG*, p. 278). Even when allowing for Conrad's customary self-deprecation, it is evident that he felt unsure of himself when dealing with literary matters. Some critics believe that he had no great critical mind: it is true that his Author's Notes in particular are disappointing, but they are usually linked with his creative decline. On the other hand, Watt remarks that his 'casual literary comments, and his letters to friends about their current manuscripts [...] reveal an impressive ease in going to the essence of critical problems', which prompts him to suggest that 'Conrad was a good literary critic who was bad at writing literary criticism'.[12] Whatever the case, it is a fact that his most memorable efforts – the Prefaces to *The Nigger of the 'Narcissus'* and *A Personal Record* – written when he was a vigorous novelist, show that he always felt the need to be guided by fellow-novelists and distinguished critics such as Pater, James, Flaubert, Maupassant and, above all, Anatole France.

# Part III

## Conrad's philosophical and aesthetic inheritance

'Conrad was obsessed by the idea of [...] a Destiny that was august, blind, inscrutable, just and above all passionless'.

Ford, p. 163

'The power of Flaubert's principles over Conrad all through his writing career and the astounding way [...] in which he stuck to those principles [...] is one of the most fascinating sights literature has to offer us.'

Edward Crankshaw, *Joseph Conrad* p. 67

# 7 Conrad and Anatole France

'Conrad's cult of Anatole France was not a case of artistic love at first sight, but a maturing intellectual appreciation', writes Paul Kirschner, who was one of the first critics to examine the close relationship between Conrad and his famous contemporary.[1] Conrad's contact with France appears to have begun in 1894 with a reading of *Le Lys rouge* (1894) which at that time left him unmoved; slowly but decisively, his commitment to France seems to have strengthened during the period 1900–8 when he read virtually all of France's writings, wrote two reviews of his fiction (in 1904 and 1908) and was even keen to send the French author a copy of his first review (*CL*, III, p. 405); with *Chance* (1914) and *Victory* (1915) France still seems a decisive living presence in Conrad's consciousness.

Unlike the impact of Flaubert and Maupassant which occurred at the very beginning of Conrad's career and constitutes something of a case of discipleship, France's influence was of a later date, slower in effect, and more diffuse. It is not for that reason of lesser importance, but simply different and more difficult to describe. For one thing, it is the *intellectual* quality of France's work that attracted Conrad in 1904 when, in his review of 'Crainquebille', he stressed that the 'proceedings of France's thought compel our intellectual admiration' (*NLL*, pp. 39–40). The adjective is revealing and points to an accord between the two writers which is indeed conspicuous, as Bendz first noted in 1923, in the 'remarkable affinity' of their ideas on a wide range of psychological, political, moral, philosophical and literary issues.[2] This being the case, it is also necessary to add – by way of qualification – that France probably attracted Conrad in different ways and for different reasons at various stages of his career. In other words, the affinity between them is not a simple and fixed one, but changed in response to Conrad's own developing needs and attitudes. Some borrowings from France in Conrad's novels prompt the conclusion that the former was at times a *maître à penser*, a decisive and formative influence upon Conrad's way of regarding the world. Elsewhere it seems truer to say that France's ideas appealed to Conrad because he had his own reasons for looking at the world in a way similar to France: hence, what he sometimes borrows are not attitudes and beliefs but primarily aphorisms and imagery which support his own deeply held convictions. Again, another reason for Conrad's intellectual attraction for France may be that the latter, as a writer superbly responsive to the mood of his times, acted as a spokesman for, and provided Conrad with access to, a whole body of late nineteenth-century opinion. In the following analysis I attempt to provide a groundplan of some of the basic affinities between the two writers in an attempt to determine which areas of France's fiction were most attractive to Conrad. I shall deal first with their view of the universe and man's position in it, his nature as an individual and social being, and finally with their response to the human predicament.

### The universe and man

Neither France nor Conrad saw the universe as the work of an intelligent deity; it invariably appeared to them to be the result of chance. In *La Vie littéraire* France says that love, the oldest of the gods, was born before there was any justice and intelligence in the world, and as he did not find in the cosmic matter the wherewithal to make a brain, eyes, or ears for himself, he was born instinctive and blind. He has produced everything but *'sans esprit, sans morale, sans intelligence'* (VI, p. 41). In a letter to Cunninghame Graham, Conrad gives his explanation of the Creation by way of a fable: 'out of a chaos of scraps of iron' a knitting machine has 'evolved itself'; he comments: 'the most withering thought is that the infamous thing has made itself; made itself' – like the demiurge of France – *'without thought, without conscience, without foresight, without eyes, without heart. It is a tragic accident'* (*CL*, I, p. 425).

The contempt in which France and Conrad held the universe and 'cette vilaine petite planète-ci' (XI, p. 389), 'this miserable planet' (*CL*, II, p. 89) in particular, is reflected in the imagery they used. France's stock image is to call the earth *'une goutte de boue'*, and so does Conrad in a letter to Cunninghame Graham of 15 June 1898, while, in 1910, in a review of George Bourne's *The Ascending Effort* he still saw it as *'one small blob of mud'* (*NLL*, p. 73).[3] But the influence of France is best felt in a letter to Cunninghame Graham of 14 January 1898 in which he speaks of *'a universe made of drops of fire and clods of mud'* (*CL*, II, pp. 16–17). In 'Rêveries astronomiques' in *La Vie littéraire* Conrad would have read: *'L'univers* que la science nous révèle est d'une désespérante monotonie. Tous les soleils sont *des gouttes de feu* et toutes les planètes *des gouttes de boue'* (VII, p. 207).

France's and Conrad's philosophical outlook was rooted in a fundamental pessimism which expressed itself in their belief in an inexorable destiny. For both, the universe is governed by irrational forces which man can neither control nor resist. The critic of *Le Temps* interprets mythology as showing that there are in man 'obscure forces' older than he, which act independently, apart from his will (VI, p. 41). The Abbé Coignard says that in the comedy of life it looks as though princes gave the orders and the people obeyed, but it is all a vain illusion, because they are all led by 'une force invisible' (VIII, p. 338). The influence of France on this subject is unmistakable in two borrowings where

Conrad speaks of '*the whole scheme of things of which we form a helpless part*' (*N*, p. 497) and '*unknown powers that shape our destinies*' (*SL*, p. 62) (see above, pp. 84-5, 135-6). They often apprehended these 'unknown powers' as a transcendental and omnipresent evil. When France said of Vigny that he had 'le sentiment profond du mal universel' (I, p. 65), he was at one with the poet, since in *Le Jardin d'Epicure* he referred on his own account to 'le mal universel' surrounding us (IX, p. 462). Conrad, too, was acutely aware of evil forces at work on this 'earth of evil' (*SA*, p. 165), and he firmly believed that the threat posed by 'the powers of darkness' (*YOS*, pp. 116–17) or 'the Dark Powers' must not be disregarded for they are 'always on the verge of triumph' (*LJ*, p. 121).

Both authors were equally gloomy about the ultimate future of our world. France argues in 'Mysticisme et Science' that all that science can tell us about the destiny of mankind is that it will perish with the death of the sun, and then, 'le grain de poussière, qui se nomme la Terre et qui n'aura plus de nom alors, roulera avec lui [le soleil] dans la nuit éternelle' (VII, p. 432). In *Le Jardin*, he paints a picture of the death of mankind and the end of the world, 'Quand *le soleil s'éteindra*'. The earth is 'froide', 'glacée', the last dying men are looking at the stars shining all day long 'dans le ciel noir, à travers l'air glacial'. After their death 'la terre continuera de rouler, emportant à travers les espaces silencieux les cendres de l'humanité, les poèmes d'Homère et les augustes débris des marbres grecs, attachés à ses flancs glacés' (IX, pp. 405-6). Conrad may well have adopted from France this thermodynamic view of a cooling sun and universe, and therefore of a dying earth. He referred to this theme on at least three occasions in letters to Cunninghame Graham: on 14 December 1897 he wrote of 'the eternal decree that will extinguish the sun, the stars one by one, and in another instant shall spread a frozen darkness over the whole universe'; a month later, he spoke of the 'fate of a humanity condemned ultimately to perish from cold' and saw the perfection attained by mankind ending 'in cold, darkness and silence'; and on 15 June 1898 he painted again the same picture, this time in French: 'Un moment, un clin d'oeil et il ne reste rien – qu'*une goutte de boue*, de boue froide, de boue morte lancée dans l'éspace noir, tournoyant autour d'*un soleil éteint*. Rien. Ni pensée, ni son, ni âme. Rien.' (*CL*, I, p. 423; II, pp. 17, 70).[4]

Since France and Conrad saw man as the product of blind creation, they naturally found fault with the design. In *Le Jardin d'Epicure* France explains his idea: had he been the demiurge, he would have created man not in the likeness of apes but in that of the insects which, from caterpillars, become butterflies that have no other care than to love and be beautiful; but, he concludes: 'Je doute, entre nous, qu'il [le démiurge] ait consulté les philosophes et les gens d'esprit' (IX, pp. 417–18). In *Lord Jim* Stein, too, sees the butterfly as an epitome of beauty, a more perfect specimen than man, who 'is amazing' but 'is not a masterpiece'; and he, like France, suggests that in the case of man the demiurge lacked vision: 'Perhaps the artist was a little mad' (p. 203).

In fact, both authors had a very limited opinion of mankind and, in their fiction, one of its main features appears to be what Conrad calls, using France's words, *'our common mediocrity'* (*V*, p. 394; see above p. 131). It is apparent in man's inability to know even what is good for him. In 'L'Humaine tragédie', Fra Giovanni, like the Abbé Coignard, reflects on this and decides that man cannot make the right choices because *'il ne connaît pas ses besoins'* (X, p. 168). In *The Secret Agent*, the Professor similarly asserts that *'Mankind [...] does not know what it wants'* (p. 305) and, for once at least, he is reflecting his author since Conrad made the same statement in a letter to Galsworthy (*LL*, II, p. 121). Man's mediocrity is also revealed in his inability to achieve anything really good or bad. The philosopher Nicias makes this point in *Thaïs*; so does Coignard who remarks that men are all alike 'également *médiocres dans le mal comme dans le bien'* (VIII, p. 455; V, p. 38). In *Chance* Marlow states categorically: 'the incapacity to achieve anything distinctly good or evil is inherent in our earthly condition. Mediocrity is our mark' (p. 23) and in his Author's Note to *Nostromo* Conrad describes his novel as a story of 'events flowing from the passions of men *short-sighted in good and evil*' (p. xvii).

One of the tragedies of man's condition is that he cannot foresee the consequences of his actions. In *Le Jardin d'Epicure* France avers that the simplest thought and the most instinctive action have *'des conséquences incalculables'* (IX, p. 533). Similarly, in *Chance* before declaring that 'Mediocrity is our mark', Marlow points out that it is 'unwise to admit any sort of responsibility for our actions, whose *consequences we are never able to foresee'* (p. 23). This uncertainty is at the root of the predicament in which most of Conrad's heroes, namely Willems, Jim, Kurtz, Nostromo, Decoud, Verloc, Razumov, and Heyst, find themselves. Remembering that some of Heyst's views on action are uttered by M. Bergeret, it may be that Conrad had France in mind, as the verbal echo suggests, in making Heyst feel, after his first meeting with Lena, that he had 'engaged himself by a rash promise to an action big with *incalculable consequences'* , and later caused him to meditate 'on the mystery of his actions' (*V*, pp. 83, 173).

Stupidity is, for France and Conrad, another prominent trait of man. *'L'imbécillité humaine'* is often on the lips of the Abbé Coignard; the order of society, he says, is stable and nothing can upset it because it rests on 'la misère et l'imbécillité humaine' (VIII, p. 380), and these are foundations which will never fail. In *The Nigger of the 'Narcissus'* the narrator states that Wait had found 'the secret of keeping for ever on the run the fundamental imbecility of mankind' (p. 37), and Conrad once blamed H. G. Wells for not taking 'sufficient account of *human imbecility* which is cunning and perfidious' (*CL*, III, p. 64).

France's and Conrad's belief in an inexorable Destiny or Fatality governing human life had far-reaching consequences for, as Baines explains in the case of

Conrad, it 'is liable to produce a sense of unreality and it may be that this expressed itself in Conrad's frequent emphasis on the illusory nature of so much experience and on the dream-like quality of life'.[5] These words also apply to France, the 'great analyst of illusions' (*NLL*, p. 33), as Conrad described him in his review of 'Crainquebille'. France asserted early in his work his conviction that man is fated to live in a world of illusory appearances; in the Preface to the 'Noces corinthiennes' (1876) he already saw the 'perpetual illusion' in which all men are plunged as 'the very condition of life' (I, p. 249). For Conrad, too, 'All is illusion' (*CL*, II, p. 98) as he wrote to Garnett, and in his review of *L'Ile des pingouins* he referred to 'that life of the earth which is but a vain and transitory illusion' (*NLL*, p. 42).

Like Maupassant, and equally under the probable influence of Schopenhauer, they affirmed that illusion is at the root of every man's conception of himself assuming as he does that he is the centre of the world. In *Le Jardin d'Epicure* France says; 'Quel être ne se croit pas la fin de l'univers et n'agit pas comme s'il l'était? C'est la condition même de la vie. Chacun de nous pense que le monde aboutit à lui' (IX, p. 441). In 'The Ascending Effort' Conrad explains that although a man believes in the Copernican system, in his everyday life 'he holds the system of Ptolemy' (*NLL*, p. 74) seeing himself and the world around him as the centre of things.

Love itself appeared to each of them as the supreme illusion and no more effective than all the other illusions with which men deceive themselves when trying to dispel the fundamental isolation to which all human beings are doomed. This perception lies at the core of their view of life, and is the central idea of their works where characters jostle against one another yet remain separate. Heyst observes, in words borrowed from Thérèse Martin, that his father's death did not trouble '*the flow of life's stream, where men and women go by* [...] revolving and *jostling* one another' (*V*, p. 175; see above, p. 131). A deep awareness of this is apparent in the conversations of the philosophers in *Thaïs* and in those of Coignard who warns his pupil Tournebroche: 'Les âmes sont presque impénétrables les unes aux autres, et c'est ce qui vous montre le néant cruel de l'amour' (VIII, pp. 207–8). 'Impénétrable': a key word in France's works: M. Bergeret uses it in *Le Mannequin d'osier*; so does Thérèse Martin when describing the feelings of Paul Vence, France's mouthpiece in *Le Lys rouge*. He recognizes, says Thérèse, that 'les âmes sont impénétrables aux âmes, et il en souffre. Il se sent seul quand il pense, seul quand il écrit. Quoi qu'on fasse, on est toujours seul au monde. [...] On s'explique toujours, on ne se comprend jamais' (IX, p. 84). No doubt Conrad found in France, as he did in Maupassant and Flaubert,[6] confirmation of his own perception of moral solitude, and France's impact is unmistakable. His assertion: '*On ne sort jamais de soi-même. C'est une vérité commune à tout le monde*, mais qui paraît plus sensible dans certaines natures, dont l'originalité est nette' (VI, p. 98) finds a distinct echo in Conrad: 'I perceived that *in common with the rest of men* nothing could deliver me from my fatal consistency. *We cannot escape from ourselves*' (*TU*, p. vii). Hence Conrad's subjectivism in literary matters, a topic on which France's mark was identified earlier.[7]

## Man as an individual

Theorists of Conrad's politics have traced his sources to Burke (Fleishman), Rousseau, or Polish romanticism (Najder). As some borrowings in *Nostromo* and *Under Western Eyes* have indicated, France represents another important and incontrovertible source of Conrad's political ideas.

Any comparison between them on this subject must take into account that it was not until around 1896 that a change gradually came into France's political thinking, a fact Kirschner seems to have overlooked when he spoke of their 'irreconcilable differences of political belief'.[8] Before he became a socialist in about 1900, the creator of Jérôme Coignard and M. Bergeret and the author of the works which most influenced Conrad was a confirmed political sceptic with whom Conrad was perfectly akin. So what we are comparing here are Conrad's views with those of France before he became a socialist.[9]

Both men shared an unyielding pessimism in their political outlook: being convinced of man's fundamental wickedness, they believed in the inevitable wickedness of society. In 'L'Abbé Jérôme Coignard' France says of his character: 'Il était persuadé que *l'homme est* naturellement *un* très *méchant animal*, et que les sociétés ne sont abominables que parce qu'il met son génie à les former' (VIII, p. 321), and in *Le Mannequin d'osier* he remarks that 'la vie ne se soutenant et ne s'accroissant que dans le meurtre, les meilleures [hommes] sont ceux qui font le plus de carnages' (XI, p. 423). Conrad was clearly receptive to France's view since he wrote to Cunninghame Graham on 8 February 1899: '*L'homme est un animal méchant*. Sa mechanceté doit être organisée. Le crime est une condition nécéssaire de l'existence organisée. La société est essentielment criminelle – ou elle n'existerait pas' (*CL*, II, p. 159).[10] (*Kirschner, p. 230)

A comparison between *Le Mannequin d'osier* and *Nostromo* further illustrates their affinity on this subject. In a discussion on barbarism and civilization, M. Bergeret remarks that men have always been 'méchants et cruels' and have always found pleasure 'à tourmenter les malheureux'. By 'tourmenter' he means psychological as well as physical torture. In the same way Conrad observes: 'At no time of the world's history have men been at a loss how to inflict mental and bodily anguish upon their fellow-creatures.' It is the Professor's contention that barbarism is less cruel than civilization and that civilized peoples show a form of ferocity which passes the imagination of savages. He concludes that a criminologist is 'plus méchant qu'un sauvage'. Conrad also feels that 'primeval man did not go to the trouble of inventing tortures. He was indolent and pure of heart,' and never killed with malice. In the course of this discussion, one of Bergeret's friends mentions the Holy Inquisition as an example of 'philanthropie spirituelle' in the name of which methods of torture unknown to 'Persia and China' were invented (XI, pp.351-2). The relevant passage in Conrad opens with a reference to the same subject: 'The priest's inquisitorial instincts suffered but little from the want of classical apparatus of the Inquisition' (pp.372-3), and indeed the tortures Father Beron had inflicted on Dr Mony-gham justify every one of Bergeret's words. France and Conrad agreed that it takes a modern man, and a philanthropist at that, to crush a human being completely.

Man's wickedness, violence and cruelty find ultimate expression in wars which they consider to be inevitable products of his violent instincts. The Abbé Coignard reaches this conclusion: 'la guerre est une des nécessités de la nature humaine' (VIII, p.423). Both he and Bergeret deplore the fact that society honours the men who take part in these massacres, and that 'la gloire du carnage' (XI, p.364), in Bergeret's words, passes all others. In *The Mirror of the Sea* Conrad acknowledges, like Coignard, the inevitability of war when he calls it 'a natural function of mankind' and he too says that we have lost this basic conception of war because 'in the evolution of sentiments and ideas, [it] has come to be regarded at last as a half-mystic and glorious ceremony' (pp.149-50).

Both authors were far more conscious of man's violent, primeval origin than of the thin veneer with which civilization tries to cover it. Throughout *Les Opinions* the Abbé voices his scepticism about the effectiveness of any change of government since it means replacing one set of men by others who will be, by their very nature, equally mediocre and stupid and even more avaricious because more avid for power. For him human nature never changes and after reforms men are just as corrupt and wretched as they were before. In a letter to Cunninghame Graham, Conrad says that in spite of his sympathy for his correspondent's 'socialistic-republican' ideas, as he calls them elsewhere, he has not 'a grain of belief' left and he remonstrates: 'Alas! What you want to reform are not institutions – it is human nature. Your faith will never move that mountain' (*CL*, II, p.25). Years later, he made clear in his review of 'Crainquebille' that he was at one with France in his 'sceptical insight into all forms of government,' adding approvingly that he 'perceives that political institutions, whether contrived by the wisdom of the few or the ignorance of the many, are incapable of securing the happiness of mankind' (*NLL*, p.33).

Because of their profound disbelief in the perfectibility of man and human institutions, France and Conrad rejected all dogmas and schemes for the better-ment of the human condition; also they despised the masses and their leaders too strongly, to have any faith in revolutions. When, in his article on 'Crainque-bille', Conrad wrote: 'M. Anatole France, who loves truth, does not love dog-ma' (*NLL*, p.37), he was voicing his own distrust of all creeds. Though, like Coignard, he was critical of social, political and religious institutions, yet, like him, he had not enough faith in man's reason to rebel against society. Just as the Abbé criticized optimism as a dangerous aberration on the ground that it usually leads to utopian fanaticism, he attacked the 'revolutionary spirit' saying: 'Its hard, absolute optimism is repulsive to my mind by the menace of fanaticism and intolerance it contains' (*PR*, pp. xix–xx). And here again Conrad felt so much at one with France that he used his very words: '*Visionaries work everlasting evil* on earth. *Their Utopias inspire in* the mass of *mediocre minds a disgust of reality*' (*UWE*, p. 95; see above, p. 104). This is the reason why France and Conrad detested Rousseau and the French Revolution which, in Conrad's words, 'was not a political movement at all, but a great outburst of morality' (*PR*, p. 95) based on the belief in the natural goodness and justice of man. France saw in that belief the source of the aberration of this movement, and noted in *Les Opinions* that the excesses of the Terror stemmed from Robespierre's conviction that men should be virtuous, because 'Quand on veut rendre les hommes bons et sages, libres, modérés, généreux, on est amené fatalement à vouloir les tuer tous' (VIII, p. 322). It is the same despair at man's imperfections which ultimately drives Kurtz to scribble at the end of his report for the International Society for the Suppression of Savage Customs 'Exterminate all the brutes' (*YOS*, p. 118). Conrad rejected the 'imbecile and atrocious answer of a purely Utopian revolutionism' because, according to him, it stems from 'the strange conviction that a fundamental change of hearts must follow the downfall of any given human institutions'; the only thing that can be effected he argues, like Coignard who views changes of government as '*de simples changements d'hommes*' (VIII, p. 455; see above, p. 105), is '*merely a change of names*' (*UWE*, p. x).[11]

In a final analysis it appears that France's and Conrad's political scepticism is based on the same conviction that, men being what they are, all thought, however noble, becomes inevitably degraded when translated into action. In 'La Morale et la Science' France makes this point: 'la pensée qui est un acte participe de la cruauté attachée à tout acte. Il n'y a pas une seule pensée absolument inoffensive. Toute philosophie destinée à régner est grosse d'abus, de violences et d'iniquités' (VII, p. 80). Conrad shows that he is in complete agreement with this idea when he writes to Cunninghame Graham that 'Into the noblest cause men manage to put something of their baseness' (*CL*, II, p. 25) and when, at the close of *Nostromo*, he makes Mrs Gould realize that 'There was something inherent in the necessities of successful action which carried with it the moral degradation of the idea' (p. 521).

## The human predicament

Conrad's outlook on life, like that of Anatole France, was rooted in a deep pessimism which, being metaphysical, moral and social, was all-pervasive. At times both leaned towards nihilism, in its philosophical sense. France, in his early work *Le Livre de mon ami* (1885), confesses that as a child he was already strongly aware of the flux of things and '*du néant de tout*' (III, p. 315) and, in the nineties, he carried his pessimistic scepticism into nearly all fields of effort and knowledge. That Conrad's scepticism equalled France's can be seen in his assertion that there is 'no morality, no knowledge and no hope' (*CL*, II, p. 30), and he was surely voicing his own view in the authorial comment on Heyst's father: 'With what strange serenity, mingled with terrors, had that man considered the *universal nothingness*' (*V*, p. 219). At its darkest extreme, the scepticism of both writers extends to the very source and end of action itself: France tersely states in *Le Puits de sainte Claire*: 'Il est également cruel et vain de penser et d'agir' (X, p. 56); Heyst's similar warning to Lena: 'Thought, action – so many snares!' (*V*, p. 193) undoubtedly reflects Conrad's own conviction, for his pessimistic verdict applies as much to Nostromo's 'audacious action' as it does to Decoud's 'intellectual audacity'. However, neither can rest easy with absolute nihilism. France confessed to having looked in the direction of 'absolute scepticism' on many occasions, but he 'never entered it' as he was frightened to put his foot 'sur cette base qui engloutit tout ce qu'on y met' (VII, p. 9). Conrad, too, always recoiled in horror from the abyss of 'moral Nihilism' (*NLL*, p. 8). In his early and major works, this meant stressing the practical necessity of 'illusions'; in the later works, accepting these 'illusions' at their practical face value. Typical of his position at the peak of his career is this often-quoted statement from 'Books' (1905): 'To be hopeful in an artistic sense it is not necessary to think that the world is good. It is enough to believe that there is no impossibility of its being made so' (*NLL*, p. 9).

Both writers made numerous indictments of all philosophical systems. In 'L'Abbé Jérôme Coignard' France recalls that his character lacked the 'esprit de système', that is, he always refused to use the sophisms which are the cement necessary to fill in the gaps between the truths in any 'vaste et belle construction mentale' (VIII, p. 314), and the Abbé himself warns Tournebroche that human reason, at its most sublime, erects its palaces and temples 'avec des nuages' (VIII, p. 75). France, for his part, never attempted to systematize his own 'philosophy'; Conrad's letter to Edward Noble on 2 November 1895 shows that from the outset of his career his attitude towards truth was similarly individualistic and pragmatic:

> Everyone must walk in the light of his own heart's gospel. No man's light is good to any of his fellows. that's my creed – from beginning to end. Thats my view of life – a view that rejects all formulas dogmas and principles of other people's making. These are only a web of illusions. We are too varied. Another man's truth is only a dismal lie to me.                                                                            (*CL*, I, p. 253)

In the preface to the second series of *La Vie littéraire*, France remarks lightheartedly that there is no reason to believe that only one doctrine is good, and that such partiality is excusable only in an inventor; for, he explains, there are very few minds with any breadth which do not harbour 'de nombreuses contradictions' (VI, p. 326). This view is characteristic of his turn of mind and was reflected in his familiar speech. Dargan quotes Corday who left this recollection: 'Whether it were a question of a thing, an idea or a human being, his thought immediately made a circuit of the object, enveloping it as in a lasso. He revealed simultaneously its strong and its weak side, its good and bad aspects – for he perceived at once *all* the aspects possible.'[12] It is striking that Curle noted this same enveloping and manifold type of discourse in Conrad: 'He never said all he thought about any one subject at any one time, and thus he often appeared to contradict himself. There was a curious caution about him, and he would walk round a subject examining it from different angles.'[13] Like France, he was contemptuous of what he considered narrow dogmatic views, as is shown by his attitude towards the 'little thoughts' of Jim's father who believes in 'one faith, one conceivable conduct of life, one manner of dying' (*LJ*, p. 341). As a result, they never aimed at consistency in their thought and never attempted to remove the ambiguities and overcome the contradictions which are sometimes found loosely side by side in their works.

Between the acceptance of dogmatic and conventional ethics and a nihilistic position, the pessimistic scepticism of France and Conrad found its natural expression in that doubt which lies at the core of their philosophical outlook. Talking about martyrs, the critic of *Le Temps* confesses that he is shocked to find that some men are so sure of certain things when he himself has searched for so long without finding anything and is finally confined to doubt (VII, p. 43). For Conrad, too, 'doubt [...] is the inseparable part of our knowledge', and we are fated to live in a 'world of doubts' (*LJ*, pp. 221, 236) since 'no explanation is final' (*PR*, p. 35). Late in life, Conrad was still voicing the same conviction towards the end of *The Rescue*: 'All the possibilities were wrapped up in doubt, uncertain, like all things pertaining to the life of men' (p. 381).[14] This attitude was rooted in what both writers saw as man's fundamental ignorance of nature's purpose, of his origin and destiny, in the complete mystery which surrounds him and the universe.

They attributed this ignorance to the inadequacy of his senses which prevent his reason from being able to interpret phenomena and therefore reach objective truth, so that illusory appearances are the only realities he will ever know. The Abbé Coignard says that the instruments scientists use only multiply their 'rapports' with nature but still keep them in ignorance of the substance of things; they discover new appearances and are thereby the toys of new illusions, which is why all human knowledge is only a progress 'dans la fantasmagorie' (VIII, pp. 405-6).[15] That Conrad, who, we recall, recognized in France 'a great analyst of illusions' (*NLL*, p. 33), shared his Abbé's view, can be seen in this statement from *A Personal Record*: 'The appearances of this perishable life are deceptive like everything that falls under the judgement of our imperfect senses' (p. 35).[16] France's account of Leconte de Lisle's 'pyrrhonic philosophy' also describes his own view of life which, as Conrad noted in his review of *L'Ile des pingouins*, is also pyrrhonic. Like the poet, France found no place for a single affirmation because he, too, believed that life is an illusion, a dream made up of meaningless images produced by the distorting mirrors of our senses. As a result, 'Nous sommes enfermés dans notre personne comme dans une prison perpétuelle' (VI, p. 6). Though this epistemological solipsism was, as Watt observes, 'an important part of the cultural atmosphere of the nineties' (as is shown by 'Le Roman' and the writings of Pater[17]), the influence of France is nevertheless easily indentifiable. 'Les Fous dans la littérature' tells how one day a flat mirror meets a convex mirror and remonstrates with it for the way it reflects nature. As the quarrel waxes between the mirrors, d'Alembert, who is walking by, tells them that they are both right and wrong and that the forms they project are perfect. And he continues: 'Un miroir concave en produirait une troisième [figure] fort différente et tout aussi parfaite. Quant à la nature elle-même, nul ne connaît sa figure véritable, et il est même probable qu'elle n'a de figure que dans les miroirs qui la reflètent' (VI, p. 170). This fable was not lost on Conrad who wrote to Cunninghame Graham on 31 January 1898: 'there is only the consciousness of ourselves which drives us about a world that whether seen in a convex or a concave mirror is always but a vain and floating appearance' (*CL*, II, p. 30). Both writers adopted certain beliefs but were often inclined to see them as the illusions of their own choice.

While deploring the minor role reason plays in the conduct of a man's life, they felt that in some ways it was better so. The writings of France and Conrad show that they shared the idea prevalent in nineteenth-century France that a close link exists between intelligence and suffering. In *Jocaste* France quotes the words of the physiologist Charles Richet: 'Il y a entre l'intelligence et la douleur un rapport tellement étroit que les êtres les plus intelligents sont ceux qui sont capables de souffrir le plus!' (II, p. 4), and he makes Pierre Nozière speak of this illusory life where 'les trois quarts de nos maux viennent de la pensée' (X, p. 381). To Lena who says 'I was thinking', Heyst makes this disillusioned sally that Conrad would certainly have endorsed: 'If you begin to think you will be unhappy' (*V*, p. 193). Thought, as France and Conrad saw it, can even be a frightful thing: 'la pensée est mauvaise' (IX, p. 528) says the first, 'reason is hateful' (*CL*, II, p. 16) echoes the second. Why this denigration of intelligence? Like Schopenhauer (and Maupassant), they believed that thought is incongruous with our animal nature, and that the fundamental evil and tragedy of man's condition lie in consciousness, in the fact that 'What makes mankind tragic is not that they are the victims of nature, it is that they are conscious of it' (*CL*, II, p. 30). They can both be found to regard consciousness as a malady which only gives man a painful awareness of his personal insignificance and weakens the impulse to action. These are France's grounds for criticizing science in *Le Jardin d'Epicure*:

[La Science] nous tourmente par d'affreuses illusions [...] elle crée notre petitesse en mesurant les astres, la brièveté de la vie en évaluant l'âge de la terre, notre infirmité en nous faisant soupçonner ce que nous ne pouvons ni voir ni atteindre, notre ignorance en nous cognant sans cesse à l'inconnaissable et notre misère en multipliant nos curiosités sans les satisfaire.                                                  (IX, p. 532)[18]

Conrad's rejection of Cunninghame Graham's suggestion of a Singleton with an education also stems from the same conviction:

Would you seriously, of malice prepense cultivate in that unconscious man the power to think. Then he would become conscious – and much smaller – and very unhappy.[...]
   Would you seriously wish to tell such a man 'Know thyself'. Understand that thou art nothing, less than a shadow, more insignificant than a drop of water in the ocean, more fleeting than the illusion of a dream.                               (CL, I, p. 423)[19]

Conrad's willingness to accept France's verdict on the danger of 'intellectual audacity' has been seen in the explanation of Decoud's end. In both cases the implication is clear: a far-seeing intellect cannot be allowed to probe too deeply into the disquieting depths of human nature or to prowl in a universe controlled by powerful evil forces without coming back from its quest bitter and disillusioned.

   For both writers a man's driving force lies in his instincts, in his passions. In Le Livre de mon ami France says that '"Tout ce qui se fait de grand en ce monde est fait par elles [les passions]"' (III, p. 352). In 'A Familiar Preface' Conrad also avers: 'It is better for mankind to be impressionable than reflective. Nothing humanely great – great, I mean, as affecting a whole mass of lives – has come from reflection' (PR, p. xi). This takes us back to Coignard's contention that the conquerors and statesmen, who have changed the face of the earth, who have 'remué le monde' (VIII, p. 452) were in fact single-minded people incapable of deep philosophical thinking, a view Conrad seems to echo when assessing the influence of Heyst the elder on his son: 'The young man learned to reflect, which is a destructive process, a reckoning of the cost. It is not the clear-sighted who lead the world. Great achievements are accomplished in a blessed, warm mental fog' (V, pp. 91-2). Whereas Heyst, with his intellect, does not possess the beliefs and hopes which are required for effective action, Lena, who is no thinker, can embark instinctively and passionately on a course of fierce resistance to the dangerous intruders, which she does precisely in a 'mental fog': 'a great vagueness enveloped her impressions' (V, p. 317) Conrad explains, following France's feminine psychology (see above, p. 130). All this is illustrated throughout his fiction: Captain MacWhirr, his only major character who triumphs – if only in a practical sense – is, in the verdict of his First Mate, 'such a stupid man' (TOS, p. 102).

   France's impact on Conrad on this subject is unmistakable, particularly in his early fiction. In Le Jardin d'Epicure he declares: 'L'ignorance est la condition nécessaire, je ne dis pas du bonheur, mais de l'existence même. Si nous savions tout, nous ne pourrions pas supporter la vie une heure. Les sentiments qui nous *la rendent ou douce, ou du moins tolérable*, naissent d'un *mensonge* et se nourrissent d'*illusions*' (IX, p. 409). In 'The Return', written in 1897, Alvan Hervey suddenly has a glimpse into 'the immensity of pain that can be contained in one short moment of human thought.' This revelation leaves him with a 'sense of loss and bitter solitude,' 'robbed and exiled.' But life must go on Conrad says and, using France's words, he adds that such revelations are followed by 'the feverish raking up of *illusions*, the cultivation of a fresh crop of *lies* ... to sustain *life, to make it supportable, to make it fair*' (*TU*, pp. 133–4).

However, for all the criticism France and Conrad levelled at reason, however much they decried it and found it weak and prone to error, they still saw it as the main attribute of man, as the sign of his greatness and dignity. France repeatedly proclaimed the 'inalienable rights of Thought' because it is 'tout ce que nous possédons en propre' (VIII, p. 320). Dargan observes that 'France's attacks on the intelligence were due to the fact that it had not done as much for the world as it should have done: he placed the mind not too low, but too high. [...] In similar sceptics like Montaigne and Bayle [...] their real onslaught is rather against the unintelligent world who will not accept her mandates'.[20] Professor Bergeret, the intellectual, irritates his fellow men and is alienated from them because he questions basic assumptions and beliefs: 'Par cela seul qu'il pensait, il était un être étrange, inquiétant, suspect à tous (XII, p. 98). Conrad's ambivalent attitude is clearly conveyed in a remark he made to his 'aunt' in 1894 about 'le privilege infernal et divin de la Pensée' (*CL*, I, p. 162). He may call reason 'hateful' and may wish to do away with 'consciousness' in his awareness of the problems it raises, but in his case too the real indictment is of the mass mentality. He once warned Norman Douglas: 'Don't forget [...] that your point of view in general is the unpopular one. It is intellectual and uncompromising. [...] People don't want intelligence. It worries them –' (*CL*, III, p. 286).

The value they placed on thought is reflected in their attitude to scepticism, which they regarded as one of the mainsprings of the critical mind. For France it was an assertion of the freedom of thought even in the thick of action. In an article in the *Univers illustré* of 14 April 1894, he confesses that in *Thaïs* he has not brought men the final truth, though this is usually what they want; he has shown the contradictions, the antinomies and has advised philosophical doubt for nothing is better: to it we owe tolerance, indulgence, pity and humane virtues (V, p. 472). In a letter to Galsworthy, Conrad refers explicitly to the saving grace of scepticism which he describes as 'the tonic of minds, the tonic of life, the agent of truth – the way of art and salvation' (*CL*, II, p. 359). Both deplored that this quality should be so scarce among men: in the article quoted above France says: 'Le doute n'est supportable qu'aux esprits cultivés' (V, p. 472); in *Nostromo* Conrad remarks: 'The popular mind is incapable of scepticism!' (p. 420). For them this is a terrible shortcoming with far-reaching consequences.

In the last analysis, man's intellectual anxiety is for both writers probably the only thing that gives meaning to life in this unconcerned universe. The critic of *Le Temps* explains: 'Et je songeai que la plus grande vertu de l'homme est peut-être la curiosité. Nous voulons savoir; il est vrai que nous ne saurons jamais rien. Mais nous aurons du moins opposé au mystère universel qui nous enveloppe une pensée obstinée et des regards audacieux' (VII, p. 84). The narrator in *Chance* echoes France's appraisal of curiosity when he describes it as 'the most respectable faculty of the human mind' (p. 40), and in *Lord Jim* Marlow clearly regards man's pursuit of truth as his *raison d'être*: 'The last word is not said, – probably shall never be said. Are not our lives too short for that full utterance which through all our stammerings is of course our only and abiding intention' (p. 225). However, in spite of this faint gleam in the darkness, for France and Conrad the prospects for the creation and mankind are gloomy. Neither shows any conception of goodness in man and in the world comparable to his conception of evil, and there is no evidence that either believed that the forces of evil would ever be overcome. In *Le Jardin* France says that hope is the greatest of all virtues, and he asks us to hope in the beings who will one day issue from man, as man issued from the brute; but he warns us that there is no hope for mankind because, in spite of 'august efforts,' it has not destroyed evil (IX, p. 463). In his first work, he had already decided that 'l'espérance est la plus grande de nos folies' (I, p. 64). Although Conrad was no nihilist, his conviction that 'there is [...] no hope' is reflected in his most important works.

What can man's attitude be 'dans l'amertume du doute, au milieu du mal universel, sous le ciel vide,' as France says in *Le Jardin*? His answer is resignation: 'Nous n'avons rien à faire en ce monde qu'à nous résigner' (IX, p. 462). In 'A Familiar Preface' Conrad also advocates resignation as being 'the only one of our feelings for which it is impossible to become a sham'. Resignation, however, is hardly a concept men can live by and he admits in the same essay that it is not 'the last word of wisdom'. France's influence in the quest for the 'last word' is conspicuous in a borrowing in which Conrad declares that we should *'will what the gods will'* and that *'in this matter of life* [...] *it is not the Why that matters so much to our happiness as the How'* (*PR*, p. xix; see above, p. 144). In other words, for both, only the existential answer is possible: since we live, live we must. Their accord is illustrated by the type of resignation they advocate, which is not that of withdrawal and despair but one which shows a positive, involved concern for humanity. France says that noble creatures give it the name of contentment because 'La charité du genre humain les échauffe' (IX, p. 462). Conrad attaches the same meaning to resignation when he defines it as 'not mystic, not detached, but [...] open-eyed, conscious, and informed by love' (*PR*, p. xix).

In 'A Familiar Preface' Conrad quotes the Frenchman's saying: *'Il y a toujours la manière'* [21] and speaks of 'those who know how to look at their kind' (*PR*, p. xix). The way France and Conrad 'looked' can be summed up in their two watchwords: Irony and Pity. In *Le Lys rouge* Paul Vence says: 'Il était sage, celui qui a dit: "Donnons aux hommes pour témoins et pour juges l'Ironie et la Pitié"' (IX, p. 360). Although this apophthegm is from Renan, France made it his own a year later in *Le Jardin d'Epicure* (IX, p. 450). When commenting on the philosophy of Jérôme Coignard, he describes it as 'empreinte d'une bienveillante ironie [...] indulgente et facile' (VIII, p. 321). Conrad's appreciation of this brand of Francian irony can be seen in the adjectives 'playful', 'charitable', 'most humane', 'delicate', with which he qualifies it in his two articles on the French master, and one cannot but agree with Bendz when he describes Conrad's irony as 'humour pointed with sarcasm, slightly insidious behind its air of dispassionate attention to mere fact, – an exquisite poking fun at things' which, he adds, 'reminds one again a little of that other master of the genre, Anatole France.'[22] But France and Conrad believed too much in human solidarity[23] to be content to look at life as detached and disdainful observers; moved by the spectacle of misery and injustice, they experienced compassion and pity for the victims. Pity, for France, is 'la plus douce, la plus naturelle, la plus utile des vertus' (V, p. 340); it reconciles him to evil and suffering. In the Prefaces to *The Nigger of the 'Narcissus'* and *A Personal Record* Conrad, echoing France, says that human affairs deserve 'wonder and pity' and 'admiration and pity', and indeed behind his uncompromising irony there undoubtedly lies a strong humane compassion for his characters in their trials. When facing Kurtz's Intended, Marlow's anger subsides before 'a feeling of infinite pity' (*YOS*, p. 161); in *Lord Jim* he feels that Jim's story calls aloud for compassion and asks: 'in what was I better than the rest of us to refuse him my pity?' (p. 129).

However, neither France nor Conrad always kept an even balance between irony and pity. The development in France's attitude is very noticeable: Coignard's considerations on man are 'mêlées de mépris et de bienveillance' (VIII, p. 313), and Bergeret inwardly thanks the story-tellers who have taught us to have 'un bienveillant mépris' for men (XI, p. 330), which he regards as the true science of life, but the professor lacks the benevolence of the Abbé and his irony is more devastating and pitiless. The trend in Conrad seems to be the reverse: in his later phase he looked less bleakly on human failings, but his attitude in his most significant works at times reflects a harshness similar to that of Bergeret. Nor do Irony and Pity hold sway over the same empire in either work: when France deals with matters concerning the Establishment or when Conrad depicts the world of Capitalists, Revolutionaries or Anarchists, irony is predominant; whenever they present poor human beings, pity tips the scales.

We are now faced with what seems to be a startling contradiction in both writers. For, having insisted scornfully on the mediocrity, stupidity, and wickedness of mankind, how can they speak of pity and even love, as in their definition of resignation? The dilemma is that of the thinker, sceptical in his outlook, who is also a man of action, deeply touched by the spectacle of men at grips with the harsh reality of life. Conrad put his finger on this in his review of 'Crainquebille': 'M. Anatole France is something of a Socialist; and in that respect he seems to depart from his sceptical philosophy', but, he adds, France is 'humane', which is why he is able to 'discard his philosophy' because 'love is stronger than truth' (*NLL*, pp. 37–8). With this in mind, we can surely accept Conrad's assertion to Wells: 'I love humanity but know they are not [to be improved].'[24]

# 8 Conrad and Gustave Flaubert

Conrad's conception of the art of the novel was not of Polish origin[1] nor was it derived from English sources, as his disparaging reference to 'The national English novelist' (*LE*, p.132) clearly indicates. In 1928, Richard Curle remarked that it was 'this preoccupation with the technical side of writing in all its aspects which differentiates him [Conrad] so profoundly from previous schools of English novelists'.[2] In that preoccupation with form, technique, and style, Conrad reflects his French background, and especially the tradition of Flaubert and Maupassant.

A continuity of aesthetic concern has long been acknowledged, of course, between Flaubert, Maupassant, James, Conrad and Ford.[3] According to Ford, he and Conrad during their collaboration were not so much interested in writing novels as in working out 'the formulation of a literary theory, Conrad seeking most of all a new form for the novel'.[4] And what brought them together in this search was 'a devotion to Flaubert and Maupassant' around whom their 'eternal technical discussions' revolved, Flaubert being the guiding spirit: 'We read nothing but French,' Ford recalled, 'you might say it was Flaubert, Flaubert, Flaubert all the way.'[5] They 'read daily together over a space of years' Flaubert's correspondence,[6] that amazing document which has been ranked 'among the very few comprehensive *arts poétiques* that have shaped as well as defined the modern novel'.[7]

Baines's view that Conrad 'served [...] no more than an apprenticeship'[8] under Flaubert and Maupassant is widely held to this day. But the Flaubertian aesthetic influence on Conrad can no longer be seen as being confined to his immature works, despite the fact that Conradian criticism has never given a comprehensive answer to the question 'What could Conrad have learned from Flaubert?' any more than Conrad himself had done in his famous letter to Walpole (see above, pp. 12-13).

The impact of Flaubert and Maupassant on him will be studied as one, since Maupassant learned his craft from Flaubert, who enjoyed calling him his 'disciple', and their opinions, even in the wording, reveal striking similarities. And given Conrad's 'saturation' with Maupassant, any study that overlooked the latter's mediating influence would be sadly incomplete. We know, for instance, that by 1897 Conrad had made use of Maupassant's essay 'Le Roman' in his own artistic credo, the Preface to *The Nigger of the 'Narcissus'*. Neverthe-

less, Flaubert, as the source of many of the most important technical innovations made since the middle of the nineteenth century, remains the
fountainhead, being in Robert Liddell's words, 'the patron saint and doctor of
the Novel'.[9]

Henry James expressed the same sentiment when he called Flaubert 'the
novelist's novelist'.[10] Indeed, of all Conrad's contemporaries, James was the
most committed to Flaubert's artistic principles. Flaubert must have been
uppermost in his mind when, in 'The Art of Fiction' (1884), he wrote of 'The
French, who have brought the theory of fiction to remarkable completeness'. [11]
It is not surprising therefore that striking similarities have been found between
James's essay and both Maupassant's 'Le Roman'[12] and Conrad's preface to
The Nigger.[13] Conrad's admiration for his 'cher maître', with whose work he
could already claim in 1905 'some twenty years of attentive acquaintance'
(NLL, p. 12), could only have strengthened his faith in the basic artistic tenets
he had derived from Flaubert and Maupassant.[14]

In general terms, what Conrad inherited was a 'clear conception of his craft'
and of the writer as 'artist', precisely what, in his eyes, the 'national English
novelist' was sadly lacking (LE, p. 132). No artist ever expended more time
and energy to achieve this aim than Flaubert did. In his correspondence, he is
seen, in letter after letter, either attempting to define a particular aspect of the
novel or evaluating the alternatives that were open to him as he was composing.
This supreme artistic awareness appealed immensely to Conrad for, as he once
declared to Davray, 'Savoir ce que l'on veut faire est le fait d'un artiste' (LF,
p. 87). Maupassant, another 'consummate' artist, also possessed 'that exact
knowledge of the means' (NLL, pp. 26, 31) which Conrad valued so highly.
Significantly, after studying Pierre et Jean 'pensée, méthode et tout' in 1894,
his comment to Mme Poradowska concentrates on the 'method': it is the 'complicated mechanism' of the novel which makes him pull his hair and weep in
rage. And when, four years later, he sends Garnett a copy of that 'amazing
masterpiece' Bel-Ami, his only comment bears again on the 'technique' of the
work which, this time, gives him 'acute pleasure' (see above, p. 13). The same
concern with 'method' is still expressed in a letter to Jean-Aubry of 26 August
1920 in which he speaks with envy of the technician and the scientist who write
for people capable of understanding not merely the subject but also 'la méthode'
(LF, p. 157). For him a book is 'a deed', 'an achievement of active life' (LE,
p. 132), the product of 'intelligent action guided by a deliberate view of the
effect to be attained' (CL, II, p. 417). Flaubert and Maupassant, his supreme
artistic mentors, played a key role in the shaping of these basic convictions
and principles, just as they inspired most of his fictional practices, if only
by providing models which crystallized and confirmed his own thoughts and
aspirations and gave him the confidence needed for self-expression.

It must be stressed, however, that influences on matters of aesthetics and
technique are bound to remain problematical compared with those which rest

primarily on incontrovertible verbal correspondences. It is not always easy to decide whether Conrad was actually following in his masters' footsteps or, as he explored new territories, progressing along a parallel path and discovering for himself principles and practices which happened to coincide with theirs. The following description of Conrad's aesthetic inheritance is in no way meant to belittle his originality. Such a description, however, must surely be a prerequisite to any attempt at defining accurately where, in the language of Barthes, he 'distorts his models', [15] that is, where his originality begins to assert itself.

## Unity

Flaubert was by no means the first exponent of unity in the novel. In his Preface to *Alwyn: or the Gentleman Comedian* (1780), Thomas Holcroft distinguished the novel in this respect from the romance: 'Unity of design is its character'; its incidents 'are made to form a whole'.[16] Nevertheless, no novelist before Flaubert had shown anything approaching his intense preoccupation with the overall structure of the work, the interrelationships of the parts, the fusion of all the elements into an integral and harmonious whole. His correspondence is peppered with references to the organization and cohesion of his, and other writers', texts: 'Tout dépend de la conception' (II, p. 339; a saying by Goethe he was fond of repeating); 'les perles ne font pas le collier; c'est le fil. [...] *Tout dépend du plan*' (II, p. 362); 'vous ne faites pas assez attention à la proportion relative de vos parties' (V, p. 180); 'tout est là: faire rentrer le détail dans l'ensemble' (III, p. 163); 'les livres [...] se font [...] comme les pyramides, avec un dessin prémédité' (IV, pp. 239–40). As a result, his verdict on his contemporaries was unequivocal: 'L'unité, l'unité, tout est là! L'ensemble, voilà ce qui manque à tous ceux d'aujourd'hui [...]. Mille beaux endroits, pas une oeuvre' (I, p. 375). Sainte-Beuve described *Madame Bovary* on its publication as 'un livre composé, médité, où tout se tient, où rien n'est laissé au hasard de la plume' (*MB*, p. 527), and it became a critical commonplace that Flaubert's books (with the notable exception of *L'Education sentimentale*) are splendidly organized entities in which the slightest detail or the apparently most casual image is part of some structural scheme or pattern of suggestion contributing to the overall impression.[17]

It has been similarly common to praise Conrad for his taut construction and carefully-timed effects. Flaubert's impact here has been all the more apparent in the sharp contrast between Conrad's novels and those of the Victorians. Curle, for instance, pointed out: 'The truth is, that the unity of the novel is an idea that has been, with the exception of Henry James and George Moore (writers much under Continental influence) upheld by few English-speaking novelists before Conrad.'[18] Both Conrad and Ford emphatically dissociated themselves from the practice of their English predecessors and contemporaries.

In *Thus to Revisit* Ford commented with amusement and bitterness on the slovenliness of the novel in the hands of the Victorians, and Conrad's most critical remark on the 'national English novelist' – mentioning Thackeray by name, and probably referring also to Dickens[19] – was centred on this point: 'He does not go about building up his book with a precise intention and a steady mind' (*LE*, p. 132). One of the main outcomes of his collaboration with Conrad, according to Ford, was the idea of the planned novel where '*every* word set on paper must carry the story forward',[20] where every step must lead towards a calculated effect, and Ford acknowledged that Conrad had the 'greater hold over the architectonics of the novel'.[21] A striking metaphor borrowed from Flaubert shows how carefully Conrad had absorbed his critical views. Flaubert, writing to Sainte-Beuve, pointed to the 'enormous' fault in *Salammbô*: '*Le piédestal est trop grand pour la statue*. Or, comme on ne pèche jamais par *le trop*, mais par *le pas assez*, il aurait fallu cent pages de plus relatives à Salammbô seulement' (V, p. 69; 'le trop' and 'le pas assez' are italicized by Flaubert). In a letter to Arnold Bennett of 19 November 1903 Conrad voiced an identical verdict on *Leonora*: 'the first criticism that occurs is that there is *not enough* of Leonora herself. The pedestal is, as it were, *too large for the statue*' (*CL*, III, p. 80).

As a confirmed organicist who viewed the novel as 'un organisme compliqué' (V, p. 155), Flaubert believed that it must grow naturally, in accordance with some inner principle of its own being.[22] Hence, for him, a good subject was an idea, one and irreducible, 'une idée mère' from which all the others follow, out of which the whole book develops 'tout d'une pièce, *d'un seul jet*' (IV, pp. 463–4). (An echo of the latter part of this statement appears in a remark Conrad made to Cunninghame Graham about his essay 'The Impenitent Thief': 'As to the form: *c'est plus d'un seul jet* if I may say so' (*CL*, II, p. 30).) This new concept of the novel heralded the disappearance of the traditional plot with its emphasis on the story-line designed to illustrate issues clearly stated in explicit commentaries. Maupassant described the change in 'Le Roman': the novelist of the realistic and naturalistic school, he says, does away with 'la ficelle unique' used by the novelist of the romantic type which was called 'l'Intrigue': 'L'habileté de son plan ne consistera donc point dans l'émotion ou dans le charme, dans un début attachant ou dans une catastrophe émouvante, mais dans le groupement adroit de petits faits constants d'où se dégagera le sens définitif de l'oeuvre' (*PJ*, pp. xii–xiii). In this way the themes and moral issues are presented through the 'small facts' which constitute the plot. This means that, however diverse and complex the story-line, the work should remain a unified whole.

Ford observed that Conrad's quest for a 'new form' was made in an effort to break away from the episodic formlessness of the Victorian serialized novel with its multiple plot; the novel in Conrad's hands, he added, gets its unity from 'one embroilment, one set of embarrassments, one human coil, one psychological progression'.[23] What better definition is there of *Madame Bovary*, *Une vie*, *Bel-Ami* and, of course, *Pierre et Jean* whose 'method' Conrad was studying so thoroughly in 1894? Watt comments that in *Almayer's Folly*, 'as in *Madame Bovary*, everything remorselessly forecloses the hopes of the protagonist and contributes to the ordained catastrophe'.[24] This ideal Conrad never abandoned: after he had finished *Lord Jim*, he wrote to Blackwood that the novel is 'the development of *one* situation, only *one* really from beginning to end' (*CL*, II, p. 282) and, years later, he described to Garnett 'the artistic purpose' of *Under Western Eyes* as 'the development of a single mood' (*LEG*, p. 234). Even *A Personal Record*, he stressed in his preface, is not made up of memories 'thrown off without system and purpose' (p. xxi), an assertion he reiterated in a letter to J. M. Dent of 29 March 1919: '*The Reminiscences* are not a collection of loose papers. The book is an elaborately planned whole in a method of my own' (*LL*, II, p. 219).[25]

It seems appropriate to examine some examples of Flaubertian and Conradian practices to determine exactly what kind of practical lessons Conrad could have learned from his predecessor. The obvious case to consider is *Madame Bovary*, that beautifully structured novel, 'tout en calcul' and full of 'profondes combinaisons' (III, pp. 201, 155), whose tightness, solidity, and inexhaustibility derive from a multiplicity of echoes, parallels and contrasts. This was the novel that Conrad was re-reading in 1892 with 'respectful admiration', of which by 1898 he knew 'immense passages by heart', which he imitated in his first work, and from which he borrowed massively during the first decade of his writing career.

*Madame Bovary* is framed by two introductory and concluding chapters from which Emma is absent and where Charles occupies the stage. It is through him that we gain access to her, and after her death we follow her influence on him. The novel consists of three parts, each one following the same movement of degradation of the initial dreams, of deterioration of the promises of satisfaction and happiness. Part I deals with Emma's romantic illusions and builds up a picture of the frustration and monotony she experiences in marital life. Her health declines; leaving Tostes, she burns her wedding bouquet. The first six chapters of part II describe her relationship with Léon and present a sentimental, platonic love affair, again full of frustration. The beginning of the liaison with Rodolphe in chapters 8 and 9 seems to bring all her coveted satisfactions. This is the apex of the pyramid (the *Comices* and the seduction scene come respectively in the seventeenth and eighteenth of the thirty-five chapters) and the period of Emma's fulfilment: 'Jamais elle n'avait eu les yeux si grands, si noirs, ni d'une telle profondeur' (p. 225) and a little later, when at the height of her beauty, 'elle s'épanouissait enfin dans la plénitude de sa nature' (p. 269). But by demanding to elope after the failure of the club-foot operation, she brings about the break with Rodolphe. The episode of carnal love ends in a second illness, serious this time. At the end of part II, Emma, convalescing, goes to the theatre in Rouen where she meets Léon. After a few exchanges during the interval, they are interrupted because 'le troisième acte commençait' (p. 315). Indeed, with the third part of the book, and her third experience with a man, a third stage in her life begins, a life increasingly characterized by duplicity, confusion and moral decay, which ends in despair and death.

The whole of Emma's life is a quest for the meaning of three key-words 'félicité', 'passion', 'ivresse', which she had repeatedly found in romantic novels. Each word is a key to a part of the book, and therefore to a stage in her life. Her progress through life is also suggested by the three cupids which are placed at the beginning of each part and which skilfully link up with the key-words. First, swinging on top of the wedding cake, there is a 'petit Amour' (p. 39), symbol of Romantic love, of the 'bliss' that Emma, whose senses 'ne sont pas encore nés', expects to enjoy in wedlock; then, in front of Guillaumin's house, 'un Amour, le doigt posé sur la bouche' (p. 98), a symbol of the 'passion' she tries to find in her 'secret' adventure with Rodolphe, an experienced man '[qui] lui remue vigoureusement le tempérament'; finally, 'un petit Cupidon de bronze, qui minaudait en arrondissant les bras sous une guirlande dorée' (p. 368) in the Hotel bedroom in Rouen where, now that she is 'mûre des sens',[26] she seeks 'ecstacy' with Léon. Love has given way to erotic desire, and the absence of authenticity suggested by 'smirking' is a link with the theatrical note which introduces this part, and the duplicity of a life which has become 'a web of lies'.[27] A fourth image of Eros, repulsive this time, comes into Emma's life at this final stage: the blind man, who, whether he is regarded as a symbol of her corruption, of death, of damnation, or of the inanity of life, is closely related, with his bawdy song, to her amorous adventures.

Furthermore, the novel is held together by many sets of contrasting characters (Charles and Emma; Léon and Rodolphe; Homais and Bournisien) and numerous contrasting scenes and episodes: the ball at la Vaubyessard and the masked ball; Rodolphe 'chauffant' Emma (Flaubert's word) at the *Comices* and Léon doing the same in Rouen Cathedral; the wedding cortège with the fiddler rosining his bow 'afin que les cordes grinçassent mieux' (p. 38) and the funeral ceremony with the coffin going down and 'les cordes' coming up again 'en grinçant' (p. 467). There are also elaborate networks of key-words, images and symbols which form so many strands in the overall fabric of the text. Thus, in order to convey the clash between dreams and reality, Flaubert contrasts a number of romantic symbols of elevation, of aspiration towards the ideal – the sea, avian imagery, colours or their adjectives, such as blue, white, and pale – with another set of terms and symbols serving to create the image of reality: the theme of the spider (with countless references to spiders, sewing, embroidering, and spinning), the theme of the baker (with important networks of associations such as wheat, flour, bread, baker – Rodolphe Boulanger lives at 'La Huchette', the 'little bread bin'[28] – and powder, dust, ashes, conveying the process of disintegration and annihilation awaiting Emma), and the figure of the circle (*tour, tourner, tournure, cercle*) epitomized in Binet's lathe (*tour*) whose 'ronflement monotone' dominates the world of Yonville, spreading over it somnolence and lethargy. In a world so clearly committed, as Binet's name indicates, to duplication, to repetition, Emma's aspirations and yearnings for change are doomed. While composing his novel, Flaubert affirmed: 'Si jamais les effets d'une symphonie ont été reportés dans un livre, ce sera là' (III, p. 365). It is clear that he made good his aim.[29]

Since Conrad was assiduously imitating and emulating such a model, it is hardly surprising that elaborate structuring and intensive patterning characterize his fiction, in particular *Lord Jim*. The parallels between Emma and Jim, and the similar use of the recurring symbols of sea and fog in both novels have already been noted (see above, pp. 64-8). With its diptych-form, *Lord Jim* constitutes a complex network of interconnections between the *Patna* and Patusan sections (beginning with the phonetic link between the two names). A dominant motif is that of the jump, with Jim leaping first instinctively as a youth from the *Patna* and later voluntarily as a mature man into Doramin's world.[30] With consummate skill Conrad suggests his imprisonment in, and escape from, the rajah's stockade as early as the trial scene, likening his mind while he is testifying to 'a creature that, finding itself imprisoned within an enclosure of high stakes, dashes round and round, distracted in the night, trying to find a weak spot, a crevice, a place to scale, some opening through which it may squeeze itself and escape' (p. 31). It is another conscious touch that Brown should say: 'There are my men in the same boat – and, by God, I am not the sort to jump out of trouble and leave them in a d.....d lurch' (pp. 382-3), thus forcing Jim to recognize that, in moral terms, he may not be better than the disreputable outlaw and cannot 'lord' it over him. The remarkable similarities between the German skipper and Doramin (both deriving from Hannon in *Salammbô*; see above, pp. 70-2) form another system of parallelisms and contrasts binding the two parts of the diptych. On pure grounds of symmetry, the master of the *Patna* is the first person Jim faces in the story proper, the chief of Patusan the last. More important, as Gysin points out, 'In the structure of the novel – in which Stein forms some kind of centre or axis – [they] represent two extreme positions, between which Jim, as a human being, is bound to move: the one, an obscene, wicked clown, is a manifestation of cowardice, temptation, and evil; the other, an imposing, reliable ruler, is an embodiment of courage, trust, and goodness.'[31] In a book built on the juxtaposition of contrasting conceptions of self and antithetical values and codes of conduct (pragmatism / romantic idealism, freedom and isolation / commitment and bondage), this kind of opposition is of paramount significance.

A comparison of two other novels further shows the kind of model provided by Flaubert's works. *Salammbô* begins and ends with a crowd scene, with all eyes focused on an isolated protagonist from the rival collectivity. In the opening scene, the feasting Mercenaries watch, fascinated, as Salammbô springs into view on the upper terrace of Hamilcar's palace and descends towards them. In the final chapter, the relation is inverted: it is the celebrating Carthaginians (some of whom, we are told, remember the Mercenaries' banquet) who watch, equally fascinated, as a vanquished Mâtho comes out of his cell at the top of the Acropolis and walks down towards them to his torture and death. And the two episodes are further linked by unmistakable verbal echoes: 'Mâtho le Libyen se penchait vers elle [Salammbô]. Involontairement elle s'en approcha' (p. 18); 'Dès le premier pas qu'il avait fait, elle s'était levée; puis involontairement, à mesure qu'il se rapprochait, elle s'était avancée' (p. 412). As an admiring student of *Salammbô*, Conrad would no doubt have noticed this structural device which is part of a general system of oppositions that underpins the whole narrative: Carthaginians versus Barbarians.[32] Interestingly, *Under Western Eyes* is also framed by the same kind of symmetrical opposition. First, there is Haldin going down the stairs of Razumov's lodgings in St Petersburg to his betrayal in the outer darkness, with Razumov looking down the staircase (p. 63). Three hundred pages later, it is Razumov who is seen, in Geneva, climbing two flights of stairs 'from the lower darkness' to confess to the revolution (p. 364). What is inscribed in *Salammbô* in the two vivid visual images is the whole story of 'The inexpiable war' between Carthage and the Barbarians and the lamentable fate of two lovers crushed by these terrible events; what is recorded in *Under Western Eyes* in those two brilliantly vivid and symbolic scenes is the whole moral development of a young man, in Claude Thomas's words 'crushed and ground down between the stones of "Absolutisme et Révolution"'.[33]

Beginnings and endings were always for Flaubert matters of the utmost concern. The skill and economy with which he introduced his essential themes are well known. Raymonde Debray-Genette has noted that in the two pages which form chapter 1 in 'Un coeur simple' the elements developed in the rest of the story are already inscribed: 'économie, fermeture, mort, religiosité, charité, dévouement, entêtement, silence, dévitalisation'.[34] In *L'Education sentimentale*, the opening sequence on board the *Ville-de-Montereau* – that 'floating microcosm of industrial society'[35] – suggests the major themes of confusion, immobility, dreams, lust, corruption, boredom and emptiness, while the boat journey itself on the impassive and unchanging Seine, becomes a symbol of the drifting quality of Frédéric's life and that of his generation. Typical in this respect, too, is the brief opening scene in *Madame Bovary* with the description of the new boy, his cap, and his attempt to name himself. Our first view of Charles skilfully suggests the dominant traits of his character: his insignificance, inelegance, clumsiness, docility, timidity, ineffectual goodwill, backwardness, and dullness. The cap, that grotesque and pitiful headgear, can be regarded primarily as a dunce's cap, and, as such, a 'compelling statement' of the chief theme of the book, 'la bêtise'.[36] With its multiplicity of odd shapes and disparate materials, this nondescript artefact is also a fitting symbol of the culture presented in the novel. Then Charles undergoes 'the ordeal of nomination', 'the traumatic entry into language' which provokes howls of derision and the further humiliation and annihilation of having to define himself, through copying and repetition (in a dead and, therefore, alienating language), as ridiculous.[37] It is clear that in these first pages Flaubert managed to set forth all his major themes: stupidity, routine, constriction, loneliness, alienation, incommunicability, failure, meaninglessness. Or, as Brombert observes: 'The entire beginning is under the triple sign of inadequacy, drowsiness, and a passively accepted necessity. The work which ends with Charles' lamentable thought, "It is the fault of fatality!" appropriately begins on a note of resignation.'[38]

According to Ford, he and Conrad realized more than most the primary importance of openings. For them, 'the opening paragraph of book or story should be of the tempo of the whole performance', and since the reader's attention 'must be gripped by that first paragraph', their 'ideal novel must begin either with a dramatic scene or with a note that should suggest the whole book'.[39] Conrad's works readily confirm this. The very first physical detail we learn about Jim suggests that, just as he misses a heroic height by 'an inch, perhaps two' (*LJ*, p. 3), he will not quite reach heroic stature either, as is soon confirmed by the training-ship episode which foreshadows a whole pattern of events. Similarly in *Nostromo* the episode of the gringoes who died in their search for a hidden treasure in the Azuera and whose 'souls cannot tear themselves away from their bodies mounting guard over the discovered treasure' (*N*, p. 5) – although, as Conrad pointed out, 'strictly speaking, [it] has nothing to do with the rest of the novel' (*LL*, II, p. 296) – prefigures the fate of all those who are going to be enslaved by the silver and destroyed by it: Nostromo, Gould, Sotillo, and the whole of Costaguana. (It is another fine instance of patterning that 500 pages later we should be made to recall this episode as the figure of Nostromo sitting 'motionless and awake' all through the night in the black gully on the Great Isabel reveals that 'the silver of San Tomé was provided now with a faithful and lifelong slave' (*N*, p. 501)). Similarly, Jean Deurbergue has shown how economically Conrad introduced his major character with his central conflict, as well as his major themes and symbols, in the first two paragraphs of *Victory*.[40]

The most famous and controversial of Flaubert's endings is undoubtedly that of *L'Education sentimentale*. Despite the critics' hostile reaction especially to the ending, Flaubert was convinced that the last chapter with the bordello incident, far from being an unfunctional appendix, encapsulated the novel as a whole. And in Brombert's words: 'The episode, as remembered by the two friends – though it occurred some time before the events of the novel itself – does in fact sum up, in miniature fashion, a whole pattern of events and meanings'. It suggests, for instance, Frédéric's timidity, his fear of judgement and humiliation, his ineffectual idealism, his tendency to see reality through a

deforming imagination, his dreamy indolence, his vague sense of guilt, his
inconclusive wavering from one woman to another, his basic inability to stick
to any course of action and impose a single direction on his life, his lasting
nostalgia for innocence.[41]

That brilliant example from his favourite book was not lost on the author of
'Heart of Darkness'. In a letter to Blackwood of 31 May 1902, Conrad made
clear that he regarded the anti-climactic scene between Marlow and the
Intended as crucial to the interpretation of the story:

> in the light of the final incident, the whole story in all its descriptive detail shall fall into
> its place – acquire its value and its significance. [...] the interview of the man and the
> girl locks in – as it were – the whole 30000 words of narrative description into one
> suggestive view of a whole phase of life and makes of that story something quite on
> another plane than an anecdote of a man who went mad in the Centre of Africa.
>
> (CL, II, p. 417)

Indeed, the way this scene fits into the thematic and verbal pattern of the
story, 'locks in' the narrative, and shifts it onto another plane is now well
established.[42]

In his overriding quest for unity, Flaubert was also concerned that all the
elements of the work – narration, description, dialogue, inner thoughts – should
fuse together. Replying to Sainte-Beuve's criticism of *Salammbô*, he stressed
the importance he attached to description for the development of both character
and action: 'Il n'y a point dans mon livre une description isolée, gratuite; toutes
*servent* à mes personnages, et ont une influence lointaine ou immédiate sur
l'action' (V, pp. 60–1).[43] The descriptions of nature, in particular, imbued as
they are with symbolic resonance, are clearly made to integrate with the major
themes. Thus, in *Madame Bovary*, *L'Education* and 'Un coeur simple' the vast,
flat, empty, monotonous countrysides on which the characters gaze become
striking symbols of their dull, empty, and wasted lives.

Conrad's fiction is also characterized by a harmonious integration of all its
elements, with natural description forwarding the narrative and the development of themes by preparing events and throwing light on characters. After
reading *The Rescue*, Gide wrote to Conrad: 'Et que dire des descriptions de
paysages? Les plus belles, me semble-t-il, que vous ayez jamais données; insép-
arables de l'action et donnant forme aux sentiments des personnages.'[44] The
'angry and muddy' river that Almayer watches with 'inattentive eyes' as it
carries 'small drift-wood and big dead logs, and whole uprooted trees' becomes,
in contrast with his 'dream of splendid future' (*AF*, pp. 3, 4), a symbol of his
helplessness and disastrous fate. Similarly, in the opening of 'The End of the
Tether', the description of the sunrays which fall 'violently' upon the calm sea
and seem 'to shatter themselves [...] into a dazzling vapour of light that blinded
the eye' (*YOS*, p. 165) foreshadows the fate awaiting Captain Whalley and the
Sofala. Physical settings, we recall, are used as images to convey the ambiguity

and elusiveness of Jim's nature (see above, p. 68). That Conrad consciously imitated his French mentors in this respect has already been illustrated by comparisons of autumn scenes in *Une vie* and 'The Idiots' and of river landscapes in *L'Education* and 'The End of the Tether' (see above, pp. 32 and 80–2).

The organic conception of the work also entailed a rigorous control of its imagery. Flaubert was most insistent on this point; when working on *Madame Bovary*, he stressed: 'Il faut ainsi que tout sorte du sujet, idées, comparaisons, métaphores, etc.' (II, p. 439); 'Il faut que les métaphores soient rigoureuses et justes d'un bout à l'autre' (III, p. 70). The aptness of some images is immediately apparent, as for instance, when, in this bovine world, Yonville, seen from a distance stretched out along the river-bank, is likened to 'un gardeur de vaches qui fait la sieste au bord de l'eau' (*MB*, p. 97). Others are more complex and require a more detailed grasp of the book. As Emma contrasts her own boring life in Tostes with the dazzling lives she imagines her convent friends to be leading, we read: 'Mais elle, sa vie était froide comme un grenier dont la lucarne est au nord, et l'ennui, araignée silencieuse, filait sa toile dans l'ombre à tous les coins de son coeur' (p. 62). One can hear Emma saying to herself: 'Ma vie, à moi, est froide, froide! … Froide comme le grenier, là-haut.' The propriety of the simile rests on the circumstances and the truth of what is 'mimed' direct speech. Flaubert then takes over, adding the realistic detail of 'the skylight looking North' and the following metaphor, which would hardly have occurred to Emma but is most appropriate as part of the elaborate network of references to spiders and spinning throughout the novel. The sentence also relates to the major theme (dreams versus reality) by carefully balancing the realism of the spider spinning its web in the cold and dark attic with the 'romantic' terms dear to Emma: 'ennui', 'silencieuse', 'ombre', 'coeur'.[45] When Proust declared that there was not a single beautiful metaphor in Flaubert, he was missing the point. Flaubert's images are not ornamental but functional. In *Madame Bovary*, Flaubert told the Goncourts, he had tried to render 'un ton gris, cette couleur de moisissure [mouldiness] d'existences de cloportes [woodlice]'.[46] In this grey, drab world, images had to be grey and drab if unity of tone was to be maintained.[47]

In Conrad's best fiction, the images cannot be judged apart from their context and the work as a whole any more than can Flaubert's, because they, too, function thematically. Marlow's vision of Kurtz as 'an animated image of death carved out of old ivory' (*YOS*, p. 134), picked up later in a reference to his 'ivory face' (p. 149), not only suggests the dehumanization of the man who has come to resemble the object of his desire, but also connects the image of death (physical and spiritual) with the colour white, symbol of Western colonialism. And Marlow's comparison of the grand piano, in the mausoleum-like drawing-room of Kurtz's Intended, to 'a sombre and polished sarcophagus' (p. 156), extends an amazingly complex network of thematic and lexical patterns binding together the Sepulchral City, Kurtz's station, and the Intended's house. Yelton, Dowden, Inamdar and many other critics have shown the skill with which Conrad's imagery is constantly brought to bear on the dominant themes and woven into elaborate patterns to create a cohesive structure.

## Selection

Despite the label 'realist' applied to him, to his exasperation, on the publication of *Madame Bovary*,[48] Flaubert always emphasized: 'l'Art n'est pas la Nature' (VIII, p. 309). He told Louise Colet, while composing *Madame Bovary*, of his desire to write all he saw, not as it was, but 'transfiguré' (III, p. 320). And near the end of his life, he compared reality to a 'springboard' from which the creative artist must rise to higher levels: 'La vérité matérielle (ou ce qu'on appelle ainsi) ne doit être qu'un tremplin pour s'élever plus haut.' *Salammbô* is not 'une vraie reproduction de Carthage' nor is '*Saint Antoine* une peinture exacte de l'Alexandrinisme'; what he has tried to express is 'l'idéal' (VIII, p. 374). And the fault he found with *L'Education sentimentale* was precisely that it was too realistic: 'C'est trop vrai et, esthétiquement parlant, il y manque: *la fausseté de la perspective*' (VIII, p. 309). A few months earlier, in a letter to Huysmans, he had made the same criticism of the latter's *Les Soeurs Vatard* – along with *L'Education* – and added that it lacked 'progression d'effet', meaning that the effect produced by the narrative was too even (VIII, p. 224; the term 'progression d'effet' already appears in connection with *Salammbô* in V, p. 69). Hence his insistence that to create the illusion of reality, the novelist must carefully select and even heighten his details, and make them fit harmoniously into the overall pattern: 'L'art n'est pas la réalité. Quoiqu'on fasse, on est obligé de choisir dans les éléments qu'elle fournit' (VIII, p. 224); 'on ne peut faire vrai qu'en choisissant et en exagérant. [...] exagérer harmonieusement' (*Supp.* II, p. 118).

Similarly, in his study of Flaubert (1884), Maupassant declared that one had only to read *Madame Bovary* 'with intelligence' to understand that nothing is further away from realism (*MB*, p. 544).[49] And in 'Le Roman' (1887) he rejected Realist and Naturalist claims to present 'the truth, the whole truth and nothing but the truth' and stressed that the principles of selection, arrangement, emphasis, in a word of interpretation, apply to the realistic novel just as they do to any form of art. Even with a 'naturalistic' writer, he said, 'la vérité dans la vie diffère de la vérité dans son livre' for, whereas life leaves everything on the same level, art on the contrary eliminates inessential events, highlights the essential ones, and gives to others a relief according to their importance in order to render the special truth that the novelist wishes to portray. 'Le réaliste, s'il est un artiste, cherchera, non pas à nous montrer la photographie banale de la vie, mais à nous en donner la vision plus complète, plus saisissante, plus probante que la réalité même' (*PJ*, pp. ix, x, xiv).

The importance Ford and Conrad attached to these ideas is well-known. In *Joseph Conrad: A Personal Remembrance* Ford recalls that they 'agreed that the whole of Art consists in selection'.[50] He also devoted a chapter to the notion of 'Progression d'effet', a term 'for which there is no English equivalent' and which they used in their discussions to designate an increase in the tempo and intensity of the narrative.[51] Although Ford claimed that they discovered it during their collaboration on *Romance*, it seems fairly obvious that the origin of their 'discovery' lies in Flaubert's correspondence, which they were assiduously reading at that time.

In describing 'the national English novelist' as being 'always at his best in denunciations of institutions, of types or of conventionalized society', Conrad – however unfairly – saw Dickens and Thackeray in their emphasis on 'rendering the disagreeable' as 'neglecting the one indispensable thing, neglecting to use their powers of selection and observation' (*LE*, pp. 132, 133). An attitude similar to Flaubert's and Maupassant's also prompted his criticism of Arnold Bennett's *Man from the North*. Just as Flaubert thought that *L'Education* lacked a summit, that the light on it was too even, Conrad found that Bennett's novel required 'a more emphatic modelling; more relief', showing how much he was at one with the French masters in his quest for a higher realism: 'You stop just short of being absolutely real because you are faithful to your dogmas of realism. Now realism in art will never approach reality. And your art, your gift should be put to the service of a larger and freer faith' (*CL*, II, p. 390).

In order to present this more comprehensive vision, the artist must shun the contingent, the relative, the ephemeral. To universalize was a tenet that constantly inspired Flaubert's artistic practice. Late in life, he confided to George Sand: 'Je me suis toujours efforcé d'aller dans l'âme des choses et de m'arrêter aux généralités les plus grandes, et je me suis détourné exprès de l'accidentel et du dramatique. Pas de monstres et pas de héros!' (VII, p. 281). Maupassant shows a similar concern when he says that the 'modern' novelist must use only 'des faits d'une vérité irrécusable et constante' (*PJ*, p. xiii), as does Conrad when he describes the aim of the work of art as 'an attempt to find [...] in the aspects of matter and in the facts of life what of each is fundamental, what is enduring and essential' (*NN*, p. vii). The artists he admired most, such as Maupassant and Turgenev, were precisely those who saw 'the essential' (*CL*, II, p. 150; *NLL*, p.48), and, in July 1923, he suggested to Curle that he begin an essay for the *Times Literary Supplement* with 'a couple of short paragraphs of general observation on authors and their material, how they transform it from particular to general, and appeal to universal emotions by the temperamental handling of personal experience' (*LRC*, p. 195).

To achieve this generalizing and universalizing aim, Flaubert, Maupassant, and Conrad exploited types. To a correspondent who had enquired about the original of Emma, Flaubert replied that no model had posed for him and that all the characters in *Madame Bovary* were completely imaginary; had he kept his eyes on individuals, his portraits would have been less lifelike; but, on the contrary, his intention had been to 'reproduire des types' (IV, p. 192). For Flaubert, who always sought the eternal in man, what distinguishes geniuses is 'la généralisation et la création'; they sum up scattered personalities in a type and bring forth new characters to the consciousness of mankind (III, p. 31). Hence the influence of *Don Quixote* on the conception of Emma, who is not merely a dreamy provincial but a type embodying a general tendency of the human psyche, never before so clearly identified but now crystallized in the concept of *bovarysme*. Although Flaubert's characters come alive as individuals, they stand for more than themselves, for 'toute individualité idéale, fortement rendue, résume' (III, p. 174). As a result, we can all recognize, in ourselves or others, something of Emma Bovary, Frédéric Moreau or Saint Antoine.

When W. L. Courtney, in his review of *The Nigger*, introduced Conrad as 'an unflinching realist', Conrad, far from being flattered, denied in his reply that Donkin was real: 'In my desire to be faithful to the ethical truth I have sacrificed the truth of the individual' (*CL*, I, p. 421). In fact, this sacrifice is not confined to Donkin in *The Nigger*. For whatever reasons, Conrad once deplored having made Kurtz 'symbolic' (*CL*, II, p. 460). Indeed, Kurtz's story is no mere case-history – with similarities to, say, Rimbaud's life – of an uncommon man going mad in the African interior, but, as Conrad was at pains to stress, 'something quite on another plane' (*CL*, II, p. 417). Inevitably, the particular has been raised to the universal, for the reason that, as he maintained, 'the nearer [a work] approaches art, the more it acquires a symbolic character' (*LL*, II. p. 205), or, as the supposedly arch-realist-and-naturalist Maupassant affirmed: 'Une oeuvre d'art n'est supérieure que si elle est, en même temps, un symbole et l'expression exacte d'une réalité' (*La Vie errante*, p. 122). Flaubert's works, like all great creations, support this view, successfully integrating as they do realism and symbolism.[52] Conrad too, in his dramas of conflicting ethical codes and ideologies, always magnifies and universalizes. (The symbolic value of characters' names in the fiction of both authors clearly shows this tendency: Bovary, Rouault (*roue, routine*), Homais (*homme*), Binet, Lheureux, Félicité; Wait, Singleton, Mahon ('pronounced Mann' (*YOS*, p. 5)), Kurtz, Whalley, Nostromo, Leggatt, Razumov, Lena, Ransome, etc.).[53]

Flaubert drew a sharp distinction between what he called 'la vérité *réelle*' and 'la vérité artistique, idéale' which he regarded as the only proper concern of the novelist.[54] He was quite content that *Salammbô* should be no more than 'probable' (IV, p. 211). What he had tried to convey was a colour ('pourpre'), and the 'ideal'.[55] It is obvious that Conrad also wrote with a transcendental idea or goal in mind. When working on *Lord Jim*, he referred to 'an idea – apart from the idea and the subject of the story – which guides me in my writing' (*CL*, II, p. 194). And he, too, made clear in a letter of March 1917 that he would have none of the labels that had been attached to him, adding:

as a matter of fact all my concern has been with the 'ideal' value of things, events and people. That and nothing else. The humorous, the pathetic, the passionate, the sentimental *aspects* came in of themselves – *mais en vérité c'est les valeurs idéales des faits et gestes humains qui se sont imposés à mon activité artistique.*                    (*LL*, II, p. 185)

It is, no doubt, this quest for a 'vérité artistique idéale' or 'les valeurs idéales' which, in Maupassant's words, enables fiction to give us a vision of life 'fuller, more vivid, and more compellingly truthful than even reality itself'. For Conrad, too, a novel is 'a form of imagined life clearer than reality' (*PR*, p. 15). And his reaction to a visit from a lady who had interrupted him as he was intensely engrossed in the world of Costaguana, shows the strength of this conviction:

Interrupted – indeed! She had robbed me of at least twenty lives, each infinitely more poignant and real than her own, because informed with passion, possessed of convictions, involved in great affairs created out of my own substance for an anxiously meditated end.                                             (*PR*, p. 102)

To attain this 'ideal' quality in his fiction, the novelist must possess equally the two great faculties of observation and imagination, because, as Flaubert put it, 'on n'est idéal qu'à la condition d'être réel et on n'est vrai qu'à force de généraliser' (V, p. 379). Unbridled imagination on its own is insufficient: he once denounced 'these masked balls of imagination' he knew only too well and from which one returns 'exhausted', having seen only 'something false' (V, p. 379). It has to be controlled by constant reference to reality in which the work must be firmly rooted. Conversely, mere observation, whether it be of oneself or others, will never lead to the discovery and presentation of general truths: 'c'est un sujet *de toi*,' he warns Louis Colet, 'et en imaginant on reproduit la généralité, tandis qu'en s'attachant à un fait *vrai*, il ne sort de votre oeuvre que quelque chose de contingent, de relatif, de restreint' (III, p. 401). This is why, on being told of her intention to visit an alms-house to write her poem 'La Servante', he again warned:

Prends garde que cette visite *n'influe trop*. Ce n'est pas une bonne méthode que de voir ainsi tout de suite, pour écrire immédiatement après. On se préoccupe trop des détails, de la couleur, et pas assez de son esprit [...]. La couleur, comme les aliments, doit être digérée et mêlée au sang des pensées.                              (III, p. 263)

For Flaubert, observation as practised by the Naturalists could only produce a mass of unconnected data. 'Il ne s'agit pas seulement de voir, il faut arranger et fondre ce que l'on a vu. La Réalité, selon moi, ne doit être qu'un tremplin' (VII, p. 359). Only imagination can 'fuse' the disparate elements provided by reality into a single, harmonious artistic form, raising the work from 'la vérité réelle' to 'la vérité artistique idéale'.

Conrad's scrupulous endeavour to do 'justice to the visible universe' (*NN*, p. vii) shows how greatly he valued that 'rare' faculty of observation he so appreciated in Maupassant (*NLL*, p. 27). Yet, like Flaubert, he adopted a detached attitude towards reality and the material which observation yielded. In 1923, he wrote to Garnett about a young writer who 'should be warned against [...] a too close contemplation of his subject' (*LEG*, p. 293). As he knew from experience, far from being a help to the creative artist, reality could be a hindrance. In the midst of writing what was then 'Two Vagabonds', he had complained to his 'aunt' about his characters being 'so true'; he knew them so well that 'they trammelled his imagination' ['ils m'entravent l'imagination'] (*CL*, I, p. 169). And later, he had faced the same problem with *The Secret Agent*: 'I had to fight hard to keep at arms-length the memories of my solitary and nocturnal walks all over London in my early days,' he recalled, 'lest they should rush in and overwhelm each page of the story as these emerged one after another' (p. xiii). His most significant works are the product of the same creative process as described by Flaubert to the 'muse': 'J'ai imaginé, je me suis ressouvenu et j'ai combiné. Ce que tu as lu n'est le souvenir de rien du tout' (I, p. 254).[56] Conrad, too, regarded imagination, the esemplastic faculty, as the greatest faculty of the novelist. In 'Books' he declared, 'Liberty of imagination should be the most precious possession of a novelist,' and concluded by inviting the artist to 'mature the strength of his imagination' (*NLL*, pp. 7–8, 10). In this respect, he regarded his two French masters as supreme exemplars: in 1904, at the height of his powers, his final appraisal of Maupassant was: 'This creative artist has the true imagination' (*NLL*, p. 31); and what already impressed him most in 1892 while re-reading *Madame Bovary* with 'respectful admiration' was the fact that there was a truly 'creative' author, endowed with 'enough imagination for two realists' (see above, p. 11).

## Impersonality

In the history of the novel Flaubert remains the greatest exponent of authorial impersonality. He believed that 'La première qualité de l'Art et son but est l'*illusion*' (III, p. 344) and that its inevitable corollary was the impersonality of the artist: 'L'illusion (s'il y en a une)' he said of *Madame Bovary* 'vient [...] de l'*impersonnalité* de l'oeuvre' (IV, p. 164). The novelist's task is to absorb the 'object' and, through some 'chimie merveilleuse' (III, p. 383), to reproduce it: 'L'art est une représentation, nous ne devons penser qu'à représenter' (III, p. 21). His only concern, therefore, should be with showing the truth: 'soyons *exposants* et non discutants' (III, p. 163). This, of course, precludes his using the novel to express his feelings or convictions. He must not put his own personality forward; he must, through mental effort, 'se transporter dans les personnages, et non les attirer à soi' (V, p. 257).[57] This anti-romantic stance, instead of equating 'inspiration' and personal emotion with artistic worth, stresses that writing a novel is essentially an intellectual procedure: 'On n'écrit pas avec son coeur, mais avec sa tête' (III, p. 30). Flaubert constantly advocates control: everything should be done 'à froid, posément' (III, p. 105) because *'Moins on sent une chose, plus on est apte à l'exprimer comme elle est* (comme elle est *toujours* en elle-même, dans sa généralité et dégagée de tous ses contingents éphémères)' (II, p. 462). His attitude is best summed up in his famous pronouncement:

> L'auteur, dans son oeuvre, doit être comme Dieu dans l'univers, présent partout, et visible nulle part. L'Art étant une seconde nature, le créateur de cette nature-là doit agir par des procédés analogues. Que l'on sente dans tous les atomes, à tous les aspects, une impassibilité cachée et infinie. L'effet, pour le spectateur, doit être une espèce d'ébahissement. *Comment tout cela s'est-il fait?* doit-on dire, et qu'on se sente écrasé sans savoir pourquoi.
> (III, pp. 61-2)[58]

This impassivity – now known as 'aesthetic distance' – made irony his privileged mode of expression. He described his ideal to Louise Colet:

> Quand est-ce donc que l'on fera de l'histoire comme on doit faire du roman, sans amour ni haine d'aucun des personnages? Quand est-ce qu'on écrira les faits au point de vue d'une *blague supérieure*, c'est-à-dire comme le bon Dieu les voit, d'en haut?
> (III, p. 37)

Significantly, in his 1876 article on Flaubert, Maupassant asserted, no doubt with his approval: 'M. Flaubert est avant tout un artiste; c'est-à-dire: un auteur impersonnel.' Flaubert, he argued, never steps forward for a chat with his public, nor does a character ever become his mouthpiece; he is 'le montreur de marionnettes humaines qui doivent parler par sa bouche, tandis qu'il ne s'accorde point le droit de penser par la leur; et il ne faut pas qu'on aperçoive les ficelles ou qu'on reconnaisse la voix'. [59] In 1884 Maupassant again recorded Flaubert's insistence that the true artist should not allow 'une seule parcelle de son opinion, rien qu'une apparence d'intention' to come through: if a book carries any kind of teaching, it must be despite its author 'par la force même des choses qu'il raconte' (*MB*, pp. 542–3).[60] Flaubert's main objections to all didactic purposes – as indeed to any form of personal outpouring – were that they are bound to lead to digressions and repetitions which are detrimental to the unity of the work,[61] and, by precluding a proper scientific approach, to impair the truth of its 'representation' and, therefore, its universality.[62]

For a long time all of Flaubert's and Maupassant's declarations, however hyperbolic, were accepted literally; exaggerated claims were made about their 'objectivity', and the principle of the total disappearance of the author from his work was erected as an absolute. As a result, in the sixties, critics like Wayne Booth and George Levine easily showed that Flaubert had failed to live up to his stated intentions and was a constant presence in his own novels, not only in overt intrusions (addresses to the reader, judgements on the characters, generalizing maxims, satirical tone) but also, more subtly, in his handling of evaluative language (as, for example, his use of imagery) down to the selection of details.[63] A more discriminating appraisal of Flaubert's intentions now prevails. His declarations, it is realized, have to be seen in their historical context. It is likely that what he advocated was a relative impersonality as compared with the practices of his contemporaries, Stendhal, Balzac or Sand. The following comments to a correspondent show him attacking the worst excesses prevalent at the time: 'Pourquoi parlez-vous en votre nom? pourquoi faites-vous des réflexions qui coupent le récit? Je n'aime pas les locutions comme celle-ci: "Notre héros, lecteur ..." Une réflexion morale ne vaut pas une analyse' (VI, p. 104). And in saying that the author must be 'like God in the universe, present everywhere, but visible nowhere' he is making a distinction between the narrator and the man: presence of the former, invisibility of the latter.[64]

Flaubert was well aware that the novelist cannot keep himself out of his work ('Madame Bovary, c'est moi!') and that total objectivity in fiction is therefore impossible. But he also knew that there are varying degrees of subjectivity, and he was convinced that new fictional standards could be achieved with the ideal of objectivity in mind. Maupassant also realized the limitations of the principle of impersonality. In 'Le Roman' he acknowledged that the novelist cannot escape from his 'moi' since nature has surrounded it with an insuperable barrier of organs, and so it is always this 'I' which shows in the characters. The skill lies in not letting it be identified by the reader 'sous tous les masques divers' which he uses to hide it (*PJ*, pp. xix-xx).[65] Both Flaubert and Maupassant recognized that the world created within the novel is the product of one perceiving mind, which cannot but communicate its 'vision personnelle du monde' (*PJ*, p. xi), and that the impersonality of the artist is primarily a matter of technique, a method of presentation, affecting not the subject-matter but the way it is expressed.[66] Flaubert knew only too well that he could not help but have his own opinion, but he was adamant: '[The artist] peut la communiquer, mais je n'aime pas à ce qu'il la dise' (V, pp. 396–7). In other words, he must express it indirectly, in a representative form. Similarly, Maupassant says that the novelist must build his work in such a way that it is impossible to discover his intentions.[67]

Both Ford and Conrad adopted impersonality as one of their chief artistic tenets; and both made it clear that in so doing they firmly placed themselves in a French tradition of fiction. The second point in Conrad's two-pronged attack on the 'national English novelist' is that he regards his work 'simply as an instinctive, often unreasoned, outpouring of his own emotions', that he is 'writing lyrically', i.e. 'expressing his own moods' (*LE*, p. 132). In the same vein, Ford portrayed the English novelist as a happy-go-lucky amateur with vine-leaves in his hair, whose novel was the recording of his 'moods of exaltation'.[68] The first lesson an author has to learn, he declared, is that of humility: 'Before everything [he] must learn to suppress himself'. Just as Flaubert had proclaimed: 'L'artiste doit s'arranger de façon à faire croire à la postérité qu'il n'a pas vécu' (II, p. 380), Ford and Conrad agreed that 'the object of the novelist

is to keep the reader entirely oblivious of the fact that the author exists'.[69] And
Ford, who repeatedly proclaimed his admiration for the impersonality he saw
in the works of French writers, acknowledged that, once again, their supreme
exemplar was Flaubert:

> It was Flaubert who most shiningly preached the doctrine of the novelist as Creator
> who should have a Creator's aloofness, rendering the world as he sees it, uttering no
> comments, falsifying no issues and carrying the subject – the Affair – he has selected for
> rendering, remorselessly out to its logical conclusion.
> There came thus into existence the novel of Aloofness.[70]

Impersonality, however, never meant aloofness for Flaubert, who had a
genuine capacity for sympathetic identification with his characters,[71] and whose
programme included having 'de la sympathie pour *tout* et pour *tous*' in order to
understand them and describe them well (IV, p. 243). There is no denying, for
instance, the sympathy with which he treats Emma and Félicité.

A letter to Unwin of 9 August 1896 already shows Conrad's strong attachment
to the notion of impersonality; what he most admires in Louis Becke as a story-
teller, he says, is 'The sacrifice of his individuality in the interest of the work.
He stands magnificently aloof from the poignancy and humour of his stories'
(*CL*, I, p. 298). Conrad's critical writings often express admiration for those
who achieved 'objectivity' (Flaubert, Maupassant, James, Crane, Turgenev)
and criticize those who indulge in subjective rhetoric (Daudet, Dostoevskii,
Thackeray, and Dickens[72] being the prime targets). Writing to Galsworthy on
11 November 1901 (at the height of his collaboration with Ford) Conrad advises
his friend: 'As against your people you must preserve an attitude of perfect
indifference, the part of creative power. A creator must be indifferent.' And
he concludes, directly in line with Flaubert's thinking, that Galsworthy's attitude to his characters should be 'purely intellectual, more independent, freer,
less rigorous than it is' (*CL*, II, p. 359), that he should not hug his 'conceptions
of right or wrong too closely' (*CL*, II, p. 359).

Conrad admonishes Galsworthy moreover, using the same 'spatial' imagery
as Flaubert and Maupassant. He warns the creator that 'directly the "Fiat!"
had issued from his lips there are the creatures made in his image that'll try to
drag him down from his eminence' (*CL*, II, p. 359). Flaubert, we recall, advocated that facts should be presented as God sees them, 'd'en haut'. And this he
did, according to Maupassant: 'Au lieu de rester au milieu des foules, il s'isole
dans une tour pour considérer ce qui se passe sur la terre'; he is 'impassible au-
dessus des passions qu'il agite'.[73] The same imagery is used in Conrad's negative
assessment of Daudet made in January 1898. Daudet did not 'affect a passive
attitude before the spectacle of life'; he 'whose business it ought to have been
to climb, in the name of Art, some elevation or other, was content to remain
below, on the plain, amongst his creations' (*NLL*, p. 21).[74]

Nothing better reveals how strongly Conrad felt on this subject than his essay on Maupassant in 1904. The previous year, Ford, in his preface to the Martindale selection, had singled out impersonality as one of the most characteristic qualities of Maupassant's fiction. He had stated that 'the first duty of an artist is not to comment and, precisely, not to moralise', and had praised 'Night' (one of those stories of which they already knew 'immense passages' by heart when they first met (see above, pp. 10, 13-14)) for its 'unerring' selection and presentation of 'concrete instances' whilst 'No moral is drawn'.[75] Conrad, in his turn, notes that Maupassant's philosophy, as it is revealed in his 'determinism, barren of praise, blame and consolation', does not matter in the case of 'so consummate an artist'. His point of view, although 'consistently preserved' is 'never obtruded for the end of personal gratification'. With his 'artistic honesty', he refuses to be led away from 'the vouchsafed vision of excellence' by the 'seductions of sentiment, of eloquence, of humour, of pathos'. Because of 'the austerity of his talent', Maupassant 'refrains from setting his cleverness against the eloquence of the facts'. And his facts are 'so perfectly rendered' that 'his high qualities appear inherent in the very things of which he speaks, as if they had been altogether independent of his presentation' (*NLL*, pp. 26–7).

'A Familiar Preface' shows that, despite the strong debt to Anatole France – who regarded Flaubert's theoretical ideal as an 'aberration' – Conrad still held to the principle of authorial self-effacement at the end of 1911. Of course, he recognizes, like Anatole France and Maupassant, that 'a novelist lives in his work' and that whatever he is writing about 'he is only writing about himself'. But, like Flaubert, who declares that the artist 'should be felt everywhere but seen nowhere' (IV, p. 164), Conrad asserts that he must be 'a suspected rather than a seen presence', and just as Maupassant sees the artist hiding behind various 'masks', Conrad sees him as 'a figure behind the veil', 'a movement and a voice behind the draperies of fiction' (*PR*, p. xiii).

The fact that Conrad's response to fellow novelists seems to have been prompted primarily by how far they attain this Flaubertian ideal gives the measure of his attachment to it. For those, like Daudet and Dickens, who are constantly seen and heard, he may have 'affection'; but his 'admiration' (and in the case of Flaubert one can even speak with Ford of his 'veneration' (see above, p. 10)) is reserved for the 'rare mortal[s]' and 'godlike' artists (*NLL*, p. 21) who have practised self-effacement. His reactions stem from another conviction he shared with Flaubert, who declared: 'L'homme n'est rien, l'oeuvre tout' (VII, p. 280). In August 1908, Conrad expressed his gratitude to Arthur Symons for 'the recognition of the work, not the man' because 'Once the last page is written the man does not count' (*LL*, II, p. 73). Flaubert's dictum that art must remain 'complet en lui-même, indépendant de son producteur' (II, p. 379) is echoed in Conrad's reference to the novelist's task as 'the independent creation of cirumstance and character' (*NLL*, p. 15).

However, it is one thing to be committed to a principle and another to put it into practice: after praising Becke for standing 'magnificently aloof', Conrad candidly and wistfully adds: 'A thing I could never do – and which I envy him' (*CL*, I, p. 298), for contradictory needs and impulses were at war in Conrad. On one hand, Flaubert's ideal of authorial invisibility must have appealed strongly to the private man for whom 'an open display of sentiment [was] repugnant' (*PR*, p. xvi), and to the dedicated artist for whom the work came first. On the other, Conrad, unlike Flaubert, never adhered to the creed of *l'art pour l'art*, no doubt because his conception of the artist's role precluded him from ever detaching himself from his fellow human beings. Flaubert, for whom Art subsumed all other passions, tended to consider any human phenomenon – even the loss of his beloved sister – as something for him to exploit ('il faut [...] *profiter de tout*' (III, p. 225)) and turn into the stuff of fiction. Conrad indirectly dissociated himself from this attitude when, in 'A Familiar Preface', he declared that as a man who started writing at the age of thirty-six, he could not 'bring himself to look upon his existence and his experience [...] as only so much material for his hands' (*PR*, pp. xiii–xiv). Again, unlike Flaubert who, with his mystical conception of 'l'Art sacro-saint' (VIII, p. 99) viewed literary creation as a godlike activity, Conrad refused 'to lay a claim of exclusive superiority' for it, regarding it as 'only one of the legitimate forms of human activity' (*NLL*, p. 7).

Indeed, whatever reservations Conrad may have had about the principle of impersonality for temperamental or moral reasons, he still attached so much importance to it that a number of his oblique techniques – such as the central narrator, the frame and the briefly dramatized narrator, the doubling of characters, the time-shifts, and possibly the symbols – can be seen as so many attempts to secure the detachment he knew a work of art requires, and thereby solve his own dilemma.[76]

According to Watson, Conrad was unable to maintain such detachment when he explored themes of considerable significance to him or in the intimate treatment of sympathetic characters. In his early stories he can be seen groping his way towards a narrative voice compatible with his own temperament, a voice that would enable him to maintain proper aesthetic distance while producing 'the deep psychic and moral resonances he was seeking in his fiction'.[77]

Crankshaw argued that in *Almayer's Folly* Conrad 'attempted to take not only the principles but the method of *Madame Bovary* to himself', that he was a failure at the 'apparatus of analysis' and was 'temperamentally incapable of revealing *objectively* [...] the train of thought of a character alien to himself'. His only option, therefore, was to create a narrator who would be both 'the impersonal author's concrete deputy or delegate'[78] and a character in his own right who, as an involved spectator, could comment, judge, philosophize and moralize as he could not do in his own name.[79]

This is the method Conrad chose in the spring of 1898 when he created Marlow as the central narrator of 'Youth', and the 'speculation' about Marlow's origins to which he refers in his Author's Note (*YOS*, p. v) still goes on. Claims have been made in favour of the three traditions Conrad knew best,[80] but it is likely that no one explanation contains the whole truth since a number of factors must have been simultaneously at work. Polish scholars see a connection between this aspect of Conrad's narrative technique and the old Polish *gawęda*, or yarn, defined by Busza as 'a loose, informal narrative, told by a speaker in the manner of someone reminiscing. It is often involved and full of digressions. Little attention is paid to chronology. At first, seemingly unimportant details and fragmentary episodes come to the fore, then gradually a coherent picture emerges. By the time the speaker has finished, everything has fallen into place'.[81] The relevance to Conrad is obvious, especially since the *gawęda* first appeared in Polish literature during the romantic period to which, through his father, he was very much attached. However, a similar practice can be observed in many tales by Maupassant. It is true that Maupassant is most famous for his swift and direct technique of narration, but he is also a master in the handling of leisurely and apparently rambling narrative when the need arises. With the tradition of the *gawęda* behind him, Conrad would not only respond to Maupassant's handling of the frame but be stimulated to try his own variations on it in 'Youth', 'Heart of Darkness', 'Amy Foster' and 'Falk'.[82] Its contribution to the creation of Marlow can hardly be doubted.[83]

Although the influence of Flaubert and Maupassant on Conrad's narrative technique seems to have been decisive during the period 1896–1898, it certainly did not end then: *Nostromo* and *The Secret Agent* have been described as his 'Flaubertian novels'.[84] One of the hallmarks of the works of the major phase is indeed that kind of 'binocular vision' that Thibaudet saw as typical of Flaubert, enabling him to present the aspirations and experiences of his characters with a running counterpoint of ironic realism. As for *The Secret Agent*, no doubt Conrad's most devastatingly ironic work, its affinities with Flaubert's art are not far to seek. Because for Flaubert irony 'dominates life', his characters often perform actions and utter statements which show them to be totally unaware of how these could be interpreted ironically. Notorious is the example of Charles urging Emma to accept Rodolphe's 'gracieuses' propositions to accompany her horse-riding, and later writing to him 'que sa femme était à sa disposition, et qu'ils comptaient sur sa complaisance' (*MB*, p. 218). This is also typical of that 'ironic treatment' on which Conrad prided himself (*SA*, p. xiii). For instance, it is Winnie herself who, unwittingly, is the first agent of Stevie's destruction when 'with her best air of inflexible calmness', she remarks to her husband: 'You could do anything with that boy, Adolf. [...] He would go through fire for you' (p. 184).

*Under Western Eyes*, too, illustrates the detachment and control which Conrad possessed in his artistic maturity. Given his antecedents it was understandable that, as he confessed in his Author's Note: 'My greatest anxiety was in being able to strike and sustain the note of scrupulous impartiality' (p. viii), and we can appreciate his exasperated protest that he was speaking with 'perfect detachment' (see above, p. 105) when Garnett accused him of having put his hatred of Russia into the novel. Recent criticism supports Gurko's judgement that Conrad managed to achieve a control which enabled him 'to present with a remarkable detachment and sympathy the soul of a nation for which he could feel no love'.[85]

Flaubert, as part of his general strategy of ironic detachment, often juxtaposed two contrasting episodes or interior monologues. A good example of the latter is the description of the dreams of Charles and Emma as they lie in bed, from which Conrad made two borrowings in 'The End of the Tether' (see above, p. 79). Also typical is the scene contrasting their thoughts during the amputation of Hippolyte's leg, which, as Kirschner has noted, finds a distinct equivalent in the scene between the Verlocs after Winnie has learned of Stevie's death. In their predicaments, both men expect assistance and comfort from their wives; when no such signs are forthcoming, they try to make contact with them but are violently rejected, each scene ending with the wife running out of the room and the dejected man falling into a chair. In both cases, language is shown to be totally inadequate, with statements such as these: 'Mais c'était peut-être un valgus?' (*MB*, p. 256), 'Do be reasonable, Winnie. What would it have been if you had lost me?' (*SA*, p. 234) revealing the gulf separating the partners. (*Kirschner, p. 185)

The *locus classicus* for such starkly ironic counterpointing is the Agricultural Show, where the amorous and inane whisperings of Rodolphe and Emma, the empty rhetoric of the pompous officials, and the bellowing of the cattle are heard simultaneously, a device repeated in the Cathedral scene as Léon courts Emma against the background of the guide's platitudes. Conrad uses the same device to portray Wait's isolation as he lies alone in his bunk in the forecastle while the jocular crew are all talking together on deck. Similarly, in the 'Malabar Gallery' where Jim tells Marlow about the Patna episode, the ironically contrasting background of indifferent, stupid, and complacent globe-trotters eating rice pudding and discussing their donkey rides, which intrudes each time he pauses in his outpourings, heightens his grief and his keen moral consciousness.[86]

The pursuit of objectivity and self-effacement led Flaubert to become, with *Madame Bovary*, the first novelist to turn free indirect style into a major mode of narration. Free indirect style can be described as a mixed form of speech- or thought-presentation which combines and superimposes the utterances (voice and linguistic forms) of the narrator and his characters, thus producing an uncanny effect of 'dual voice'. As a result, it can be made into a subtle, flexible and efficient distancing device offering great possibilities for irony, and also for ambiguity, since the reader is often left wondering whose voice it is he is hearing. As Stephen Ullman has pointed out, it is 'the exact equivalent' on the linguistic plane of the withdrawal of the author advocated by Flaubert.[87]

Flaubert, therefore, was the first to make systematic use of it because it met one of his basic needs as a novelist. His lesson was not lost on Conrad. Charles Jones, after recalling Ullmann's comment on Flaubert, notes 'what appears to be at least a very similar use and even, perhaps, an imitation of Flaubert's method of speech presentation' by Conrad.[88] We can now be a little less tentative: Conrad's attentive study of Flaubert's works and his deliberate imitation of their style is bound to have entailed a close examination of Flaubert's method of speech and thought presentation, and Conrad would no doubt have felt the need to emulate the Frenchman in that regard since he shared his ideal of impersonality. It is in the works of his mature period, especially in *Nostromo* and *The Secret Agent*, that Conrad used the free indirect mode most extensively. And, as Werner Senn has shown, he did so, like Flaubert, 'with great versatility and to masterful effect'.[89]

Finally, if teaching and moralizing were unacceptable encroachments on the work of art, it followed that the worst offence the artist could commit was to set out to prove a thesis or preconceived theory about the meaning of life. Flaubert protested throughout against what he considered to be the mania of man for conclusions obviously beyond his scope: hence his famous dictum 'L'ineptie consiste à vouloir conclure' (II, p. 239). He saw there a real danger for the artist because 'On fausse toujours la réalité quand on veut l'amener à une conclusion qui n'appartient qu'à Dieu seul' (V, p. 111), and accordingly he flatly rejected 'la littérature probante' with the terse comment: 'du moment que vous prouvez, vous mentez' (II, p. 379). Conrad was no less forceful than Flaubert on this subject: at many years' interval he asserted that the aim of art 'is not in the clear logic of a triumphant conclusion' (*NN*, p. xi), and stressed: 'Art for me *is* an end in itself. Conclusions are not for it.'[90]

Jonathan Culler has examined this 'thematic indeterminacy' in Flaubert:

Flaubert had set out to frustrate, by the construction of the novels, the working out of those themes which are explicitly posed and carried by the general movement of the plot. Attention is deflected from the problems which the novels raise and we find ourselves drawn into a puzzling inconclusiveness as soon as we try to take them seriously as thematic statements.

The greatness of *Madame Bovary*, he argues, derives from 'those areas of maximum indeterminacy', while *L'Education sentimentale*, a 'puzzling and exasperating masterpiece, [...] is the most striking, most challenging example of thematic indeterminacy'.[91] Many critics would agree with the latter statement.[92]

Like Flaubert – arguably even more than Flaubert – Conrad strove to preserve the uncertainty necessary to leave open all points of view. A letter to Norman Douglas shows that he, too, considered the 'full close', 'the nail hit on the head' a falsifying novelistic convention kept up only to satisfy 'the ordinary reader' who, with his 'inconceivable stupidity', expects it (*LL*, II,

p. 68). At the beginning of 'Heart of Darkness', the narrator realizes that he is fated to hear about one of Marlow's 'inconclusive experiences', and Marlow straightaway warns his audience that what he is going to narrate was 'not very clear' although 'it seemed to throw a kind of light' (*YOS*, p. 51). In *Lord Jim* he emphasizes again the inconclusiveness of his story, which is due to the central enigma posed by Jim's character, life and destiny. Marlow finds himself unable to decide whether his sudden departure from his various jobs 'amounted to shirking his ghost or to facing him out', whether it was 'flight' or 'a mode of combat' (p. 197), and his final comment contains the same ambivalence: 'He goes away from a living woman to celebrate his pitiless wedding with a shadowy ideal of conduct' (p. 416). Is this the recognition of ultimate victory or the avowal of ultimate defeat? Should we condemn Jim for being misguided and irresponsible, or admire him for his courage and untainted sense of honour? The moral point of view of the novel is deliberately confusing and disconcerting, as witnessed by the wide array of critical evaluations of Jim, who has been seen as noble, ridiculous, bewildering, the hero of a boy's book, or a failure.[93] As one of Marlow's statements reminds us, a 'full utterance' about Jim is beyond our reach (*LJ*, p. 225); like any of us, he is bound to remain something of an enigma. Conrad has achieved this by making the problematic nature of experience the work's central theme. Hence the narrative technique which brings to bear a variety of perspectives on the central figure and the issues he raises, with each perspective being offered as valid but limited, and none as fully adequate and final.[94] These characteristics are by no means confined to *Lord Jim*. It is difficult to imagine a less committed, more open-ended novel than *Nostromo*, which, despite a couple of pronouncements on the value of work, defies all attempts to formulate any positive ethic. We are left with Dr Monygham's prediction that, for lack of 'a moral principle', all that the Gould Concession stands for shall soon 'weigh as heavily upon the people as the barbarism, cruelty, and misrule of a few years back' (*N*, p. 511). As for *Victory*, the mass of widely divergent interpretations it has generated shows that it too offers no straightforward answers to the questions it raises. Gordon Thompson makes this point:

Is Lena's nature truly spiritual? Yes and no. Has there been a real victory in the novel? Yes and no. Is 'Victory' an ironic title? Yes and no. Conrad wants to leave the reader torn between belief and negation, between commitment and detachment, between vision and open-eyed realism. The world of *Victory* is thoroughly ambiguous and any response to it is likely to be insufficient and uncertain.[95]

If Flaubert said that the writer should forgo any conviction, it was because for him there was no objective reality, every man's vision was an illusion proper to himself, and therefore 'le doute absolu' (III, p. 183) was the only truth. When Maupassant complained to him that reality was monotonous, that events were not varied enough, he asked: 'Avez-vous jamais cru à l'existence des choses? Est-ce que tout n'est pas une illusion? Il n'y a de vrai que les "rapports", c'est-à-dire la façon dont nous percevons les objets' (VIII, p. 135). Maupassant heeded the lesson: in 'Le Roman' he declared that it is childish to believe in reality since we each carry our own in our minds and senses and thus create our own 'illusion' of the world (*PJ*, p. xvi). Conrad shared all these views (see above, pp. 158-9). He, too, believed that 'All is illusion' (*CL*, II, p. 198); he, too, rejected 'all formulas dogmas and principles' as 'only a web of illusions' (*CL*, I, p. 253). And, no doubt, the description of Stephen in *The Sisters*: 'He set off on his search for a creed – and found only an infinity of formulas' (p. 33) applies to his own experience. As a result, E. M. Forster complained that we are not able 'to write him down philosophically. No creed, in fact. Only opinions'.[96]

The rise of objectivity in nineteenth-century literature is related to the erosion of the old certainties, particularly in religious and ethical matters.[97] Indeed, the connection with philosophical doubt is clearly made in a letter to Flaubert from Alfred le Poittevin (*c.* 1845), when they were formulating the doctrine of impersonality: 'La vie étant reconnue pour une énigme [...] se réduire à l'immobilité impassible.'[98] In 1838, the seventeen-year-old Flaubert had already declared to his closest childhood friend: 'J'en suis venu maintenant à regarder le monde comme un spectacle et à en rire' (I, p. 30), thus showing that, for him, the universe could not be explained in philosophical or ethical terms. His attitude anticipates that of Conrad in *A Personal Record*:

> The ethical view of the universe involves us at last in so many cruel and absurd contradictions, where the last vestiges of faith, hope, charity, and even of reason itself, seem ready to perish, that I have come to suspect that the aim of creation cannot be ethical at all. I would fondly believe that its object is purely spectacular: a spectacle for awe, love, adoration, or hate [...] Those visions, delicious or poignant, are a moral end in themselves. (p. 92)

This conception of an enigmatic and purely spectacular universe accounts for the view of Conrad and Flaubert that the task of the artist must be to give as truthful, as accurate a 'representation' of the universe as lies in his power, and therefore 'to bear true testimony to the visible wonder, [...] to [...] the abiding mystery of the sublime spectacle' (*PR*, p. 92). For them, objectivity was part of a philosophy of 'not knowing' or 'half knowing' in which they foreswore the privilege of omniscience to preserve intact the mystery of human life and destiny while conducting tentative probings into the nature of reality and truth. In Flaubert's words, 'Exactitude et mystère!' (IV, p. 427).

## Visibility

Watt's statement: 'Perhaps the most distinctive quality of Conrad's own writing [...] is its strong visual sense'[99] represents a commonly held view. Many critics have accordingly explored analogies between Conrad's writing and the visual arts,[100] and Impressionism[101] has provided the major hunting ground. Although many early reviewers had associated him with the movement, the view of Conrad as an impressionist was made popular by Ford in his essay 'On Impressionism', published in 1913, and his memoir in 1924; then it was taken up by Joseph Warren Beach and Edward Crankshaw in the thirties. Recently a number of critics have reopened the case,[102] and despite his rejection of all 'isms', the impressionist label is now firmly pinned on Conrad.[103]

Although these studies have produced valuable insights, they are disappointing on two grounds. First, they force the conclusion reached by Watt that 'it is very unlikely that Conrad either thought of himself as an impressionist or was significantly influenced by the impressionist movement'.[104] Secondly, they fail to present the technical innovations of Conrad and Ford in an accurate historical perspective, since most of their theories and practices, whether evolved before they met or in the course of their collaboration, derived primarily from the fictional and critical models offered by Flaubert and Maupassant.

It is worth recalling that impressionism in literature is older than in painting, and that Flaubert, without being a pure impressionist like the Goncourts, is regarded as its founder (as Ford was well aware). Indeed, Flaubert, who was keenly stimulated by paintings and whose intention while composing *Madame Bovary* was 'peindre couleur sur couleur et sans tons tranchés' (III, p. 86), clearly stands, with his insatiable passion for description, his fondness for colours, and fascination with the play of light, as a forerunner of the Impressionist painters. Pierre Danger has analysed the many correspondences that can be found between Flaubert's landscape descriptions and Impressionist paintings not only in 'the general spirit' but also in 'the very detail of certain devices'.[105] Helmut Hatzfeld notes that Flaubert was 'capable of giving a consistent picture, and not merely fragments [like Balzac], of an early impressionistic landscape' and that, like Corot, he tried 'to catch, but by literary means, the atmospheric colors of a Spring evening'.[106] Furthermore, this kind of correspondence does not apply to Flaubert alone. Only uninformed views could have led some critics to oppose the practices of the so-called French 'realists' in which Conrad was steeped to the Impressionists' aims and methods. The Impressionists thought of themselves as realists, and the realists and naturalists exploited some of the Impressionists' discoveries. Friendships between members of both groups, like that between Zola and the painters Manet and Cézanne, show that they found inspiration in each other's works.[107]

Failure to remember some of these points has led to misleading comparisons. Hay, after noting that in 'L'Impressionnisme dans le roman' Brunetière had praised Daudet's use of 'the picturesque imperfect tense' instead of the usual narrative preterite, 'thus immobilising a scene in a painterly tableau, while allowing other actions to overtake it and pass out of sight', comments: 'One thinks of Conrad's group immobilised aboard the *Nellie*, listening to Marlow's

Congo story.'[108] The comparison may be valid but it fails to record the important fact that it was Flaubert, 'l'homme de l'imparfait' as Thibaudet called him, who gave the imperfect prominence over the past historic in creating, among other things, the new value mentioned by Brunetière.[109] And Roger Huss has pointed out that the predilection for painting tableaux led Flaubert at times to turn 'away from narrative to a contemplation of what is more static and more lasting', presenting events 'not in their dynamic aspect but in their descriptive aspect' and that as a result, 'characters often appear to be striking attitudes rather than performing actions'.[110] The scene where Emma drinks a liqueur with Charles (quoted by Ford in *The March of Literature*, p. 812) offers a vivid illustration of an action described in such a painterly fashion that it seems arrested:

Elle [...] atteignit deux petits verres, emplit l'un jusqu'au bord, versa à peine dans l'autre, et, après avoir trinqué, le porta à sa bouche. Comme il était presque vide, elle se renversait pour boire: et, la tête en arrière, les lèvres avancées, le cou tendu, elle riait de ne rien sentir, tandis que le bout de la langue, passant entre ses dents fines, léchait à petits coups le fond du verre.                                        (*MB*, pp. 29–30)

Narrative flow is similarly arrested by descriptive amplification in the following scene from *The Rescue:*

Shaw approached the table and began to help himself, handling the bottles in profound silence and with exaggerated caution, as if he had been measuring out of fragile vessels a dose of some deadly poison. Carter, his hands in his pockets, and leaning back, examined him from head to foot with a cool stare. The mate of the brig raised the glass to his lips, and glaring above the rim at the stranger, drained the contents slowly. (p. 35)

Whatever reservations we may have about Conrad's overall assessment of his debt to Flaubert, in acknowledging his influence 'from the point of view of the rendering of concrete things and visual impressions' where he found him 'marvellous' (see above, p. 12), Conrad was recognizing the doctrine of visual clarity, arguably Flaubert's greatest contribution to the art of the novel,[111] as one of the most important aesthetic tenets that he and Ford had inherited from the French master. Ford explained:

There was painting before Cézanne and there has been painting since Cézanne, but the objectives of the two modes of painting have scarcely any connection. A similar cesura is observable in the aesthetics of creative writing. There was writing before Flaubert; but Flaubert and his coterie opened, as it were, a window through which one saw the literary scene from an entirely new angle. Perhaps more than anything else it was a matter of giving visibility to your pages: perhaps better than elsewhere, Conrad with his 'It is above all to make you see!' expressed the aims of the New World. And your seeing things became an integral part of your story.[112]

Conrad probably found the best formula to express this new aim, which, according to James's distinction, emphasizes narrative as 'showing' rather than 'telling', and comes as no surprise from an admiring student of Flaubert's art and correspondence. Flaubert said that when reading Shakespeare 'On n'est plus homme, on est *oeil*' (I, p. 339), for him, the hallmark of genius. His first approach to writing was to see and to 'see well': '*voir*, avoir le modèle devant soi, qui pose' (II, p. 462). Before starting to write 'Hérodias', he could exclaim: '*je vois* (nettement, comme *je vois* la Seine) la surface de la mer Morte scintiller au soleil' (VII, p. 341). He even coined an expression for this intense visualization: 'pénétration, de l'objectif' (III, p. 269), a seeing through the object of the sensation, a total intimacy which he regarded as a prerequisite to reproducing it well and communicating his vision faithfully. For there lay his ultimate aim: 'faire sentir presque *matériellement* les choses qu'il reproduit' (II, p. 344); 'faire voir' (IV, p. 227). This was of such importance to him that his critical judgements are often simply an appraisal of the visual clarity of the characters, scenery, and events depicted, praise or blame ensuing accordingly.

This intense concern with the visual soon extended to what Ford calls Flaubert's 'coterie' and became part of the French literary climate. More important from our point of view, Flaubert first passed on his concern to his 'disciple', who described in 'Le Roman' the training he had received: 'il me forçait à exprimer, en quelques phrases, un être ou un objet de manière à le particulariser nettement, à le distinguer de tous les autres êtres ou de tous les autres objets de même race ou de même espèce', culminating with the injunction '*faites-moi voir, par un seul mot*' (*PJ*, p. xxiv) which inspired Conrad's famous declaration of intent (see above, p. 139). And Conrad made it clear that he admired Maupassant's fiction mainly because Maupassant's facts were 'perfectly rendered' (*NLL*, p. 27).[113] The concern of Conrad and Ford with the accurate rendering of concrete reality is reflected in their bilingual efforts, when driving over 'a country of commonplace downlands', to 'render a field of ripe corn, a ten-acre patch of blue-purple cabbage, a hopoast'.[114]

Flaubert prided himself on his acute visual sense: 'Je sais voir et voir comme voient les myopes, jusque dans les pores des choses' (II, p. 343) – remember the beads of sweat on Emma's shoulders. Surface solidity, or 'solidity of specification' as James has it, produced by the use of definite particulars is indeed the most immediately identifiable characteristic of his writings: Bovary senior is not simply sunk in a perpetual torpor in front of his fire: we see him smoking and spitting in the ashes; Félicité is not merely 'thrifty': we see her slowly eating her bread from a twelve-pound loaf and picking up the crumbs from the table. Conrad undoubtedly learned his lesson. On 23 July 1901, we find him chiding Ford for leaving his treatment of *Seraphina* 'too much in the air', for failing to give it a sense of 'hard *reality*' (*CL*, II. p. 343). And at the peak of his career, he imitates Flaubert in the specificity of his descriptions: as Deslauriers, after walking from Villenauxe to Nogent to see Frédéric, arrives with his shoes 'blancs de poussière' (*ES*, p. 22), so Gould, after walking from town to announce to Doña Emilia the news of his father's death, meets her 'dusty with the white dust of the road lying on his boots' (*N*, p. 61).

The concomitant of this emphasis on the visual is Maupassant's 'objective' method, according to which 'la psychologie doit être cachée dans le livre comme elle est cachée en réalité sous les faits dans l'existence' (*PJ*, p. xvii).[115] (Again, Maupassant is merely echoing Flaubert, who used the same words in a letter to his niece: after recounting the events of the previous day, he asks her to guess '*la psychologie sous les faits*' (VI, p. 434).) Eschewing psychological analysis, the author undertakes to reveal the character's inner life through visual or dramatic equivalents, in particular the small, seemingly casual surface details which suggest psychological depths. When Emma goes to the Banneville beech grove with her greyhound, a sea breeze sometimes brings its salt freshness far inland; the rushes whistle, the beech leaves shake with a rapid shivering, the tree-tops sway ceaselessly with a high continuous murmur; Emma 'serrait son châle contre ses épaules et se levait' (*MB*, p. 63). Her reaction to the disquieting effects of the wind objectifies her feelings of unease and isolation, building up the picture of her increasing disenchantment with married life. Conrad achieves a similar effect when Donkin leaves Wait's cabin after his death and is 'astounded to find the world outside as he had left it': 'He shuddered a little in the penetrating freshness of the air, and hugged himself forlornly' (*NN*, p. 155). The last word, and the context, make Conrad's sentence more explicit than Flaubert's, but Donkin's gesture, like Emma's, aptly suggests his uneasiness and alienation. In each case, the detail is both an observed fact and a metaphorical correlative of the action. Because of his emphasis on the visual, Flaubert also made an innovative use of sensory images to present mental states.[116] This procedure, whereby, as Faguet defined it, 'on représente un état d'âme par un paysage' or rather 'un état d'âme *se représente à lui-même* par un paysage',[117] is best exemplified in the rendering of Emma's expectations, after she has given herself to Rodolphe:

Elle entrait dans quelque chose de merveilleux où tout serait passion, extase, délire; une immensité bleuâtre l'entourait, les sommets du sentiment étincelaient sous sa pensée, et l'existence ordinaire n'apparaissait qu'au loin, tout en bas, dans l'ombre, entre les intervalles de ces hauteurs.                    (*MB*, p. 225)

Conrad adopted the same method in Jim's day-dreams, and, as Kirschner has suggested,[118] this passage may well have inspired Marlow's description of him 'high in the sunshine on the top of that historic hill of his', dominating 'the forest, the secular gloom, the old mankind', as Jim ecstatically assesses his achievement: 'it was immense! Immense!' (*LJ*, pp. 265, 271).

As Proust observed: 'ce qui jusqu'à Flaubert était action devient impression. Les choses ont autant de vie que les hommes'.[119] Reality in Flaubert is to be found not so much in the events being narrated as in the things which signify them and the impressions that those things create: Bovary's cap, Emma's wedding cake and wedding bouquet, Binet's lathe, his napkin rings and 'indescrib-able' carvings typify Flaubert's mode of expression. Because of their suggestiveness, these objects acquire symbolic value, making *Madame Bovary*, the greatest of French 'realist' novels, paradoxically a source of both naturalistic and symbolic interpretations. Let us examine some examples Conrad found in the works of his French mentors involving three important sets of symbolic objects: headgear, statues, and pictures.

On his first visit to Rosanette Bron,[120] Frédéric, left by himself in the dining-room, notices on the table in the middle a man's hat, 'un vieux feutre bossué, gras, immonde. A qui donc ce chapeau? Montrant impudemment sa coiffe décousue, il semblait dire: "Je m'en moque après tout! Je suis le maître!"' Rosanette comes in, takes the hat, opens the conservatory, throws it inside, shuts the door, and then takes him into her dressing room (*ES*, p. 188). The hat belongs to Oudry, the rich old man who keeps her. Its description, its position, and her gesture tell us all we need to know about the sort of man he is, his position in the household, and the fate awaiting him now that Frédéric has appeared on the scene. Equivalents are easily found in Conrad. Peter Ivano-vitch, the great feminist and 'noble archpriest of Revolution' who dominates Château Borel, leaves his black silk top hat rim upwards upon the white marble balustrade on the landing, where it is seen by those below and where it, too, 'asserted itself extremely' (*UWE*, p. 226). The hat, in its elevated position, takes on psychological significance. So does Verloc's shapeless, greasy old black bowler which cannot be separated from him, and symbolizes his shabby and sordid existence.[121]

Statue symbolism plays a significant part in *Madame Bovary*. Besides the role of the three cupids, already analyzed (see above, pp. 170), the cold haughty statue of a woman 'draped to the chin' which gazes motionless on the sumptuous dinner being served at la Vaubyessard (p. 68) implies severe moral judge-ment.[122] There is also the plaster curé seen scaling away in the garden at Tostes and later reduced to smithereens on the 'pavé de Quincampoix' in the move to Yonville, which objectifies the gradual decay of Emma's spiritual life and suggests, together with the burning of her wedding bouquet, that her past is being left behind. Counterparts of these symbols can be found in 'The Return', in the 'marble' woman which underscores visually the coldness, rigidity, blind-ness and lifelessness of the 'decent' life of a society couple (*TU*, p. 123), and in *Under Western Eyes*, in Spontini's 'Flight of Youth' (p. 43), expressing the poignancy of Razumov's situation, and, of course, in the statue of Rousseau.[123]

Flaubert and Maupassant also made a remarkable use of pictures. This is a conspicuous feature of *Madame Bovary* with the 'head of Minerva' drawn by Emma on the kitchen wall at Les Bertaux,[124] her 'two small pencil sketches' in their 'very large frames' which Bovary shows with pride in their sitting-room at Tostes, the 'Fame blowing her trumpets' cut out from 'some perfumer's pro-spectus' that Emma notices in the nurse's poor dwelling, and the few coarsely

coloured bills representing four scenes from *La Tour de Nesle*, with a motto in
Spanish and French, in the hotel room in Rouen. Typical, too, are Schopin's
Potiphar and Steuben's Esmeralda which decorate the dining-room where
Emma has to suffer Guillaumin's libidinous proposals.[125] *L'Education, Fort
comme la mort* and *Bel-Ami* offer other interesting examples, in Pellerin's portrait of Rosanette, Bertin's portrait of Mme de Guilleroy, and Marcowitch's
religious masterpiece 'Jésus marchant sur les flots'. Typical of Maupassant's
procedure is the detailed description of the tapestry representing the story of
Pyramus and Thisbe in Jeanne's room which prefigures her entire life, and that
of the four engravings in Mme Rosémilly's apartment in *Pierre et Jean*, whose
characters and stories create a complex interplay of parallelisms and displace-
ments with the characters and situations depicted in the novel.[126] When studying *Pierre et Jean* Conrad could hardly have missed the subtle effect of 'mise
en abyme' produced by these engravings. Indeed, his work offers striking
examples of such symbolic images, such as the sketches, water-colours and
engravings in Alvan Hervey's apartments (*TU*, pp. 123–4), Kurtz's small
sketch in oils 'representing a woman, draped and blindfolded, carrying a lighted
torch' against a 'sombre – almost black' background (*YOS*, p. 79),[127] Mrs
Gould's water-colour sketch of the San Tomé gorge 'hanging alone' in its 'black
[...] frame' (*N*, p. 209), and the portrait of Heyst senior, 'quill pen in his
hand' (*V*, p. 195), which, when it is presented 'a little above [Heyst's] head; a
wonderful presence in its heavy frame [...] looking [...] out of place and
masterful' (pp. 218–19) makes us grasp visually the 'heavy' philosophical
influence he is exerting on his son.[128]

Flaubert's passion for description and lack of interest in narrative – 'L'histoire, l'aventure d'un roman', he confessed to the Goncourts, 'ça m'est bien
égal'[129] – was bound to undermine traditional narrative structures. So did Conrad's and Ford's realization that 'Life did not narrate, but made impressions
on our brains',[130] a dictum which is directly in line with Flaubert's attitude and
practice.[131] Take, for instance, the description of the new flax mill which is
visited by the Bovarys, Homais and Léon:

> Rien pourtant n'était moins curieux que cette curiosité. Un grand espace de terrain
> vide où se trouvaient pêle-mêle, entre des tas de sable et de cailloux, quelques roues
> d'engrenage déjà rouillées, entourait un long bâtiment quadrangulaire que perçaient
> quantité de petites fenêtres. Il n'était pas achevé d'être bâti            (*MB*, p. 140)

Tanner's comment, 'Some rusty wheels in an empty landscape – such indeed
will be the most accurate memorial to the society depicted by Flaubert, the
most appropriate comment on the variety of futile and finally self-destroying
circlings that made up its organizing momentum'[132] might apply, *mutatis
mutandis*, to 'Heart of Darkness' where the general desolation, degradation,
and utter meaninglessness resulting from colonialism is stated in terms of a
French gunboat shelling a continent, derelict machinery, useless blasting, and

wasted shapes of men huddled in death.[133] The conventional narrative has indeed been abandoned in favour of a succession of small scenes which function like images in an imagist poem. In 1924, Edwin Muir observed appreciatively: 'Mr. Conrad writes in pictures, for the pictures come, and what he shows us is not action, but a progression of dissolving scenes, continuous and living, which in the end reflect action and give us a true apprehension of it.'[134] Fifty-five years earlier, French critics were unable to accept such absence of narrative continuity in *L'Education sentimentale*, and condemned it as a mere collection of tableaux, medallions, and photographs (cf. *ES*, pp. 613, 696, 698).[135]

The visual intensity Flaubert, Maupassant and Conrad so anxiously aimed for no doubt accounts for the hallucinatory quality that often characterizes their writings[136] and their constant preoccupation with hallucinatory phenomena.[137] It is interesting to note the similarity, whether fortuitous or not, that exists between Emma's hallucination – '*Tout* ce qu'il y avait dans sa tête de réminiscences, d'idées, *s'échappait à la fois, d'un seul bond, comme les mille pièces d'un feu d'artifice*' (*MB*, p. 432) – and that of Winnie Verloc who sees 'smashed branches, torn leaves, gravel, bits of brotherly flesh and bone, *all spouting up together in the manner of a firework*' (*SA*, p. 260); or between the hallucinations of old Rouault who, riding to Emma's funeral, keeps seeing her '*devant lui, étendue sur le dos, au milieu de la route*' (*MB*, p. 463) and that of Razumov who, on his way to the police bureau to betray Haldin, sees him '*stretched on his back, right across his path*' (*UWE*, p. 36).[138]

It remains to show that a number of Conrad's techniques currently associated with the impressionist movement in painting or in literature have their source in Flaubert.

The aim of impressionism, Ford said, is to capture, in whatever art form, 'the impression of a moment'.[139] Ford and Conrad only had to turn to *Madame Bovary* to formulate this objective. Allen Tate has observed that when Emma reads Rodolphe's letter in the attic, Flaubert, using Binet's lathe, gives us 'a direct *impression* of Emma's sensation at a particular moment (which not even the drama could accomplish), and thus by rendering audible to us what Emma alone could hear he charged the entire scene with actuality'. But why confine this effect to the lathe when, as Tate himself points out, 'we see nothing that she does not see, hear nothing that she does not hear', and every single sensation, visual, auditory, synaesthetic, is made to give us a 'direct impression' of what Emma is experiencing? For an amazing complex of sensations is at work here, the heavy heat gripping her temples and stifling her, the dazzling sunlight, the open country, the empty village square, the pebbles glittering, the weathercocks standing motionless, her heart pounding like a battering-ram, the ray of light dragging her down, the ground swaying up the walls, the floor dipping on end, all culminating in the air whirling in her hollow head, 'The humming vertigo that draws the street towards her [which] is rendered audible to us by the correlative sound of the lathe',[140] that ceaseless whirring 'like a voice furiously calling her' (pp. 284–5). Similarly, when Ford said that impressionism exists to render 'those queer effects of real life', those 'superimposed emotions' which derive from the fact that 'we are almost always in one place with our minds somewhere quite other', he mentioned as a model 'Emma's love scene at the cattle show',[141] a scene Conrad also knew intimately (see above, pp. 76-7 and below, p. 267 (n. 23)). What Ford had in mind is the passage where the smell of the pomade on Rodolphe's hair brings back to Emma memories of the Viscount with whom she had waltzed at La Vaubyessard and whose beard had exhaled the same perfume, while the sight of the *Hirondelle* in the distance reminds her of Léon. Then everything blurs: 'il lui sembla qu'elle tournait encore dans la valse, sous le feu des lustres, au bras du vicomte, et que Léon n'était pas loin, qu'il allait venir ... et cependant elle sentait toujours la tête de Rodolphe à côté d'elle. La douceur de cette sensation pénétrait ainsi ses désirs d'autrefois' (*MB*, p. 204). Such scenes admirably produce that 'illusion of reality' which, according to Ford, it is 'the business of Impressionism to produce'.[142]

Conrad's and Ford's desire to present what is seen or felt in a passing moment is also linked to the 'witness technique' – the use of a restricted point of view or limited field of vision – which forms an integral part of Flaubert's strategy of authorial impersonality and contributes a great deal to the original texture of *Madame Bovary*. R. J. Sherrington has given an excellent illustration of this procedure in the gradual introduction of Emma through Charles's eyes:

We follow [Charles] into Les Bertaux, noticing, as he does, the external (misleading, but we do not know that yet) signs of a well-to-do establishment. Then 'une jeune femme, en robe de mérinos bleu garnie de trois volants' – this is all that Charles notices about his future wife – takes him into the kitchen, then upstairs to attend the patient. Only when he is forced to interrupt his work to wait for her does he notice anything more, and then in the most natural way: she is sewing, pricks her finger, and as she brings it to her mouth, Charles sees her hands and her eyes, which are then described. As usual, it is made clear that it is in Charles's mind that the description first occurs, that the author is merely recording: 'Charles fut surpris de la blancheur de ses ongles.' Some time later, he has the opportunity of noticing one or two more details: her lips, [her neck], her hair, her cheeks. Again it is noted that the details are given because of Charles's interest: 'avec un mouvement ondé vers les tempes, *que le médecin de compagne remarqua là* pour la première fois de sa vie'. Moreover, the point of view is emphasized throughout the passage by Emma's being referred to as 'Mlle Emma' or 'Mlle Rouault' while Charles is simply 'Charles'. The reader already knows Charles, whereas he is still on somewhat formal terms – as Charles is – with Emma.[143]

Conrad frequently used the 'witness technique' to present his characters, for instance in gradually revealing Lena's appearance through Heyst's eyes. During an interval in a performance by the Zangiacomo band, Heyst first notices 'two white muslin dresses and crimson sashes' that have not left the platform. One of these dresses is motionless on a chair:

On the lap of that dress there lay, unclasped and idle, a pair of small hands, not very white, attached to well-formed arms. The next detail Heyst was led to observe was the arrangement of the hair – two thick brown tresses rolled round an attractively shaped head.

'A girl, by Jove!' he exclaimed mentally.                                        (V, p. 70)

He then notices the outline of the shoulders, the slender white bust, the feet in white shoes crossed prettily. Impulsively, he goes up to the girl, but, unaware of his presence, she remains looking down, without colour, without glances, without voice and movement. After a brief exchange, they sit at a table, saying very little, looking at each other in amazement. Because of Heyst's interest in her 'physiognomy', her expression is described and analysed at some length, again reflecting the impression it makes on him: 'the features had more fineness than those of any other feminine countenance he had ever had the opportunity to observe so closely'.[144]

Perhaps the most conspicuous of impressionistic devices consists in recording sense impressions in the order of their occurrence and interpreting them only when the mind has made out their meaning. Two examples in Conrad have been singled out by a number of critics: Marlow's slow elucidation of the incomprehensible sensations he experiences as he finds himself in the air after the final explosion on the *Judea* in 'Youth' (*YOS*, pp. 22–3), and, in 'Heart of Darkness', his belated understanding of what is happening on his boat when it is attacked because of his failure, while navigating, to identify straightaway first the arrows, then the spear, which are flung at them (*YOS*, pp. 109–12). Watt calls this device 'delayed decoding', and describes it as 'the verbal equivalent of the impressionist painter's attempt to render visual sensation directly'. No doubt, but it was not derived from the Impressionists, nor can it be regarded as 'one of the minor innovations of [Conrad's] narrative technique'.[145] So assiduous a reader of *Salammbô* as Conrad was could not have failed to note a device which appears in it about a dozen times. One example will suffice:

Tout à coup il [Schahabarim] aperçut à l'horizon, derrière Tunis, comme des brouillards légers, qui se traînaient contre le sol; puis ce fut un grand rideau de poudre grise perpendiculairement étalé, et, dans les tourbillons de cette masse nombreuse, des têtes de dromadaires, des lances, des boucliers parurent. C'était l'armée des Barbares qui s'avançait sur Carthage.                               (*Sal*, p. 65)[146]

That Flaubert's example, as set in this passage, had not been lost on Conrad is evident from his rendering, in 'Prince Roman', of the Prince's perception of an approaching army:

One afternoon, it happened that the Prince after turning his horse's head for home remarked a low dense cloud of dark dust cutting off slantwise a part of the view. He reined in on a knoll and peered. There were slender gleams of steel here and there in that cloud, and it contained moving forms which revealed themselves at last as a long line of peasant carts full of soldiers, moving slowly in double file under the escort of mounted Cossacks.                                                    (*TH*, p. 38)

The 'delayed decoding' shows once again, Conrad refining upon an already existing Flaubertian technique.[147]

The preceding arguments prove that the aim 'to make you see' should not imply that Conrad adopted a specifically impressionistic position. Previous studies by Hay and Watt have shown that early in his career he reacted unfavourably to both pictorial and literary impressionism. No doubt he shared the reservations expressed by Brunetière, who had accused impressionist writers of confining themselves to appearances, of trifling as dilettantes 'à la surface ondoyante et multiple des choses' instead of going 'au fond', like the masters of the past. Similarly, in the Preface to *The Nigger* early in 1897, Conrad emphasizes the need to pay attention both to surfaces 'to render the highest kind of justice to the visible universe' and to depths 'by bringing to light the truth [...] underlying its every aspect' (p. vii) (like Brunetière's 'et de là [le fond] ramenaient quelqu'une de ces vérités générales') (see below, p. 251). We have already noted how Conrad, emulating Flaubert and Maupassant, rejected the restricted, the contingent, the ephemeral, in favour of the general, the fundamental, the enduring. He could not, therefore, identify with a movement which he saw as concerned primarily with transient visual appearances. His assessments of Crane and Daudet made during the same period bear this out: in December 1897, he wrote to Garnett that Crane was '*the only* impressionist and *only* an impressionist' (*CL*, I, p. 416), and, in his article on Daudet (the main object of Brunetière's strictures) written the following month, he showed that he did not believe it sufficient for an author's creations to be 'seen', as he acknowledged Daudet's to be, because if, like Daudet's, they are deficient in meaning, 'their fate is [...] of not the slightest consequence' (*NLL*, p. 24).

The truth is that Conrad's double aim of outward clarity and inward depth derives from Flaubert and Maupassant. Flaubert's predilection for the visual was not that of a mere impressionist: 'Il faut faire des tableaux, [...] mais des tableaux complets, *peindre le dessous et le dessus*' (III, p. 158). He always insisted that minute attention to particulars was a means of penetrating to the underlying nature of things, of apprehending their essence.[148]

This dual concern for 'le dessous et le dessus' is particularly evident in our authors' attitude to characterization. On the face of it, Flaubert has merely painted a vivid picture of Emma drinking a glass of curaçao with Charles, but the picture is so suggestive that avidity and sensuousness are firmly established as her main attributes. He trained Maupassant not merely to show him the physical appearance of this or that greengrocer or concierge but also 'indiquée par l'adresse de l'image, toute leur nature morale' (*PJ*, p. xxiv). Maupassant accordingly explains that the aim of the 'modern' writer is to make his character behave in such a way that all his actions and all his movements are 'le reflet de sa nature intime' (*PJ*, p. xvii). Like Flaubert and Maupassant, and unlike the impressionists, Conrad was equally concerned with both appearance and meaning, that is with the 'inner truth' which he, too, saw 'foreshadowed' 'in the features and character of a human face' (*PR*, p. xix).

Maupassant and Conrad attached great importance to the art of reading faces, and a key word they used in this connection was 'penetrate'. In 'Les Soeurs Rondoli', Pierre Jouvenet is speaking for his creator when he says that whenever he finds himself in front of a new face, he has 'l'obsession de deviner quelle âme, quelle intelligence, quel caractère se cachent derrière ces traits' (*SR*, p. 12). This obsession Maupassant transferred to many of his characters who gaze long and deeply into each other's eyes in desperate attempts to 'penetrate' into each other's minds and souls, an attitude Conrad adopted for his own characters on at least three occasions.[149] Conversely, an authorial comment on Captain Mitchell deplores the fact that he 'had not much penetration of any kind; characteristic, illuminating trifles of expression, action, or movement, escaped him completely' (*N*, p. 338). Nothing could better illustrate the impact that Flaubert and Maupassant made on Conrad in this respect than his adoption of their ideal which combined acute observation of the phenomenal world with its intuitive and imaginative penetration (see above p. 140).

To sum up, just as 'the *example* of Flaubert', as Yelton observed, 'is much more implicated in the formation of [Conrad's] aesthetic than any conjectured influence of *Symboliste* doctrine',[150] the example of Flaubert and Maupassant is much more implicated in any analogy that can be found between Conrad's art and painting than a conjectured influence of painting in general and Impressionism in particular. The emphasis on the visual, the use of terms related to the making of pictures such as 'vision', 'form', 'colour', in the Preface to *The Nigger*, the reliance on visual procedures (scenes, tableaux, objects, imagistic details), the presentation of a visual work of art (painting, sculpture) functioning as a symbolic image, the adoption of the 'witness technique' and the device of 'delayed decoding' to render experience as it is lived, then finally, the insistence that the depiction of the surface goes hand in hand with plumbing the depths, all this, instead of revealing 'Conrad's special awareness of painting', as Gillon would have it,[151] reveals his special awareness of the art and doctrines of his French mentors to whom he repeatedly paid the highest forms of tribute: borrowing and close imitation.[152]

Why did Conrad abandon the predominantly analytical approach of his early works to adopt the objective method? After the uncertain results of the first two novels, it was the total failure of *The Sisters* which prompted him to try the objective method in *The Rescuer* in March or April 1896. In a letter to Garnett of 8 October 1897, he said he wanted 'to make it a kind of glorified book for boys [. . .]. No analysis. No damned mouthing. Pictures – pictures – pictures' (*CL*, I, p. 392). But, after two years of 'acute distress and worry', as Garnett recalled (*LEG*, p. 18), when foundering once more in June 1898, he wrote to him: 'In the matter of R. I have lost all sense of form and I can't see *images*'

(*CL*, II, p.66), and soon ground to a halt. Meanwhile, from June 1896 to February 1897 Conrad had written *The Nigger*, and this time he showed a remarkable mastery of objective realism and produced his first great achievement. However, despite this success, he returned once more to the analytical approach in 'The Return' in April 1897. It was only with its devastating failure after five months of bitterness and frustration that he finally learned his lesson and admitted to Garnett: 'It is evident that my fate is to be descriptive and descriptive only. There are things I must leave alone' (*CL*, I, p.387).[153]

Joseph Martin has attributed the fundamental shift in Conrad's approach largely to 'the continuing critical pressure of Edward Garnett during the years 1895–1897'. He notes: 'One sees in Garnett's reader's reports and published essays of the early and mid-nineties the same distrust of direct analysis and the same belief that the novelist should be a "hidden psychologist" presenting his ideas through the objective surface of life as are found in Maupassant's "Le Roman"'.[154] Indeed, Garnett's reaction to the opening chapter of *The Rescuer* in a letter of 26 May 1896: 'The situation grips one with great force. It is as clearly and forcibly *seen* as if one had spent a month on those seas – (that is the highest praise)',[155] is strikingly similar to Flaubert's praise of 'Boule de Suif', Maupassant's first successful effort: 'Le paysage et les personnages se voient' (VIII, p.364).

But, of course, no amount of encouragement and advice from Garnett and theorizing from Maupassant could have shown the still unsure and self-doubting novice Conrad was in the latter half of 1896 how to write certain scenes in *The Nigger*. Fortunately, *Salammbô*, *Madame Bovary* and *Bel-Ami* provided magnificent models and invaluable sources of material. Again, what better indication of Conrad's debt to Flaubert and Maupassant than the presence of these novels in his first major work, and, in particular, the last two in the death of Wait, one of the key scenes in the book? It is significant that Garnett, when reading the manuscript, 'devoted five marginal bravos to the death scene alone',[156] and that Crane also singled it out for praise, even mentioning that he 'felt ill over that red thread lining from the corner of the man's mouth to his chin', a visual detail he found 'frightful with the weight of a real and present death', which, as Kirschner has shown, came straight from Maupassant.[157]

### The 'mot juste'

Conrad, the artist who described himself as 'haunted, mercilessly haunted by the *necessity* of style' (*CL*, II, p.50), acknowledged his debt to 'French culture' in respect of style and the 'mot juste'. Davray recalled:

Combien de fois, de vive voix, ne m'a-t-il pas répété tout ce qu'il devait à sa culture française, en particulier son souci du style et de l'expression; sa recherche du mot juste, de l'équilibre de la phrase; son emploi des mots pour leur sonorité ou leur musique, leur force ou leur charme, leur puissance de signification ou de séduction.[158]

As was the case with 'unity', this concept of the 'mot juste' is of interest to us because Flaubert, Maupassant, Conrad, Ford, and James all believed in it and were inspired by it.

As a confirmed organicist, Flaubert rejected the old view of language as a mere 'dress of thought', as Dr Johnson called it: 'ces gaillards-là s'en tiennent à la vieille comparaison: la forme est un manteau. Mais non! La forme est la chair même de la pensée, comme la pensée en est l'âme, la vie' (III, p. 141). As a result, he regarded any distinction between substance and form, matter and manner, idea and style, as arbitrary and meaningless: 'ces distinctions de la pensée et du style sont un sophisme' (II, p. 339).[159] For him, the perfect polish of the sentence was not an end in itself: there was no divorcing the idea, the vision from its expression, since style alone was 'une manière absolue de voir les choses' (II, p. 346). Conrad echoed this view when he said that in writing *Chance* his intention was 'to interest people in [his] vision of things which is indissolubly allied to the style in which it is expressed' (*C*, p. x).

Flaubert believed that 'Everything depends on the conception', because the conception governs the harmony between the substance and the form of the work. Their identity meant that the quest for style, for form, was first and foremost a process of clarification of his own thoughts. It is the conception, the vision which must first be made perfect for, as he explained to Louise Colet, 'il est fort difficile de rendre clair par les mots ce qui est obscur encore dans votre pensée' (II, p. 361). This is precisely the view Conrad develops when discussing Maupassant's 'first feeble drafts'. Maupassant, the acknowledged 'master of the *mot juste*', has never been 'a dealer in words:'

what has been matured, improved, brought to perfection by unwearied endeavour is not the diction of the tale, but the vision of its true shape and detail. Those first attempts are not faltering or uncertain in expression. It is the conception which is at fault. The subjects have not yet been adequately seen.                                        (*NLL*, p. 28)

When the subject is seen, the artist can communicate his vision to his reader only through the right word, for, since no two objects are alike, only one word can adequately describe each object in its uniqueness and individuality. More fundamentally, however, the whole concept of the *mot juste* rests on the assumption that exact correlations exist beween the world of ideas and the world of words which it is the artist's task to find, whatever the cost. In 'Le Roman', Maupassant faithfully voiced his master's views when he made his well-known pronouncement: 'Quelle que soit la chose qu'on veut dire, il n'y a qu'un mot pour l'exprimer, qu'un verbe pour l'animer et qu'un adjectif pour la qualifier. Il faut donc chercher, jusqu'à ce qu'on les ait découverts, ce mot, ce verbe et cet adjectif, et ne jamais se contenter de l'à peu près' (*PJ*, pp. xxiv–v).[160] In the perfect blending of the idea and the form that suits it, sound and sense coalesce and the reader can apprehend the subject directly as it has been seen, in its essence. It is again significant that Conrad should praise Maupassant along those lines: 'His vision by a more scrupulous, prolonged and devoted attention to the aspects of the visible world discovered at last the right words as if miraculously impressed for him upon the face of things and events' (*NLL*, p. 28).

According to this view of language, Strother Purdy explains, 'it is the writer's proper study to direct his reader's attention away from his words as words, and to keep his reader in the same kind of unawareness of language that characterizes ordinary speech'.[161] Our authors shared this ideal of transparency of language. Flaubert made the connection between the right word and the invisible word early in his career: 'plus l'expression se rapproche de la pensée, plus le mot colle dessus et disparaît' (II, p. 345). As Maupassant recalled, he believed that style should be 'impersonnel', taking on its quality from the quality of the writer's thought and the power of his vision, which meant that he rejected the idea of a book's originality as deriving from 'la singularité du style' (*MB*, p. 546). (In 'Le Roman' Maupassant did not hide his aversion to the Goncourts' 'vocabulaire bizarre, compliqué, nombreux et chinois' (*PJ*, p. xxv) which prevailed in his days under the name of 'écriture artiste'.) Conrad, praising James's *The Spoils of Poynton* in a letter to Garnett of 13 February 1897, also shows he valued transparency of language: 'It is like a great sheet of plate glass [...]. It's [...] as *pellucid* as clean plate glass' (*CL*, I, p. 339). Later, Ford clearly indicated that he and Conrad had made this a cardinal concept in their pursuit of style:

we set out to search for a formula for the *Mot Juste*. [...] We wanted to write [...] as simply as the grass grows. We desired to achieve a style – the *habit* of a style – so simple that you would notice it no more than you notice the unostentatious covering of the South Downs. [...]

Our most constant preoccupation, then, was to avoid words that stuck out of sentences either by their brilliant unusualness or their 'amazing aptness.' For either sort of word arrests the attention of a reader, and thus 'hangs up' both the meaning and the cadence of a phrase. We wanted the Reader to forget the Writer – to forget that he was reading. We wished him to be hypnotised into thinking that he was living what he read – [162]

But how is the author to identify the word that is the one and only one, that will seem so natural to the reader that he will be thus 'hypnotized'? First, it is the objectively accurate one, that is, the one which renders truthfully the phenomenon he wishes to depict: 'Si je mets *bleues* après *pierres*' Flaubert explained to Sainte-Beuve à propos of *Salammbô*, 'c'est que *bleues* est le mot juste, croyez-moi, et soyez également persuadé que l'on distingue très bien la couleur des pierres à la clarté des étoiles' (V, pp. 67–8). But more than that,

quand on sait la valeur exacte des mots, et quand on sait modifier cette valeur selon la place qu'on leur donne, quand on sait attirer tout l'intérêt d'une page sur une ligne, mettre une idée en relief entre cent autres, uniquement par le choix et la position des termes qui l'expriment [...] on est vraiment un artiste, le plus supérieur des artistes, un vrai prosateur.                                                      $(MB, p. 548)^{163}$

That Flaubert was thinking in terms of both the intrinsic and contextual proper-ties of words is confirmed in an anecdote related by Maupassant. To meet the criticism of a ten-line passage in 'Un coeur simple' by a circle of friends, Flaubert spent a night trying to change a sentence but finally kept it as it was because he had been unable to build another with satisfying harmony (*MB*, p. 547). Because the order of words determines their interaction and, therefore, modifies their value, changing a single word could ruin a whole passage: 'tout se tient et, quand je dérange un mot, il faut quelquefois détraquer plusieurs pages' (III, p. 223). Thus, the 'mot juste' is not merely the denotative word, but rather the word which, to use the pictorial term Flaubert himself employed, fits into the general colour he wished to render (see above, pp. 175, 178), or, if conveyed in a musical analogy, the word which is part of the total orchestration of the work.[164]

Predictably, 'precision' is a key-word in both men's critical thinking and artistic practice. For Flaubert, Art must strive for 'la précision de la science' (V, p. 397) because 'C'est la précision qui fait la force' (II, p. 471); it is the hallmark of perfection (III, p. 249). His successive drafts reveal his intense struggle to attain greater visualization of his material and a corresponding sharpening of his diction.[165] Conrad's similar attitude is reflected in his com-ment that the sailor's phrase to watch 'the growth of the cable' has 'the force, precision, and imagery of technical language', a language which 'created by simple men with keen eyes for the real aspect of the things they see in their trade, achieves the just expression seizing upon the essential, which is the ambition of the artist in words' (*MS*, p. 21). Indeed, his basic criticism of Mrs E. L. Sanderson's South African sketches in a letter of September 1910 is that her expression 'is not always sufficiently precise', and his amendments and suggestions all bear on this point: he has erased a few words because they 'detract from the *actuality* of the impression'; he has added the word '*wonder*' for 'Greater precision' because 'wonder is one of the conditions of the childhood of the world'; he finds fault with 'Something truly pagan' because it is 'too vague', and stresses that 'In letters suggestiveness itself, – a great quality – must be obtained by precise expression' (*LL*, II, pp. 116–18). His own revisions were aimed primarily at curbing his natural tendency to prolixity and vague-ness, in favour of greater conciseness and specificity.[166] And late in life, Conrad, although not often self-congratulatory, declared: 'as to precision of images and analysis my artistic conscience is at rest' (*LL*, II, p. 205).

Yet with both authors the 'mot juste' is not always precise in the sense of having a clearly defined referent. The blind man's voice, we read, 'se traînait dans la nuit, comme l'indistincte lamentation d'une vague détresse'; there was something remote in it which upset Emma: 'Cela lui descendait au fond de l'âme comme un tourbillon dans un abîme, et l'emportait parmi les espaces d'une mélancolie sans bornes' (*MB*, p. 370). The 'mot juste', in such contexts, can only be the one which, because it conveys the proper degree of imprecision, exerts the greatest power of suggestion. Margaret Tillett speaks of the 'unforgettable effect' created in Flaubert's works by 'the combination of the clear and definite with the vague and elusive'.[167] The relevance to the author of 'Heart of Darkness' needs no labouring: nothing is more typical of Conrad's art than this combination of scenes of amazing vividness and, at times, hallucinatory intensity with the evocation of human profundities and unfathomable mysteries. All that Marlow can first say of the 'round knobs' in front of Kurtz's hut is that they were 'expressive and puzzling, striking and disturbing'. No doubt these four adjectives, although they convey no concrete information, are no less 'justes' and precise in their factual imprecision than the adjectives 'black, dried, sunken' with which he then describes objectively one of those 'heads on the stakes' (*YOS*, p. 130).[168]

It is again striking that on this issue our two authors should hold identical views. As is well-known, Flaubert was strenuously opposed to the illustration of his own works – despite the visual character of his genius and his dependence on pictorial sources for information and stimulation – for he was convinced that any visual image would have a harmful effect by making explicit what the text was intended to evoke or suggest. His publisher's idea of an illustrated edition of *Salammbô* filled him with 'indescribable fury': 'Ce n'était guère la peine d'employer tant d'art à laisser tout dans le vague pour qu'un pignouf [a lout] vienne démolir mon rêve par sa précision inepte!' (V, p. 24). This is exactly the point Conrad made in April 1922 when Curle in an article entitled 'Conrad in the East'[169] named the port of landing in 'Youth' as Muntok. Conrad called it 'a damned hole' and complained: 'It is a strange fate that everything that I have, of set artistic purpose, laboured to leave indefinite, suggestive [...] should have that light turned on to it' (*LRC*, p. 142). Flaubert rejected all illustrations of Emma because a drawn woman resembles one woman whereas 'une femme écrite fait rêver à mille femmes' (V, p. 26). For him, the highest aim of Art was indeed 'de *faire rêver*' (III, p. 322), an aim which can be achieved only by creating an 'illusion' (III, p. 344). Similarly, Conrad went on to explain to Curle: 'Explicitness, my dear fellow, is fatal to the glamour of all artistic work, robbing it of all suggestiveness, destroying all illusion.'

This strong belief in the quasi-magical power of words accounts for the uncompromising attitude Flaubert and Conrad adopted towards language. Conrad concludes the letter to Mrs Sanderson, previously quoted, with an injunction, already traced to 'Le Roman', to 'guard oneself against the "*à peu près*"' (*LL*, II, p. 118; see above, p. 138). Just as Flaubert advises Louise Colet: 'Médite donc plus avant d'écrire et attache-toi au *mot*. Tout le talent d'écrire ne consiste après tout que dans le choix des mots' (II, p. 471),[170] Conrad cautions Galsworthy: '*every* word is an object to be considered anxiously with heart searchings and in a spirit of severe resolution. Don't write them (words) hurriedly' (*CL*, II, p. 178) (original emphasis).

Why should Conrad, on his own admission, 'perspire in incertitude over every word' (*CL*, I, p. 293);[171] why was he 'always worrying about the right phrase',[172] as his illustrious predecessor had done? The answer lies in his concern for Truth and his conviction that Truth cannot be dissociated from its expression. Here again Flaubert had set a precedent. As Auerbach has noted, Flaubert believed that 'the truth of the phenomenal world is also revealed in linguistic expression'; as a result, his artistic practice rested 'on a profound faith in the truth of language responsibly, candidly, and carefully employed'.[173] A letter to Hugh Clifford makes it clear that Conrad shared this faith:

words, groups of words, words standing alone, are symbols of life, have the power in their sound or their aspect to present the very thing you wish to hold up before the mental vision of your readers. The things 'as they are' exist in words; therefore words should be handled with care lest the picture, the image of truth abiding in facts should become distorted – or blurred.                                            (*CL*, II, p. 200)

Thus, despite his warm feelings for Miss Haldin, the language teacher objects as much to her 'mystic phrases' which 'clothe a naïve and hopeless cynicism' (*UWE*, p. 104) as he does to the loquacious and 'disconnected' speech (p. 4) of most of her compatriots, no doubt because they, too, distort and blur 'the image of truth'.[174]

Flaubert and Conrad, however, also shared a belief in epistemological solipsism: Truth, for them, had no objective reality. Flaubert said to George Sand: 'j'écris les choses comme je les sens, c'est-à-dire comme je crois qu'elles existent' (V, p. 385) and Conrad declared that his aim had always been to render 'the naked form of truth, such as one conceives it, such as one feels it' (*PR*, pp. 111–12). Their concern with language, like their belief in authorial impersonality, sprang from a desire to present their private perception of human experience as faithfully as possible. Just as Maupassant says that the writer of 'realistic' fiction has no other mission than to 'reproduire fidèlement' his own 'illusion' of the world (*PJ*, p. xvi), Conrad defines the first part of his twofold task as 'to depict faithfully [...] that innermost world as one apprehends it, and to express one's own real sense of that inner life' (*CL*, III, p. 90). Both his critical writings and correspondence are peppered with references to 'sincerity',[175] and twice in a letter to Francis Warrington Dawson of 20 June 1913 he speaks of the 'remorseless fidelity to the truth of his own sensations' which is 'the whole Credo of the artist' and in which 'the artist's salvation' lies.[176]

However, for all their passion for the truth, Conrad and Ford did not see it as the ultimate goal of their endeavours. Their wrestling with language was, above all, the expression of their faith in the ideal of beauty, of absolute formal perfection which, if it was to be attained, also meant that every word had to be tested and justified. In this quest for the Beautiful, Flaubert, once more, was the supreme exemplar. Indeed, Flaubert viewed the novel as a poetic structure to be endowed with the tightness of form of a poem and elaborated with all the resources of poetic language, which meant that artistic prose, in order to be 'souple et véhémente, pleine et imagée, musicale toujours' (VI, p. 481) as he envisaged it, must have all the attributes of verse, like 'precision' and 'sonority' (II, p. 448), 'consistency' (II, p. 468), 'rhythm', while remaining 'prose, et très prose' (III, pp. 142–3). He was the first to realize that, as Mallarmé was later to point out, it is language, not life, which is the novelist's medium.[177]

As early as 1846, answering the critics who found fault with novelists who are supposedly only concerned with style to the neglect of 'l'Idée, le but moral', Flaubert exclaimed: 'comme si le but de l'Art n'était pas le Beau avant tout' (I, p. 321). Thirty years later, although he went well beyond the requirements of novelistic verisimilitude in his fidelity to facts, he made it clear to George Sand that he considered the technical detail, the local piece of information, the historical and exact side of things – in other words, documentary accuracy – as 'très secondaire', and he stressed again that, above everything else, he sought 'la *beauté*' (VII, p. 281). Echoing him, Maupassant in 'Le Roman' urged the novelist to ignore the clamour of the multitude who demand to be consoled, amused, saddened, moved, etc., and to listen only to the few 'esprits d'élite' who say 'Faites-moi quelque chose de beau' (*PJ*, p. ix). Conrad paraphrased this passage in the Preface to *The Nigger* (see above p. 138) but made no reference there to that last injunction. However, fourteen years later, in 'A Familiar Preface', he declared (this time using the words of Anatole France) that he had '*never sought in the written word anything else but a form of the Beautiful*' (*PR*, p. xvii; see above, p. 144).

Flaubert took from Plato the idea that the True, the Beautiful, and the Good are one and eternal.[178] Beauty, for him, as for all the devotees of *l'art pour l'art* (Gautier, Baudelaire, the Parnassians) resulted from the perfect unity of the artist's vision and the form he gave it, a view from which he never budged. Soon after the publication of *Madame Bovary* he rejected a correspondent's charge that 'he paid too much attention to form' saying: 'Plus une idée est belle, plus la phrase est sonore [...]. La précision de la pensée fait (et est elle-même) celle du mot' (IV, p. 243). Nearly twenty years later, he explained to George Sand that his concern for beauty was '*une méthode*', the discovery of a bad assonance or a repetition warning him that he was 'dans le faux'; by dint of searching, he concluded, he always found the right expression, which was 'la seule' and was, at the same time, 'l'harmonieuse' (VII, p. 290). His statement that his main difficulty remained 'le style, la forme, le Beau indéfinissable *résultant de la conception même* et qui est la splendeur du Vrai comme disait Platon' (IV, pp. 164–5) can be regarded as a key to his art. Absorbing the lesson, Maupassant, in his 1884 study of Flaubert, said that when, through sheer probity, the form puts all the means available at the service of the idea, style reaches this sovereign beauty which comes from 'une accordance absolue de l'expression avec l'idée, d'une sensation d'harmonie, de beauté secrète' (*MB*, p. 545).[179] And Conrad too, from the outset of his career, was fully committed to 'complete, unswerving devotion to the perfect blending of form and substance', to 'an unremitting never-discouraged care for the shape and ring of sentences' (*NN*, p. ix). Without being Platonists like Flaubert, Maupassant and Conrad also placed an equal emphasis on Truth and Beauty.

But for Flaubert and Conrad this ideal could be attained only through an agonisingly slow and frustrating creative process with long periods of stagnation ('Les stérilités des écrivains nerveux')[180] and fits of depression – what Flaubert called 'les *affres* de l'Art' (II, p. 339) and which Barthes defined as 'the "Flaubertization" of writing',[181] that is, the substitution of labour and compositional ordeal for genius and Romantic inspiration. It is revealing that Conrad, who never gave much away about his relationship with Flaubert, singled out 'the desperate heart-breaking toil and effort of the writing' as a point of resemblance between himself and 'that great man' (see above, p. 12). Countless statements from their letters would bear this out: Flaubert's statement: 'Peu d'hommes, je crois, auront autant souffert que moi par la littérature' (IV, p. 231) finds its counterpart in Conrad's own assessment: 'Believe me, no man paid more for his lines than I have' (*LL*, II, p. 73).[182]

Indeed, both approached their art with a quasi-religious devotion and sacrificed everything to it. It was precisely this characteristic which Conrad stressed in the opening paragraph of *A Personal Record* by referring to the author who in 'his unworldly, almost ascetic, devotion to his art [was] a sort of literary, saint-like hermit' (p. 3). Significantly, he also saw himself in this character when he became a professional novelist: 'I live like a silly hermit', he wrote to Mrs Bontine on 22 November 1898, 'and can be of no good to my friends. Je ne suis pas dans le mouvement' (*CL*, II, p. 122). And a month later, in a letter to Aniela Zagórska, he showed (in terms which sound like a direct echo from Flaubert's correspondence) that for him, as for Flaubert, artistic creation did not allow for relaxation: 'the hermit is severe and dyspeptic et n'entend pas la plaisanterie en matière d'Art' (*CL*, II, p. 132).[183] (Compare Flaubert's remark to George Sand that he continues 'à n'entendre point la plaisanterie sur sa religion' [Art, of course] (VII, pp. 162–3)).

Such dedication reflected both writers' strong belief that aesthetics and ethics were complementary aspects of a single reality. Because he equated the quest for Beauty with the quest for Truth, Flaubert maintained, 'La morale de l'Art consiste dans sa beauté même' (IV, p. 136). Having turned Art into a religion, he considered artistic creation as a kind of priesthood which demanded a quasi-ascetic life. When in his early thirties, he confided to Louise Colet that he was not writing for money, or celebrity, or immortality, and that what supported him was '*la conviction que je suis dans le vrai*, et si je suis dans le vrai, je suis dans le bien, j'accomplis un devoir, j'exécute la justice' (III, p. 165). In a letter to George Sand written as he was finishing 'La Légende de Saint Julien l'Hospitalier', he once more rejected the idea of stating his personal opinion but declared that an intelligent reader will always see in a book 'la moralité qui doit s'y trouver' provided the book is not '*faux*', for, he added, 'du moment qu'une chose est vraie, elle est bonne' (VII, p. 285).[184]

Conrad agreed with Flaubert that ethics and aesthetics are one. In the letter to Hugh Clifford previously quoted, after stating that 'the expression should be studied in the interest of veracity', he adds: 'This is the only morality of *art* apart from *subject*' (*CL*, II, p. 200). Like Flaubert, who regarded ethics as the 'fundamental condition' of aesthetics (IX, p. 3), Conrad stated his 'primary conviction that truth alone is the justification of any fiction which makes the least claim to the quality of art' (*UWE*, p. viii). And just as Flaubert believed that the reader should draw from a book 'the morality' it is bound to contain if the picture is true, Conrad makes his language teacher look for some 'key-word' which, 'if not truth itself, may perchance hold truth enough to help the moral discovery which should be the object of every tale' (*UWE*, p. 67). Between the didacticism of the Victorians and the artistic anarchy of the *fin de siècle* writers, Conrad, thanks primarily to the heroic example of the 'literary, saint-like hermit' for whom he had such 'veneration', found refuge, as Karl put it, in 'that devotion to craft wherein art and morality meet in commitment, responsibility and lawfulness'.[185]

As a result, just as Flaubert had raised the status of the French novel, by insisting on and demonstrating its supreme artistic seriousness, Conrad – together with James and Ford – brought a new conception to the English novel which gave it a new aesthetic dimension.

# Part IV

---

# Conclusion

'No poet, no artist of any art, has his complete meaning alone. His significance, his appreciation is the appreciation of his relation to the dead poets and artists'.
                    T. S. Eliot, 'Tradition and the Individual Talent' (1919)

# 9    Conclusion

This study has, I hope, clearly demonstrated the extent to which French literature held a special place in Conrad's affections and career. The detailed evidence points to a profound Conradian debt, over his two most creative decades, to the modes, methods and traditions of French novelists – particularly Flaubert, Maupassant and Anatole France. Now the time has come to face some of the general issues and problems underlying the detailed evidence, and this will be done in three stages. In a first section, I examine the general questions of Conrad's literary traditions and the relative importance of personal experience and books in order to propose that our terms of critical reference need to be radically widened and redefined. I shall then examine the possible reasons which led Conrad to borrow as much as he did and, in broader terms, to make such extensive use of books. A coda suggests that the concept of 'borrowing' is too limited as a way of describing Conrad's varied engagement with books and writers and goes on to suggest other, richer, ways of describing the relationship between creative originality and literary dependency in his work.

## Conrad's triple identity

Over the past two decades a number of studies have set out to explore, with varying degrees of success, the cultural origins and background of Conrad's imaginative vision. Let us first consider some representative critical views of Conrad's place in English literary traditions. In *Conrad's Romanticism* (1974), David Thorburn has analysed his roots in English Romanticism with a special focus on Wordsworth and Stevenson. The book stems from the conviction that 'Conrad was in fundamental ways a man of the nineteenth century' who employed 'Romantic modes of storytelling' and who, with his 'stoic Romanticism grounded in a sense of human sharing and continuity', was closer to Wordsworth than any other modern 'prophets of our disorder'.[1] There are, no doubt, some psychic and structural affinities between Conrad and Wordsworth (although some mentioned by Thorburn seem forced), and it is helpful to be reminded of the Stevensonian complexion of a good deal of Conrad's fiction and its affinities with Kipling, Haggard, and other late Victorian writers. Yet no analysis of Conrad's romanticism should ignore, as this one does, either the influence of the works of the great Polish romantic poets and playwrights[2] or

213

that of the early French Romantics: Vigny, Hugo, Constant, Mérimée, not to mention half the writings of Flaubert, 'the last of the Romantics'. Thorburn makes interesting comparisons between Conrad and Wordsworth on the basis of their use of narrators and styles of narration, but again no account can be reliable which overlooks the much more important influence of the Polish *gawęda* and that of Maupassant. Put briefly, Conrad's romanticism requires a far wider context than the one offered in this book. John Batchelor's *The Edwardian Novelists* (1982) was initiated, we are told, by the question 'why does Conrad look so isolated a figure?' and tries to dispel the illusion of this 'apparent isolation' by relating him to a context which includes Ford, Wells, Bennett, Galsworthy, and Forster.[3] But this it achieves only partially. As Jeremy Hawthorn points out, the book is a 'creative failure' because 'it ends up establishing far more links between the writers other than Conrad than it does between them and him'. There is good reason for that: despite his strong feelings for some English writers, such as Shakespeare and Dickens, English literature was not Conrad's favourite, and English novelists, Victorian and Edwardian, were not his masters. As a result, Batchelor 'succeeds in establishing many links between Conrad and his British contemporaries' – which, no doubt, fully justify the existence of his book – 'but one is left with the feeling that perhaps the major part of his greatness resides in his distance from them'.[4]

Then there is the image of Conrad as seen in relation to Poland and his Polish heritage. Over the years, Polish scholars – Najder, Busza, Gillon, Morf, Tarnawski, to name only a few of the best known – have given us detailed descriptions of the formative influence of Conrad's Polish background, and of the impact made on his art by the rich and distinctive Polish cultural and literary traditions he inherited. Such descriptions are, of course, indispensable, and make it obvious that, as Leszek Prorok puts it, the Polish background 'affords the basic key to the interpretation of many special or mysterious features of his work'.[5] Unfortunately, some of them are marred by a tendency to over-simplify and make excessive claims.[6] For example, in *The Polish Shades and Ghosts of Joseph Conrad* (1976) Gustav Morf starts from 'the *duplex* personality of Conrad' and attempts 'to show how most of Conrad's themes ultimately derive from his Polish background, and that he was never far away from Poland when writing'.[7] But, as Batchelor comments, in order to prove his point Morf 'works too hard to find Polish "shades and ghosts" throughout the Conrad canon', and as a result 'some of his judgements seem wildly askew'. For instance, Batchelor challenges Morf's assertion that 'all the really important events [in *Nostromo* ... ] can be traced back to Conrad's Polish or Mediterranean days', and his claim that Giorgio Viola ('a gruff stoic') is based on Conrad's father ('a hysterical immature romantic').[8] In a similar way, Douglas Hewitt accepts that 'here and there we may find scraps of Polish experience incorporated in novels about other places and other situations' but, he adds, 'this is a very different matter from suggesting that an allegorization of Polish history and his own feelings about it lies at the centre of his work'.[9]

The rationale of these – and other – contextual studies is that what is still perceived as the isolated, mysterious character of Conrad's fiction can be explained in terms of the particular tradition which constitutes the subject of the inquiry. What they all make clear, however, is that, while they may shed light on certain aspects of his work, they cannot account satisfactorily for its multiple and elusive affiliations. No doubt the Polish background in particular is a valuable, an indispensable key; but a master-key it is not.

A general conclusion which compels recognition is that not only, as Batchelor asserts, 'to read Conrad in isolation is obviously to distort him',[10] but also that the same applies to any attempt to tie him securely to any one cultural and literary tradition. Conrad is no more 'in' the English tradition, 'in and of it', as Leavis would have it, than he is 'in and of' the French tradition, as some of Ford's comments may have suggested, although, in fairness to Ford, it must be said that he often stressed the cosmopolitan status of Conrad's fiction. Nor is he purely and simply, despite his strong links with the great Polish Romantic movement in poetry and drama, some kind of 'late Romantic', an offshoot of that movement using the medium of English prose, as Prorok presents him.[11] In the light of present-day scholarship, there can be no excuse for losing sight of the fact that, as Knowles put it, 'The perpetual fascination of Conrad's fiction is that it stands in suggestive relationship to so many European literary traditions – English, Polish and French – without ultimately belonging to any single one'.[12] Indeed, Conrad, the displaced Pole who wrote in English while constantly engaged in some kind of dialogue with writers from other nationalities, was never able to work – as, say, Dickens or Flaubert were able to do – from a well-established position within a given culture. Never did he enjoy that position of confidence and strength based on the writer's knowledge of values and assumptions shared between himself and his readers, which derived from common roots within the same cultural soil. With his complex background Conrad could never feel 'at home' anywhere. Conversely, it would be a grave misconception – of which he has long been the victim – to view him as rootless. The man who was once insulted by being called a man 'without either country or language'[13] turns out to have had three countries and three languages; the cosmopolitan déraciné had, after all, strong intellectual and artistic roots in three great literary traditions; the isolated novelist whom 'No one could help', according to Galsworthy, and who, in Watt's view, was 'too proud to owe very much to anyone'[14] had, in fact, contracted an enormous debt to writers belonging to all these traditions and others beyond. The 'great novelist unclassified'[15] will always be unclassifiable because, as he was well aware, he was not a 'national' writer (LF, p. 87) but a truly European writer endowed with a triple inheritance, a triple identity, a triple imagination and vision. His apparent isolation cannot be dispelled and his elusiveness explained by relating him to only one or even two cultural and literary contexts. The Polish–English duality, which has been the prevalent view of him so far ('a Polish nobleman, cased in British tar' (*CL*, I, p. 52)) has been proved inadequate. From now on, only Conrad's 'triple image' will ever be acceptable.

As if inspired by Conrad's own tendency to minimize his indebtedness to other writers while emphasizing the importance of 'real-life',[16] Conrad criticism has always taken a dim view of all literary influences – witness the remarks above by Galsworthy and Watt, made at some fifty years' interval – and preferred to dwell on the biographical aspects of his fiction. The perspective on this subject again remained basically the same for decades. Just as in 1941 M. C. Bradbrook confidently asserted: 'All Conrad's work is based on his personal reminiscences [...] every book he wrote is founded upon real people and incidents of real life',[17] so Karl states in the same vein in his biography: 'his work was embedded in past experience, both the actual events and people and the imagination working on them'. Karl justifies his intense concentration on Conrad's Polish life by saying that 'it informed every aspect of his later years' and was 'the matrix for his ideas'. As a result, Conrad as a novelist is seen engaged in a 'retrieval of past memories' and is presented as 'a Proustian of sorts'.[18]

The attempt to link Conrad firmly with his Polish past calls for a few more remarks. Justification for this approach is not far to seek: 'One's literary life,' Conrad said, 'must turn frequently for sustenance to memories and seek discourse with the shades' (*PR*, p. xv). Nevertheless, if one may be excused for stating a truism, life does not end at sixteen (in the Preface to his biography, Najder has a timely warning for 'Poles who are apt to see in Conrad a Polish Romantic writer and forget about his later life'[19]). After the sombre experiences of his family and national environment, he embarked in Marseilles on his colourful life as a sailor: 'In Marseilles I did begin life,' he confided to Galsworthy on 8 May 1905, 'It's the place where the puppy opened his eyes' (*CL*, III, p. 240). Conrad's development as an adult, accomplished in other countries, mainly in two different languages, cannot be regarded, despite a distinct measure of continuity, as a mere extension of a process started in Poland, nor can the work of his maturity be seen purely as a fulfilment of his youth. 'Sailing towards Poland',[20] therefore, can be regarded as a fruitful enterprise only if we do not lose sight of the fact that Conrad, despite his 'fidelity to a special tradition' (*PR*, p. 36), sailed away from Poland and discovered new horizons.

The findings made about Conrad's use of his experiences as a sailor must also be put into their proper perspective. Najder has already corrected the overall impression left by many biographical critics when he points out that 'the detailed research, particularly by Norman Sherry, of tracing presumed prototypes of characters and sources of plots, the persistent search for analogies between the lives of actual people and those of the characters in Conrad's works, all reveal that the connections and similarities are vague'. And later he adds:

Conrad used the names of people met at that time [i.e. in Borneo], and occasionally their external appearance, in his writings only as fulcra for raising his new fictional world from the vast magma of reminiscences, the books he had read, and his own imagination. Sherry asserts that Conrad's 'contact with the Berau trading post was crucial. From it came *Almayer's Folly*, *An Outcast of the Islands*, the second part of *Lord Jim*, and *The Rescue*'. This claim seems exaggerated even in the light of his own findings. Books by travelers and diarists played a more significant role as a source of raw material for fiction.[21]

What further complicates this whole issue is that his works differ greatly in this respect. Watt mentions six works – *The Nigger of the 'Narcissus'*, 'Youth', 'Heart of Darkness', 'Typhoon', 'The Secret Sharer' and *The Shadow-Line* – which 'are alike in that they are more immediately and exclusively rooted in remembered experience than Conrad's other fiction'. Conrad's creative method in these stories is aptly described as 'characteristically personal without being directly autobiographical'. But even then, as Watt points out, despite this common basis, they show considerable variations in the extent to which they approach autobiography, with 'Youth' and 'Heart of Darkness', for instance, being 'much closer' to 'particular events' in Conrad's life and to his 'main personal preoccupations' than *The Nigger*.[22] This is in accordance with the respective reliance on literature – and reading generally – discovered so far in these stories: it is important in all of them, but in *The Nigger* it is truly remarkable.

Futhermore, these six works represent only a part of Conrad's total *oeuvre*, and the conclusions to be drawn from them about his creative process have only limited validity. Does Watt's assertion that with Conrad memory dominated creation and that he 'could only construct his imaginative edifice on the foundation of some preexistent real features in the landscape of memory'[23] really apply to the longer novels of the major phase from *Lord Jim* to *Victory*? Clearly, the indiscriminate insistence on Conrad's use of past experience as the basis of his fiction fails to register the 'subtle change in the nature of [his] inspiration' (*N*, p. xv) which took place at the beginning of 1903 as he was embarking on *Nostromo*, and which led him for a full decade to turn repeatedly to secondary sources – both non-fiction and fiction – as he treated subjects no longer drawn from his own experience.

As a result, Conrad's fiction presents a complex mixture of elements gathered from his rich and varied life or his vast and eclectic readings. Countless illustrations of this have been shown in his work, whether it be description of nature (a night in the tropics, an evening on the Essex marshes, the *Patna* on the Arabian sea), characterization (the portrayal of Jim, Captain Whalley, Decoud, Alice, Heyst and Lena), or general outlook and treatment of individual themes. Let us take a brief look at a few of these themes. While recognizing the likelihood of an innate predisposition towards pessimism, it is certainly possible, as Najder believes,[24] that an important source of Conrad's 'deep scepticism, frequently tinged with pessimism' lies in Bobrowski's 'exhortations'. But the company he constantly kept with nineteenth-century French writers probably played an even more influential role in his attitude as a mature artist, as his adoption of some of their most sceptical and pessimistic statements indicates. Morf may have a point when, after saying that in *Nostromo* 'we hear of civil war, repression and pacification, imprisonment and torture, military tyranny, deeds of valor and deeds of atrocity', he observes: 'it is the Polish history of the years 1814 to 1867 all over again'.[25] At the same time, one is also entitled to point out that Conrad's most obvious literary models, *Salammbô* and *L'Education sentimentale* – together with the writings of Anatole France – present a similarly bleak view of history. Although the theme of moral solitude probably stems from his loneliness as a child and his situation as an expatriate, it was also fostered by his immersion in nineteenth-century French literature where it is a dominant motif. Conrad found in the lives and works of some lonely sceptics of the early part of the century, such as Constant and Mérimée, a reflection of his own predicament. Characteristically, as Knowles has shown, he discovered important roots 'in a tradition of writing which deals with rootless cosmopolitanism and dangerously unfettered isolation'. The same paradoxical 'sense of fellowship-in-isolation', the same 'kind of moral support in the very perception of solitude',[26] Conrad also found in the works of his favourite writers of the second half of the century – Flaubert, Maupassant and Anatole France. Again, Conrad's personal life can well account for his preoccupation with death, but so does his familiarity with French authors. It may be that, in Meyer's words, his 'witnessing the slow dying of his mother and later his father' was the source of Wait's death,[27] but, although death from tuberculosis was bound to have strong resonances for him since both his parents had died of it, the treatment of Wait's illness and death ultimately derives from Flaubert and Maupassant (whose character, Forestier, also dies of this disease).

There is obviously much more to Conrad's fiction than can be explained by his biography, and Schwarz's contention that 'More than we have realised, Conrad's work must be read as an expression of his own personal life'[28] is no longer tenable. For an artist like Conrad, the reality of the outside world and the reality of books ('Books are an integral part of one's life' (*PR*, p. 73)) constituted, on equal terms, a vast quarry of raw material from which he could draw at will. This is why any attempt at too closely interlinking his art and his life is bound to produce dubious interpretations and cause serious distortions. The proper assessment of the balance between personal elements and elements derived from books in any given work requires a prudent and discriminating approach, and a mind free from preconceived theses. Indeed the various ingredients are often so inextricably mixed that there is no distinguishing between the spontaneous expression of a very genuine and deeply-felt experience on Conrad's part and his deliberate borrowing of another man's perceptions for carefully calculated artistic purposes. Conrad's works are intensely personal, rooted deep in the rich soil of their author's psyche; but they are also, and no less importantly, cultural artefacts with equally deep roots in the rich soil of remote and diverse cultural and literary traditions.

## Why did Conrad borrow?

As early as 1940, with the publication of Gordan's *Joseph Conrad: The Making of a Novelist*, it became clear that Conrad relied considerably on factual sources when writing his early fiction. And since it was known at that time that he had also made use of factual material for 'The Duel' and *Suspense*, Gordan was in a position to state that 'Conrad's habit of drawing inspiration from his reading lasted throughout his life'.[29] However, until the mid-sixties, that is before the publication of the work of Kirschner, Yelton and Busza, practically the only literary sources to have been found were confined to the early works (*Almayer's Folly*, 'The Idiots') or the late *Victory*. Understandably, these influences and textual borrowings were interpreted as signs of early inexperience or late creative decline. Thus, Walpole saw the influence of Flaubert (and the French language) as a 'crutch' which Conrad used in his early writing 'before he could walk alone'.[30] Gradually, as more factual borrowings and verbal influences were discovered, other reasons for Conrad's reliance on books came to be invoked such as ill health and mental stress. This is how Kirschner and Karl have explained his massive debt to 'Les Soeurs Rondoli' in 'A Smile of Fortune', the first work after his breakdown in early 1910.[31] And Knowles has interpreted the presence of an extensive borrowing from *Le Lys rouge* towards the end of *Victory* on the same grounds, saying that Conrad, 'under pressure and over-tired at this late stage of the novel, decided to take the shortest and quickest route to his final destination'.[32] Indeed, since Conrad's life as a professional novelist was constantly plagued with hardships – health problems, family tension, financial worries, artistic doubts, and so on – it could be reasonably argued that his life-long practice stems from a pressing need for assistance at times of great duress. Even more fundamental, perhaps, is the fact that, while enjoying contact with Ford, James, Galsworthy, Wells, Garnett, Cunninghame Graham and others, he lived and worked in relative isolation. His constant reliance on books may well be the sign – contrary to Karl's assertion that he 'needed little [...] intellectual stimulation' – that he was permanently looking for stimulating communication.[33]

Other fairly obvious reasons spring to mind readily. It may be the case that he borrowed from factual sources to obtain the raw material – geographical, historical, social, political – which he needed to build his stories and with which he was not familiar. As already noted, his reliance, in his critical writings, on fellow-novelists and distinguished critics can be attributed to a lack of both critical ability and self-confidence in handling formal critical conventions. His dependence on some 'authority' like Maupassant or France, when dealing with his 'uncongenial subject', can be explained in terms of his limited experience with women. And without being facetious, it could even be suggested that Conrad, who came late to his writing career, tackled his new craft in a sailor-like spirit, 'se debrouillant avec les moyens du bord', making do with the means at his disposal.[34] It is likely that all these factors played a part, but Conrad's practice, it would seem, goes deeper than this and calls for a deeper understanding. Why then did he borrow so extensively?

As a preliminary, a basic question needs to be answered: was this a conscious procedure on Conrad's part? Kirschner, on the evidence available to him, came to the conclusion that it was. Conrad, he suggested, perhaps 'referred to Maupassant while he wrote', or 'perhaps he immersed himself in a scene from Maupassant before writing a thematically related scene of his own'. Whatever the case may be, he translated, 'and translating is a conscious operation'.[35] Despite this sensible assessment, the above view is still regarded sceptically by some critics. Watt's response to Kirschner's findings, for instance, is that these borrowings 'look like unconscious residues of Conrad's remarkable but erratic memory', that 'he probably forgot that he was remembering'.[36] No doubt his continuous immersion in Flaubert, Maupassant, France, and other authors may account for a few unobtrusive phrases and images slipping unnoticed into his writings as a result of some quirk of subconscious memory. But his borrowings are so obvious, numerous, and varied that it is abundantly clear that, whether or not French works were on his desk, Conrad was highly conscious of those original texts; in short we are faced with a deliberate mode of composition.

When trying to account for Conrad's adoption of such a method, four reasons emerge as being particularly relevant: his linguistic situation, his psychology, his creative make-up, and his conception of the nature of fiction.

Conrad's persistent creative ordeal was to a large extent, and this is too easily forgotten, the result of his difficulties with the linguistic medium. Kirschner rightly stressed: 'We tend perhaps to take too much for granted the strain on Conrad of habitually expressing himself in a foreign language'.[37] Conrad is largely responsible for this, having referred in 1918 to his 'subtle and unforeseen accord' with English (*LL*, II, p. 206), and stating the following year: 'my faculty to write in English is as natural as any other aptitude with which I might have been born' (*PR*, p. v). The truth, however, is that this kind of 'official' pronouncement, like others made late in life, is part of his personal mythologizing. The reality was likely to have been less glamorous. Ford recorded Conrad's intense dissatisfaction with English when he was working on *Nostromo*,[38] and indeed the man who could produce in that novel such glaring gallicisms as 'the *lecture* of the letters' (p. 57); 'the man seemed *to find his account in it*' (p. 93); 'Father Beron had been *adjoined* to the commission' (p. 371), could not have been thinking wholly in English. Later confirmation comes in January 1907, when Conrad wrote to Mme Poradowska: 'Et puis l'Anglais m'est toujours une langue etrangère qui demande un effort formidable pour être maniée' (*CL*, III, p. 401). And as late as January 1911, he still admitted to Joseph de Smet: 'In writing I wrestle painfully with that language which I feel I do not possess but which possesses me, – alas!' (*LL*, II, p. 125).[39] If that is the way he responded to English at the peak of his career, with some of the greatest novels in the English language to his credit, the question arises as to how he reacted to it when he started writing *Almayer's Folly*?

Whatever Conrad's personal feelings for English may have been, it is obvious that he experienced a considerable degree of uncertainty when handling it, and understandably so. After all, he had started learning it in his early twenties, in the company of 'fishermen, shipwrights and sailors', and this absence of any formal learning resulted in the fact that he 'never opened an English grammar' (*LL*, II, pp. 124, 125). His literary English he acquired through his vast and eclectic reading in, for example, the Bible, Shakespeare, Dickens, Marryat, and Fenimore Cooper. He also acquired it through the time-honoured process of translation – possibly from Polish, definitely from French, the latter a language he knew from childhood and which had given him access directly or through translation to European literature in general. Ford gave an interesting glimpse of Conrad serving his apprenticeship in the English language, forging the tool he would later use as an artist: 'Tormented with the curiosity of words, even at sea, on the margins of the French books he made notes for the translation of phrases'. And, we recall, Ford mentioned having seen copies of *Pêcheur d'Islande* and *Madame Bovary* which Conrad had 'annotated' in this way.[40]

The collaboration with Ford, initiated by Conrad himself primarily on linguistic grounds, with a view to becoming better acquainted with English usage and the associations and connotations of English words, far from weaning him from this linguistic reliance on French authors during the crucial years 1898–1904 (at a time when one would have expected him to gain total confidence with his medium) consolidated it. Not only did they often converse in French and read French books together ('We never read anything but French in those days'),[41] they also used French in the process of composition and, more importantly, they made Flaubert and Maupassant their 'chief masters in style', deliberately producing stylistic imitations of them. Since both men had indulged in this kind of exercise before they met, they no doubt found it natural to make it into a regular procedure. Thus, stylistic considerations, rooted in their desire to emulate their favourite authors, reinforced a practice which was also rooted, in Conrad's case, in linguistic need.

Bernard Meyer has said that Conrad 'suffered from an uncertain sense of his own identity' and that this 'very wavering of Conrad's sense of self was indeed one of the most important features of his personality'.[42] That Conrad harboured a fragile sense of personal identity and self-belief, he conveyed on a number of occasions. Writing to Stephen Crane on 16 November 1897, he shows his pleasure at another craftsman's appreciation of *The Nigger*, but then asks himself if Crane really meant what he said. Apologetically, Conrad adds: 'The mistrust is not of you – it is of myself' and explains: 'I am not more vile than my neighbours but this disbelief in oneself is like a taint that spreads on everything one comes in contact with' (*CL*, I, p. 410).[43] A letter to Galsworthy of 9 April 1906 shows him to be still plagued with the same problem. After referring to his days of creative sterility, 'those days without a line, nay, without a word', he writes: 'I doubt not only my talent (I was never so sure of that) but my character' (*CL*, III, pp. 327–8). It is surely significant that in the course of his literary career, both before and after the Ford era, he proposed collaboration with at least four other writers – Mme Poradowska, Crane, Edward Noble, and Richard Curle. As Karl points out, 'Conrad's desperate need for support is made clear by his willingness to work with someone fifteen years his junior'[44] – who, one could add, had no great achievement to his credit. The fact is that Conrad required considerable propping throughout his career. To complete *Nostromo*, for instance, he needed 'Pinker financially, Ford for dictation and possible writing of copy, Galsworthy for correction of galleys and for loans, and, of course, Jessie for routine typing', just as, throughout its composition, he had relied on countless factual and fictional sources. His dependence on other authors was clearly part of the same overall 'dependency pattern that seems intrinsic to [his] way of working and surviving'.[45] For a man riddled with psychological, intellectual, aesthetic and linguistic doubts, for whom writing was a frustratingly slow and painful process ('I had to work like a coal miner in his pit quarrying all my English sentences out of a black night' (*LL*, II, p. 82)), which entailed an enormous expenditure of intellectual and nervous energy ('if you knew the wear and tear of my writing' (*CL*, I, p. 293)), books, as we have seen, provided rich seams from which valuable materials and models could be extracted speedily and economically. And who knows? Perhaps the act of borrowing, while leaving him open to what Harold Bloom calls 'the anxiety of influence',[46] paradoxically helped to boost his shaky sense of self-confidence. After all, what could be more soul-destroying for Conrad, after a day's work, than a blank sheet of paper, that 'vide papier que la blancheur défend' which equally haunted Mallarmé?[47]

Since this kind of dependence is by no means unique in the annals of literature (although, admittedly, the scale of Conrad's borrowings seems to be), it may be helpful to recall the case of another inveterate borrower, Samuel Coleridge, with which Conrad's case presents some analogy. In his review of Norman Fruman's *The Damaged Archangel*, a book which constitutes 'an unrelenting assault upon Coleridge' recapitulating the charges of plagiarism which have been restated at intervals against him, Thomas McFarland writes that 'all Coleridge's plagiarisms exist as testimony to his compulsive intellectual symbiosis'. After pointing out that borrowings 'so honeycomb his work as to form virtually a mode of composition', he stresses that these 'were not the thefts of a poverty-stricken mind, but the mosaic materials of a neurotic technique of composition'. In other words, Coleridge was 'a deeply neurotic man' and his 'compulsive plagiarisms' are viewed as 'a neurotic manifestation'.[48] Conrad, as we know, was hypersensitive, self-pitying, over-scrupulous, psychologically and professionally insecure, and these factors may account for a neurotic element in his compositional practice. Indeed, why should he have felt the need to echo the words of Mickiewicz's *Konrad Wallenrod*: '"It has set at last," said Alf to Halban, / Pointing to the sun from the window of his crenelle' in order to write, in *Almayer's Folly*, something as simple as '"It has set at last," said Nina to her mother pointing towards the hills behind which the sun had sunk' (147)?[49] And if amateurism can be invoked at this early stage, why should he follow Flaubert, often verbatim, when describing the appearance of the German skipper, Doramin, Old Swaffer, Captain Whalley and Linda Viola? Most puzzling of all, why should the British Master Mariner turn to Maupassant, the freshwater sailor, to describe the voyage of the *Patna* on a route with which he was familiar? Conrad's reliance on books may, like Coleridge's, testify to a kind of 'compulsive intellectual symbiosis', with the exact wording of another writer being, in his case too, 'some sort of talisman that allayed his anxieties'.[50]

Many of Conrad's borrowings can also be attributed to general characteristics in his creative make-up. First, its deficiencies. In the letter to Walpole of 7 June 1918 containing the misleading assessment of his debt to Flaubert, he dismissed the suggestion that he had ever hesitated between English and French 'as a writing langue', and then denied having ever thought in French during the process of composition. He explained: 'When I wrote the first words of *Almayer's Folly*, I had been already for years and years *thinking* in English. [...] Is it thinkable that anybody possessed of some effective inspiration should contemplate for a moment such a frantic thing as translating it into another tongue?' (*LL*, II, p. 206). As we know, this argument does not stand up on linguistic grounds. Neither does it stand on the other grounds invoked, that of 'effective inspiration', since one of his major problems lay precisely in persistent bouts of creative paralysis. In this predicament, he turned to those sources which could provide not only 'inspiration' but also concrete material, in particular the works of his favourite authors, even though, since most of them were French, this involved such a 'frantic thing' as translation.

Conrad was also handicapped by a general lack of inventiveness – as he put it himself, he was 'not a facile inventor' (*LL*, II, p. 139), a limitation he deplored throughout his career. On 5 August 1896, in the midst of his difficulties with *The Rescue*, he wrote to Garnett: 'I begin to fear that I have not enough imagination – not enough power to make anything out of the situation; that I cannot invent an illuminating episode that would set in a clear light the persons and feelings' (*CL*, I, p. 296). Two decades later, in his Author's Note to 'An Outpost of Progress' (1919), he commented: 'As for the story itself it is true enough in its essentials. The sustained invention of a really telling lie demands a talent which I do not possess' (*TU*, p. vii). And a recollection by Curle shows that Conrad was very open on this subject, since he often admitted that 'he had no gift for invention' (*N*, p. viii).[51]

In this light, Gordan's remarks that Conrad's 'power lay not in invention but in recollection' and that 'creation came to him easily – at times came only – when he had some personal experience or some observation to elaborate'[52] seem justified. Indeed, Conrad's imagination, as is well-known, needed a firm foundation of facts, and when memories were inadequate he was threatened by stagnation. As he was grinding to a halt with *The Rescue*, 'sitting down before the blank page' day after day to find that he 'could not put one sentence together', he confessed to Garnett: 'I am frightened when I remember that I have to drag it all out of myself', adding by way of explanation that his 'impressions and sensations' were 'all faded' (*CL*, I, pp. 288–9). And when working on *Nostromo*, he complained to Cunninghame Graham that his memories of Central America, of which he had only had a glimpse twenty-five years earlier, seemed to 'slip away' and were 'not enough pour bâtir un roman dessus' (*CL*, III, p. 45). Under such circumstances, books were again indispensable to him. So the whole truth is more complex than is suggested by the statement that Conrad's power lay 'in recollection' since books, in varying degrees, were always indispensable to him, not merely when he was elaborating subjects remote from personal experience but even when working on autobiographical material.

Nonetheless, Conrad's psychological and creative make-up, need I say, also had its positive aspects, such as – and this is of particular relevance here – his general receptiveness[53] and adaptability: adaptability to different countries, languages, careers, types of fiction, styles, and above all to individual people. Both Garnett and Meyer have referred to the 'chameleon-like quality' of his letters,[54] and this is one of the keynotes struck by Laurence Davies in his introduction to *The Collected Letters*:

> Reading such an edition, one is conscious, above all, of the range of personalities at Conrad's disposal. While remaining essentially Conrad, he seems to reshape himself for each correspondent: subversively cynical for Garnett; sympathetic, encouraging, upright, rather respectable for Ted Sanderson and Helen Watson; soulful for the Briquels; Byronic for Marguerite Poradowska; provocatively nihilistic for Cunninghame Graham; fussily professional for Unwin; good-natured for the Polish cousins; frank for Janina de Brunnow. In these letters, often so personal, yet so much of a performance, an impersonation, we hear not one but many voices.          (*CL*, I, p. lviii)

At a more sophisticated level, Conrad's mimetic gift and artistic versatility are clearly shown by his obvious talent as a 'pasticheur' who could write at will in the styles of Flaubert, Maupassant, Zola, Dickens, and others.

This mimetic ability can be related to the linguistic considerations already raised. After all, the acquisition of a foreign language, in both its spoken and written forms, entails a great deal of learning by rote, and in particular the assimilation of set phrases which can be re-used fairly safely and with a minimum of change in given situations. In other words, it entails 'aping' native speakers and writers. Thanks to his amazingly retentive memory, Conrad must have gleaned a vast pool of phrases and sentences from his immense English reading, and this habit may also explain many of his borrowings from, and allusions to, French writers. For instance, in Maupassant's 'Menuet', a story selected for the Martindale edition, Conrad had read: 'certaines choses [...] nous *laissent à l'âme comme une trainée de* tristesse' (*Contes de la Bécasse*, p. 62), and the phrase reappears, suitably adapted, in his appraisal of Cunninghame Graham's *Mogreb-el-Acksa. A Journey in Morocco* in a letter to Mrs Bontine of 4 December 1898: 'Cette oeuvre brilliante *laisse dans l'âme* du lecteur *comme une trainée de* lumière' (*CL*, II, p. 125). Similarly, in *La Vie littéraire*, Conrad had read, in an essay on the young Russian exile Marie Bashkirtseff, of '*cette vie* déracinée et *jetée à tous les vents de* l'Europe' (VI, p. 163), a phrase which, because of its relevance to his own life, must have made a deep impression on him, and so, in a letter to Cunninghame Graham of 8 February 1899, he applies it to himself: 'J'ai *jété ma vie a tous les vents du* ciel' (*CL*, II, p. 160), and years later, again suitably adapted, to Razumov: 'He does not *throw* his soul *to the winds*' (*UWE*, p. 15).

The 'chameleon-like quality' Conrad so often displays in his fiction must also be connected with the fluidity and uncertainty already noted in his psychological make-up. Meyer interprets his 'identifications with heroic figures [which] can be repeatedly demonstrated in both the factual and the fictional aspects of Conrad's life' – Ford's recollection that he amused himself by discovering presumed resemblances between himself and distinguished historical figures being an obvious example – as a sign of his 'constant search for a distinct image of his very identity'.[55] Conrad's willingness to adopt the views of other writers on a wide variety of subjects of fundamental importance is probably another aspect of this search. The French novelist Georges Perec, who, unlike Conrad, has not felt the need to be reserved about his debt to Flaubert, has attributed his 'systematic borrowings' from *L'Education sentimentale* in *Les Choses* to 'un accaparement' [an appropriation], 'un vouloir-être Flaubert'.[56] Because Conrad was, in Ford's words, 'so immensely... impressed – and depressed' (see above, p. 10) by Flaubert's writings, the same process of identification and assimilation, the same desire 'to be Flaubert' – or for that matter to be Maupassant, Anatole France, and so on – may also have been at work in his case.

Another important reason for Conrad's borrowings probably lies in his conception of the nature of fiction and what, for him, constituted reality. The novel, as we have seen, Conrad defined as 'a form of imagined life clearer than reality' (*PR*, p. 15). He regarded 'Liberty of imagination' as 'the most precious possession of a novelist' (*NLL*, p. 7) because 'Only in men's imagination does every truth find an effective and undeniable existence' (*PR*, p. 25). And in June 1924, only a few weeks before his death, he stressed his imaginative freedom in a discussion with Jean-Aubry: 'I do not write history, but fiction, and I am therefore entitled to choose as I please what is most suitable in regard to characters and particulars to help me in the general impression I wish to produce' (*LL*, I, p. 77). His quest was indeed for a higher realism. Probably the best illustration of his achievement in this respect was provided by Conrad himself who, in a letter to Edmund Gosse of 1918, emphasized that 'Sulaco is a synthetic product', a synthesis of many Central and South American countries, and added: 'The historical part is an achievement in mosaic too, though, personally, it seems to me much more true than any history I ever learned.'[57] Conrad's method of composition finds here its full justification, for 'it is precisely the quintessence of his talent', as Hans van Marle once commented, 'that he created a new functional reality of a higher order out of bits and pieces of the reality of everyday life'.[58]

So clearly, on the face of it, Conrad kept his distance from so-called reality. But there is another side to the coin. Fiction, he argued, 'puts to shame the pride of documentary history' (*PR*, p. 15) because, whereas history is based on printed material, 'on second-hand impression', fiction (which is 'human history') 'stands on firmer ground, being based on the reality of forms and the observation of social phenomena [...]. Thus fiction is nearer truth' (*NLL*, p. 17). And 'truth alone', he also affirmed 'is the justification of any fiction which makes the least claim to the quality of art' (*UWE*, p. viii). So, the demarcation line between reality and fiction is not clearly defined after all. Fiction must be true, and invention discarded. We are reminded in this connection of Flaubert and Maupassant scouring the Normandy countryside in search of the proper setting for *Bouvard et Pécuchet*, a setting Flaubert already carried in his head, and indeed, Conrad's greatest praise for Maupassant was that he was endowed with 'the true imagination' and never condescended 'to invent anything' (*NLL*, p. 31). After saying that he does 'not write history, but fiction', Conrad made clear, nevertheless, that his own fiction, too, is firmly rooted in reality: 'Most of the personages I have portrayed actually belonged to the crew of the real *Narcissus*' (*LL*, I, p. 77), he explained, and we now know that, with typical scrupulousness, he followed in his story 'the wind patterns normally prevailing from June to October on the course of the *Narcissus*'.[59] And when accused of showing a lack of 'fair play' in making the gunboat which shells the African bush French, he retorted that he had been faithful to the facts and merely recorded an observed reality (*CL*, III, p. 93).

Similarly, Conrad's use of documentary sources must also be linked with his concern for this kind of specificity. How else is one to explain, for instance, that a passage of the letter Jim receives from his father, who is a parson, was taken verbatim from a letter of the Reverend William Hazlitt to his own son?

Conrad's immense reading of books on Malayan, African, and South American backgrounds, on the worlds of revolutionaries and anarchists, on the Napoleonic era, was intended to supply him with fully authentic detail. In this respect, his working method was again no different from that of Flaubert. The prodigious work of authentication that went into the making of Flaubert's Carthage (the preparation itself included reading ninety-eight volumes within five months on subjects as varied as ethnography, public life, military art, religion, medicine, and commerce), finds its equivalent in the intensive reading that went into the creation of Costaguana. As a result, just as Flaubert could quote his sources when challenged by Sainte-Beuve about the authenticity of, say, the carbuncles formed by the urine of lynxes, so Conrad, had he been similarly challenged about presenting the 'Emaciated greybeards' of Pedro Montero's army riding into Sulaco 'with strips of raw beef twined round the crowns of their hats' (*N*, pp. 384–5), would also have been able to show that he had 'invented' nothing.[60] In fact, this is precisely what happened when Hugh Clifford accused him of having no knowledge of the Malays. On 13 December 1898, he pointed out to Blackwood:

> I am inexact and ignorant no doubt (most of us are) but I don't think I sinned so recklessly. Curiously enough all the details about the little characteristic acts and customs which they hold up as proof I have taken out (to be safe) from undoubted sources – dull, wise books. [...] In *Karain*, for instance, there's not a single action of my man (and good many of his expressions) that can not be backed by a traveller's tale – I mean a serious traveller's.                                              (*CL*, II, p. 130)

## Creativity and tradition

Our new knowledge of Conrad's compositional practices prompts another set of awkward questions: is his integrity, whether artistic or intellectual, compromised? Should his originality be impugned? What is the relationship, in his case, between individual talent, creative dependency and less creative forms of indebtedness?

In the first place, it should be stressed that the concept of 'borrowing', because it refers primarily to a covert use of sources, is too narrow a term to apply to Conrad's extraordinarily varied engagement with previous books and writers. The current passion for originality is a modern attitude only 200 years old, and our perception of Conrad's practice might benefit from being seen in a larger historical perspective. 'The writers of antiquity' Alexander Lindey writes, 'deemed innovation hazardous, and imitation both necessary and laudable'.[61] Imitation was recognized as a literary method, in particular as a method of perfecting one's own style by composing detailed imitations from one or more models. In the Middle Ages, poets were so wary of originality that they used to invent sources for their material in an attempt to authenticate it. Classical and Renaissance writers expected to study their predecessors for inspiration, subjects, material, and style. They therefore regarded it as a matter of pride to acknowledge models and sources. Both Ancient and Classical writers, however, saw imitators as emulators who were expected to change the original and add something of their own. Thus the 'busy bee', for its assimilating and metamorphosing activity, came to epitomize the classical attitude towards imitation: imitators, in K. K. Ruthven's words, are 'busy bees who ransack the profusion of flowers in the Muses' garden and transform the stolen pollen into honey'.[62] This image makes it clear that for these writers the good imitator gathers the best from the best models and undermines the claim of Meyer – made, no doubt, for the charitable purpose of exonerating Conrad – that 'He picked up a pebble and changed it into a diamond'.[63] Far from being pebbles, Conrad's borrowings represent some of the finest passages which the greatest nineteenth-century masters could offer. And since the bee was regarded as a symbol of eclecticism and universality, could a more suitable emblem be found to express Conrad's practice?[64]

Although the shift from the ideal of imitative art to that of invention through imagination goes back to the Renaissance, it is only towards the mid eighteenth century that the word 'imitation' became pejorative and the theory of originality was formulated by a growing number of critics who agreed that no matter how creative an imitation might be, it was necessarily inferior to an original work. Then it was in the Romantic period, with its emphasis on individuality, novelty, and flamboyance, that this notion came to be associated with the concept of 'genius' and acquire the prestige it still enjoys nowadays.

But critics and historians of literature have often overstressed the need for originality, which is not the obligatory hallmark of greatness. And so the concept of influence has been under attack, chiefly since the 1950s. Tracing influences and source-hunting has been presented as a futile pastime (often with good reason) and even as a somewhat disreputable exercise, for it suggests, on the part of the influenced author, servile dependence and an unacceptable lack of originality. It is necessary, therefore, to remind ourselves of some of the ways in which, to quote T. S. Eliot, 'No poet, no artist of any art, has his complete meaning alone'.[65]

First, originality can only be relative. Writers read all the time and borrowing is bound to be, and indeed always has been, an integral part of the creative process. And this is true, of course, for all the arts: 'the plain fact', Lindey writes, 'is that the titans who have, since the birth of civilization, given us the best in literature, the arts and music have been indefatigable borrowers'.[66] Indeed, as Eliot reminds us, an artist can build only on a tradition, and creative imitation is a *sine qua non* of artistic inspiration. Conrad was disingenuous when he advised Norman Douglas: 'Before all, *imitate no one*!!' (*LL*, II, p. 68), for, judging by his own practice, he clearly knew better.

It should also be remembered that there can be no influence without affinity, without a kinship in psychological and intellectual make-up. No germination can take place without propitious soil. And that does not mean helpless passivity. Affinities, in this context, mean 'elective affinities'.[67] One is impressed only by what is already latent in oneself and what one wants to develop: 'Les oeuvres qui nous exaltent', Valéry said, 'nous indiquent aussi *ce qui veut croître en nous*'.[68] In that sense, an artist chooses his influences. As already noted, Conrad assimilated Flaubert because he wanted to be Flaubert, and this was also the best way of becoming himself, for, as Théophile Gautier points out, originality finds its truest source in imitation.[69] And because Conrad was successful in his enterprise, he is both the inheritor and the continuator of Flaubert.

Influence is also a misleading concept in that, except in the case of the most servile and, therefore, sterile plagiarism, the sources and the models always undergo a transformation; as Malraux was fond of saying, 'l'héritage' is always 'une métamorphose'.[70] Influence is not a one-way activity and ultimately, the one issue of real interest is not so much the material the author has used as what he has done with it. The true test of his appropriations, and the only warrant for them lie in the quality and originality of his own work. His borrowings and imitations can be judged only in the light of his total achievement. Here is the vindication of source-hunting and influence-tracing, for the knowledge of the way an author uses, transforms and departs from his sources provides us with the best possible insight into the working of his own creative faculty, into his personal concerns, and into the nature of his independent contribution to the art.

We can now safely dispose of a second misconception about originality. Goethe once exclaimed: 'People are always talking about originality; but what do they mean? [...] If I could give an account of all that I owe to great predecessors and contemporaries, there would not be much left over.'[71] He was voicing the prevalent belief that the originality of a work is the residue from which all debts have been subtracted. This is perhaps the main reason why critics have shied away from investigating Conrad's debt to French writers, desiring to present him as 'original'. But the use of books as sources, it must be stressed again, does not invalidate an author's originality. The fact that Goethe wrote *Werther* after close perusal of *La Nouvelle Héloïse* did not prevent him from producing, despite striking similarities, a completely different book, any more than Conrad's use of Flaubert, Maupassant, Melville and others in *The Nigger of the 'Narcissus'* – the 'story by which, as creative artist', Conrad declared himself to 'stand or fall'[72] – prevented him from writing a novel which, as Yelton aptly defined it, is 'quintessentially Conradian as to both mythos and ethos'.[73] Indeed, Conrad was not boasting when, in the letter just quoted, he went on to say that *The Nigger* was 'A landmark in literature [...] for nothing like it has been ever done before'. And he was perfectly justified in pointing out to his agent in July 1907: 'One may read everybody and yet in the end want

to read me – for a change if for nothing else. For I don't resemble anybody'
(*CL*, III, p. 460). The fairly obvious notion that influences and originality
are in no way incompatible counters decades of misunderstanding in Conrad
criticism, where the view commonly held is the one expressed by Karl that the
French influence which 'was particularly strong in Conrad's early work [...]
diminished somewhat as he began to find his own voice in those distinctive
years between 1899 and 1904'.[74] It is an incontrovertible fact that Conrad's
triumphant originality in his major phase, far from precluding the use of
models, actually depended on them. But here we must pause and try to understand the nature and extent of this dependence.

Although the process of literary composition is just as elusive as the concept
of originality, a few aspects of Conrad's own practice seem distinct. His creative
impetus was triggered, we recall, by some 'definite images', images of people
(Olmeijer, A. P. Williams, some idiot children), images drawn from some lived
experience ('Youth', 'Heart of Darkness', *The Shadow-Line*), images evoked
by an anecdote read or heard (the desertion of the *Jeddah*, the stealing of a
lighter full of silver, the Greenwich Bomb outrage). But the real moment of
conception must have occurred, as Watt has suggested in connection with *Lord
Jim*,[75] when he was able to link up these images with whatever particular
problem or theme was of major concern to him at the time. His account of the
genesis of *Nostromo* bears witness to this.[76] After a period of gestation, he must
have had a fairly clear idea about his choice of characters, the moral problem
or theme he wished to explore, and the broad outline of the work. Conversely,
as we know, he was often in the dark even at an advanced stage in the writing
about the scope of the work and lines of development to be adopted, and when
he had eventually decided on a course of action his problem was how to carry
it out. This seems to suggest: comparative clarity of conception, but great
uncertainty about its execution. With the following corollary: autonomy in
terms of the general design of the work, with heavy reliance on countless models
in its crafting. The second proposition needs no labouring, but let us briefly
consider the first. A few years ago, Bill Strutton claimed that Thomas Keneal-
ly's novel *Season in Purgatory* was based on his own novel *The Island of Terrible
Friends*.[77] No such accusation could be levelled at any major work by Conrad.
Only some of his decidedly inferior products, such as 'The Inn of the Two
Witches', are open to this kind of criticism. Even 'The Idiots', 'The Return',
and 'A Smile of Fortune', highly derivative though they are, do not repeat the
pattern of other stories. On the face of it, *Under Western Eyes* seems to be the
exception, since it is based on *Crime and Punishment*. But what characterizes
Conrad's novel is not the way it is like Dostoevskii's, but the way it is not.
The so-called influence, in this case, far from being an act of dependence and
acceptance, is an act of challenge and rejection – a clear case of what Gide called
influence 'par protestation'[78] – in fact, a refusal to be influenced. So there can

be no question about the uniqueness of the overall design of Conrad's works or, therefore, of the profound originality of the vision they convey.

The above distinction may serve as a clue to a fundamental paradox in Conrad's fiction. Watt states that 'In a sense, Conrad is the least derivative of writers; he wrote very little that could possibly be mistaken for the work of anyone else'.[79] The other truth is that Conrad is probably one of the most derivative of major modern writers. Indeed, his use of literary texts was often overt, and the notions of intertextuality and hypertextuality have to be brought into play here if we are to do full justice to his mode of composition and the way his own texts function.[80] As we have seen, 'Heart of Darkness', *Lord Jim*, *Under Western Eyes*, and *Victory* are complex cultural artefacts, echo-chambers constantly reverberating intertextually with innumerable borrowings, quotations and allusions, and the same applies to most of his best works in varying degrees. And although it may not always be easy to decide exactly what Conrad intended his reader to identify, there can be no doubt that he was expected to see the relevance of many of these intertextual connections. It is also clear that Conrad wished the presence of other texts in his own text to operate on the reader and, consciously or otherwise, to deepen his experience simply by virtue of their provenance. Such may also apply to the allusions to newspaper accounts of Stanley's speeches and to rhetorical proclamations by King Leopold about the civilizing mission of Europe in 'Heart of Darkness', to echoes of Lombroso, Nordau, and Nietzsche in *The Secret Agent*, and to veiled references to Russian revolutionary writers in *Under Western Eyes*. Whatever Conrad's intentions, these intertextual connections contribute considerably to the density and complexity of his stories, and also to their effectiveness in lifting them from the particular to the generality and universality which are characteristic of all great art.

The idea that the literature of the past may provide aesthetic models or be exploited for didactic or moral purposes is not new. But, since the end of the nineteenth century, intertextuality has become more conscious and systematic, with the modern literary text overtly proclaiming its relation to a host of other texts. In this evolution towards a 'literature of the intertextual', Flaubert, with *La Tentation de saint Antoine* and *Bouvard et Pécuchet* in particular, occupies a key position. As Michel Foucault has observed about the former work: 'It is a work which, from the start, takes its shape in the field of learning: it has its being in a fundamental relationship with books [...]. It belongs to the kind of literature which exists only in and through the network of the already written: a book in which the fiction of books is acted out.'[81] Such is the case with *The Waste Land*, *Ulysses*, and Pound's *Cantos*, and also, undoubtedly, with 'Heart of Darkness', *Under Western Eyes*, and *Victory*. For a full appreciation, these works demand not only a close and attentive reading, but also a 'relational' reading, what Philippe Lejeune has called a 'lecture palimpsestueuse', whereby two or several texts are read, each one in terms of the others. This is, of course, an exacting exercise, but one to be welcomed as a constant source of refined pleasure for, as Genette remarks: 'If one really enjoys texts, one must surely wish, now and again, to enjoy (at least) two at the same time.'[82]

The fascinating question is: how can a work by Conrad be so uniquely Conradian when it so often gives an impression of *déjà lu*? Another look at Conrad's creative process may help to elucidate the paradox. Conrad, we recall, described the historical part of *Nostromo* as 'an achievement in mosaic' (see above, p. 226). It would appear from the complex mixture of personal and printed elements detected in most of his books that the formula applies to Conrad's work as a whole, his novels indeed being composed like mosaics from innumerable details drawn from a huge variety of sources. Ford gave an illuminating example of the way Conrad's mind worked: 'He could suddenly produce an incident from the life of Lord Shaftesbury and work it into *Nostromo*: which was the political history of an imagined South American Republic. That was one of the secrets of his greatness.'[83] The explanation for the amazing achievement represented by his major works must surely lie in the quality of his imagination which, needless to say, must not be understood in its popular sense of inventiveness in matters of plot and setting, but as an integrating faculty, what Coleridge called in his *Biographia Literaria* (chapter 10) 'esemplastic': the shaping and unifying power. And here must also be the source of Conrad's originality for, as T. S. Eliot defined it, 'poetic originality is largely an original way of assembling the most disparate and unlikely material to make a new whole'.[84] The fragments of Conrad's mosaics may be borrowed, but the designs are his own. It is indeed fascinating to see how, thanks to this remarkable gift, the mass of 'disparate and unlikely' elements stored in Conrad's consciousness was transmuted and fused into richly patterned and vitally new artistic entities.

# Appendix

# Conrad's knowledge of French writers

**Novelists having a significant impact on Conrad's fiction***

*Benjamin Constant (1767–1830)*

See above, pp. 122-35 for Conrad's debt to Constant in the creation of *Victory*.

*Stendhal (1783–1842)*

In 'Books' (1905) Conrad, castigating the 'high priests who have proclaimed Stendhal for a prophet of Naturalism', gave this warm appreciation:

> But Stendhal himself would have accepted no limitation of his freedom. Stendhal's mind was of the first order. His spirit above must be raging with a peculiarly Stendhalesque scorn and indignation. For the truth is that more than one kind of intellectual cowardice hides behind the literary formulas. And Stendhal was pre-eminently courageous. He wrote his two great novels, which so few people have read, in a spirit of fearless liberty.
> *(NLL*, p. 8)[1]

Although Retinger asserted that Conrad found the *Forsyte Saga* 'too grey' because it 'conformed too much [...] to Stendhal's definition of a novel: *un miroir qui se promène sur la grande route*',[2] Conrad does not seem to have been indifferent to Stendhal's technique. Ford recollected hearing Conrad 'read with enthusiasm, commenting as he went on the technique there employed, at least half of *Le Rouge et le Noir*', and claimed that Stendhal 'did very much inspire Joseph Conrad, at any rate during the earlier periods of his writing career'.[3] (See above, pp. 107-8 for the impact of *Le Rouge et le noir* (1830) on *Under Western Eyes*.)

*Alfred de Vigny (1797–1863)*

In the Author's Note to *A Personal Record* Conrad tells of his father's admiration for the author of *Chatterton*, a play Apollo translated and for which he wrote

---

* This list excludes Flaubert, Maupassant and Anatole France, who, because of their exceptional influence, have been discussed separately in the main text (see above, pp. 10-15 and 149-210).

'an eloquent preface' extolling 'the poet's deep humanity and his ideal of noble stoicism' (p. ix).[4] Late in life Conrad himself, reviewing his childhood, concluded: 'if my mind took a tinge from anything it was from French romanticism, perhaps' (*LL*, II, p. 289), and he may well have been thinking of Vigny. The affinity between their outlooks on life struck Gide as it did Jean-Aubry, who noted that their works had 'plusieurs points de contact'.[5]

Both were disillusioned romantics, solitaries and stoics, acutely aware of evil forces at work in the world. Like Conrad, Vigny loved man, whose fate is to suffer and die: his ethics rest on pity. For Vigny, man was a prisoner of Destiny, and he admired those who fought against it. In his *Journal d'un poète* (1867), he wrote: '*Tous ceux qui luttèrent contre le ciel injuste ont eu l'admiration et l'amour secret des hommes.*'[6] Conrad uses these lines in drawing the character of d'Alcacer in *The Rescue*:

Mr. d'Alcacer [...] preferred to look upon himself as the victim not of a swindle but of a rough man naïvely engaged in a contest with heaven's injustice. D'Alcacer did not examine his heart, but some lines of a French poet came into his mind, to the effect that in all times *those who fought with an unjust heaven had possessed the secret admiration and love of men.* (p. 346)

Gide, after asking if the poet in question were Vigny, told Conrad that if he were ever to write an article about him, it would be to Vigny, alone 'que je voudrais vous apparenter'.[7]

The work by Vigny which most readily establishes this kinship is the collection of three tales published in 1835 under the title *Servitude et grandeur militaires*; they illustrate the devotion to duty and the self-sacrifice of Napoleon's armies. Captain Renaud, who finds solace 'dans le plus humble et le plus austère devoir', is akin to many of Conrad's heroes, and Vigny's statement in his peroration that, in the universal wreck of all creeds, the only sacred thing left is 'ce sentiment de l'Honneur qui veille en nous comme une dernière lampe dans un temple dévasté',[8] would undoubtedly have struck a responsive chord in Conrad.[9]

### Honoré de Balzac (1799–1850)

In 'A Preface to Thomas Beer's "Stephen Crane"', Conrad related amusingly how, after tramping the streets of London with Crane at their first meeting, he was forced to talk 'in particular detail all about the "Comédie Humaine", its contents, its scope, its plan, and its general significance, together with a critical description of Balzac's style'.[10] We also know from Galsworthy that Conrad had 'a great liking' for Balzac,[11] and Davray recorded how 'he dissected' his characters.[12] According to Curle, Conrad 'admired the intense vitality of Balzac',[13] whilst Retinger stressed that 'Among the French, Balzac seemed to him [Conrad] the most incomparable creator of life'. Retinger also mentions Balzac as one of the two French authors who had especially influenced Conrad, the other being Flaubert.[14] Indeed, on 7 June 1918 Conrad admitted to Hugh Walpole: 'One can learn something from Balzac' (*LL*, II, p. 206). But what could he have learned?

One obvious answer might be the art of characterization.[15] Compare, for instance, the portrayal of Poiret in *Le Père Goriot* (1834) – a novel read by Kayerts and Carlier in Africa (*TU*, p. 94) – with that of Captain Robinson in *Lord Jim*:

> Monsieur Poiret était une espèce de mécanique. En l'apercevant s'étendre comme une ombre grise le long d'une allée au Jardin-des-Plantes, la tête couverte d'une vieille casquette flasque, tenant à peine sa canne à pomme d'ivoire jauni dans sa main, laissant flotter les pans flétris de sa redingote qui cachait mal une culotte presque vide, et des jambes en bas bleus qui flageolaient comme celles d'un homme ivre, montrant son gilet blanc sale et son jabot de grosse mousseline recroquevillée qui s'unissait imparfaitement à sa cravate cordée autour de son cou de dindon, bien des gens se demandaient si cette ombre chinoise appartenait à la race audacieuse des fils de Japhet qui papillonnent sur le boulevard Italien. Quel travail avait pu le ratatiner ainsi?[16]

> An emaciated patriarch in a suit of white drill, a solah topi with a green-lined rim on a head trembling with age, joined us after crossing the street in a trotting shuffle, and stood propped with both hands on the handle of an umbrella. A white beard with amber streaks hung lumpily down to his waist. He blinked his creased eyelids at me in a bewildered way. 'How do you do? how do you do?' he piped, amiably, and tottered.
>
> (*LJ*, p. 163)

> [Chester] squared his shoulders and stroked his dumpy moustache, while the notorious Robinson, coughing at his side, clung more than ever to the handle of the umbrella, and seemed ready to subside passively into a heap of old bones. (p. 166)

(Interestingly, just as Vautrin prides himself on being a realist – 'Voilà la vie telle qu'elle est' (p. 333) – as he tries to overcome the moral objections of a still idealistic Rastignac, so does Chester who flaunts his cynical maxim 'You must see things exactly as they are' (*LJ*, p. 162) as he scornfully repudiates Jim's romantic conscience.)

Conrad's intimacy with Balzac also suggests that he could hardly have been impervious to his ideas and his vision of mankind. 'L'homme est imparfait' (p. 333) says Vautrin; 'Man [. . .] is not a masterpiece' (*LJ*, p. 208) affirms Stein. Neither writer had any illusions about human motives. In *Le Père Goriot* Balzac observes: 'Ce que les moralistes nomment les abîmes du coeur humain sont uniquement les décevantes pensées, les involontaires mouvements de l'intérêt personnel. Ces péripéties, le sujet de tant de déclamations, ces retours soudains sont des calculs faits au profit de nos jouissances' (p. 341), exactly the point made by Conrad on 15 June 1898 in a letter to Cunninghame Graham: 'Il n y a pas des convertis aux idées de l'honneur, de la justice, de la pitié, de la liberté. Il n y a que des gens qui sans savoir, sans comprendre, sans sentir s'extasient sur les mots, les repètent, les crient, s'imaginent y croire – sans croire a autre chose qu'au gain, a l'avantage personel, a la vanité satisfaite' (*CL*, II, pp. 69–70). A few years later he made Decoud argue: 'We have no political reason; we have political passions – sometimes. What is a conviction? A particular view of our personal advantage either practical or emotional' (*N*, p. 189).

Baines has noted that the time-shifts in *Almayer's Folly* 'almost exactly parallel those in *Le Curé de Tours*'[17] and Arthur Symons believed that Conrad 'learnt one of his secrets from Balzac: the method of doubling or trebling the interest by setting action within action.'[18] R. L. Mégroz says that Symons called this method 'Balzac's "Chinese boxes"'', and he acknowledges that, although it goes back to *The Thousand and One Nights*, Balzac 'was perhaps the first novelist to use it extensively to increase the psychological interest in human behaviour'. Conrad made frequent use of the method: 'An Anarchist' provides what Mégroz calls 'a very simple model'[19] of it; in *Chance* Karl finds that it is 'at its furthest development in a Conrad novel'.[20]

*Victor Hugo (1802–1885)*

In *A Personal Record* Conrad states that *Les Travailleurs de la mer* (1866) was his 'first introduction to the sea in literature' (p. 72), and some images Conrad uses in *The Mirror of the Sea* have their origin in it. In the description of a hurricane, Hugo refers to frigates which leaked 'comme des paniers' (p. 633); Conrad, recalling a gale in the Mediterranean, says of his old ship: 'She leaked fully [...] like a basket' (p. 153). In another passage describing the movement of the wind in gales, Hugo writes: 'Les spirales indéfinies et fuyantes du vent sifflaient en tordant le flot; les vagues, devenues *disques* sous ces tournoiements, étaient lancées contre les brisants comme des *palets* gigantesques par des athlètes invisibles' (p. 728). Conrad pictures the West Wind at play with cloud and water 'as if in sport'; the wind speaks: 'Let me play at *quoits* with cyclonic gales, flinging the *discs* of spinning cloud and whirling air from one end of my dismal kingdom to the other' (p. 93).

A number of critics have noted the probable influence of *Les Travailleurs de la mer* on Conrad's fiction. Baines points out that Conrad and his father would have seen Gilliat's position, isolated in a hostile society, as a reflection of their own fate,[21] and draws a parallel between the hostile attitude of the villagers to Yanko Goorall in 'Amy Foster' and 'the treatment of the mysterious but kindly Gilliatt.'[22] Edward Visiak has noted a parallel with 'Freya of the Seven Isles':

In *Les Travailleurs*, Mess Lethierry, the father of Déruchette, has two loves, his daughter and his steam-boat. In *Freya*, Jasper Allen loves Freya in conjunction with his brig. In *Les Travailleurs*, Clubin, a malignant character, deliberately wrecks Lethierry's steam-boat on rocks. In *Freya*, Heemskirk, with fiendish jealousy, deliberately wrecks Jasper Allen's brig on a rock.[23]

But the most spectacular suggestion comes from Wallace Watson who has argued that Hugo's novel was probably in Conrad's mind during the composition of *Nostromo* (see above, pp. 94-5).

## Prosper Mérimée (1803–1870)

According to Galsworthy Conrad had 'a great liking' for Mérimée.[24] In a letter to Jean-Aubry of 26 August 1920, Conrad gave his reaction to Mérimée's short story 'Tamango' (1833):

Cela est assez bien. Quant à moi je n'aurai jamais pu l'écrire de cette façon là ni d'aucune autre. Je me serai perdu dans les technicalités de la situation. Du reste, je pense que 'Tamango' est plutôt un morceau philosophique dans le genre des écrivains du 18ème siècle. Du moins c'est l'impression qui m'est restée depuis des années que j'ai lu cela.

(*LF*, p. 157)

(For Conrad's debt to Mérimée in *Nostromo* and 'The Planter of Malata', see above, pp. 86-8 and 120-2.)

## Emile Zola (1840–1902)

While Conrad's references to Zola show that he knew at least some of his works, they give the impression that he had no liking either for them or for the school of Naturalism. In a letter to Mme Poradowska of 8 September 1894, he says that her idea of a novel based on a pilgrimage is excellent, but cautions: 'Seulement n'est-ce pas trop tôt après "Lourdes" [which had just been published]. On dira que Vous suivez la mode'. (*CL*, I, p. 174), which reveals how closely he followed the literary scene in France. In 'His War Book', the preface to a new edition of *The Red Badge of Courage*, published in 1925, Conrad recalls that critics had mentioned *La Débâcle* (1892) in connection with Crane's book, but, he continues, 'Zola's main concern was with the downfall of the imperial régime he fancied he was portraying' (*LE*, p. 123). More interesting is his comment to Angèle Zagórska at Christmas 1898 on the British literary scene: 'George Moore has published the novel *Evelyn Innes* – un succès d'estime. He is supposed to belong to the naturalistic school and Zola is his prophet. Tout ça, c'est très vieux jeu' (*CL*, II, p. 138). Whatever Conrad's feelings were about Zola, there can be no question that he borrowed from him in both 'The Idiots' and *The Secret Agent* (see above, pp. 34-6 and 97-100).[25]

## Alphonse Daudet (1840–1897)

Writing to Mme Poradowska on 23? February 1895, while *Almayer's Folly* was in the press, Conrad showed his intimate acquaintance with, and attachment to, Daudet's works: 'Vous connaissez mon culte Daudet. Croyez Vous que ce serait ridicule de ma part de lui envoyer mon livre – moi qui a lu tous les

siens sous tous les cieux? Ce n'est pas pour qu'il le lise – simplement un acte
d'hommage car après tout il est un de mes enthousiasmes de jeunesse qui a
survecu – même qui a grandi' (*CL*, I, p. 201). Emilie Briquel recorded at
Champel that Conrad had advised her to read *Fromont jeune et Risler aîné* (1874)
and *Le Nabab* (1877) (see above, p. 9), and it was from Champel that, on 12
May 1895, Conrad remarked to Garnett, while reporting on his progress with
*An Outcast of the Islands*: 'I am working every day: – tolerably bad work. Like
poor Risler the Elder's cashier "I haf' no gonfidence"' (*CL*, I, p. 216), an
allusion to the Alsatian Sigismond Planus's repeated complaint 'chai bas gonfi-
anze'. Jean-Aubry recalled that *Fromont jeune et Risler aîné* was one of the works
from which, late in life, Conrad could quote whole sentences by heart.

However, Conrad's interest in Daudet was apparently a 'youthful enthusiasm'. Although Ford relates that, at the beginning of their collaboration in
1898, 'Conrad was still then inclined to have a feeling for Daudet – for such
books as *Jack*' (1876), [26] it is clear that in three years the 'worship' had worn
thin, as can be judged from the obituary tribute Conrad wrote for *Outlook* early
in 1898. He highly commends Daudet for his spontaneity, animation, honesty,
tolerance, and for his tenderness towards his characters and humanity at large.
He speaks of Tartarin, the Nabob, the Duc de Mora, Félicia Ruys, and Monsieur de Montpavon with affectionate familiarity. [27] But he has decided that their
fate, however 'poignant' and 'interesting' is 'of not the slightest consequence'
because, despite all his wonderful qualities, their creator was 'not an artist'
(*NLL*, pp. 20–4). [28]

Nevertheless, whatever Conrad's feelings may have been later in life, [29] it
seems likely that Daudet influenced his earliest writing. Lawrence Graver feels
that Daudet stands behind 'The Black Mate', Conrad's first piece of fiction,
which he entered unsuccessfully in a competition set by *Tit-Bits* in 1886 and
which he rewrote twenty-two years later for the *London Magazine*: he sees
this influence in the motif of harmless deception and the trick ending, and
concludes:

> Conrad's first story leans heavily on sentimental irony, steady suspense, mechanically
> developed characters, a colloquial style, a whimsical plot, and a surprise ending – traits
> which are found in Daudet, in *Tit-Bits*, and in the *London Magazine*, but rarely in
> Conrad's best work. [30]

Ford detected the same influence on *Almayer's Folly* which, he felt, was
'written too much in the style of Alphonse Daudet'. He affirmed that while
Conrad was ice-bound in Rouen (in December 1893 and January 1894), he 'was
reading [...] Daudet's *Jack*, which immensely fascinated him'. [31] And Baines
also notes, as does Graver about 'The Black Mate', that '*Almayer's Folly*, unlike
Conrad's subsequent work, does show traces of that brand of sentimental irony
in which Daudet specialised'. [32]

*Pierre Loti (1850–1923)*

Ford mentioned Loti as one of the writers that Conrad read at sea (according to Emilie Briquel, Conrad still read Loti with pleasure in 1895) and recalled seeing a copy of *Pêcheur d'Islande* that he had 'annotated'. As a budding novelist anxious to achieve popular success, Conrad must have felt a special attraction to a writer who had pursued a successful career as an officer in the French navy, and whose very popular novels were usually set at sea or in exotic places.[33] (For Loti's possible influence on *An Outcast of the Islands* and *The Nigger of the 'Narcissus'* see above, pp. 29-31 and 47-9.)

Baines's assertion – often repeated but never examined – that 'Conrad's descriptive writing at its worst reflects Loti's inflated and rhetorical phraseology'[34] is indeed easy to demonstrate. Compare, for instance, the following phrases from *Le Roman d'un spahi* (1881): 'des couchers de soleil inimaginables' (p. 30), 'une lumière invraisemblable' (p. 31), 'd'indéfinissables effluves de mort' (p. 63), 'un infini de solitudes mystérieuses' (p. 131), 'les immobilités stupéfiantes du sommeil d'un monde' (p. 198), 'des profondeurs cosmiques, vagues, infinies' (p. 199), 'ces immobilités inexprimables' (p. 199)[35] and these from *An Outcast*: 'he fought with the impalpable' (p. 157), 'the everlasting and invincible shadows' (p. 324), 'an immense and impenetrable silence' (p. 327), 'two incomprehensible and sombre outcasts' (p. 328), 'the silence of a solitude impenetrable and immense' (p. 357). Similarly, Leavis's complaint that in 'Heart of Darkness' the 'same vocabulary, the same adjectival insistence upon inexpressible and incomprehensible mystery, is applied to the evocation of human profundities and spiritual horrors'[36] can equally be levelled at Loti, as the two following examples from *Ramuntcho* clearly show:

En lui, le chaos des choses *autres*, des *ailleurs* lumineux, des splendeurs ou des épouvantes étrangères à sa propre vie, s'agitait confusément, cherchant à se démêler ... Mais non, tout cela, qui était l'insaisissable et l'incompréhensible, restait sans lien, sans suite et sans forme, dans des ténèbres ... (p. 15)

elle se rappelait ses vagues paroles de lassitude infinie, d'incompréhensible désespérance; il avait l'air de voir toujours, au-delà de son horizon à elle, des lointains de gouffres et de ténèbres. (p. 21)[37]

The matter, however, is more complex, since the tendency to use vague words was not confined to Loti, but characterized much late nineteenth- and early twentieth-century French literature, starting with the *symbolistes*, who made vagueness one of their basic aesthetic principles. It is embodied, for instance, in Verlaine's 'Art poétique':

> Il faut aussi que tu n'ailles point
> Choisir tes mots sans quelque méprise:
> Rien de plus cher que la chanson grise
> Où l'Indécis au Précis se joint.[38]

and Mallarmé took up the same idea in 'Toute l'âme résumée':

> Le sens trop précis rature
> Ta vague littérature.[39]

Gide related that, under the influence of Symbolism, he used to be fond of words 'qui laissent à l'imagination pleine licence tels que *incertain, infini, indicible*'.[40] Similarly, impressionist writers complained bitterly about the precision of their linguistic medium ('Mais les mots, si vagues qu'ils soient, restent encore trop précis pour exprimer ces choses' (*Pêcheur d'Islande*); 'Je ne dispose que de mots trop clairs, trop précis' (Barrès, *Le Mystère en pleine lumière*)), and systematically sought words with ill-defined contours. Hence the enormous use that many novelists from Hugo onwards (the Goncourts, Daudet, Huysmans, Loti, Barrès, Estaunié, Proust) made of nominalized adjectives and past participles such as 'l'inconnu', 'l'inconnaissable', 'l'impalpable', 'l'impossible', 'l'inexprimé', 'l'inexprimable', 'l'indéfini', 'l'irréalisé', 'l'innommable', 'l'inaccessible', 'l'illimité', and so on. This kind of vocabulary was an attempt, by symbolist and impressionist writers alike, to express the inexpressible, to seize 'l'insaisissable', to register 'l'absence', to suggest 'le mystère'.[41] Conrad's fondness for polysyllabic privative adjectives and their nominalized forms ('the cry of inconceivable triumph and of unspeakable pain'; 'to live in the midst of the incomprehensible' (*YOS*, pp. 162, 50)) was fostered not only by Loti but by late nineteenth-century French literature as a whole.

### Other writers of fiction with whose work Conrad was acquainted

*François Rabelais (c. 1483–1553)*

During his honeymoon in Brittany, Conrad seems to have read Rabelais with pleasure, for on 22 May 1896 he wrote to Garnett from Ile-Grande: 'Don't you read the Resc[uer]: read nothing but Rabelais – if you must read' (*CL*, I, p. 280).

*Madame de Staël (1766–1817)*

See below, p. 276, n. 60 for the relevance of the reference in *Under Western Eyes* to 'the gifted author of *Corinne*' (*UWE*, p. 142).

*Paul de Musset (1804–1880)*

Andrzej Tretiak has pointed out that *A Set of Six* and Paul de Musset's collection of short stories *La Table de nuit* (1832) have the same number of tales, with analogous subtitles: Histoire inconvenante, mystérieuse, sentimentale, exagérée, triste, fashionable; A Romantic, A Desperate, An Indignant, A Military, An Ironic, A Pathetic Tale. In a letter to Davray of 14 March 1908, Conrad explains that *A Set of Six* will appear with subtitles to warn the readers about 'l'intention *artistique*' of the book and, after enumerating them, he adds that they give 'le *ton*' of each tale (*LF*, p. 91). Musset's volume had been re-edited in 1884 and Tretiak plausibly suggests, 'When putting together his six stories in a "set", Conrad took over – consciously or unconsciously – the form of the subtitle from P. de Musset, as it was an exquisite artistic means of enhancing the dramatic impression of the contents'.[42]

## *Pétrus Borel (1809–1859)*

See above p. 110 for the relevance of Conrad's choice of the name Borel for the château in *Under Western Eyes*. (But see also Kirschner, 'Making you *see* Geneva', p. 112, n. 21.)

## *Théophile Gautier (1811–1872)*

The two references Ford has left to Conrad reading Gautier in Marseilles (see above, p. 8) and at sea[43] suggest, since he is mentioned among other French novelists, that Conrad knew primarily his novels rather than his poems.

## *Elémir Bourges (1852–1925)*

Conrad read two of Bourges's novels, *Le Crépuscule des dieux* (1884) and *Les Oiseaux s'envolent et les fleurs tombent* (1893) sent to him by Gide. Thanking Gide on 1 December 1913, he claimed to have a strong admiration for Bourges, but showed that he was keenly aware of the limitations of his art (*LF*, pp. 128–9).

## *Paul Bourget (1852–1935)*

According to Retinger, Conrad 'admired P. Bourget'.[44]

## *Maurice Barrès (1862–1923)*

Gide said that Conrad 'ne prisait que médiocrement Barrès'.[45]

## *Marcel Prévost (1862–1941)*

When Prévost expressed his interest in translating 'The Secret Sharer', Conrad, in a letter to Edith Wharton of 24 December 1912, showed 'great pleasure in the words of a fellow author of "such great and distinctive gifts"'.[46]

*André Gide (1869–1951)*

It was Retinger's impression that Conrad was 'sceptical about the preciousness of A. Gide'.[47] His correspondence with Gide suggests a warmer appreciation, but it is well known that he was inclined to be over-warm and over-generous. On 26 December 1911, he wrote to Gide:

> Je vous avoue enfin que j'ai lu et admiré *L'Immoraliste* [1902]; il y a bien deux ans de ça. [...] Quant au volume de critique [*Prétextes* (1903)], tout ce que je puis vous dire, c'est que je me sens tellement d'accord avec le sentiment de ce livre, que ma sympathie – permettez-moi de dire: l'affection – que j'ai ressentie pour vous dès le premier moment, en est infiniment augmentée.                                                          (*LF*, p. 113)

On 20 August 1919, Conrad told Gide that he was 'fort impressionné' by his *Journal sans dates* (1919) (*LF*, p. 147). And his two comments on *Les Caves du Vatican* (1914), written at seven years' interval (8 January 1914 and 5 August 1921) also show a definite liking: 'Quelle belle entrée en matière! Que de choses vous avez mises dans les pages si caractéristiques et si intéressantes de ce beau commencement'; 'Justement, il y a quelques jours, j'ai relu les *Caves de Vatican*, toujours avec le même intérêt, mais avec une admiration qui croît à chaque nouvelle lecture. C'est vraiment merveilleux, l'infinité de choses que vous avez mises dans ce livre, où la main est si légère et la pensée si profonde.' (*LF*, pp. 130, 165–6).[48]

*Marcel Proust (1871–1922)*

Jean–Aubry reported in his 'Souvenirs' that Conrad was the first person (except for Ortega y Gasset) to assess with great insight 'les qualités, la place, la portée, les faiblesses de l'oeuvre de Marcel Proust'.[49] In a letter to Sir John Collings Squire after Proust's death on 18 November 1922, Conrad indicates that he first heard of him in 1913 or 1914, that is, on the appearance of the first volumes of *A la recherche du temps perdu*, and that he admired him immensely.[50] On 22 September 1922 he announced to Jean–Aubry that Scott Moncrieff had sent him the English translation of *Du côté de chez Swann* which had just been published and adds: 'Nous verrons!' (*LF*, p. 174). On 21 November of the same year, he wrote to C. Sandeman: 'I've lately read nothing but Marcel Proust' (*LL*, II, p. 287), and three months later he was still reading him since, on 26 February 1923, he thanked Jean–Aubry for sending him the volumes of *Sodome et Gomorrhe* for which he had asked (*LF*, p. 181).[51] That he read Proust with considerable enjoyment we know from the latter, who recorded some of his reactions as he savoured *Pastiches et mélanges* (1914),[52] and from Hugh Walpole, who recorded in his diary on 20 October 1923: 'jolly talk in the evening, mostly damning everyone, but Conrad's eyes lit over Fenimore Cooper and over Proust, who stirred him to deep excitement.'[53] Indeed, Conrad's contribution to the English memorial tribute to Proust, written in a letter to

Scott Moncrieff on 17 December 1922, reveals his intense admiration for Proust's 'great art':

The important thing is that whereas before we had analysis allied to creative art, great in poetic conception, in observation, or in style, his is a creative art absolutely based on analysis. It is really more than that. He is a writer who has pushed analysis to the point when it became creative.                           (*LL*, II, pp. 291-2)[54]

### Marcelle Tinayre (1872–1948)

On 21 May 1903 Conrad gave Cunninghame Graham his reaction to Tinayre's *La Maison du péché* (1902):

The book [...] has arrived and is now half read. Without going further my verdict is that it is good, but is not 'fort'. For that sort of thing *no matter how good* I always feel a secret contempt for the reason that it is just *what I can do* myself – essentielment. Fundamentally I believe that sort of fiction (I *don't* mean the *subject* of course) is somehow wrong. Too easy. Trop inventé; never *assez vécu*. There is a curse on the descriptive analysis of that sort.                           (*CL*, III, p. 35)

### Colette (1873–1954)
### Charles-Louis Philippe (1874–1909)

Conrad's dislike for Naturalism appears again in Retinger's recollection that 'he deprecated the return to naturalism shown by Charles-Louis Philippe or Colette'.[55]

### Valery Larbaud (1881–1957)

Even if Retinger had not mentioned that 'V. Larbaud was quite a favourite with [Conrad]',[56] we would know it from a letter he wrote to Larbaud on 2 December 1913 welcoming the just-published *Journal intime d'A. O. Barnabooth*:

Il est difficile de vous exprimer la joie que m'a donnée l'arrivée des oeuvres complètes de M. Barnabooth.

Je vous prie de croire en mon admiration. La première lecture du 'Journal Intime' est une impression inoubliable. Je vous assure que je ne suis guère enthousiaste de tempérament, mais la simplicité artistique du livre, la valeur esthétique, la force créatrice et la subtile analyse m'ont conquis du premier coup et définitivement.

Nous sommes là une petite bande dont vous avez fait les délices.      (*LF*, p. 129)

By remarking to Gide on 8 January 1914, that he had not told Larbaud 'tout le bien' he thought of his book for fear that too marked an enthusiasm might have appeared suspect (*LF*, p. 131), Conrad confirmed that his appreciation was heartfelt.

**Poets**

In his own words, Conrad was 'in general insensible to verse' (*CL*, II, p. 172), whether French or English. Apart from Vigny and Hugo, whose poetry he knew from childhood,[57] and a few *symbolistes*, the only major French poet with whom he seems to have been well acquainted was Baudelaire.

*Charles Baudelaire (1821–1867)*

Although there are some indications that Conrad knew Baudelaire from the beginning of his writing career,[58] Edward Said may be right when he notes 'the extraordinary, quite sudden appearance of a Baudelairean strain in Conrad's writing and thinking during the period (1905–1912)'[59] (clearly the last date should read 1915). Indeed, in a letter to Edmund Gosse of 23 March 1905, Conrad speaks of 'those difficult moments which Baudelaire has defined happily as "*les stérilités des écrivains nerveux*"' (*CL*, III, p. 224), an allusion to 'Edgar Poe, sa vie et ses oeuvres' where Baudelaire (clearly thinking of himself) says that Poe was often struck momentarily by '*une de ces stérilités que connaissent les écrivains nerveux*'.[60]

It has also been suggested that Baudelaire could have provided him with the title of his first avowedly autobiographical work, *The Mirror of the Sea*, on which he was working from early 1904 to early 1906.[61] Yelton points out that it is recurrent in Baudelaire, and 'most explicitly developed in "L'Homme et la mer"':[62]

> Homme libre, toujours tu chériras la mer!
> *La mer est ton miroir*; tu contemples ton âme
> Dans le déroulement infini de sa lame,[63]

In a letter of 29 August 1908 to Arthur Symons (the leading exponent of French Symbolism in England), Conrad, after stressing that he has approached the object of his task 'things human, in a spirit of piety', says: '*The earth is a temple* where there is going on a mystery play' (*LL*, II, p. 83). He could hardly have written this without having in mind what must be Baudelaire's most famous lines, the first quatrain in 'Correspondances', the poem which makes him the undisputed precursor of the *symbolistes*:

> *La Nature est un temple* où de vivants piliers
> Laissent parfois sortir de confuses paroles;
> L'homme y passe à travers des forêts de symboles
> Qui l'observent avec des regards familiers.[64]

What is more, the metaphor of the temple reappears in a description of an evening in 'A Smile of Fortune' written two years later (from May to August 1910) but, this time, the metaphor of the garden as 'an enormous censer' is reminiscent of the famous pantoum 'Harmonie du soir':

Voici venir les temps où vibrant sur sa tige
Chaque fleur s'évapore ainsi qu'un *encensoir*;
Les sons et les parfums tournent dans l'air du soir;
Valse mélancolique et langoureux vertige![65]

The evening closed upon me. The shadows lengthened, deepened, mingled together into a pool of twilight in which the flower-beds glowed like coloured embers; whiffs of heavy scent came to me as if the dusk of this hemisphere were but the dimness of a temple and the garden an enormous *censer* swinging before the altar of the stars.

*(TLS*, p. 76)[66]

Conrad must have been sensitive to the vision of the author of *Les Fleurs du mal* (1857) whose world is a prey to chaos and evil and in which demonic forces are seen as superior to divine forces. In *Victory* (April 1912–July 1914) he makes Heyst the father say: 'It is not poets alone who dare descend into the abyss of infernal regions' (p. 219). Although the statement refers to poets in general, the image of 'descending into the abyss' seems to apply with particular aptness to the author of 'Le Voyage' who wanted to dive 'au fond du gouffre' in order to discover something new.[67] In fact, the obsessive nature of the 'gouffre' in Baudelaire, for whom 'tout est abîme',[68] can be said to have its counterpart in Conrad who also displays something of an obsession in his frequent use of the image of the abyss.[69]

The presence of Baudelaire in Conrad's mind at about this time can again be seen in a light-hearted remark from a 1914 interview: 'So you want to learn something about my life? Hm ... I have nothing to hide, and I have told and will tell everything. [...] Yes, everything except some murder or other, or imprisonment, as Baudelaire says.'[70] And the following year, he chose the concluding lines of 'La Musique' as the epigraph to *The Shadow-Line* (February–December 1915), thus showing again that, like Baudelaire, he regarded the sea as a symbol of the human psyche. Music, the initial subject of the poem, takes hold of the poet 'comme une mer', and he is then transformed into a ship responding to the sea's various moods:

Je sens vibrer en moi toutes les passions
    D'un vaisseau qui souffre;
Le bon vent, la tempête et ses convulsions

    Sur l'immense gouffre
Me bercent. D'autres fois, calme plat, grand miroir
    De mon désespoir![71]

Said has also noted a link between the two writers in the way Conrad renders himself in *The Mirror of the Sea* as a 'clearly defined *homo duplex*',[72] man of action and man of reflection:

Then there is the portrait of himself as a double man, sailor and writer, strikingly similar to and probably inspired by the well-known passage in Baudelaire's 'De l'essence du rire': 'l'artiste n'est artiste qu'à la condition d'être double et de n'ignorer aucun phénomène de sa double nature.'[73]

Another aspect of the 'homo duplex', Baudelaire's famous statement in 'Mon coeur mis à nu' that any man, at any time, is solicited by 'deux postulations simultanées, l'une vers Dieu, l'autre vers Satan',[74] finds its equivalent in Stein's diagnosis of man's predicament: 'He wants to be a saint, and he wants to be a devil' (*LJ*, p. 213).

## The Symbolist movement

(See also pp. 239–40) There is apparently only one reference by Conrad to the French Symbolists and in it he dissociates himself from them. On 4 May 1918, he explained to Barrett Clark, who had inquired about the 'final effect' of a work of art:

a work of art is very seldom limited to one exclusive meaning and not necessarily tending to a definite conclusion. And this for the reason that the nearer it approaches art, the more it acquires a symbolic character. This statement may surprise you, who may imagine that I am alluding to the Symbolist School of poets or prose writers. Theirs, however, is only a literary proceeding against which I have nothing to say. I am concerned here with something much larger.                                        (*LL*, II, p. 205)

However, both Yelton[75] and Watt[76] have noted striking similarities between Conrad's aesthetic ideas and those of the French Symbolists. Watt points out that Conrad 'often speaks of the mysteriously evocative power of words with an emphasis somewhat reminiscent of Mallarmé. Thus in November 1898, just before starting *Heart of Darkness*, he wrote [to Ford]: "How fine it could be [...] if the idea had a substance and words a magic power, if the invisible could be snared into a shape." [*CL*, II, p. 119] It sounds like a Symbolist prayer'.[77] In fact Conrad was apparently echoing Moreas's statement in *Un manifeste littéraire* (1886) that symbolist poetry 'cherche à *vêtir l'Idée* d'une *forme* sensible'. Two other quotations also suggest that he knew it. Two years earlier, he had written in *The Sisters*: 'he [Stephen] murmured indistinctly: "Nature", as if he had been ashamed of using the profaned word [...] to *clothe* the august *form* of the terrible, of the immense and tormenting *Idea*' (pp. 56–7) (note that both 'l'Idée' and 'the Idea' are capitalized), and, in a letter to Ford of 24 April 1902, he used the same key terms, saying that there is an excitement 'in giving *form* to an *idea*, in *clothing* the breath of our life with day' (*CL*, II, p. 409).

Watt concludes that the plot of 'Heart of Darkness' is 'based on a simple symbolic quest', its structure is 'very largely based on naturally symbolic actions and objects', and it

shares many of the characteristic preoccupations and themes of the French Symbolists: the spiritual voyage of discovery, especially through an exotic jungle landscape, which was a common symbolist theme, in Baudelaire's 'Le Voyage' and Rimbaud's 'Bâteau ivre', for instance; the pervasive atmosphere of dream, nightmare and hallucination, again typical of Rimbaud; and the very subject of Kurtz also recalls, not only Rimbaud's own spectacular career, but the typical symbolist fondness for the lawless, the depraved, and the extreme modes of experience.[78]

Both Yelton and Watt, however, discount any direct influence of the Symbolists on Conrad. And as has been made abundantly clear, Yelton is surely right to conclude that 'the *example* of Flaubert, as intuitively apprehended by Conrad and articulated in his own quasi-*Symboliste* terms, is much more implicated in the formation of his aesthetic than any conjectured influence of *Symboliste* doctrine'.[79]

## Arthur Rimbaud (1854–1891)

Aniela Kowalska has suggested that *Une saison en enfer* (1873) was a source for Kurtz.[80] The parallel between Rimbaud and Kurtz is unmistakable: Rimbaud turned his back on European civilization in 1875 and became an explorer and a trader in ivory, gold-dust, perfumes, and even arms, establishing himself first at Aden, then at Harar where he lived like a native chief. Kurtz, a poet, painter, and political thinker, becomes a trader in ivory in the heart of Africa where he turns native, finally indulging in the total liberation from all the constraints of the civilization he has come to promote. Rimbaud was held by his family to be an ideal hero, just as Kurtz is so regarded by his Intended. Conrad had undoubtedly some knowledge of Rimbaud when he started writing 'Heart of Darkness' in December 1898. On 27 August of that year, to Cunninghame Graham who wanted to know his opinion of Rimbaud, he made this typically evasive answer: 'Can't understand Rimbaud at all. You overrate my intelligence' (*CL*, II, p. 89). This statement, however, does not tally with his response, on 8 February 1899, to Charles Whibley's essay on Rimbaud 'A Vagabond Poet', which appeared in *Blackwood's Magazine*[81] simultaneously with the publication of the first chapter of 'Heart of Darkness'. In his letter to the editor, Conrad praised it as 'very interesting – very appreciative very fair', adding 'I happen to know Rimbaud's verses' (*CL*, II, p. 162).

Kowalska points out that Whibley had ascribed a place of highest merit to *Une saison en enfer*, a volume which, as Resink has indicated, was included in the copy of Rimbaud's works owned by Conrad.[82] She claims that 'the very suggestive visions of *Une Saison en enfer* could have had an influence on the creative concept in "Heart of Darkness", especially in the context of Kurtz's infernal night'.[83]

Further evidence of Conrad's interest in Rimbaud at that time appears in his description to E. L. Sanderson on 12 October 1899 of the unearthly nature of fiction writing: 'It is strange. The unreality of it seems to enter one's real life

[...]. One's will becomes the slave of hallucinations, responds only to shadowy impulses, waits on imagination alone. A strange state, a trying experience, a kind of fiery trial of untruthfulness' (*CL*, II, p. 205). This is reminiscent of Rimbaud's theory of the *voyant*-poet, with its injunction that, to get beyond good and evil and express the inexpressible (which Conrad had obviously attempted to do in 'Heart of Darkness'), the poet must develop his creative faculty by experimenting with self-induced states of delirium, a methodical 'dérèglement de tous les sens'.[84]

## *Henri de Régnier (1864–1936)*

This *symboliste* poet is mentioned by Jean-Aubry among the more recent writers with whom Conrad was familiar, and a link has been established between his 'Monsieur D'Amercourt' and 'The Planter of Malata' (see below p. 277, n. 17).

## *Jules Laforgue (1860–1887)*

In December 1922, Conrad discovered the poetry of Laforgue in the selection introduced by Jean-Aubry, but it made no great impression on him, judging by his casual comment: 'Le texte de votre auteur est curieux. On en sent le charme à travers les faits' (*LF*, p. 180)

## *Paul Claudel (1868–1955)*

Retinger said that he regarded Claudel and Valéry as 'too strong medicine for him'.[85]

## *Paul Valéry (1871–1945)*

According to Valéry, he and Conrad met only twice and very briefly. The first meeting, arranged by Jean-Aubry, took place in the London salon of Lady Colefax where Valéry had given a talk. Ravel was present. Conrad was obviously delighted with the meeting: 'The two of them were charming to me', he told Gide, 'The moment I saw Valéry I felt a real affection for him', and he invited the poet to Oswalds,[86] where in October of the following year – again in the company of Ravel and Jean-Aubry – the two men had a lively discussion on the fighting qualities of the British and French navies at the time of Napoleon.[87] In February Conrad had asked Jean-Aubry to send him 'les vers de Valéry' (*LF*, p. 181). He probably did not respond to them as warmly as he did to the man if we are to believe Retinger (see Claudel above).

**Dramatists**

*Molière (1622–1673)*

Reminiscing about his stay at Capel House in the summer of 1912, Saint-John Perse (Alexis Léger) wrote to Conrad from Peking in February 1921: 'Et vous me surprenez encore en m'avouant que vos auteurs français les plus familiers sont Molière et Zola',[88] and on 19 September 1947 he wrote to Jean-Aubry on the publication of his biography of Cônrad: 'Vous souvenez-vous de son goût inattendu pour Molière et pour Zola?'[89] Even if Conrad's words about Zola must be taken with a pinch of salt, given the views he expressed above (see p. 237), a genuine knowledge and appreciation of Molière may lie behind the following allusions. In 'The Censor of Plays' Conrad speculated: 'He [the Censor] may call his cook (Molière used to do that) from below and give her five acts to judge every morning' (*NLL*, p. 79), while in *Suspense* he likened Count Montevesso to 'a character out of a Molière comedy: "Le Jaloux". The elderly jealous husband' (p. 204). In his correspondence, he also alluded more than once to Molière's famous line 'Que diable allait-il faire dans cette galère?' to describe the hard condition of a writer (*LF*, p. 131, 8 Jan. 1914; *CL*, II, pp. 69, 75).

*Jean Racine (1639–1699)*

Conrad undoubtedly knew the works of Racine. Ford recalled how in the thick of a fierce argument about 'French verse-theories', with his face clouding over, he 'would snatch up a volume of Racine and read half a dozen lines' to make his point.[90] A reference to 'a tragedy of Racine' appears in 'A Smile of Fortune' (*TLS*, p. 35), and Razumov, during his last meeting with Natalia, when he refers to '*a breast unwarmed* by any affection' (p. 344), might just possibly allude to a line from *Mithridate*:

> Ah! qu'il eût mieux valu, plus sage et plus heureux,
> Et repoussant les traits d'un amour dangereux,
> Ne pas laisser remplir d'ardeurs empoisonnées
> *Un coeur déjà glacé par* le froid des années! (IV. v. 39–42)

*Eugène Scribe (1791–1861), Victorien Sardou (1831–1908), Edouard Pailleron (1834–1899)*

A reference in a letter to Garnett of March 1911 shows that Conrad knew the works of these three playwrights:[91] 'Why not read up Scribe and Sardou (the two good mechanics) a little, and give us a play about *Le Monde où l'on Ecrit* – the world where they write!' (*LEG*, p. 228). (*Le Monde où l'on s'amuse* (1868) is one of Pailleron's comedies.)

*Philippe Auguste Villiers de l'Isle-Adam (1838–1889)*

The only French play known so far to have left a tangible mark on Conrad's work is his drama *Axël* (1890; produced in Paris in 1894), which has been described as the epitome of the *symboliste* movement and is regarded as a source for *Victory*. (See above, p. 133)

*Maurice Maeterlinck (1862–1949)*

Conrad had apparently nothing but disdain for Maeterlinck's symbolist dramas. Writing to Galsworthy on 24 October 1907, he calls the Belgian dramatist a 'farceur who has been hiding an appalling poverty of ideas and hollowness of sentiment in wistful baby-talk' (*CL*, III, p. 503), and four years earlier, he had referred, in a letter to Garnett, to 'the pretty-pretty of Maeterlinck' (*LEG*, p. 227).

*Edmond Rostand (1868–1918)*

On 19 July 1898 Conrad thanked Cunninghame Graham for sending him *Cyrano de Bergerac* (1897),[92] which he dismissed a few weeks later in a letter to the same friend: 'Je ne suis bon qu'a lire Cyrano and such like coglionerie' (*CL*, II, pp. 79, 89).

**Critics**

Because of its importance, Conrad's debt to Anatole France and to Maupassant in his critical writings has been given a chapter to itself (see above, pp. 137–45).

*Ferdinand Brunetière (1849–1906)*

Conrad seems to have had little time for Brunetière. In a letter of 23? February 1895 to Mme Poradowska, he inveighed against this critic, who, as the new head of the *Revue des deux mondes*, had demanded important cuts to be made in her book *Marylka*: 'Chère et bonne, Vous avez massacré ce pauvre livre! Et Brunetière – qui est le seul coupable – est aussi un imbecile. [...] j'aimairais bien abreger Brunetière disons: d'une tête. (L'imbecile!)' (*CL*, I, p. 201).[93] And his evocation of a 'sparring match' between Brunetière and France in *A Personal Record* over 'the principles and rules of literary criticism' makes it clear that he rejected the former's dogmatism and believed, like France, that there are 'no rules and no principles' (pp. 95–6).

Eloise Knapp Hay has argued that Conrad must have known Brunetière's review 'L'*Impressionnisme* dans le roman' if not as an article then as a chapter in his book *Le Roman naturaliste* (1883). She points out that the key phrase in

Conrad's disclaimer to Lenormand towards the end of his life: 'Je ne veux pas *aller au fond* [...]. Je veux considérer la réalité comme une chose rude et rugueuse sur laquelle je promène mes doigts. Rien de plus' (original emphasis),[94] was precisely the memorable phrase Brunetière had used to describe the power wanting in impressionism. The great writers of the past, he had affirmed, did not trifle as artists with the shimmering and multiple surface of things: '*ils allaient au fond* d'abord'.[95] (Brunetière continued: '*et de là ramenaient quelqu'une de ces vérités générales* qui sont comme un jour jeté, comme une lueur d'éclair brusquement faite sur l'éternelle nature humaine.' That Conrad would have responded more directly to this comment is obvious in the light of his own definition of art, in the Preface to *The Nigger of the 'Narcissus'*, as an attempt 'to render the highest kind of justice to the visible universe, *by bringing to light the truth*, manifold and one, underlying its every aspect' (p. vii).)

### Jules Lemaître (1853–1914)

Gide asserted that Conrad especially appreciated Jules Lemaître,[96] a statement borne out by the following passage from 'The Censor of Plays' in which Conrad contrasts the function of the Censor with that of the French critic. After reproducing the picture Lemaître gives of himself, with his pen poised in his hand, hesitating and whispering to himself: 'What if I were perchance doing my part in killing a masterpiece', Conrad continues:

> Such were the lofty scruples of M. Jules Lemaître – dramatist and dramatic critic, a great citizen and a high magistrate in the Republic of Letters; a Censor of Plays exercising his august office openly in the light of day, with the authority of a European reputation. But then M. Jules Lemaître is a man possessed of wisdom, of great fame, of a fine conscience (*NLL*, p. 80)

### Henri Ghéon (1875–1944)

A medical practitioner and prolific dramatist, poet and critic, Ghéon was a co-founder in 1909 of the prestigious *Nouvelle Revue Française*, and one of its most respected critics. The book for which Conrad warmly thanked him in a letter dated 22 November 1911 is *Nos directions: réalisme et poésie*,[97] consisting of a series of literary essays which had previously appeared in the *Nouvelle Revue Française*. Jean-Pierre Cap, who has published Conrad's letter to Ghéon, notes that Conrad 'finds himself in full agreement with the aesthetics championed by his French friends'.[98]

**Moralists, psychologists, philosophers**

*François, duc de La Rochefoucauld (1613–1680)*

Conrad admired the *Maximes* (1665) of this famous sceptic: 'The Maxims of La Rochefoucauld are concise enough. But they open horizons; they plumb the depths; they make us squirm, shudder, smile in turn; and even sigh – at times' (*LE*, p. 39).[99]

*Blaise Pascal (1623–1662)*

For the use of *pensée 347* in *Under Western Eyes* see above, p. 108. No doubt Conrad had the same *pensée* in mind when, shortly after the publication of *Lord Jim*, he wrote to Garnett: 'Like the philosopher who crowed at the Universe I shall know when I am utterly squashed. This time I am only very bruised, very sore, very humiliated' (*CL*, II, p. 303) 12 Nov. 1900).[100]

*Jean de La Bruyère (1645–1696)*

The epigraph for *The Arrow of Gold* comes from *Les Caractères*: 'De l'homme', p. 156 (1688).

*Voltaire (1694–1778)*

We know from Jean-Aubry that Conrad had 'une grande sympathie pour [l'esprit] de Voltaire et son oeuvre' (*LF*, p. 144). For Voltaire's presence in *Under Western Eyes*, see above, pp. 109–10.

*Jean-Jacques Rousseau (1712–1778)*

Jean-Aubry said that Conrad 'détestait l'esprit de Rousseau' (*LF*, p. 144). The judgement he passed on him in *A Personal Record* supports that statement:

> The matter in hand, however, is to keep these reminiscences from turning into con-
> fessions, a form of literary activity discredited by Jean-Jacques Rousseau on account of
> the extreme thoroughness he brought to the work of justifying his own existence; for
> that such was his purpose is palpably, even grossly, visible to an unprejudiced eye. But
> then, you see, the man was not a writer of fiction. He was an artless moralist [...]. He
> had no imagination, as the most casual perusal of 'Emile' will prove. (pp. 94-5)

However, as Fleishman remarks, his 'archness toward Rousseau's egoism and idealism does not [...] disqualify Rousseau's works [...] from his close examination',[101] as is borne out by the references to *Les Confessions* (1781–1788) and *L'Emile* (1762)[102] in the above passage, and to *Le Contrat social* (1762) in

*Under Western Eyes*. For the impact of Rousseau's ideas on Conrad, see above, pp. 108–9.

## *Joseph de Maistre (1753–1821)*

See above, p. 109.

## *Henri Frédéric Amiel (1821–1881)*

Conrad attributed the epigraph of *Almayer's Folly* to this Swiss professor of aesthetics and philosophy. David Leon Higdon has pointed out that the passage appears in Amiel's *Fragments d'un journal intime* (28 April 1852) first published in 1883, whereas Ian Watt says that the original is from his 'little-known collection of poems and prose meditations *Grains de Mil* (Paris, 1854), p. 196', the sentence occurring in a brief chapter entitled 'Les Visions de jeunesse'.[103] Although Conrad's wording 'Qui de nous n'a eu sa terre promise' is not identical to either version, it is closer to the wording in the former ('Lequel de nous n'a sa Terre promise') than in the latter ('Lequel de nous n'a sa terre de promission'). A brief study by Owen Knowles *'Under Western Eyes*: a note on two sources' (see below, p. 274, n. 48) suggests that Amiel's *Journal intime* may have acted as a catalyst in the evolution of parts of this book, influencing its form and content.

## *Théodule Ribot (1839–1916)*

John E. Saveson argues that Conrad's psychological assumptions in *The Nigger of the 'Narcissus'* show the influence of this Utilitarian psychologist: 'To the identity of analytical points in Conrad's and Ribot's psychology, it may be added that Conrad's phrasing recalls Ribot's'. He traces in the characters of Wait, Donkin and Podmore, 'the contemporary pathology of the conservative instinct, especially as it is set down in Ribot'.[104]

## *Henri Bergson (1859–1941)*

Wolfgang Fleischmann has suggested that *Le Rire* (1900) is 'a likely source' for Marlow's theories of the ludicrous in *Chance*.[105]

## Memoirists, historians, political writers

Jean-Aubry regarded Conrad as having an amazing knowledge of French political and historical writings, while Ford recalled reading with Conrad the memoirs of Maxime Du Camp, and added that 'somewhere in the past Conrad had read every imaginable and unimaginable volume of politicians' memoirs,

Mme de Campan, the Duc d'Audiffret Pasquier, Benjamin Constant, [...]
Napoleon the Great, Napoleon III'.[106] And, late in life, we find him preparing
to read Saint-Simon's famous *Mémoires* (1829–1831) with keen anticipation: on
17 March 1920 he wrote to Jean–Aubry: 'Merci du Saint-Simon arrivé ce matin,
à ma grande joie. [...] Demain, je me plonge en ce Saint-Simon' (*LE*, p. 153).
Ford also recorded that Conrad 'liked to amuse himself with resemblances
between himself and other great men [...]. Or he would find in memoirs
accidental traits of resemblance between himself and Napoleon, Louis XVIII,
Theophile Gautier or General Gallifet'.[107] The recurrence throughout his fiction, correspondence and critical writings of the phrase 'as the Frenchman says'
testifies to this extensive political and historical reading: '"*Le temps*", as a
distinguished Frenchman has said, "*est un galant homme*"' (*MS*, p. 193).[108] And
'she had what some Frenchman has called the "terrible gift of familiarity"'[109]
(*AG*, p. 25). He quotes the saying of Louis-Philippe 'The people are never in
fault', the Abbé Sieyès's '*J'ai vécu*' (*PR*, pp. 37, 94), and Gambetta's '*immanente
justice des choses*' (*NLL*, p. 95).[110] He makes Decoud compare Antonia as a
young girl to 'a sort of Charlotte Corday in a schoolgirl's dress; a ferocious
patriot' (*N*, p. 180), and has Blunt likening Doña Rita to Louise de la Vallière
(*AG*, p. 24), while in an early draft she was compared to 'a Mancini', another
favourite of Louis XIV.[111] He evokes the medieval French knight Bayard '*sans
peur et sans reproche*' in a letter to R. B. Cunninghame Graham of 16 February
1905 (*CL*, III, p. 217), in the essay entitled 'Books' of the same year (*NLL*,
p. 3) and in 'Prince Roman' where he refers to 'a fidelity without fear and
without reproach' (*TH*, p. 52). Writing to Sir Sidney Colvin on 21 April 1917
Conrad shows the extent of his familiarity with the French political scene:

If I shocked you by flying out against Gambetta I am sorry. He *was* a great man, especially
in regard of the other makers of the 3rd Republic. Freycinet, Léon Say, Challemel-
Lacour were most distinguished personalities – but rather *hommes de cabinet*. Of the
others (with perhaps the exception of the golden-tongued Jew, Jules Simon) the best
that can be said is that they were politicians. They are now decently forgotten. But the
greatest figure of the times through which we have lived was The People itself, *La
Nation*. For 150 years the French people has been always greater (and better) than its
leaders, masters and teachers.                                        (*LL*, II, p. 190)

Two periods of French history, the First and Second Empire, always had a
particularly strong attraction for Conrad. Curle declared: 'to hear him discuss,
for example, the intricate European politics of the Napoleonic eras – either
First or Second Empire – was to listen to a masterly and detailed survey.'[112]
Ford said that 'his favourite political character was Louis Napoleon as Adven-
turer, and even Napoleon III, Emperor of the French, roused some of his
admiration'.[113] The latter part of this statement seems to conflict sharply with
the presentation of the Emperor's court in *Nostromo* as despicable. But the
strong appeal of the period for him never waned, as a remark he made in

November 1922 clearly shows: 'the Second Empire. What an astonishing atmosphere that time had' (*LL*, II, p. 287). Curle's account of the evening he spent with Conrad two days before his death is eloquent:

– in connection with an article in the current number of the *Times Literary Supplement* – he slipped into a kind of monologue about the Second Empire. As though he had been concerned in it himself, he discussed, with graphic asides, its tortuous policies and outstanding figures. [...] it would really be impossible to convey the feeling of inside knowledge which his conversation suggested. He had read all the contemporary authorities, and he had dramatised for himself the characters and the scenes in such a manner as to make the whole thing emerge in quite a new light.[114]

Yet it was the First Empire which fascinated him most. In his introduction to *Suspense* Curle wrote: 'All his life Conrad was a student of the Napoleonic era. He had absorbed the history, the memoirs, the campaigns of that period with immense assiduity and unflagging interest' (p. vi). This interest was, so to speak, inherited, as Conrad explained to Davray on 14 March 1908 in connection with 'The Duel':

j'avoue une faiblesse pour cette petite machine où j'ai taché de mettre un peu de l'esprit militaire de l'époque. J'ai deux officiers de Napoléon parmi mes ancètres. Mon grand' oncle maternel et mon grand'père paternel. Donc c'est une affaire de famille comme qui dirait.                                                                                  (*LF*, p. 91)

Indeed, Conrad recalled having heard 'a good deal of the great Napoleonic legend' (*SS*, p. viii) in his boyhood, and his recollections in *A Personal Record* show that his imagination must have been stirred in particular by the tales his Uncle Nicholas told of the Retreat from Russia, although he often drew more on Bobrowski's *Memoirs* than on his own memories. He painted the Retreat vividly in a scene in 'The Duel', and later it became the background for 'The Warrior's Soul', the hint for which he said he had found in Philippe de Ségur's *Mémoires*.[115]

Throughout his career, Conrad was haunted by the idea of writing a Napoleonic novel,[116] for which he did a prodigious amount of background reading. For instance, on 25 January 1907, he wrote to J. B. Pinker that he was visiting the Town Library at Montpellier with a view to 'reading up all I can discover there about Napoleon in *Elba*' (*CL*, III, p. 409).[117] However, it was not until June 1920 that he eventually started to write *Suspense*, and early in 1921 he spent two months in Corsica to saturate himself in Napoleonic atmosphere, revive memories of harbours and sailors, and do further background reading, as the list of books he borrowed from the Ajaccio library, recorded by Jean-Aubry, indicates.[118] In addition, the Hodgson sale catalogue of 13 March 1925, which lists some of the books in Conrad's library at the time of his death, shows that he possessed a great many on Napoleon and the Napoleonic era.[119]

However, it was the *Mémoires de la Comtesse de Boigne* which, as Jean-Aubry first pointed out, finally provided him with the basis of the plot, a number of characters and incidents, and even a few substantial passages.[120]

# Notes

## Introduction

1. For example, F. R. Leavis who, although he saw Conrad 'significantly "in" the tradition – in and of it', admitted that 'we can't [...] neatly and conclusively relate him to any one English novelist', and felt that 'Rather, we have to stress his foreignness' (*The Great Tradition* (London: Chatto & Windus, 1960), p. 17).
2. Edward W. Said, 'Conrad and Nietzsche', in *Joseph Conrad: A Commemoration*, ed. Norman Sherry (London: Macmillan, 1976), p. 65.
3. Gustav Morf, *The Polish Heritage of Joseph Conrad* (London: Sampson Low, Marston, 1930). Morf made a second attempt in *The Polish Shades and Ghosts of Joseph Conrad* (New York: Astra Books, 1976). [Abbreviated Morf]
4. Frederick R. Karl, *Joseph Conrad: The Three Lives* (London: Faber and Faber, 1979), p. 974. [Abbreviated Karl]
5. Leavis, *The Great Tradition*, p. 189.
6. In 'Conrad's double image', *Sunday Times*, 24 May 1964, 35, a review of Zdzisław Najder's *Conrad's Polish Background*, Jerzy Peterkiewicz wrote: 'Mr. Najder, quite rightly, frowns on the perpetuated myth of Conrad's French culture' and concluded by referring to his 'dual identity'.
7. Cedric Watts, *A Preface to Conrad* (London: Longman, 1982), p. 7
8. Gérard Jean-Aubry, 'Joseph Conrad et la France', *Chronique des lettres françaises*, 1 (1923), 425.
9. Hugh Walpole, *Joseph Conrad*, new and revised edn (London: Nisbet, 1924), p. 78.
10. Richard Curle, *The Last Twelve Years of Joseph Conrad* (London: Sampson Low, Marston, 1928), pp. 115, 116. [Abbreviated Curle]
11. Jocelyn Baines, *Joseph Conrad: A Critical Biography* (London: Weidenfeld and Nicolson, 1960), pp. 145, 148. [Abbreviated Baines]
12. Zdzisław Najder (ed.), *Conrad's Polish Background* (London: Oxford University Press, 1964), p. 28.
13. Andrzej Busza, 'St. Flaubert and Prince Roman', *L'Epoque conradienne* (February 1980), 2.
14. Ian Watt, *Conrad in the Nineteenth Century* (London: Chatto and Windus, 1980), pp. 48, 203. [Abbreviated Watt]
15. Robert L. Caserio, 'Joseph Conrad, Dickensian novelist of the nineteenth century: a dissent from Ian Watt', *Nineteenth-Century Fiction*, 36 (1981), 337.
16. Ford Madox Ford, *Thus to Revisit* (London: Chapman & Hall, 1921), p. 88. Many more valuable hints were to follow three years later in his memoir, *Joseph Conrad: A Personal Remembrance* (London: Duckworth, 1924). [Abbreviated Ford] Indeed, as Bernard Meyer points out, 'a careful inquiry into [the Ford–Conrad collaboration

controversy] has led Morey to the conclusion that although Hueffer's "impressions may be exaggerated... they are essentially true"' (*Joseph Conrad: A Psychoanalytic Biography* (Princeton University Press, 1967), p. 151). The reference to J. Morey is to his PhD thesis, 'Joseph Conrad and Ford Madox Ford: a study in collaboration', Cornell University, 1960, p. 94. It is now clear that as regards Conrad's French influences, Ford, far from exaggerating, clearly understated their importance: he never said that Conrad had borrowed from Flaubert and Maupassant but merely that he wrote 'in their spirit', and he failed to mention the influence of Anatole France.

## Chapter 1

1. H.-R. Lenormand, 'Il y a quatre ans, en Corse avec Joseph Conrad, coureur de mers', *Transatlantic Review*, 2 (1924), 339, and 'Note sur un séjour de Conrad en Corse', *Hommage à Joseph Conrad, Nouvelle Revue Française*, 23 no. 135 (1924), 670. [Abbreviated *NRF*]
2. André Gide, 'Joseph Conrad', *NRF*, p. 661.
3. John Galsworthy, 'Reminiscences of Conrad' in *Castles in Spain* (London: Heinemann, 1927), p. 79.
4. Ernest Dawson, 'Some recollections of Joseph Conrad', *Fortnightly Review*, 130 (1928), 208.
5. Joseph H. Retinger, *Conrad and his Contemporaries* (London: Minerva, 1941), p. 90. [Abbreviated Retinger]
6. In 'The intellectual relations between France and Poland' (*Poland*, 6 (1925), 69), M. J. Rudwin writes:

> Intellectual relations between France and Poland have been uninterrupted from the early Middle Ages to the present day. French thought and Polish thought, throughout the ages, have been closely allied. French influence is dominant in every domain of mental activity in Poland.

7. Georg Brandes, *Poland: A Study of the Land, People and Literature* (London: Heinemann, 1903), p. 31.
8. Retinger, p. 20.
9. In fact, it would seem that Conrad could already read French when he was only just five years old: 'For the new year 1863, [he] received from Uncle Tadeusz a beautiful book on the lives of outstanding and virtuous people, *Les Anges de la terre*, by A. E. de Saintes'. (Zdzisław Najder, *Joseph Conrad: A Chronicle* (Cambridge University Press, 1983), p. 18). [Abbreviated Najder] For a detailed study of Conrad's French, see 'Le Français de Joseph Conrad' by René Rapin in *Lettres de Joseph Conrad à Marguerite Poradowska* (Geneva: Droz, 1966), pp. 15–53. [Abbreviated *LMP*] The use Conrad made of French both in his everyday life (in his speech and correspondence) and as a novelist (in his fiction and process of composition) is examined in my 'Joseph Conrad and the French language, part one', *Conradiana*, 11 (1979), 229–51; the influence French had on his English is analysed in 'part two', *Conradiana*, 14 (1982), 23–49.

10. Apollo's interest in Hugo (his 'favorite' writer according to Jean-Aubry and Najder) can be judged from this comment in a letter to a friend dated 4 March 1866:

> Did I write to you that for a long time now Victor Hugo and his function as poet and citizen have been the subject of a major work of mine? I am sending you the translation of the introduction and the conclusion of the *Chansons des Rues et des Bois*. They show admirably the scope of the mind of this poet whose hair has grown white; his views on the destiny of inspiration and on the responsibilities that weigh upon the poet. This Victor Hugo is a very learned gentleman. Note how in these songs everything is tastefully arranged, with supreme mastery.

And Jean-Aubry notes that in his *Memoirs* Tadeusz Bobrowski says that Apollo was 'unrivaled as a translator of Victor Hugo, whose style he admirably rendered'. (All quotations are from Gérard Jean-Aubry, *The Sea-Dreamer* (London: Allen and Unwin, 1957), pp. 31, 38, 45.)

11. For instance, in 'Geography and Some Explorers' Conrad recalls that, at the age of ten, he read Sir Leopold McClintock's *The Voyage of the 'Fox' in the Arctic Seas* 'probably in French' (*LE*, p. 11).

12. Najder, p. 31. We do know, however, that his uncle and guardian, Tadeusz Bobrowski, had an excellent command of French and probably a fair knowledge of the French classics, as suggested by his allusions to Molière's *Les Fourberies de Scapin* and *George Dandin* (see *MS*, p. 153, and Najder's *Conrad's Polish Background*, pp. 130, 133).

13. In his account of his stay in Cracow in 1914, Conrad mentions his visit to the Jagiellonian library with Borys which, he says, he had not seen since he was fourteen years old (*NLL*, p. 175). In answer to my query, Mgr Janina Tyszkowska, Vice-Director of the library, has kindly informed me that the name Józef Korzeniowski is not entered in the register of readers who used the reading room from 20 February 1869 to August 1873. But that shows only that Conrad did not read books on the spot; obviously, he could have borrowed them. Unfortunately, whether he did or not remains obscure. But it is clear from the old catalogue, which still survives, that the library then contained a rich collection of books in French, preserved to this day.

14. Avrom Fleishman, *Conrad's Politics* (Baltimore: Johns Hopkins Press, 1967), p. 12. On 'Young Poland', see Czesław Miłosz, *The History of Polish Literature* (London: Collier-Macmillan, 1969), pp. 322–79.

15. Najder, p. 35.

16. Ford, pp. 70–1, and p. 56 for the following quotation.

17. Ford, *Thus to Revisit*, p. 86.

18. Curle, p. 114. Clearly, Conrad's complaint to Garnett in 1923 that he left the sea possessing 'Not even one single piece of "cultural" luggage' (*LEG*, p. 294) does not stand.

19. Quoted in Najder, p. 178. This unflagging interest in French literature is corroborated by the correspondence beween Conrad and Mme Poradowska (née Gachet), herself a novelist, from February 1890 to June 1895 – a crucial time in his life. It is thanks to this correspondence that we know many of Conrad's reactions to the works of French authors.

20. Henry-D. Davray, 'Joseph Conrad', *Mercure de France*, 175 (1 October 1924), 34.
21. G. Jean-Aubry, 'Joseph Conrad', *Fortnightly Review*, 122 (1924), 306. The same statement appears in French in *NRF*, p. 675.
22. Curle, p. 136.
23. Paul Wiley, *Conrad's Measure of Man* (Madison: University of Wisconsin Press, 1954), p. 28.
24. Conrad's familiarity with French cultural life was not confined to the world of letters. Gillon writes: 'According to Lyman Owen [...] Conrad's old Doyen in *The Arrow of Gold* was probably drawn after Gustav Doré. There was a Gustave Doyen, a *peintre de genre*, born in 1837 in Festieux, who exhibited his work in the Salon de Paris. There was another painter called Eugene Doyen, member of the *Société des Artistes Français* in Paris.' ('Conrad as painter', *Conradiana*, 10 (1978), 266). Conrad was also well acquainted with the work of Rodin (see Thomas R. Dilworth, 'Conrad's secret sharer at the Gate of Hell', *Conradiana*, 9 (1977), 203–17). Towards the end of his life Conrad met Ravel on three occasions, and, as he put it, they 'got rather thick together' (*LL*, II, p. 303).
25. *NRF*, p. 661.
26. *NRF*, p. 679; Dawson, 'Some recollections', p. 208.
27. Galsworthy, 'Reminiscences of Conrad' in *Castles in Spain*, p. 89.
28. Henry-D. Davray, 'Lettres anglaises', *Mercure de France*, 31 (July–September 1899), 266. Davray also recorded: 'Bientôt, il nous récita quelques-uns des plus magnifiques morceaux de Flaubert, et sa mémoire en possédait bien d'autres. Comme il avait compris et comme il savait!' ('Lettres anglaises', *Mercure de France*, 38 (April–June 1901), 262).
29. Arthur Symons, '*A Set of Six*', in George T. Keating, *A Conrad Memorial Library* (Garden City, NY: Doubleday, Doran, 1929), p. 180.
30. Ford, pp. 36, 35, 36. Dawson heard him 'declaim admirably a sonorous passage from Julien l'Hospitalier' ('Some recollections', p. 208).
31. Douglas Goldring, *South Lodge* (London: Constable, 1943), pp. 24, 25.
32. Ford Madox Ford, 'Techniques', *Southern Review*, 1 (July 1935), 25. Reprinted in *Critical Writings of Ford Madox Ford*, ed. Frank MacShane (Lincoln: University of Nebraska Press, 1964), pp. 56–71.
33. Ford, p. 31.
34. Yves Guérin, 'Huit lettres inédites de Joseph Conrad à Robert d'Humières traducteur du *Nigger of the "Narcissus"* en français', *Revue de littérature comparée*, 44 (1970), 372.
35. Conrad had probably gleaned this information from Maxime Du Camp's memoirs which he and Ford had read together (see Ford, p. 59).
36. Lenormand, 'Il y a quatre ans, en Corse avec Joseph Conrad, coureur de mers', p. 339.
37. Arnold T. Schwab, 'Joseph Conrad's American friend: correspondence with James Huneker', *Modern Philology*, 52 (1955), 224. Najder says that 'he became acquainted with Flaubert, through *Salammbô*' during his stay in Australia (Najder, p. 62) (that is, between January and July 1879). (The key-word in the quotation is 'communion' and not 'commission' as recorded in Karl, p. 669.)
38. Guérin, p. 372.

39. In his essay 'Gustave Flaubert' published in 1893 James had already said that in *Salammbô* 'We breathe the air of pure aesthetics' (*Selected Literary Criticism*, ed. Morris Shapira (London: Heinemann, 1963), p. 148). Had this appreciation stayed in Conrad's mind?

40. Watts points out: 'Aubry identifies them as *Typhoon and Other Stories* (*LL*, I, p. 315). However, as that volume contains four tales, the reference here is to *Youth: a Narrative; and Two Other Stories* (Blackwood, London, 1902)' (*LCG*, p. 145).

41. Conrad means Félicité in 'Un Coeur simple'. He had already alluded to the death march of Mâtho in a letter to Galsworthy of 6 January 1908. Describing himself as a victim of gout, he had written: '*Et le misérable écrivait toujours*' (*LL*, II, p. 64), which, as Jean-Aubry pointed out, is an allusion to the sentence '*et le misérable marchait toujours*' (*Salammbô*, p. 412).

42. Donald C. Yelton, *Mimesis and Metaphor* (The Hague: Mouton, 1967), p. 104. [Abbreviated Yelton]

43. In *Egoists: A Book of Supermen* (New York: Scribner, 1909), which Huneker had sent to Conrad, he had described Flaubert 'toiling like a titan over his books' (p. 111).

44. Schwab, 'Joseph Conrad's American friend', pp. 224–5. When writing the last sentence, Conrad probably had in mind this statement from the *Correspondance*: 'je n'ai point peur de la mort. L'hypothèse du néant absolu n'a même rien qui me terrifie. Je suis prêt à me jeter dans le grand trou noir avec placidité' (IV, p. 170). When, late in life, he read Huneker's comment that 'J.C. makes the fifth of a quintette of the world's greatest writers of fiction: Flaubert, Turgenev, Tolstoy, *and* Dostoievski [*sic*]', characteristically, his reaction was: 'Dear Huneker had Russians on the brain. Tolstoy and Dostoievski deny everything for which I stand. I hate to hear my name pronounced in the same breath with theirs. To be classed with Flaubert is, of course, a great compliment' (Schwab, 'Joseph Conrad's American friend', pp. 229–30).

45. Conrad also described himself as one of 'the last of the romantics'; see Marian Dabrowski, 'An interview with Joseph Conrad' (translated by Bronislas A. Jezierski), *American Scholar*, 13 (1944), 374.

46. A probable allusion to *La Tentation de Saint Antoine* (chapter 2) can be seen in this comment on Maupassant:

> He will not be led into perdition by the seductions of sentiment, of eloquence, of humour, of pathos; of all that splendid pageant of faults that pass between the writer and his probity on the blank sheet of paper, like the glittering cortège of deadly sins before the austere anchorite in the desert air of Thebaïde.
>
> (*NLL*, pp. 26–7)

47. Józef Ujejski, *Joseph Conrad*, trans. Pierre Duméril (Paris: Société Française d'Editions Littéraires et Techniques, 1939), p. 191.

48. Published under the title *Stories from de Maupassant*, translated by E. M. [Elsie Martindale], with a preface by Ford Madox Hueffer (London: Duckworth, 1903).

49. Ford, p. 195. Describing how he worked out cadences for sentences and paragraphs in the first draft of what was to become *Romance*, Ford recalls:

> Every sentence had a dying fall and every paragraph faded out. The last sentences of that original draft ran: *Above our heads a nightingale* (did something: *poured out*

*its soul*, as like as not, or *poured out its melody on the summer air*, the cadence calling
there for eleven syllables). *As it was June it sang a trifle hoarsely*. . . . The reader
will observe that the writer had then already read his *Trois Contes* [. . .]. The last
cadences, then, of Herodias run: 'Et tous trois, ayant pris la tête de Jokanaan s'en
allaient vers Galilé. Comme elle était très lourde, ils la portaient alternativement.'. . . As cadence the later sentences are an exact pastiche of the former.
In each the first contains nineteen syllables; the concluding one commences with
*As it was*, and is distinguished by the *u* sounds of '*June*' and '*lourd*' and the *or*
sounds of '*hoarse*' and '*portaient*'. It was in that way that, before the writer and
Conrad met, they had studied their Flaubert.                         (Ford, pp. 14–15)

50. Ford, p. 200.
51. Symons, '*A Set of Six*', p. 180. For a valuable addition to this assessment of Conrad's
    relationship with Maupassant, see Paul Kirschner, 'Some notes on *Conrad in the
    Nineteenth Century*', *Conradiana*, 17 (1985), 32–4.
52. The *Catalogue of Second-Hand Books, no. 267*, which lists the 'Books from Joseph
    Conrad's library' sold by W. Heffer & Sons Ltd., Cambridge, in 1926, shows that
    Conrad owned also a copy of France's *La Révolte des anges* (1914). I am greatly
    indebted to Mr F. R. Collieson of Heffers Booksellers for kindly sending me xeroxes
    of all the Conrad entries in their sale catalogues.
53. Curle, p. 119.

## Chapter 2

1. Ford, p. 94.
2. Jules de Gaultier, *Le Bovarysme*, new edn (Paris: Mercure de France, 1921).
3. Albert J. Guerard, *Conrad the Novelist* (Cambridge, Mass.: Harvard University
   Press, 1958), p. 77. He also notes that 'One of the better pictures of the royal
   household [i.e. when Lakamba asks Babalatchi to play a hand-organ] recalls, in fact,
   the organ-grinding scene of *Madame Bovary*, that brilliant forestatement of Emma's
   squalid destiny'.
4. Baines, p. 146. The most relevant passages from Flaubert read:

   Quelquefois pourtant, un curieux se haussait par-dessus la haie du jardin, et
   apercevait avec ébahissement cet homme à barbe longue, couvert d'habits sor-
   dides, farouche, et qui pleurait tout haut en marchant.              (*MB*, p. 479)

   Il avait la tête renversée contre le mur, les yeux clos, la bouche ouverte, et tenait
   dans ses mains une longue mèche de cheveux noirs.                    (*MB*, p. 481)

5. Watt, p. 52.
6. The relationship between *Madame Bovary* and *Une vie* is very well documented.
   See, for instance, *Analyses & réflexions sur 'Une vie' de Guy de Maupassant et le
   pessimisme* (Liguçé: Edition Marketing, 1979), pp. 118–20.
7. The passage by Amiel reads: 'Who among us does not have his Promised Land, his
   day of ecstasy and his end in exile? And so how pallid a counterfeit of that once-
   glimpsed life is actual existence, and how those fiery lightning flashes of the pro-

phetic visions of our youth serve to cast a yet duller shade on the twilight of our shabby and monotonous adulthood!' (Quoted in Watt, p. 66).

8. Paul Kirschner, *Conrad: The Psychologist as Artist* (Edinburgh: Oliver and Boyd, 1968), pp. 208–11. [Abbreviated Kirschner]

9. Compare also the following parallels:

l'arrière [du bateau], *relevé, semblait jeter vers le ciel, comme un cri d'appel désespéré*, ces deux mots [...] *Marie-Joseph.*                ('L'Epave', *La Petite Roque*, p. 79)

The tree [...] began to move down stream again [...] raising upwards a long, denuded branch, like a hand *lifted in mute appeal to heaven*                (*AF*, p. 4)

*la Méditerranée, sans une ride,* [...] semblait une plaque de métal polie
                (*Contes du jour et de la nuit*, p. 77)

*the polished steel* of the *unwrinkled sea*                (*AF*, p. 186)

10. John Dozier Gordan, *Joseph Conrad: The Making of a Novelist* (Cambridge Mass: Harvard University Press, 1940), p. 178.

11. Gordan says that 'Ford himself somewhat discredited his anecdote' that 'the first words of Conrad's first book were pencilled on the flyleaves and margins of *Madame Bovary* [...] by later adding *L'Education sentimentale* to *Madame Bovary* (*Return to Yesterday*, p. 246)' (Gordan, p. 380). Clearly Ford did nothing of the kind.

12. Lawrence Thornton, 'Beyond *Le Mot juste*', unpublished PhD thesis, University of California, Santa Barbara, 1973, pp. 136–40.

13. Jean-Pierre Richard, *Littérature et sensation* (Paris: Seuil, 1954), pp. 128–9 (my translation).

14. Baines, p. 443.

15. Kirschner, p. 216. Quotation from 'Le Bonheur', *Contes du jour et de la nuit*, p. 83.

16. On 20 July? 1894, three months before confessing to Mme Poradowska his fear of being 'trop sous l'influence de Maupassant' (*CL*, I, p. 183), Conrad wrote: 'Il faut *trainer le boulet* de son individualité jusqu'a la fin' (*CL*, I, p. 162). This sounds like an echo of a comment Maupassant had made in *Gil Blas* of 10 June 1884: 'Nous sommes emprisonnés en nous-mêmes, sans parvenir à sortir de nous, condamnés à *traîner le boulet* de notre rêve sans essor' (*Chroniques*, 10/18 (Paris: UGE, 1980), II, p. 402).

17. In *Guy de Maupassant et l'art du roman* (Paris: Nizet, 1954), p. 129, André Vial notes:

Maupassant pouvait lire, dès 1879, dans la traduction qu'A. Burdeau donnait du *Fondement de la morale* de Schopenhauer:

Du point de vue tout subjectif où reste nécessairement placée notre conscience, chacun est à lui-même l'univers entier: tout ce qui est objet n'existe pour lui qu'indirectement, en qualité de représentation du sujet; si bien que rien n'existe, sinon en tant qu'il est dans la conscience. Le seul univers que chacun de nous connaisse réellement, il le porte en lui-même comme une représentation qui est à lui; c'est pourquoi il en est le centre. (Paris, Germer-Baillière, p. 105)

Although Conrad had a first-hand knowledge of the great pessimistic philosopher

(Galsworthy recalled in 1924: 'Schopenhauer used to give him satisfaction twenty years or more ago' (Galsworthy, p. 91)), he must have absorbed many of his ideas via Maupassant and Anatole France, who were both strongly influenced by Schopenhauer (see, for instance, A. Baillot, *Influence de la philosophie de Schopenhauer en France, 1860–1900* (Paris: Vrin, 1927); G. Hainsworth, 'Schopenhauer, Flaubert, Maupassant: conceptual thought and artistic "truth"', in *Currents of Thought in French Literature*, ed. T. V. Benn (Oxford: Blackwell, 1965), pp. 165–90; René-Pierre Colin, *Schopenhauer en France* (Lyon: Presses Universitaires de Lyon, 1979), ch. 5, 'Maupassant et le "saccageur de rêves"'.

18. See Norman Sherry, *Conrad's Eastern World* (Cambridge University Press, 1966), pp. 139–70.

19. Although Garnett's adverse criticism probably helped persuade Conrad to abandon his third attempt at a novel, Ford claimed that the reason had to do with a problem arising from Maupassant's influence:

> The difficulty – the literary, not the material difficulty – was the figure of the priest. I don't know whether Conrad began the story before he had read *Une Vie* or the other story of Maupassant's ['Le Saut du berger'] in which a fanatical priest murders the guilty couple. I rather think that must have been the case. Or he may have begun the story with the idea that he could sufficiently differentiate his priest from Maupassant's. Or he may even have thought of treating the priest in a spirit of rivalry to the author of *La Maison Tellier*. I know we both vaingloriously and only half in earnest talked of treating one or other of Maupassant's subjects and indeed, I did eventually have a shot at it.
>
> But that abbé was the real snag – the question of how to treat him similarly and yet differently seemed too difficult and I daresay that reluctance to face that problem was what really made him put the manuscript once again away.
>
> (*The Sisters* (Milan: Mursia, 1968), pp. 20–1)

20. Gordan, *Joseph Conrad: The Making of a Novelist*, p. 53.

21. Daniel Schwarz points out that Conrad uses the setting here 'to reinforce moral meaning or implicitly comment on the quality of life in Ploumar', the bleak aspect of the area, for instance, suggesting the moral wasteland prevailing in the parish (Daniel R. Schwarz, 'Moral bankruptcy in Ploumar parish: a study of Conrad's "The Idiots"', *Conradiana*, 1 (1969), 115).

22. Milton Chaikin, 'Zola and Conrad's "The Idiots"', *Studies in Philology*, 52 (1955), 503.

23. Thornton, 'Beyond *Le Mot juste*', pp. 144, 145.

24. Chaikin, 'Zola and Conrad's "The Idiots"', p. 504.

25. References to *La Terre* are to *Les Rougon-Macquart*, La Pléiade (Paris: Gallimard, 1966), IV.

26. Chaikin notes: 'We find Zola's sardonic treatment of characters of all classes, of the intriguing aristocrat, the fat priest, the greedy merchant, the besotted villager. Conrad's skepticism and anticlericalism here are typically Zolaesque' ('Zola and Conrad's "The Idiots"', p. 505).

27. References to *La Joie de vivre* are to *Les Rougon-Macquart*, La Pléiade (Paris: Gallimard, 1964), III.

28. The same simile reappears in 'Karain': 'The bay was like a bottomless *pit* of intense light' (*TU*, p. 5).
29. Zola's description also inspired later touches in 'Karain': '*Ragged edges of black clouds* peeped over the hills' (*TU*, p. 20); and in *The Mirror of the Sea:* 'Clothed in a mantle of dazzling gold or draped in *rags of black clouds* like a beggar, the might of *the Westerly Wind* sits enthroned' (*MS*, p. 81).
30. Graver in *Conrad's Short Fiction* (Berkeley: University of California Press, 1969) noted that this passage 'parallels a fine scene' where 'Bouvard and Pécuchet mention Richelieu and read Dumas and Balzac in an uncomprehending way' (*BP*, pp. 165, 168–9). He also points out that 'Kayerts' daughter Mélie has the same name as the provocative maid from whom Pécuchet [...] contracts gonorrhea' (Graver, p. 11).
31. Wallace Watson, '"The shade of old Flaubert" and Maupassant's "Art impeccable (presque)"': French influences on the development of Conrad's Marlow', *Journal of Narrative Technique*, 7 (1977), 41–2. Watson feels that Conrad 'failed markedly' in his efforts to emulate the master of Croisset and that, although he was 'apparently quite happy at first with his ability to so mimic the Flaubertian manner' he must have soon realized that the style of 'An Outpost' was 'by no means limited to those "new rhythms" of crisp Flaubertian satire' he prided himself on having captured in the Author's Note for the 1898 *Tales of Unrest*.
32. Watt, p. 75.

### Chapter 3

1. This echo is an addition to Kirschner.
2. The following parallel is also of note: '*Une barque à voile*, au milieu de la rivière, ayant tendu sur ses deux bords deux grands triangles de toile blanche pour cueillir les moindres souffles de brise, *avait l'air d'un énorme oiseau prêt à s'envoler*' (*BA*, p. 308); '*The ship* rose to it [the coming wave] *as though she had soared on wings*, and for a moment rested poised upon the foaming crest *as if she had been a great sea-bird*' (p. 57).
3. Guérin, pp. 384–92.
4. Richard Curle, 'Joseph Conrad', *Rhythm*, 2 (1912), 242–55. Curle wrote: 'The sailors in the forecastle of the "Narcissus" in the first chapter are filled in with a similar touch to the barbarians in the garden of Hamilcar in the beginning of *Salammbô*. These sharp, little sentences remind me exactly of Flaubert in a certain mood' (p. 246). Lest his assertions should seem unfounded, Curle pointed out these resemblances to Conrad who told him that on seeing his article 'he had suddenly remembered that he had just been reading *Salammbô* before he sat down to write the *Nigger*' (Curle, p. 116).
5. Roger Bismut, 'Quelques problèmes de création littéraire dans "Bel-Ami"', *Revue d'histoire littéraire de la France*, 67 (1967), 577–89.
6. elle prétendit qu'elle allait mieux et qu'elle se lèverait tout à l'heure.

(MB, pp. 436–7)

– Oui, ça va mieux, j'ai repris des forces. [...]

– Non, je vais beaucoup mieux.                    (*BA*, pp. 268, 269) de grosses larmes lui découlèrent des yeux.                    (*MB*, pp. 447–8)

De grosses larmes coulaient de ses yeux                         (*BA*, p. 276)

Un grand frisson lui secouait les épaules                        (*MB*, p. 436)

Soudain il tressaillit d'un frisson brusque qu'on vit courir d'un bout à l'autre de son corps                                                              (*BA*, p. 277)

et ses pauvres mains se traînaient sur les draps avec ce geste hideux et doux des agonisants qui semblent vouloir déjà se recouvrir du suaire.      (*MB*, p. 446)

Il traînait toujours ses doigts maigres sur le drap comme pour le ramener vers sa face                                                                    (*BA*, p. 278)

Sa poitrine aussitôt se mit à haleter rapidement. [...] l'effrayante accélération de ses côtes, secouées par un souffle furieux                      (*MB*, p. 448)

L'haleine de Forestier était plus rapide que celle d'un chien qui vient de courir, si pressée qu'on ne la pouvait point compter [...]. Il restait immobile, hagard et haletant.                                                        (*BA*, p. 277, 278)

ses yeux [...] pâlissaient comme deux globes de lampes qui s'éteignent
                                                                 (*MB*, p. 448)

[Duroy] ouvrit les yeux juste à temps pour voir Forestier fermer les siens comme deux lumières qui s'éteignent.                                  (*BA*, p. 278)

7. Albert Thibaudet, *Gustave Flaubert* (Paris: Gallimard, 1935), p. 236.
8. H. G. Wells, review of *An Outcast of the Islands* in *Saturday Review*, 81 (1896), 509–10.
9. In 'Conrad criticism and *The Nigger of the "Narcissus"'*, Ian Watt says that the opening paragraph of the fourth chapter – which Mudrick had attacked as an example of Conrad's 'unctuous thrilling rhetoric' – can be explained in terms of 'the influence of the stylistic aims of French romanticism, the only specific literary influence on his work which he [Conrad] admitted. The passage is, in part, an attempt to write "la belle page" – to achieve the grandiose richness of verbal and rhythmic suggestion found, for example, in Victor Hugo's *Les Travailleurs de la mer*' (*Nineteenth-Century Fiction*, 12 (1958), 263).
10. Chwalewik suggested that 'in all probability' Conrad was 'merely paraphrasing his father's noble rendering of this passage in his Polish versified translation of De Vigny's prose original' (Witold Chwalewik, 'Conrad and the literary tradition', *Kwartalnik Neofilologiczny*, 5 (1958), 33).
11. The possibility of an influence was mentioned by Ernest A. Baker, *History of the English Novel* (London: Witherby, 1936), X, p. 28.
12. All references to *Mon frère Yves* are to the Calmann-Lévy edition.
13. For a detailed comparison between the two descriptions, see my 'Aspects of Flaubertian influence on Conrad's fiction', *Revue de littérature comparée*, 57 (1983), 19–21.
14. Thibaudet said that in the course of a description or narration, the 'et de mouvement' accompanies or signifies the move to a more important or more dramatic moment, a progression; it introduces 'la fin du tableau, le trait décisif' (*Flaubert*, pp. 265–6).

Proust has also commented on this 'et' which is 'comme l'indication qu'une autre partie du tableau commence' ('A propos du "style" de Flaubert', *Nouvelle Revue Française*, 14 (1920), 79). In this respect Ramón Fernández saw the Flaubertian influence as somewhat negative. In his tribute, he wrote that 'Flaubert n'a pas toujours eu sur lui la meilleure influence. Ses phrases sont souvent trop écrites, et l'inévitable *et* qui précède la dernière proposition les rend quelque peu monotones' ('L'Art de Conrad', *NRF*, p. 737) Yelton comments: 'The last sentence exaggerates the incidence in Conrad's prose of a Flaubertian stylistic device which he never rejected, but which ceases to be very conspicuous in the works written after about 1900' (Yelton, p. 101).

15. See Thibaudet, *Flaubert*, pp. 231–6.
16. Quoted with an illustration by René Dumesnil, *Gustave Flaubert: l'homme et l'oeuvre* (Paris: Desclée de Brouwer, 1932), pp. 432–3.
17. James Huneker, 'The genius of Joseph Conrad', in his *Ivory Apes and Peacocks* (New York: Scribner's Sons, 1921), pp. 6–7. To illustrate his formula he quotes the second half of the opening paragraph from 'Karain', in which, he says, 'There is no mistaking the *coda* [...] beginning at "and' ['and green islets scattered'] which 'suggests the author of *Salammbô*'. Yelton, who noticed the parallel between the two critical judgements, says that 'It seems more than likely that Huneker appropriated the formula, without acknowledgement, from Hennequin', and adds 'but if so it would still be significant that he should think that a musical analogy cut to Flaubert's measurements should fit Conrad with no alterations' (Yelton, pp. 101–2).
18. A detailed comparison of the two sequences can be found in Horst Gödicke, 'Der Einfluß Flauberts und Maupassants auf Joseph Conrad', Dissertation of the Philosophy Faculty, University of Hamburg, 1969, pp. 70–3.
19. See Watt, p. 203, and Watson, '"The shade of old Flaubert"', p. 46.
20. Edward D. Sullivan, *Maupassant the Novelist* (Princeton University Press, 1954), pp. 86, 87.
21. The 'brilliant idea', as Baines sees it (p. 193), of using a dressing-table with three mirrors finds a precedent in Maupassant's *Notre coeur*.
22. Watson, '"The shade of old Flaubert"', pp. 49–50.
23. Ford recollected Conrad's saying that when the *Adowa* was frozen fast in Rouen harbour, he translated 'phrases from the scene between Rodolphe and Emma at the cattle-show' (Ford, p. 102).
24. See Norman Sherry, *Conrad's Western World* (Cambridge University Press, 1971), and M. M. Mahood, *The Colonial Encounter* (London: Collings, 1977).
25. See Betsy C. Yarrison, 'The symbolism of literary allusion in *Heart of Darkness*, *Conradiana*, 7 (1975), 155–64.
26. Mahood, *The Colonial Encounter*, p. 26.
27. Baker, *History of the English Novel*, X, p. 31. Other sources and influences have also been suggested. See, in particular, Bruce Johnson, '"Heart of Darkness" and the problem of emptiness' (*Studies in Short Fiction*, 9 (1972), 387–400) (which discusses the nature of Kurtz's hollowness and suggests the influence of Schopenhauer and Kipling's 'The man who would be king'); Merrill Harvey Goldwyn, 'Nathaniel Hawthorne and Conrad's *Heart of Darkness*', *Conradiana*, 16 (1984), 72–8; G. Peter Winnington, 'Conrad and Cutcliffe Hyne: a new source for *Heart of Darkness*',

*Conradiana*, 16 (1984), 163–82. In 'Conrad and Mark Twain: a newly-discovered essay', David Leon Higdon says that 'it is highly likely that the episode of running chutes on the Mississippi was the fictional inspiration for writing about the great river and its shoals in *Heart of Darkness*' and points out that 'Marlow's meditations on navigation closely echo several passages in *Life on the Mississippi*' (*Journal of Modern Literature*, 12 (1985), 354–61).

28. Watson, '"The shade of old Flaubert"', p. 50.

29. Quoted by Morf (Morf, p. 299). For example, Najder points out that 'the main character of Mickiewicz's greatest work *Pan Tadeusz*, Jacek Soplica, alias Father Robak, is shown as trying to atone, by many years of heroic service to Poland, for a moment of weakness in his youth when his private feelings made him forget his national obligations: a perfect fore-runner of Conrad's Jim' (*Conrad's Polish Background*, p. 15), and Adam Gillon observes that 'the sense of mission and the dream of hero leadership, which are largely responsible for Lord Jim's actions, are strikingly similar to those of Mickiewicz's *Konrad Wallenrod*' ('Some Polish literary motifs in the works of Joseph Conrad', *Slavic and East European Journal*, 10 (1966), 429). See also Wit Tarnawski, *Conrad the Man, the Writer, the Pole* (London: Polish Cultural Foundation, 1984), pp. 80–97.

30. In *James & Conrad* (Athens: University of Georgia Press, 1977), Elsa Nettels presents *Lord Jim* as 'the novel in which Conrad seems to share most fully the central concerns of James' (p. 46).

31. See Frank D. McConnell, 'Félicité, passion, ivresse: the lexicography of *Madame Bovary*', *Novel*, 3 (1970), 159.

32. Jean Rousset, '*Madame Bovary* ou le livre sur rien', in his *Forme et signification* (Paris: Corti, 1964), pp. 109–33.

33. As Gillon remarks, Jim occupies 'both a central and a higher position than anyone else even higher than that of his penitent judge – Brierly himself' ('Conrad as painter', p. 260).

34. At one stage in her life, we read of Emma: 'Avec [...] sa démarche d'oiseau [...] ne semblait-elle pas *traverser l'existence en y touchant à peine*' (148–9); Brown taunts Jim with a similar remark: 'you talk as if you were one of those people that should have wings so as *to go about without touching the* dirty *earth*' (*LJ*, p. 383).

35. Flaubert's use of these symbols is analysed by James Trammell Cox in 'The finest French novel in the English language', *Modern Fiction Studies*, 9 (1963), 79–93, which examines the influence of *Madame Bovary* on Ford's *The Good Soldier*.

36. As Thornton comments: 'The fact that this passage is embedded in a morass of romantic clichés only serves to heighten the irony associated with Emma's distorted ideas and ideals' (Thornton, 'Beyond *Le Mot juste*', p. 169). Thornton has examined many of the similarities between *Madame Bovary* and *Lord Jim*.

37. See D. A. Williams, 'Water imagery in *Madame Bovary*', *Forum for Modern Language Studies*, 13 (1977), 70–84 and in particular 78–9.

38. Harold Brooks argues that the metaphor derived from a poem by Browning. See Brooks, '*Lord Jim* and *Fifine at the Fair*', *Conradiana*, 3 (1971), 9–25.

39. Of the romantic, Stein says: '*He wants to be a saint*, and he wants to be a devil – and every time he shuts his eyes he sees himself as a very fine fellow – so fine as he can never be.... In a dream' (p. 213). This verdict applies to Emma with particular

aptness: *'Elle voulut devenir une sainte'* (*MB*, p. 296) but she also wants to be a courtesan, and she is convinced all the time of her uniqueness, always 'in a dream'.

40. Guerard, *Conrad*, p. 164.

41. Tony Tanner, *Adultery in the Novel* (Baltimore: Johns Hopkins University Press, 1979), p. 313.

42. As Wilfred S. Dowden points out, the reasons for Jim's inability to act in the training ship episode are 'as dimly perceived as the ships, shore, and boats which are seen intermittently through the breaks in the mist' (*Joseph Conrad: The Imaged Style* (Nashville: Vanderbilt University Press, 1970), p. 59).

43. Yelton, p. 116.

44. Fritz Gysin has pointed out that the captain's 'voice and parts of his body are connected with images of dead matter' and said that this image 'strongly suggests a corpse and a coffin and processes taking place at the undertaker's' ('The vitality of distortion and decay: the grotesque skipper in *Lord Jim*', *English Studies*, 59 (1978), 426).

45. Gysin, 'The vitality of distortion and decay', p. 431. On the live models (the Rajah of Goa, Nakhoda Trong) Conrad used to create Doramin, see Sherry, *Conrad's Eastern World*, pp. 158–61.

46. Apart from Gysin's article, see Elsa Nettels, 'The grotesque in Conrad's fiction', *Nineteenth-Century Fiction*, 29 (1974), 144–63 and chapter seven entitled 'The grotesque' in her *James and Conrad*, pp. 159–93.

47. A few examples of ternary structures from Maupassant and Conrad are quoted in my 'Joseph Conrad and the French language, part one', pp. 248–9. Nevertheless, the device frequently appears in the works of some Polish writers (see I. P. Pulc, 'The imprint of Polish on Conrad's prose', in *Joseph Conrad: Theory and World Fiction*, ed. Wolodymyr T. Zyla and Wendell M. Aycock (Lubbock: Texas Tech University, 1974), p. 117–39). Conrad undoubtedly adopted it primarily as a result of his imitation of Flaubert and Maupassant (see pp. 120–1).

48. Sherry, *Conrad's Eastern World*, p. 49.

49. *Correspondance inédite de l'abbé Ferdinand Galiani* (Paris: Treuttel et Würtz, 1818), II, p. 426. Thomas Schultheiss has pointed out that this phrasing of 'the question' is identical to Camus's in *Le Mythe de Sisyphe*: 'L' important, disait l'abbé Galiani à Mme d'Epinay, n'est pas de guérir, mais de vivre avec ses maux' (Schultheiss, 'Lord Hamlet and Lord Jim', *Polish Review*, 11 (1966), 105–6. See Albert Camus, *Essais*, La Pléiade (Paris: Gallimard, 1965), p. 126). Camus seems to have been quoting from memory.

50. Jean-Aubry misquotes the title calling it *Récits, aventures et combats* (*LF*, p. 184).

51. Kirschner notes an interesting parallel between Conrad's determination when a boy to leave his home and country to go to sea and Garneray's own rebellion as narrated in the opening of his book. (Kirschner, pp. 11–12)

52. On 14 May 1923 he wrote to Jean-Aubry: 'je suis infiniment touché par les offres de mes amis français de me procurer l'oeuvre de Garneray' (*LF*, p. 184). The W. Heffer sale catalogue contains the following item: Albert Savine, *Abordages d'un marin de la République* (*Souvenirs de Louis Garneray*) (Paris: 1912). The volume is inscribed: 'Pour l'admirable auteur Joseph Conrad, cette réédition de l'oeuvre qui le passionna, à défaut de l'introuvable édition originale, cherché vainement jusqu'à

270 Notes to pages 75–82

ce jour. Un admirateur de votre oeuvre. – Robert Télier, Libraire, Paris, 12 rue de l'Université.'
53. Louis Garneray, *Voyages, aventures et combats* (Paris: Nelson, [n.d.]), p. 29.
54. Sherry, *Conrad's Eastern World*, p. 141.
55. Patricia Dale, 'Conrad: a borrowing from Hazlitt's father', *Notes and Queries*, new series 10, (1963), 146.
56. Carl Nelson, 'The ironic allusive texture of *Lord Jim*: Coleridge, Crane, Milton and Melville', *Conradiana*, 4 (1972), 47–59.
57. Brooks, '*Lord Jim* and *Fifine at the Fair*'.
58. Christopher Ricks, 'The pink toads in *Lord Jim*', *Essays in Criticism*, 31 (1981), 142–4.
59. Leo A. Lensing, 'Goethe's *Torquato Tasso* in *Lord Jim*: a note on Conrad's use of literary quotation', *English Literature in Transition*, 19 (1976), 101–4, and Paul Kirschner, 'Conrad, Goethe and Stein: the romantic fate in *Lord Jim*', *Ariel*, 10 (1979), 65–81.
60. Schultheiss, 'Lord Hamlet and Lord Jim', and Gillon, pp. 53–69.
61. Andrzej Busza has shown that when relating the predicament of his Carpathian peasant, Yanko Goorall, he was using 'a type of "emigrant story" which was in vogue in Poland in the last decade of the nineteenth century' (Busza, 'Conrad's Polish literary background and some illustrations of the influence of Polish literature on his work', *Antemurale*, 10 (1966), 224).
62. Richard Herndon, 'The genesis of Conrad's "Amy Foster"' *Studies in Philology*, 57 (1960), 560, 562. See also Peter G. Beidler, 'Conrad's "Amy Foster" and Chaucer's Prioress', *Nineteenth-Century Fiction*, 30 (1975), 111–15.
63. When, a few years later, he made the teacher of languages say of Mrs Haldin: 'her facial immobility had in it *something monachal*' (*UWE*, p. 101), it is as though these passages were still lingering in his mind.
64. Baines, p. 271.
65. David Thorburn, *Conrad's Romanticism* (New Haven/London: Yale University Press, 1974), p. 36.
66. Sherry, *Conrad's Eastern World*, p. 203.
67. Yelton, pp. 55–6.
68. Yelton, p. 55.
69. Christopher Prendergast, 'Flaubert: writing and negativity', *Novel*, 8 (1975), 197.
70. I use these terms as defined by Doris Y. Kadish in 'Two semiological features of four functions of description: the example of Flaubert', *Romanic Review*, 70 (1979), 278–98.
71. Leo Gurko, *Joseph Conrad: Giant in Exile* (London: Collier Macmillan, 1979), p. 84. The last sentence may hold the clue to the major link that Conrad perceived between his story and Flaubert's, since Frédéric's failure also lies in his inability to move in an age of change symbolized by the *Ville-de-Montereau*, that microcosm of nineteenth-century industrial society.

Chapter 4

1. Sherry, *Conrad's Western World*, p. 148. Rosemary Freeman in 'Conrad's *Nostromo*: a source and its use', *Modern Fiction Studies*, 7 (1961/62), 317–26, and Sherry in *Conrad's Western World*, p. 156 have also shown that, when writing *Nostromo*, Conrad made considerable use of the *Mémoires de Garibaldi* (1860), which gave him materials for the characterization of old Viola, the 'Garibaldino', background material on South America, and valuable hints for the narrative. Freeman shows, too, that Conrad had the *Mémoires* in mind when composing 'The End of the Tether'.

2. Leavis, *The Great Tradition*, p. 210.

3. Edgar Wright, who discovered (at the same time as Ivo Vidan) that G. F. Masterman's *Seven Eventful Years in Paraguay* (1869) was one source of *Nostromo*, says that the Montero brothers are 'a divided portrait' of the ruthless President Francisco Solano Lopez, and that 'there is no doubt of the Lopez origin' ('Joseph Conrad: his expressed views about technique and the principles underlying them, with a study of their relevance to certain novels', unpublished MA thesis, University of London, 1955, p. 290). Masterman says:

> I believe the origin of the war may be traced to the time when Lopez visited France, namely, in the year 1854. He, suddenly emerging from the semi-barbarism of a remote and almost unknown republic, was dazzled by the parade and glitter, the false glory and proud memories of wars and warriors he found around him, and was fired with the ambition of making the brave and devoted people he knew he would be one day called upon to rule, a nation to be feared and courted as the dominant power of South America. (p. 84)

It is understandable that Wright might regard this passage as the single source for Conrad's Pedrito; however, without being the only source, it may have given Conrad the idea of causing Pedrito to go and stay in France during the Second Empire, an idea which, in turn, reminded him of this episode from *L'Anneau d'améthyste*.

4. Karl, p. 656.

5. Thomas Moser, *Joseph Conrad: Achievement and Decline* (Cambridge, Mass.: Harvard University Press, 1957), p. 87. [Abbreviated Moser]

6. Sherry, *Conrad's Western World*, pp. 165, 169. For a detailed analysis of the precise nature of Conrad's ambiguous relationship with Decoud, see Martin Ray, 'Conrad and Decoud', *Polish Review*, 29 (1984), 53–64.

7. Owen Knowles, 'Conrad, Anatole France, and the early French romantic tradition: some influences', *Conradiana*, 11 (1979), 41–61. [Abbreviated Knowles]

8. This borrowing was first shown in my PhD thesis, 'French linguistic and literary influences on Joseph Conrad', Leeds University, 1971, pp. 267–9.

9. Knowles, pp. 42, 43.

10. Knowles, p. 45.

11. For instance, Cunninghame Graham confessed to Garnett on 31 October 1904: 'I do not like either, the explanation of the end of Decoud' (*LCG*, p. 159).

12. Guerard, *Conrad*, p. 199.

13. Knowles, p. 48.

14. Kingsley Widmer, 'Conrad's Pyrrhonistic conservatism: ideological melodrama

around "simple ideas"', *Novel*, 7 (1973), 141, 142. Similar views have been expressed by a number of critics (see Ray, 'Conrad and Decoud', pp. 57–8).

15. Wit Tarnawski, '*Nostromo* and Flaubert's *Salammbô*' in *Wit Tarnawski: The Man, the Writer, the Pole*, ed. John Crompton (London: The Joseph Conrad Society (UK), 1976), p. 20.

16. Like that of Conrad, Flaubert's political scepticism extended to the concepts of progress and civilization for he, too, had no faith in man's ability to improve himself and create a better future. His cry, during the Franco-Prussian war: 'quelle dérision que les mots "humanité, progrès, civilisation"' (VI, p. 188), was not the reflection of a transient mood, understandable in the circumstances, but the expression of a deep-seated conviction. In this connection, the significance of the presence of *Bouvard et Pécuchet* in 'An Outpost of Progress' needs no further stressing.

17. Curle, p. 115.

18. Frederick R. Karl, *A Reader's Guide to Joseph Conrad* (London: Thames and Hudson, 1960), p. 149.

19. Najder, p. 88.

20. Roger Huss, 'Some anomalous uses of the imperfect and the status of action in Flaubert', *French Studies*, 31 (1977), 145.

21. E. Stegmaier, 'The "would-scene" in Joseph Conrad's "Lord Jim" and "Nostromo"', *Modern Language Review*, 67 (1972), 517.

22. Huss, 'Some anomalous uses', pp. 144, 146.

23. Stegmaier, 'The "would-scene"', pp. 522, 517.

24. Arnold Kettle, *An Introduction to the English Novel* (London: Hutchinson, 1953), II, p. 67.

25. Kirschner, pp. 213–14. In 'L'Epreuve', a suspicious husband becomes obsessed by his doubts about his wife's faithfulness: 'Déjà il devenait agité, il marchait plus vite et perdait son calme. *On ne peut rien contre l'Idée. Elle est imprenable*, impossible à chasser, impossible à tuer' (*L'Inutile beauté*, p. 149). Conrad makes a similar analysis when Karain, after the death of his faithful servant, becomes the victim of a fixed idea. His face, the narrator says, showed 'the tormented weariness, the anger and the fear of a struggle against a thought, *an idea* – against *something that cannot be grappled*, that never rests – a shadow, a nothing, unconquerable and immortal, that preys upon life' (*TU*, p. 23).

26. Wallace S. Watson, 'Joseph Conrad's debts to the French', unpublished PhD thesis, Indiana Unversity, 1966, pp. 254–7. Watson also notes:

> a sentence [from Hugo's novel] that seems to have been consciously echoed by Conrad: 'Il y a trois Hanois, le grand Hanois, le petit Hanois, et la Mauve' [p. 614] (Compare Conrad's 'There is the Great Isabel; the Little Isabel, which is round; and Hermosa, which is the smallest' [p. 7]. (p. 348)

On 22 April 1965, the anonymous author of 'Hugo turns the tables' had deplored the fact that *Nostromo* was studied without reference to 'its glaring debt to *Les Travailleurs de la mer*' (*TLS*, 24 April 1965, 308).

27. Sherry, *Conrad's Western World*, p. 227.

28. Baker, *History of the English Novel*, X, p. 36.

29. Baines, p. 323.

30. Frederick R. Karl, 'Conrad's debt to Dickens', *Notes and Queries*, new series 4 (1957), 398–400, and James Walton, 'Conrad, Dickens and the detective novel', *Nineteenth-Century Fiction*, 23 (1969), 446–62.

31. Elisabeth Gerver, 'Fact into fiction: Conrad's creative process. [Review of Sherry's *Conrad's Western World*]', *Dalhousie Review*, 52 (1972), 299, 301. In '"The Princess Casamassima" between Balzac and Conrad' (*Studia Romanica et Anglica Zagrabiensia*, 21–22 (1966), 259–76), Ivo Vidan had also claimed that 'the presence of *The Princess Casamassima* in *The Secret Agent* cannot be denied' by pointing out a number of analogies between the two novels. Conrad's 'allusions to significant murders in Shakespeare's major tragedies' are briefly examined in Daniel R. Schwarz's *Conrad: Almayer's Folly to Under Western Eyes* (Ithaca, NY: Cornell University Press, 1980), pp. 172–3.

32. Norman Sherry (ed.), *Conrad: The Critical Heritage* (London: Routledge & Kegan Paul, 1973), p. 186.

33. Wiley, *Conrad's Measure of Man*, p. 14.

34. James Walton, 'Conrad and naturalism: *The Secret Agent*', *Texas Studies in Literature and Language*, 10 (1967), 290.

35. Walton, 'Conrad and naturalism', pp. 292–3.

36. See Robert G. Jacobs, 'Comrade Ossipon's favourite saint: Lombroso and Conrad', *Nineteenth-Century Fiction*, 23 (1968), 74–84; Sherry, *Conrad's Western World*, pp. 275–6; John E. Saveson, 'The criminal psychology of *The Secret Agent*' in his *Joseph Conrad: The Making of a Moralist* (Amsterdam: Rodopi NV, 1972), pp. 117–36, and 'Conrad, *Blackwood's*, and Lombroso', *Conradiana*, 6 (1974), 57–62; Martin Ray, 'Conrad, Nordau, and other degenerates: the psychology of *The Secret Agent*', Conradiana, 16 (1984), 125–40.

37. R. M. Spensley, 'Zola and Conrad: the influence of *Pot-Bouille* on *The Secret Agent*', *Conradiana*, 11 (1979), 185.

38. Spensley, 'Zola and Conrad', p. 186. All references to Zola's novel are to *Les Rougon-Macquart*, La Pléiade (Paris: Gallimard, 1964), IV.

39. Spensley, 'Zola and Conrad', pp. 187–8. Spensley also notes:

> At a certain point in both journeys, one of the occupants of the cab vaguely realizes that progress is not as rapid as it might be. The movement of the passages is similar; a description of the apparent lack of motion of the cab is followed by a brief, banal comment.

> Le fiacre ne marchait plus. Il semblait rouler depuis des heures sur un pont, lorsque Trublot [Auguste's guide], sortant le premier de sa rêverie, risqua cette remarque judicieuse: 'Cette voiture ne va pas fort.' (p. 308)

> Later on, in the wider space of Whitehall, all visual evidences of motion became imperceptible. The rattle and jingle of glass went on indefinitely in front of the long Treasury building and time itself seemed to stand still. At last Winnie observed: 'This isn't a very good horse.' (pp. 156–7)

In '"The Last Cab" in James's "The Papers" and in *The Secret Agent*: Conrad's cues from the Master' (*Modern Fiction Studies*, 29 (1983), 227–33), Daniel Mark Fogel argues that Conrad may have been inspired with the idea of a 'last cab' episode

by Henry James's long tale 'The papers', a possibility which he says 'must be
assigned a high probability'. Fogel is overstating his case for, as Owen Knowles
comments in a review: 'Many of Fogel's examples suggest affinity (or "cues") rather
than influence' ('The year's work in Conrad studies, 1983: a survey of periodical
literature', *The Conradian*, 9 (1984), 42). Furthermore, Conrad's highly probable
reliance on *Pot-Bouille* makes the possibility of a debt to James even more remote.

40. C. B. Cox, 'Joseph Conrad's "The Secret Agent": the irresponsible piano', *Critical
Quarterly*, 15 (1973), 211.

41. For a brief comparison between Zola's *Le Ventre de Paris* and 'An Anarchist' and
*The Secret Agent*, see R. M. Spensley, 'A note on Conrad and Zola', *Journal of the
Joseph Conrad Society (UK)*, 4 (1978), 16–17.

42. Walton, 'Conrad and naturalism', p. 300.

43. An anonymous reviewer of *Almayer's Folly* said: 'Mr Conrad has, we imagine, studied Zola to some purpose, as witness the following overloaded, but powerful description of a Bornean forest: [quotes: In a moment [...] from which they sprang, ch. 5,
p. 71]', in *Conrad: The Critical Heritage*, ed. Sherry, p. 52, while in 'Zola and Conrad's "The Idiots"', Chaikin suggested that Zola's influence on Conrad's early
fiction was not confined to his 'descriptive writing and atmospheric painting' but
that 'There is ground for belief that Zola influenced his early style in a general way'
(Chaikin, pp. 507, 503).

44. Finally, as Sylvère Monod has pointed out to me, when Conrad writes that Winnie
was surprised at her mother's 'sudden *mania for locomotion*' (*SA*, p. 152) as the latter
goes in search of an almshouse to retire to, he seems to be echoing the famous cab-
ride scene in *Madame Bovary* with the driver who could not conceive 'quelle *fureur
de la locomotion*' (p. 338) possessed his passengers. (Conrad had also come across
the phrase '*une telle rage de locomotion*' in the opening paragraph of Maupassant's
'L'Abandonné' (*Yvette*, p. 167).)

45. Conrad, however, was better acquainted with things Russian than he maintained,
as the first 1980 issue of *Conradiana* makes clear.

46. See, for instance, Tarnawski, '*Under Western Eyes* and *Crime and Punishment*' in
*Conrad the Man, the Writer, the Pole*, pp. 175–8.

47. David Leon Higdon, 'Pascal's *Pensée* 347 in *Under Western Eyes*', *Conradiana*, 5
(1973), 81–3. References to Dostoevskii, Tolstoi, Rousseau and Borel are given in
his note 1. On Turgenev, see Kirschner, pp. 249–52. On Poe, see Harriet Gilliam,
'The daemonic in Conrad's *Under Western Eyes*', *Conradiana*, 9 (1977), 219–36. On
Shakespeare, see Gillon, pp. 69–77. Also, on the Biblical allusions in the novel, see
Dwight H. Purdy, '"Peace that passeth understanding": the Professor's English
Bible in *Under Western Eyes*', *Conradiana*, 13 (1981), 83–93.

48. To this list must now be added Henri Frédéric Amiel and the likely influence of his
*Journal intime*. For fuller details, see Owen Knowles, '*Under Western Eyes*: a note
on two sources', *The Conradian*, 10 (1985), 154–61.

49. Eloise Knapp Hay, *The Political Novels of Joseph Conrad* (University of Chicago
Press, 1963), p. 279. In '*Under Western Eyes*: Conrad's diary of a writer?', *Conradiana*, 9 (1977), 269–74, Jeffrey Berman and Donna Van Wagenen show that Conrad
apparently took Ivanovitch's speeches on the future of democracy in Russia and on
the subject of women from Dostoevskii's *The Diary of a Writer* (published in French

in 1904). And in 'Peter Ivanovitch's escape: a possible source overlooked', Margaret Ann Rusk White suggests that 'Souvenirs d'un Sibérien', the French translation of the autobiographical account of escape from Siberian exile written by the Polish political convict Rufin Piotrowski, which appeared serially in the *Revue des deux mondes* in the spring of 1862, 'could have been one of Conrad's inspirations for the story of Peter Ivanovitch's escape from a similar situation', *Conradiana*, 12 (1980), 72–80. See also Knowles, *'Under Western Eyes'*, 154–7.

50. Anatole France is quoting the famous formula used by Napoleon in a speech on 1 January 1814: 'Le trône lui-même, qu'est-ce? Quatre morceaux de bois doré recouverts de velours.' Also quoted as a remark he made to Lainé in L. Rozelaar, 'Le *Mémorial de Sainte-Hélène* et Victor Hugo en 1827', *French Quarterly*, 9 (1927), 58. I am indebted to Dr Keith Wren for these references.

51. Note the similarity between Vence's condemnation of the anarchist 'Li n'est pas humain parce qu'il n'est pas sensuel' (IX, p. 58) and Conrad's comment that Tolstoi's 'anti-sensualism is suspect to me' (*LEG*, p. 244).

   This survey does not claim to have exhausted all that Conrad could have derived from *Le Lys rouge*. For example, Thérèse, looking at herself in a distant mirror, follows 'les ondulations de *sa forme longue* dans le fourreau de satin *noir*' (p. 5); Razumov, back in his room after denouncing Haldin, sees him in a distant corner appearing 'like *a dark and elongated shape*' (p. 55). After a few weeks away from her first lover, Robert Le Ménil, Thérèse *'n'était plus la même femme. Ils étaient séparés maintenant par des choses imperceptibles* et fortes comme ces influences de l'air qui font vivre ou mourir' (p. 159); Razumov explains to Haldin that something apparently trivial can be momentous: a man goes for a walk and when he returns *'he is no longer the same man. The most unlikely things* have a secret power over one's thoughts' (p. 59).

52. Gillon, p. 190. For instance, see Zdzisław Najder, 'Conrad and Rousseau: concepts of man and society' in *Joseph Conrad: A Commemoration*, ed. Sherry, p. 85.

53. Kirschner, pp. 214–15.

54. References to *Le Rouge et le noir* are to the Collection Folio (Paris: Gallimard, 1972).

55. Richard Curle, *Joseph Conrad and his Characters* (London: Heinemann, 1957), p. 164.

56. Higdon, 'Pascal's *Pensée* 347', p. 81. Higdon explains that the numbering of the *pensée* presents difficulties and that he has 'used the number 347 because the edition most familiar to an English audience, the W. F. Trotter translation (London: Dent, 1904), follows the numbering provided in the older scholarly edition, *Blaise Pascal: opuscules et pensées*, ed. Léon Brunschvicg (Paris: Hachette, 1897)' (p. 83).

57. Najder, 'Conrad and Rousseau', pp. 83, 80, 81, 84.

58. Najder, 'Conrad and Rousseau', p. 85. The same critic detects, among the many Polish and Russian writers whose views the novel reflects, the presence of the Marquis de Custine, author of the famous *La Russie en 1839*, which, he feels, Conrad had certainly read. He notes that 'both mention, for example, the conservative temper of the nation, resignation as a Russian national trait, drunkenness, cynicism' (pp. 85, 90).

59. In his *Anatole France et Voltaire* (Geneva: Droz, 1960), Jean Sareil states that France received from Voltaire 'l'héritage de la grande tradition sceptique' (p. 432).

60. In his presentation of Madame de S——, the narrator says: 'Her loud pretensions to be one of the leaders of modern thought and of modern sentiment, she sheltered (like Voltaire and Mme. de Staël) on the republican territory of Geneva' (p. 125). Later, he compares Château Borel, her residence, to that of 'that other dangerous and exiled woman, Madame de Staël, in the Napoleonic era' but, he adds, 'Madame de S—— was very far from resembling the gifted author of *Corinne*' (p. 142). The epithet 'gifted', together with his description of her as 'that intellectual woman', suggests that this reference was not prompted merely by the geographical location. When we recall that the leading theme of *Corinne* (1807) is the intellectual woman's fundamental loneliness and misery, we can appreciate the particular aptness of this reference in a novel which, as Tony Tanner states, portrays the tragedy of 'a man with a mind'. ('Nightmare and complacency: Razumov and the western eye', *Critical Quarterly*, 4 (1962), 213).

61. 'Quoi que vous fassiez, écrasez l'infâme, et aimez qui qui vous aime.' Letter to M. d'Alembert, 28 November 1762. ('L'infâme' could be defined as superstition, fanaticism, intolerance and persecution, embodied in any dogmatic religion – especially in the Roman Catholic church of the time – and, in more general terms, as privileged and persecuting orthodoxy.)

62. This is a close summary of David Leon Higdon's 'Château Borel, Petrus Borel and Conrad's *Under Western Eyes*', *Studies in the Novel*, 3 (1971), 99–102.

63. Letter to Basil MacDonald Hastings, 24 December 1916. Quoted by Roderick Davis, '*Under Western Eyes*: "The most deeply meditated novel"', *Conradiana*, 9 (1977), 74, 75.

64. At the same time, Conrad confided to Jessie his fear that his novel might be considered derivative by critics: 'They will be trying to drag in comparisons with Russian writers of a certain kind' (Jessie Conrad, *Joseph Conrad as I Knew Him* (Garden City, NY: Doubleday Page, 1926), p. 56).

65. Jacques Darras, *Joseph Conrad and the West* (London: Macmillan, 1982), p. 132.

66. Hay, *The Political Novels*, p. 278.

## Chapter 5

1. Kirschner, pp. 220–9.
2. 'Pierre Jouvenet' and not 'Guy' as Kirschner calls him (Kirschner, p. 221).
3. Ford, p. 172.
4. Kirschner, p. 227.
5. Wiley, *Conrad's Measure of Man*, p. 137.
6. Guerard, *Conrad*, p. 51.
7. Guerard, *Conrad*, p. 51.
8. Guerard, *Conrad*, p. 52.
9. Ford, p. 73. Another comment by Ford also throws an interesting light on the title:

   it is characteristic that Mr. Conrad translates the French phrase *Une Bonne Fortune* by the words A SMILE OF FORTUNE; and that the comment of the Second Mate, in this case, is 'A wonderful piece of luck!' ... But those words apply to the price at which the hero sells his potatoes, not to the unconsummated embrace.

   (Ford, *Thus to Revisit*, pp. 97–8)

10. Watt, p. 69.
11. Karl, p. 259.
12. Meyer, p. 77.
13. Thomas C. Moser, 'Conrad, Ford, and the sources of *Chance*', *Conradiana*, 7 (1975), 207.
14. Moser, 'Conrad, Ford, and the sources of *Chance*', pp. 213–14, 215, 216.
15. The parallels between the two Anthonys and the two Patmores are shown by Moser, 'Conrad, Ford, and the sources of *Chance*', p. 208.
16. E. E. Duncan-Jones, 'Some sources of *Chance*', *Review of English Studies*, new series 20 (1969), 470. For other source-studies, see William B. Bache, '"Othello" and Conrad's "Chance"', *Notes and Queries*, new series 2 (1955), 479; and Julie M. Johnson, 'The damsel and her knights: the goddess and the grail in Conrad's *Chance*', *Conradiana*, 13 (1981), 221–8.
17. To this list we must now add the name of a minor French writer, Henri de Régnier. Mario Maurin has recently shown that Régnier's 'Monsieur d'Amercourt', a story included in his prose collection, *La Canne de Jaspe* (1894), provided Conrad with substantial detail for the content of Renouard's long dream on board his schooner. While Maurin acknowledges a degree of anglicization in Conrad's adaptation, he persuasively shows that this appropriation can hardly be a case of unwitting reminiscence or unconscious borrowing. Indeed he suggests that the problem is complicated by a larger web of literary reminiscence which links the plot of 'The Planter' to that of another French work, *Le Temps d'aimer* (1908), by Gérard d'Houville (the pseudonym of Régnier's wife). For fuller details, see Maurin's 'The Planter's French connection: an appropriation by Joseph Conrad', *Modern Philology*, 82 (1985), 304–9.
18. Owen Knowles, 'Conrad and Mérimée: the legend of Venus in "The Planter of Malata"', *Conradiana*, 11 (1979), 178–9, 180–1, 183. All references to 'La Vénus d'Ille' are to *Romans et nouvelles de Prosper Mérimée* (Paris: Garnier, 1967), II, pp. 97–8.
19. On *Victory*'s contentious critical history, see Gordon W. Thompson, 'Conrad's women', *Nineteenth-Century Fiction*, 32 (1978), 445, n. 11.
20. Katherine Haynes Gatch, 'Conrad's Axel', *Studies in Philology*, 48 (1951), 98–106; Kirschner, pp. 193–8; Knowles, pp. 49–58.
21. David Lodge, 'Conrad's *Victory* and *The Tempest*: an amplification', *Modern Language Review*, 59 (1964), 195–9; Arthur Sherbo, 'Conrad's "Victory" and "Hamlet"', *Notes and Queries*, 198 (1953), 492–3; Seymour L. Gross, 'Hamlet and Heyst again', *Notes and Queries*, new series 6 (1959), 87–8; Gillon, pp. 85–116; Busza, 'Conrad's Polish literary background', 216–23; Norman Page, 'Dickensian elements in *Victory*', *Conradiana*, 5 (1973), 37–42; Jean E. Kennard, 'Emerson and Dickens: a note on Conrad's *Victory*', *Conradiana*, 6 (1974), 215–19; Dwight H. Purdy, 'Paul and the Pardoner in Conrad's *Victory*', *Texas Studies in Literature and Language*, 23 (1981), 197–213; G. J. Resink, 'Samburan Encantada', *English Studies*, 47 (1966), 35–44, reprinted in *Conradiana*, 1 (1969), 37–44 [on Melville's 'The Encantadas' in *The Piazza Tales* (1856)]; J. C. Maxwell, 'Conrad and Turgenev: a minor source for "*Victory*"' *Notes and Queries*, new series 10 (1963), 372–3.
22. Conrad's analysis of Willems's predicament: 'He was not, of course, able to discern

clearly the causes of his misery; but there are [...] none so simple as not to feel and *suffer from the shock of warring impulses' (OI*, p. 129), suggests that as early as 1894 or 1895 he was already making use of France's psychology.

23. Voltaire had said: 'Ils [les hommes] ne se servent de la pensée que pour autoriser leurs injustices', ('Dialogue du chapon et de la poularde', *Dialogues et entretiens philosophiques*, no. 14).

24. Conrad had previously applied Maupassant's comparison not only to Donkin (see above, p. 100) but also to Razumov: 'Razumov, in his chair, leaning his head on his hand, *spoke as if from the bottom of an abyss' (UWE*, p. 23).

25. H. T. Webster, 'Conrad's changes in narrative conception in the manuscripts of *Typhoon and Other Stories* and *Victory'*, *PMLA*, 64 (1949), 958. Webster points out that Heyst shows 'a greater objective awareness of [his] emotional evolution in the MS than in the novel', and feels that in the original passage he was led 'to reconsider the whole perplexing relationship in words which make it so understandable that one almost wishes them in the printed *Victory'* (pp. 958-9).

26. This and all the subsequent passages from the manuscript are quoted from Karl, '*Victory*: its origin and development', *Conradiana*, 15 (1983), 42, 31, 32, 31, 32.

27. This borrowing from Maupassant casts serious doubt on Gillon's attempt to see behind this passage lines from *Macbeth* ('all our yesterdays have lighted fools / The way to *dusty* death' and life is now 'a tale / Told by an idiot full of sound and *fury*, / Signifying *nothing'* (V.v.22–8)) (Gillon, p. 110). This inappropriate link shows the arbitrariness of his procedure.

28. Dwight H. Purdy, 'The manuscript of *Victory* and the problem of Conrad's intentions', *Journal of Modern Literature*, 10 (1983), 99.

29. Knowles, p. 61.

30. Knowles, p. 61. Benjamin Constant, *Adolphe* (Paris: Garnier, 1960), pp. 304, 56. Maxwell ('Conrad and Turgenev', p. 372) suggests a connection between Heyst's exclamation and Lavretsky's 'Woe to the heart that has not loved in youth!' in Turgenev's *A House of Gentlefolk*.

31. Gurko, *Joseph Conrad*, p. 213.

32. In addition to the literary sources indicated in note 3, reference must be made to the scriptural allusions (see Dowden, *Joseph Conrad: The Imaged Style*, pp. 156–66; Purdy, 'Paul and the Pardoner in Conrad's *Victory'* pp. 203–7 and 'The manuscript of *Victory* and the problem of Conrad's intentions', pp. 100–4), and the use of classical mythology (see John Saveson, *Conrad: The Later Moralist* (Amsterdam, Rodopi NV, 1974), pp. 126–9).

33. Edmund Wilson, *Axel's Castle* (New York: Scribner's Sons, 1931), p. 264. This figure of the hermit, tormented in his solitude, is a familiar symbol of withdrawal from ordinary life in the works of Flaubert, Baudelaire, Huysmans, and Villiers de l'Isle-Adam, and when adapting it, Conrad was again reflecting his French culture. Its importance for these writers lay in its embodiment of a complex psychological situation, divided as the hermit is between action and detachment, mind and passion, virtue and vice, morality and instinct.

34. Gatch, 'Conrad's Axel', p. 101.

35. Knowles, pp. 49, 50.

36. Knowles, pp. 52, 53.

37. Karl, '*Victory*: its origin and development', p. 31.
38. Knowles, p. 56. It is worth bearing in mind, however, Karl's observation that 'in the manuscript, we view [Lena] as a multi-dimensional person trying to comprehend what is incomprehensible, more as a complicated woman than the victim and martyr of the revised version' ('*Victory*: its origin and development', p. 33).
39. Knowles, pp. 54–8.
40. Gatch, 'Conrad's Axel', pp. 98–9.
41. Similarly, Busza points out: 'it seems likely that Jones and Ricardo owe more to Żeromski's villains than to the two characters, mentioned by Conrad in his preface' ('Conrad's Polish literary background', p. 223), and Purdy thinks that the resemblances between Jones and the character of the Pardoner suggest that 'Chaucer is a source for the Jones plot of *Victory*' ('Paul and the Pardoner in Conrad's *Victory*', p. 201).
42. Karl, p. 777.
43. Watts has analysed the influence of Coleridge's 'visionary, nightmarish poem of the sea, "The Rime of the Ancyent Marinere"' on *The Shadow-Line* (*A Preface to Conrad*, pp. 106–8). Meyer has put forward the hypothesis that 'a number of elements' in *The Arrow of Gold* were 'inspired' by Sacher-Masoch's *Venus in Furs* (Meyer, pp. 310–16). Finally, a number of sources have been discovered for *Suspense*. In 'Fenimore Cooper and Conrad's *Suspense*' (*Notes and Queries*, new series 10 (1963), 373–5), Manfred MacKenzie has examined the influence of *The Prairie*, and, according to Franco Marenco, the design which emerges from the unfinished work resembles that of *La Chartreuse de Parme*, which suggests to him that Conrad had Stendhal's novel in mind when he began writing his own (Joseph Conrad, *Ultimi Romanzi: Vittoria e romanzi mediterranei* (Milano: Mursia, 1977)). In addition, he made use of the *Mémoires de la Comtesse de Boigne* (see above p. 256).
44. This borrowing was first pointed out by Jacques Mouradian in 'Conrad and Anatole France', *TLS*, 30 October 1930, 890.

## Chapter 6

1. See also the section on Brunetière, *Appendix*, pp. 250-1.
2. Wright, 'Joseph Conrad', p. 117.
3. Wright, 'Joseph Conrad', p. 134. 'Dévoiler' is Maupassant's standard word in this context (see n. 115 in chapter 8).
4. George J. Worth, 'Conrad's debt to Maupassant in the Preface to *The Nigger of the "Narcissus"*', *Journal of English and Germanic Philology*, 54 (1955), 704.
5. This echo was first noted by Baines, p. 148.
6. Throughout his career, Conrad held to the ideal depicted by Maupassant (whom he described as 'a great artist, who sees the essential in everything' (*CL*, II, p. 150)). In an essay written in 1917, he saw Turgenev, as Maupassant saw Lamarthe, endowed with '*the clearest vision*', '*penetrating insight*', 'an exquisite perception of the visible world and *an unerring instinct* for the significant, for *the essential in the life of men*' (*NLL*, p. 48) and, two years later, he saw Crane possessed of the same ability: 'He had indeed a wonderful power of *vision*, which he applied to the things of this

earth and of our mortal humanity with *a penetrating force* that seemed to reach, within life's appearances and forms, the very spirit of *life's truth*' (*NLL*, p. 50).

7. Kirschner has argued that in the case of the Preface there is 'a much greater debt to Schopenhauer' than to Maupassant (Kirschner, p. 272). This can no longer be maintained, but that one can detect Schopenhauerian resonances is not surprising in the light of the influence he exerted on both Maupassant and France.

8. Maupassant also viewed the novelist as the historian of human experience. In 'Le Roman', he contends that, unlike his predecessors who recorded the crises of life, the extreme states of heart and soul, the 'modern' novelist writes 'l'histoire du coeur, de l'âme et de l'intelligence' in a normal state (*PJ*, p. xiii).

9. It is possible that Marlow's view of Kurtz as 'the remarkable man who had pronounced a judgement upon the *adventures of his soul* on this earth' (*YOS*, p. 150) contains a reminiscence from France.

10. This borrowing was first shown by J. H. Stape in 'Conrad as journalist: further borrowings from Anatole France', *The Conradian*, 8 (1983), 39. Stape has also pointed out that Conrad, in his reviews of both France's *Crainquebille, Putois, Riquet et plusieurs autres récits profitables* (1904) and *L'Ile des pingouins* (1908), adopts the practice of using the writer's own words (translated) to give a summary or *compte rendu* of the original work. For his analysis of several such examples, see Stape, 'Conrad as journalist', pp. 39–43.

11. Conrad's heavy indebtedness to *La Vie littéraire* in his fiction and critical writings suggests that from this source he derived numerous other references and allusions. In the preface to the second series of *La Vie littéraire*, France says that the happiest of mortals at times produce works which may become masterpieces 'avec l'aide du temps, qui est un galant homme, comme disait Mazarin' (VI, pp. 330–1), a sentiment echoed in *The Mirror of the Sea*: '"Le Temps", as a distinguished Frenchman has said, "est un galant homme"' (p. 193). The nursery rhyme Conrad used as an epigraph to *A Set of Six* is one with which France concludes his article 'M. Guy de Maupassant et les conteurs français' (IV, p. 61). The first section of 'Poland revisited' (1915) ends with an obvious reminiscence from 'La Morale et la science': '*Quand de l'arbre de la science un fruit tombe, c'est qu'il est mûr. Nul ne pouvait l'empêcher de tomber*' (VII, p. 83); '*For when the fruit ripens on a branch it must fall. There is nothing on earth that can prevent it*' (*NLL*, p. 147). This verbal echo, as Stape comments, 'attests again to Conrad's good memory for a memorable phrase' (Stape, 'Conrad as journalist', p. 39). In *La Vie littéraire* and *Les Opinions de M. Jérôme Coignard* France relates the apologue of Zemire, the king of Persia, who was most anxious to learn the history of mankind. On his death-bed, he complains to his chief historian:

> – Je mourrai donc sans savoir l'histoire des hommes!
> – Sire, répondit le doyen, [...] je vais vous la *résumer* en trois mots: *Ils naquirent, ils souffrirent, ils moururent.*                              (VI, p. 222; VIII, p. 465)

These words evidently made a strong impression on Conrad: he would often use them in conversation (as remembered by Richard Curle), and again in his Author's Note to *Chance* (1920) (note the gallicism 'resumed'): 'The history of men on this earth since the beginning of ages may be *resumed* in one phrase of infinite poignancy: *They were born, they suffered, they died*' (p. viii).

12. Watt, p. 77. An early instance of Conrad's critical insight can be seen in his reaction to *Pierre et Jean* in 1894: 'Ça n'a l'air de rien mais c'est d'un compliqué comme mécanisme qui me fait m'arracher les cheveux. On a envie de pleurer de rage en lisant cela' (*CL*, I, p. 183). Eighty-seven years later, Mary Donaldson-Evans comes to the conclusion that this novel reveals that 'the "simple" and "obvious" Maupassant has proven himself capable of weaving an unexpectedly intricate web, whose fine mesh has ensnared many a reader, blissfully unaware of all but the most obvious strands' ('Maupassant *ludens*: a re-examination of *Pierre et Jean*', *Nineteenth-Century French Studies*, 9 (1981), 219). Conrad was anything but 'blissfully unaware'.

## Chapter 7

1. Kirschner, p. 229.
2. Ernst Bendz wrote: 'one cannot help noticing the remarkable affinity of intellect that betrays itself, on so many points, between Conrad and "the most eloquent and just of French prose writers," whom he so frequently paraphrases or alludes to.' (*Joseph Conrad: An Appreciation* (Gothenburg: Gumpert, 1923), p. 89)
3. France also views the earth as a 'grain de poussière' (VII, p. 432), and so does Conrad who refers to it as a 'mote of dust' (*LJ*, p. 305; *YOS*, p. 225).
4. France is presented as the most likely source of Conrad's views on this subject because of the latter's habit of extracting material from him, and particularly from *La Vie littéraire* and *Le Jardin d'Epicure*. But, of course, this 'astrophysical pessimism', to use Watt's phrase, was a commonplace in the latter half of the nineteenth century. It all began in 1824 with 'Carnot's demonstration of the necessary loss of energy in any and all mechanical systems' (George Steiner, 'Has truth a future?', *The Listener*, 12 January 1978, 43), a discovery which led to the formulation of the second law of thermodynamics by William Thomson (later Lord Kelvin). The principle of the dissipation of energy, first stated in 1851 and briefly summarized in this law, seemed to suggest that the universe is running down, that the sun must inevitably burn itself out, and that 'like all else, the earth would end in cold and drought' (Watt, p. 152). On this subject, see also 'Darkness and the dying sun' in Watts, *A Preface to Conrad*, pp. 86–8, and O'Hanlon, *Joseph Conrad and Charles Darwin* (Edinburgh: The Salamander Press, 1984), pp. 17–19, 160.
5. Baines, p. 448.
6. Flaubert's correspondence shows how deep and permanent was his sense of the impossibility of communication between human beings and of the fundamental isolation and loneliness of the individual, as the two following statements made respectively in May 1852 and December 1878 clearly indicate: 'L'âme a beau faire, elle ne brise pas sa solitude, elle marche avec lui [le néant]. On se sent fourmi dans un désert et perdu, perdu' (II, p. 411); 'Nous sommes tous dans un désert, personne ne comprend personne' (VIII, p. 175).
7. Although the theme of moral solitude is primarily a link between Conrad and Maupassant, it must be stressed that it is also an important link with many of his favourite nineteenth-century French authors (Vigny, Constant, Mérimée, Baudelaire, Flaubert, Loti, and France) and, arguably, with French literature in general. (See Victor Brombert, *La Prison romantique* (Paris: Corti, 1975).)

 8. Kirschner, p. 229.
 9. The following chapter headings in Carter Jefferson's *Anatole France: The Politics of Skepticism* (New Brunswick, NJ: Rutgers University Press, 1965) show the evolution of France's political thinking: 1. The conservative (1844–1888), 2. The anarchist (1888–1898), 3. The crusader (1898–1906), 4. The socialist (1906–1917), 5. The 'bolshevick' (1917–1924). It must be added, however, that France's views did not change as radically as might be assumed from these headings.
10. Najder thinks that Conrad's pronouncement 'ought to be taken as a caustic satire and not as a serious philosophical evaluation' (Najder, p. 251).
11. Conrad's political conservatism – or should one say fatalism? – is encapsulated in this recollection by Retinger: 'any kind of conversation on politics he used to close with the formula *"Il ne faut pas aller contre le courant des choses"*' (Retinger, p. 65). Interestingly, France had used practically the same formula in a political context in *Sur la pierre blanche*, a work mentioned in Conrad's correspondence: 'Il est certain du moins qu'*ils n'allèrent pas contre le cours des choses*' (XIII, p. 535).
12. E. P. Dargan, *Anatole France (1844–1896)* (New York: Oxford University Press, 1937), p. 550.
13. Curle, pp. 12–13.
14. During his stay in Corsica in 1921, Conrad urged Lenormand to write a novel on 'le déclin des hommes parvenus à la certitude' (*NRF*, p. 670).
15. All this, of course, repeats Schopenhauer, who was himself following the Kantian distinction between phenomenal appearances as the product of the activity of the perceiving mind and the underlying noumenal reality, or the thing as it is in itself, which, being beyond all possible experience, must remain unknowable. All that science can do, Schopenhauer believed, is to connect up and order appearances. One more example of the way France, like Maupassant, acted as a relay for the philosopher's ideas is of interest here. In his reply to W. L. Courtney for his review of *The Nigger*, Conrad, after defining his aim and disclaiming 'all allegiance to realism, to naturalism', commented: 'There is joy and sorrow; there is sunshine and darkness – and all are within the same eternal smile of the inscrutable Maya' (David R. Smith, '"One word more" about *The Nigger of the "Narcissus"*', *Nineteenth-Century Fiction*, 23 (1968), 208). This, as Watt points out, gives his aim 'a Schopenhauerian note' (Watt, p. 186, n. 33). However, steeped as he was in *La Vie littéraire*, Conrad may well have been echoing France. In a review of Zola's *Le Rêve*, France takes up Zola's thought 'Tout n'est que rêve' as the only philosophical reflection he ever made; he then adds that he, too, firmly believes that 'l'éternelle illusion nous berce et nous enveloppe' and that 'la vie n'est qu'un songe', but finds it difficult to imagine the author of *Pot-Bouille* anxiously interrogating 'le sourire de Maïa' and casting the lead into 'l'océan des apparences' (VI, p. 592).
16. Needless to say, on this point as on many others, France and Conrad were not original thinkers. The limitation of our senses and, therefore, of our intelligence is a theory expounded in Spencer, Hamilton, Schopenhauer, Taine, and Maupassant, where it becomes a real leitmotif.
17. Watt, p. 172. In 1868, in the 'Conclusion' to *The Renaissance*, Walter Pater already referred to 'the individual in his isolation, each mind keeping as a solitary prisoner its own dream of a world' (London: Macmillan, 1910), p. 235). And in *Marius the*

*Epicurean* (1885) – which Conrad read in 1897 – there is a passage where Marius reflects that 'all that is real in our experience [is] but a series of fleeting impressions: [...] given, that we are never to get beyond the walls of the closely shut cell of one's own personality; that the ideas we are somehow impelled to form of an outer world, and of other minds akin to our own, are, it may be, but a day-dream' (London: Macmillan, 1910), I, p. 146).

18. There is little doubt that, as many echoes and parallels have already indicated, Conrad's scepticism towards the claims of nineteenth-century science derived to a large extent from his close familiarity with France. Under 'Ideological perspectives', Watt has a section entitled 'The material universe', and practically every major point he makes (Watt, pp. 152–3) can be related to France. As note 4 on Conrad's 'astrophysical pessimism' has already made clear, the new knowledge gained in astronomy and physics brought him no consolation. These recent developments, Watt says, forced man 'to confront his infinitely minute and equally transitory role in the total scheme of things', which is precisely the point made in *Le Jardin*. Similarly, Conrad's view of individual consciousness as 'inevitably separate from its environment and the fate which it dictates' (see the parallel preceding the quotation from *Le Jardin*), his reference to the convex or concave mirror (see above, p. 159), his interpretation of the creation (see above, p. 150), could all have come to him via France. And the same applies to the idea that the Laws of Nature 'really dealt with matters that are essentially irrelevant to the deepest human concerns', and Conrad's assertion that '[Reason] demonstrates [...] that [...] the fate of a humanity condemned ultimately to perish from cold is not worth troubling about' (*CL*, II, pp. 16–17), since both points are made in 'Mysticisme et science' (see above, p. 151).

19. The whole weight of the French tradition Conrad knew best can be seen here shaping his views. Chapter 19 in Book I of *Le Rouge et le noir* is entitled 'Penser fait souffrir'. Flaubert often says it in his correspondence: 'Penser, c'est le moyen de souffrir' (I, p. 213), and one of the most famous sentences in *Bouvard et Pécuchet* is 'Et ayant plus d'idées, ils eurent plus de souffrances' (p. 13). Maupassant, too, believed that thought engenders suffering because it alienates man from the rest of nature. For him, it is a 'petit accident' to which we owe 'd'être très mal en ce monde qui n'est pas fait pour nous' (*L'Inutile beauté*, p. 28).

20. Dargan, *Anatole France*, p. 548.

21. The source of the quotation here is Henri Lavedan and his play *Prince d'Aurec* (1892).

22. Bendz, *Conrad: An Appreciation*, p. 108.

23. In their concern with solidarity in the 1890s, France and Conrad show how sensitive they were to the social preoccupations of their day. Watt explains that in 1896 'the term solidarity was very much in the air, partly because it had been popularized as the name of a French political movement, with which Durkheim was loosely associated, that advocated measures to ameliorate the various conflicts which prevented solidarity; and the political leader of the movement, Léon Bourgeois, published a much discussed book, *La Solidarité*, in 1896' (Watt, p. 144).

24. Rupert Hart-Davis, *Hugh Walpole* (London: Macmillan, 1952), p. 168. From Walpole's diary, January 1923.

Chapter 8

1. Najder observes, 'In [Conrad's] Polish literary heritage the novel was practically nonexistent' (Najder, p. 117).
2. Curle, p. 116.
3. Describing the novel's transition from Victorian to modern, Hugh Kenner refers to 'The transplantation of the French novel to English [which] was undertaken, early in the present century, by Ford Madox Ford and Joseph Conrad' (Hugh Kenner, *The Poetry of Ezra Pound* (London: Faber and Faber, 1951), p. 264).
4. Ford Madox Ford, 'On Conrad's vocabulary', *Bookman*, New York, 57 (1928), 405.
5. Ford, *Thus to Revisit*, p. 39.
6. Ford, p. 59. Charpentier published *Lettres de Gustave Flaubert à George Sand* in 1884 and a four-volume edition of his *Correspondance* 1887-93 (cf. *Flaubert, extraits de la correspondance*, ed. Geneviève Bollème (Paris: Seuil, 1963), p. 18). The correspondence to which Conrad and Ford had access was less than half of that now available, but it comprised much of the most valuable material, including the all-important letters to Louise Colet written during the composition of *Madame Bovary*. (The new Pléiade edition by Jean Bruneau (Paris: Gallimard, 1973–   ) will eventually supersede all previous collections.)
7. Haskell Block, 'Theory of language in Gustave Flaubert and James Joyce', *Revue de littérature comparée*, 35 (1961), 198.
8. Baines, p. 148.
9. Robert Liddell, *A Treatise on the Novel* (London: Cape, 1947), p. 37.
10. Henry James, 'Gustave Flaubert' (1902), in *Selected Literary Criticism*, p. 239. All references to James's criticism are to this volume.
11. James, 'The art of fiction' in *Selected Literary Criticism*, p. 59.
12. See Philip Grover, *Henry James and the French Novel* (London: Elek, 1973), p. 117.
13. See Karl, p. 397.
14. For an account of the personal relationship between Conrad and James, a comparative study of their main aesthetic principles, and an interpretation of their fiction, see Nettels, *James & Conrad*.
15. Roland Barthes, 'The two criticisms' in his *Critical Essays*, translated by Richard Howard (Evanston, Ill.: Northwestern University Press, 1972), p. 252.
16. Quoted by Miriam Allott, *Novelists on the Novel* (London: Routledge and Kegan Paul, 1959), pp. 46–7.
17. Typical in this respect is James's comment in his 'Gustave Flaubert' (1902) that it was 'a wonderful success' that Flaubert who was 'so the devotee of the phrase' yet was never 'its victim'; that it is 'always related and associated', 'properly part of something else that is in turn part of something other, part of a reference, a tone, a passage, a page' (*Selected Literary Criticism*, p. 230). And so is the following appreciation by Ford from *The March of Literature* (London: Allen & Unwin, 1939), p. 712:

> every detail of that amazing book, *Madame Bovary*, has been worked out with the same awareness. The most casual detail – the shouting of a beggar in the street, the operations by the doctor, the conversation of a pompous druggist – is recorded only because it inevitably carries the story forward and hangs on the inevitable

tragedy at the end. [...] in *Madame Bovary* every minutest detail must have its reason.

18. Richard Curle, *Joseph Conrad: A Study* (London: Kegan Paul, Trench, Trübner, 1914), p. 96.

19. For instance, Retinger recorded that Conrad 'disliked the lack of structural cohesion in the works of the author of *David Copperfield*' (Retinger, p. 104). In his response to English writers in general, and Dickens in particular, Conrad was at one with Flaubert who thought that they all, apart from Shakespeare, Scott, and Byron up to a point, lacked a sense of composition. After reading *The Pickwick Papers* he wrote to George Sand: 'Il y a des parties superbes; mais quelle composition défectueuse! Tous les écrivains anglais en sont là. Walter Scott excepté, ils manquent de plan' (VI, p. 394).

20. Ford, p. 210.

21. Ford, p. 169. Corroborating evidence can be found in Retinger's recollection that Conrad's 'first and principal care was given to the structure and the technique of the novel and short story' (Retinger, p. 90).

22. James developed the same organic conception of the novel in 'The art of fiction': 'A novel is a living thing, all one and continuous, like any other organism, and in proportion as it lives will it be found, I think, that in each of the parts there is something of each of the other parts' (*Selected Literary Criticism*, p. 58).

23. Ford, *Thus to Revisit*, p. 44.

24. Watt, p. 53.

25. Conrad's concern with the overall organization of his works is also illustrated by his concept of the pivot. When writing *Under Western Eyes*, he stressed to Garnett that he 'wanted a pivot for the action to turn on' (*LEG*, p. 234); in 'To My Readers in America', he presented Wait as 'the centre of the ship's collective psychology and the pivot of the action' (*NN*, Preface (Garden City, NY: Doubleday Page, 1914)); and in 1923, he pointed out to Bendz that the silver of the San Tomé mine is 'the pivot of the moral and material events' (*LL*, II, p. 296). However, Conrad, unlike Flaubert, seldom built his works with a 'dessein prémédité' in mind. He was often still in the dark about their general outline and overall scope when they were well on their way, as the many short stories that turned into full-bodied novels bear witness. His unfinished *Suspense* shows that this habit stayed with him to the last since, on the day before he died, he confided to Curle that he saw 'five or six different lines of treatment' (*S*, p. vi).

26. The three sentences without reference appear in Flaubert's notes and plans.

27. See William Bysshe Stein, '*Madame Bovary* and Cupid unmasked', *Sewanee Review*, 73 (1965), 197–209.

28. In *Towards the Real Flaubert* (Oxford: Clarendon Press, 1984), p. 88, Margaret Lowe also points out that Rodolphe who is a '*chasseur* – ancient metaphor for Death – [...] lives at La Huchette, a name evocative of the hunting horn used to *hucher* (that is, call) in the death-hunt'. (A *huchet* is a hunting-horn.)

29. On these various structural schemes and patterns of imagery, see in particular: James Trammel Cox, 'The finest French novel in the English language', pp. 85–7, Jean-Luc Mercié, 'Leurres et discours du texte: le système des oiseaux dans *Madame Bovary*', *Travaux de linguistique et de littérature*, 18 (1980), 181–91; Stirling Haig,

'The *Madame Bovary* blues', *Romanic Review*, 61 (1970), 27–34; Ole Wehner Rasmussen, 'La Signification de l'adjectif *pâle* dans *Madame Bovary*', *Revue romane*, 7 (1972), 26–31; A. M. Lowe, 'Emma Bovary, a modern Arachne', *French Studies*, 26 (1972), 30–41; Robert Goodhand, 'Emma Bovary, the baker's paramour', *Rice University Studies*, 59 (1973), 37–41; Tony Tanner, 'Monsieur Binet and his lathe' in his *Adultery in the Novel*, pp. 254–65; Claudine Gothot-Mersch, *La Genèse de* Madame Bovary (Paris: Corti, 1966), chapter 4, 'Une symphonie'.

30.  A detailed analysis of this figure can be found in Robert F. Haugh's 'The structure of "Lord Jim"', *College English*, 13 (1951), 137–41.

31.  Gysin, 'The vitality of distortion and decay', p. 432.

32.  See Jean Rousset, 'Positions, distances, perspectives dans "Salammbô"', *Poétique*, no. 6 (1971), 145–8.

33.  Claude Thomas, 'Structure and narrative technique of *Under Western Eyes*' in *Studies in Joseph Conrad*, ed. Claude Thomas (Montpellier: CERVE, 1975), p. 208.

34.  Raymonde Debray-Genette, 'Les figures du récit dans "Un coeur simple"', *Poétique*, no. 3 (1970), 363.

35.  Gerhard C. Gerhardi, 'Romantic love and the prostitution of politics: on the structural unity of *L'Education sentimentale*', *Studies in the Novel*, 4 (1972), 413.

36.  Martin Turnell, '*Madame Bovary*' in *Flaubert: A Collection of Critical Essays*, ed. Raymond Giraud (Englewood Cliffs, NJ: Prentice Hall, 1964), p. 100. In *The March of Literature* (p. 802) Ford commented:

> The matchless description of Charles Bovary's hat in the opening pages of *Madame Bovary* is not a mere example of descriptive gusto: It is the measure and prophecy of the fusionlessness that throughout the story Charles is to display. Parents sufficiently ill-omened to provide their offspring with a headpiece so mournful and grotesque could only beget a son who should be as mournful and grotesque in his career as in his hat.

37.  Tony Tanner, 'Charles Bovary goes to school, drops his cap, and tries to say his name', in his *Adultery in the Novel*, pp. 236–54.

38.  Victor Brombert, *The Novels of Flaubert* (Princeton University Press, 1966), p. 44.

39.  Ford, p. 171.

40.  Jean Deurbergue, 'The opening of *Victory*' in *Studies in Joseph Conrad*, ed. Thomas, pp. 239–70. (For example, by the end of the first paragraph the conflict in Heyst between the 'practical' and the 'mystical', already suggested in the contrast between 'coal' and 'diamonds', is clearly stated, along with the predicament of modern man in industrial society. In the second paragraph elements are introduced of Heyst's passivity, lofty idealism, withdrawal and isolation. And the parallel between Heyst puffing at his cheroot before going to bed and his neighbour the 'indolent' volcano 'levell[ing] at him', a dull red glow introduces the threat of firearms and the element of fire, anticipating the *dénouement*.)

41.  Brombert, *The Novels of Flaubert*, pp. 126–8.

42.  See, for instance, Bruce R. Stark, 'Kurtz's Intended: the heart of *Heart of Darkness*', *Texas Studies in Literature and Language*, 16 (1974), 535–55, David M. Martin, 'The function of the Intended in Conrad's "Heart of Darkness"', *Studies in Short Fiction*,

11 (1974), 27–33, and especially Jan Verleun, 'Conrad's *Heart of Darkness*: Marlow and the Intended', *Neophilologus*, 67 (1983), 623–39.

43. In 'The art of fiction' James declared that he could not 'conceive, in any novel worth discussing at all, of a passage of description that is not in its intention narrative' (*Selected Literary Criticism*, p. 58).

44. Vidan, 'Thirteen letters of André Gide to Joseph Conrad', *Studia Romanica et Anglica Zagrabiensia*, 24 (1967), 163.

45. This sentence is analysed by Pierre A. Clamens, ' "D'un mot mis en sa place..." ': étude sur le mot juste dans *Madame Bovary*', *Romanic Review*, 45 (1954), 45–54.

46. Edmond et Jules de Goncourt, *Journal: mémoires de la vie littéraire* (Paris: Fasquelle [et] Flammarion, 1956), I, p. 889 (17 March 1861).

47. We can see Flaubert worrying over this problem as he writes to Louise Colet when working on *Bovary*: 'je viens de sortir d'une *comparaison soutenue* [...]. Mais peut-être est-ce trop pompeux pour la couleur générale du livre' (III, p. 232).

48. 'On me croit épris du réel, tandis que je l'exècre; car c'est en haine du réalisme que j'ai entrepris ce roman [*Madame Bovary*]' (IV, p. 134).

49. Maupassant wrote a number of studies of Flaubert. The most important one was published in 1884 as an introduction to his *Lettres à George Sand*. An extract can be found in the Conard edition of *Madame Bovary*, taken from the 1885 Quantin edition, which is quoted here. The study appears in its entirety in the Conard edition of Maupassant's works (*Oeuvres posthumes*, II), and is easily accessible in Maupassant's *Chroniques 3*, 10/18 (Paris: Union Générale d'Editions, 1980).

50. Ford, p. 182. Similarly, in 'The art of fiction' James asserts: 'Art is essentially selection', but he adds that 'it is a selection whose main care is to be typical, to be inclusive' (*Selected Literary Criticism*, p. 62).

51. Ford, p. 210.

52. A story like 'Hérodias', C. H. Wake notes, 'exists completely adequately on the realistic level, but the undercurrent of symbolism gives it the universal application Flaubert always sought in his work' ('Symbolism in Flaubert's *Hérodias*: an interpretation', *Forum for Modern Language Studies*, 4 (1968), 329).

53. For a detailed analysis of most of these and other names, see Watts, *A Preface to Conrad*, pp. 176–9.

54. Flaubert, *Correspondance*, La Pléiade (Paris: Gallimard, 1980), II, p. 197. See also B. F. Bart, 'Flaubert's concept of the novel', *PMLA*, 80 (1965), 84–9.

55. Goncourt, *Journal*, I, p. 889 (17 March 1861).

56. This is an early statement; to be more accurate with regard to both authors it should also include 'J'ai lu'.

57. The following comment by Erich Auerbach (in *Mimesis* (Princeton University Press, 1968), p. 487) throws light on Flaubert's innovatory attitude in this field:

> a comparative interpretation of Flaubert's *Notre coeur ne doit être bon qu'à sentir celui des autres*, and Rousseau's statement at the beginning of the Confessions, *Je sens mon coeur, et je connais les hommes*, could effectually represent the change in attitude which had taken place.

58. It may be a reminiscence from this passage which made Conrad write in his praise of Hudson: 'son style est comme une herbe à qui Dieu a commandé de croître et

lorsqu'elle a grandi, personne ne pourrait dire *comment cela s'est fait* (quoted by Ujejski, *Conrad*, p. 192).

59. Maupassant, 'Gustave Flaubert' in *Chroniques 1*, pp. 20–1.

60. Flaubert's attitude is typical of a devotee of art for art's sake. The first known use of the phrase, as recorded in Benjamin Constant's *Journal intime* on 10 February 1804, reads: '*L'art pour l'art* without purpose, for all purpose perverts art' (*Journal intime de Benjamin Constant* (Paris: Ollendorf, 1895), p. 7)). The idea that the novel must not be a speaker's rostrum or a pulpit is, of course, in direct contrast to the Victorian convention as illustrated, for instance, by Trollope who wrote in *An Autobiography* (London: Blackwood, 1883) that he had ever thought of himself as 'a preacher of sermons' (ch. 8).

61. Flaubert made this point in a letter to Louise Colet: 'lorsqu'on écrit quelque chose de *soi*, la phrase peut être bonne par *jets* (et les esprits lyriques arrivent à l'effet facilement et en suivant leur pente naturelle), mais l'*ensemble manque*' (III, p. 321).

62. Most of the cogent generalizations in *Madame Bovary* seem to grow naturally out of the action and are usually related to the work's major themes. Thus, when analysing Rodolphe's jaded response to Emma's repeated protestations of love in conventional words, the narrator comments:

> comme si la plénitude de l'âme ne débordait pas quelquefois par les métaphores les plus vides, puisque personne, jamais, ne peut donner l'exacte mesure de ses besoins, ni de ses conceptions, ni de ses douleurs, et que la parole humaine est comme un chaudron fêlé où nous battons des mélodies à faire danser les ours, quand on voudrait attendrir les étoiles'.                    (*MB*, p. 265).

Clearly, this kind of generalization on the theme of the inadequacy of language and human incommunicability (introduced in the opening sequence with the 'Charbovari' episode), by opening up a dimension which goes far beyond that created by the dramatized events, contributes to the universalizing of Emma's story. It may be regarded as an infringement of the ideal of authorial invisibility – unless, of course, one makes a sharp distinction between author and narrator – but it does not impair the unity of the work as 'preaching' does. (For a detailed discussion of the problems posed by generalizations, see D. A. Williams, 'Generalizations in *Madame Bovary*', *Neophilologus*, 62 (1978), 492–503.)

63. See Wayne C. Booth, *The Rhetoric of Fiction* (University of Chicago Press, 1961), chapter 3, and George Levine, '*Madame Bovary* and the disappearing author', *Modern Fiction Studies*, 9 (1963), 103–19.

64. These points are raised in Jean Bruneau's 'La Présence de Flaubert dans *L'Education sentimentale*', and the ensuing discussion, in *Langages de Flaubert*, ed. Michael Issacharoff (Paris: Lettres Modernes, Minard, 1976), pp. 33–51. For a detailed examination of this question, see R. J. Sherrington, *Three Novels by Flaubert* (Oxford: Clarendon Press, 1970), pp. 26–48.

65. In 'Guy de Maupassant' James wrote: 'M. de Maupassant is remarkably objective and impersonal, but he would go too far if he were to entertain the belief that he has kept himself out of his books. They speak of him eloquently, even if it only be to tell us how easy [...] he has found this impersonality' (*Selected Literary Criticism*, p. 96). Clearly Maupassant never entertained any such belief.

66. Marianne Bonwit demonstrated this in her early monograph *Gustave Flaubert et le principe d'impassibilité*, University of California Publications in Modern Philology, 33 (Berkeley: University of California Press, 1950). In *The Rhetoric of Fiction* Booth says that his distinction among the three forms of objectivity, i.e. 'neutrality', 'impartiality', '*impassibilité*' was derived in part from this study (p. 68).

67. Perhaps the most helpful distinction to bear in mind here is the one made by Geoffrey Leech and Michael Short in *Style in Fiction* (London/New York: Longman, 1981), p. 287:

> The difference between the 'interfering' author and the 'disappearing' one is not that the one exists in the novel while the other does not, but rather that the one conveys his presence directly, while the other does so only through the inferences we inevitably draw from the way the fiction is presented. It is simply a question of different styles of discourse.

68. Ford, *Thus to Revisit*, pp. 8–9.

69. Ford, pp. 194, 186.

70. Ford, *The English Novel* (London: Constable, 1930), p. 123.

71. Without going to the other extreme, it is worth remembering that Flaubert spoke of his 'faculté panthéiste' and described the intense pleasure he experienced when 'moving about' in his creation. He also recorded that, when describing Emma's death, he actually felt the taste of arsenic in his mouth and was physically sick. Conrad claimed the same kind of identification with, of all people, his anarchists: 'there had been moments during the writing of the book when I was an extreme revolutionist' (*SA*, p. xiv).

72. Retinger recorded that Conrad 'was irritated by his [Dickens's] moralizing tone and the unending preaching attitude' (Retinger, p. 104).

73. Maupassant, *Chroniques 1*, p. 21.

74. Conrad may have listened to Brunetière on some questions (see above pp. 250-1), but not on this one. Brunetière had praised Daudet who, far from affecting towards his characters the 'disdainful impassibility' adopted by contemporary writers, such as the author of *Madame Bovary*, 'lives and suffers with them'. He 'takes an interest' in all of them, whether they be ridiculous or odious, always finding some words of admiration or sympathy. At times, he 'intervenes himself' as if the soul of the character 'vibrated and palpitated in him' (Brunetière, 'L'*Impressionisme* dans le roman', in his *Le Roman naturaliste* (Paris: Calmann Lévy, 1883), pp. 92–94). Conrad makes all these points about Daudet: he 'cares immensely' for his characters; he 'take[s] an eager part in [their] disasters, weaknesses, and joys'; he 'vibrates together with his universe'. But Conrad declares that he 'cannot forgive him [...] the constant whisper of his presence', and his final verdict leaves us in no doubt as to whose side he is on. Whereas Brunetière was convinced that Daudet was 'an artist', Conrad, who, like his masters, obviously saw impersonality as a prerequisite for artistic excellence, was no less convinced to the contrary: Daudet's creations 'are *seen*', he acknowledges, 'and the man who is not an artist is seen also, commiserating, indignant, joyous, human and alive in their very midst' (*NLL*, pp. 21–4).

75. *Stories from de Maupassant*, p. xvi.

76. This, though he puts it more emphatically, is the central idea of Wallace S. Watson's

doctoral thesis 'Joseph Conrad's debts to the French' (1966), the 'primary focus' of which is upon 'that principle of impersonality, which subsumes virtually all the particulars of Conrad's theoretical esthetic and of his authorial techniques' (p. iii).

77. Watson, '"The shade of old Flaubert"', pp. 39–47.

78. Henry James, Preface to *The Golden Bowl* (London: The Bodley Head, 1971), p. 15.

79. Edward Crankshaw, *Joseph Conrad* (London: John Lane, The Bodley Head, 1936), pp. 67, 85, 71.

80. Watt recalls that 'Several critics have suggested that Conrad may have developed Marlow from James's use of a central observer', a view for which he finds 'some circumstantial support' (Watt, p. 204). The influence of Anatole France may also have been involved. In *The Intellectual Hero* (London: Faber and Faber, 1962), p. 89, Victor Brombert writes:

> Bergeret is to some extent a *new* character: he has sired a whole progeny of non-heroic commentator-heroes who, within the novel of which they are the moral center, comment on an action in which they can never wholly participate. [...]
>
> Haakon M. Chevalier, in *The ironic temper*, p. 99, points to the 'serene, worldly-wise, witty, disillusioned, detached and unimpassioned' characters that appeared in European literature after 1900 (the ironic 'commentators' of Schnitzler, Proust, Pirandello, Gide, Mann, Huxley) who are, he feels, to some extent derivative from France's prototype.

It would seem to be no accident, in the light of the irrefutable influence France exerted on Conrad as early as 1897, that his 'ironic commentator' in *L'Orme du Mail* (1896) and *Le Mannequin d'osier* (1897) first reappears in Conrad's work in June 1898.

81. Busza, 'Conrad's Polish literary background', p. 208. See also Najder, *Conrad's Polish Background*, pp. 16–17, Najder, p. 230, and Tarnawski, *Conrad the Man, the Writer, the Pole*, pp. 27–31.

82. See Kirschner, p. 206, n. 48. A good example is 'Un soir' in which Conrad showed an active interest when writing 'The Return' in 1897. On his way back to Paris from Africa, the first-person narrator meets an old school friend, Trémoulin, now settled at a port east of Algiers. Trémoulin invites him to his home and, after dinner, the two men go fishing by the light of a huge brazier lit on the bow of the boat. Trémoulin shows himself to be a skilled and avid fisherman, and his joy reaches a paroxysm when he spears a large octopus with his long three-pronged fork. But, most disturbingly, he then sadistically tortures it by dangling its tentacles over the fire. At this stage, half-way through the tale, we still have no idea of what it is about. Only when the two men return and Trémoulin begins to relate his own life do we realize that all this was a frame for a grim story of jealousy and deceit, and only when Trémoulin confesses how he would like to have tortured his wife ('je lui aurais brûlé les doigts sur le feu... [...] Je les aurais tenus sur les charbons, ils auraient été grillés, par le bout') (*La Main gauche*, pp. 148–9) in order to make her speak, do we realize that the episode with the octopus, together with other details, the relevance of which only emerges later, is part of an elaborate, if seemingly casual, thematic preparation, creating a subtle interplay between frame and story proper which adds resonance and depth to the tale. This should suffice to show that the influence of Conrad's

early Polish readings and that of Maupassant, far from being mutually exclusive, would reinforce each other.

The device of the *gawęda*, which consists in gathering a group of people around a table to tell one or many stories, is, of course, an old one. But between 1895 and 1910 it was Maupassant who dominated the literary horizon (especially Conrad's) and who held the attention of short-story tellers.

83. Watson has cogently argued that Conrad's 'complex experiments in narrative point of view [...] had their roots in his efforts in the period 1896–1898 to apply the lessons of Flaubert and Maupassant to his own intense struggle to find a compatible narrative voice'. Flaubert's artistry proved more frustrating than practicable. On the other hand, 'Maupassant's indirect narrative techniques lent themselves much more readily to adaptation by Conrad than those of the magisterial Flaubert'. When Conrad's 'groping efforts' came to fruition in the voice of Marlow 'it was Maupassant – whose indirect approaches to narration seem to have been the main inspiration for his earlier experiments with dramatized narrators – who provided the primary model for that voice, balancing sympathy and ironic detachment in progressively more complex ways in "Youth", "Heart of Darkness" and *Lord Jim*'. Indeed, we now know that during the composition of 'Youth' Conrad found in 'L'Epave' – among other things – 'a helpful model for that oblique narrative approach' (Watson, '"The shade of old Flaubert"', pp. 53, 44, 46–7, 49).

84. Marvin Mudrick (ed.), *Conrad: A Collection of Critical Essays* (Englewood Cliffs, NJ: Prentice Hall, 1966), pp. 7–8. An analysis of Conrad's 'supreme control and detachment' in *Nostromo* can be found in William S. Saunders's 'The unity of *Nostromo*', *Conradiana*, 5 (1973), 27–36. Kettle has noted the 'subtle dissociation' from the character of Dr Monygham in Conrad's description of the doctor's ideal conception of his disgrace as 'a conception eminently fit and proper for an officer and a gentleman' (*N*, p. 375)), and 'the artistic and moral control' exercised by Conrad to 'permit himself the irony of [that] sentence without jeopardising the compassion which informs the whole description' (Kettle, *An Introduction to the English Novel*, II, pp. 70–71).

85. Gurko, *Giant in Exile*, p. 189. More recent work by Marcus Wheeler confirms that, although Conrad loathed Russian autocracy, he was not biased in his portrayal of the Russian people ('Russia and Russians in the works of Conrad', *Conradiana*, 12 (1980), 23–36).

86. A few more examples of 'discordant juxtaposition' are given by Watts in *A Preface to Conrad*, p. 105. Cleanth Brooks has pointed out that Flaubert's device of 'incongruous juxtaposition became the "Time-Shift" developed by Conrad and Ford' (William K. Wimsatt, Jr and Cleanth Brooks, *Literary Criticism*, Vol. 4: *Modern Criticism* (London: Routledge and Kegan Paul, 1957), p. 685).

87. Stephen Ullmann, *Style in the French Novel* (Oxford: Blackwell, 1957), p. 118. Valuable observations on Flaubert's use of free indirect style can also be found in John Porter Houston, *Fictional Technique in France, 1802–1927* (Baton Rouge: Louisiana State University Press, 1972), pp. 64–9; Pierre Guiraud, 'Modern linguistics looks at rhetoric: free indirect style', in *Patterns of Literary Style*, ed. Joseph Strelka (Pennsylvania State University Press, 1971), pp. 86–9, and Dominick LaCapra, *Madame Bovary on Trial* (Cornell University Press, 1982), pp. 126–49.

88. Charles Jones, 'Varieties of speech presentation in Conrad's "The Secret Agent"', *Lingua*, 20 (1968), 164.
89. Werner Senn, *Conrad's Narrative Voice* (Bern: Francke, 1980), p. 166.
90. *JCWD*, p. 159. In 'The art of fiction' James's advice to the 'young novelist' is: 'If you must indulge in conclusions, let them have the taste of a wide knowledge' (*Selected Literary Criticism*, p. 67).
91. Jonathan Culler, *Flaubert: The Uses of Uncertainty* (Cornell University Press, 1974), pp. 136, 139, 147.
92. P. M. Wetherill points out that 'Any attempt to work out what is so often being discussed just out of Frédéric Moreau's earshot [...] is misguided' because *L'Education* puts over 'an *experience* of uncertainty, mystery, confusion and underhand dealing' (*The Literary Text*, (Oxford: Blackwell, 1974), p. 130). And the ending of the novel, which strongly disconcerts the reader, 'refuses', in Marianna Torgovnick's words, 'to offer either climax, or moral, or insight, or comfort, or even a stable vantage point from which to regard the novel' (Torgovnick, *Closure in the Novel* (Princeton University Press, 1981), p. 118).
93. See, for instance, Alex Spalding, '*Lord Jim*: the result of reading light holiday literature', *Humanities Association Bulletin*, 19 (1968), 14–22.
94. Most relevant in this respect are Jean Deurbergue's '*Lord Jim*, roman du nébuleux?', *Etudes anglaises*, 25 (1972), 147–61, and Bernard J. Paris's 'The dramatization of interpretation: *Lord Jim*' in *A Psychological Approach to Fiction* (Bloomington/London: Indiana University Press, 1974), pp. 215–74.
95. Thompson, 'Conrad's women', p. 450. Similarly, Suresh Raval argues that the novel 'invites contradictory readings at crucial moments and generates a textual ambiguity that is not resolvable into a final thematic meaning' ('Conrad's *Victory*: skepticism and experience', *Nineteenth-Century Fiction*, 34 (1980), 416). The open-endedness of Conrad's fiction is explored by Norman Sherry in 'The essential Conrad', *Essays and Studies*, 27 (1974), 98–113, and Senn (in *Conrad's Narrative Voice*) has shown how he created the narrative mood of uncertainty, ambivalence and indeterminacy by a skilful manipulation of linguistic devices. In *Conrad's Endings* (Ann Arbor, Mich.: UMI Research Press, 1984), Arnold Davidson demonstrates that Conrad's novels end in two different ways simultaneously since the endings both bring about closure and establish the impossibility of concluding. Finally, mention should be made here of the concept of 'janiformity' – that is, the ability of a text to look in opposite ways at the same time because of its paradoxical or self-contradictory nature – which Watts has proposed in 'Janiform novels', *English*, 24 no. 119 (1975), 40–9, as an alternative to the notion of organic whole, and which he repeatedly applies in *A Preface to Conrad* and *The Deceptive Text* (Sussex: Harvester / New Jersey: Barnes & Noble, 1984).
96. E. M. Forster, 'Joseph Conrad: a note' in his *Abinger Harvest* (London: Arnold, 1936), p. 160.
97. Jean Rousset asked: 'Is not such an experience [i.e. that all is uncertain] of a nature to put into question the privileged position of the omniscient author endowed with the absolute vision of God?' (Rousset, '*Madame Bovary* ou le livre sur rien', translated as '*Madame Bovary* or the book about nothing' in *Flaubert: A Collection of*

*Critical Essays*, ed. Raymond Giraud (Englewood Cliffs, NJ: Prentice-Hall, 1964), p. 114).

98. Quoted by Bonwit, *Flaubert et le principe d'impassibilité*, p. 305.

99. Watt, p. 174. In the *Academy* of 15 October 1898, in what, according to Sherry, was 'the first general article on Conrad to appear', Garnett already singled out 'his particular gift of flashing a scene or episode upon us in a dozen lines', and gave this appraisal: 'His power of making us *see* a constant succession of changing pictures is what dominates the reader' (*Conrad: The Critical Heritage*, ed. Sherry, pp. 104, 107). Similarly, Kirschner examined Conrad's use of eidetic memory-images of Geneva for artistic purposes in *Under Western Eyes* ('Making you *see* Geneva: the sense of place in *Under Western Eyes*', *L'Epoque conradienne* (1988), 101–27.

100. Gillon asks, mainly with reference to *Lord Jim*, 'In what sense can his representations of people, nature and things inanimate be seen as verbal paintings, snapshots, or the moving pictures of a roving camera?' (Gillon, 'Conrad as painter', p. 254).

101. 'Impressionism' and 'Impressionist' are spelled with a capital only when referring to painting.

102. See, in particular, Eloise Knapp Hay, 'Impressionism limited', in *Joseph Conrad: A Commemoration*, ed. Norman Sherry (London: Macmillan, 1976), pp. 54–64; Todd K. Bender, 'Conrad and literary impressionism', *Conradiana*, 10 (1978), 211–24; Watt, pp. 169–80; and Bruce Johnson, 'Conrad's impressionism and Watt's "delayed decoding"' in *Conrad Revisited*, ed. Ross C. Murfin (University of Alabama Press, 1985), pp. 51–70.

103. For a salutary warning on 'the problem of literary impressionism', see J. Theodore Johnson, Jr's 'Literary impressionism in France: a survey of criticism', *L'Esprit créateur*, 13 (1973), 271–97. Johnson comments: 'Critical studies on literary impressionism are not lacking, but what emerges from a survey of these studies is that there is not an agreement as to who the literary impressionists are and what in fact constitutes literary impressionism' (p. 274). He later quotes the conclusion reached by Calvin S. Brown in his 'How useful is the concept of impressionism' (*Yearbook of Comparative and General Literature*, 19 (1968), 53–9): 'ninety years after Brunetière's prophecy ['Le mot d'*impressionnisme*, à son tour, disparaîtra'], the time has come to fulfil it by dropping *impressionism* and *impressionist* from the musical and literary vocabulary. We have nothing to lose but confusion' (p. 283), a verdict he recalls and endorses in his own conclusion: 'Certainly the present critical vagueness about the term invites this sort of drastic action' (p. 297). A valuable attempt to define impressionism as a critical term may be found in James Nagel's *Stephen Crane and Literary Impressionism* (Pennsylvania State University Press, 1980).

104. Watt, p. 179. Similarly, Karl demonstrates how sharply Conrad diverged from the impressionists (Karl, pp. 408–10 and part VI), and so does Elsa Nettels in the last section of her 'Conrad and Stephen Crane', *Conradiana*, 10 (1978), 277–81.

105. Pierre Danger, *Sensations et objets dans le roman de Flaubert* (Paris: Colin, 1973), p. 86. (See also Martine Dunet, 'Flaubert, artiste et précurseur de l'impressionnisme', *Les Amis de Flaubert*, 46 (1975), 25–36.) Danger explains:

> Sans être intimement lié, comme le sera Zola, à des peintres de son époque et

sans s'intéresser particulièrement aux idées qu'ils défendent, Flaubert devance pourtant, en quelque sorte instinctivement, les premiers impressionnistes tant il est proche d'eux par sa conception de l'art et le regard qu'il pose sur les choses.

Remarks comparing Flaubert's descriptions to painting abound. As early as 1880, Brunetière described his practice of presenting those aspects of a scene which reflect or refract the incident light as a 'procédé de peintre' ('Gustave Flaubert', *Revue des deux mondes*, 15 June 1880, 831). Commenting on the description which opens the third chapter of *Salammbô*, Gustave Lanson observed: 'C'est la lumière qui est l'objet de sa description, qui en fait l'unité [...]. La plume a voulu être, ici, un pinceau' (*L'Art de la prose* (Paris: Nizet, [1968], pp. 278–9). A remark Flaubert made in 1850 during his trip in the Near East: 'Axiome: c'est le ciel qui fait le paysage' (*Notes de voyage* (Paris: Conard, 1910), II, p. 19), shows that, before starting work on *Madame Bovary*, he was fully conscious of the influence of light on our perceptions.

106. Helmut Hatzfeld, *Literature through Art* (University of North Carolina Press, 1969), pp. 168, 169. Interestingly, the passage from *Madame Bovary* quoted by way of illustration is the one which, in all likelihood, inspired Conrad in the opening of 'Heart of Darkness', where he, too, tried to capture the atmospheric aspects of the Essex marshes on a beautiful evening (see above p. 63).

107. See, for instance, Joy Newton, 'Emile Zola impressionniste', *Cahiers naturalistes*, 13 no. 33 (1967), 39–52, and 13 no. 34 (1967), 124–38, and 'Emile Zola and the French impressionist novel', *Esprit créateur*, 13 (1973), 320–8. As J. Theodore Johnson, Jr shows: 'Work on Zola and his relation to the Impressionists and literary impressionism is overwhelming', ('Literary impressionism in France', p. 291).

108. Hay, 'Impressionism limited', p. 56. See Brunetière, 'L'*Impressionnisme* dans le roman', pp. 84–5.

109. In 'L'Imparfait de Flaubert et des romanciers naturalistes du XIXᵉ siècle', *Acta Linguistica Academiae Scientiarum Hungaricae*, 20 (1970) Jolán Kelemen writes:

> Avec Flaubert, nous venons de rencontrer la première grande rupture dans l'emploi traditionnel du passé simple comme temps principal de la narration, emploi qui se maintenait depuis des siècles. *C'est Flaubert qui, le premier, a écrit un roman où l'imparfait domine par rapport au passé simple, qui a inventé une manière d'écrire permettant d'user abondamment de l'imparfait*, par l'usage conséquent de procédés stylistiques comme la description, le style indirect et indirect libre, le monologue intérieur, etc. (p. 73, original emphasis)

110. Huss, 'Some anomalous uses of the imperfect', pp. 141, 142.

111. According to Alan Spiegel, the reification of the narrative form, a trend he sees beginning with *Madame Bovary*, represents 'one of the defining characteristics of much of the fiction we designate as modern'. He lists seven characteristics of the reified narrative, the last one, 'of special importance', being defined as 'Action that is often understood in terms of what is seen (that is, transmitted in words that evoke expressive visual images)'. The 'intensive visualization in reified form', he claims, 'establishes a link between the reified art of Flaubert and such modern

reificationalists as Conrad, Joyce, Faulkner, Nabokov, and Robbe-Grillet' ('Flaubert to Joyce: evolution of a cinematographic form', *Novel*, 6 (1973), 229.

112. Ford, *The March of Literature*, pp. 801–2.

113. Similarly, in 'Guy de Maupassant' James had praised the use Maupassant made of his 'powerful' visual sense: 'His eye *selects* unerringly, unscrupulously, almost impudently – catches the particular thing in which the character of the object or the scene resides, and, by expressing it with the artful brevity of a master, leaves a convincing, original picture.' In his best stories, which are 'gems of narration', 'the whole thing is real, observed, noted, and represented, not an invention or a castle in the air' (*Selected Literary Criticism*, pp. 91–2, 99).

114. Ford, p. 31.

115. Maupassant attached so much importance to this point that he made it on a number of occasions. In his 'Etude sur Gustave Flaubert' (1884), he had explained: 'Au lieu d'étaler la psychologie des personnages en des dissertations explicatives, [Flaubert] la faisait simplement apparaître par leurs actes. Les dedans étaient ainsi *dévoilés* par les dehors, sans aucune argumentation psychologique' (*MB*, p. 543). And in 'Romans' published in the *Gil Blas* of 26 April 1882, he had already asked: 'montrer les personnages si puissamment que tous leurs dessous soient devinés rien qu'à les voir; les faire agir de sorte qu'on *dévoile* au lecteur, par les actes seulement, tout le mécanisme de leurs intentions [...] ne serait-ce pas là faire du vrai roman [...]?' (*Chroniques 2*, p. 42). My italicizing of 'dévoiler' is explained in note 3 to chapter 6.

116. Wiley points out that Paul Bourget credited Flaubert with 'having invented a procedure of capital importance to literature in making use in *Madame Bovary* of [...] a system of exhibiting mental activity through images on the theory that they represent the content of the mind in accordance with the doctrine of association of ideas' (Wiley, p. 33).

117. Emile Faguet, *Gustave Flaubert* (Paris: Hachette, 1899), p. 156. (Original emphasis)

118. Kirschner, pp. 185–6.

119. Proust, 'A propos du "style" de Flaubert', p. 75.

120. Jean-Aubry suggested to Conrad that it was perhaps a reminiscence which had made him choose the same name for Scevela Bron in *The Rover*. Conrad said the idea had not occurred to him (*'The Rover'*, in Keating, *A Conrad Memorial Library*, p. 331).

121. See Frances Dodson Rhome, 'Headgear as symbol in Conrad's novels', *Conradiana*, 2 (1970), 180–6.

122. Andrew Lytle, 'In defense of a passionate and incorruptible heart', *Sewanee Review*, 73 (1965), 594.

123. See Karl, *A Reader's Guide to Joseph Conrad*, pp. 215–17.

124. See Richard B. Grant, 'The role of Minerva in *Madame Bovary*', *Romance Notes*, 6 (1965), 113–15 and Lowe, 'Emma Bovary, a modern Arachne'.

125. See Jean Seznec, 'Flaubert and the graphic arts', *Journal of the Warburg and Courtauld Institutes*, 8 (1945), 179–81.

126. See Jean Verrier, 'Questions sur une lecture de *Pierre et Jean*', *Le Français dans le monde*, 146 (1979), 18–23.

127. For a detailed interpretation of this sketch, see Stark, 'Kurtz's Intended', p. 551.
128. See Gillon, 'Conrad as painter', p. 265.
129. Goncourt, I, p. 888 (17 March 1861).
130. Ford, p. 182.
131. According to Ezra Pound, 'what Flaubert had done to change French prose, Conrad and Ford did to transform English prose', a transformation he defined as 'the piling up of imagistic details which replaced, in part at least, a direct narrative' (quoted in Karl, *A Reader's Guide to Joseph Conrad*, p. 43).
132. Tanner, *Adultery in the Novel*, p. 302.
133. R. W. Stallman has also drawn a parallel between the two works: 'Flaubert's summoning-up of a complex of feelings by a set of images is the method of Conrad in "The Heart of Darkness", the atmosphere in that story being engendered by a structure of sense-impressions which objectify the atmosphere and evoke it' ('Flaubert's *Madame Bovary*', *College English*, 10 (1949), 196).
134. Edwin Muir, 'A note on Mr Conrad' in his *Latitudes* (New York: Huebsch, 1924), p. 50. Quoted by Yelton, p. 27.
135. It is easy to see why critics have explored the relation between both authors' practices and cinematic techniques. Danger writes:

> L'oeuvre de Flaubert est [...] exactement conçue comme une oeuvre cinématographique, c'est-à-dire que tout est exprimé par l'image, le son et la perception du mouvement, sans qu'aucune analyse psychologique, aucun commentaire de l'auteur ne vienne jamais se superposer à la simple vision de la scène décrite, si ce n'est, à de rares occasions, quelques rapides lumières sur le discours intérieur qui se déroule dans la conscience claire du personnage. Et tous les procédés par lesquels se construisent et s'enchaînent ces images sont ceux que nous retrouverons dans le septième art. Il y a là une préfiguration tout à fait remarquable de cette nouvelle technique d'écriture que l'on allait bientôt découvrir.
>
> (Danger, *Flaubert*, p. 186)

Other critics have shown that Flaubert used many cinematic symbols in *Madame Bovary* (Harry Levin, '*Madame Bovary*: the cathedral and the hospital', *Essays in Criticism*, 2 (1952), 6) and in *La Tentation* (Brombert, *The Novels of Flaubert*, p. 206), while Hanna Charney in 'Images of absence in Flaubert and some contemporary films' (*Style*, 9 (1975), 490) selects as almost 'entirely cinematic' the passage from *Madame Bovary* showing Charles returning home after the funeral of his first wife, part of which Conrad used in 'The End of the Tether' (see above, p. 80). Although the criticism devoted to the 'cinematic' aspects of Conrad's fiction is slim by comparison, valuable comments have been made by Yelton (p. 26) and more systematically by Spiegel ('Flaubert to Joyce') and Kirschner ('Conrad and the film', *Quarterly of Film, Radio, and Television*, 11 (1957), 343–53) Conrad himself initiated this kind of comparison when, on 9 April 1923, he described his forthcoming talk at the Long Island house of Mrs Curtiss James, developing 'on the (apparently) extravagant lines of the imaginative literary art being based fundamentally on scenic motion, like a cinema' (*LL*, II, p. 302). See also Conrad's notes for this talk, headed 'Author and cinematograph', in which he wrote: 'fundamentally the creator in letters aims at a moving picture – moving to the eye, to the

mind, and to our complex emotions which I will express with one word – heart'
(Donald W. Rude, 'Joseph Conrad's speeches in America: his texts recovered',
*L'Epoque conradienne* (1987), 26.

136. See Faguet, *Gustave Flaubert*, p. 163; Vial, *Guy de Maupassant*, p. 234; André
Chevrillon, 'Conrad', *NRF*, p. 705; and Spiegel, 'Flaubert to Joyce', p. 238.

137. John Lapp comments that 'of all Flaubert's works *Madame Bovary* reflects the
hallucinations most prominently' ('Art and hallucination in Flaubert', *French
Studies*, 10 (1956), 332); Charney ('Images of absence in Flaubert and some contemporary films', p. 491) notes that 'in *L'Education sentimentale* (as well as in other
later works) one dominant mode of perception is hallucinatory'; *La Tentation* is
overtly about Saint Antoine's hallucinated visions; in 'Un coeur simple' Félicité
dies seeing a gigantic parrot/paraclete soaring above her head. In Maupassant,
hallucination is too frequent a phenomenon for any meaningful inventory to be
drawn in a few lines.

138. Conclusive evidence of literary influence is shown in Almayer's distraction at the
sight of the corpse of the supposed Dain Maroola, closely modelled on one of the
three hallucinations experienced by Frédéric Moreau (see above pp. 22-3).

139. Ford, 'On Impressionism', in *Critical Writings of Ford Madox Ford*, ed. Frank
MacShane (Lincoln: University of Nebraska Press, 1964), p. 41.

140. Allen Tate, 'Techniques of fiction' in his *Collected Essays* (Denver: Swallow, 1959),
pp. 144, 143, 145.

141. Ford, 'On Impressionism', pp. 41, 42.

142. Ford, 'On Impressionism', p. 43. Yelton has suggested that in the scene of the
assembly held in the sala of the Casa Gould (*N*, pp. 173–206) Conrad was emulating
Flaubert's 'symphonic' movement in the *Comices* in which 'Rodolphe's verbal
assault upon Emma's conjugal fidelity, conducted behind a window on the second
floor of the *mairie* overlooking the square, alternates with fragments of official
rhetoric wafted from the platform below and with the announcements of awards'.
He hastens to add that 'Conrad attempted nothing like an imitation of the *Comices*',
but 'under a like impulsion towards a "musical" structure, has attempted something at once perfectly distinct in execution and markedly similar in conception'
(Yelton, pp. 97–8). It must be remembered, however, that when writing this 'memorable scene', Conrad did rely on a scene from Maupassant's 'L'Héritage' (see
above pp. 91-2).

143. Sherrington, *Three Novels by Flaubert*, pp. 81-2. It is only during a later visit that
we get a fuller portrait of Emma, again as she is seen by Charles, in a particular
setting, during a few fleeting moments:

> On s'était dit adieu, on ne parlait plus; le grand air l'entourait, levant pêle-mêle
> les petits cheveux follets de sa nuque, ou secouant sur sa hanche les cordons de
> son tablier, qui se tortillaient comme des banderoles. Une fois, par un temps de
> dégel, l'écorce des arbres suintait dans la cour, la neige sur les couvertures des
> bâtiments se fondait. Elle était sur le seuil; elle alla chercher son ombrelle, elle
> l'ouvrit. L'ombrelle, de soie gorge de pigeon, que traversait le soleil, éclairait
> de reflets mobiles la peau blanche de sa figure. Elle souriait là-dessus à la chaleur
> tiède; et on entendait les gouttes d'eau, une à une, tomber sur la moire tendue.
> (*MB*, pp. 22-3)

The motionlessness of the characters, the silence, the smile, the warm air, the snow melting off the roofs and the trees, the sunlight, coloured as it passes through Emma's sunshade and playing on her face, this, as Sherrington concludes, 'is not a description, but an impression', the impression, we sense, of a man falling in love. It is natural to think of the Impressionists, but what painting by Manet, Monet or Renoir could have taught Conrad and Ford as much about verbal portrait-painting as did Flaubert?

144. In like manner, it is only gradually that we get to know Jim and form in our minds a certain portrait of him. Conrad, Gillon explains, never gives us a 'completed verbal canvas': 'With each scene, each narrative point of view, a significant detail is added to the fictional canvas, either by filling up a blank spot or by superimposing a new layer of color upon the earlier surface. It is these little additions, at first hardly noticeable, to the initial visual impression of the protagonist that finally determine both his outward appearance and his inner essence.' By the end of the novel, the reader has been presented with 'a veritable gallery of pictures as well as reels of film, showing fragmentary glimpses, views, and movements of his protagonist', and it is left to him 'to emulate Marlow's example by fitting the fragments together to form his own intelligible picture' (Gillon, 'Conrad as painter', p. 258). Conrad's method is a natural extension of Flaubert's.

145. Watt, pp. 176, 174.

146. See also the whole page given to the detailed description of the Barbarians' impressions as they look uncomprehendingly at what finally turns out to be the approaching Carthaginian army (pp. 198–9).

147. However admirable Ramón Fernández's 'L'Art de Conrad' (*NRF*, p. 733), I find him misleading when he, too, presents an example of 'delayed decoding' drawn from *The Shadow-Line* as something specifically Conradian. This story was written in 1915, and we find exactly the same kind of thing in 'Combray', the first volume of *A la recherche*, published in 1913, which Conrad read, as he recalled, in 1913 or 1914:

> Un petit coup au carreau, comme si quelque chose l'avait heurté, suivi d'une ample chute légère comme de grains de sable qu'on eût laissés tomber d'une fenêtre au-dessus, puis la chute s'étendant, se réglant, adoptant un rythme, devenant fluide, sonore, musicale, innombrable, universelle: c'était la pluie.
>
> (Marcel Proust, *A la recherche du temps perdu*, La Pléiade, (Paris: Gallimard, 1954), I, pp. 101–2)

> I became bothered by curious, irregular sounds of faint tapping on the deck. They could be heard single, in pairs, in groups. While I wondered at this mysterious devilry, I received a slight blow under the left eye and felt an enormous tear run down my cheek. Raindrops. Enormous. Forerunners of something. Tap. Tap. Tap. . . .                                           (*SL*, p. 113)

The comparison beween the dates is not meant to suggest an influence, but to underline the fact that by then the device had become the common property of novelists. (In *A la recherche*, Proust attributes the same primacy of the impression characteristic of Elstir's painting to both Mme de Sévigné and Dostoevskii: 'Mme de Sévigné est une grande artiste de la même famille qu' [. . .] Elstir. Je me rendis compte à Balbec que c'est de la même façon que lui qu'elle nous présente les choses, dans l'ordre de nos perceptions, au lieu de les expliquer d'abord par leur cause' (I, p. 653); 'Il est arrivé que Mme de Sévigné, comme Elstir, comme Dostoïevsky, au lieu de présenter les choses dans l'ordre logique, c'est-à-dire en commençant par la cause, nous montre d'abord l'effet, l'illusion qui nous frappe' (III, p. 378).

148. The attic scene in *Madame Bovary* is more than just a fine example of impressionistic writing, for, as Albert Cook points out:

> Not only the lathe is a metaphor: the heavy heat of the tiles morally as well as physically grips [Emma's] temples and stifles her. What the light dazzles is a moral darkness ensconced in her physical solitude. There is no end to the physical countryside, nor to the moral monotony she feels. The real emptiness of the village square reflects her metaphorical condition: she is alone because she feels so, and also because no one knows of her love. No one, that is, except perhaps Binet, whose lathe, then, is metaphorically heard. ('Flaubert: the riches of detachment',                                    *French Review*, 32 (1958), 123)

149. Meyer comments that 'in "The Return" the notion of "penetration" attains the rank of an obsession' (Meyer, p. 291). The influence of Maupassant is clearly implicated here, as is corroborated by the examples already quoted comparing the reactions of Dain and Nina with those of Jeanne and Julien (pp. 35–6) and the reactions of Willems and Aïssa with those of Duroy and Madeleine (pp. 47–8).

150. Yelton, p. 30.

151. Gillon, 'Conrad as painter', p. 265. Neither the memories of Conrad's friends nor his own letters reveal any such awareness. Ernest Dawson recalled that Conrad was 'not much interested' in the other arts, adding that his [Dawson's] memory was 'empty [...] of anything said by him about pictures'. He also made it clear that Conrad's reactions were totally unsophisticated: 'For him [...] a picture was a record of its subject; just that and no more. [...] If the subject had charm or interest for him, and the record seemed accurate, he liked the picture' ('Some recollections of Joseph Conrad', pp. 208–9). All this is confirmed by Watt's comment: 'Conrad's tastes in painting, as in music, were distinctly old-fashioned; he apparently disliked Van Gogh and Cézanne, and the only painter he ever mentioned as a model for his own writing was the peasant realist Jean-François Millet: in a letter to Quiller-Couch, Conrad wrote 'It has been my desire to do for seamen what Millet (if I dare pronounce the name of that great man and good artist in this connection) has done for peasants' (Watt, p. 173).

152. A short borrowing encapsulates this point: when Conrad wrote of Karain's domain: '*All that had* [...] *the* suspicious *immobility of a painted scene*' (*TU*, p. 7), his prime source of inspiration was not painting but Flaubert's description of Rouen in *Madame Bovary* (see above p. 50).

153. It has also been surmised that the obvious difficulty Flaubert encountered when writing passages of psychological analysis may have had something to do with his adoption of an objective technique (see *Madame Bovary*, ed. C. Gothot-Mersch (Paris: Garnier, 1971), p. xliii–xliv).

154. Joseph Martin, 'Edward Garnett and Conrad's plunge into the "destructive ele-

ment"', *Texas Studies in Literature and Language*, 15 (1973), 519, 520. Martin also writes: 'Both Garnett's early novel, *Light and Shadow* (1889), which markedly shows Maupassant's influence, and his critical writings from the 1890s through the 1930s indicate that Maupassant's essay became quite early, and remained, the cornerstone of Garnett's literary philosophy' (p. 520, n. 10).

155. Martin, 'Edward Garnett and Conrad's plunge', p. 527.
156. Martin, 'Edward Garnett and Conrad's plunge', p. 533, n. 43.
157. Kirschner, p. 205.
158. Davray, 'Joseph Conrad', pp. 54–5.
159. Flaubert never budged from this view. Thirty years later we find him writing to Louise Colet: 'tu n'ôteras pas la forme de l'Idée, car l'Idée n'existe qu'en vertu de sa forme' (I, p. 321), and to George Sand: 'je crois la forme et le fond deux subtilités, deuxentités qui n'existent jamais l'une sans l'autre' (VII, p. 290). In 'Style' Walter Pater quoted Flaubert and Maupassant at some length on this subject. James, too, was a firm believer in the inseparability of form and content throughout his life, as can be seen from statements he made in 'The art of fiction' (*Selected Literary Criticism*, p. 63) and in a letter to Hugh Walpole of May 1912 in which he stressed that 'Form *is* [...] substance to that degree that there is absolutely no substance without it' (quoted by Allott, *Novelists on the Novel*, p. 235). Whereas, in the same letter, he described the works of Tolstoi and Dostoevskii as 'fluid puddings', in his 1902 essay on Flaubert, he had observed that *Madame Bovary* has a perfection 'that makes it stand almost alone', a perfection resulting from the fusion of form and content: 'The form is in *itself* as interesting, as active, as much of the essence of the subject as the idea, and yet so close is its fit and so inseparable its life that we catch it at no moment on any errand of its own' (*Selected Literary Criticism*, p. 221).
160. Maupassant had already recorded Flaubert's views in his 1884 essay (cf. *MB*, p. 546). One suspects that Flaubert was echoing La Bruyère's statement:

> entre toutes les différentes expressions qui peuvent rendre une seule de nos pensées, il n'y en a qu'une qui soit la bonne. On ne la rencontre pas toujours en parlant ou en écrivant; il est vrai néanmoins qu'elle existe, que tout ce qui ne l'est point est faible, et ne satisfait point un homme d'esprit qui veut se faire entendre.
>
> ('Des ouvrages de l'Esprit', in *Oeuvres complètes*,
> La Pléiade (Paris: Gallimard, 1951), p. 69,)

James adopted this idea. Whether he took it from La Bruyère or from Flaubert, he wrote in 1878: 'We believe there is a certain particular phrase, better than any other, for everything in the world, and the thoroughly accomplished writer ends by finding it.' (*French Poets and Novelists* (New York: Grosset and Dunlap, 1964), p. 202.)
161. Strother B. Purdy, 'Henry James, Gustave Flaubert, and the ideal style', *Language and Style*, 3 (1970), 173–4. This, he goes on, is 'historically part of the concept of Attic or "plain style"', and La Bruyère was close to paraphrasing Cicero's description of the Attic orator when he described '"la bonne expression" as "celle qui

était la plus simple, la plus naturelle, qui semblait devoir se présenter d'abord et sans effort"'. Cicero's description reads: 'He is restrained and plain, he follows the ordinary usage [...]. All noticeable ornament will be excluded [...] only elegance and neatness will remain. The language will be pure Latin, plain and clear; propriety will always be the chief aim' (George Williamson, *The Senecan Amble* (London: Faber and Faber, 1951), p. 18.

162. Ford, *Thus to Revisit*, pp. 51, 52–3. In *The March of Literature* Ford again asserted his belief that 'A too startling epithet, however vivid, or a simile, however just, is a capital defect, because the first province of style is to be unnoticeable' (p. 843). In *Joseph Conrad: A Personal Remembrance* he recorded Conrad's desire 'to write a prose of extreme limpidity' (p. 214) and in 'On Conrad's vocabulary', p. 405, he declared that in the course of their collaboration he himself was after 'a limpidity of expression that should make prose seem like the sound of some one talking in rather a low voice into the ear of a person that he liked.'

163. Maupassant is again echoing his master when, in 'Le Roman', he stresses the need to discern 'avec une extrême lucidité toutes les modifications de la valeur d'un mot suivant la place qu'il occupe' (*PJ*, p. xxv).

164. See Block, 'Theory of language in Gustave Flaubert and James Joyce', p. 200, and Clamens, '"D'un mot mis en sa place..."', p. 45.

165. Compare, for instance, the six different descriptions of Rouen (five drafts followed by a final version) in Antoine Albalat, *Le Travail du style enseigné par les corrections manuscrites des grands écrivains* (Paris: Colin, 1903), pp. 72–80.

166. In 'On Conrad's vocabulary', p. 407, Ford examined some alterations in the manuscript of *The Sisters* and showed that they had been made 'in the interests of precision' (Conrad changed 'ancient' into 'mediaeval' because 'the connotations of words must always be considered' and the word 'ancient' to some extent connotes classical antiquity) or 'in the interests of his cadence'. Similarly, in his examination of the revisions Conrad made to the 'Dollars' manuscript for the printed text of *Victory*, Karl has shown how he moved repeatedly 'from descriptive vagueness to narrative firmness'. Karl also points out that the *Nostromo* manuscript 'demonstrates, as does "Dollars", that Conrad aimed at visual sharpness, concrete expression, pointed narrative' ('*Victory*: its origin and development', p. 45). His painstaking search for achieving what Roderick Davis calls 'a progressively colder effect' in describing Razumov's final encounter with Natalia is shown by the variants following 'she advanced towards him a step or two' (*UWE*, pp. 337–8):

> Then his expression changed. It was with lowered eyelids that he took the hand she offered him; just touched it – no more.
> Then his expression changed. He did not notice the hand she offered him. He did not notice the hand she put out.
> He disregarded the hand she put out.    (Davis, '*Under Western Eyes*', p. 73)

167. Margaret Tillett, *On Reading Flaubert* (London: Oxford University Press, 1961), p. 11.

168. This emphasis on the importance Conrad attached to 'precision' must not make us lose sight of the equally strong pull he felt towards 'vagueness', to be analysed in connection with Loti (pp. 239-40).

169. *Yale Review*, new series 12 (1923), 497–508.
170. Ford also made this point: 'The proof of prose is in the percentage of right words' (Ford, p. 105).
171. This 'incertitude' – aggravated no doubt by the use of a foreign medium – must have increased his tendency to use too many words. As J. W. Beach remarked: 'It is as if in his search for the *mot juste* he tried out three or four or a dozen words, and then, instead of keeping the one which just suited his need, he kept them all' (*The Twentieth Century Novel* (New York: Appleton-Century-Crofts, 1932), p. 341).
172. Rodolphe L. Mégroz, *Joseph Conrad's Mind and Method* (London: Faber & Faber, 1931), p. 40.
173. Auerbach, *Mimesis*, p. 429. Flaubert's practice, he adds, is a 'very old, classic French tradition'. Indeed, in *Novelists on the Novel* Allott remarks: 'A feeling of responsibility for truth in handling words characterizes almost every pronouncement on style made by French novelists' (p. 221).
174. In a deleted passage from the manuscript of *Under Western Eyes*, Conrad had made the language teacher point to Tekla's disillusionment as Peter Ivanovitch's scribe: 'It seems that she thought that teaching and invective and lofty mystic preaching ought to have been poured out in an inspired stream; whereas she had discovered that great phrases were built up laboriously, word by word, not in the heat of conviction but with a cold regard for effect.' (Davis, '*Under Western Eyes*', p. 69). Behind such a statement 'the shade of old Flaubert', warning the 'muse' to be on guard against that kind of overheating ['échauffement'] called inspiration and stressing that everything should be done coldly, with poise ['à froid, posément'] (III, p. 105), is again unmistakable.
175. See, for instance, *NN*, p. x; *CL*, I, p. 252; II, p. 445; III, p. 90. In 'The art of fiction' James asserts that 'the only condition [...] attaching to the composition of the novel is [...] that it be sincere' (*Selected Literary Criticism*, p. 67).
176. *JCWD*, pp. 160–1. The phrase 'an absolute truth to my sensations' already appears in a letter to Blackwood of 31 May 1902 (*CL*, II, p. 418).
177. The resistance to the ensuing birth of artistic consciousness in the English novel was strong. Ford said that for the Victorians, even in the dying years of the reign, the novel was 'fiction', which meant that it had 'sometimes a purpose, sometimes a key', and that, for them, 'the conception of the novel as a work of Art was unthinkable' (Ford, *Return to Yesterday*, pp. 185–6). And he added that he owed a great deal to Conrad on this question of aesthetic awareness.
178. This point is developed by B. F. Bart in 'Flaubert's concept of the novel', p. 84.
179. It is clear who Walter Pater had in mind when, in 'Style', he said that 'beauty is, after all, truth', and affirmed that this principle has 'one sole purpose – that absolute accordance of expression to idea' (*Appreciations* (London: Macmillan, 1910), p. 34).
180. Charles Baudelaire, 'Edgar Poe, sa vie et ses oeuvres', in *Oeuvres complètes*, La Pléiade (Paris: Gallimard, 1975–76), II, p. 308.
181. Roland Barthes, *Writing Degree Zero*, translated by Annette Lavers and Colin Smith (London: Cape, 1967), p. 72.
182. However, Conrad realized that these unproductive spells probably had their posi-

tive side (as was the case with Flaubert): 'And yet perhaps those days without a line, nay, without a word, the hard, atrocious, agonizing days are simply part of my *method* of work, a decreed necessity of my production' (*CL*, III, p. 327).

183. H. G. Wells reported, somewhat ironically, how Conrad 'had gone literary with a singleness and intensity of purpose that made the kindred concentration of Henry James seem lax and large and pale' (*Experiment in Autobiography* (London: Gollancz/Cresset Press, 1934), II, p. 617).

184. Benjamin Bart, in examining the transformation the original legend underwent in Flaubert's hands, has shown that in his effort to create the true and the beautiful, Flaubert was inevitably writing a moral tale ('The moral of Flaubert's *Saint-Julien*', *Romanic Review*, 38 (1947), 33. In 'The art of fiction' James explains:

> There is one point at which the moral sense and the artistic sense lie very near together; that is in the light of the very obvious truth that the deepest quality of a work of art will always be the quality of the mind of the producer. In proportion as that intelligence is fine will the novel, the picture, the statue partake of the substance of beauty and truth'.          (*Selected Literary Criticism*, p. 66)

185. Karl, *A Reader's Guide to Joseph Conrad*, p. 36.

## Chapter 9

1. Thorburn, *Conrad's Romanticism*, pp. x–xi.
2. In 'The concept of Romanticism in literary history' (*Concepts of Criticism* (New Haven: Yale University Press, 1963), p. 195), René Wellek says: 'Polish romantic literature is the most romantic of all minor literatures: Mickiewicz and Slowacki share fully the romantic view of nature, the romantic concept of the imagination, the use of symbol and mythology, and express them even extravagantly.'
3. John Batchelor, *The Edwardian Novelists* (London: Duckworth, 1982), p. vii.
4. Jeremy Hawthorn's review of *The Edwardian Novelists* in *Conradiana*, 15 (1983), 72. Mention must be made here of two attempts to show the relationship between Conrad and Shakespeare and Conrad and Dickens. In his long title-essay in *Conrad and Shakespeare* (New York: Astra Books, 1976), Adam Gillon aimed to trace all Conrad's borrowings – verbal and thematic – from Shakespeare. Critics have viewed his findings with considerable scepticism and, after taking Ian Watt to task for asserting the importance of French influences, Robert Caserio points out: 'By Conrad's express admission [...] the connection that matters most is Dickens. In *A Personal Record* [...] Conrad names Dickens as the patron of his literary career and shapes the memoir to give Dickens a climactic place in his life' ('Joseph Conrad, Dickensian novelist', p. 338). Conrad had great affection for Dickens whose influence on some of his work is undeniable, but he clearly repudiated his conception of the novelist's craft. So, unfortunately, Caserio is another victim of Conrad's personal myth-making. His admission and artistic shaping in his reminiscences are no more reliable than the 1918 assessment of his debt to Flaubert, and must surely be part of his attempt to be viewed as a classic of the English literary tradition.
5. Leszek Prorok, 'A big book about Conrad', *The Conradian*, 6 (1981), 24. Conrad

himself indicated this in his interview with Marian Dabrowski of 1914: 'English critics – since I am an English writer – when speaking of me, always add that there is in me something incomprehensible, inexplicable, unfathomable. You alone can understand what they mean by "incomprehensible". That is the quality of being a Pole' ('An interview with Joseph Conrad', p. 373).

6. Probably the least satisfactory in this respect is Robert Hodges's *The Dual Heritage of Joseph Conrad* (The Hague: Mouton, 1967), which presents Conrad's personality and art exclusively in the light of his Polish background, as a product of the conflicting influences of his father and uncle. (For a sensible refutation of this approach, see Andrew Busza's 'A trip into the Polish interior: a review', *English Literature in Transition*, 11 (1968), 222–6.)

7. Morf, p. 299.

8. John Batchelor's review of Morf's *The Polish Shades and Ghosts of Joseph Conrad* in *Notes and Queries*, new series 27 (1980), 383, 384.

9. Douglas Hewitt's review of *The Polish Shades* in *Review of English Studies*, new series 32 (1981), 354. The same criticism can be levelled at Tarnawski's *Conrad the Man, the Writer, the Pole*, which is over-rigorous and too schematic in its pursuit of Polish strains in Conrad's fiction.

10. Batchelor, *The Edwardian Novelists*, p. vii.

11. Prorok says that, although Conrad was using the English language, he 'filled in' for the Poles 'a big gap in Polish Romanticism', offering them 'several great Romantic novels', and he concludes with 'the image of Conrad as a late Romantic' ('A big book about Conrad', pp. 23, 25).

12. Knowles, p. 58.

13. Robert Lynd's review of *A Set of Six* in the *Daily News*, 10 August, 1908. Reprinted in *Conrad: The Critical Heritage*, ed. Sherry, pp. 210—12.

14. Galsworthy, 'Reminiscences of Conrad', in *Castles in Spain*, p. 89; Watt, p. 50.

15. Crankshaw, *Joseph Conrad*, p. 1.

16. Many examples of the latter tendency are quoted by David Goldknopf, 'What's wrong with Conrad', *Criticism*, 10 (1968), 56–8.

17. M. C. Bradbrook, *Joseph Conrad: Poland's English Genius* (Cambridge University Press, 1941), p. 14.

18. Karl, pp. xiv, xiii.

19. Najder, p. vii.

20. Title of a review article by Jean M. Szczypień in the *Polish Review*, 29 (1984), 89–96.

21. Najder, pp. 99, 100.

22. Watt, p. 93.

23. Watt, p. 93.

24. Najder, p. 19.

25. Morf, p. 300.

26. Knowles, pp. 58, 59; Kirschner, p. 229.

27. Meyer, p. 120.

28. Schwarz, *Conrad*: Almayer's Folly *to* Under Western Eyes, p. 214.

29. Gordan, p. 73.

30. Walpole, *Joseph Conrad*, p. 78. Baines repeats the same image in connection with

*Suspense* which he describes as 'the work of a man whose mind had to proceed on crutches' (*Joseph Conrad: A Critical Biography*, p. 438).

31. See Kirschner, p. 221 and Karl, p. 687n.

32. Knowles, p. 55.

33. Karl, p. 387. After all, his letters are full of complaints about his 'mental impotence' and 'the irresolution and sluggishness of [his] intellect' (*CL*, II, p. 425; III, p. 150).

34. Interestingly, Retinger already noted that Conrad '*prenait son bien où il le trouvait*' (Retinger, p. 90).

35. Kirschner, p. 204.

36. Watt, p. 50 (and p. 93). See also Najder, pp. 205, 394. In their desire to exonerate Conrad from the charge of plagiarism, critics have advanced the most charitable and ingenious speculations. After noting the similarity between the passages describing Ewa's death in Żeromski's *The History of a Sin* and Lena's death in *Victory* – a similarity in content and phrasing 'so remarkable that it precludes mere coincidence' – Busza explains:

> Moreover, the virtual identity of the last sentence suggests, either careful memorial reconstruction, or even some form of direct copying, possibly through an intermediary note. It does not necessarily follow that, at the time of the writing of *Victory*, Conrad was fully aware of the fact that he was plagiarising or, at least, of the extent to which he reproduced Żeromski's text. He could have, for instance, jotted down at some point the final paragraph of Żeromski's novel and used it several years later, having, in the meantime, forgotten completely the origin of the jotting.                     ('Conrad's Polish literary background', p. 217)

37. Kirschner, p. 265 n. 17.

38. Ford, p. 211.

39. This corroborates Ford's statement that Conrad 'was convinced that he would never master English' (Ford, p. 213).

40. Captain Craig of the *Vidar* told Jean-Aubry that when he went down to his chief's cabin for a chat, he usually found him writing (*LL*, I, p. 98). Conrad, it has been suggested, could have been writing letters, or a diary, or trying his hand at creative writing (see Baines, p. 90 and Najder, p. 101). However, Ford's statement that these phrases from the Agricultural Show in *Madame Bovary* were translated when the *Adowa* was immobilized in Rouen harbour suggests that he could also have spent his leisure time at sea doing translations.

41. Ford Madox Ford, *Portraits from Life* (Chicago: Henry Regnery, 1937), p. 83. See also my 'Joseph Conrad and the French language, part one', pp. 245–7.

42. Bernard C. Meyer, '*Language and Being: Joseph Conrad and the Literature of Personality* by Peter J. Glassman', *Literature and Psychology*, 26 (1976), 181.

43. Writing to Garnett on 10 June 1902, Conrad speaks of having lost 'utterly all faith in myself, all sense of style, all belief in my power of telling the simplest fact in a simple way' (*CL*, II, p. 424).

44. Karl, p. 411.

45. Karl, pp. 544, 537–8.

46. Harold Bloom, *The Anxiety of Influence* (New York: Oxford University Press, 1973).

See also Jane Ford, 'James Joyce and the Conrad connection: the anxiety of influence', *Conradiana*, 7 (1985), 3–18.

47. Mallarmé, 'Brise marine' in *Oeuvres complètes: poésies*, critical edn by Carl Paul Barbier and Charles Gordon Millan (Paris: Flammarion, 1983), p. 176.

48. Thomas McFarland, 'Coleridge's plagiarisms once more: a review essay', *Yale Review*, 63 (1974), 252, 268, 272.

49. Quoted by Adam Gillon, 'Some Polish literary motifs in the works of Joseph Conrad', p. 433.

50. McFarland, 'Coleridge's plagiarisms', p. 273.

51. See also *N*, p. xvii. Clearly Conrad endowed his teacher of languages with this personal characteristic when he made him stress that 'to invent the mere bald facts of [Razumov's] life would have been utterly beyond [his] powers' (*UWE*, p. 3; see also *UWE*, p. 100).

52. Gordan, *Joseph Conrad: The Making of a Novelist*, pp. 29, 30.

53. As an example of Conrad's 'susceptibility to his uncle's influence', Meyer quotes his reference, in *A Personal Record*, p. 42, to 'entering a Carthusian monastery', an expression Bobrowski had used in a letter to him of 26 October 1876 (Meyer, p. 29).

54. See *LEG*, p. 20 and Meyer, p. 98. After noting how Conrad, when he learned of Doctor Johnson's habit of collecting dried orange peel, passed through a phase of engaging in that strange practice, Meyer observes: 'This chameleon-like quality was also reflected in his letters in which he colored his language in order to harmonize with the image of his correspondent'.

55. Meyer, pp. 31, 97. See Ford, p. 88.

56. Georges Perec, 'Emprunts à Flaubert', *L'Arc*, 79 (1980), 50.

57. Letter published in the magazine *Thoth*, Syracuse University, Spring 1969. Quoted by Watts, *A Preface to Conrad*, p. 160.

58. Hans van Marle, 'Young Ulysses ashore: on the trail of Konrad Korzeniowski in Marseilles', *L'Epoque conradienne* (May 1976), 28.

59. Watt, p. 89.

60. Sherry, *Conrad's Western World*, p. 177.

61. Alexander Lindey, *Plagiarism and Originality* (Westport, Conn.: Greenwood Press, 1974), p. 66.

62. K. K. Ruthven, *Critical Assumptions* (Cambridge University Press, 1979), p. 106. For instance, Ben Jonson used this image when discussing *imitatio* in *Timber* (1641). 'Imitation' – one of the four requisites in a true poet – he defined as the capacity 'to convert the substance or Riches of another *Poet* to his owne use. [...] Not, to imitate servilely, as *Horace* saith, and catch at vices, for vertue, but to draw forth out of the best, and choisest flowers, with the Bee, and turne all into Honey'. (Quoted by Harold Ogden White, *Plagiarism and Imitation during the English Renaissance* (Harvard University Press, 1935), p. 200.) For a historical survey of the bee as a symbol, see James W. Johnson, 'That neo-classical bee', *Journal of the History of Ideas*, 22 (1961), 262–6.

63. Meyer, p. 362. This is the reply made by the publisher Novello to the charge that Handel had engaged in plagiarism.

64. Possibly at the back of his mind Conrad used as a point of reference Anatole France's 'Apologie pour le plagiat'. France, who prided himself on borrowing from everyone,

argued that while in the seventeenth century plagiarism meant taking the bad along with the good, the chaff with the grain, the real offence was not to take, but to take indiscriminately. The plagiarist is the man 'qui pille sans goût et sans discernement les demeures idéales. [...] Mais quant à l'écrivain qui ne prend chez les autres que ce qui lui est convenable et profitable, et qui sait choisir, c'est un honnête homme.' And his verdict on Molière, who also took from everyone, was: 'tout ce qu'il prend lui appartient aussitôt, parce qu'il y met sa marque'. (VII, pp. 535, 550)

65. T. S. Eliot, 'Tradition and the individual talent' in *Selected Essays*, 3rd enlarged edn (London: Faber and Faber, 1951), p. 15.

66. Lindey, *Plagiarism and originality*, p. 20.

67. English translation of Goethe's *Die Wahlverwandtschaften* (1809).

68. Paul Valéry, 'Stéphane Mallarmé' in *Oeuvres*, La Pléiade (Paris: Gallimard, 1962), I, p. 675. (Original emphasis)

69. Théophile Gautier, *La Préface de Mademoiselle de Maupin* (Paris: Droz, 1946).

70. André Malraux, *Psychologie de l'art*, 3 vols. (Genève: Skira, 1949–50).

71. Quoted by McFarland, 'Coleridge's plagiarisms', p. 269.

72. Quoted in Karl, p. 725.

73. Yelton, p. 114.

74. Karl, p. 341.

75. Watt, p. 268.

76. 'It was only when it dawned upon me that the purloiner of the treasure need not necessarily be a confirmed rogue, that he could be even a man of character, an actor and possibly a victim in the changing scenes of a revolution, it was only then that I had the first vision of a twilight country which was to become the province of Sulaco' (*N*, p. xvii).

77. Philip Oakes, 'Novelists battle for the spoils of war', *Sunday Times*, 18 November 1979, 37.

78. André Gide, *Journal, 1889–1939*, La Pléiade (Paris: Gallimard, 1951), p. 902.

79. Watt, p. 42.

80. Unfortunately, there is no consensus on the meaning and the use of the term 'intertextuality'. In his introduction to *Texte*, 2 (1983), a volume entirely devoted to 'l'intertextualité, intertexte, autotexte, intratexte', Andrew Oliver refers to 'L'anarchie terminologique et conceptuelle' which we all deplore (p. 10). In the opening to *Palimpsestes*, Poétique (Paris: Seuil, 1982), Gérard Genette gives a narrow definition of the term as 'la présence effective d'un texte dans un autre', and he then quotes Riffaterre's much wider definition: 'L'intertexte est la perception, par le lecture, de rapports entre une oeuvre et d'autres qui l'ont précédée ou suivie' (p. 8). By 'hypertextualité' Genette means: 'toute relation unissant un texte B (que j'appellerai *hypertexte*) à un texte antérieur A (que j'appellerai, bien sûr, *hypotexte*) sur lequel il se greffe d'une manière qui n'est pas celle du commentaire' (pp. 11–12).

81. Michel Foucault, Preface to *La Tentation de saint Antoine* (Paris: Livre de Poche, 1971), pp. 11–12 (my translation).

82. Genette, *Palimpsestes*, p. 452 (my translation).

83. Ford. p. 59.

84. T. S. Eliot, *On Poetry and Poets* (London: Faber and Faber, 1957), p. 108. Eliot's

comment was made in connection with John Livingston Lowes's *The Road to Xanadu* (1927), a famous piece of literary detection in respect of Coleridge's borrowings.

**Appendix**

1. This appreciation is confirmed by Dawson's testimony: 'Stendhal he ranked very high; the only book he ever lent me was *Le Rouge et le Noir*', 'Some recollections', 208. Item 58 in the W. Heffer sale catalogue is *La Chartreuse de Parme*.
2. Retinger, p. 107. This definition appears twice in *Le Rouge et le noir*: in v. I, ch. 13 and II, ch. 19.
3. Ford Madox Ford, *The March of Literature*, pp. 783, 782.
4. A distinct reminiscence from *Chatterton*, or probably from Apollo's translation, has been found in *The Nigger of the 'Narcissus'* (see above, p. 47).
5. Jean-Aubry, 'Souvenirs', *NRF*, p. 679.
6. Alfred de Vigny, *Oeuvres complètes*, La Pléiade (Paris: Gallimard, 1960), II, p. 1001.
7. Ivo Vidan, 'Thirteen letters of André Gide to Joseph Conrad', p. 163. (Letter dated 16 October 1921)
8. Alfred de Vigny, *Oeuvres complètes*, II, p. 677.
9. According to André Levinson these tales form the 'breviary' of a doctrine which was also Conrad's: 'Abdiquer sa liberté pour suivre un drapeau, se taire, servir, c'est bien en quoi réside, pour Conrad, la vocation du véritable marin' ('Joseph Conrad est-il un écrivain polonais?' *Nouvelles littéraires*, 7 (4 August 1928), 8).
10. Schwab writes about the episode: 'Thomas Beer, Crane's first biographer, who probably obtained the information directly from Huneker, states that it was Huneker who "ordered" Crane to read Balzac and that "only the contrary opinion of another authority stopped him". This "authority" may well have been Conrad' ('Joseph Conrad's American friend', p. 223).
11. Galsworthy, 'Reminiscences of Conrad' in *Castles in Spain*, p. 91. See letter to Galsworthy, 9 April 1906 (*CL*, III, p. 327).
12. Davray, 'Joseph Conrad', p. 34.
13. Curle, p. 119.
14. Retinger, pp. 108, 102.
15. Ironically, Baines says that, in *Victory*, Heyst's description to Lena of the trio Mr Jones, Ricardo and Pedro 'Here they are before you – evil intelligence, instinctive savagery, arm in arm. The brute force is at the back' (p. 329) is 'reminiscent of Hugo, or Balzac at his worst', when his characters are not individuals but mere abstractions, forces typified as in the following sentence from *La Dernière incarnation de Vautrin*: 'Ces deux hommes, le CRIME et la JUSTICE, se regardèrent' (Baines, p. 398) quoted from Honoré de Balzac, *Oeuvres complètes* (Paris: Conard, 1949), XVI, p. 253).
16. Balzac, *Oeuvres complètes*, VI, pp. 231–2.
17. Baines, p. 145.
18. Symons, '*A Set of Six*', in Keating, *A Conrad Memorial Library*, p. 180.
19. Mégroz, *Joseph Conrad's Mind and Method*, p. 204.
20. Frederick R. Karl, *A Reader's Guide to Joseph Conrad*, p. 56. See also L. J. Morris-

sey, 'The tellers in *Heart of Darkness*: Conrad's Chinese boxes', *Conradiana*, 13 (1981), 141–8.
21. Baines, p. 18. He then quotes the following passage:

> Les volcans lancent des pierres et les révolutions des hommes. Des familles sont ainsi envoyées à de grandes distances, des destinées sont dépaysées, des groupes sont dispersés et s'émiettent, des gens tombent des nues [...]. Ils étonnent les naturels du pays. [...] S'ils restent, on les tolère: s'ils s'en vont, on est content. [...] J'ai vu une pauvre touffe d'herbe lancée éperdument en l'air par une explosion de mine. [...]
> La femme qu'à Guernesey on appelait *la Gilliat* était peut-être cette touffe d'herbe-là.
> La femme vieillit, l'enfant grandit. Ils vivaient seuls, et évités.
> (Victor Hugo, *Oeuvres complètes* (Paris: Le Club français du livre, 1969), XII, pp. 559–60)

22. Baines, p. 267.
23. Visiak, *The Mirror of Conrad* (London: Werner Laurie, 1955), p. 26.
24. Galsworthy, 'Reminiscences of Conrad', in *Castles in Spain*, p. 91. Galsworthy also recorded that Conrad's fondness for Bizet's *Carmen* was almost 'a vice' (p. 110), and Jean-Aubry recalled a letter in which Conrad asked him for 'the libretto of Carmen', the reason for his request being 'his desire that one of his books should form the subject-matter of a lyrical drama' and, as a result, 'he intended looking through several libretti of operas with the literary themes of which he was acquainted, as in the case of Mérimée's *Carmen*' (G. Jean-Aubry, 'Joseph Conrad and music', *The Chesterian*, 6 (1924), 41, quoted by E. C. Bufkin, 'Conrad, grand opera, and *Nostromo*', *Nineteenth-Century Fiction*, 30 (1975), 212.)
25. 'Falk' (January–May 1901) 'is almost pure Zola', according to Karl, who quotes a passage 'which seems to derive from *Germinal*' [cf. *TOS*, pp. 223–4] (Karl, p. 513).
26. Ford, p. 35.
27. These characters, together with Conrad's reference to Daudet's 'Nabobs, his kings, his book-keepers, his Colettes, and his Saphos' (*NLL*, p. 23) make clear that, in addition to the works already cited, he had read the *Tartarin* stories, *Les Rois en exil* (1879), *L'Immortel* (1880), and *Sapho* (1884). It may also be pointed out that Jean Peyrol, the name of the old rover, may be a reminiscence from an episodic character of the same name in *Le Petit Chose* (1868).
28. Jean-Aubry says that what led Conrad to write for *The Outlook* was 'the indignation aroused in him by a derogatory article, published in London' after Daudet's death (*The Sea Dreamer*, p. 233).
29. We only know from Jean-Aubry that Conrad 'reread Daudet' during his stay in Montpellier in 1906 (*The Sea Dreamer*, p. 250), and Curle gathered the impression that he 'was charmed by the artistry of Daudet, although he did not consider Daudet a great figure' (Curle, p. 120). The 'distinguished French writer' whom Conrad quotes in 'Books' and in the Author's Notes to *Chance* and *Within the Tides* complaining that the art of the novelist was 'un art trop difficile' is Daudet, as he explained to Jean-Aubry on 26 August 1920: '"Le roman est un art trop difficile". Cette phrase a été dit par A. Daudet à Henry James au cours d'une discussion

plus ou moins technique, qu'ils ont eu pendant la visite d'Alphonse Daudet en Angleterre' (*LF*, p. 157).

30. Lawrence Graver, *Conrad's Short Fiction*, p. 4.
31. Ford, pp. 16, 103.
32. Baines, p. 145.
33. On 25 June 1908, in a letter to E. Dawson, Conrad contrasted his fate with that of Loti: 'I don't think of the sea now. No one cares about it really, or I would have had as much success here as Loti in France' (*LL*, II, p. 70).
34. Baines, p. 145.
35. All references to *Le Roman d'un spahi* are to the edition published Paris: Calmann-Lévy, [1947].
36. Leavis, *The Great Tradition*, pp. 196–7.
37. All references to *Ramuntcho* are to the edition published Paris: Calmann-Lévy, 1959.
38. Paul Verlaine, *Oeuvres poétiques complètes*, La Pléiade (Paris: Gallimard, 1962), pp. 326–7.
39. Mallarmé, *Oeuvres complètes: poésies*, p. 432.
40. André Gide, *Si le grain ne meurt* (Paris: Editions de la *Nouvelle Revue Française*, 1928), p. 246.
41. For illustrations of all these words and further analysis, see Henri Godin, *Les Ressources stylistiques du français contemporain* (Oxford: Blackwell, 1964), pp. 91–4.
42. Andrzej Tretiak, 'A note on Joseph Conrad', *Revue anglo-américaine*, 12 (1934), 46-7.
43. Ford, p. 94.
44. Retinger, p. 108.
45. *NRF*, p. 661.
46. Karl, p. 725.
47. Retinger, p. 108.
48. The W. Heffer sale catalogue lists the four following items by Gide: *Incidences* (1924); *Isabelle* (1911); *Souvenirs de la Cour d'Assises* (1913); *La Symphonie pastorale* (1919).
49. *NRF*, pp. 679–80.
50. Quoted in Karl, p. 879, which contains a facsimile of this letter of 30 November 1922 between pp. 722 and 723.
51. The W. Heffer sale catalogue shows that Conrad possessed the first five sections of *A la recherche*: *Du côté de chez Swann* (first published by Grasset in 1913; reprinted by the NRF in 1917); *A l'ombre des jeunes filles en fleurs* (1918); *Le Côté de Guermantes* (1920–21); *Sodome et Gomorrhe* (1921–22); *La Prisonnière* (1923). The last two sections, *Albertine disparue* and *Le Temps retrouvé*, were published after Conrad's death, in 1925 and 1927.
52. *NRF*, p. 679.
53. Hart-Davis, *Hugh Walpole*, p. 236.
54. The relevant part of Conrad's letter was published by G. K. Scott Moncrieff in *Marcel Proust: an English tribute* (London: Chatto & Windus, 1923), pp. 126–8, under the title 'Proust as creator'. In view of Conrad's interest in Proust in the last years of his life, the following comments by Albert Guerard on *The Arrow of Gold* (written from November 1917 to June 1918) seem particularly interesting: 'The rich

material in a way seems Proustian rather than Conradian: a story of passions and reticences in a vivid setting of Legitimist conspirators and against a *mondain* past of successful artists and wealthy, corrupt aristocrats.' Guerard then describes obvious differences between the art of the two writers, and concludes: 'These references to Proust, otherwise impertinent, suggest how far afield Conrad went, fictionally, when he tried to dramatize (or tried to understand) the most "romantic" moment of his youth' (*Conrad the Novelist*, p. 279).

55. Retinger, p. 108.

56. Retinger, pp. 108–9.

57. We recall that in 1895 Conrad told Emilie Briquel that he liked Hugo's poetry. The epigraph for *Romance*: 'C'est toi qui dors dans l'ombre, ô sacré Souvenir' is the last line of his 'Tristesse d'Olympio'. Also quoted by Ford as the epigraph for Part One in *Joseph Conrad: A Personal Remembrance*.

58. As Yelton points out (Yelton, p. 274), the reference to *victime et bourreau* in his letter of 20 July? 1894 to Mme Poradowska (*CL*, I, p. 162) looks like an echo of the poet's remark in 'Mon coeur mis à nu' that 'Il serait peut-être doux d'être alternativement *victime et bourreau*' (Baudelaire, I, p. 676). Karl has also suggested (Karl, p. 365) that Conrad may have been alluding to Baudelaire when, in *The Sisters* (September 1895–April 1896), he wrote of Stephen: 'He resolved to return to the cities, amongst men; not because of what the poet said about solitude in a crowd; but from an inward sense of his difference from the majority of mankind' (pp. 60–1). In his 'Edgar Poe, sa vie et ses oeuvres', Baudelaire refers to 'Certains esprits, solitaires au milieu de la foule' (Baudelaire, II, pp. 307–8).

59. Edward W. Said, *Joseph Conrad and the Fiction of Autobiography* (Cambridge, Mass.: Harvard University Press, 1966), p. 124. [Abbreviated Said]

60. Baudelaire, II, p. 308.

61. Apparently, the first reference to this title comes in a letter to George Harvey dated 15 April 1904: 'For title I thought of: *A Seaman's Sketches* or if a more general effect is desired *Mirror of the Sea*' (*CL*, III, p. 132).

62. Yelton, pp. 274, 303. The poem is *Spleen et idéal*, p. 14.

63. However, it is fair to add that Conrad could have come across the metaphor 'le miroir de la mer' more than once in *Pêcheur d'Islande*. (See above p. 239)

64. *Spleen et idéal*, p. 4.

65. *Spleen et idéal*, p. 47.

66. Conrad also read in *Salammbô*: 'Sur les montagnes, de grandes fleurs, pleines de parfums qui fument, se balancent comme d'éternels encensoirs' (p. 265), a simile which may well derive from Baudelaire.

67. *La Mort*, p. 126.

68. 'Le Gouffre', Baudelaire, I, pp. 142–3. See 'Le gouffre de Baudelaire', in Pierre Guiraud, *Essais de stylistique* (Paris: Klincksieck, 1969), pp. 87–94.

69. The importance of the imagery of the fall and the abyss in Conrad's early and middle work has often been commented upon (see, for instance, Albert Cook, 'Conrad's void', *Nineteenth-Century Fiction*, 12 (1958), 326–7; Tony Tanner, 'Mountains and depths: an approach to nineteenth-century dualism', *Review of English Literature*, 3 (1962), 51–61; Yelton, chapter 7; Sanford J. Smoller, 'A note on Joseph Conrad's fall and abyss', *Modern Fiction Studies*, 15 (1969), 261–4). Tanner is particularly

helpful in reminding us that, in the nineteenth century, 'the mountain-depths meta-phor' is not merely part of the texture of the mind of a few individuals, like Baude-laire and Conrad (and Flaubert, from whom Conrad borrowed twice the image of the abyss, see above, pp. 20 and 101), but is an expression of 'the Cartesian dichotomy of mind and matter [which] has become part of the landscape of the nineteenth–century mind' ('Mountains and depths', pp. 60, 61).

70. Dabrowski, 'An interview with Joseph Conrad', p. 372.

71. *Spleen et idéal*, p. 69. Yelton has pointed out the relevance of the epigraph: '"le bon vent" may be taken to identify the natural agency which shatters, in the novel, the enchanted mirror, the "calme plat" which lies at the center of the work and which reflects, if not Baudelaire's "désespoir", then something very like it – a "sense of life-emptiness" whose "evil influence" and "bitter plausibility" define the narrator's state at the outset of his adventure (p. 49), and which finds its objective correlative in the becalmed sea and the ship immobilized or capriciously tossed about without direction' (Yelton, pp. 303-4).

72. In a letter to K. Waliszewski of 5 December 1903, Conrad said: 'Homo duplex has in my case more than one meaning' (*CL*, III, p. 89). The fact which prompted this confidence is that although his point of view on both land and sea was English, he himself was not. Apart from the obvious Polish-English duality and the dualities already mentioned, Conrad could have had in mind such oppositions as practical man and dreamer, romantic and realist, conservative and sceptic.

73. Said, p. 124.

74. Baudelaire, I, p. 682.

75. Yelton, p. 30.

76. Watt, p. 185.

77. Watt, p. 186.

78. Watt, pp. 198–9.

79. Yelton, p. 30.

80. Aniela Kowalska, *Conrad 1896–1900: strategia wrażeń i refleksji w narracjach Marlowa* [*Patterns of Impressions and Reflections in Marlow's Narratives*] (Lódź: Society of Arts and Science', 1973), pp. 35, 43–81.

81. Charles Whibley, 'A vagabond poet', *Blackwood's Magazine*, 165, (1899), 402–12.

82. The W. Heffer sale catalogue mentions that the copy of Rimbaud's *Oeuvres* (pub-lished in the spring of 1898), 'wants binding'. This may be an example of 'Conrad's carelessness in his treatment of books', as the catalogue records in connection with France's *La Révolte des anges*, or an indication that the book had been well used.

83. Kowalska notes 'the striking presence of an "infernal" imagery in Conrad's letters of the period when the idea of *Heart of Darkness* was emerging ("May all the infernal Gods look upon You with favour; and may all the men who are food for Hell shake their heads at your words and gestures" [*CL*, II, pp. 133–4])'. The quotations from this critic's *Conrad 1896–1900* are taken from her summary in English, pp. 127–8.

84. Indeed, a few years later, Conrad referred in *A Personal Record* to 'the poet as the seer *par excellence*' (p. 93).

85. Retinger, p. 109.

86. Conrad to Gide, 28 December 1922, Bibliothèque Doucet, Paris, quoted in Najder,

p. 472. In 'Des heures anglaises ...' (*Cahiers du Sud*, 1946, 135), Jean-Aubry recollected:

> Un soir, Joseph Conrad, auquel j'avais prêté *Charmes* qui l'avait vivement frappé, vint lui rendre visite, après dîner chez ses hôtes qui étaient également des amis du grand romancier. Une sympathie immédiate et vive fut la conséquence de cette première rencontre et les deux hommes se séparèrent sur la promesse, en un prochain voyage, d'une visite à Bishopsbourne où vivait Conrad.

87. Jean-Aubry, 'Des heures anglaises ...', p. 136, and Paul Valéry, 'Sujet d'une conversation avec Conrad', *NRF*, pp. 663–5. The precise and difficult problem Conrad and Valéry were discussing was: 'Pourquoi et comment la France n'a-t-elle pu jamais s'assurer la suprématie de la mer?' Valéry explains:

> Conrad avait sur cette question une opinion singulière. Il remarquait que dans un grand nombre de combats *individuels* c'est-à-dire de navire isolé à navire isolé, – livrés à la fin de l'ancien Régime et sous l'Empire, quand les forces des deux navires engagés étaient comparables, le Français avait pris généralement le dessus.
>
> Il observait le contraire dans les rencontres d'escadres. Il en déduisait que *quelque chose* dans ces engagements collectifs venait gêner la valeur personnelle de nos hommes, et l'empêcher de développer sa supériorité. Il accusait les instructions de Versailles. Nos amiraux, selon lui, recevait du pouvoir central des recommendations expresses de ménager les oeuvres vives de l'ennemi et d'en capturer les vaisseaux plutôt que de viser à les détruire. En conséquence, nous envoyions nos bordées dans les gréements et les batteries. Mais l'Anglais tirait à couler ...
>
> Je ne sais où Conrad avait puisé ce renseignement. J'ignore ce qu'il vaut. (p. 664)

But for the reference to the 'instructions de Versailles', Conrad could have drawn this information from *La Bataille navale: études sur les facteurs tactiques* (Paris: Berger-Levrault, 1912) by A. Baudry – the book which heads the list of volumes from his library in the Heffer catalogue. For instance, on page 100 he could have read: 'Il semble que toujours, sur mer, l'attitude offensive nous fut plus favorable, nous mit mieux en valeur, que le long combat traînant. Les Anglais craignaient fort notre abordage: bateau à bateau, le long du bord, ils ne se sentaient plus à égalité.' On page 147, Baudry refers to 'les méthodes "à démâter" du tir franco-espagnol' [at Trafalgar], and on page 158 he explains: 'A Trafalgar, les Anglais tirent en plein bois, en pleine coque, en pleine masse humaine; les Français à démâter, aux goélands, ou à couler bas, aux scombres,' and he mentions Nelson's familiar signal: 'combattre à toucher!'. These points are again taken up on page 234.

88. Saint-John Perse, *Oeuvres complètes*, La Pléiade (Paris: Gallimard, 1972), p. 886.

89. Roger Little, 'Saint-John Perse and Joseph Conrad: some notes and an uncollected letter', *Modern Language Review*, 72 (1977), 813.

90. Ford, p. 201.

91. Baines suggests he may have seen the first two performed in Marseilles (Baines, p. 35). E. C. Bufkin notes that Jean-Aubry was more certain than Baines about this matter: Conrad 'often found delight in recalling the evenings he had spent [...] at the Marseilles Opera. [...] Although 50 years, or very nearly, had elapsed since

then, he had kept of that time most accurate recollections and he retained a very correct impression of Meyerbeer's or Verdi's operas, as well as of Offenbach's operettas which were then in the fashion and which he had had an opportunity of hearing.' Conrad never lost his taste for Giacomo Meyerbeer (1791–1864), the principal composer of grand opera, for, in June 1910, he confessed to Galsworthy: 'I suppose that I am now the only human being in these Isles who thinks Myerbeer a great composer' (*LL*, II, p. 110). It is noteworthy that the libretti of the four operas, *Robert le Diable*, *Les Huguenots*, *Le Prophète*, *L'Africaine*, on which Meyerbeer's reputation rests, were all written by Scribe. (See Bufkin, 'Conrad, grand opera, and *Nostromo*', pp. 208, 209.)

92. A translation of Rostand's *Cyrano de Bergerac* had been published in July 1898 by William Heinemann, so Conrad may have read that and not the original.

93. However, Conrad's familiarity with Brunetière's writings through the copies of the *Revue des deux mondes* sent to him by his 'chère Tante' gives weight to Said's suggestion that Conrad probably knew his 'La Philosophie de Schopenhauer et les conséquences du pessimisme', in *Essais sur la littérature contemporaine* (1892), although it was not necessarily, as Said also suggests, his first encounter with Schopenhauerian ideas (Said, p. 102).

94. *NRF*, p. 669.

95. Eloise Knapp Hay, 'Impressionism limited', p. 62. See Ferdinand Brunetière, *Le Roman naturaliste*, p. 102.

96. *NRF*, p. 661. Lemaître's brilliant, impressionistic, and often ironical articles were published in collected form in *Les Contemporains* (vols. 1–7, Paris, 1886–99; vol. 8, 1918) and *Impressions de théâtre* (vols. 1–10, Paris, 1888–98; vol. 11, 1920).

97. Henri Ghéon, *Nos directions* (Paris: Editions de la *Nouvelle Revue Française*, 1911), recorded as item 28 in the W. Heffer sale catalogue. Item 27 is Ghéon's *Le Pain: tragédie populaire* (Paris, 1912).

98. Jean-Pierre Cap, 'A Conrad letter to Henri Ghéon', *Conradiana*, 8 (1976), 220.

99. J. M. Kertzer says that Conrad, whose 'skepticism often recalls the [Frenchman's] epigrams', 'must have found in them a kindred but subtly different spirit'. Conrad, he finds, is 'less bitter than La Rochefoucauld, and more compassionate' (Kertzer, '"The bitterness of our wisdom": cynicism, skepticism and Joseph Conrad', *Novel*, 16 (1983), 128–31).

100. See Bruce Johnson's discussion of Pascal as one of Conrad's 'existential models' in *Conrad's Models of Mind* (Minneapolis: University of Minnesota Press, 1971).

101. Fleishman, *Conrad's Politics*, p. 231.

102. In a letter to Emilie Briquel of 14 November 1895 Conrad sends his regards to 'ce brave "Notaire Savoyard"', obviously a person who 'must have reminded [him] and his friends of the unctuously benevolent Vicaire Savoyard' in *L'Emile* (*CL*, I, p. 255).

103. See David L. Higdon, 'Conrad and Amiel', *Joseph Conrad Today*, 3 (1977), 66–7, and Watt, p. 66.

104. John E. Saveson, *Joseph Conrad: The Making of a Moralist* (Amsterdam: Rodopi NV, 1972), pp. 109, 110, 114. The chapter is entitled 'Contemporary psychology in *The Nigger of the "Narcissus"*' and was first published under that title in *Studies in Short Fiction*, 7 (1970), 219–31. The relevant work by Ribot is *La Psychologie*

*des sentiments* (Paris: Alcan, 1896) translated as *The Psychology of the Emotions* (London: Walter Scott, 1897). A number of assertions made by Ribot in this work are examined in Redmond O'Hanlon's *Joseph Conrad and Charles Darwin*. Also of interest here are Watt's pages on contemporary sociology. For instance, he points out that 'The tensions between conflicting group allegiances on board the *Narcissus* are [...] treated in a way which is very close to the thought of [...] Emile Durkheim, and particularly that of his first book, *De la division du travail social*' (Paris, 1893), and that 'Conrad's treatment of the psychology of the crew of the *Narcissus* is also similar to yet another celebrated work of the period, Gustave Le Bon's *La Psychologie des foules* (1895)' (Watt, pp. 113, 115).

105. Wolfgang B. Fleischmann, 'Conrad's *Chance* and Bergson's *Laughter*', *Renascence*, 14 (1962), 66–71.
106. Ford, p. 59.
107. Ford, p. 88.
108. Quotation from Mazarin.
109. 'Don terrible de la familiarité', Mirabeau, *Letters*. On 27 June 1904, Conrad had already adapted the phrase in his wry comment to William Rothenstein, who was raising money to support him: 'Je n'ai pas le don terrible de la popularité' (*CL*, III, p. 147).
110. Conrad concluded 'Autocracy and War' with Gambetta very much in mind: 'the once-famous saying of poor Gambetta, tribune of the people (who was simple and believed in the "immanent justice of things") may be adapted in the shape of a warning that, so far as a future of liberty, concord, and justice is concerned: "*Le Prussianisme – voilà l'ennemi!*"' (*NLL*, pp. 113–14). Gambetta's formula was '*Le cléricalisme, voilà l'ennemi!*' (According to *Bentham's Book of Quotations* (London: Harrap, 1962, p. 746b) the formula was coined by Alphonse Peyrat in a speech, 1859).
111. See Meyer, p. 310.
112. Richard Curle, 'Joseph Conrad: ten years after', *Virginia Quarterly Review*, 10 (1934), 421. (Reprinted in the *Fortnightly Review*, new series 136 (1934), 189–99.)
113. Ford, pp. 60–1.
114. Curle, p. 223. Sherry has discovered notes made by Conrad on 12 February 1898 on the Siege and Fall of Paris in 1870–71, which closely follow contemporary accounts of this historical event, such as those of Henry Labouchère: *Diary of the Besieged Resident in Paris* (London, 1872). It is not clear what he intended to do with these notes, but Sherry speculates that he took them with him when visiting the Cranes at 'Ravensbrook' a week later 'in the hope that they might collaborate on a novel centred round this subject' ('A Conrad manuscript', *TLS*, 25 June 1970, 691).
115. See Baines, p. 406. (Letter to Colvin, 2 April 1917, Yale.) In *Un aide de camp de Napoléon (de 1800 à 1812): mémoires du Général Comte de Ségur* (Paris: Firmin-Didot, 1895) translated by H. A. Patchett-Martin (London: Hutchinson, 1895), Philippe-Paul de Ségur narrates how, during the battle of Austerlitz, when a wing of the Russian Army was retreating across a frozen lake, thousands of men fell through the ice; then comes what could be the relevant passage:

Indeed, we who were charging them, stopped short in pity at the sight of this terrible and novel spectacle; some of us even holding out a helping hand to those drowning men. As I passed by I pulled out a Cossack from the frozen water. Little did I then think that the following year, after having first taken part in the conquest of Naples and the Calabrias, then in that of Prussia, very far from these lakes I should meet with him again, and that, wounded myself, and a prisoner in the centre of Poland, I should be recognised and succoured in my turn by this Tartar! (pp. 255–6)

116. According to Ford, they even 'contemplated' and 'talked for years' of a collaboration 'which was to have been about the execution – or rather the escape – of Marshal Ney after Waterloo' (*Return to Yesterday* (London: Gollancz, 1931), p. 198).

117. During this stay in Montpellier Conrad wrote 'The Duel'. In his Author's Note (1920) he declared that the story stemmed from 'a ten-line paragraph in a small provincial paper published in the South of France' and that he had had to 'invent' everything else, including the 'futile pretext' (*SS*, p. viii) for the series of duels between two officers in Napoleon's Grand Army which forms the basis of the story. However, J. De Lancey Ferguson has drawn a revealing parallel between 'The Duel' and the version of the episode that appeared in *Harper's Magazine* in September 1858, which was 'obviously a close paraphrase from some French newspaper', providing incontrovertible evidence that Conrad had found in print not only 'the mere germ of the story but its whole outline' including the 'futile pretext'. ('The plot of Conrad's *The Duel*', *Modern Language Notes*, 50 (1935), 385–90).

In 'Conrad's "The Duel"', Donald Cross demonstrates that the original source was *L'Audience*, 1858. He concludes that whether Conrad first saw the story in French or English still remained an open question (*TLS*, 15 August 1968, 881).

118. Jean-Aubry, *The Sea Dreamer* (p. 279) mentions: G. Gourgaud, *Sainte-Hélène* (1889); Stendhal, *Vie de Napoléon* (1876); M. Pellet, *Napoléon à l'île d'Elbe* (1888); P. Gruyer, *Napoléon, roi de l'île d'Elbe* (1906); J. Rapp, *Mémoires écrits par lui-même* (1823); L. Lanzac de Laborie, *Paris sous Napoléon*, 8 vols. (1905–13).

119. Lots 102 to 106. In addition, the W. Heffer sale catalogue shows that Conrad owned Benjamin Constant's *Mémoires sur la vie privée de Napoléon, sa famille et sa cour* (Paris, n.d.).

120. Mildred Atkinson is often wrongly credited with this discovery. Jean-Aubry was first alerted by Conrad himself who revealed the source of the characters of Marquis d'Armand and his daughter Adèle. In 'The inner history of Conrad's *Suspense*', he wrote:

> Even if I had not myself had the assurance of these facts in the course of several conversations with Joseph Conrad himself, it would be easy to determine by the precision of the details for whom these two personages as well as the Count of Montevesso stand. The novelist obviously borrowed them from the *Mémoires de la Comtesse de Boigne* (*Bookman's Journal*, 13 no. 49 (1925), 7).

Jean-Aubry took up this subject again in '*Suspense*', in Keating, *A Conrad Memorial Library*, pp. 351–7. See also Mildred Atkinson, 'Conrad's *Suspense*', *TLS*, 25 February 1926, 142; Léonie Villard, 'A Conrad heroine in real life', *Living Age*, 328

(1926), 637–9, and 'Joseph Conrad et les mémorialistes (à propos de *Suspense*)', *Revue anglo-américaine*, 3 (1926), 313–21; Miriam H. Wood, 'A source of Conrad's *Suspense*', *Modern Language Notes*, 50 (1935), 390–4; Baines, pp. 436–8.

# Bibliography

**Primary literature**

*Joseph Conrad*

*Collected Edition of the Works of Joseph Conrad*, 21 vols. London: Dent, 1947–55.

*The Collected Letters of Joseph Conrad*, I – III [1861–1907] (and in progress), edited by Frederick R. Karl and Laurence Davies. Cambridge: Cambridge University Press, 1983–8. [Abbreviated *CL*]

*Conrad to a Friend: 150 Selected Letters from Joseph Conrad to Richard Curle*, edited with an introduction and notes by Richard Curle. London: Sampson Low, Marston, 1928. [Abbreviated *LRC*]

*Conrad's Polish Background: Letters to and from Polish Friends*, edited by Zdzisław Najder and translated by Halina Carroll. London: Oxford University Press, 1964

'Huit lettres inédites de Joseph Conrad à Robert d'Humières traducteur du *Nigger of the "Narcissus"* en français', edited by Yves Guérin, *Revue de littérature comparée*, 44 (1970), 367–92. [Abbreviated Guérin]

*Joseph Conrad and Warrington Dawson: The Record of a Friendship*, edited by Dale B. J. Randall. Durham, NC: Duke University Press, 1968. [Abbreviated JWCD]

*Joseph Conrad: Life & Letters*, by G. Jean-Aubry, 2 vols. London: Heinemann, 1927. [Abbreviated *LL*]

*Joseph Conrad's Letters to R. B. Cunninghame Graham*, edited by C. T. Watts. Cambridge: Cambridge University Press, 1969. [Abbreviated *LCG*]

*Letters from Joseph Conrad, 1895–1924*, edited with an introduction and notes by Edward Garnett. Indianapolis: Bobbs-Merrill, 1928. [Abbreviated *LEG*]

*Letters to William Blackwood and David S. Meldrum*, edited by William Blackburn. Durham, NC: Duke University Press, 1958. [Abbreviated *LBM*]

*Lettres de Joseph Conrad à Marguerite Poradowska*, edited by René Rapin with a study of the French of Joseph Conrad. Genève: Droz, 1966 (Publns de la Faculté des Lettres de l'Université de Lausanne, 17) [Abbreviated *LMP*]

*Lettres françaises*, with introduction and notes by G. Jean-Aubry. Paris: Gallimard, 1930 (nrf) [Abbreviated *LF*]

*The Nigger of the 'Narcissus'*. Garden City, NY: Doubleday, Page, 1914. (Incl. 'To my readers in America', pp. ix–x)

'Proust as creator' in *Marcel Proust: An English Tribute*, collected by G. K. Scott Moncrieff (London: Chatto & Windus, 1923), pp. 126–8

*The Sisters: An Unfinished Story*, with an introduction by Ford Madox Ford, edited by Ugo Mursia. Milan: Mursia, 1968

*Ultimi romanzi: Vittoria e romanzi mediterranei*, edited by Ugo Mursia, introduction by

Franco Marenco. Milano: Mursia, 1977. (Tutte le opere narrative di Joseph Conrad, 4)
*Youth: A Narrative; and Two Other Stories.* London: Blackwood, 1902


*Other writers in English*

Labouchère, Henry, *Diary of the Besieged Resident in Paris*, 3rd edn. London: Macmillan, 1872. [Reprinted from *The Daily News* (August 1870 – January 1871), with several new letters and a preface]
Masterman, George Frederick, *Seven Eventful Years in Paraguay.* London: Sampson Low, Son, and Marston, 1869
Trollope, Anthony, *An Autobiography*, 2 vols. Edinburgh and London: Blackwood, 1883
Wells, H. G., *Experiment in Autobiography*, 2 vols. London: Victor Gollancz/Cresset Press, 1934


*French writers*

Balzac, Honoré de, *La Dernière incarnation de Vautrin.* Paris: Conard, 1949 (Oeuvres complètes, XVI)
*Le Père Goriot.* Paris: Conard, 1949 (Oeuvres complètes, VI)
Baudelaire, Charles, *Oeuvres complètes*, edited by Claude Pichois, 2 vols. Paris: Gallimard, 1975–76. (La Pléiade)
Baudry, A., *La Bataille navale: études sur les facteurs tactiques.* Paris: Berger-Levrault, 1912
Constant, Benjamin, *Adolphe*, edited with introduction by Jacques Henry Bornecque. Paris: Garnier, 1960. (Classiques Garnier)
*Journal intime de Benjamin Constant, et lettres à sa famille et à ses amis*, with an introduction by D. Melagari. Paris: Ollendorf, 1895
Durkheim, Emile, *De la division du travail social: étude sur l'organisation des sociétés supérieures.* Paris: Alcan, 1893
Flaubert, Gustave, *Correspondance*, 4 vols. Paris: Charpentier, 1887–93
*Correspondance*, edited by Jean Bruneau, vol. 1– (in progress). Paris: Gallimard, 1973– (La Pléiade)
*Extraits de la correspondance ou Préface à la vie d'écrivain*, edited by Geneviève Bollème. Paris: Seuil, 1963
*Lettres de Gustave Flaubert à George Sand*, with a study by Guy de Maupassant. Paris: Charpentier, 1884
*Madame Bovary*, edited by C. Gothot-Mersch. Paris: Garnier, 1971
*Oeuvres complètes*, 28 vols. Paris: Conard, 1921–54. (Incl. *Correspondance*)
*La Tentation de saint Antoine*, with a preface by Michel Foucault. Paris: Livre de Poche, 1971
France, Anatole, *Oeuvres complètes illustrées*, 25 vols. Paris: Calmann-Lévy, 1925–35
Galiani, Ferdinando, *Correspondance inédite de l'abbé Ferdinand Galiani*, 2 vols. Paris: Treuttel et Würtz, 1818
Garneray, Louis, *Voyages, aventures et combats.* Paris: Nelson, [n.d.]
Gautier, Théophile, *La Préface de Mademoiselle de Maupin.* Paris: Droz, 1946

Ghéon, Henri, *Nos directions: réalisme et poésie*. Paris: Editions de la *Nouvelle Revue Française*, 1911

Gide, André, *Journal, 1899–1939*. Paris: Gallimard, 1951. (La Pléiade)

*Si le grain ne meurt*. Paris: Editions de la *Nouvelle Revue Française*, 1928

'Thirteen letters of André Gide to Joseph Conrad', edited by Ivo Vidan, *Studia Romanica et Anglica Zagrabiensia*, 24 (1967), 145–68

Goncourt, Edmond et Jules de, *Journal: mémoires de la vie littéraire*, edited by Robert Ricatte. Paris: Fasquelle [et] Flammarion, 1956. (Vol. 1: 1851–1863)

Hugo, Victor, *Oeuvres complètes*, edited under the direction of Jean Massin, 18 vols. Paris: Le Club français du livre, 1967–70. (Vol. 12 incl. *Les Travailleurs de la mer*, pp. 483–821)

La Bruyère, Jean de, *Oeuvres complètes*, edited by Julien Benda. Paris: Gallimard, 1951. (La Pléiade)

Le Bon, Gustave, *Psychologie des foules*. Paris: Alcan, 1895

Lemaître, Jules, *Les Contemporains: études et portraits littéraires*, 8 vols. Paris: Lecène et Oudin, 1886–1918

*Impressions de théâtre*, 11 vols. Paris: Lecène et Oudin, 1888–1920

Loti, Pierre, *Mon frère Yves*. Paris: Calmann-Lévy, 1965

*Pêcheur d'Islande*. Paris: Calmann-Lévy, 1962

*Ramuntcho*. Paris: Calmann-Lévy, 1959

*Le Roman d'un spahi*. Paris: Calmann-Lévy, [1947]

Mallarmé, Stéphane, *Oeuvres complètes: poésies*, edited by Carl Paul Barbier and Charles Gordon Millan. Paris: Flammarion, 1983. (Incl. 'Brise marine', p. 176, and 'Toute l'âme résumée', p. 432)

Maupassant, Guy de, *Chroniques*, 3 vols. Paris: Union Générale d'Editions, 1980. (10/18) (Incl. 'Gustave Flaubert' [reprinted from *La République des lettres*, 22.10.1876] I, pp. 17–23; 'Par-delà', II, pp. 399–407; 'Gustave Flaubert' [reprinted from Gustave Flaubert, *Lettres à George Sand* (Paris: Charpentier, 1884)], III, pp. 77–124)

'Etude sur Gustave Flaubert' (1885), in *Madame Bovary*, by Gustave Flaubert (Paris: Conard, 1930), pp. 540–55. [Alternative title to 'Gustave Flaubert (1884)']

*Oeuvres complètes*, 29 vols. Paris: Conard, 1909–30.

*Stories from de Maupassant*, translated by E[lsie] M[artindale], preface by Ford M. Hueffer. London: Duckworth, 1903. (Greenback library, 8)

Mérimée, Prosper, *Romans et nouvelles de Prosper Mérimée*, edited by Maurice Parturier, 2 vols. Faris: Garnier, 1967

Pascal, Blaise, *Opuscules et pensées*, with introduction and notes by M. Léon Brunschvicg. Paris: Hachette, 1897

Perse, Saint-John, *Oeuvres complètes*. Paris: Gallimard, 1972. (La Pléiade)

Proust, Marcel, *A la recherche du temps perdu*, edited by Pierre Clarac and André Ferré, 3 vols. Paris: Gallimard, 1954. (La Pléiade)

Ribot, Théodule, *La Psychologie des sentiments*. Paris: Alcan, 1896. [Translated as *The Psychology of the Emotions* (London: Walter Scott, 1897)]

Rostand, Edmond, *Cyrano de Bergerac*, translated from the French by Gladys Thomas and M. F. Guillemard. London: Heinemann, 1898

Savine, Albert, *Abordages d'un marin de la République: souvenirs de Louis Garneray*. Paris: Louis-Michaud, 1912

Ségur, Philippe-Paul, comte de, *Un aide de camp de Napoléon (de 1800 à 1812): mémoires du Général Comte de Ségur*, new edition. Paris: Firmin-Didot, 1895. [Translated as *An Aide-de-camp of Napoleon (from 1800 to 1812): Memoirs of General Count de Ségur*, new edition translated by H. A. Patchett-Martin. London: Hutchinson, 1895]

Stendhal, *Le Rouge et le noir*. Paris: Gallimard, 1972. (Colln Folio)

Valéry, Paul, *Oeuvres*, edited by Jean Hytier, 2 vols. Paris: Gallimard, 1962. (La Pléiade) (Vol. I incl. 'Lettre sur Mallarmé', pp. 633–43; 'Stéphane Mallarmé, pp. 660–80; 'Fragments des Mémoires d'un poème', pp. 1,464–91)

Verlaine, Paul, *Oeuvres poétiques complètes*, edited by Y.-G. Le Dantec, completed and revised edition by Jacques Borel. Paris: Gallimard, 1962. (La Pléiade) (Incl. 'Art poétique', pp. 326–7)

Vigny, Alfred de, *Oeuvres complètes*, edited by F. Baldensperger, 2 vols. Paris: Gallimard, 1960–64. (La Pléiade)

Zola, Emile, *Les Rougon-Macquart*, edited under the direction of Armand Lanoux, 5 vols. Paris: Gallimard, 1960–67. (La Pléiade)


## Secondary literature

### Books

Albalat, Antoine, *Le Travail du style enseigné par les corrections manuscrites des grands écrivains*. Paris: Colin, 1903

Allott, Miriam, *Novelists on the Novel*. London: Routledge and Kegan Paul / New York: Columbia University Press, 1959

*Analyses & réflexions sur "Une vie" de Guy de Maupassant et le pessimisme*, by Marcel Desportes [and others]. Ligugé: Edition Marketing, 1979

Auerbach, Erich, *Mimesis: The Representation of Reality in Western Literature*, translated from the German by Willard R. Trask. Princeton, NJ: Princeton University Press, 1968

Baillot, Alexandre, *Influence de la philosophie de Schopenhauer en France, 1860–1900: étude suivie d'un essai sur les sources françaises de Schopenhauer*. Paris: Vrin, 1927

Baines, Jocelyn, *Joseph Conrad: A Critical Biography*. London: Weidenfeld and Nicolson, 1960. [Abbreviated Baines]

Baker, Ernest A., *History of the English Novel*. London: Witherby, 1936. Vol. 10: *Yesterday*.

Barthes, Roland, *Critical Essays*, translated from the French by Richard Howard. Evanston, Ill.: Northwestern University Press, 1972. (Incl. 'The two criticisms', pp. 249–54)

*Writing Degree Zero*, translated from the French by Annette Lavers and Colin Smith. London: Cape, 1967

Batchelor, John, *The Edwardian Novelists*. London: Duckworth, 1982

Beach, J. W., *The Twentieth Century Novel: Studies in Technique*. New York: Appleton-Century-Crofts, 1932

Bendz, Ernst, *Joseph Conrad: An Appreciation*. Gothenburg: Gumpert, 1923

Bloom, Harold, *The Anxiety of Influence: A Theory of Poetry*. New York: Oxford University Press, 1973

Bonwit, Marianne, *Gustave Flaubert et le principe d'impassibilité*. Berkeley: University of California Press, 1950. (University of California Publns in Modern Philology, 33)

Booth, Wayne C., *The Rhetoric of Fiction*. Chicago: University of Chicago Press, 1961

Bourgeois, Léon, *Solidarité*. Paris: Colin, 1896

Bradbrook, M. C., *Joseph Conrad: Poland's English Genius*. Cambridge: Cambridge University Press, 1941

Brandes, Georg, *Poland: A Study of the Land, People, and Literature*. London: Heinemann, 1903

Brombert, Victor, *The Intellectual Hero*. London: Faber and Faber, 1962

*The Novels of Flaubert*. Princeton, NJ: Princeton University Press, 1966

*La Prison romantique: essai sur l'imaginaire*. Paris: Corti, 1975

Bruneau, Jean, 'La Présence de Flaubert dans *L'Education sentimentale*', in *Langages de Flaubert*, edited by Michael Issacharoff (Paris: Lettres Modernes, Minard, 1976), pp. 33–51

Brunetière, Ferdinand, *Essais sur la littérature contemporaine*, 2nd edn. Paris: Calmann Lévy, 1892. (Incl. 'La Philosophie de Schopenhauer et les conséquences du pessimisme', pp. 57–80)

*Le Roman naturaliste*. Paris: Calmann Lévy, 1883. (Incl. 'L'*Impressionisme* dans le roman', pp. 75–104)

Camus, Albert, *Essais*, edited by R. Quilliot and L. Faucon. Paris: Gallimard, 1965. (La Pléiade) (Théâtre, récits, nouvelles, 2)

Chevalier, Haakon M., *The Ironic Temper: Anatole France and his Time*. New York: Oxford University Press, 1932

Colin, René-Pierre, *Schopenhauer en France: un mythe naturaliste*. Lyon: Presses Universitaires de Lyon, 1979

Conrad, Jessie, *Joseph Conrad as I Knew Him*, with an introduction by Richard Curle. London: Heinemann / Garden City, NY: Doubleday Page, 1926

Conard, Mark, *Modernism and Authority: Strategies of Legitimation in Flaubert and Conrad*. Baltimore and London: Johns Hopkins University Press, 1985 ·

Crankshaw, Edward, *Joseph Conrad: Some Aspects of the Art of the Novel*. London: John Lane, The Bodley Head, 1936. [Reprinted New York: Russell & Russell, 1963]

Crompton, John ed., *Wit Tarnawski: The Man, the Writer, the Pole*. London: The Joseph Conrad Society (UK), 1976. (Incl. Wit Tarnawski, '*Nostromo* and Flaubert's *Salammbô*', pp. 18–21)

Culler, Jonathan, *Flaubert: The Uses of Uncertainty*. London: Elek / Ithaca, NY: Cornell University Press, 1974

Curle, Richard, *Joseph Conrad: A Study*. London: Kegan Paul, Trench, Trübner / Garden City, NY: Doubleday, Page, 1914

*Joseph Conrad and his Characters: A Study of Six Novels*. London: Heinemann, 1957. [Reprinted New York: Russell & Russell, 1968]

*The Last Twelve Years of Joseph Conrad*. London: Sampson Low, Marston / Garden City, NY: Doubleday Page, 1928. [Reprinted New York: Russell & Russell, 1968] [Abbreviated Curle]

*Currents of Thought in French Literature: Essays in Memory of G. T. Clapton*, edited by T. V. Benn and others. Oxford: Blackwell, 1965. (Incl. G. Hainsworth, 'Schopenhauer, Flaubert, Maupassant: conceptual thought and artistic "truth"', pp. 165–90)

Danger, Pierre, *Sensations et objets dans le roman de Flaubert*. Paris: Colin, 1973

Dargan, E. P., *Anatole France, 1844–1896*. New York and Toronto: Oxford University Press, 1937

Darras, Jacques, *Joseph Conrad and the West: Signs of Empire*, translated from the French by Anne Luyat and Jacques Darras. London: Macmillan, 1982

Davidson, Arnold E., *Conrad's Endings*. Ann Arbor, Michigan: UMI Research Press, 1984

Deurbergue, Jean, 'The opening of *Victory*', in *Studies in Joseph Conrad*, edited by Claude Thomas (Montpellier: CERVE, 1975), pp. 239–70

Dowden, Wilfred S., *Joseph Conrad: The Imaged Style*. Nashville, Tenn.: Vanderbilt University Press, 1970

Dumesnil, René, *Gustave Flaubert: l'homme et l'oeuvre*. Paris: Desclée de Brouwer, 1932

Eliot, T. S., *On Poetry and Poets*. London: Faber and Faber, 1957

*Selected Essays*, 3rd enlarged edn. London: Faber and Faber, 1951. (Incl. 'Tradition and the individual talent', pp. 13-22)

Faguet, Emile, *Gustave Flaubert*. Paris: Hachette, 1899

Fleishman, Avrom, *Conrad's Politics: Community and Anarchy in the Fiction of Joseph Conrad*. Baltimore, Md: Johns Hopkins Press, [1967]

Ford, Ford Madox, *Critical Writings*, edited by Frank MacShane. Lincoln: University of Nebraska Press, 1964

*The English Novel from the Earliest Days to the Death of Joseph Conrad*. London: Constable, 1930

*Joseph Conrad: A Personal Remembrance*. London: Duckworth, 1924. [Abbreviated Ford]

*The March of Literature*. London: Allen and Unwin, 1939

*Portraits from Life*. Chicago: Henry Regnery, 1937

*Return to Yesterday: Reminiscences 1894–1914*. London: Gollancz, 1931

*Thus to Revisit: Some Reminiscences*. London: Chapman & Hall, 1921

Forster, E. M., *Abinger Harvest*. London: Arnold, 1936. (Incl. 'Joseph Conrad: a note', pp. 159–64)

Foucault, Michel, *Préface à La Tentation de saint Antoine*, by Gustave Flaubert. Paris: Livre de Poche, 1971

Galsworthy, John, *Castles in Spain & Other Screeds*. London: Heinemann, 1927. (Incl. 'Reminiscences of Conrad', pp. 74–95)

Gaultier, Jules de, *Le Bovarysme*, new edition. Paris: Mercure de France, 1921

Genette, Gérard, *Palimpsestes: la littérature au second degré*. Paris: Seuil, 1982. (Poétique)

Gillon, Adam, *Conrad and Shakespeare and Other Essays*. New York: Astra Books, 1976. [Abbreviated Gillon]

Giraud, Raymond ed., *Flaubert: A Collection of Critical Essays*. Englewood Cliffs, NJ: Prentice-Hall, 1964. (Incl. Martin Turnell, '*Madame Bovary*', pp. 97–111, and Jean Rousset, '*Madame Bovary* or the book about nothing', pp. 112–31)

Godin, Henri, *Les Ressources stylistiques du français contemporain*. Oxford: Blackwell, 1964

Goldring, Douglas, *South Lodge: Reminiscences of Violet Hunt, Ford Madox Ford and the English Review Circle*. London: Constable, 1943

Gordan, John Dozier, *Joseph Conrad: The Making of a Novelist*. Cambridge, Mass.: Harvard University Press, 1940 [Reprinted New York: Russell & Russell, 1963]

Gothot-Mersch, Claudine, *La Genèse de* Madame Bovary. Paris: Corti, 1966

Graver, Lawrence, *Conrad's Short Fiction*. Berkeley: University of California Press, 1969

Grover, Philip, *Henry James and the French Novel: A Study in Inspiration*. London: Elek, 1973

Guerard, Albert J., *Conrad the Novelist*. Cambridge, Mass.: Harvard University Press, 1958

Guiraud, Pierre, *Essais de stylistique*. Paris: Klincksieck, 1969. (Incl. 'Le Gouufre de Baudelaire', pp. 87–94)

'Modern linguistics looks at rhetoric: free indirect style', in *Patterns of Literary Style*, edited by Joseph Strelka (University Park: Pennsylvania State University Press, 1971), pp. 77–89

Gurko, Leo, *Joseph Conrad: Giant in Exile*, with a new introduction. London: Collier Macmillan / New York: Collier Books, 1979

Hainsworth, G., 'Schopenhauer, Flaubert, Maupassant: conceptual thought and artistic "truth"', in *Currents of Thought in French Literature: Essays in Memory of G. T. Clapton*, edited by T. V. Benn [and others] (Oxford: Blackwell, 1965), pp. 165–90

Hart-Davis, Rupert, *Hugh Walpole: A Biography*. London: Macmillan, 1952

Hatzfeld, Helmut, *Literature through Art: A New Approach to French Literature*. Chapel Hill: University of North Carolina Press, 1969. (Studies in the Romance languages and literatures, 86) [First published New York: Oxford University Press, 1952]

Hay, Eloise Knapp, 'Impressionism limited', in *Joseph Conrad: A Commemoration*, edited by Norman Sherry (London: Macmillan, 1976), pp. 54–64

*The Political Novels of Joseph Conrad*. Chicago: University of Chicago Press, 1963

Heffer (W.) & Sons Ltd. 'Books from Joseph Conrad's Library', in *Catalogue of Second-Hand Books, no. 267* (Cambridge: Heffer, 1926), pp. 1–3

Hodges, Robert, *The Dual Heritage of Joseph Conrad*. The Hague: Mouton, 1967

Hodgson & Co., *A Catalogue of Books, Manuscripts and Corrected Typescripts from the Library of the Late Joseph Conrad to be Sold by Auction [. . .] on Friday March 13th 1925*. London: Hodgson, 1925

Houston, John Porter, *Fictional Technique in France, 1802–1927*. Baton Rouge: Louisiana State University Press, 1972. (Incl. 'Flaubert his disciples and impersonal narration', pp. 62–94)

Hueffer, Ford Madox *see* Ford, Ford Madox

Huneker, James, *Egoists: A Book of Supermen*. London: T. Werner Laurie / New York: Scribner, 1909

*Ivory Apes and Peacocks*. New York, Scribner's Sons, 1921 (Incl. 'The genius of Joseph Conrad', pp. 1–21)

Issacharoff, Michael ed., *Langages de Flaubert*. Paris: Lettres Modernes, Minard, 1976. (Situation, 32) (Incl. Jean Bruneau, 'La Présence de Flaubert dans *L'Education sentimentale*', pp. 33–51)

James, Henry, *French Poets and Novelists*. New York: Grosset and Dunlap, 1964

James Henry, *The Golden Bowl*. London: The Bodley Head, 1971. (The Bodley Head Henry James, vol. 9)

*Selected Literary Criticism*, edited by Morris Shapira. London: Heinemann, 1963. (Incl. 'Gustave Flaubert' (1893), pp. 138–54; 'The art of fiction', pp. 49–67; 'Guy de Maupassant', pp. 87–111; 'Gustave Flaubert' (1902), pp. 212–39)

Jean-Aubry, G., *Joseph Conrad: Life & Letters*, 2 vols. London: Heinemann, 1927. [Abbreviated *LL*]

*The Sea-Dreamer: A Definitive Biography of Joseph Conrad*, translated by Helen Sebba. London: Allen & Unwin, 1957

'*Suspense*', in *A Conrad Memorial Library*, by George T. Keating (Garden City, NY: Doubleday, Doran, 1929), pp. 351–7

Jefferson, Carter, *Anatole France: The Politics of Skepticism*. New Brunswick, NJ: Rutgers University Press, 1965

Johnson, Bruce, 'Conrad's impressionism and Watt's "delayed decoding"', in *Conrad Revisited*, edited by Ross C. Murfin (University of Alabama Press, 1985), pp. 51–70

*Conrad's Models of Mind*. Minneapolis: University of Minnesota Press, 1971

Karl, Frederick R., *Joseph Conrad: The Three Lives. A Biography*. London: Faber & Faber, 1979. [Abbreviated Karl]

*A Reader's Guide to Joseph Conrad*. London: Thames and Hudson / New York: Noonday Press, 1960

Keating, George T., *A Conrad Memorial Library: The Collection of George T. Keating*. Garden City, NY: Doubleday, Doran, 1929

Kenner, Hugh, *The Poetry of Ezra Pound*, 2 vols. London: Faber & Faber, 1951–53

Kettle, Arnold, *An Introduction to the English Novel*, 2 vols. London: Hutchinson, 1951–53.

Kirschner, Paul, *Conrad: The Psychologist as Artist*. Edinburgh: Oliver and Boyd, 1968. [Abbreviated Kirschner]

Kowalska, Aniela, *Conrad 1896–1900: strategia wrażeń i refleksji w narracjach Marlowa* [Patterns of Impressions and Reflections in Marlow's narratives]. Łódź: Society of Arts and Sciences, 1973. ('Summary', pp. 127–8)

Lacapra, Dominick, *Madame Bovary on Trial*. Ithaca, NY and London: Cornell University Press, 1982

Lanson, Gustave, *L'Art de la prose*. Paris: Nizet, [1968]

Leavis, F. R., *The Great Tradition: George Eliot, Henry James, Joseph Conrad*, new edition. London: Chatto & Windus, 1960. [First published 1948]

Leech, Geoffrey N. and Michael H. Short, *Style in Fiction*. London and New York: Longman, 1981

Liddell, Robert, *A Treatise on the Novel*. London: Cape, 1947

Lindey, Alexander, *Plagiarism and Originality*. New York: Harper, 1952. [Reprinted Westport, Conn.: Greenwood Press, 1974]

Lowe, Margaret, *Towards the Real Flaubert*. Oxford: Clarendon Press, 1984

Lowes, John Livingston, *The Road to Xanadu*. London and Cambridge, Mass.: Constable, 1927

Mahood, M. M., *The Colonial Encounter: A Reading of Six Novels*. London: Collings, 1977

Malraux, André, *Psychologie de l'art*, 3 vols. Genève: Skira, 1949–50.

Mégroz, Rodolphe L., *Joseph Conrad's Mind and Method: A Study of Personality in Art*. London: Faber & Faber, 1931. [Reprinted New York: Russell & Russell, 1964]

Meyer, Bernard C., *Joseph Conrad: A Psychoanalytic Biography*. Princeton, NJ: Princeton University Press, 1967. [Abbreviated Meyer]

Miłosz, Czesław, *The History of Polish Literature*. London: Collier-Macmillan, 1969

Moncrieff, G. K. Scott ed., *Marcel Proust: An English Tribute*. London: Chatto & Windus, 1923

Morf, Gustav, *The Polish Heritage of Joseph Conrad*. London: Sampson Low, Marston, 1930

*The Polish Shades and Ghosts of Joseph Conrad*. New York: Astra Books, 1976. [Abbreviated Morf]

Moser, Thomas, *Joseph Conrad: Achievement and Decline*. Cambridge, Mass.: Harvard University Press, 1957. [Reprinted Hamden, Conn.: Archon Books, 1966] [Abbreviated Moser]

Mudrick, Marvin ed., *Conrad: A Collection of Critical Essays*. Englewood Cliffs, NJ: Prentice-Hall, 1966

Muir, Edwin, *Latitudes*. New York: Huebsch, 1924. (Incl. 'A Note on Mr. Conrad', pp. 47–56)

Murfin, Ross C. ed., *Conrad Revisited: Essays for the Eighties*. Alabama: University of Alabama Press, 1985. (Incl. Bruce Johnson, 'Conrad's impressionism and Watt's "delayed decoding"', pp. 51–70)

Nagel, James, *Stephen Crane and Literary Impressionism*. University Park: Pennsylvania State University Press, 1980

Najder, Zdzisław, 'Conrad and Rousseau: concepts of man and society', in *Joseph Conrad: A Commemoration*, edited by Norman Sherry. (London: Macmillan, 1976), pp. 77–90

*Conrad's Polish Background: Letters to and from Polish Friends*, edited by Zdzisław Najder and translated by Halina Carroll. London: Oxford University Press, 1964

*Joseph Conrad: A Chronicle*, translation by Halina Carroll-Najder. Cambridge University Press, 1983. [Abbreviated Najder]

Nettels, Elsa, *James & Conrad*. Athens: University of Georgia Press, 1977

O'Hanlon, Redmond, *Joseph Conrad and Charles Darwin: The Influence of Scientific Thought on Conrad's Fiction*. Edinburgh: The Salamander Press, 1984

Paris, Bernard J., *A Psychological Approach to Fiction: Studies in Thackeray, Stendhal, George Eliot, Dostoevsky, and Conrad*. Bloomington and London: Indiana University Press, 1974

Pater, Walter, *Appreciations, with an Essay on Style*. London: Macmillan, 1910

*Marius the Epicurean*, 2 vols. London: Macmillan, 1910.

*The Renaissance: Studies in Art and Poetry*. London: Macmillan, 1910. (Incl. 'The School of Giorgione', pp. 130–54)

Pulc, I. P., 'The imprint of Polish on Conrad's prose', in *Joseph Conrad: Theory and World Fiction*, edited by Wolodymyr T. Zyla and Wendell M. Aycock. (Lubbock: Texas Tech University, 1974), pp. 117–39

Rapin, René, 'Le Français de Joseph Conrad', in *Lettres de Joseph Conrad à Marguerite Poradowska* (Genève: Droz, 1966), pp. 15–53

Ray, Martin, *Joseph Conrad and his Contemporaries: An Annotated Bibliography of Inter-*

*views and Recollections*. London: Joseph Conrad Society (UK), 1988. (JCS Monographs, 1)

Retinger, Joseph H., *Conrad and his Contemporaries: Souvenirs*. London: Minerva, 1941. [Abbreviated Retinger]

Richard, Jean-Pierre, *Littérature et sensation*. Paris: Seuil, 1954

Rousset, Jean, *Forme et signification: essais sur les structures littéraires de Corneille à Claudel*. Paris: Corti, 1964. (Incl. '*Madame Bovary* ou le livre sur rien', pp. 109–33)

'*Madame Bovary* or the book about nothing', in *Flaubert: A Collection of Critical Essays*, edited by Raymond Giraud (Englewood Cliffs, NJ: Prentice-Hall, 1964), pp. 112–31

Ruthven, K. K., *Critical Assumptions*. Cambridge: Cambridge University Press, 1979.

Said, Edward W., 'Conrad and Nietzsche', in *Joseph Conrad: A Commemoration*, edited by Norman Sherry. (London: Macmillan, 1976), pp. 65–76

*Joseph Conrad and the Fiction of Autobiography*. Cambridge, Mass.; Harvard University Press, 1966. [Abbreviated Said]

Sareil, Jean, *Anatole France et Voltaire*. Genève: Droz, 1960

Saveson, John E., *Conrad: The Later Moralist*. Amsterdam: Rodopi NV, 1974.

*Joseph Conrad: The Making of a Moralist*. Amsterdam: Rodopi NV, 1972. (Incl. 'Contemporary psychology in *The Nigger of the "Narcissus"*', pp. 109–15, and 'The criminal psychology of *The Secret Agent*', pp. 117–36)

Schwarz, Daniel R., *Conrad: Almayer's Folly to Under Western Eyes*. Ithaca, NY: Cornell University Press, 1980

Senn, Werner, *Conrad's Narrative Voice: Stylistic Aspects of his Fiction*. Bern: Francke, 1980

Sherrington, R. J., *Three Novels by Flaubert: A Study of Techniques*. Oxford: Clarendon Press, 1970

Sherry, Norman ed., *Conrad: The Critical Heritage*. London: Routledge & Kegan Paul, 1973. (Incl. Edward Garnett, 'Academy portraits: xxxix. – Mr Joseph Conrad', *Academy* (15 October 1898, 82–3). pp. 104–8; Robert Lynd, 'Review of *A Set of Six*', *Daily News* (10 August 1908, 3), pp. 210–12)

Sherry, Norman, *Conrad's Eastern World*. Cambridge: Cambridge University Press, 1966

*Conrad's Western World*. Cambridge: Cambridge University Press, 1971

Sherry, Norman ed., *Joseph Conrad: A Commemoration*. London: Macmillan, 1976. (Incl. Eloise Knapp Hay, 'Impressionism limited', pp. 54–64; Edward W. Said, 'Conrad and Nietzsche', pp. 65–76; Zdzisław Najder, 'Conrad and Rousseau', pp. 77–90)

Strelka, Joseph ed., *Patterns of Literary Style*. University Park: Pennsylvania State University Press, 1971. (Incl. Pierre Guiraud, 'Modern linguistics looks at rhetoric', pp. 77–89)

Sullivan, Edward D., *Maupassant the Novelist*. Princeton, NJ: Princeton University Press, 1954. [Reprinted Westport, Conn.: Greenwood Press, 1978]

Symons, Arthur, '*A Set of Six*', in *A Conrad Memorial Library*, by George T. Keating (Garden City, NY: Doubleday, Doran, 1929), pp. 170–81

Tanner, Tony, *Adultery in the Novel: Contract and Transgression*. Baltimore and London:

Johns Hopkins University Press, 1979. (Incl. 'Charles Bovary goes to school', pp. 236–54 and 'Monsieur Binet and his lathe', pp. 254–65)

Tarnawski, Wit M., *Conrad the Man, the Writer, the Pole: An Essay in Psychological Biography*, translated by Rosamund Batchelor. London: Polish Cultural Foundation, 1984. (Incl. 'The idea in *Lord Jim*', pp. 80–97 and '*Under Western Eyes* and *Crime and Punishment*', pp. 175–8)

'*Nostromo* and Flaubert's *Salammbô*', in *Wit Tarnawski: The Man, the Writer, the Pole*, edited by John Crompton (London: The Joseph Conrad Society (UK), 1976), pp. 18–21

Tate, Allen, *Collected Essays*. Denver: Swallow, 1959. (Incl. 'Techniques of fiction', pp. 129–45)

Thibaudet, Albert, *Gustave Flaubert*. Paris: Gallimard, 1935

Thomas, Claude ed., *Studies in Joseph Conrad*. Montpellier: Centre d'Etudes Victoriennes et Edouardiennes, 1975. (Cahiers, 2) (Incl. Claude Thomas, 'Structure and narrative technique of *Under Western Eyes*', pp. 205–22, and Jean Deurbergue, 'The opening of *Victory*', pp. 239–70)

Thorburn, David, *Conrad's Romanticism*. New Haven and London: Yale University Press, 1974

Tillett, Margaret, *On Reading Flaubert*. London: Oxford University Press, 1961

Torgovnick, Marianna, *Closure in the Novel*. Princeton, NJ: Princeton University Press, 1981

Turnell, Martin, '*Madame Bovary*', in *Flaubert: A Collection of Critical Essays*, edited by Raymond Giraud (Englewood Cliffs, NJ: Prentice-Hall, 1964), pp. 97–111

Ujejski, Józef, *Joseph Conrad*, translated from the Polish by Pierre Duméril. Paris: Société Française d'Éditions Littéraires et Techniques, 1939

Ullmann, Stephen, *Style in the French Novel*. Oxford: Blackwell, 1957

Vial, André, *Guy de Maupassant et l'art du roman*. Paris: Nizet, 1954

Visiak, E. H., *The Mirror of Conrad*. London: T. Werner Laurie, 1955

Walpole, Hugh, *Joseph Conrad*, new and revised edn. London: Nisbet, [1924]

Watt, Ian, *Conrad in the Nineteenth Century*. London: Chatto & Windus, 1980. [Abbreviated Watt]

Watts, Cedric, *The Deceptive Text*. Sussex: The Harvester Press / New Jersey: Barnes & Noble, 1984

*A Preface to Conrad*. London and New York: Longman, 1982

Wellek, René, *Concepts of Criticism*. New Haven and London: Yale University Press, 1963. (Incl. 'The concept of Romanticism in literary history', pp. 128–98)

Wetherill, P. M., *The Literary Text*. Oxford: Blackwell, 1974

White, Harold Ogden, *Plagiarism and Imitation during the English Renaissance: A Study in Critical Distinctions*. Cambridge, Mass.: Harvard University Press, 1935. [Reprinted New York: Octagon Books, 1965]

Wiley, Paul L., *Conrad's Measure of Man*. Madison: University of Wisconsin Press, 1954

Williamson, George, *The Senecan Amble: A Study in Prose Form from Bacon to Collier*. London: Faber & Faber, 1951

Wilson, Edmund, *Axel's Castle: A Study in the Imaginative Literature of 1870-1930*. New York: Scribner's Sons, 1931

Wimsatt, William K., Jr and Cleanth Brooks, *Literary Criticism*, Vol. 4: *Modern Criticism*. London: Routledge and Kegan Paul, 1957
Yelton, Donald C., *Mimesis and Metaphor: An Inquiry into the Genesis and Scope of Conrad's Symbolic Imagery*. The Hague: Mouton, 1967 [Abbreviated Yelton]
Zyla, Wolodymyr T. and Wendell M. Aycock eds., *Joseph Conrad: Theory and World Fiction*. Lubbock: Texas Tech University, 1974 (Proceedings of the Comparative Literature Symposium, vol. 7) (Incl. I. P. Pulc, 'The imprint of Polish on Conrad's prose', pp. 117–39, and N. Sherry, 'The essential Conrad', pp. 141–9)


*Articles*

Atkinson, Mildred, 'Conrad's *Suspense*', *TLS*, 25 February 1926, 142 [Reprinted in *Saturday Review of Literature*, 2 (1926), 666]
Bache, William B., '"Othello" and Conrad's "Chance"', *Notes and Queries*, new series 2 (1955), 478–9
Bart, B. F., 'Flaubert's concept of the novel', *PMLA*, 80 (1965), 84–9
   'The moral of Flaubert's *Saint-Julien*', *Romanic Review*, 38 (1947), 23–33
Batchelor, John, '[Review of *The Polish Shades and Ghosts of Joseph Conrad*, by Gustav Morf]', *Notes and Queries*, new series 27 (1980), 383–4
Beidler, Peter G., 'Conrad's "Amy Foster" and Chaucer's Prioress', *Nineteenth-Century Fiction*, 30 (1975), 111–15
Bender, Todd K., 'Conrad and literary impressionism', *Conradiana*, 10 (1978), 211–24
Berman, Jeffrey, 'Introduction to Conrad and the Russians', *Conradiana*, 12 (1980), 3–12
Berman, Jeffrey and Donna Van Wagenen, '*Under Western Eyes*: Conrad's diary of a writer?', *Conradiana*, 9 (1977), 269–74
Bismut, Roger, 'Quelques problèmes de création littéraire dans "Bel-Ami"', *Revue d'histoire littéraire de la France*, 67 (1967), 577–89
Block, Haskell, 'Theory of language in Gustave Flaubert and James Joyce', *Revue de littérature comparée*, 35 (1961), 197–206
Brooks, Harold, '*Lord Jim* and *Fifine at the Fair*', *Conradiana*, 3 (1971), 9–25
Brown, Calvin S., 'How useful is the concept of Impressionism', *Yearbook of Comparative and General Literature*, 19 (1968), 53–9
Brunetière, Ferdinand, 'Gustave Flaubert', *Revue des deux mondes* (15 June 1880), 828–57
Bufkin, E. C., 'Conrad, grand opera, and *Nostromo*', *Nineteenth-Century Fiction*, 30 (1975), 206–14
Busza, Andrzej, 'Conrad's Polish literary background and some illustrations of the influence of Polish literature on his work', *Antemurale*, 10 (1966), 109–255
   'St. Flaubert and Prince Roman', *L'Epoque conradienne* (February 1980), 1–23
   'A trip into the Polish interior: a review', *English Literature in Transition*, 11 (1968), 222–6
Cap, Jean-Pierre, 'A Conrad letter to Henri Ghéon', *Conradiana*, 8 (1976), 219–24
Caserio, Robert L., 'Joseph Conrad, Dickensian novelist of the nineteenth century: a dissent from Ian Watt', *Nineteenth-Century Fiction*, 36 (1981), 337–47

Chaikin, Milton, 'Zola and Conrad's "The Idiots"', *Studies in Philology*, 52 (1955), 502–7. [Abbreviated Chaikin]

Charney, Hanna, 'Images of absence in Flaubert and some contemporary films', *Style*, 9 (1975), 488–501

Chevrillon, André, 'Conrad', *Nouvelle Revue Française*, 23 no. 135 (1924), 704–7

Chwalewik, Witold, 'Conrad and the literary tradition', *Kwartalnik Neofilologiczny*, 5 (1958), 29–37

Clamens, Pierre A., '"D'un mot mis en sa place ..."': étude sur le mot juste dans *Madame Bovary*', *Romanic Review*, 45 (1954), 45–54

Cook, Albert, 'Conrad's void', *Nineteenth-Century Fiction*, 12 (1958), 326–30

'Flaubert: the riches of detachment', *French Review*, 32 (1958), 120–9

Cox, C. B., 'Joseph Conrad's "The Secret Agent": the irresponsible piano', *Critical Quarterly*, 15 (1973), 197–212

Cox, James Trammell, 'The finest French novel in the English language', *Modern Fiction Studies*, 9 (1963), 79–93

Cross, Donald, 'Conrad's "The Duel"', *TLS*, 15 August 1968, 881

Curle, Richard, 'Conrad in the East', *Yale Review*, new series 12 (1923), 497–508

'Joseph Conrad', *Rhythm*, 2 (1912), 242–55

'Joseph Conrad: ten years after', *Virginia Quarterly Review*, 10 (1934), 420–35. [Reprinted in the *Fortnightly Review*, new series 136 (1934), 189–99]

Dabrowski, Marian, 'An interview with Joseph Conrad, translated by Bronislas A. Jezierski', *American Scholar*, 13 (1944), 371–5. [Reprinted in *Polish-American Studies*, 17 (1960), 66–71]

Dale, Patricia, 'Conrad: a borrowing from Hazlitt's father', *Notes and Queries*, new series 10 (1963), 146

Davis, Roderick, '*Under Western Eyes*: "The most deeply meditated novel"', *Conradiana*, 9 (1977), 59–75

Davray, Henry-D, 'Joseph Conrad', *Mercure de France*, 175 (1 October 1924), 32–55

'Lettres anglaises', *Mercure de France*, 31 (July-September 1899), 263–9

Lettres anglaises', *Mercure de France*, 38 (April-June 1901), 262

Dawson, Ernest, 'Some recollections of Joseph Conrad', *Fortnightly Review*, 130 (1928), 203–12

Debray-Genette, Raymonde, 'Les figures du récit dans "Un coeur simple"', *Poétique*, no. 3 (1970), 348–64

Deurbergue, Jean, '*Lord Jim*, roman du nébuleux?', *Etudes anglaises*, 25 (1972), 147–61

Dilworth, Thomas R., 'Conrad's secret sharer at the Gate of Hell', *Conradiana*, 9 (1977), 203–17

Donaldson-Evans, Mary, 'Maupassant *ludens*: a re-examination of *Pierre et Jean*', *Nineteenth-Century French Studies*, 9 (1981), 204–19

Duncan-Jones, E. E., 'Some sources of *Chance*', *Review of English Studies*, new series 20 (1969), 468–71

Dunet, Martine, 'Flaubert, artiste et précurseur de l'impressionisme', *Les Amis de Flaubert*, 46 (1975), 25–40

Ferguson, J. DeLancey, 'The plot of Conrad's *The Duel*', *Modern Language Notes*, 50 (1935), 385–90

Fernández, Ramon, 'L'Art de Conrad', *Nouvelle Revue Française*, 23 no. 135 (1924), 730–7

Fleischmann, Wolfgang B., 'Conrad's *Chance* and Bergson's *Laughter*', *Renascence*, 14 (1962), 66–71

Fogel, Daniel Mark, '"The last cab" in James's "The Papers" and in *The Secret Agent*: Conrad's cues from the Master', *Modern Fiction Studies*, 29 (1983), 227–33

Ford, Ford Madox, 'On Conrad's vocabulary', *Bookman*, 67 (1928), 405–8

'Techniques', *Southern Review*, 1 (July 1935), 20–35. [Reprinted with one cut in *Critical Writings of Ford Madox Ford* (Lincoln: University of Nebraska Press, 1964), pp. 56–71]

Ford, Jane, 'Conrad's *Cloche fêlée*', *Explicator*, 35 (1976), 21–2

'James Joyce and the Conrad connection: the anxiety of influence', *Conradiana*, 17 (1985), 3–18

Freeman, Rosemary, 'Conrad's *Nostromo*: a source and its use', *Modern Fiction Studies*, 7 (1961/62), 317–26

Garnett, Edward, 'Academy portraits: xxxix. – Mr Joseph Conrad', *Academy* (15 October 1898), 82–3. [Reprinted in *Conrad: The Critical Heritage*, edited by Norman Sherry (London: Routledge & Kegan Paul, 1973), pp. 104–8]

Gatch, Katherine Haynes, 'Conrad's Axel', *Studies in Philology*, 48 (1951) 98–106

Gerhardi, Gerhard C., 'Romantic love and the prostitution of politics: on the structural unity of *L'Education sentimentale*', *Studies in the Novel*, 4 (1972), 402–15

Gerver, Elisabeth, 'Fact into fiction: Conrad's creative process: [review of *Conrad's Western World*, by Norman Sherry]', *Dalhousie Review*, 52 (1972), 295–302

Gide, André, 'Joseph Conrad', *Nouvelle Revue Française*, 23 no. 135 (1924), 659–62

Gilliam, Harriet, 'The daemonic in Conrad's *Under Western Eyes*', *Conradiana*, 9 (1977), 219–36

Gillon, Adam, 'Conrad as painter', *Conradiana*, 10 (1978), 253–66

'Some Polish literary motifs in the works of Joseph Conrad', *Slavic and East European Journal*, 10 (1966), 424–39

Goldknopf, David, 'What's wrong with Conrad: Conrad on Conrad', *Criticism*, 10 (1968), 54–64

Goldwyn, Merrill Harvey, 'Nathaniel Hawthorne and Conrad's *Heart of Darkness*', *Conradiana*, 16 (1984), 72–8

Goodhand, Robert, 'Emma Bovary, the baker's paramour', *Rice University Studies*, 59 (1973), 37–41

Grant, Richard B., 'The role of Minerva in *Madame Bovary*', *Romance Notes*, 6 (1965), 113–15

Gross, Seymour L., 'Hamlet and Heyst again', *Notes and Queries*, new series 6 (1959), 87–8

Guérin, Yves, 'Huit lettres inédites de Joseph Conrad à Robert d'Humières traducteur du *Nigger of the "Narcissus"* en français', *Revue de littérature comparée*, 44 (1970), 367–92. [Abbreviated Guérin]

Gysin, Fritz, 'The vitality of distortion and decay: the grotesque skipper in *Lord Jim*', *English Studies*, 59 (1978), 425–33

Haig, Stirling, 'The *Madame Bovary* blues', *Romanic Review*, 61 (1970), 27–34

Haugh, Robert F., 'The structure of "Lord Jim"', *College English*, 13 (1951), 137–41

Hawthorn, Jeremy, '[Review of *The Edwardian Novelists*, by John Batchelor]' *Conradiana*, 15 (1983), 22, 52, 72

Herndon, Richard, 'The genesis of Conrad's "Amy Foster" ', *Studies in Philology*, 57 (1960), 549–66

Hervouet, Yves, 'Aspects of Flaubertian influence on Conrad's fiction', *Revue de littérature comparée*, 57 (1983), 5–24 and 185–207

'Conrad and Anatole France', *Ariel*, 1 (1970), 84–99

'Conrad and Maupassant: an investigation into Conrad's creative process', *Conradiana*, 14 (1982), 83–111

'Conrad's debt to French authors in *Under Western Eyes*', *Conradiana*, 14 (1982), 113–25

'Conrad's relationship with Anatole France', *Conradiana*, 12 (1980), 195–225

'Joseph Conrad and the French language', *Conradiana*, 11 (1979), 229–51, and 14 (1982), 23–49

'Why did Conrad borrow so extensively?', *The Conradian*, 9 (1984), 53–68

Hewitt, Douglas, '[Review of *The Polish Shades and Ghosts of Joseph Conrad*, by Gustav Morf]', *Review of English Studies*, new series 32 (1981), 353–4

Higdon, David L., 'Conrad and Amiel', *Joseph Conrad Today*, 3 (1977), 66–7

'Conrad and Mark Twain: a newly-discovered essay', *Journal of Modern Literature*, 12 (1985), 354–61

'Château Borel, Petrus Borel and Conrad's *Under Western Eyes*', *Studies in the Novel*, 3 (1971), 99–102

'Pascal's *Pensée* 347 in *Under Western Eyes*', *Conradiana*, 5 (1973), 81–3

'Hommage à Joseph Conrad 1837–1924', *Nouvelle Revue Française*, 23 no. 135 (1924) [Abbreviated *NRF*]

Huss, Roger, 'Some anomalous uses of the imperfect and the status of action in Flaubert', *French Studies*, 31 (1977), 139–48

Jacobs, Robert G., 'Comrade Ossipon's favourite saint: Lombroso and Conrad', *Nineteenth-Century Fiction*, 23 (1968), 74–84

Jean-Aubry, G., 'Des heures anglaises ...', *Cahiers du Sud* (1946), 132–7

'The inner history of Conrad's *Suspense*: notes & extracts from letters', *Bookman's Journal*, 13 no. 49 (1925), 3–10

'Joseph Conrad and music', *The Chesterian*, 6 (1924), 37–42

'Joseph Conrad et la France', *Chronique des lettres françaises*, 1 (1923), 425. [Reprinted in *Nouvelles littéraires*, 7 (11 February 1928), 7]

'Joseph Conrad (6 December 1857 – 3 August 1924)', *Fortnightly Review*, 122 (1924), 303–13. [English version of 'Souvenirs', *q.v.*]

'Souvenirs (fragments)', *Nouvelle Revue Française*, 23 no. 135 (1924), 672–80

Johnson, Bruce, ' "Heart of Darkness" and the problem of emptiness', *Studies in Short Fiction*, 9 (1972), 387–400

Johnson, J. Theodore, Jr, 'Literary impressionism in France: a survey of criticism', *L'Esprit créateur*, 13 (1973), 271–97

Johnson, James W., 'That neo-classical bee', *Journal of the History of Ideas*, 22 (1961), 262–6

Johnson, Julie M., 'The damsel and her knights: the goddess and the grail in Conrad's *Chance*', *Conradiana*, 13 (1981), 221–8

Jones, Charles, 'Varieties of speech presentation in Conrad's "The Secret Agent"', *Lingua*, 20 (1968), 162–76

Kadish, Doris Y., 'Two semiological features of four functions of description: the example of Flaubert', *Romanic Review*, 70 (1979), 278–98

Karl, Frederick R., 'Conrad and Gide: a relationship and a correspondence', *Comparative Literature*, 29 (1977), 148–71

'Conrad's debt to Dickens', *Notes and Queries*, new series 4 (1957), 398–400

'*Victory*: its origin and development', *Conradiana*, 15 (1983), 23–51

Kelemen, Jolán, 'L'Imparfait de Flaubert et des romanciers naturaliste du XIX$^e$ siècle', *Acta Linguistica Academiae Scientiarum Hungaricae*, 20 (1970), 63–85

Kennard, Jean E., 'Emerson and Dickens: a note on Conrad's *Victory*', *Conradiana*, 6 (1974), 215–19

Kertzer, J. M., '"The bitterness of our wisdom": cynicism, skepticism and Joseph Conrad', *Novel*, 16 (1983), 121–40

Kirschner, Paul, 'Conrad and the film', *Quarterly of Film, Radio, and Television*, 11 (1957), 343–53

'Conrad, Goethe and Stein: the romantic fate in *Lord Jim*', *Ariel*, 10 (1979), 65–81

'Making you *see* Geneva: the sense of place in *Under Western Eyes*', *L'Epoque conradienne* (1988), 101–27.

'Some notes on *Conrad in the Nineteenth Century*', *Conradiana*, 17 (1985), 31–6

Knowles, Owen, 'Conrad, Anatole France, and the early French romantic tradition: some influences', *Conradiana*, 11 (1979), 41–61. [Abbreviated Knowles]

'Conrad and Mérimée: the legend of Venus in "The Planter of Malata"', *Conradiana*, 11 (1979), 177–84

'*Under Western Eyes*: a note on two sources', *The Conradian*, 10 (1985), 154–61

'The year's work in Conrad studies, 1983: a survey of periodical literature', *The Conradian*, 9 (1984), 37–43

Lapp, John C., 'Art and hallucination in Flaubert', *French Studies*, 10 (1956), 322–34

Lenormand, H.-R., 'Il y a quatre ans, en Corse avec Joseph Conrad, coureur de mers', *Transatlantic Review*, 2 (1924), 338–40

'Note sur un séjour de Conrad en Corse', *Nouvelle Revue Française*, 23 no. 135 (1924), 666–71

Lensing, Leo A., 'Goethe's *Torquato Tasso* in *Lord Jim*: a note on Conrad's use of literary quotation', *English Literature in Transition*, 19 (1976), 101–4

Levin, Harry, '*Madame Bovary*: the cathedral and the hospital', *Essays in Criticism*, 2 (1952), 1–23

Levine, George, '*Madame Bovary* and the disappearing author', *Modern Fiction Studies*, 9 (1963), 103–19

Levinson, André, 'Joseph Conrad est-il un écrivain polonais?', *Nouvelles littéraires*, 7 (4 August 1928), 8

Little, Roger, 'Saint-John Perse and Joseph Conrad: some notes and an uncollected letter', *Modern Language Review*, 72 (1977), 811–4

Lodge, David, 'Conrad's *Victory* and *The Tempest*: an amplification', *Modern Language Review*, 59 (1964), 195–9

Lowe, A. M., 'Emma Bovary, a modern Arachne', *French Studies*, 26 (1972), 30–41

Lynd, Robert, 'Review of *A Set of Six*', *Daily News* (10 August 1908), 3 [Reprinted in *Conrad: The Critical Heritage*, edited by Norman Sherry, pp. 210–12]

Lytle, Andrew, 'In defense of a passionate and incorruptible heart', *Sewanee Review*, 73 (1965), 593–615

McConnell, Frank D., 'Félicité, passion, ivresse: the lexicography of *Madame Bovary*', *Novel*, 3 (1970), 153–66.

McFarland, Thomas, 'Coleridge's plagiarisms once more: a review essay', *Yale Review*, 63 (1974), 252–86

MacKenzie, Manfred, 'Fenimore Cooper and Conrad's *Suspense*', *Notes and Queries*, new series 10 (1963), 373–5

McLauchlan, Juliet, 'The "something human" in *Heart of Darkness*', *Conradiana*, 9 (1977), 115–25

Marle, Hans van, 'Young Ulysses ashore: on the trail of Konrad Korzeniowski in Marseilles', *L'Epoque conradienne* (May 1976), 22–34

Martin, David M., 'The function of the Intended in Conrad's "Heart of Darkness"', *Studies in Short Fiction*, 11 (1974), 27–33

Martin, Joseph, 'Edward Garnett and Conrad's plunge into the "destructive element"', *Texas Studies in Literature and Language*, 15 (1973), 517–36

Maurin, Mario, 'The Planter's French connection: an appropriation by Joseph Conrad', *Modern Philology*, 82 (1985), 304–9

Maxwell, J. C., 'Conrad and Turgenev: a minor source for "Victory"', *Notes and Queries*, new series 10 (1963), 372–3

Mercié, Jean-Luc, 'Leurres et discours du texte: le système des oiseaux dans *Madame Bovary*', *Travaux de linguistique et de littérature*, 18 (1980), 181–91

Meyer, Bernard C., 'Conrad and the Russians', *Conradiana*, 12 (1980), 13–21

'*Language and Being: Joseph Conrad and the Literature of Personality* by Peter J. Glassman', *Literature and Psychology*, 26 (1976), 181–4

Morrissey, L. J., 'The tellers in *Heart of Darkness*: Conrad's Chinese boxes', *Conradiana*, 13 (1981), 141–8

Moser, Thomas, 'Conrad, Ford, and the sources of *Chance*', *Conradiana*, 7 (1975), 207–24

Mouradian, Jacques, 'Conrad and Anatole France: [letter to the editor]', *TLS*, 30 October 1930, 890

Nelson, Carl, 'The ironic allusive texture of *Lord Jim*: Coleridge, Crane, Milton and Melville', *Conradiana*, 4 (1972), 47–59

Nettels, Elsa, 'Conrad and Stephen Crane', *Conradiana*, 10 (1978), 267–83

'The grotesque in Conrad's fiction', *Nineteenth-Century Fiction*, 29 (1974), 144–63

Newton, Joy, 'Emile Zola and the French impressionist novel', *Esprit créateur*, 13 (1973), 320–8

'Emile Zola impressioniste', *Cahiers naturalistes*, 13 no. 33 (1967), 39–52, and 13 no. 34 (1967), 124–38

Oakes, Philip, 'Novelists battle for the spoils of war', *Sunday Times*, 18 November 1979, 37

Oliver, Andrew, 'Introduction', *Texte*, 2 (1983), 5–11

Page, Norman, 'Dickensian elements in *Victory*', *Conradiana*, 5 (1973), 37–42

Perec, Georges, 'Emprunts à Flaubert', *L'Arc*, 79 (1980), 49–50

Peterkiewicz, Jerzy, 'Conrad's double image [: review of *Conrad's Polish Background*, edited by Zdzisław Najder]', *Sunday Times*, 24 May 1964, 35

Prendergast, Christopher, 'Flaubert: writing and negativity', *Novel*, 8 (1975), 197–213

Prorok, Leszek, 'A big book about Conrad', *The Conradian*, 6 (1981), 23–5

Proust, Marcel, 'A propos du "style" de Flaubert', *Nouvelle Revue Française*, 14 (1920), 72–90

Purdy, Dwight H., 'The manuscript of *Victory* and the problem of Conrad's intentions', *Journal of Modern Literature*, 10 (1983), 91–108

'Paul and the Pardoner in Conrad's *Victory*', *Texas Studies in Literature and Language*, 23 (1981), 197–213

'"Peace that passeth understanding": the Professor's English Bible in *Under Western Eyes*', *Conradiana*, 13 (1981), 83–93

Purdy, Strother B., 'Henry James, Gustave Flaubert, and the ideal style', *Language and Style*, 3 (1970), 163–84

Rasmussen, Ole Wehner, 'La Signification de l'adjectif *pâle* dans *Madame Bovary*', *Revue romane*, 7 (1972), 26–31

Raval, Suresh, 'Conrad's *Victory*: a skepticism and experience', *Nineteenth-Century Fiction*, 34 (1980), 414–33

Ray, Martin, 'Conrad and Decoud', *Polish Review*, 29 (1984), 53–64

'Conrad, Nordau, and other degenerates: the psychology of *The Secret Agent*', *Conradiana*, 16 (1984), 125–40

Resink, G. J., 'Samburan Encantada', *English Studies*, 47 (1966), 35–44. [Reprinted in *Conradiana*, 1 (1969), 37–44]

Rhome, Frances Dodson, 'Headgear as symbol in Conrad's novels', *Conradiana*, 2 (1970), 180–6

Ricks, Christopher, 'The pink toads in *Lord Jim*', *Essays in Criticism*, 31 (1981), 142–4

Rousset, Jean, 'Positions, distances, perspectives dans "Salammbô"', *Poétique*, no. 6 (1971), 145–54

Rozelaar, Louis A., '*Le Mémorial de Sainte-Hélène* et Victor Hugo en 1827', *French Quarterly*, 9 (1927), 53–68

Rude, Donald W., 'Joseph Conrad's speeches in America: his texts recovered', *L'Epoque conradienne* (1987), 21–32

Rudwin, M. J., 'The intellectual relations between France and Poland', *Poland*, 6 (1925), 69–72

Saunders, William S., 'The unity of *Nostromo*', *Conradiana*, 5 (1973), 27–36

Saveson, John E., 'Conrad, *Blackwood's*, and Lombroso', *Conradiana*, 6 (1974), 57–62

'Contemporary psychology in *The Nigger of the "Narcissus"*', *Studies in Short Fiction*, 7 (1970), 219–31. [Reprinted in Saveson, *Joseph Conrad: The Making of a Moralist* (Amsterdam: Rodopi NV, 1972), pp. 109–15]

Schultheiss, Thomas, 'Lord Hamlet and Lord Jim', *Polish Review*, 11 (1966), 101–33

Schwab, Arnold T., 'Joseph Conrad's American friend: correspondence with James Huneker', *Modern Philology*, 52 (1955), 222–32.

Schwarz, Daniel R., 'Moral bankruptcy in Ploumar parish: a study of Conrad's "The Idiots"', *Conradiana*, 1 (1969), 113–17

Seznec, Jean, 'Flaubert and the graphic arts', *Journal of the Warburg and Courtauld Institutes*, 8 (1945), 175–90

Sherbo, Arthur, 'Conrad's "Victory" and "Hamlet" ', *Notes and Queries*, 198 (1953), 492–3

Sherry, Norman, 'A Conrad manuscript', *TLS*, 25 June 1970, 691

'The essential Conrad', *Essays and Studies*, 27 (1974), 98–113 [Reprinted in *Joseph Conrad: Theory and World Fiction*, edited by Wolodymyr T. Zyla and Wendell M. Aycock (Lubbock: Texas Tech University, 1974), pp. 141–9]

Smith, David R., ' "One word more" about *The Nigger of the "Narcissus"* ', *Nineteenth-Century Fiction*, 23 (1968), 201–16

Smoller, Sanford J., 'A note on Joseph Conrad's fall and abyss', *Modern Fiction Studies*, 15 (1969), 261–4

Spalding, Alex, '*Lord Jim*: the result of reading light holiday literature', *Humanities Association Bulletin*, 19 (1968), 14–22

Spensley, R. M., 'A note on Conrad and Zola', *Journal of the Joseph Conrad Society (UK)*, 4 (1978), 16–17

'Zola and Conrad: the influence of *Pot-Bouille* on *The Secret Agent*', *Conradiana*, 11 (1979), 185–9

Spiegel, Alan, 'Flaubert to Joyce: evolution of a cinematographic form', *Novel*, 6 (1973), 229–43

Stallman, R. W., 'Flaubert's "Madame Bovary" ', *College English*, 10 (1949), 195–203

Stape, J. H., 'Conrad as journalist: further borrowings from Anatole France', *The Conradian*, 8 (1983), 39–43

'Conrad to an unidentified correspondent, 1916: an unpublished letter', *The Conradian*, 13 (1988), 203–4

Stark, Bruce R., 'Kurtz's Intended: the heart of *Heart of Darkness*', *Texas Studies in Literature and Language*, 16 (1974), 535–55

Stegmaier, E., 'The "would-scene" in Joseph Conrad's "Lord Jim" and "Nostromo" ', *Modern Language Review*, 67 (1972), 517–23

Stein, William Bysshe, '*Madame Bovary* and Cupid unmasked', *Sewanee Review*, 73 (1965), 197–209

Steiner, George, 'Has truth a future?', *The Listener*, 12 January 1978, 42–6

Szczypień, Jean M., 'Sailing towards Poland', *Polish Review*, 29 (1984), 89–96

Tanner, Tony, 'Mountains and depths – an approach to nineteenth-century dualism', *Review of English Literature*, 3 (1962), 51–61

'Nightmare and complacency: Razumov and the western eye', *Critical Quarterly*, 4 (1962), 197–214

Thompson, Gordon W., 'Conrad's women', *Nineteenth-Century Fiction*, 32 (1978), 442–63

Tretiak, Andrzej, 'A note on Joseph Conrad', *Revue anglo-américaine*, 12 (1934), 46–7

Valéry, Paul, 'Sujet d'une conversation avec Conrad', *Nouvelle Revue Française*, 23 no. 135 (1924), 663–5

Verleun, Jan, 'Conrad's *Heart of Darkness*: Marlow and the Intended', *Neophilologus*, 67 (1983), 623–39

Verrier, Jean, 'Questions sur une lecture de *Pierre et Jean*', *Le Français dans le monde*, 146 (1979), 18–23

Vidan, Ivo, ' "The Princess Casamassima" between Balzac and Conrad', *Studia Romanica et Anglica Zagrabiensia*, 21–22 (1966), 259–76

Vidan, Ivo, 'Thirteen letters of André Gide to Joseph Conrad', *Studia Romanica et Anglica Zagrabiensia*, 24 (1967), 145–68

Villard, Léonie, 'A Conrad heroine in real life', *Living Age*, 328 (1926), 637–9

'Joseph Conrad et les mémorialistes (à propose de *Suspense*)', *Revue anglo-américaine*, 3 (1926), 313–21

Wake, C. H., 'Symbolism in Flaubert's *Hérodias*: an interpretation', *Forum for Modern Language Studies*, 4 (1968), 322–9

Walton, James, 'Conrad and naturalism: *The Secret Agent*', *Texas Studies in Literature and Language*, 10 (1967), 289–301

'Conrad, Dickens and the detective novel', *Nineteenth-Century Fiction*, 23 (1969), 446–62

Watson, Wallace, '"The Shade of Old Flaubert" and Maupassant's "Art impeccable (presque)": French influences on the development of Conrad's Marlow', *Journal of Narrative Technique*, 7 (1977), 37–56

Watt, Ian, 'Conrad criticism and *The Nigger of the "Narcissus"*', *Nineteenth-Century Fiction*, 12 (1958), 257–83

Watts, Cedric, 'Janiform novels', *English*, 24 no. 119 (1975), 40–9

Webster, H. T., 'Conrad's changes in narrative conception in the manuscripts of *Typhoon and Other Stories* and *Victory*', *PMLA*, 64 (1949), 953–62

Wells, H. G., '[Review of *An Outcast of the Islands*]', *Saturday Review*, 81 (1896), 509–10

Wheeler, Marcus, 'Russia and Russians in the works of Conrad', *Conradiana*, 12 (1980), 23–36

Whibley, Charles, 'A vagabond poet', *Blackwood's Magazine*, 165 (1899), 402–12

White, Margaret Ann Rusk, 'Peter Ivanovitch's escape: a possible source overlooked', *Conradiana*, 12 (1980), 72–80

Widmer, Kingsley, 'Conrad's Pyrrhonistic conservatism: ideological melodrama around "simple ideas"', *Novel*, 7 (1973), 133–42

Williams, D. A., 'Generalizations in *Madame Bovary*', *Neophilologus*, 62 (1978), 492–503

'Water imagery in *Madame Bovary*', *Forum for Modern Language Studies*, 13 (1977), 70–84

Winnington, G. Peter, 'Conrad and Cutcliffe Hyne: a new source for *Heart of Darkness*', *Conradiana*, 16 (1984), 163–82

Wood, Miriam H., 'A source of Conrad's *Suspense*', *Modern Language Notes*, 50 (1935), 390–4

Worth, George J., 'Conrad's debt to Maupassant in the Preface to *The Nigger of the "Narcissus"*', *Journal of English and Germanic Philology*, 54 (1955), 700–4

Yarrison, Betsy C., 'The symbolism of literary allusion in *Heart of Darkness*', *Conradiana*, 7 (1975), 155–64

Zabierowski, Stefan, 'Conrad and Żeromski', *The Conrad News* (1986), 7–32


*Theses*

Gödicke, Horst, 'Der Einfluß Flauberts und Maupassants auf Joseph Conrad'. Dissertation of the Philosophy Faculty, University of Hamburg, 1969

Hervouet, Yves, 'French linguistic and literary influences on Joseph Conrad'. Unpublished PhD thesis, Leeds University, 1971

Morey, John Hope, 'Joseph Conrad and Ford Madox Ford: a study in collaboration'. Unpublished PhD thesis, Cornell University, 1960

Thornton, Lawrence, 'Beyond *Le mot juste*'. Unpublished PhD thesis, University of California, Santa Barbara, 1973

Watson, Wallace S., 'Joseph Conrad's debts to the French'. Unpublished PhD thesis, Indiana University, 1966

Wright, Edgar, 'Joseph Conrad: his expressed views about technique and the principles underlying them, with a study of their relevance to certain novels'. Unpublished MA thesis, London University, 1955

# General name index

Page numbers in bold refer to main sections.

# Index of Conrad's links with other writers

Each work by Conrad is followed by sub-entries which indicate any kind of connection with other writers or thinkers, whether an affinity, influence, source, textual borrowing, quotation or reference.